HOW TO BUILD MODERN FURNITURE

MARIO DAL FABBRO

VOL. I   PRACTICAL CONSTRUCTION METHODS

PUBLISHED BY F. W. DODGE CORPORATION, NEW YORK

A PATHFINDER BOOK REPRINT EDITION
Printed in the United States of America
ISBN: 979-8-8691-1454-9

FOREWORD

WHEN IT WAS DECIDED THAT I SHOULD PREPARE THIS VOLUME ON THE CONSTRUCTION OF FURNITURE I WAS GREATLY PLEASED. I SAW THE OPPORTUNITY TO EXPLAIN MY IDEAS IN A FIELD THAT IS PARTICULARLY DEAR TO ME. IN PREPARING THIS BOOK I HAD THE FULL COOPERATION OF MR. JEFFREY LIVINGSTONE, EDITOR OF THE BOOK DEPARTMENT OF THE F. W. DODGE CORP. WITH HIS ASSURANCE THAT THERE WAS A NEED FOR SUCH A BOOK, I PROCEEDED IN ITS PREPARATION GIVING THE BEST KNOWLEDGE WITHIN ME, A KNOWLEDGE GAINED FROM LONG EXPERIENCE IN THIS WORK IN EUROPE AND MORE RECENTLY IN AMERICA. DUE TO MY LIMITED KNOWLEDGE OF THE ENGLISH LANGUAGE, DR. RUDOLPH PAROLA OF NEW YORK CITY TRANSLATED MY ORIGINAL TEXT, SO THAT I MIGHT MORE FULLY EXPLAIN WHAT I HAD IN MIND.

I BEGAN MY TASK BY FINDING OUT WHO WOULD BE MOST INTERESTED IN A BOOK OF THIS SORT. AFTER CONTACTING PEOPLE IN DIFFERENT BRANCHES OF THE FURNITURE FIELD I FOUND THAT THERE WAS A KEEN INTEREST AMONG ARCHITECTS, DRAFTSMEN, INTERIOR DECORATORS, CABINET MAKERS, AMATEURS, HOBBYISTS, AND COLLEGE STUDENTS.

TO PREPARE A VOLUME THAT WOULD SERVE THOSE INTERESTED IN THE VARIOUS BRANCHES OF THE FURNITURE DESIGN WAS NOT AN EASY ACCOMPLISHMENT. I DISCARDED ONE METHOD AFTER ANOTHER. I REALIZED THAT A BOOK WITH TOO MUCH WRITTEN MATERIAL WOULD NOT SERVE THE INTENDED PURPOSE, SO I THOUGHT IT WOULD BE BEST IF I CONFINED MYSELF TO ILLUSTRATIVE MATERIAL WHERE POSSIBLE. IN THIS WAY I WAS SURE THAT THE ILLUSTRATIONS WOULD EXPLAIN THE DESIGNS SIMPLY WHILE THE SHORT FOOTNOTES UNDER EACH WOULD GIVE A BRIEF BUT DETAILED EXPLANATION.

IN THIS BOOK I HAVE TRIED TO GIVE A STEP BY STEP COVERAGE OF ALL PHASES OF FURNITURE CONSTRUCTION. MANY METHODS OF JOINING PLANKS, RAILS AND FRAMES HAVE BEEN EXPLAINED. IN OTHER SECTIONS VENEERS, PLYWOODS, CURVES AND DOORS ARE DESCRIBED. HARDWARE IS THE SUBJECT OF ANOTHER PART. METHODS OF JOINING WOOD TO OTHER MATERIALS SUCH AS GLASS, METAL AND PLASTICS ARE SHOWN. UPHOLSTERING PROCEDURES ARE ILLUSTRATIVELY DESCRIBED IN A WAY THAT THE AMATEUR WILL BE ABLE TO FOLLOW.

THE LAST 15 PAGES OF THE TEXT HAVE BEEN DEVOTED TO DRAWINGS OF FURNITURE PIECES WHICH MAY BE BUILT BY THE HOME CRAFTSMAN. THIS SECTION IS ESSENTIALLY A PRELUDE TO VOLUME TWO.

IN THE SECOND VOLUME WHICH I HAVE UNDERTAKEN TO DO FOR THE F. W. DODGE CORPORATION I WILL FULLY DESCRIBE THE TOOLS WHICH SHOULD BE USED IN FURNITURE CONSTRUCTION, THE STANDARD MEASUREMENTS OF FURNITURE AND A SERIES OF FURNITURE DESIGNS WHICH WILL ENABLE THE UNSKILLED TO ACHIEVE SUCCESS IN WHAT HE BUILDS. THIS SECOND VOLUME WILL ALSO SHOW EXAMPLES OF ASSEMBLED FURNITURE IN MODERN GROUPINGS.

IT IS MY PERSONAL BELIEF THAT A BOOK OF THIS TYPE WILL BE FOUND USEFUL BY ALL THOSE INTERESTED IN FURNITURE. FOR THOSE WHO HAVE A DESIRE TO BUILD, THIS VOLUME IS AN INDISPENSABLE ASSET. IT IS MY HOPE AND DESIRE THAT ALL THOSE WHO USE THIS BOOK ARE SUCCESSFULLY SERVED.

Mario Dal Fabbro

THE AUTHOR

MARIO DAL FABBRO WAS BORN IN ITALY IN 1913. AFTER COMPLETING HIS STUDIES AT THE R. SUPERIOR INSTITUTE FOR DECORATIVE AND INDUSTRIAL ARTS AT VENICE, HE ATTENDED THE R. MAGISTERO ARTISTICO, FROM WHICH HE WAS GRADUATED WITH HIGH HONORS IN 1937.

FOLLOWING A LONG-ESTABLISHED TRADITION, MARIO WORKED FROM CHILDHOOD IN HIS FAMILY'S FURNITURE DESIGN SHOP. THIS EARLY EXPERIENCE PROBABLY ACCOUNTS FOR HIS SUCCESS IN THE TECHNICAL AND CREATIVE FIELD OF FURNITURE DESIGN, FOR HE HAS ALWAYS BEEN ABLE TO COMBINE THE THEORETICAL WITH THE PRACTICAL ASPECTS OF CONSTRUCTION. MARIO HAS ALSO BEEN AFFILIATED WITH ONE OF THE LARGEST FURNITURE HOUSES IN ITALY.

BETWEEN 1938 AND 1948 MARIO CREATED DESIGNS FOR PRIVATE INDIVIDUALS AND VARIOUS FURNITURE HOUSES IN MILAN. HE HAS CONTRIBUTED TO THE ITALIAN MAGAZINES *DOMUS* AND *STILE*, AND THE FRENCH MAGAZINE *L'ARCHITECTURE D'AUJOURD'HUI*, AND IS THE AUTHOR OF SEVERAL BOOKS ON FURNITURE CONSTRUCTION PUBLISHED BY HOEPLI AND GORLICH IN MILAN. IN 1939 AND 1947 HE PARTICIPATED IN THE TRIENALI INTERNATIONAL COMPETITION AND WON THE GARZANTI CONTEST FOR THE STANDARDIZATION OF FURNITURE.

IN 1948 HE TRANSFERRED HIS DESIGN ACTIVITIES TO THE UNITED STATES. HIS FIRST WORK PUBLISHED IN THIS COUNTRY WAS MODERN FURNITURE, A BOOK WHICH HAS ACHIEVED INTERNATIONAL RECOGNITION. THE AUTHOR NOW DESIGNS FURNITURE FOR MASS PRODUCTION. HE HAS ALSO CONTRIBUTED TO VARIOUS NEWSPAPERS AND MAGAZINES, INCLUDING *THE NEW YORK TIMES* AND *HOUSE AND GARDEN*.

CONTENTS

GENERAL NOTES ABOUT WOOD

IN ORDER TO SELECT THE TYPE OF WOOD BEST ADAPTED TO SPECIFIC NEEDS, IT IS ESSENTIAL TO UNDERSTAND THE CHARACTERISTICS OF THE MATERIAL. I HAVE, THEREFORE, OUTLINED SOME BASIC INFORMATION REGARDING ITS STRUCTURE AND DEFECTS, AS WELL AS METHODS OF SAWING AND HANDLING.

STRUCTURE OF WOOD

WOOD IS DERIVED FROM A TREE. IT IS MADE UP OF BUNDLES OF FIBERS OR LONG TUBES THAT RUN PARALLEL TO THE STEM OF THE TREE. THESE ARE CROSSED BY OTHER FIBERS THAT FORM THE MEDULLARY RAYS. THESE MEDULLARY RAYS PASS FROM THE CENTER OR PITH TO THE BARK AND SERVE TO BIND THE UNITS TOGETHER. THE ARRANGEMENT OF THE WOOD IN CONCENTRIC RINGS IS DUE TO THE TREE'S GRADUAL FORMATION. ONE LAYER OR RING IS ADDED EACH YEAR, AND FOR THIS REASON THE LAYERS ARE CALLED ANNUAL RINGS.

NATURE OF WOOD

SHOWN BELOW IS A PARTIAL SECTION OF A TREE. NOTE THE LOCATION OF ITS PARTS AS DESCRIBED BELOW. MEDULLA OR PITH: THIS IS THE CENTER OF THE TREE. IT IS LIGHTER IN COLOR AND LESS STRONG THAN HEARTWOOD.

HEARTWOOD: LOCATED BETWEEN THE MEDULLA AND SAPWOOD, THIS PART OF THE TREE ALWAYS GIVES US THE BEST BUILDING MATERIAL.

SAPWOOD: THIS PART OF THE TREE CONTAINS THE RECENT ANNUAL RINGS. IT IS SITUATED BETWEEN THE HEARTWOOD AND CAMBIUM.

CAMBIUM: THIS IS THE MOST RECENT ANNUAL RING.

BARK: THIS EXTERNAL LAYER SERVES AS A PROTECTION TO THE TREE.

DEFECTS IN WOOD

THE VARIOUS DEFECTS IN WOOD MAY BE DIVIDED INTO TWO CLASSES. FIRST ARE THOSE WHICH COME

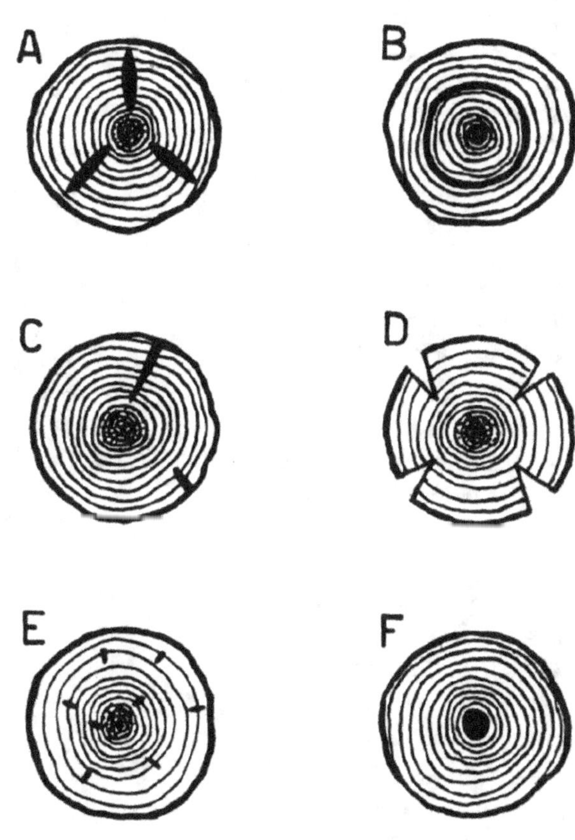

FROM ABNORMAL GROWTH SUCH AS HEART SHAKES, WIND OR CUP SHAKES AND KNOTS. SECOND ARE THOSE CAUSED BY DETERIORATION SUCH AS DRY AND HEART ROT. IN THE SECTIONS ABOVE YOU WILL NOTE THE FOLLOWING DEFECTS:

A — HEART SHAKES	D — STAR SHAKES
B — WIND OR CUP SHAKE	E — DRY ROT
C — HARD KNOTS	F — HEART ROT

SAWING THE TREE INTO PLANKS

A TREE IS USUALLY CUT DURING THE WINTER SEASON WHEN THERE IS LITTLE SAP IN THE WOOD. AT THIS TIME THE WOOD IS LESS SUBJECT TO FUNGI ATTACK. AFTER THE BARK HAS BEEN STRIPPED, THE TRUNK IS WASHED TO PREVENT FUNGI, MOLD OR OTHER GROWTH. THIS PROCESS ALSO HELPS TO SEASON THE WOOD. AT THE END OF THE SEASONING PERIOD THE TRUNK MAY BE SAWED INTO PLANKS IN A NUMBER OF DIFFERENT WAYS. ONE OF THE MOST PRACTICAL METHODS IS SAWING PARALLEL TO THE GRAIN. ANOTHER METHOD WHICH IS USED FOR BETTER WORK IS QUARTER SAWING.

A — PLAIN (OR BASTARD) SAWING OF A TRUNK INTO PLANKS PARALLEL TO THE GRAIN.

B — CURVATURE OF PLANKS AFTER THEY HAVE BEEN SAWED.

C — SAWING OF PLANKS PARALLEL TO THE GRAIN FROM A TRUNK THAT HAS HAD TWO SIDES REMOVED.

D — SAWING A TRUNK INTO PLANKS AFTER REMOVING THE PITH PLANK.

E — SAWING OF PLANKS FROM TRUNK THAT HAS BEEN SQUARED AND PITH PLANK REMOVED.

F — SAWING A TRUNK INTO PLANKS BY FOLLOWING THE MEDULLARY RAYS.

A

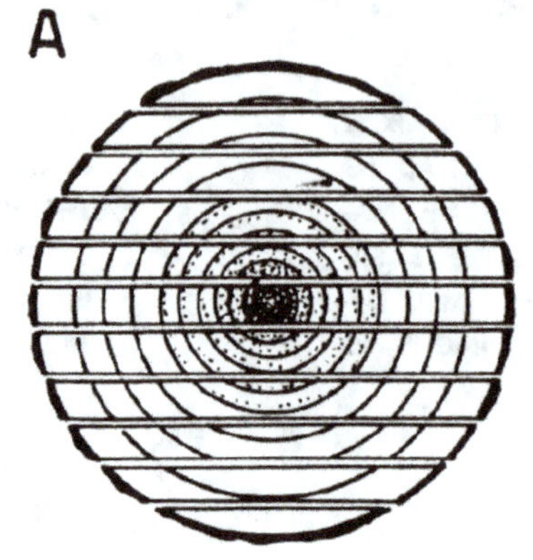

B

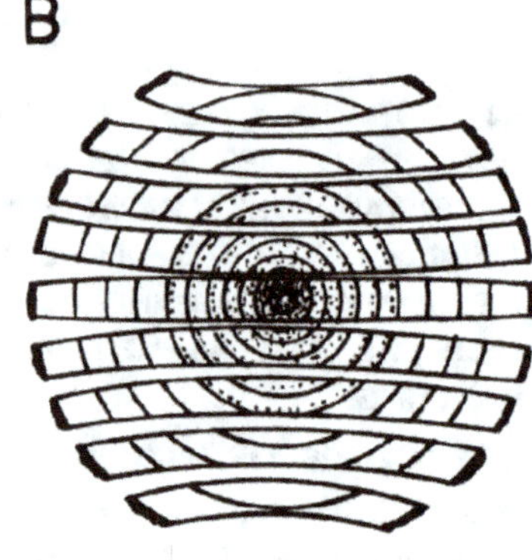

C

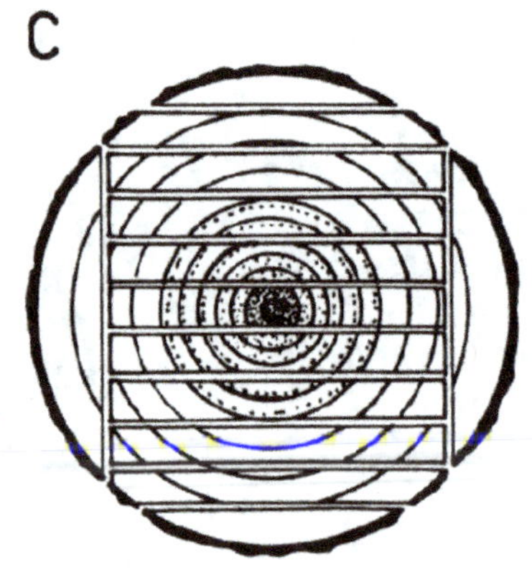

D

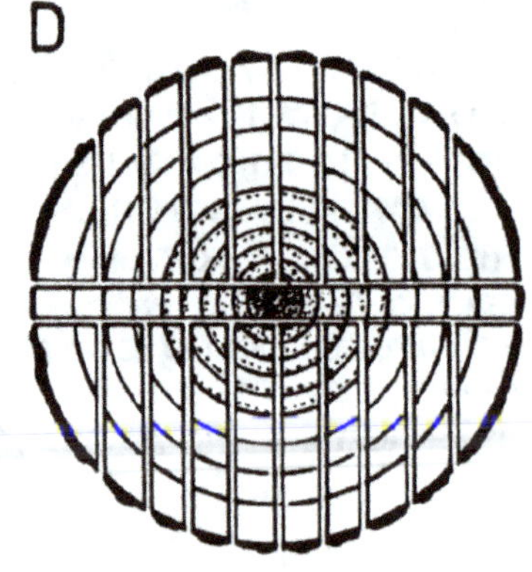

E

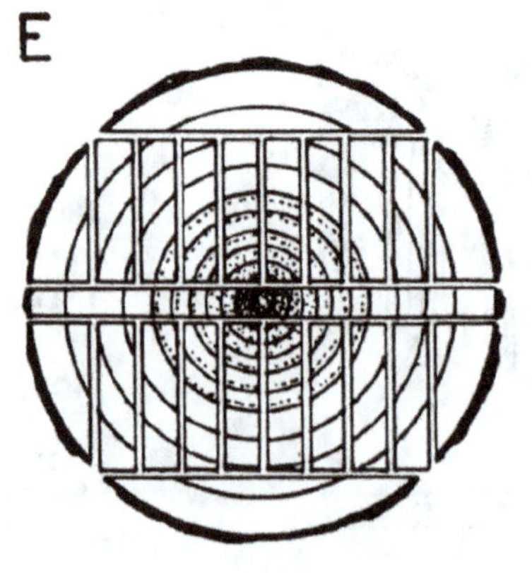

F

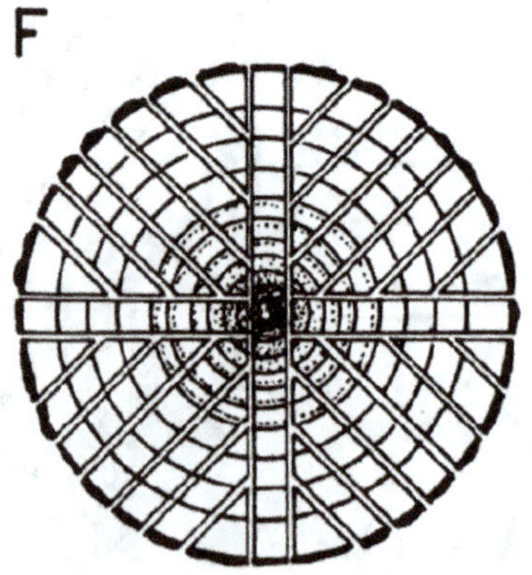

WOOD CHANGES

PLANKS UNDERGO SOME CHANGES DURING THE SEASONING PROCESS. THESE CHANGES ARE CALLED WARPING AND SHRINKING. SHRINKING IS MOST NOTICEABLE AT THE OUTER EDGES OF THE PLANK BECAUSE THE ANNUAL RINGS OF THE SAPWOOD ARE FRESHER AND LESS DENSE. THE GENERAL CHANGE THE PLANK UNDERGOES AFTER BEING CUT IS CALLED WARPING.

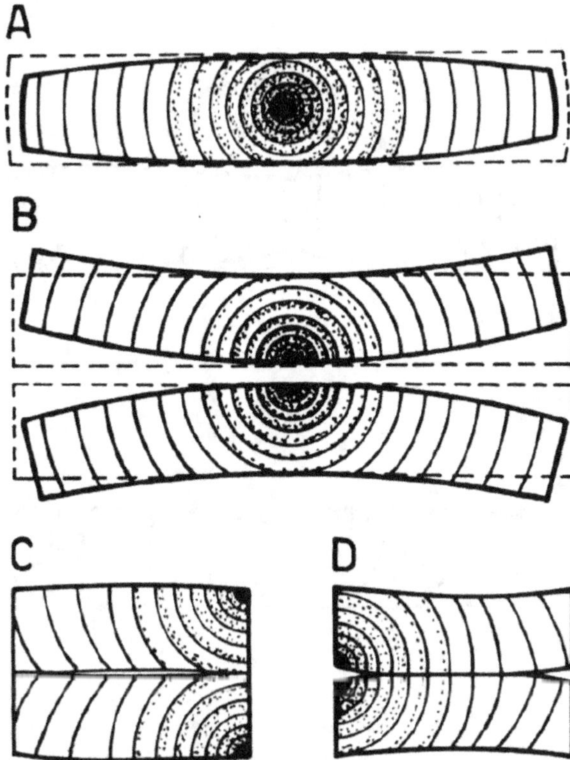

A — WARPING WHICH TAKES PLACE IN A PLANK WHICH INCLUDES THE PITH.

B — WARPING AND CURVATURE OF PARALLEL SAWED PLANKS. NOTE HOW THE CURVATURE RUNS IN A DIRECTION OPPOSITE TO THE ARC FORMED BY THE ANNUAL RINGS.

C — ALIGNING OR JOINING OF TWO PLANKS MUST BE DONE ON THEIR CONCAVE SIDES.

D — JOINING TWO PLANKS ON THEIR CONVEX SIDES WILL PRODUCE A WEAK JOINT.

SEASONING OF LUMBER

IT IS ESSENTIAL THAT LUMBER BE WELL SEASONED BEFORE IT IS USED. THE USUAL METHODS ARE AS FOLLOWS:

NATURAL SEASONING: IN THIS METHOD SAWED LUMBER IS EXPOSED TO FREE AIR AFTER IT HAS BEEN CAREFULLY STACKED. WHILE THE PROCEDURE IS SLOW, THE LUMBER PROCESSED IN THIS WAY IS THE LEAST SUBJECT TO SPLIT OR DECAY.

WATER SEASONING: A SOMEWHAT QUICKER METHOD OF SEASONING CONSISTS OF IMMERSING THE LUMBER IN RUNNING WATER FOR ABOUT ONE MONTH. THE WATER ENTERING THE PORES OF THE WOOD WASHES OUT THE SAP. THE LUMBER IS DRIED IN THE OPEN AIR.

ARTIFICIAL SEASONING: IN THIS METHOD THE LUMBER IS PLACED IN A DRYING KILN. A CURRENT OF HOT AIR IS ALLOWED TO CIRCULATE CONTINUOUSLY BETWEEN THE LAYERS OF LUMBER. IN SOME CASES STEAM IS USED. THIS IS THE QUICKEST METHOD.

GLUING WOOD

ONE OF THE ADVANTAGES OF WOOD IS THAT PIECES MAY BE JOINED TOGETHER BY GLUE.

AMONG THE OLDER ADHESIVES STILL USED IN WOODWORKING ARE THE PROTEIN ADHESIVES WHICH ARE WATER SOLUBLE, NON-STAINING AND EASY TO HANDLE. CASEIN GLUE MADE FROM SKIM MILK IS ALSO USED. FISH BASE AND BLOOD ALBUMIN GLUES ARE SUITABLE, BUT REQUIRE HEATING TO 140° TO 180° F BEFORE APPLICATION.

AMONG THE SYNTHETIC GLUES NOW USED ARE THE PHENOLS, RESORCINOL, MALAMINE AND UREA ADHESIVES. RUBBER BASE ADHESIVES, ANOTHER GROUP, ARE OFTEN USED TO JOIN WOOD AND METAL.

IN ORDER TO JOIN TWO PIECES OF WOOD IT IS NECESSARY THAT THEY BE PLACED TOGETHER SO THAT THE GRAIN IS PARALLEL. AFTER THE PIECES ARE PREPARED, THE GLUE IS APPLIED TO THE SURFACE OF EACH PIECE AND IN TURN THEY ARE CLAMPED OR PRESSED TOGETHER FOR FOUR TO TWELVE HOURS ACCORDING TO THE TYPE OF GLUE USED.

COLORING WOOD

BEST RESULTS DEPEND UPON THE ABILITY OF THE PERSON APPLYING THE COLOR. AFTER INITIAL SANDPAPERING, A STAIN MAY BE USED TO CHANGE THE NATURAL COLORING OF THE WOOD. THIS COLORING MATERIAL MAY BE MADE BY ADDING CHROMA IN TUBES, POWDER OR GRANULES TO WATER OR ALCOHOL. THIS MATERIAL IS THEN BRUSHED, RUBBED OR SPRAYED ON THE WOOD SURFACE.

FINISHING WOOD

GENERALLY, WOOD IS FINISHED WITH LACQUER APPLIED BY SPRAY IN THIN LAYERS OVER THE PREPARED SURFACE. WHEN DRY, THE LACQUER WILL FORM A SOLID TRANSPARENT LAYER. A FINAL FINISH MAY BE ADDED BY RUBBING WITH A PREPARED COMPOUND EITHER BY HAND OR BY USE OF A BUFFING WHEEL. ONE OF THE OLDEST METHODS OF FINISHING IS FRENCH POLISHING, WHICH CONSISTS OF RUBBING A MIXTURE OF ONE PART SHELLAC TO THREE PARTS ALCOHOL OVER THE SURFACE WITH A RUBBER BLOCK.

METHODS OF JOINING BOARDS

PARALLEL BUTT JOINT

WHEN PLANKS ARE SAWED FROM THE TRUNK, IT IS OFTEN FOUND THAT THEY ARE NOT LARGE ENOUGH FOR THE PARTICULAR WORK INVOLVED. IN ORDER TO OBTAIN THE DESIRED WIDTH OR LENGTH IT IS NECESSARY TO GLUE ONE OR MORE PIECES TOGETHER WITH WHAT IS CALLED A SIDE OR END JOINT.

IN ORDER TO OBTAIN AN INVISIBLE JOINT IN EXPOSED PANELS IT IS NECESSARY THAT A UNION OF PARALLEL JOINTS BE MADE BY AN ACCURATE ALIGNMENT OF THE GRAIN. AS IN ALL OTHER TYPES OF JOINTS, THERE ARE MANY WAYS OF JOINING THESE PARTS. EACH METHOD HAS ITS OWN PARTICULAR USE, DEPENDING ON THE TYPE OF WORK INVOLVED.

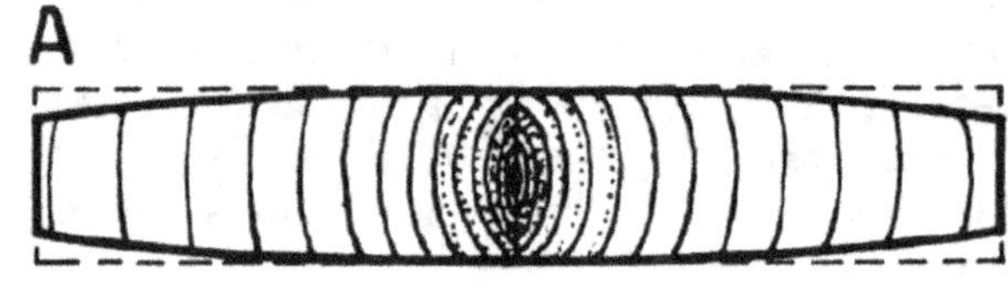

A — BECAUSE THE PLANKS SAWED FROM THE CENTER OF THE TREE TRUNK ARE CONSIDERED THE WEAKEST, IT IS ADVISABLE TO SAW THEM IN TWO AND GLUE THEM TOGETHER TO GIVE THEM STABILITY AND STRENGTH.

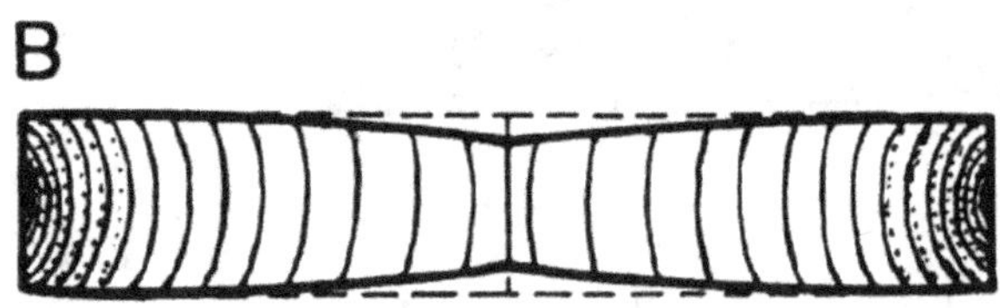

B — TO OBTAIN BEST RESULTS, THE JOINING OF TWO PLANKS SHOULD BE ACCOMPLISHED BY MATCHING THE EXTERNAL RINGS, OR INTERIOR RINGS, IN ORDER TO EQUALIZE WHATEVER SHRINKING OR WARPING TAKES PLACE.

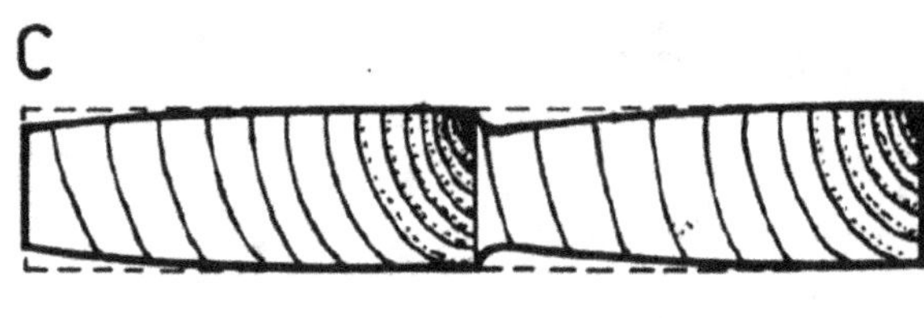

C — IF THE EXTERNAL PART OF THE LUMBER IS CONNECTED WITH THE INTERNAL PART, A VERY BAD JOINT MAY BE THE RESULT. THERE WILL BE NO PROPER SEASONING OF THE TWO PIECES AND AFTER A PERIOD OF TIME THERE WILL BE A NOTICEABLE DEMARCATION OF THE WHOLE JOINT.

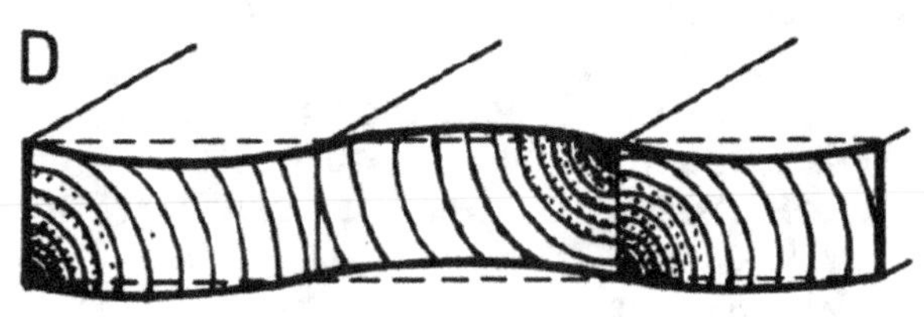

D — TO OBTAIN BEST RESULTS IN A SOLID PANEL IT IS NECESSARY TO HAVE THE EDGE STRAIGHT TO FORM A PERFECT JOINT. IT IS OF UTMOST IMPORTANCE TO SEE THAT THE GRAIN OF EACH PLANK IS ALTERNATED WITH THE NEXT IN ORDER TO EQUALIZE THE STRAIN MADE BY THE ANNUAL RINGS.

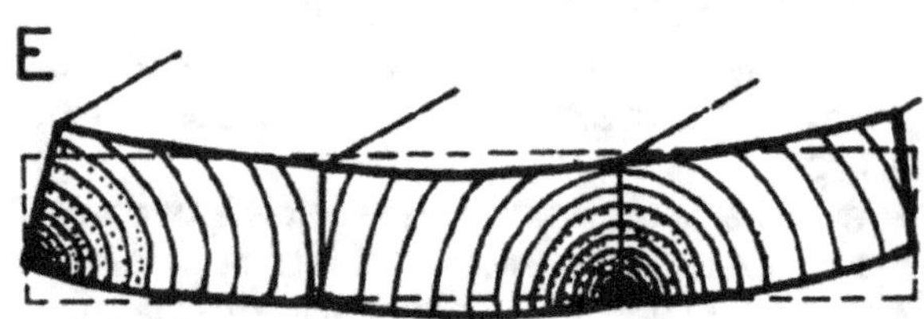

E — HERE IS AN EXAMPLE OF WHAT WOULD HAPPEN IF ATTENTION WERE NOT PAID TO PARAGRAPH D. THE PLANK WOULD HAVE A TENDENCY TO CURVE.

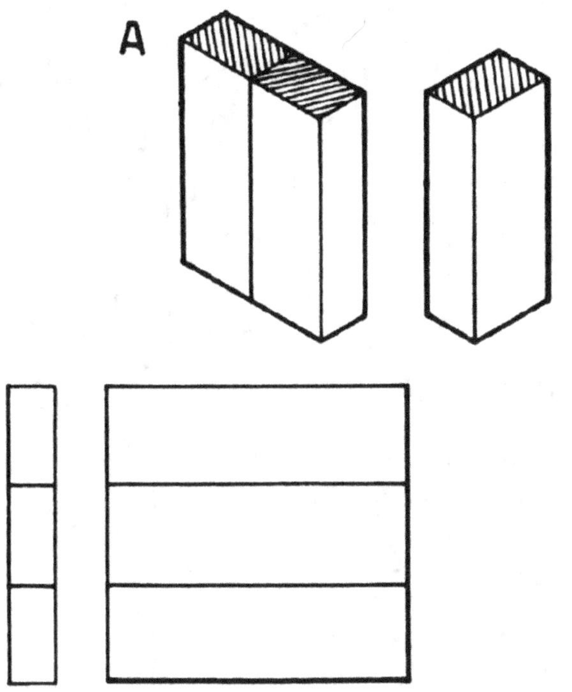

STRAIGHT JOINT: THIS IS ONE OF THE SIMPLEST AND MOST FREQUENTLY USED JOINTS.

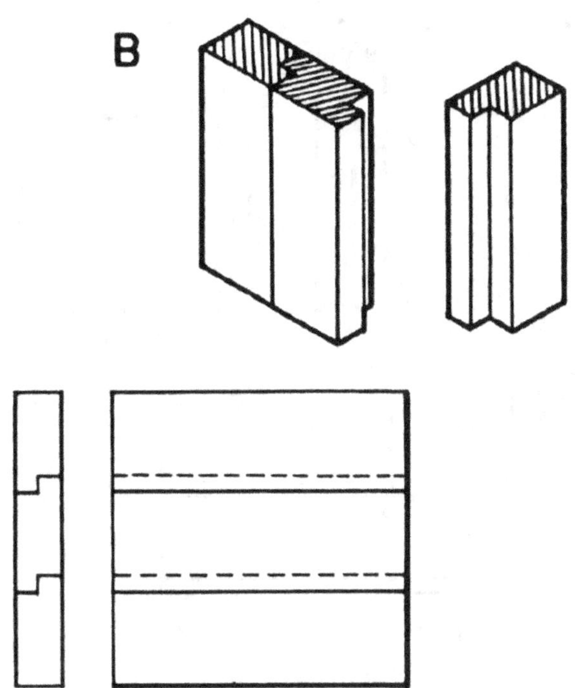

RABBET JOINT: SIMILAR TO THE PRECEDING METHOD, BUT SELDOM USED BECAUSE IT IS MORE DIFFICULT.

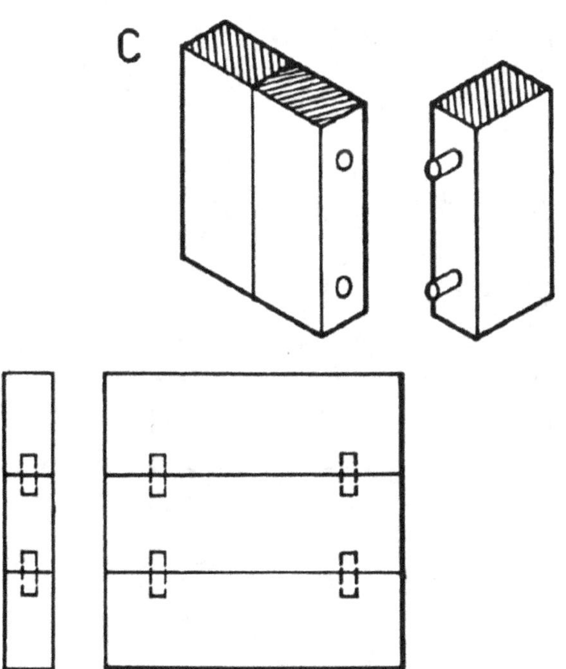

DOWEL JOINT: A COMMON METHOD, OFTEN USED WHERE THE TOTAL AREA IS LARGE.

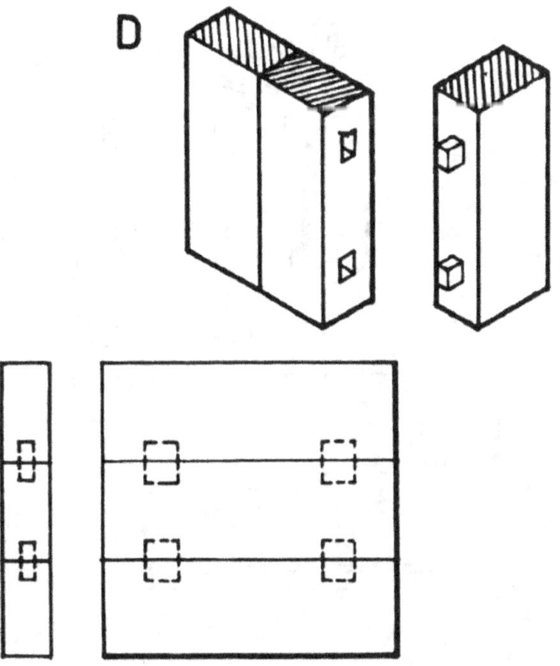

MORTISE AND TENON JOINT: THIS METHOD IS LESS OFTEN USED THAN THE JOINT AT LEFT.

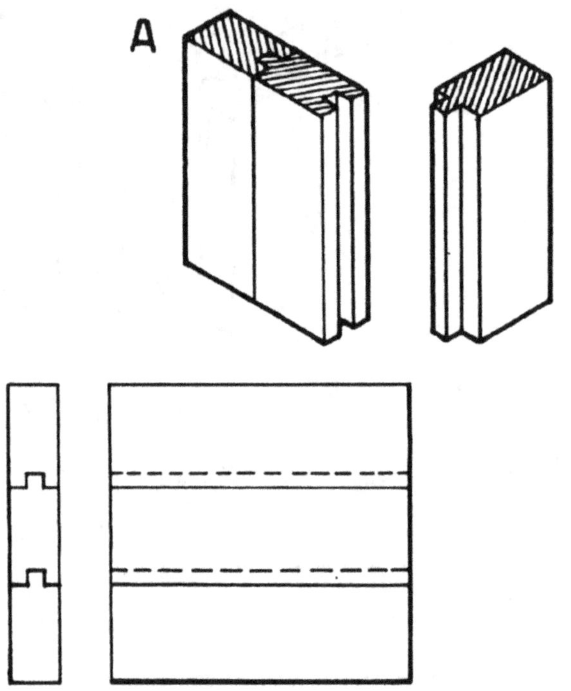

TONGUE AND GROOVE: FLOORING IS USUALLY MADE
THIS WAY. IT IS ALSO PRACTICAL IN FURNITURE WORK.

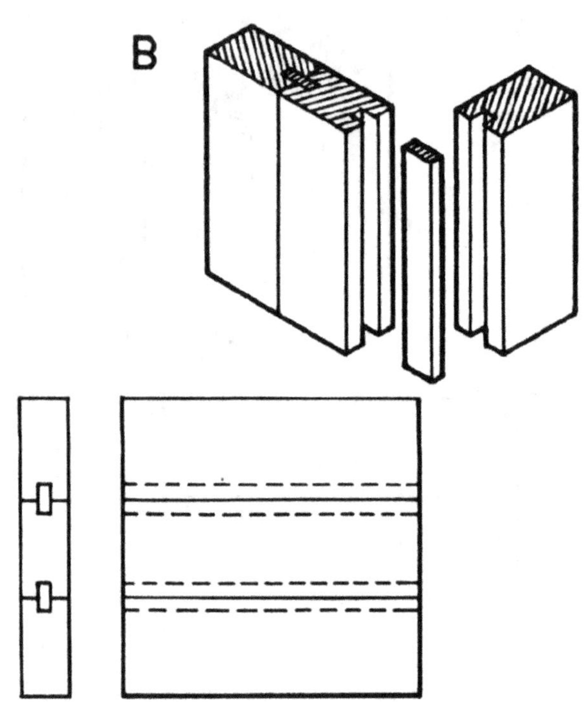

FEATHER JOINT: THIS IS ONE OF THE BEST AND MOST
PRACTICAL WAYS OF JOINING PARALLEL PLANES.

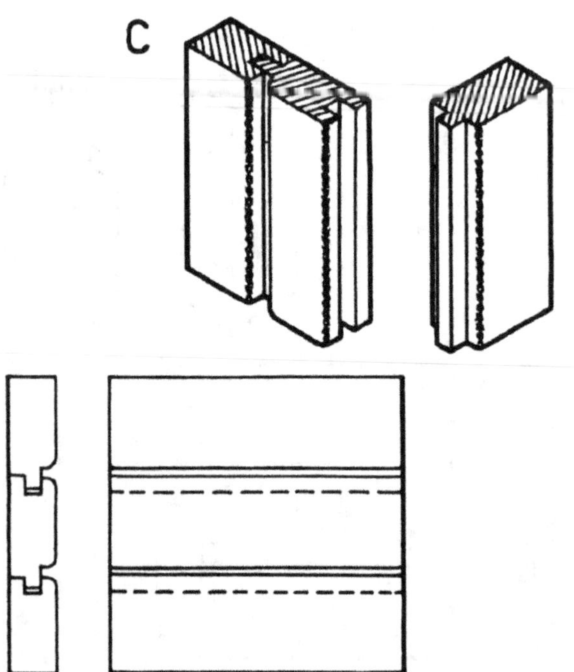

LOOSE TONGUE AND GROOVE: WITH ROUNDED OR
BEVELED EDGES, THIS JOINT IS OFTEN USED IN WALL
PANELING.

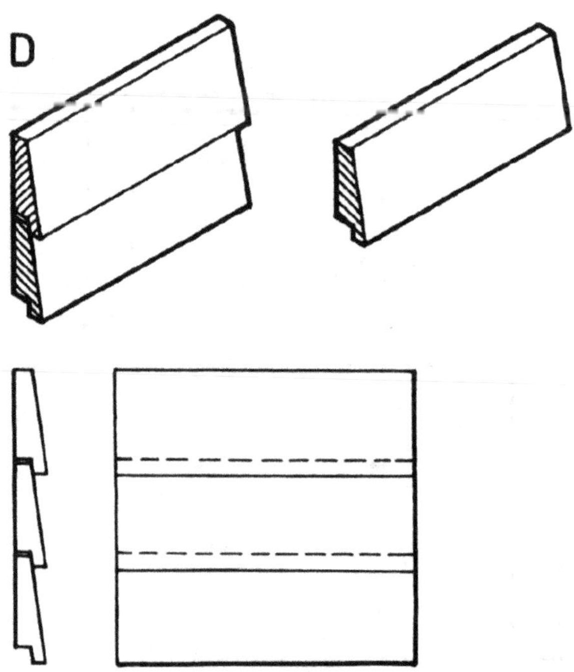

SHIP LAP JOINT: THIS METHOD IS USED EXTENSIVELY
FOR SIDING ON HOMES. IT IS EASY TO MAKE A WATER-
TIGHT JOINT IN THIS WAY.

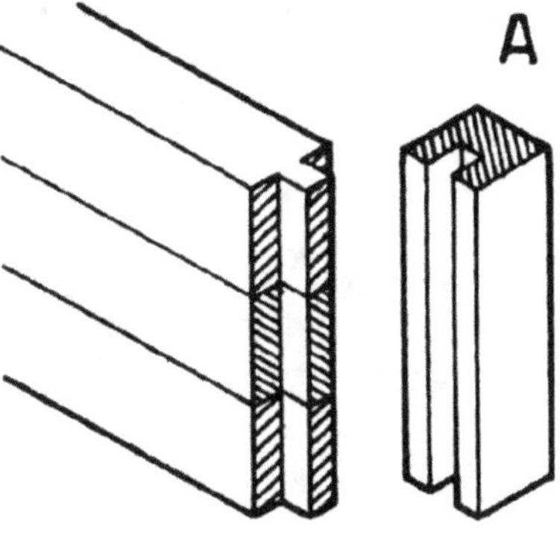 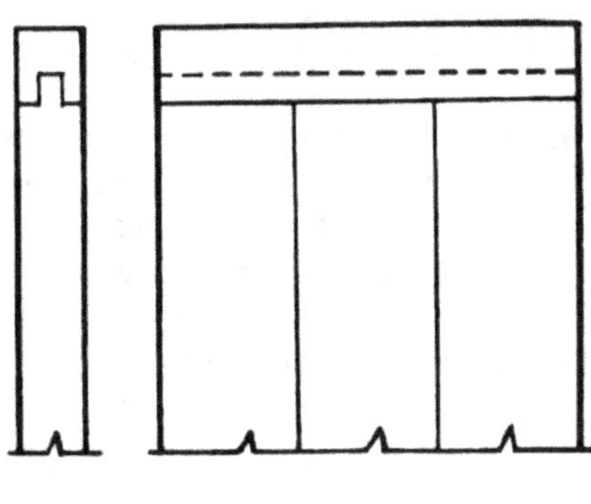

DRAWING BOARD USING A TONGUE AND GROOVE JOINT. THE TRANSVERSE RAIL IS USED TO AVOID WARPING IN THE PLANK.

A

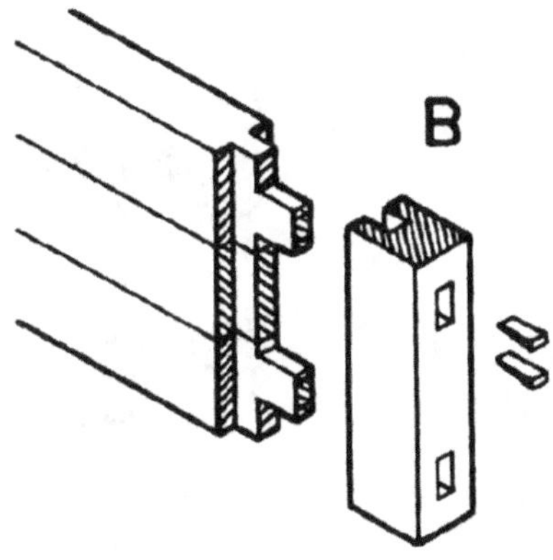 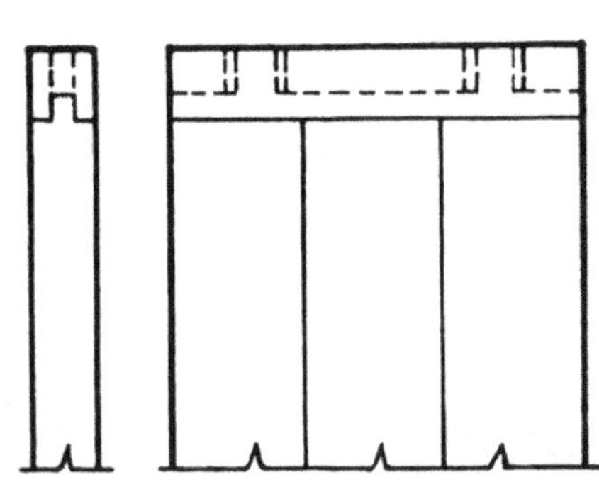

WEDGE MORTISE AND TENON: THIS METHOD IS USED WHEN WORK IS TO BE EXPOSED TO INCLEMENT WEATHER.

B

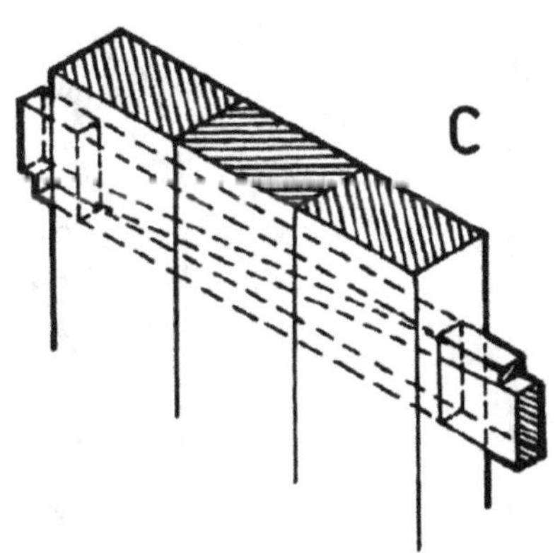 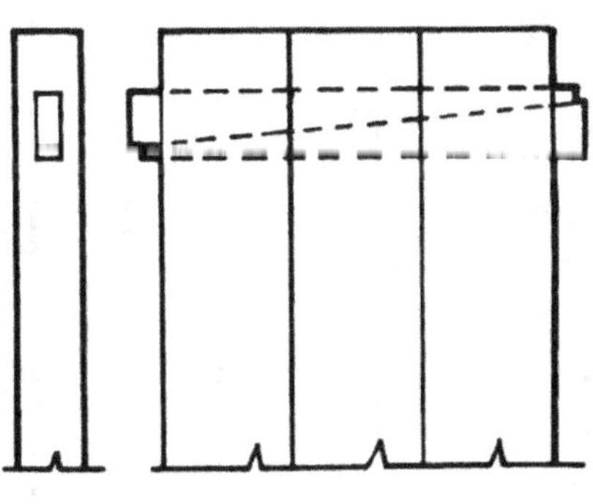

STRAIGHT JOINT WITH WEDGES.

C

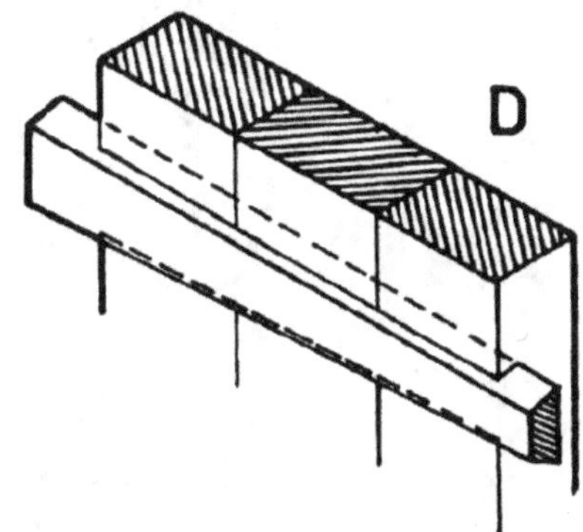 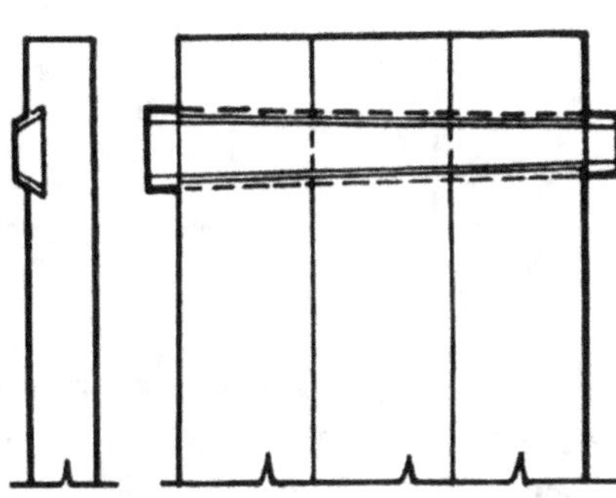

STRAIGHT JOINT WITH DOVE-TAIL WEDGE: THIS IS A GOOD METHOD TO USE WITH A STRAIGHT JOINT AND FOR OUTSIDE WORK.

D

BUTT JOINTS

THE END BUTT JOINT IS NOT OFTEN USED IN FURNITURE WORK FOR PRACTICAL REASONS: IT IS NOT STRONG, GLUE WILL NOT ADHERE EASILY TO ITS SURFACES, AND THE JOINT IS ALWAYS VISIBLE. WHEN POSSIBLE, IT IS BEST TO AVOID THIS TYPE OF CONSTRUCTION IN CABINET WORK.

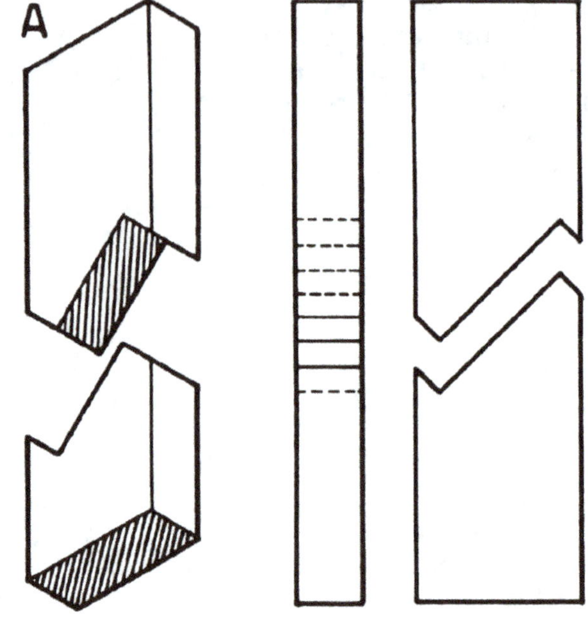

ZIG ZAG BUTT JOINT: THIS JOINT HAS GREATER CONTACT WITH THE WOOD GRAIN AND IS, THEREFORE, STRONGER THAN A RIGHT ANGLE BUTT JOINT.

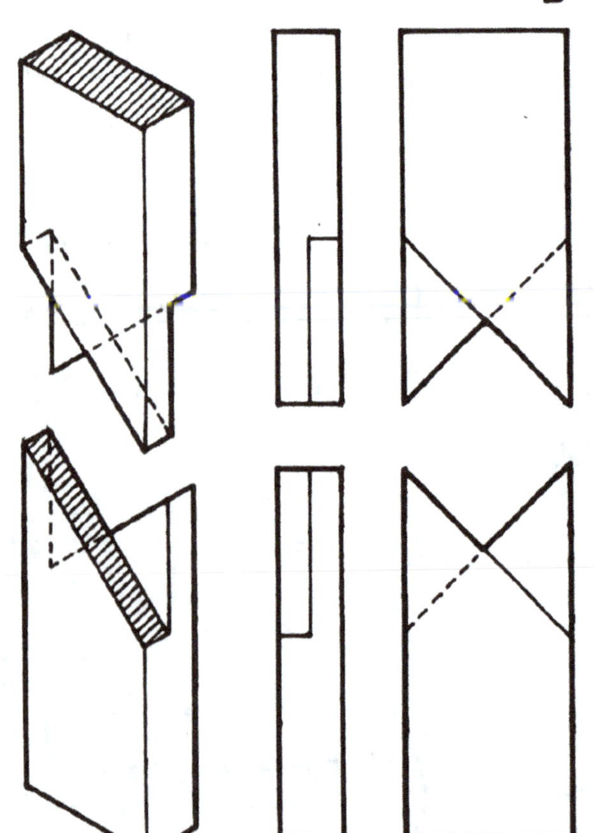

FORK BUTT JOINT: A GOOD JOINT IS OBTAINED BECAUSE THE NATURAL CONTACT OF THE SURFACES PERMITS GOOD GLUE ADHESION.

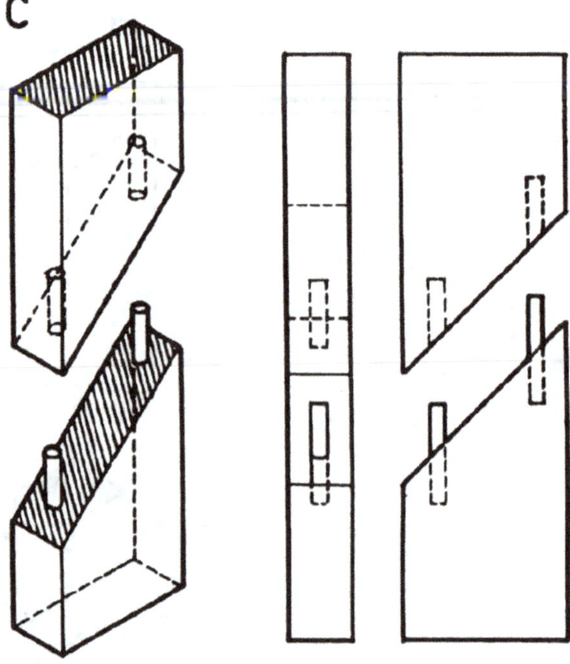

DOWEL BUTT JOINT: THE DOWELS STRENGTHEN THE JOINT. GLUE IS USED WITH ALL OF THESE JOINTS.

DOUBLE DOVETAIL BUTT JOINT: THIS IS USED IN CASES WHERE THE JOINT IS SUBJECT TO STRAIN.

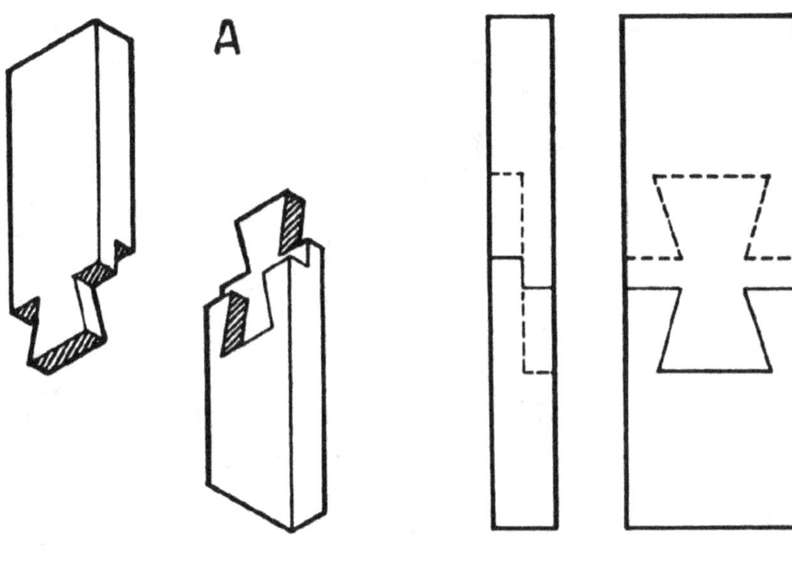

TENSION SCARF JOINT: THIS JOINT IS HELD IN PLACE BY WOODEN WEDGES, AND IS USED MOSTLY IN ORDINARY CARPENTRY.

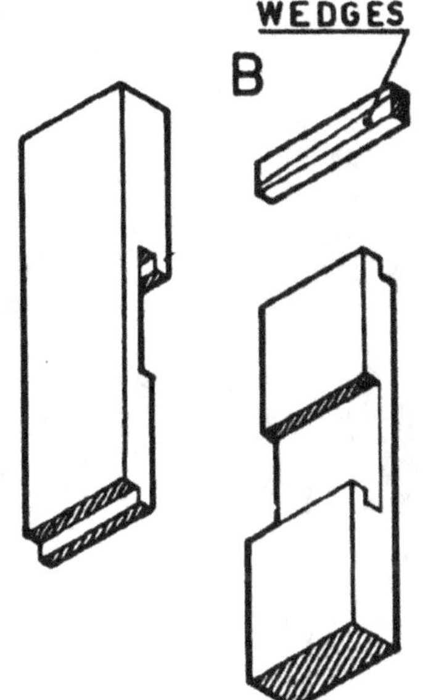

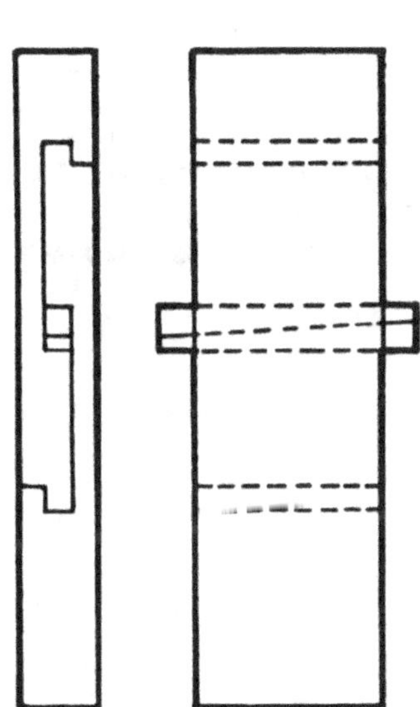

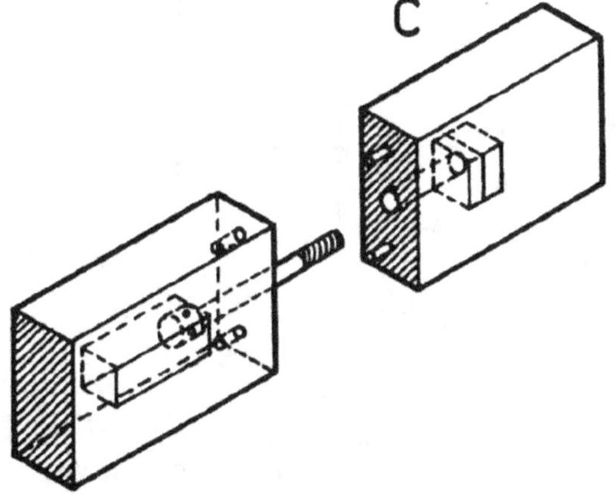

DOWEL AND BOLT BUTT JOINT: THIS IS DONE WITH DOWELS AND CLOSED WITH BOLTS INCASED IN THE WOOD.

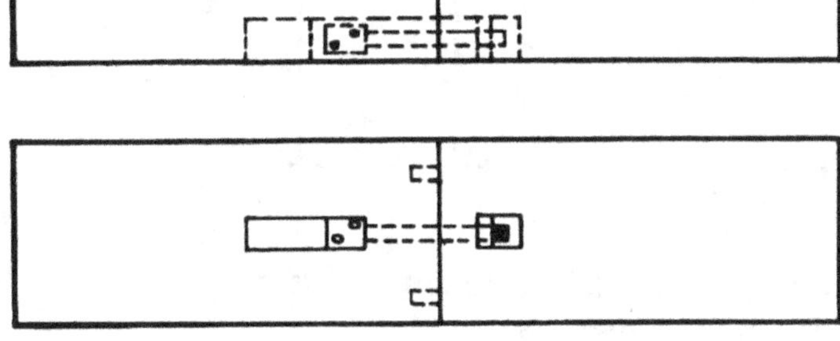

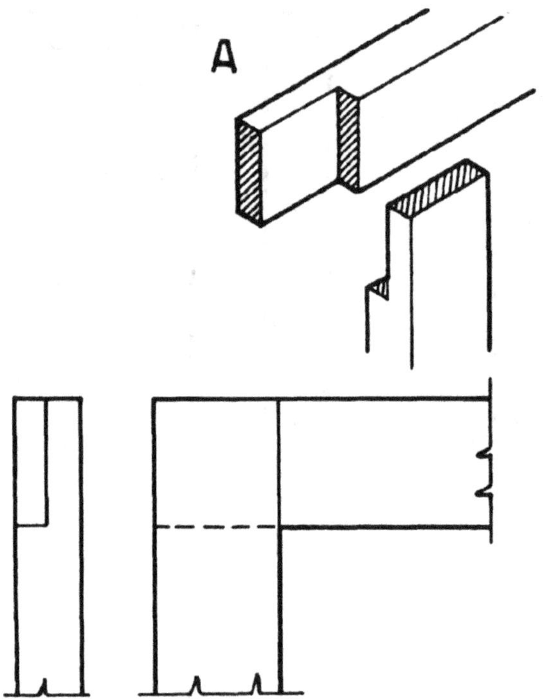

ANGLE RAIL JOINTS

THE PREPARATION FOR ANGLE RAIL JOINTS IS OF GREAT IMPORTANCE. THEY REPRESENT THE BASIC ELEMENT IN THE CONSTRUCTION OF FURNITURE PIECES. VARIOUS TYPES OF STRAIGHT RAILS AND TRANSVERSE RAILS MAY BE USED TO FORM VARIOUS TYPES OF FRAMES. EACH OF THESE JOINTS HAS INDIVIDUAL CHARACTERISTICS WHICH NECESSITATE CHOOSING THE RIGHT TYPE FOR THE WORK TO BE DONE. YOU MUST CONSIDER THE THICKNESS OF THE STRAIGHT AND TRANSVERSE RAILS, THE QUALITY OF WOOD, AND THE POSITION OF THE FRAME — WHETHER VISIBLE OR OBSCURED. AT TIMES A MIDDLE RAIL IS ADDED TO THE STRAIGHT AND TRANSVERSE RAILS FOR EXTRA SUPPORT. THE SERIES OF ILLUSTRATED EXAMPLES WILL GIVE YOU AN IDEA OF THE VARIOUS TYPES, AND EXPLAIN THE INDIVIDUAL CHARACTERISTICS OF EACH.

END HALF LAP JOINT: THIS JOINT IS EASILY CONSTRUCTED. UNLESS REINFORCED WITH PINS AND BOLTS OR SCREWS, IT DOES NOT MAKE A VERY DURABLE JOINT. IT IS USED MOSTLY IN REPAIR WORK.

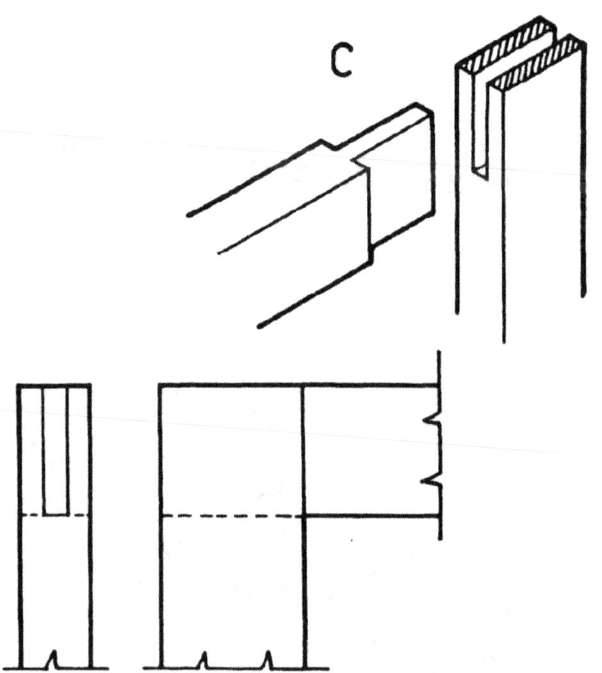

DOWEL JOINT: A COMMON JOINT AND USED IN ORDINARY REPAIR WORK.

THROUGH MORTISE AND TENON JOINT: THIS IS A JOINT OFTEN USED BY THE AMATEUR CRAFTSMAN.

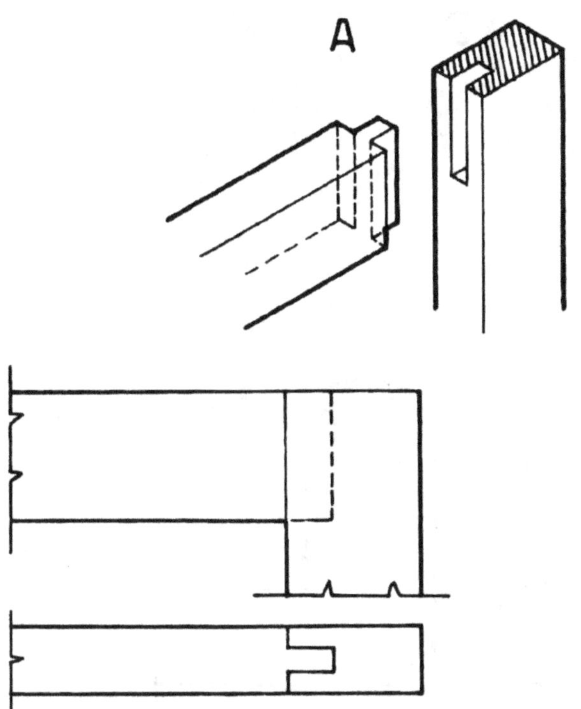

OPEN MORTISE AND TENON JOINT: THIS JOINT IS EASY TO MAKE AND IS USED FOR ORDINARY WORK.

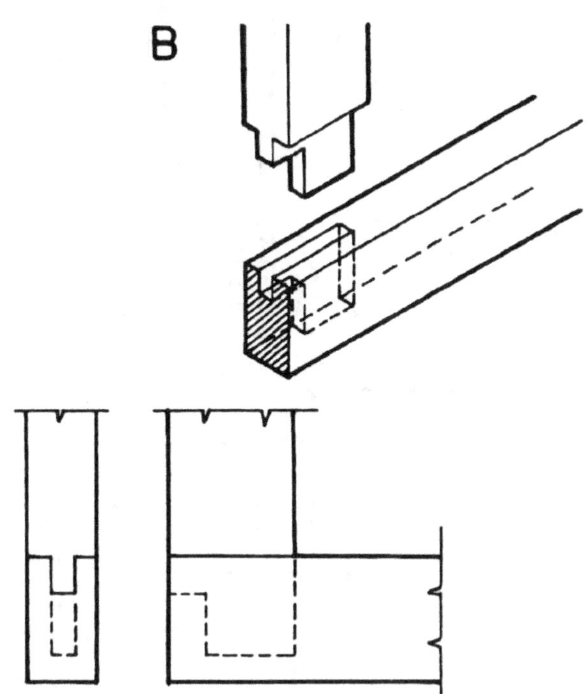

RABBET MORTISE AND STUB TENON JOINT: THIS IS THE MOST USED JOINT IN THE FURNITURE FIELD. IT HAS ALL THE REQUISITES OF THE PERFECT JOINT.

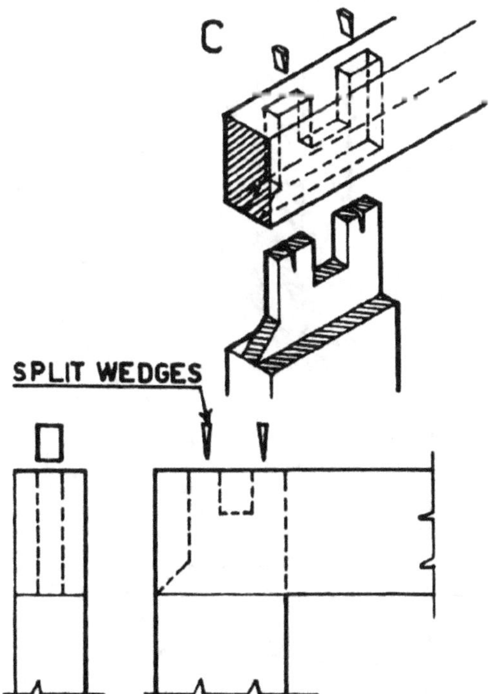

DOUBLE MORTISE AND TENON WITH MITER RABBET: THESE JOINTS ARE VERY STRONG AND PREFERRED WHERE THE WORK IS EXPOSED TO THE ELEMENTS.

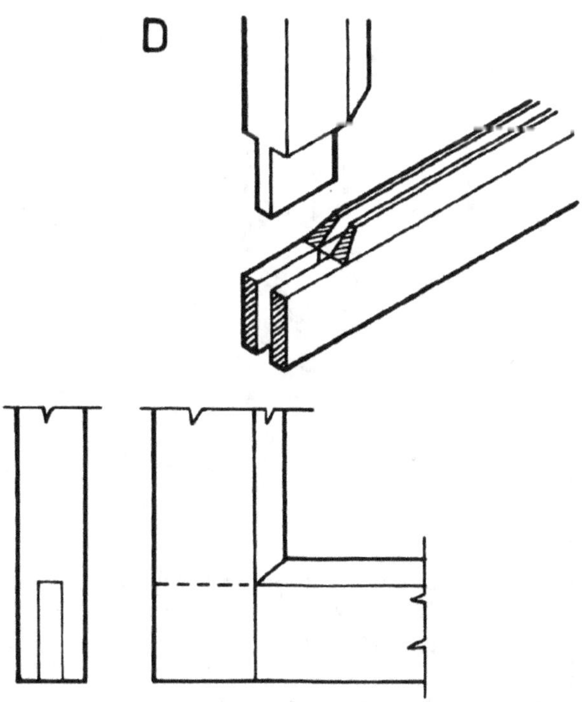

THROUGH MORTISE AND TENON WITH GROOVE END MITER ON THE INNER EDGE.

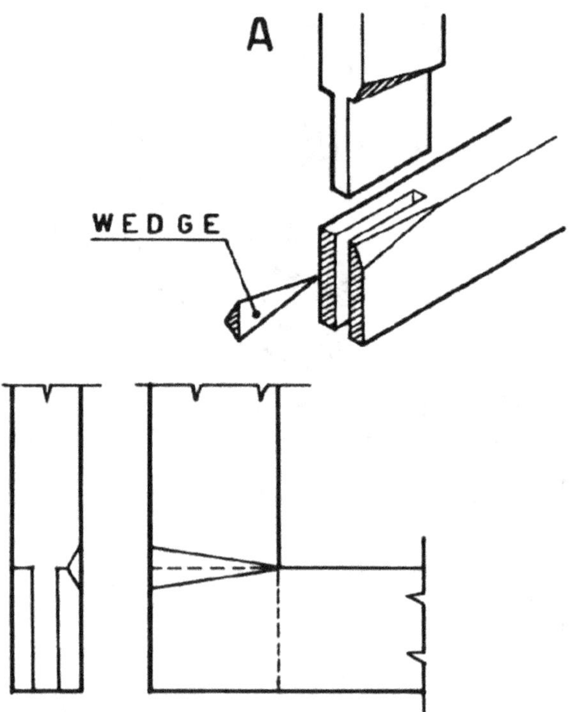

THROUGH MORTISE AND TENON WITH WEDGE IN THE SIDE JOINT USED FOR VENEER COVER. THE WEDGE ELIMINATES ANY MARK ON THE OUTSIDE OF THE VENEER.

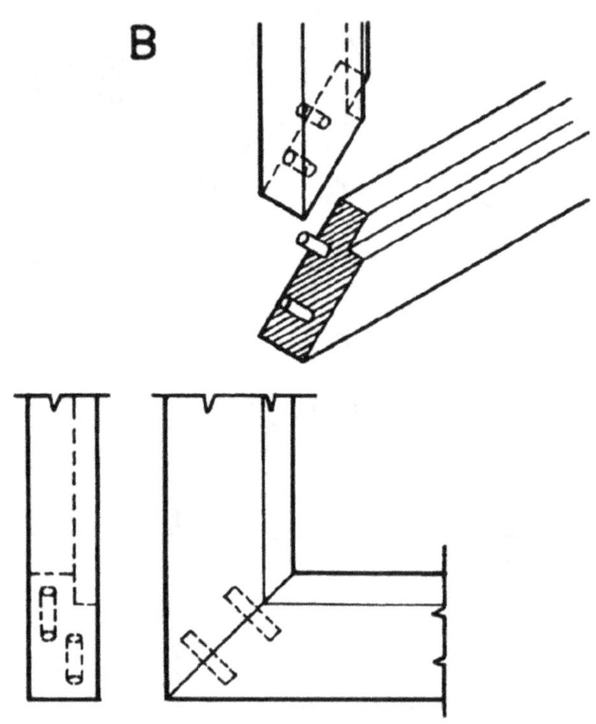

DOWEL MITER JOINT IS USED IN EVERY TYPE OF WORK.

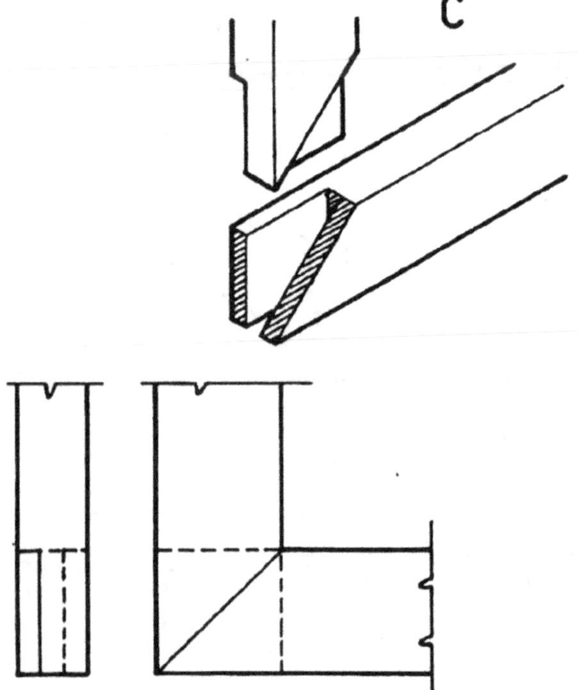

OPEN MORTISE AND TENON WITH MITER.

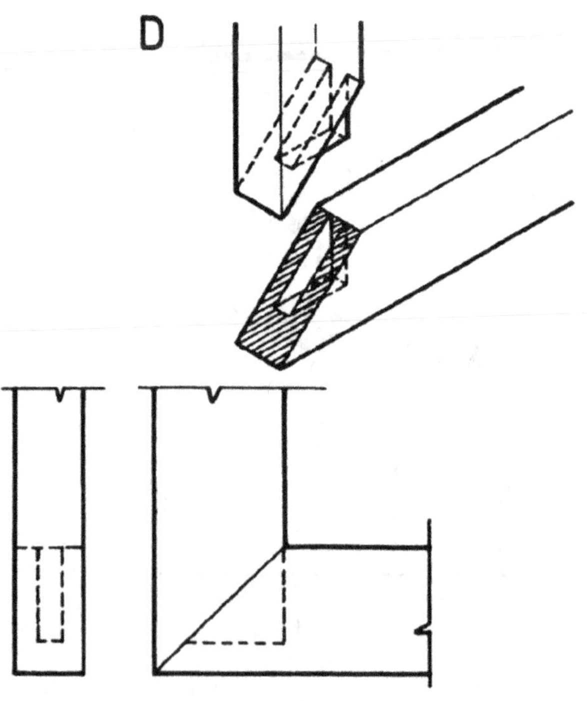

MITER WITH BLIND MORTISE AND TENON.

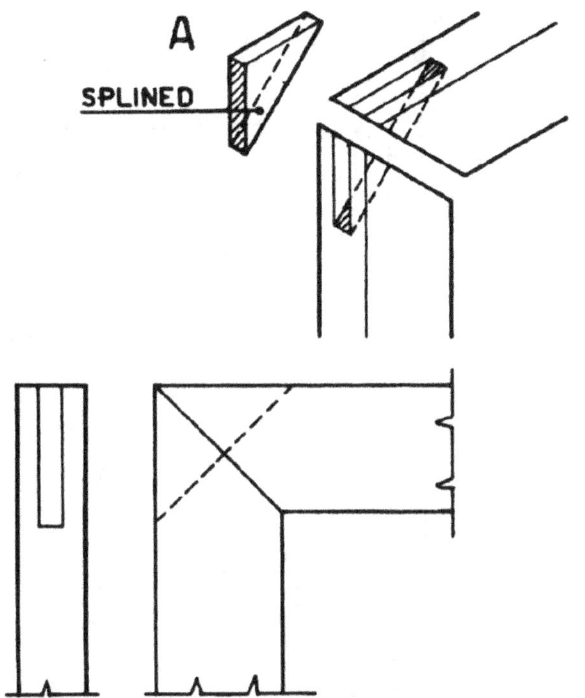

MITER JOINT WITH SPLINE: THIS JOINT IS EASY TO MAKE AND USED IN WORK DONE BY THE AMATEUR CRAFTSMAN.

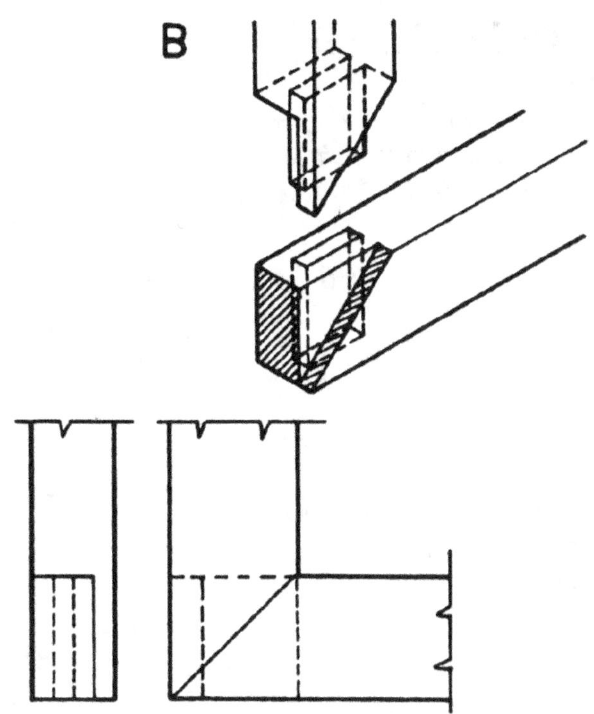

MITER MORTISE AND TENON JOINT: A VERY STRONG JOINT USED FOR WORK EXPOSED TO HUMIDITY.

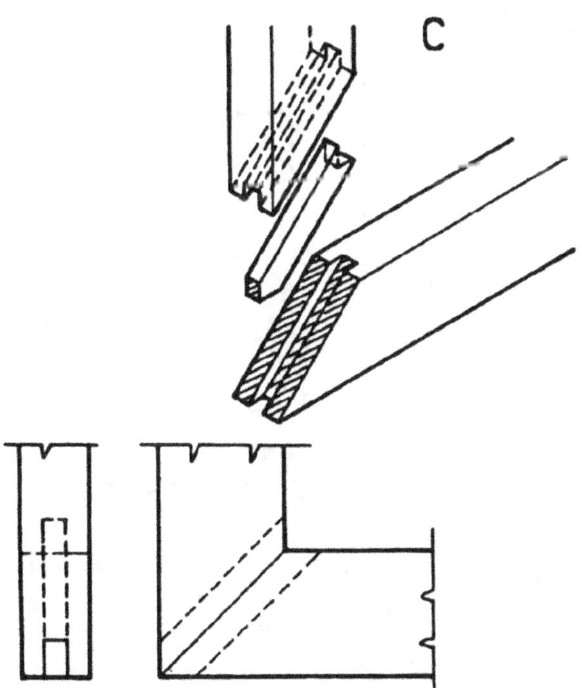

MITER TONGUE JOINT: THIS IS VERY COMMON IN STANDARD PRODUCTION.

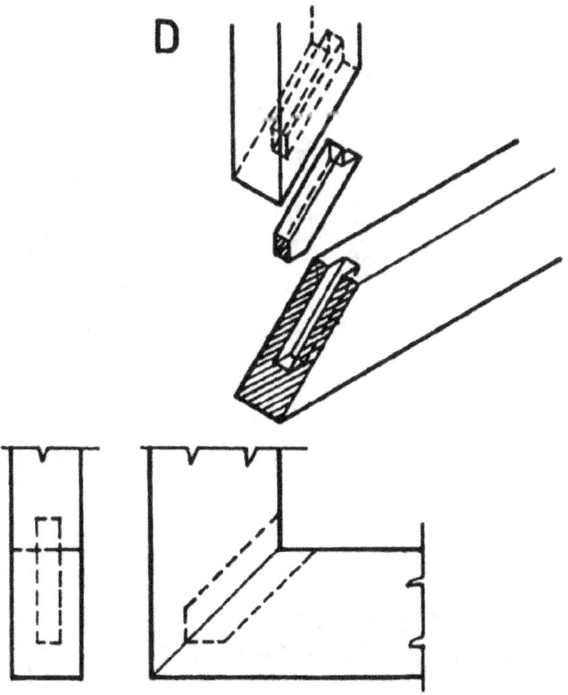

MITER STUB TONGUE JOINT: SAME AS PRECEDING ONE EXCEPT THAT FEATHER JOINT IS INVISIBLE.

MIDDLE RAIL JOINTS

LAP TEE JOINT: OFTEN USED BY THE AMATEUR CRAFTSMAN; ALSO IN REPAIR WORK.

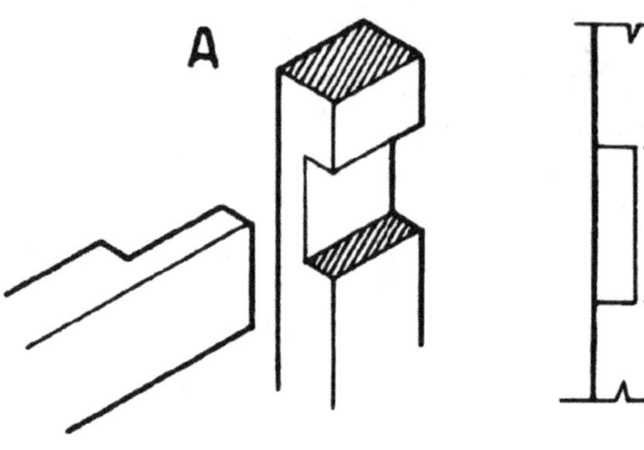
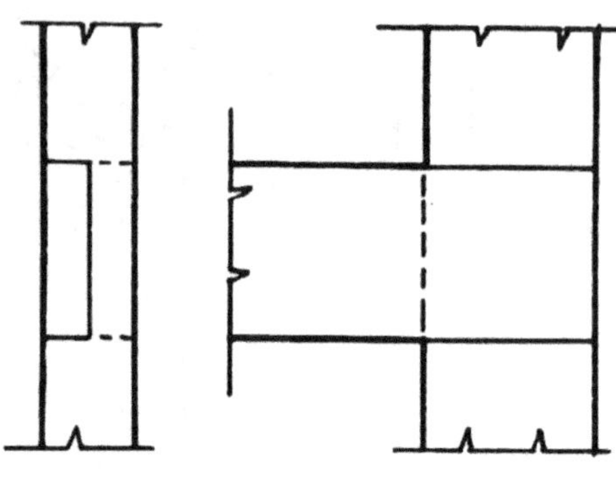

DOWEL JOINT: VARIOUS TYPES OF WORK REQUIRE THIS TYPE OF JOINT.

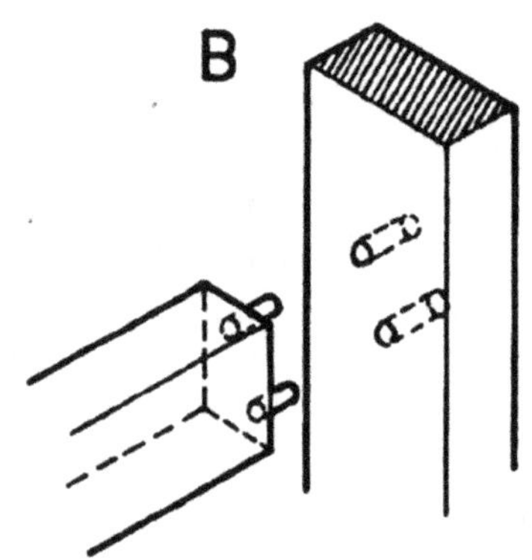
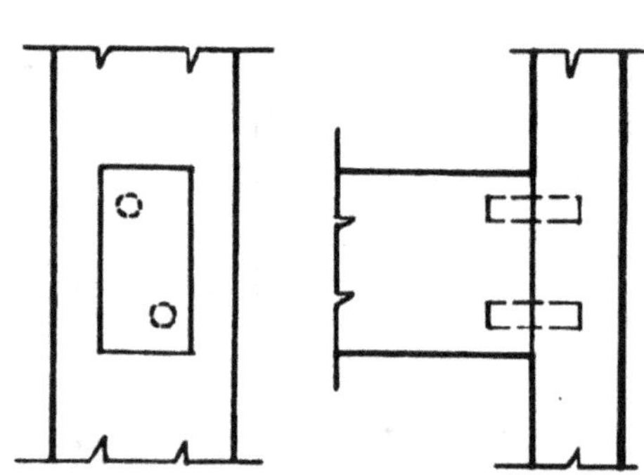

BLIND MORTISE AND TENON: THIS IS AN EASILY MADE JOINT THAT IS USED EXTENSIVELY.

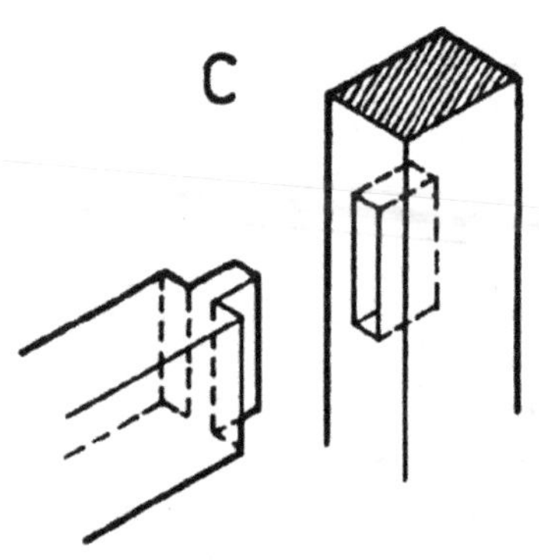
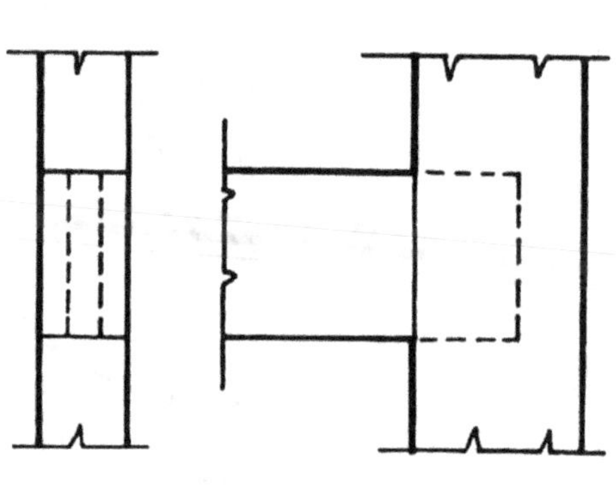

THROUGH MORTISE AND TEN-ON JOINT: WITH THE ADDI-TION OF THE WEDGE THIS IS A VERY STRONG JOINT. IT IS USED IN WORK EXPOSED TO WEATHER.

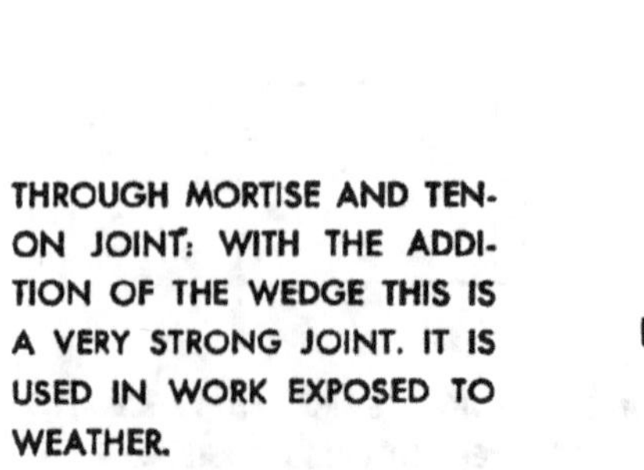
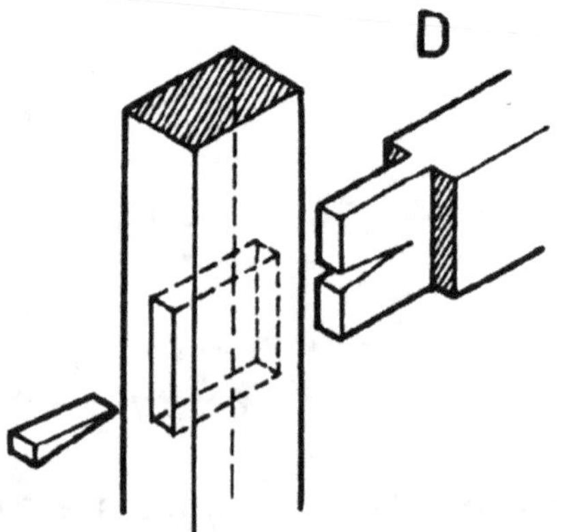
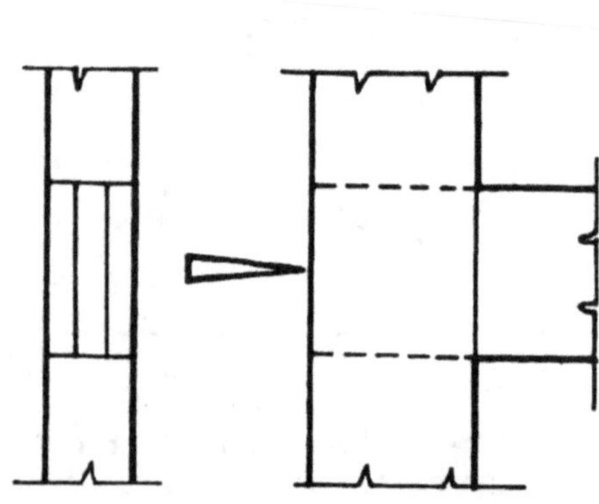

DOVETAIL STUB JOINT: THIS METHOD IS USED TO STRENGTHEN THE FRAME WHERE UNUSUAL STRAIN TAKES PLACE.

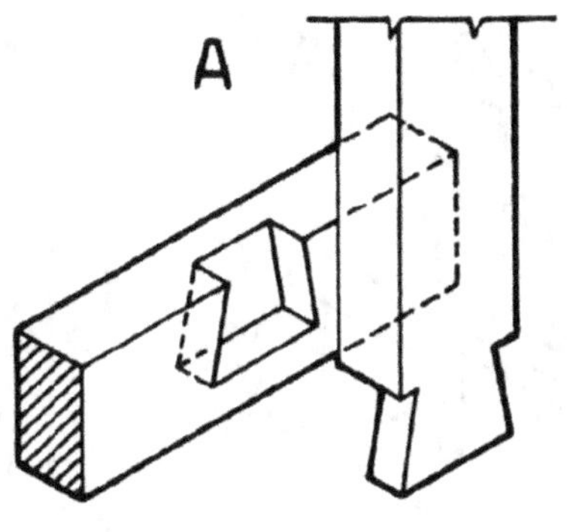

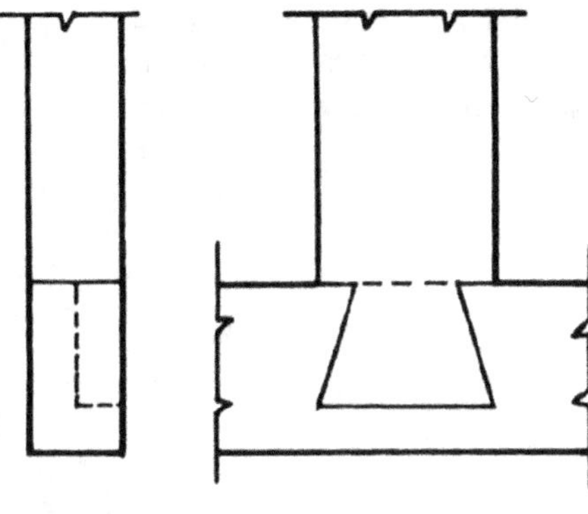

OBLIQUE DOVETAIL JOINT: SAME AS ABOVE EXCEPT THAT TONGUE RUNS THROUGH AND JOINT IS IN OBLIQUE POSITION.

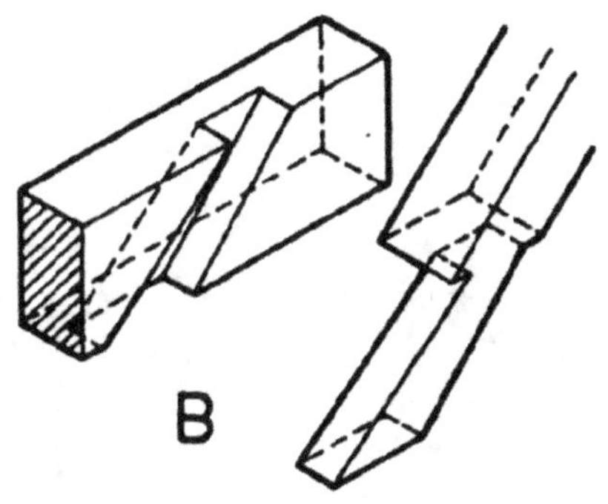

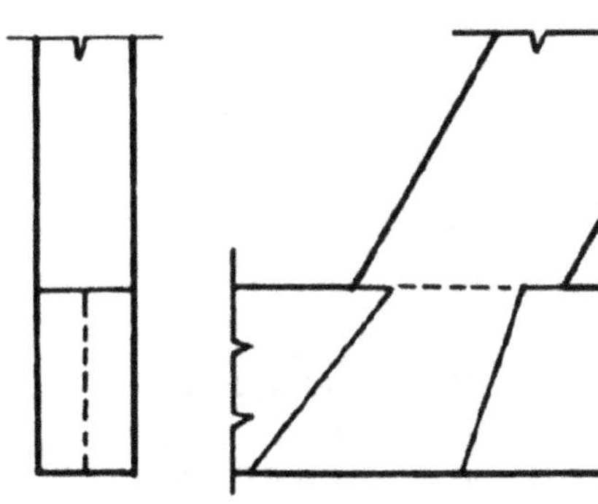

SPECIAL DOVETAIL JOINT: THIS IS DIFFICULT TO MAKE AND IS USED ONLY WHEN PRECISION WORK IS REQUIRED.

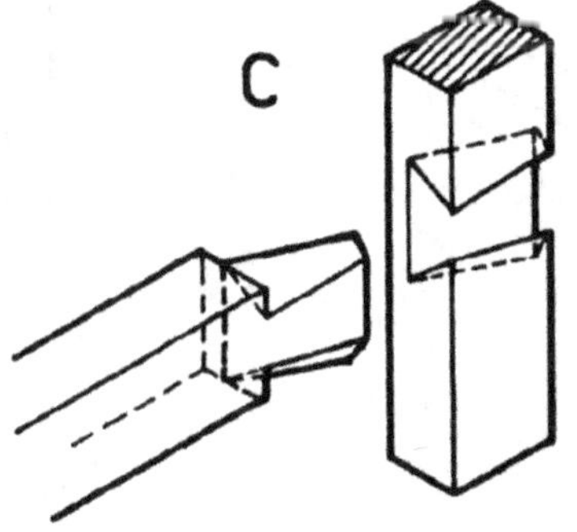

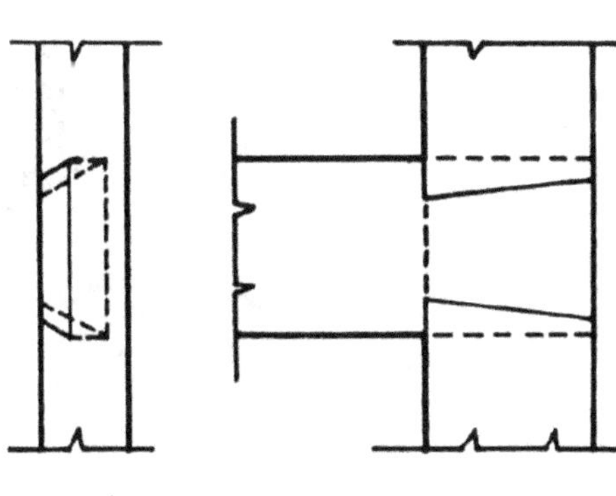

DOUBLE DOVETAIL JOINT: THE PRINCIPLE HERE IS THE SAME AS IN A SINGLE DOVETAIL JOINT. BOTH SYSTEMS ARE USED WHERE THERE IS GREAT STRAIN.

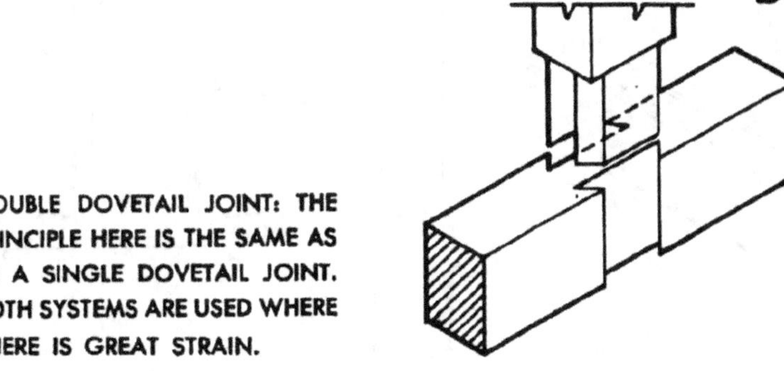

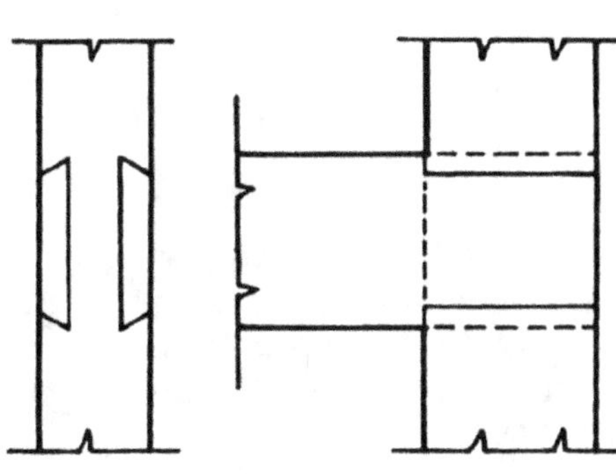

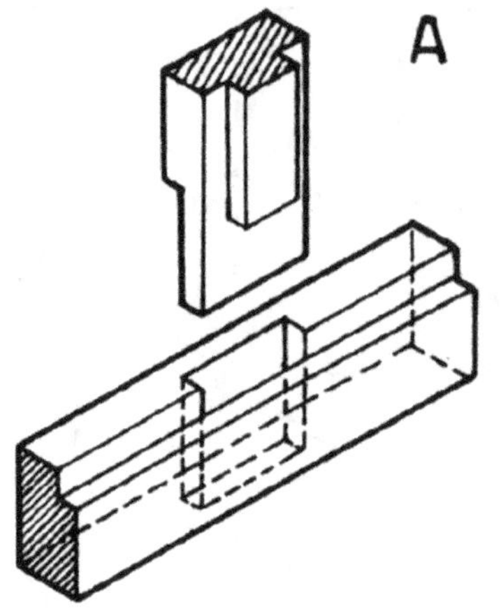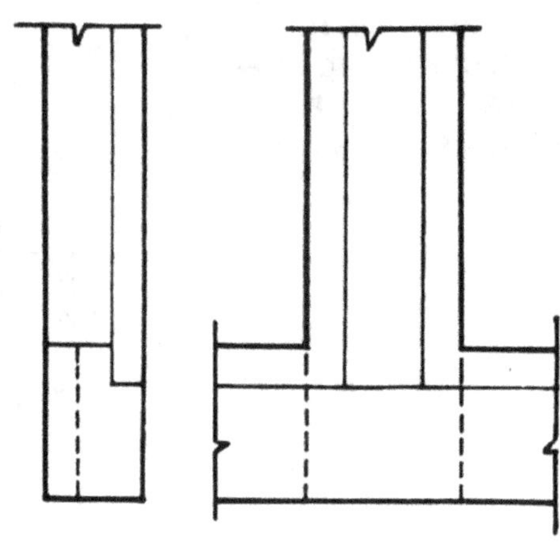

MORTISE AND TENON WITH RABBET: HERE IS ONE WAY OF JOINING A RAIL AND A PANEL.

A

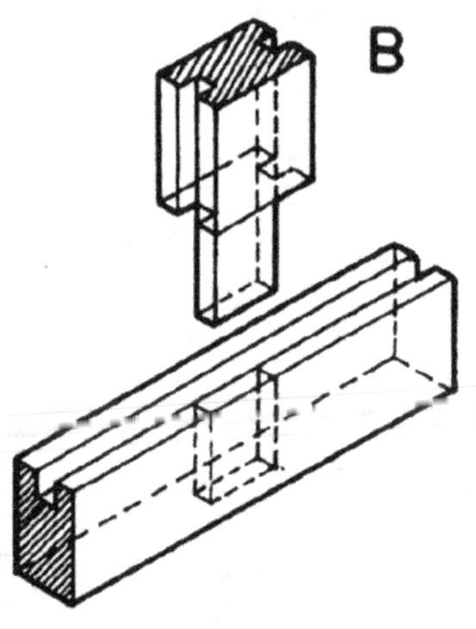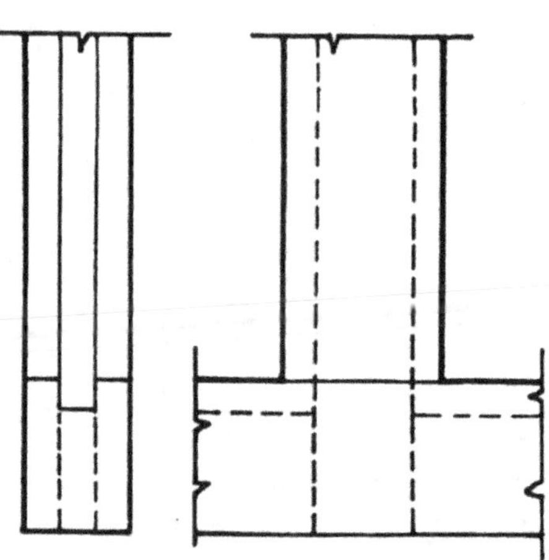

MORTISE AND TENON JOINT WITH GROOVE: SAME AS PRECEDING METHOD BUT WITH GROOVE FOR PANEL. NOTE THAT THE MORTISE AND TENON ARE REDUCED IN WIDTH.

B

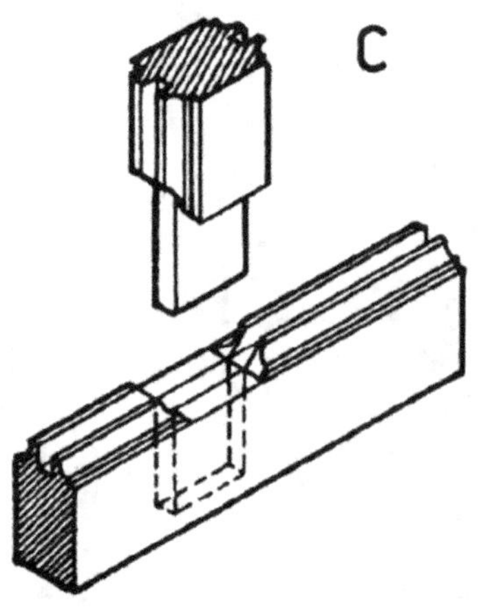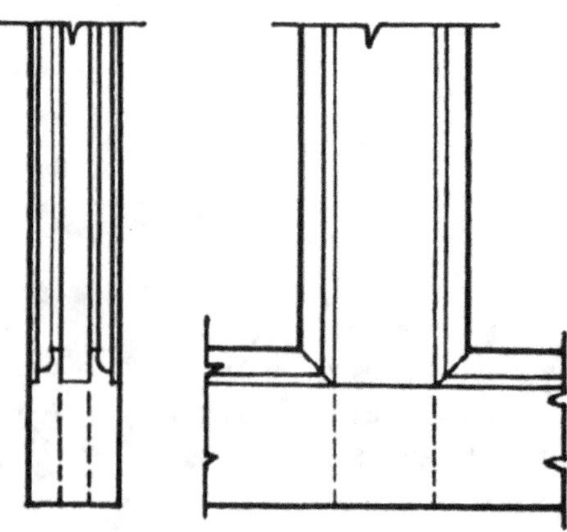

MORTISE AND TENON WITH MITERED RAIL AND FRAME: SAME AS ABOVE BUT SQUARED AT INTERSECTION. THE ANGLE JOINT MUST BE MITERED.

C

CROSS LAP JOINT: EASY TO
MAKE AND USED IN ALL TYPES
OF WORK; ONE OF THE MOST
COMMONLY USED ELEMENTS IN
FURNITURE CONSTRUCTION.

CROSS LAP JOINT: THE SAME
METHOD AS ABOVE WITH JOINT
IN DIFFERENT POSITION.

MORTISE AND TENON: THIS
CROSS RAIL JOINT HAS MANY
APPLICATIONS AND USES.

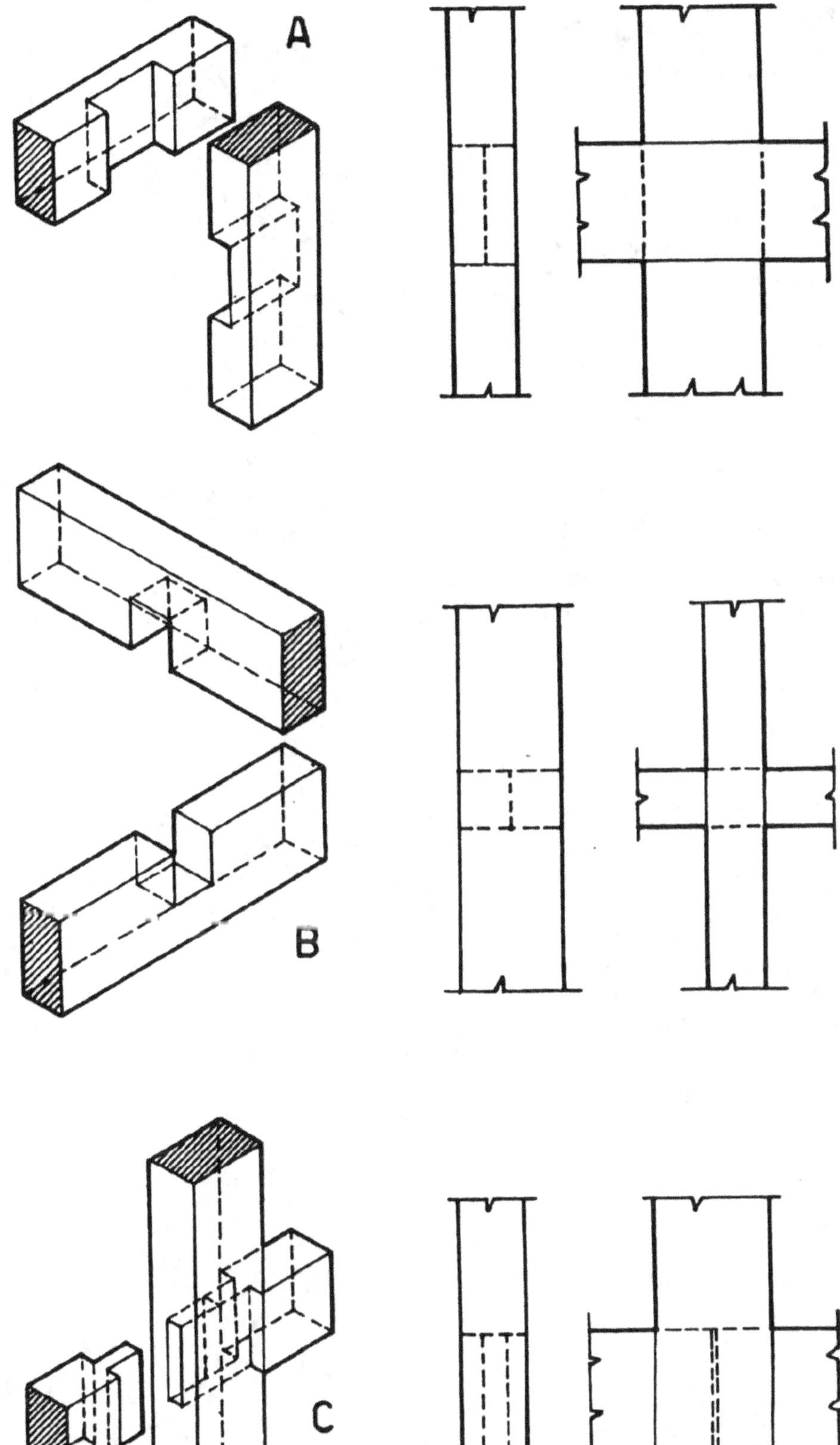

RAIL TO FRAME JOINTS

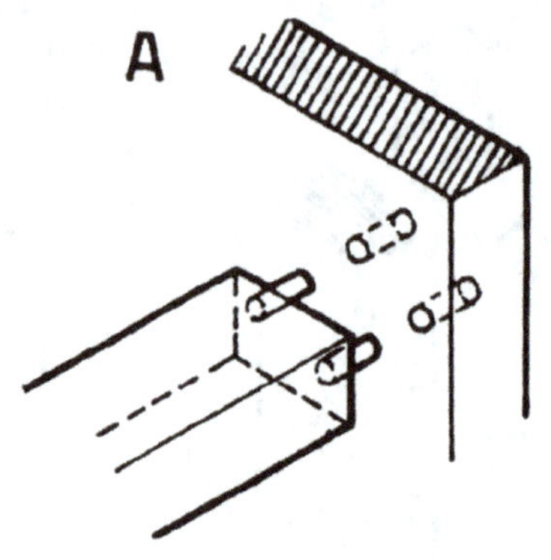

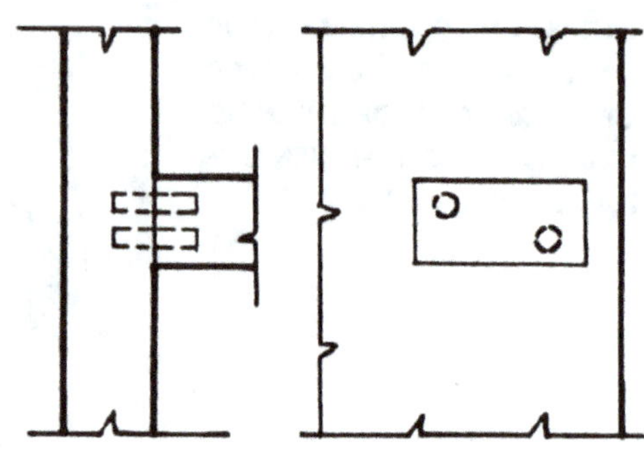

DOWEL JOINT: THIS IS ONE OF THE EASIEST UNIONS TO MAKE.

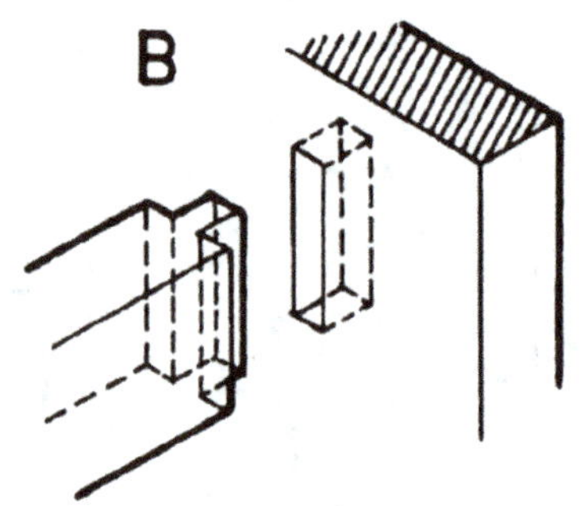

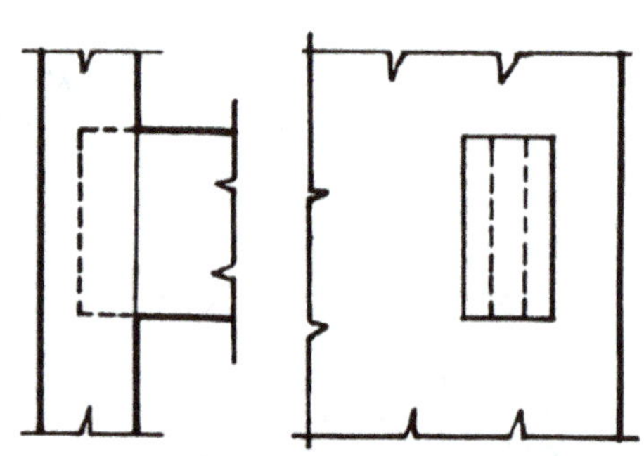

MORTISE AND TENON JOINT: GOOD RESULTS ARE OBTAINED BY THIS METHOD. THE JOINT MAY BE GLUED AT THE ENDS.

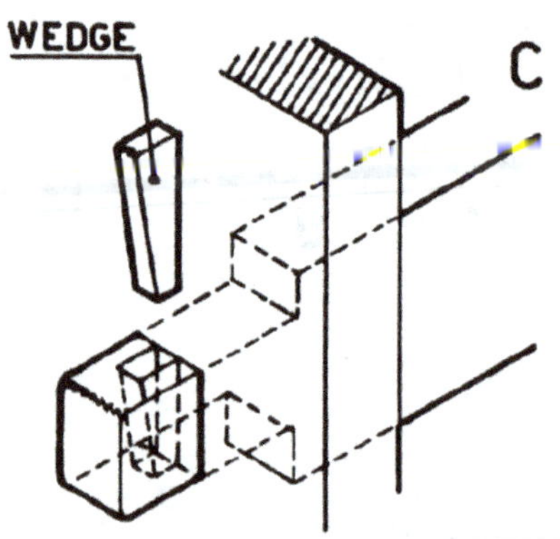

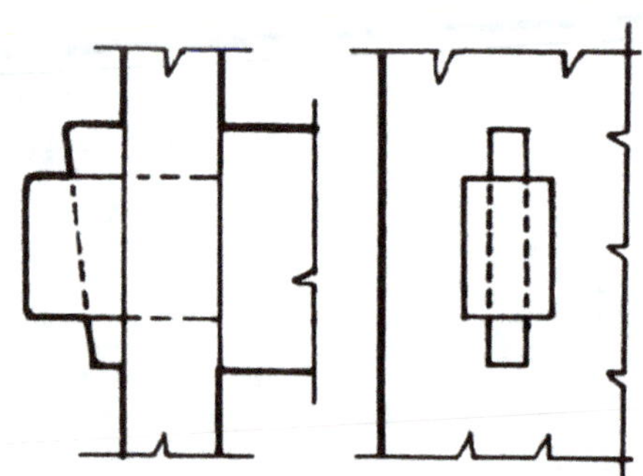

EXPOSED WEDGE JOINT: THE WEDGE TIGHTENS THE RAIL AND PANEL TOGETHER, MAKING A VERY SOLID JOINT.

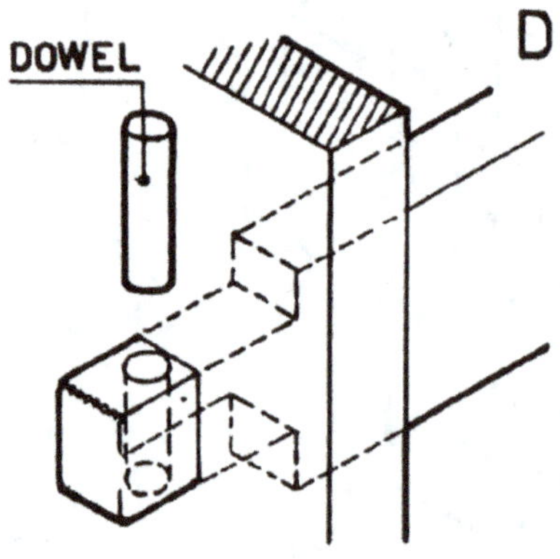

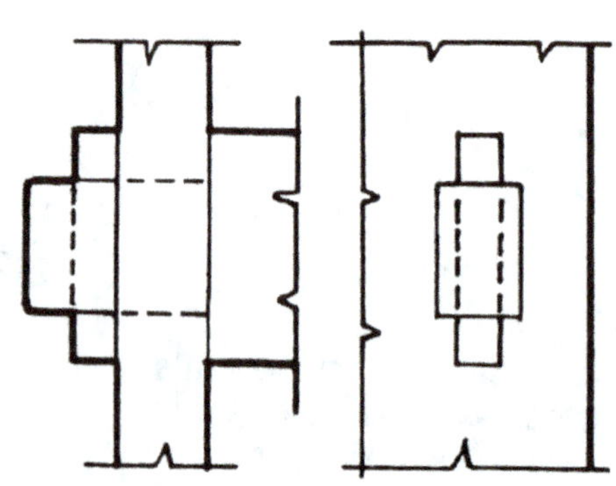

EXPOSED DOWEL JOINT: SIMILAR TO THE WEDGE JOINT (ABOVE) EXCEPT THAT THE DOWEL DOES NOT TIGHTEN THE PANEL AND RAIL.

PANEL TO FRAME JOINTS

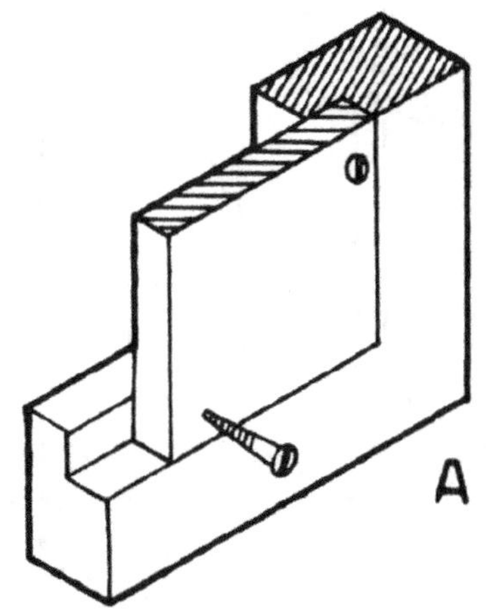

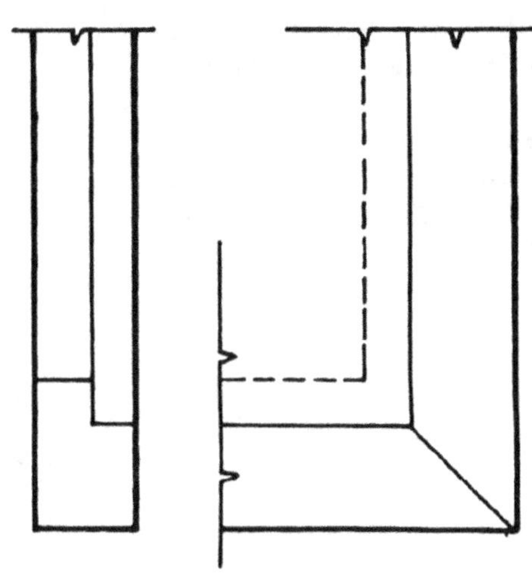

PANEL IN RABBET: PANEL IS AT-TACHED TO FRAME WITH SCREWS. THIS IS A SATISFAC-TORY METHOD OF JOINING A PANEL AND FRAME.

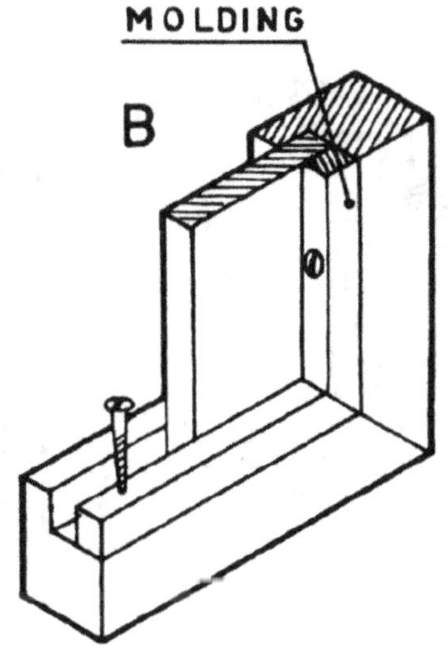

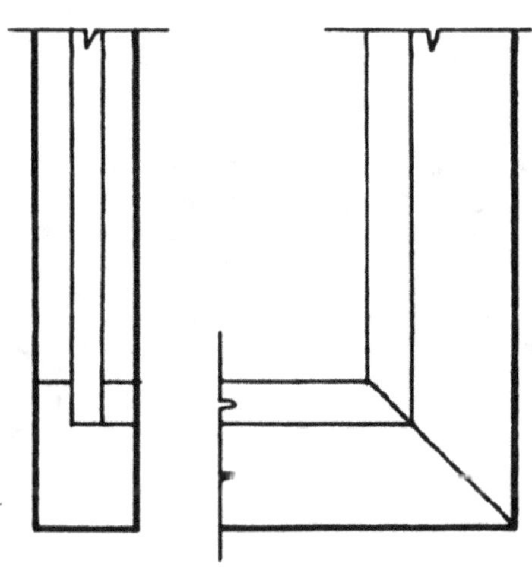

PANEL IN RABBET WITH MOLD-ING: THE MOLDING IS ATTACH-ED WITH SCREWS OR NAILS AFTER THE PANEL IS IN PLACE.

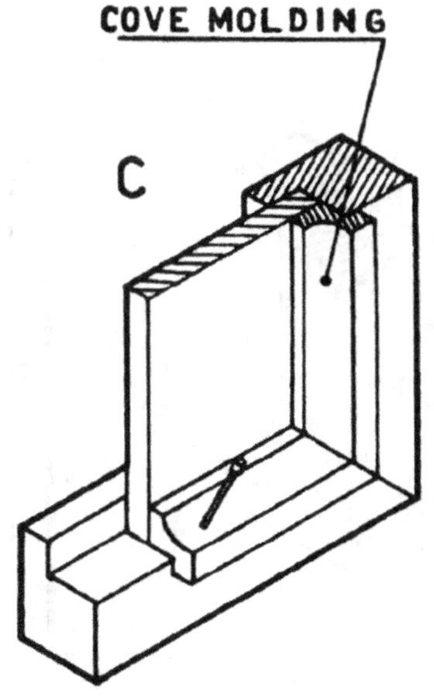

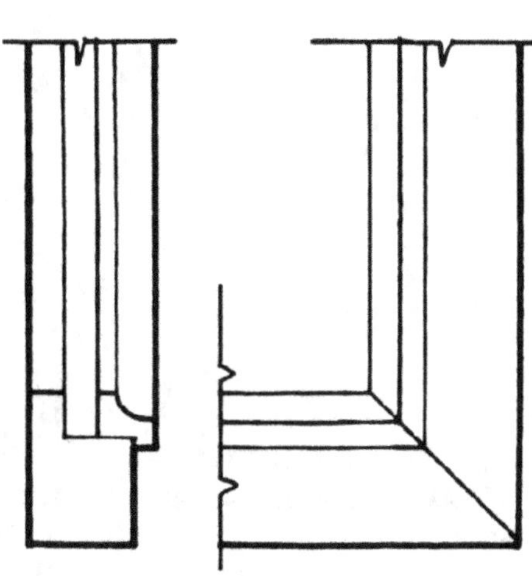

PANEL IN RABBET WITH COVE MOLDING: THIS IS SIMILAR TO "B" ABOVE, EXCEPT FOR THE TYPE OF MOLDING USED.

PANEL IN DADO GROOVE: THIS IS A SIMPLE METHOD OF JOINING A PANEL AND FRAME. THE FRAME MUST REMAIN INDEPENDENT OF THE PANEL TO ALLOW FREE MOVEMENT IN THE **WOOD**.

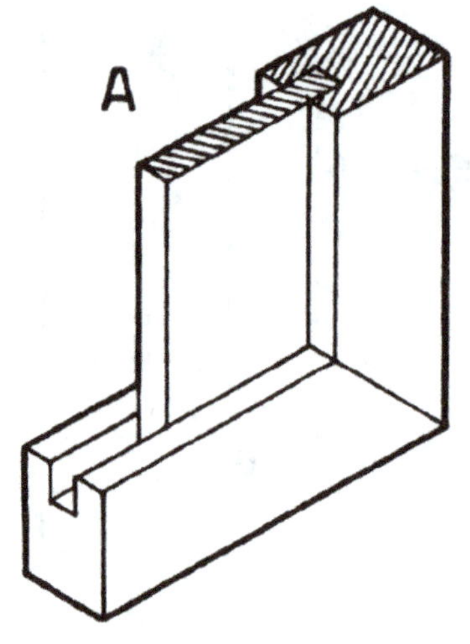

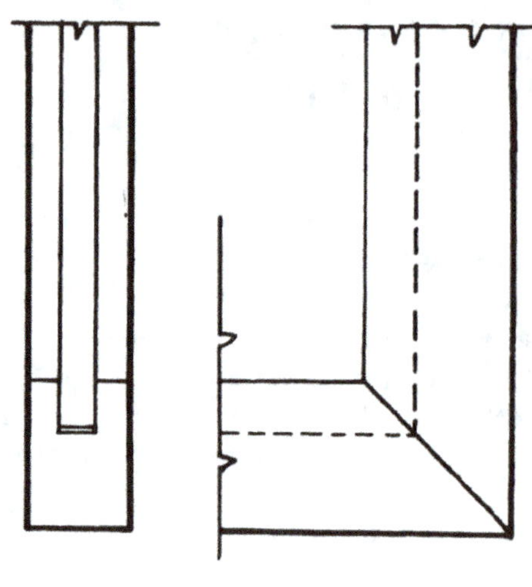

BEVELED PANEL IN DADO GROOVE: THE BEVELING OF THE PANEL PERMITS GREATER STABILITY. PANEL WILL NOT RATTLE AS ONE WALKS ACROSS THE FLOOR.

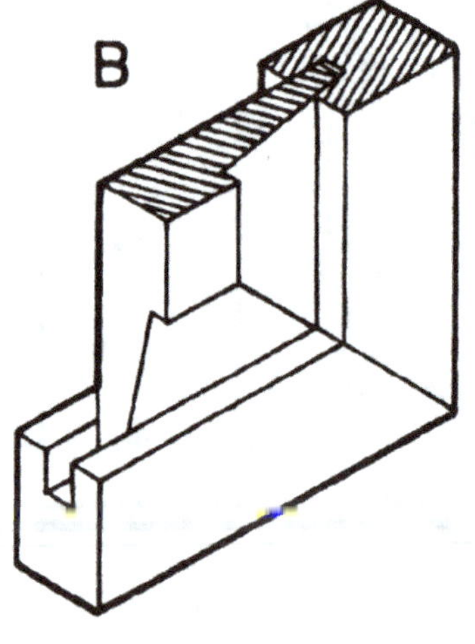

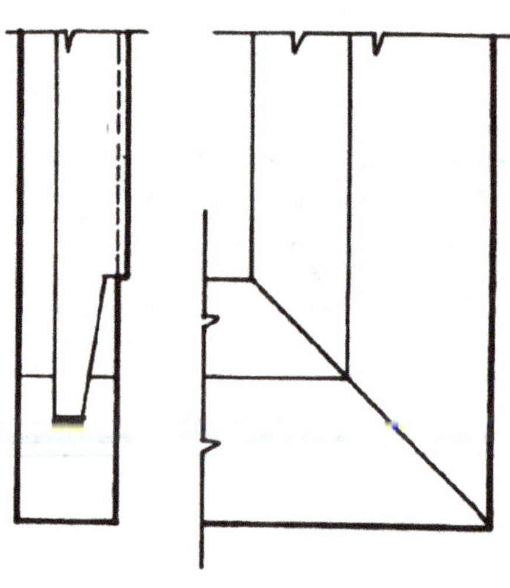

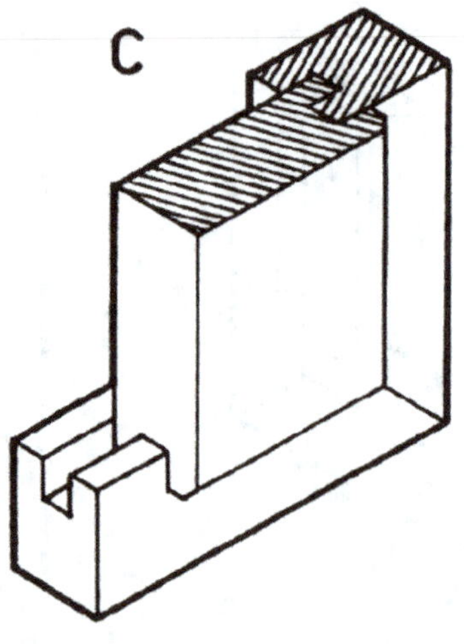

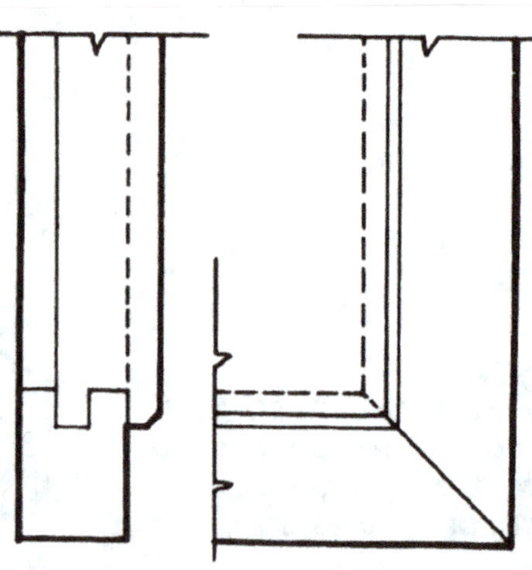

PANEL LOCK JOINT: THE PANEL AND FRAME ARE INDEPENDENT MEMBERS.

ANGLE FRAME JOINTS

JOINING FRAME MEMBERS IS ONE OF THE MOST IMPORTANT PHASES OF FURNITURE CONSTRUCTION. AFTER MAKING THE FRAME PIECES TO THE DESIRED SIZE, YOU WILL WANT TO ASSEMBLE THEM. ALWAYS BEAR IN MIND THAT SOLID WOOD SECTIONS HAVE A TENDENCY TO SHRINK, AND THAT SHRINKAGE CAUSES CRACKS IN THE DIRECTION OF THE GRAIN. YOU WILL WANT TO SELECT THE PROPER JOINT IN ACCORDANCE WITH THE CHARACTER OF THE WORK AND THE STRENGTH REQUIRED FOR THE FINAL PIECE OF FURNITURE.

IN LARGE FURNITURE PIECES WHICH WILL BE DIFFICULT TO MOVE, IT IS ADVISABLE TO USE JOINTS THAT CAN BE EASILY REASSEMBLED (SOMETIMES REFERRED TO AS DEMOUNTABLE JOINTS). IN THESE CASES THE FRAME WILL PROBABLY HAVE TO BE CONSTRUCTED WITH SPECIAL BOLTS OR DOVETAIL JOINTS. BELOW ARE SEVERAL EXAMPLES SHOWING WAYS THIS CAN BE DONE.

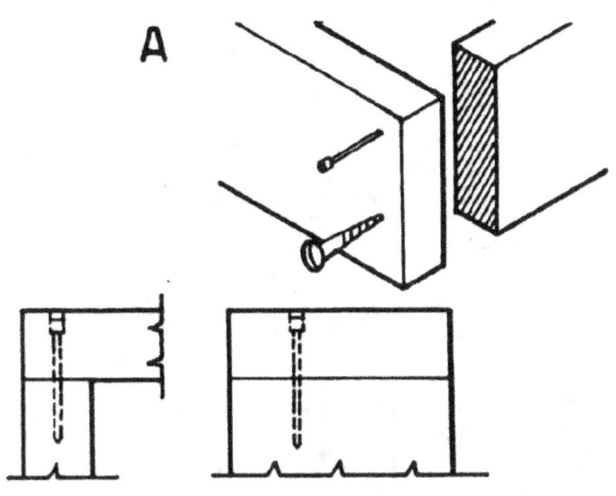

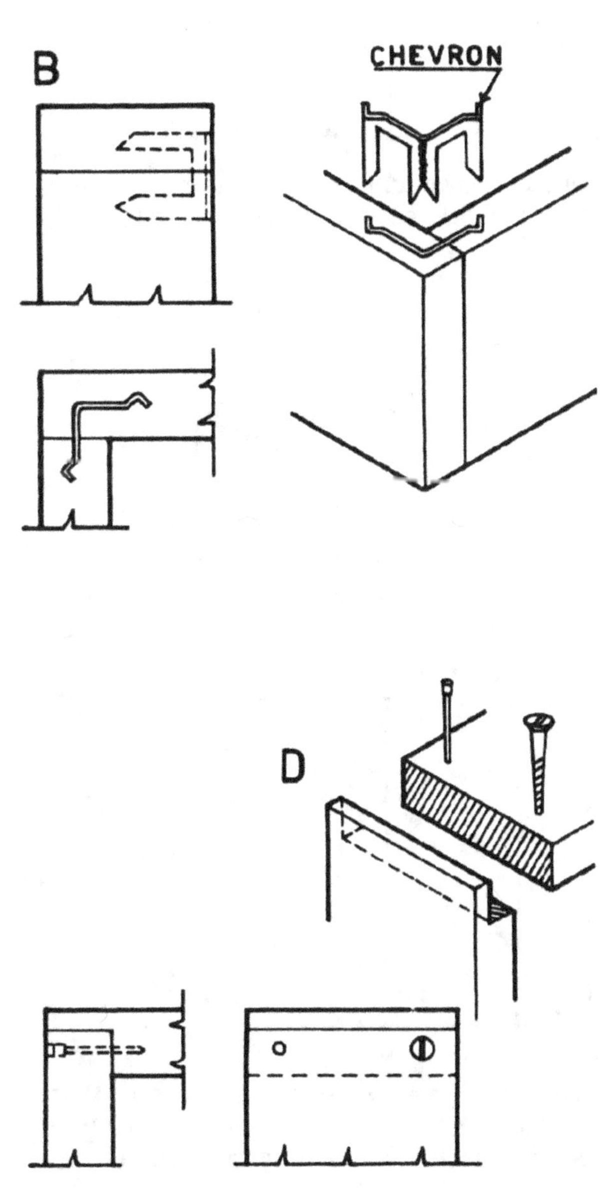

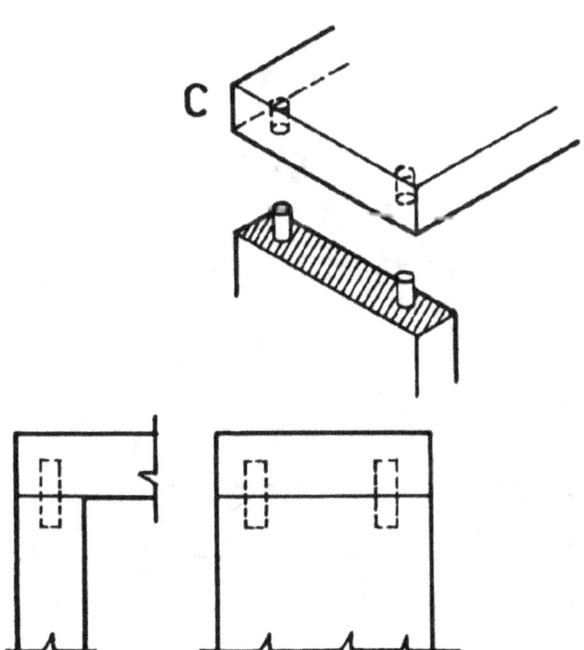

A — BUTT JOINT ATTACHED WITH NAILS OR SCREWS.
B — BUTT JOINT ATTACHED WITH CHEVRONS ON THE BOARD.
C — DOWEL JOINT WHICH IS COMMONLY USED IN THIS TYPE WORK.
D — RABBET JOINT ATTACHED WITH GLUE AND NAILS OR SCREWS.

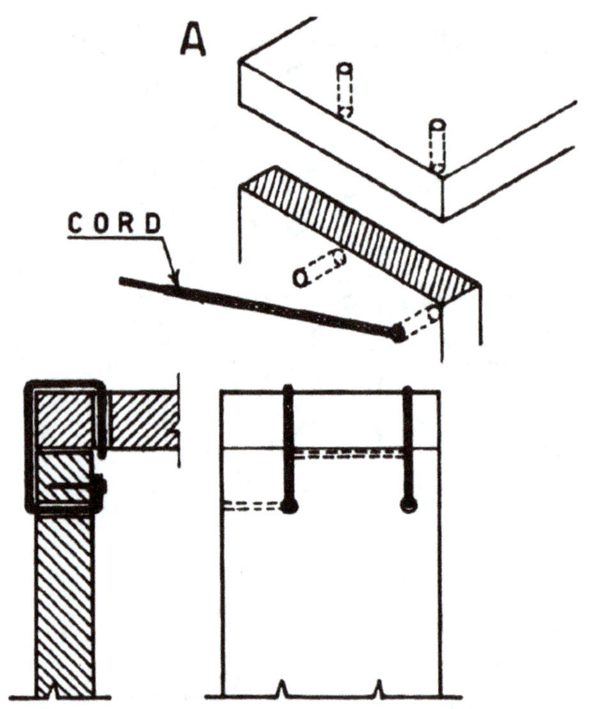

BUTT JOINT WITH CORD OR LEATHER: USED IN SPECIAL CONSTRUCTION SUCH AS CHILDREN'S FURNITURE.

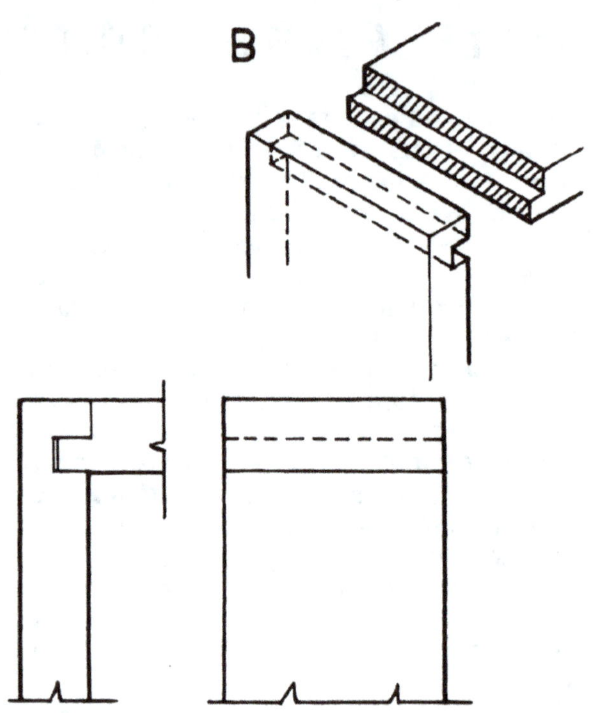

BOX CORNER JOINT: THIS JOINT IS LESS USED DUE TO POSSIBILITY OF CRACKS AT EDGES.

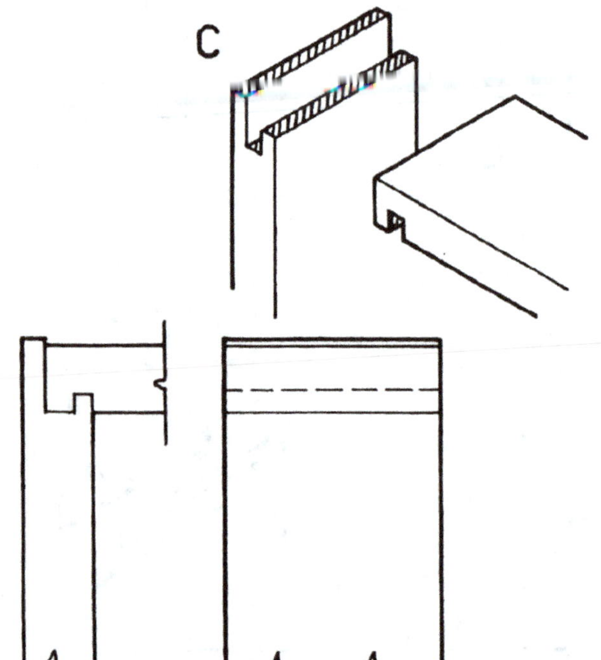

MILLED CORNER JOINT: EXTENSIVELY USED IN BUILDING DRAWERS. IT DIFFERS FROM THE PRECEDING JOINT IN HAVING CLOSED EDGES, WHICH AVOID CRACKS.

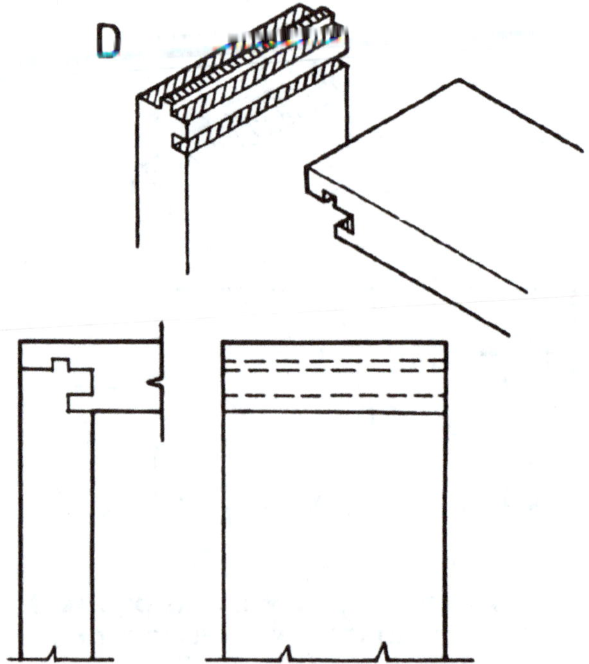

LOCK BUTT JOINT: EXCELLENT WHERE ACCURATE WORK IS DESIRED.

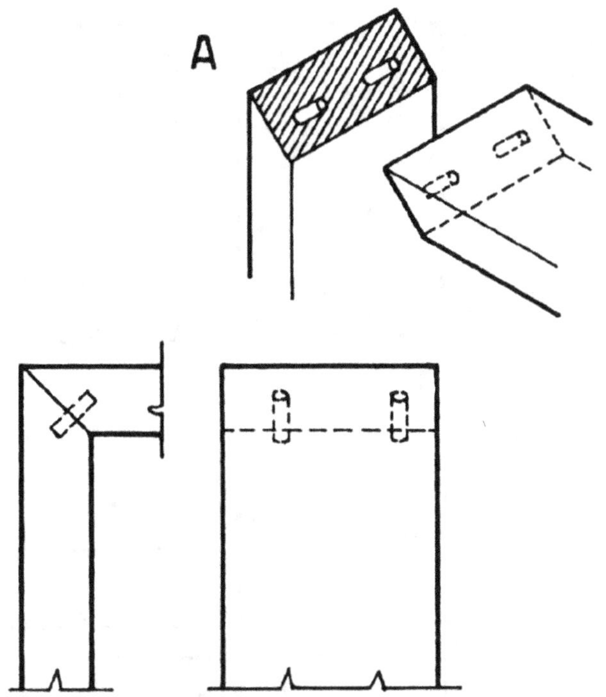

DOWEL MITER JOINT: OFTEN USED BY THE AMATEUR CRAFTSMAN AND CARPENTERS.

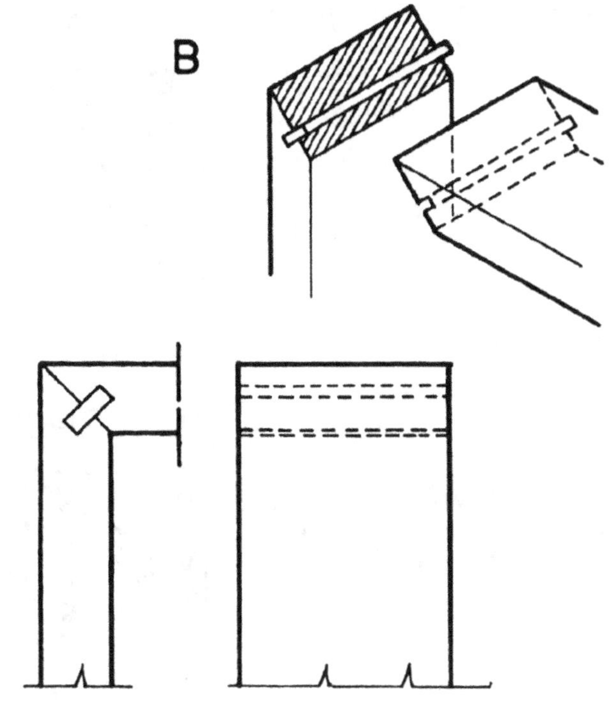

FEATHER MITER JOINT: USED IN MANUFACTURED WORK.

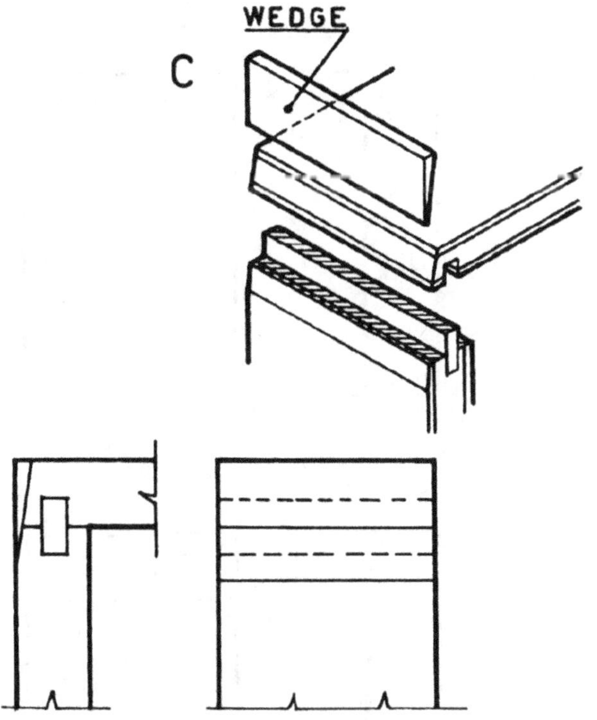

FEATHER JOINT: COVERED WITH A WEDGE AND USED WHEN VENEER IS APPLIED. THE WEDGE ELIMINATES ANY MARK ON THE VENEER OUTSIDE.

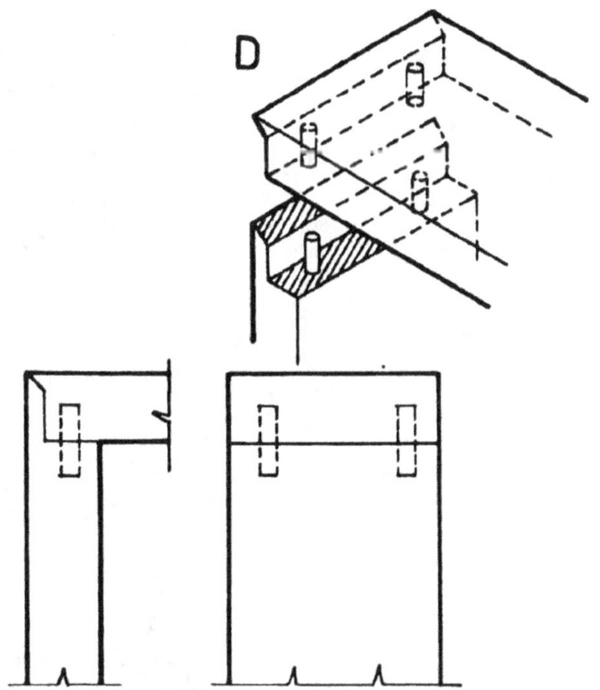

DOWEL MITER JOINT: THIS METHOD IS COMMON IN MANUFACTURED PIECES.

SPLINED MITER JOINT: USED BY
AMATEUR CRAFTSMEN.

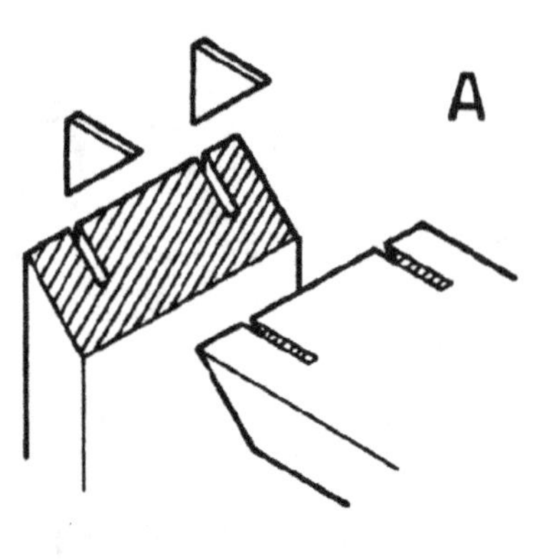
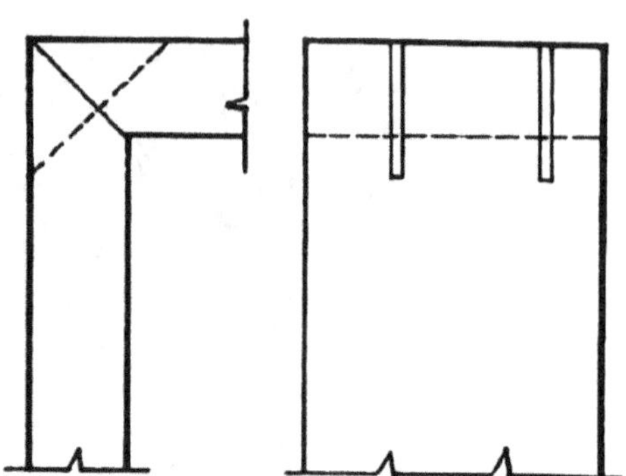

A

MITER WITH METAL CLAMP: THIS
CLAMP IS EASY TO APPLY AND
GIVES GOOD RESULTS.

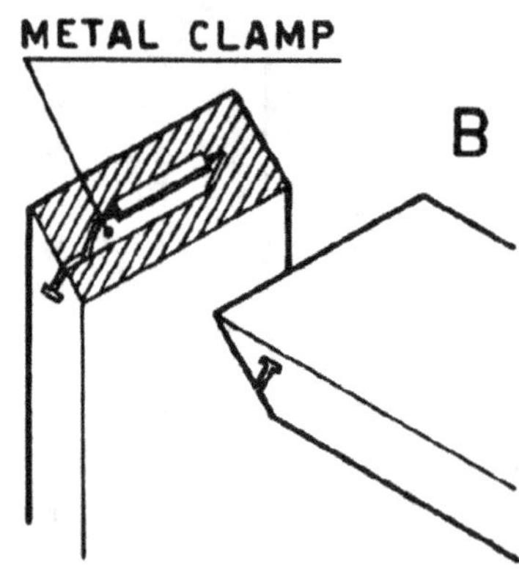

METAL CLAMP
B

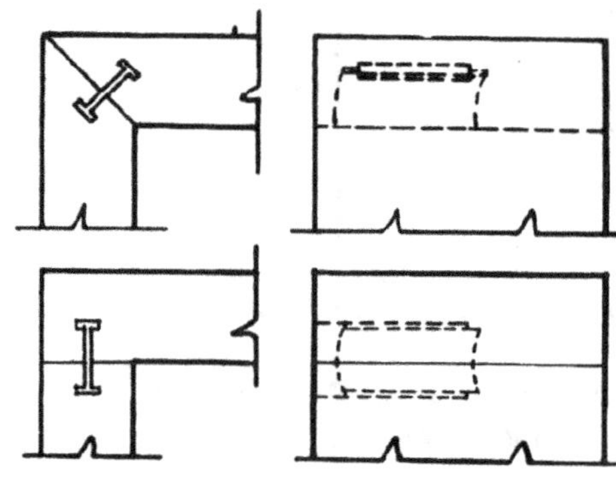

MITER TONGUE AND GROOVE
JOINT USED IN GOOD STANDARD
PRODUCTION.

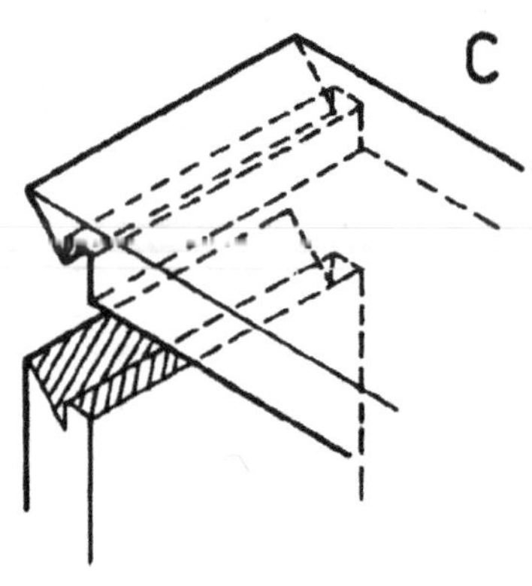

C

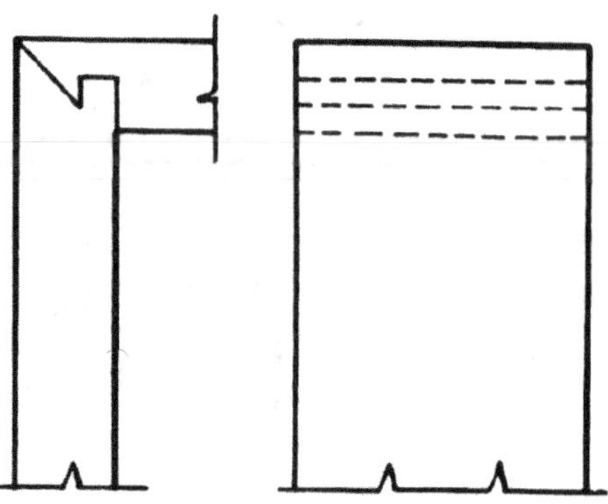

LOCK MITER JOINT IS ONE OF
BETTER CONSTRUCTION.

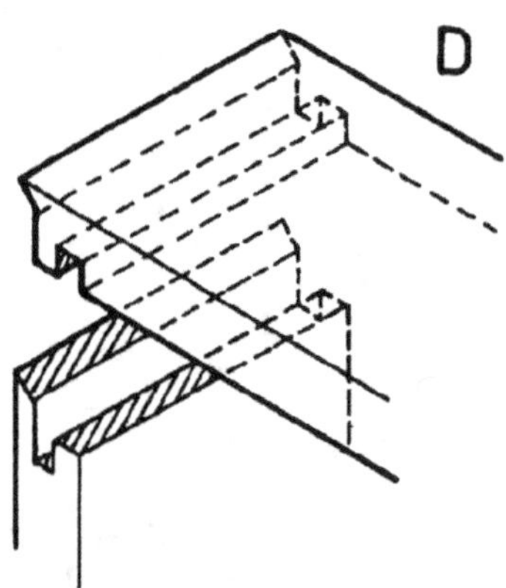

D

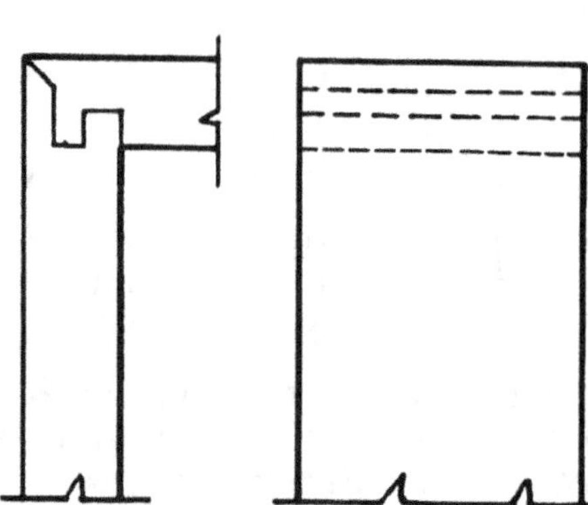

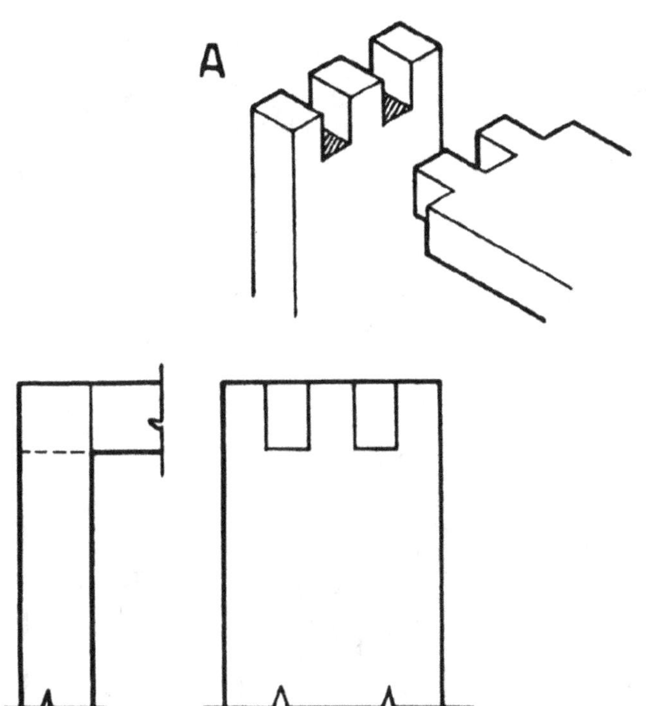

BOX JOINT: AN EASY TO MAKE AND VERY STRONG
JOINT.

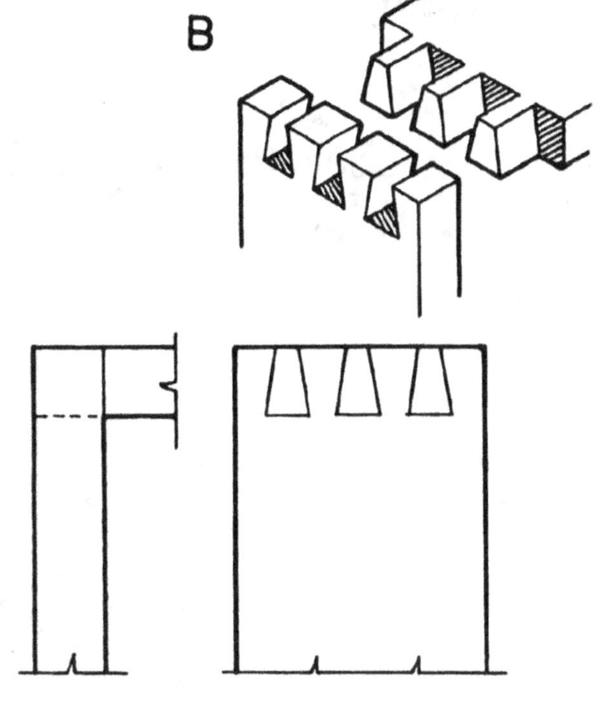

DOVETAIL JOINT: THIS IS ONE OF THE STRONGEST
TERMINAL TYPE JOINTS.

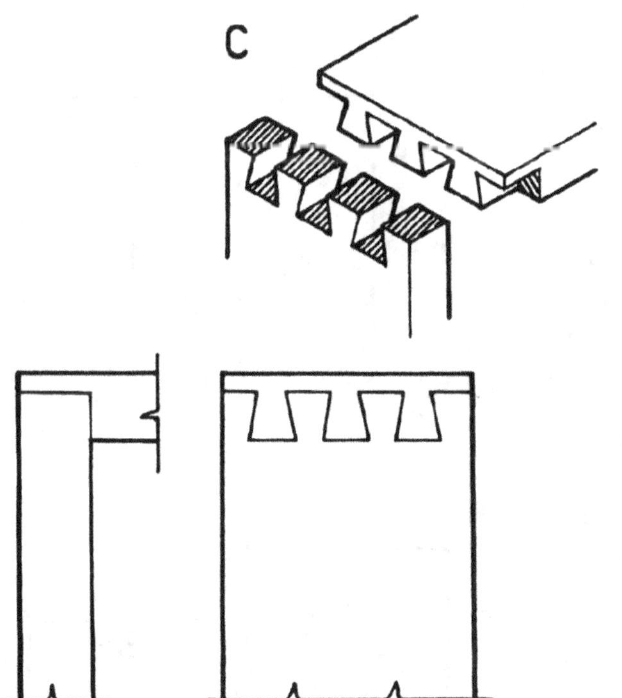

HALF BLIND DOVETAIL JOINT.

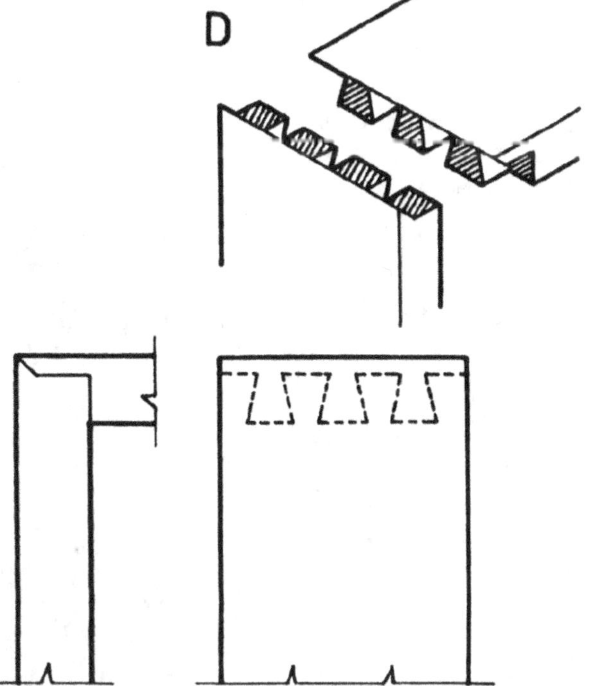

BLIND DOVETAIL JOINT: USED WHEN THE TWO SIDES
ARE TO BE LEFT EXPOSED.

DEMOUNTABLE JOINTS

OLD TYPE OF DEMOUNTABLE JOINT. THIS TYPE IS SELDOM USED ANY MORE IN STANDARD PRODUCTION.

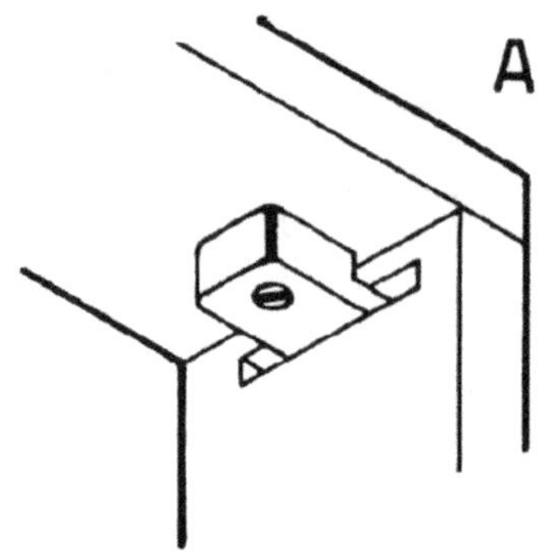
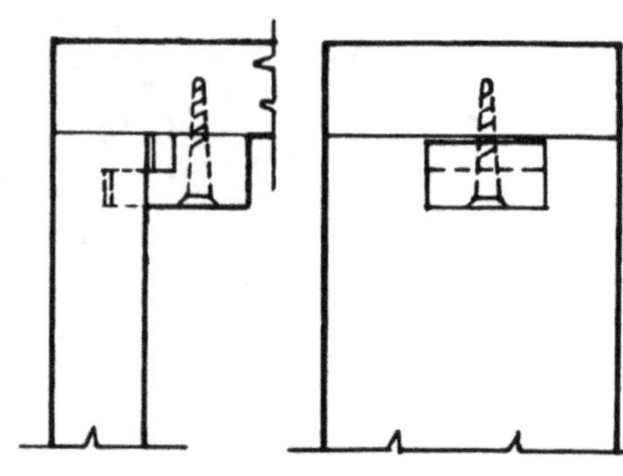

BUTT JOINT USING EXPOSED HARDWARE.

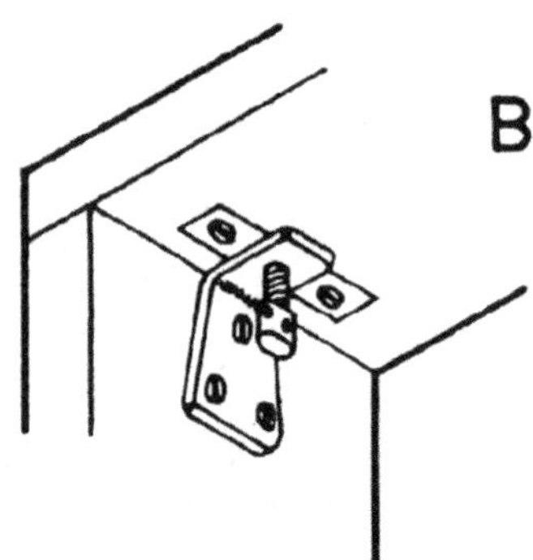
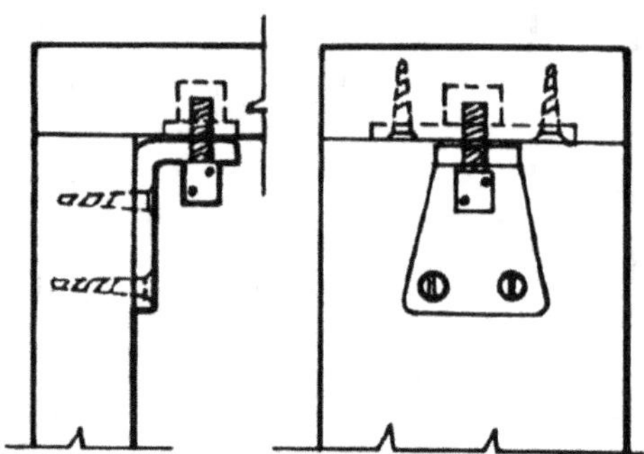

ENCASED BOLT: NOTE THAT HOLE MUST BE CUT SO THAT BOLT MAY BE TIGHTENED.

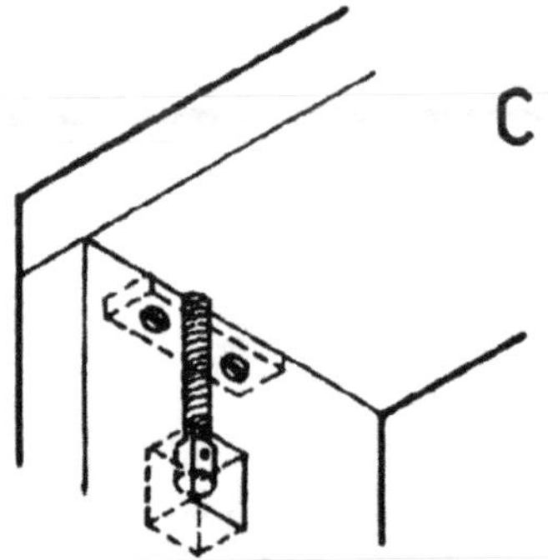
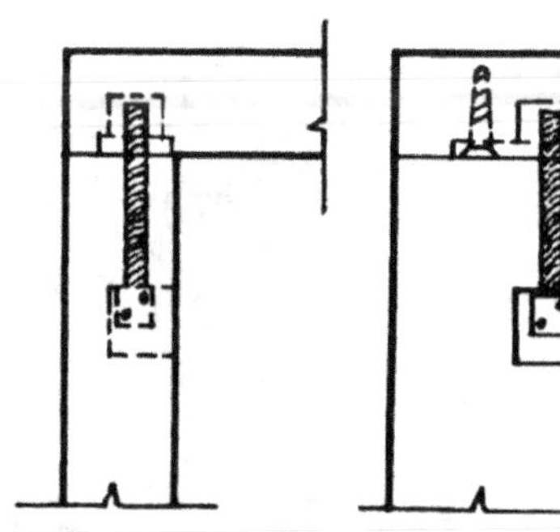

MITER JOINT WITH BLIND ANGLE IRON: ONLY TWO SCREWS ARE NEEDED AT EACH JOINT.

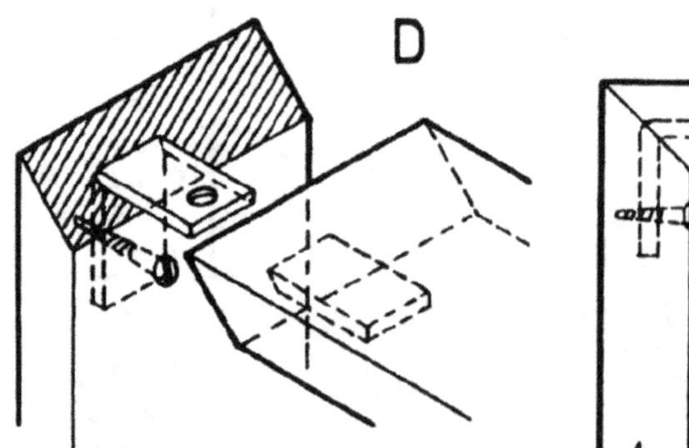
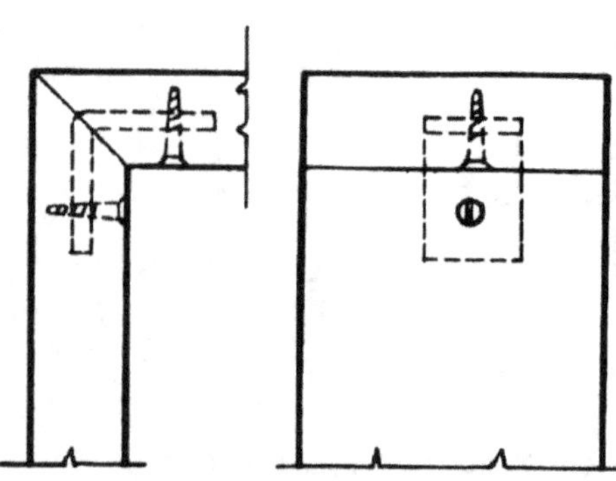

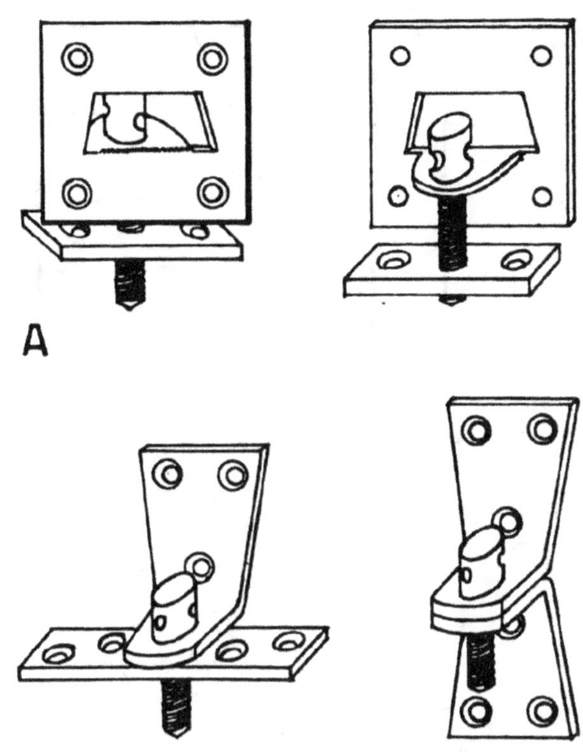

VARIOUS TYPES OF BOLTS USED WITH FURNITURE WHICH MUST BE REASSEMBLED OCCASIONALLY.

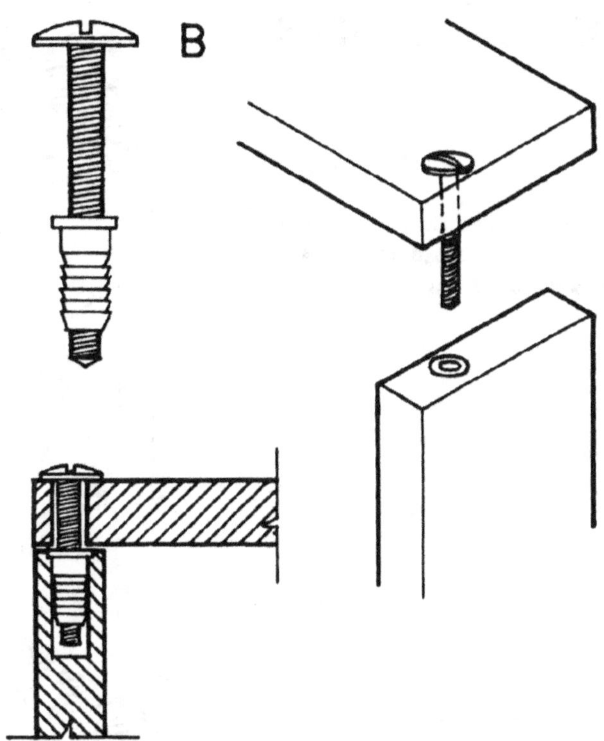

BUTT JOINT WITH AN ENCASED BOLT: NOTE THAT BOLT HEAD WILL BE EXPOSED.

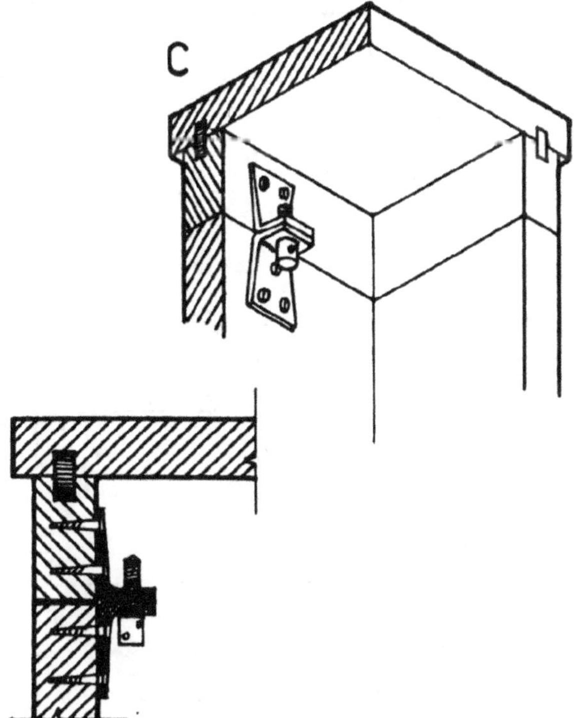

SIDE JOINT WITH EXPOSED BOLTING ARRANGEMENT: THIS IS A SIMPLE METHOD FOR THE NOVICE.

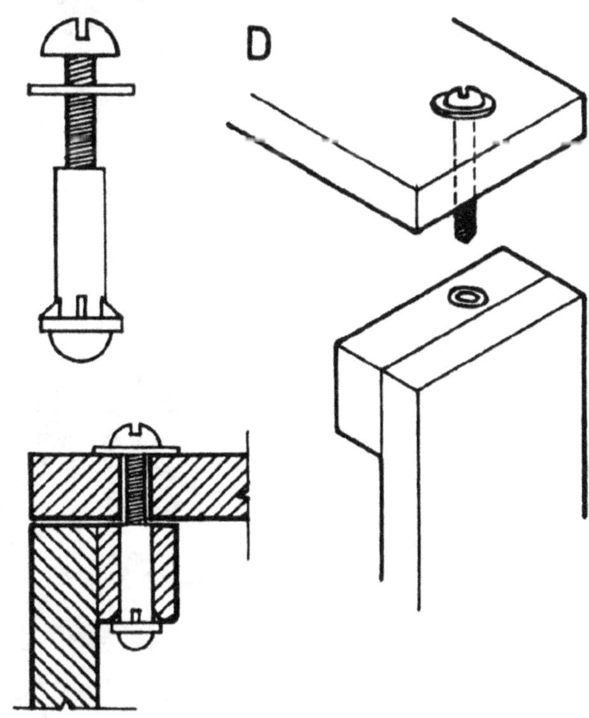

BOLT TO RAIL JOINT: RAIL SHOULD BE FIRMLY ATTACHED TO SIDE BEFORE BOLT IS INSTALLED.

MIDDLE FRAME JOINTS

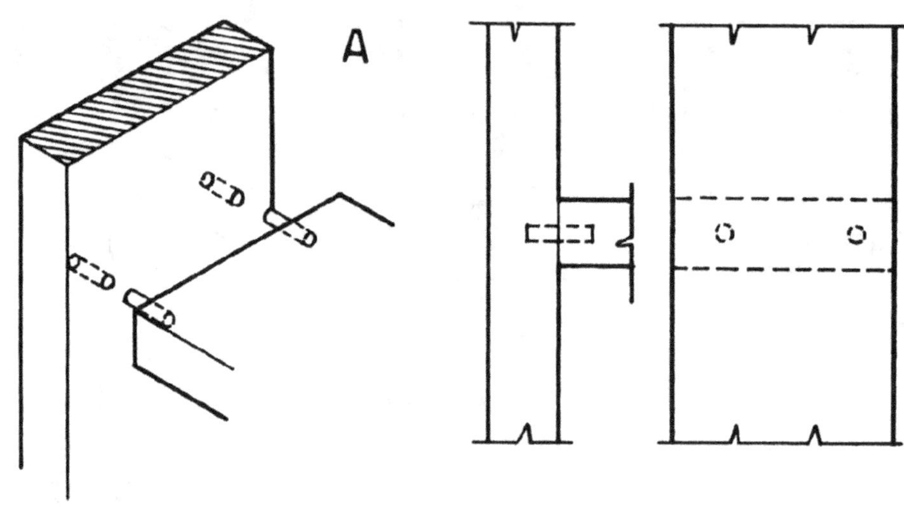

DOWEL JOINT: THIS IS AN EASY JOINT OFTEN USED BY THE AM-ATEUR CRAFTSMAN.

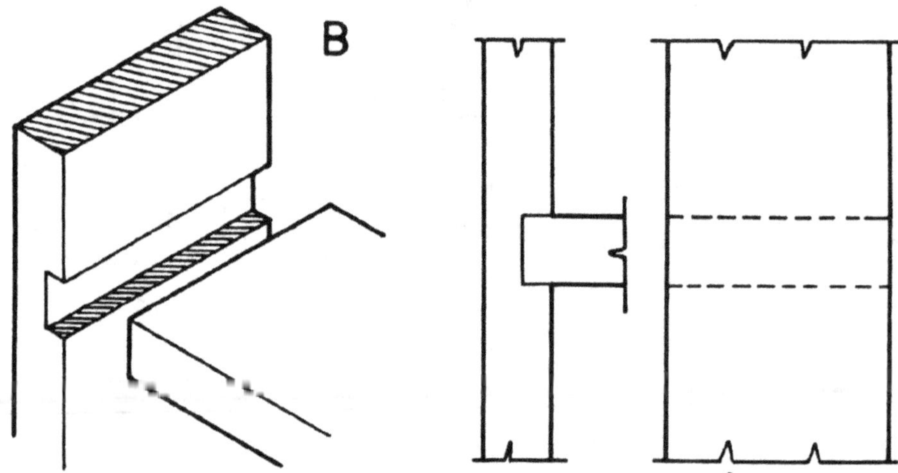

DADO JOINT: USED IN ORDINARY WORK, ESPECIALLY WHERE PROD-UCT IS TO BE PAINTED.

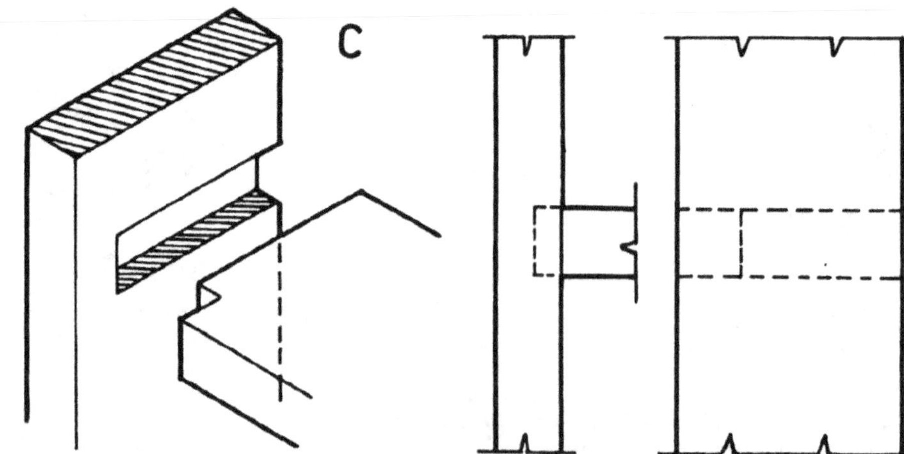

STOPPED DADO JOINT: EXCELLENT METHOD OF JOINING CERTAIN TYPES OF WOODWORK.

THROUGH AND STOPPED FEATHER JOINT: WHEN PROPERLY GLUED, THIS IS A GOOD JOINT.

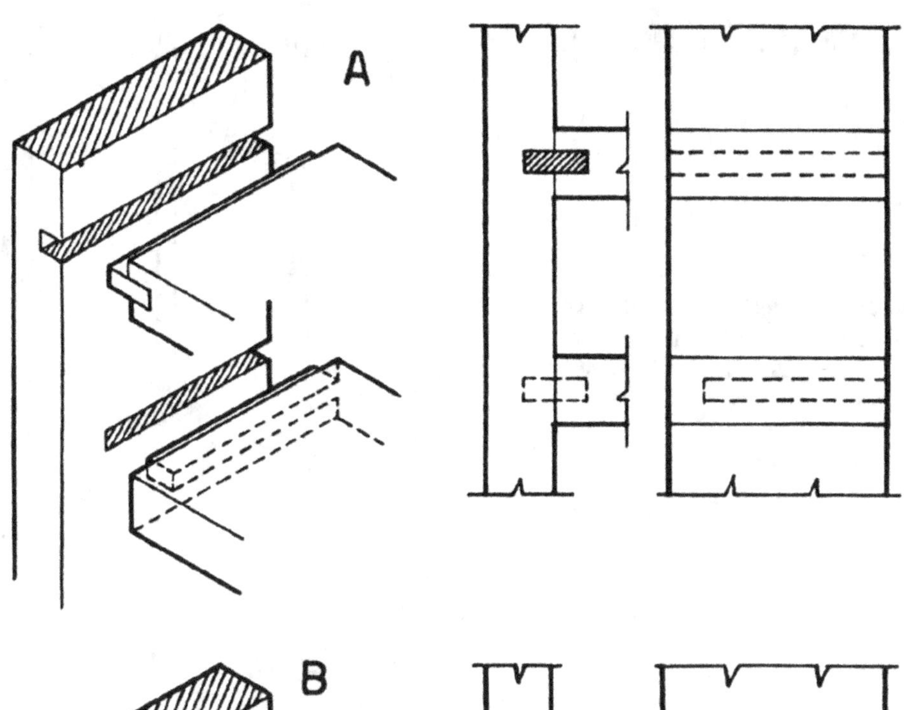

DOVETAIL SLIP JOINT: SIDES JOINED BY THIS METHOD CANNOT PULL APART.

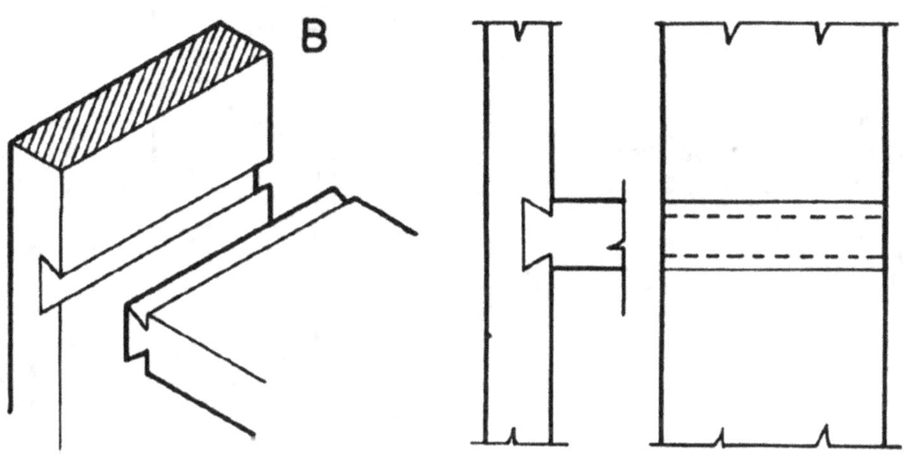

METAL CLAMP JOINT: THIS IS A PATENTED CLAMP THAT IS EASY TO INSTALL.

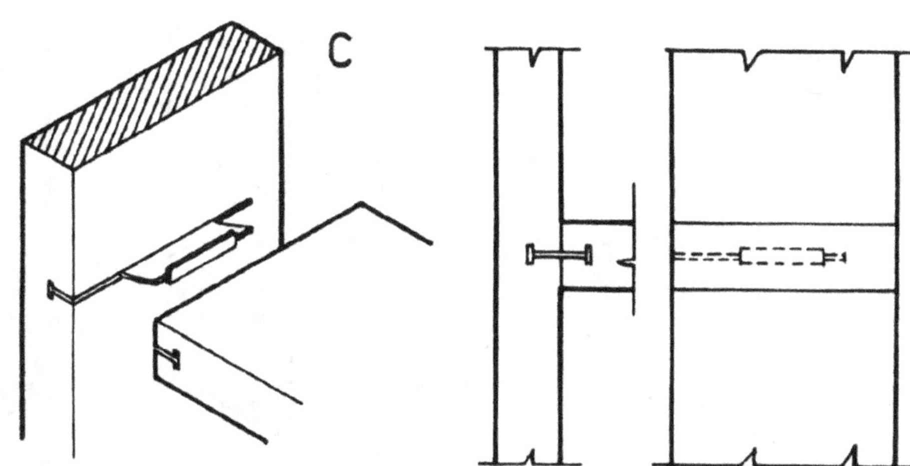

BACK PANEL JOINTS

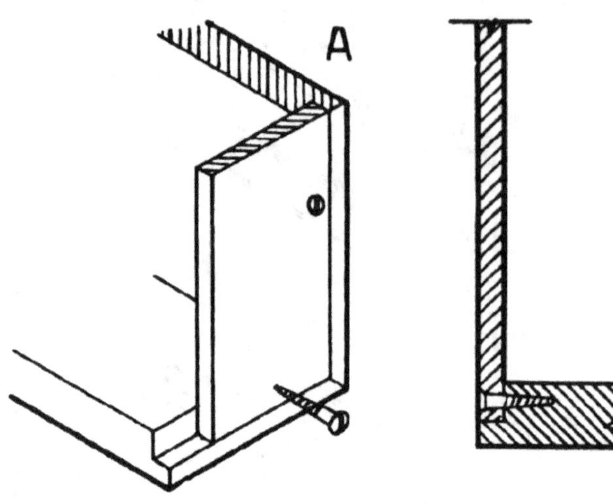

BACK IN RABBET JOINT: THIS IS A COMMON METHOD OF ATTACHING A BACK PANEL BY MEANS OF NAILS OR SCREWS.

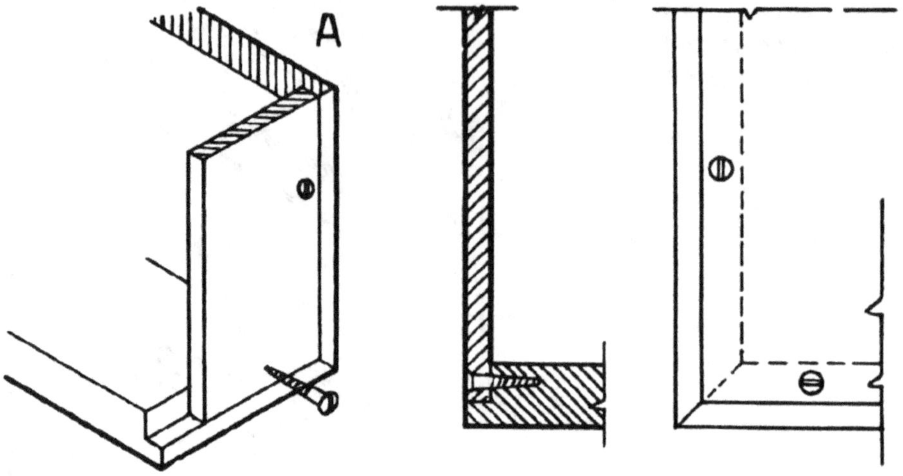

BACK IN GROOVE: NOTE THAT THE BOTTOM OF THE PANEL IS HELD IN PLACE WITH SCREWS.

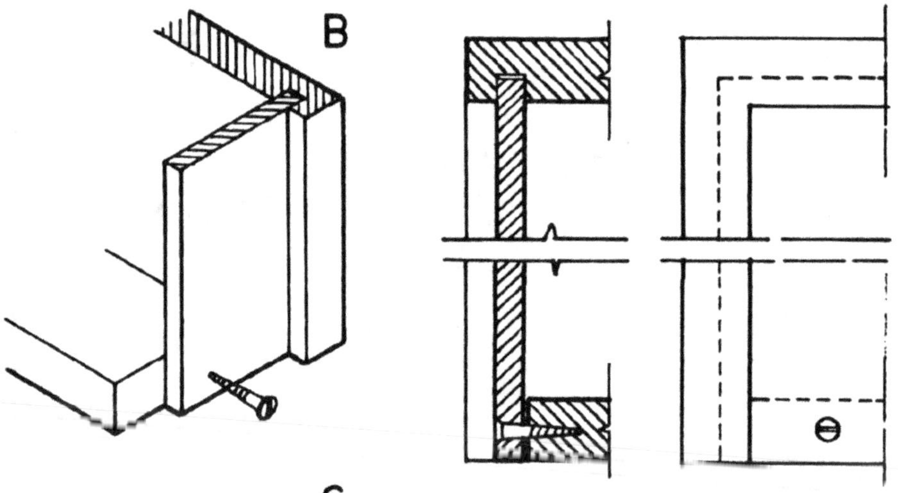

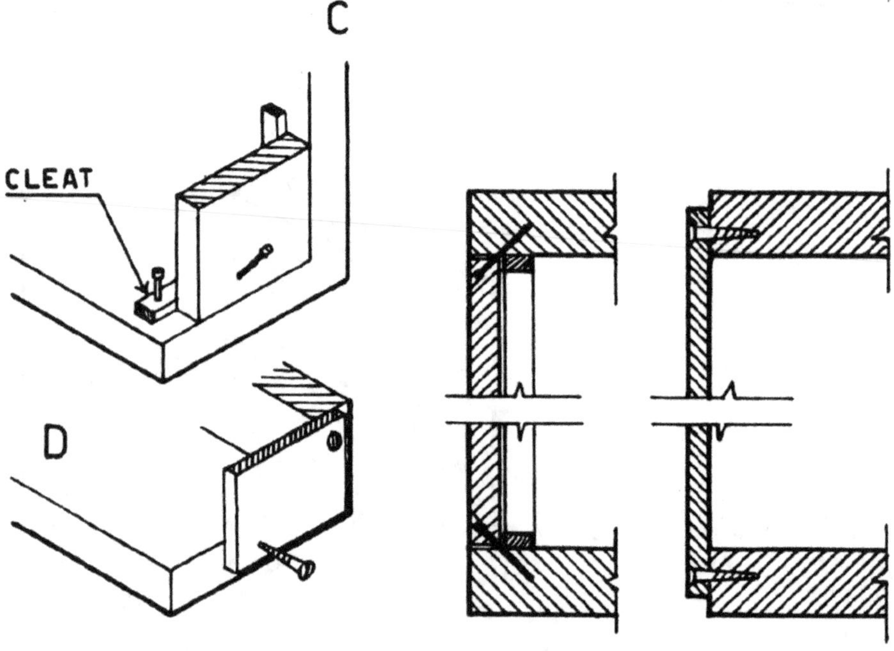

THESE TWO METHODS OF ATTACHING THE BACK PANEL ARE IDEAL FOR AMATEUR CRAFTSMEN.

JOINING OF THREE PIECES

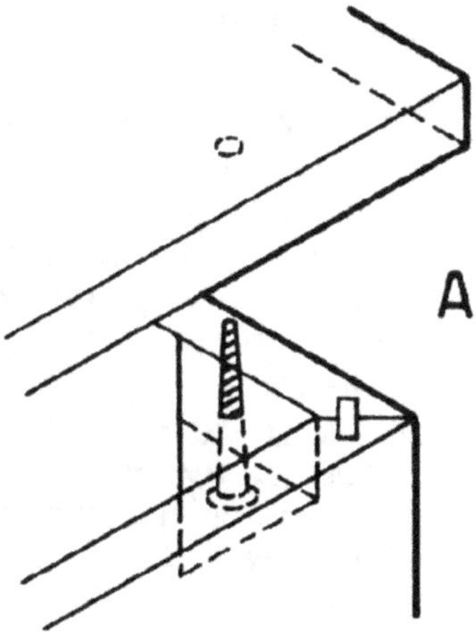

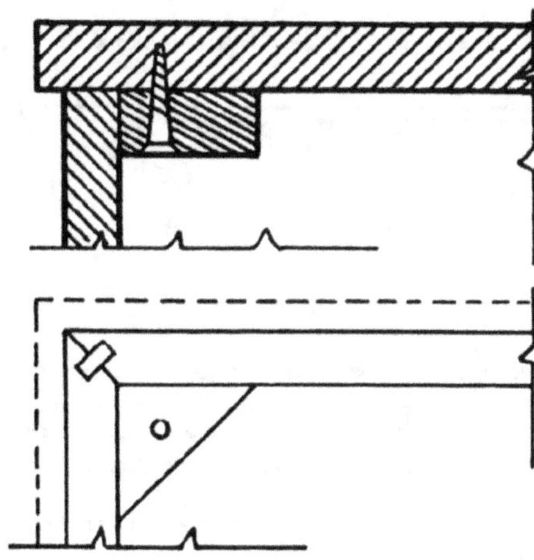

TOP ATTACHED WITH SCREWS FROM UNDER SIDE. BOLTS OR DOWELS MAY BE SUBSTITUTED FOR SCREWS.

A

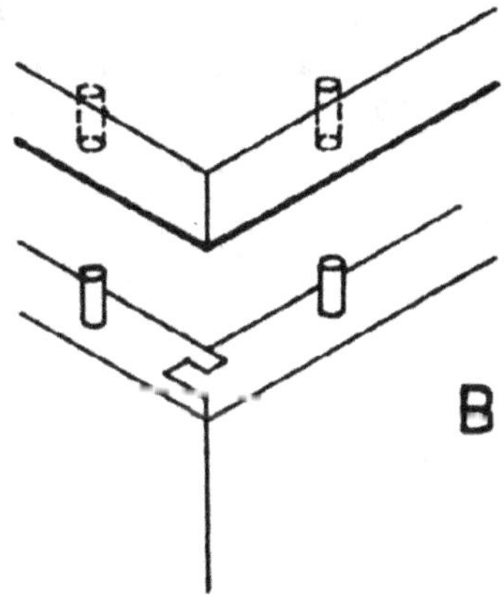

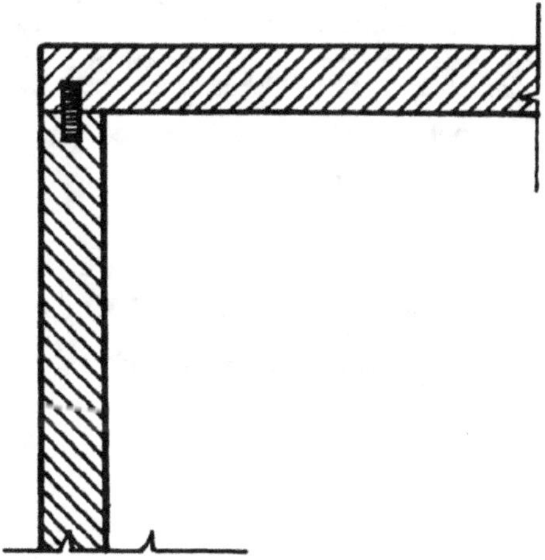

TOP ATTACHED TO SIDES WITH DOWELS.

B

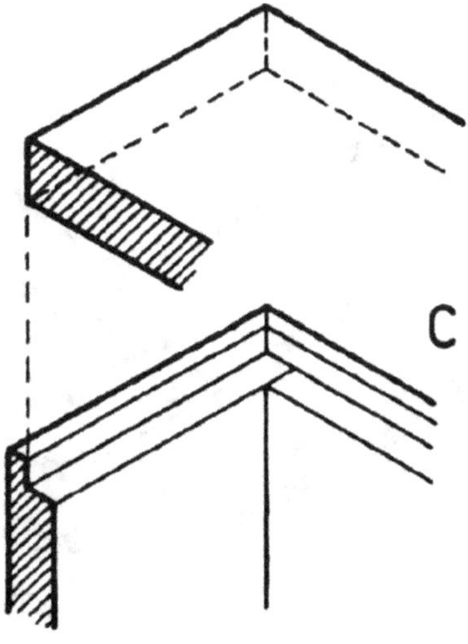

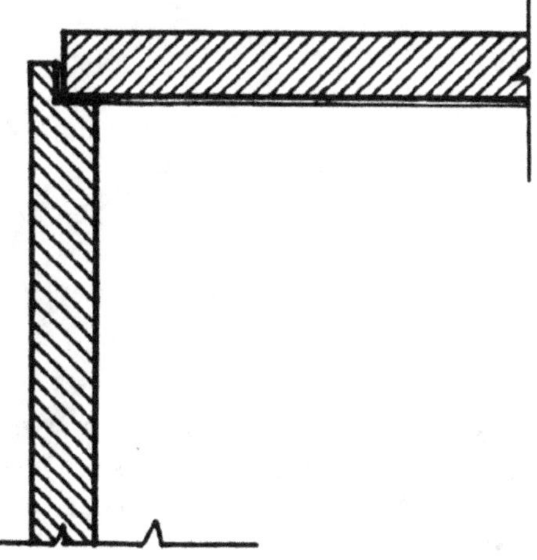

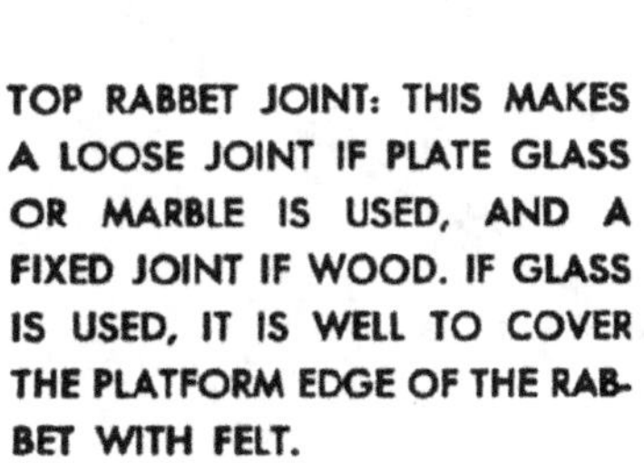

TOP RABBET JOINT: THIS MAKES A LOOSE JOINT IF PLATE GLASS OR MARBLE IS USED, AND A FIXED JOINT IF WOOD. IF GLASS IS USED, IT IS WELL TO COVER THE PLATFORM EDGE OF THE RABBET WITH FELT.

C

PLYWOOD, LUMBER CORE PLYWOOD, AND LAMINATED WOOD

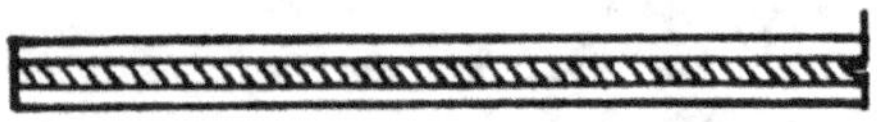

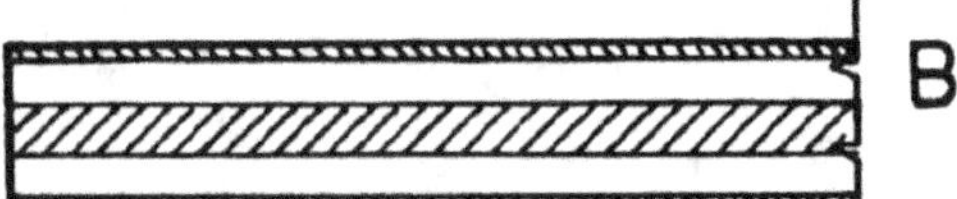

A — FORMATION OF A PANEL OF PLYWOOD WITH THREE-PLY VENEER.

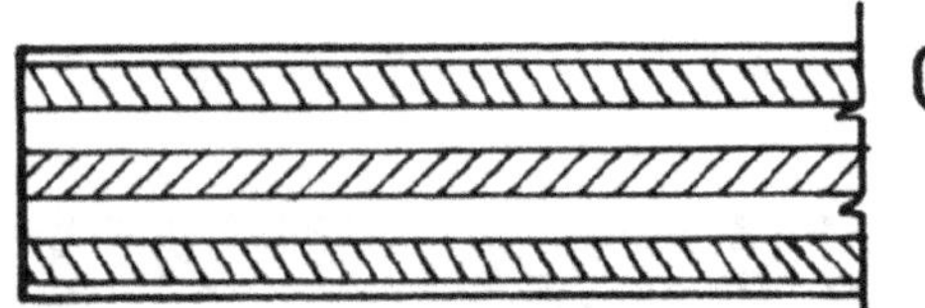

B — FORMATION OF PLYWOOD WITH FIVE-PLY VENEER.

C — FORMATION OF PLYWOOD WITH SEVEN-PLY VENEER.

PLYWOOD IS PRODUCED BY PLACING 3-5-7 OR MORE LAYERS OF WOOD ONE ON TOP OF THE OTHER WITH GRAIN CROSSED. EACH LAYER IS GLUED TO THE PREVIOUS LAYER AND PUT UNDER HEAVY PRESSURE. THE FACE VENEER GENERALLY IS IN ONE CONTINUOUS SHEET STRIPPED OR PEELED FROM THE SURFACE OF A SINGLE LOG AFTER THE LOG HAS BEEN REDUCED TO UNIFORM DIAMETER.

LUMBER CORE PLYWOOD CONSISTS OF GLUED STRIPS OF SOLID HEARTWOOD COVERED ON EACH SIDE WITH A THIN PANEL OF PLYWOOD. THIS METHOD HAS DONE MUCH TO CHANGE FURNITURE CONSTRUCTION.

IN ADDITION TO PLYWOOD AND LUMBER CORE PLYWOOD WE HAVE TODAY THE POSSIBILITY OF PRODUCING DIFFERENT TYPES OF PANELS BY GLUING WITH SPECIAL GLUES ONE OR MORE LAYERS OF WOOD AND UNITING THEM WITH VARIOUS OTHER MATERIALS SUCH AS LIGHT METAL (page 107 D.E.; page 108 fig. A), AND PLASTIC MATERIALS, EACH HAVING ITS OWN PARTICULAR CHARACTERISTIC.

LAMINATED WOOD IS PRODUCED BY GLUING THIN SHEETS OF HARDWOOD WITH THE GRAIN RUNNING IN THE SAME DIRECTION. IT IS USED TO OBTAIN A SOLID CURVATURE IN THE WOOD (see page 46, fig. A).

GRAIN DIRECTION

D

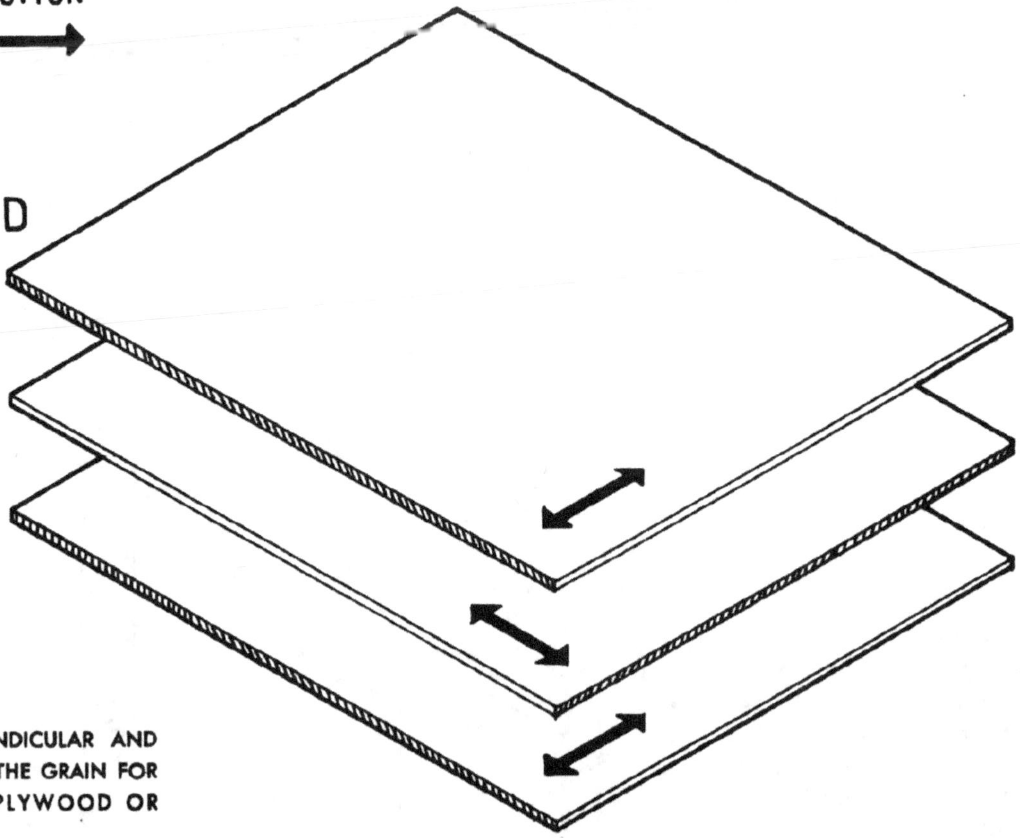

ILLUSTRATION OF PERPENDICULAR AND CROSSED DIRECTION OF THE GRAIN FOR THE FORMATION OF PLYWOOD OR VENEER CORE PANEL.

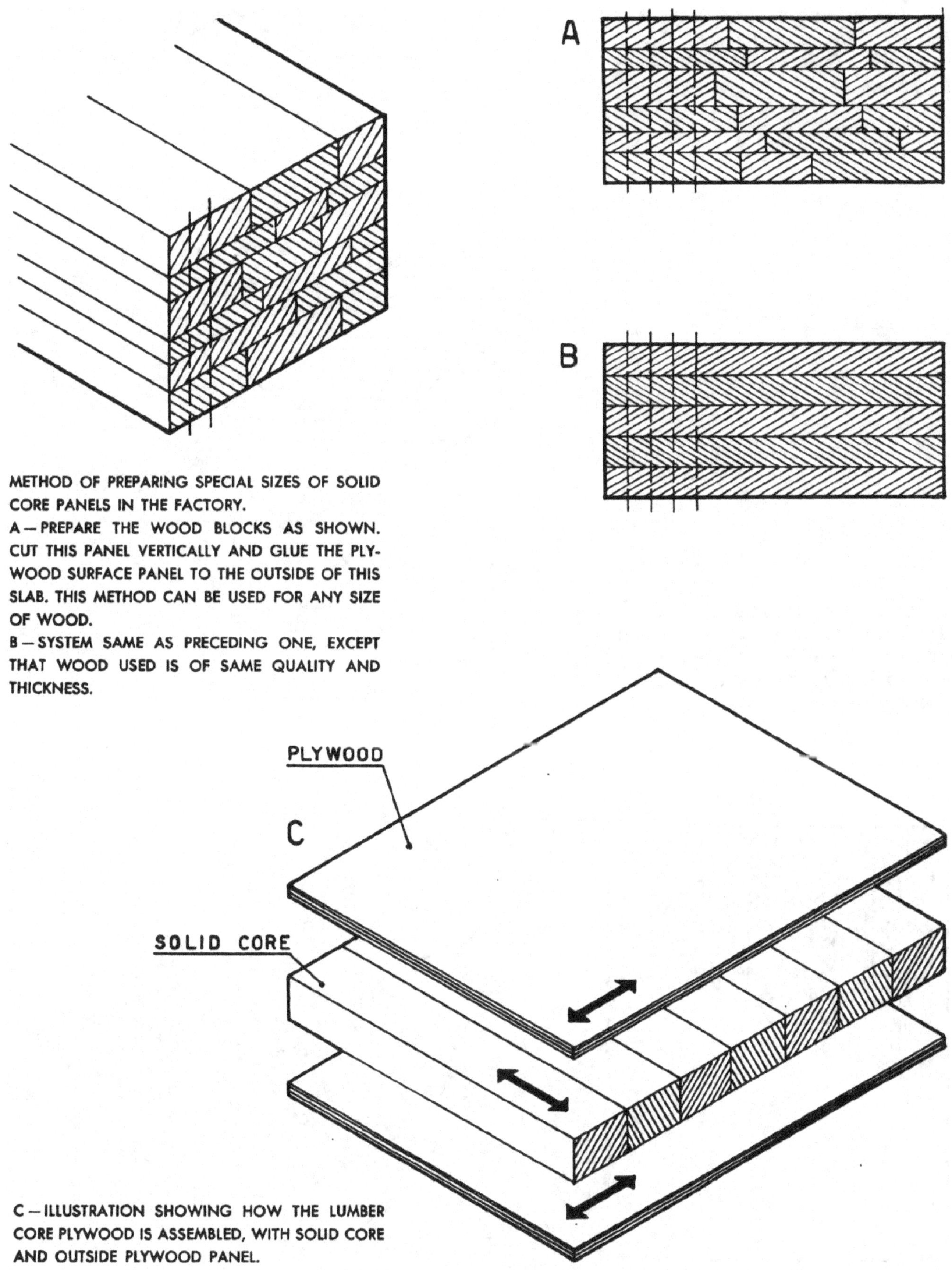

METHOD OF PREPARING SPECIAL SIZES OF SOLID
CORE PANELS IN THE FACTORY.
A — PREPARE THE WOOD BLOCKS AS SHOWN.
CUT THIS PANEL VERTICALLY AND GLUE THE PLY-
WOOD SURFACE PANEL TO THE OUTSIDE OF THIS
SLAB. THIS METHOD CAN BE USED FOR ANY SIZE
OF WOOD.
B — SYSTEM SAME AS PRECEDING ONE, EXCEPT
THAT WOOD USED IS OF SAME QUALITY AND
THICKNESS.

C — ILLUSTRATION SHOWING HOW THE LUMBER
CORE PLYWOOD IS ASSEMBLED, WITH SOLID CORE
AND OUTSIDE PLYWOOD PANEL.

THICK LUMBER CORE PLYWOOD. FOR BEST RE-
SULTS IT IS NECESSARY TO MAKE A CROSS
SAW KERF TO TAKE CARE OF ANY MOVEMENT
IN THE GRAIN.

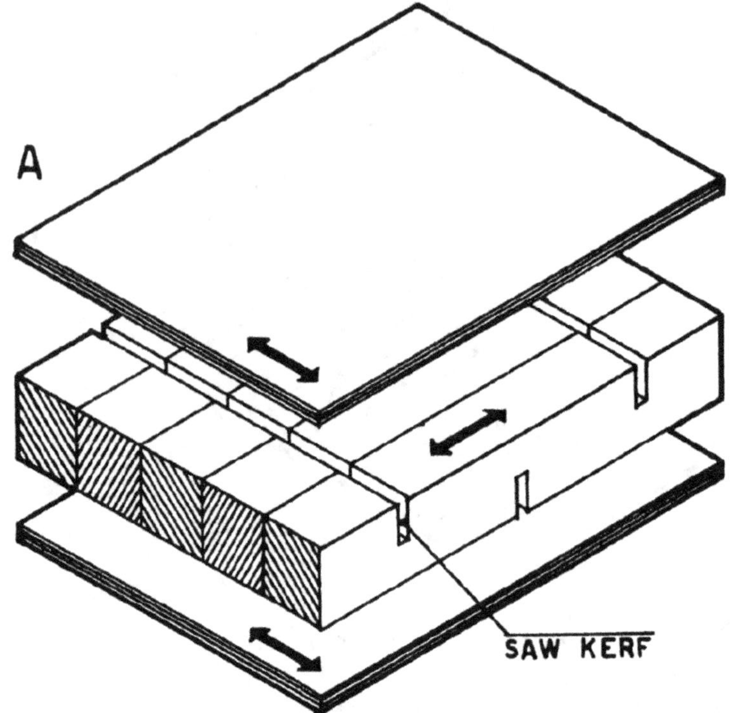

CORRUGATED PANEL FORMED BY CELLULAR
CARDBOARD PLACED IN FRAME AND GLUED
BETWEEN TWO SHEETS OF PLYWOOD. THIS
TYPE OF CONSTRUCTION IS OFTEN USED IN
MAKING FLUSH PANEL DOORS.

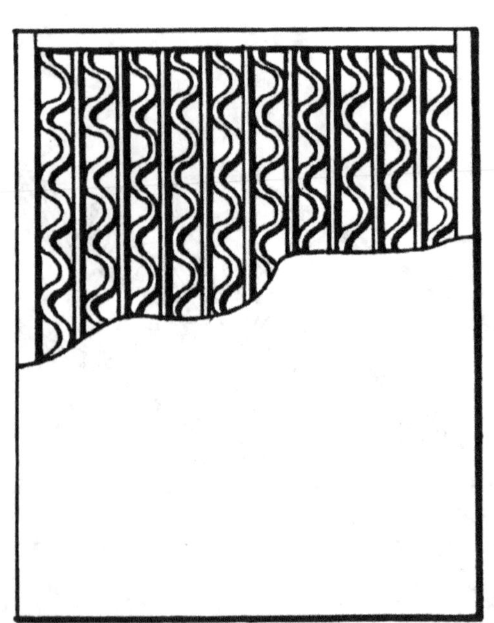

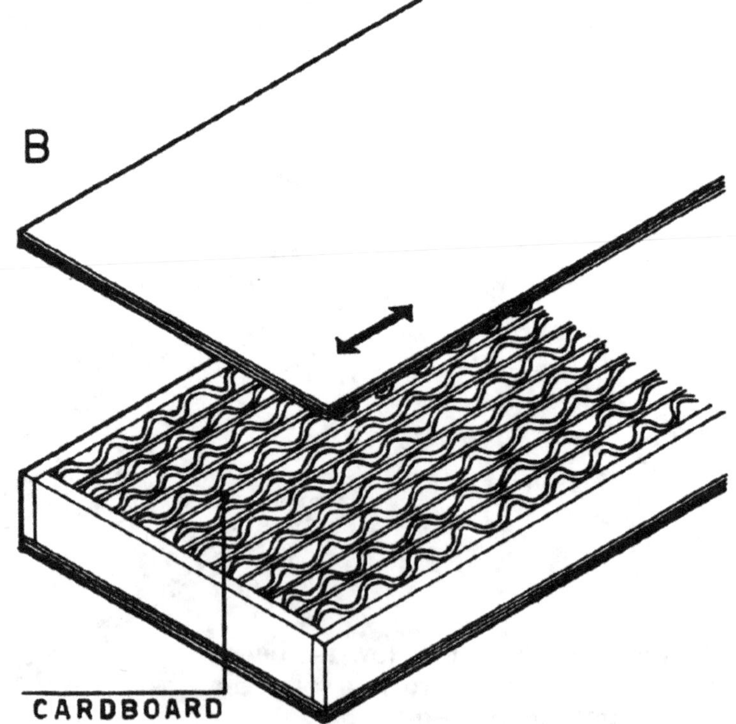

STANDARD THICKNESSES OF PLYWOOD AND LUMBER CORE PLYWOOD

LUMBER CORE PLYWOOD OF ½".

A

¼" PLYWOOD FORMED BY THREE LAYERS OF WOOD.

B

⅛" PLYWOOD FORMED BY THREE LAYERS.

C

³⁄₁₆" PLYWOOD FORMED BY THREE LAYERS.

D

¼" PLYWOOD FORMED BY THREE LAYERS.

E

⅜" PLWOOD FORMED BY THREE LAYERS.

F

⅜" PLYWOOD FORMED BY FIVE LAYERS.

G

½" PLYWOOD FORMED BY FIVE LAYERS.

H

¾" PLYWOOD FORMED BY FIVE LAYERS.

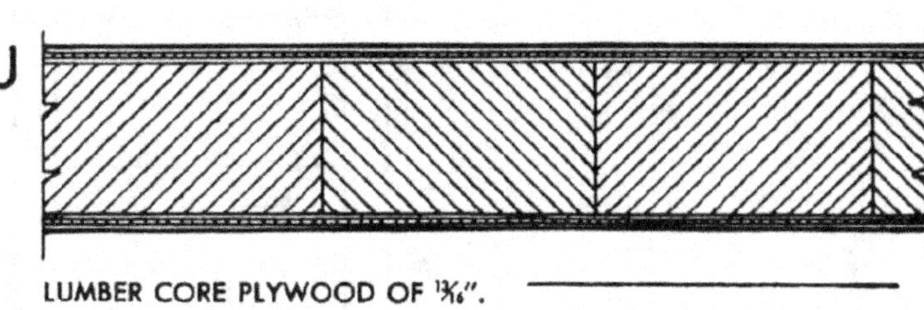

J

LUMBER CORE PLYWOOD OF ¹³⁄₁₆".

SPECIAL PLYWOOD AND LUMBER CORE PLYWOOD

FOR SPECIAL WORK REQUIRING WOOD OF GREAT STRENGTH IT IS OFTEN ADVISABLE TO USE THIS METHOD OF FORMING PANELS OF PLYWOOD. LAYERS OF WOOD OF UNIFORM THICKNESS WITH THE GRAIN RUNNING IN CROSS DIRECTION WILL PROVIDE A STRONG BOARD.

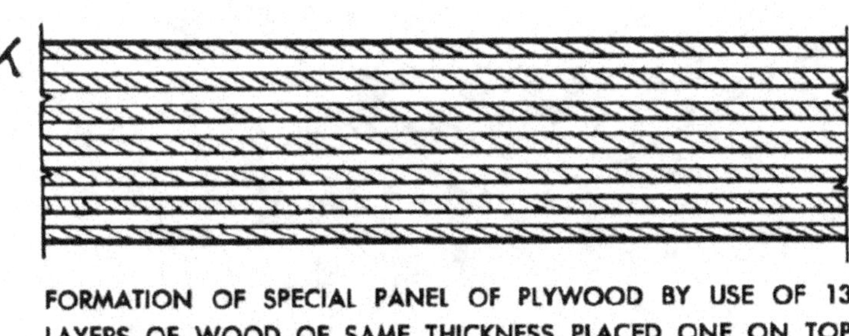

K

FORMATION OF SPECIAL PANEL OF PLYWOOD BY USE OF 13 LAYERS OF WOOD OF SAME THICKNESS PLACED ONE ON TOP OF THE OTHER WITH THE GRAINS RUNNING PERPENDICULAR.

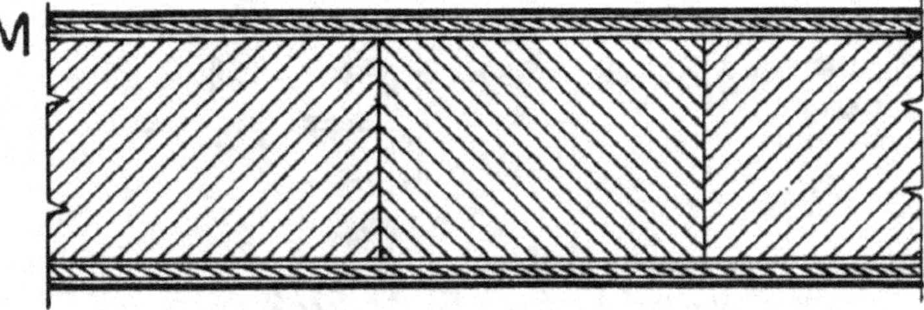

M

LUMBER CORE PLYWOOD WITH EXTRA THICKNESS. ITS FORMATION IS INDICATED ON PAGE 33, FIG. A-B.

PLYWOOD HOLLOW FRAME

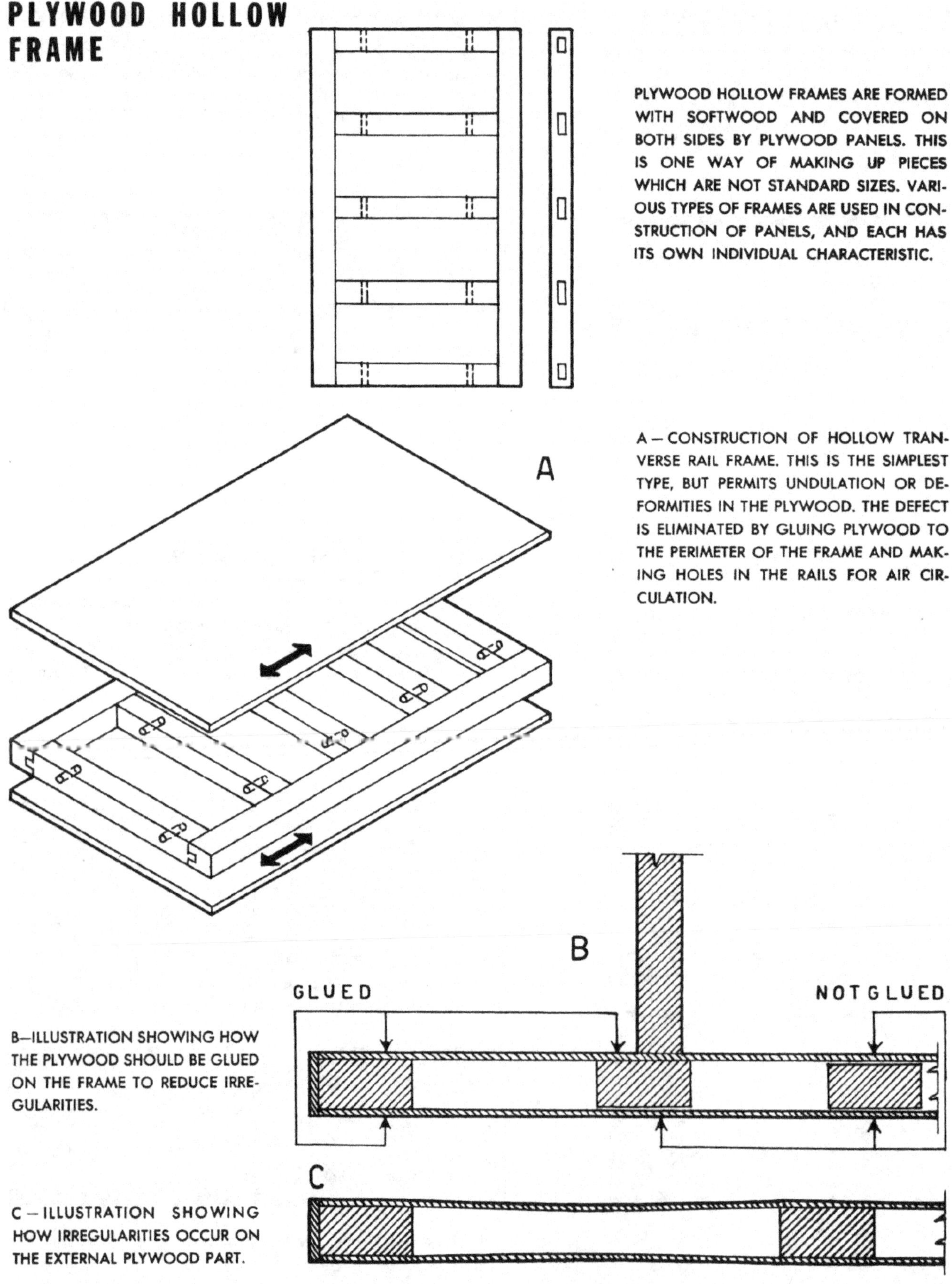

PLYWOOD HOLLOW FRAMES ARE FORMED WITH SOFTWOOD AND COVERED ON BOTH SIDES BY PLYWOOD PANELS. THIS IS ONE WAY OF MAKING UP PIECES WHICH ARE NOT STANDARD SIZES. VARIOUS TYPES OF FRAMES ARE USED IN CONSTRUCTION OF PANELS, AND EACH HAS ITS OWN INDIVIDUAL CHARACTERISTIC.

A — CONSTRUCTION OF HOLLOW TRANVERSE RAIL FRAME. THIS IS THE SIMPLEST TYPE, BUT PERMITS UNDULATION OR DEFORMITIES IN THE PLYWOOD. THE DEFECT IS ELIMINATED BY GLUING PLYWOOD TO THE PERIMETER OF THE FRAME AND MAKING HOLES IN THE RAILS FOR AIR CIRCULATION.

B—ILLUSTRATION SHOWING HOW THE PLYWOOD SHOULD BE GLUED ON THE FRAME TO REDUCE IRREGULARITIES.

C—ILLUSTRATION SHOWING HOW IRREGULARITIES OCCUR ON THE EXTERNAL PLYWOOD PART.

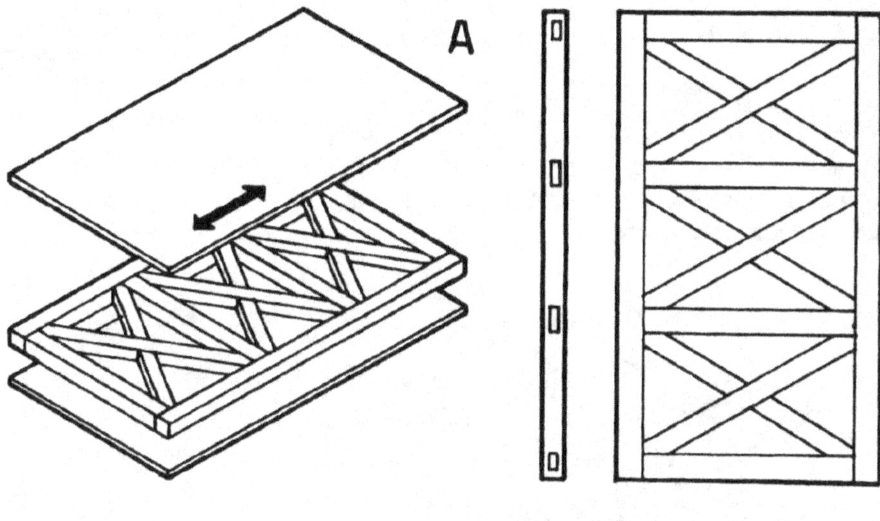

CROSS RAIL FRAME. WITH THIS METHOD YOU CAN OBTAIN GOOD CONSTRUCTION OF THE FRAME WITH LIMITED DEFORMITIES IN THE PLYWOOD.

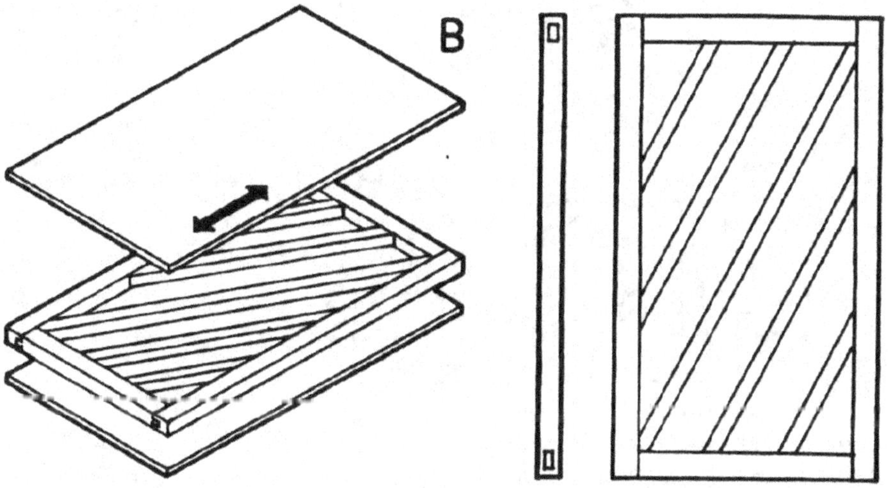

DIAGONAL RAIL FRAME USED IN GOOD CONSTRUCTION.

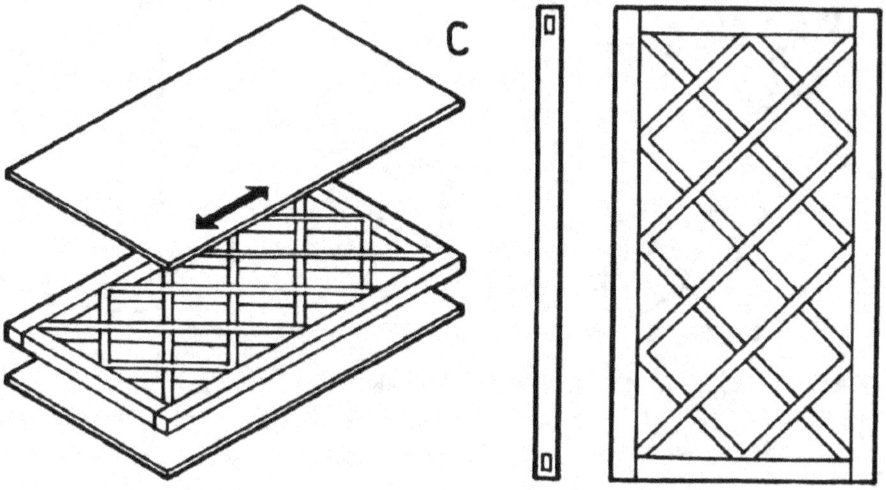

THE LOOSE CELLULAR FRAME IS THE TYPE BEST SUITED TO PLYWOOD.

VENEER

VENEER IS FORMED BY STRIPPING A CONTINUOUS SHEET FROM THE LOG. THIS SHEET IS APPLIED WITH GLUE TO OTHER WOODS TO CREATE A RICH SURFACE EFFECT. THE APPLICATION IS MADE DURING THE PROCESS OF CONSTRUCTION.

VENEER MUST BE APPLIED ACROSS THE GRAIN.

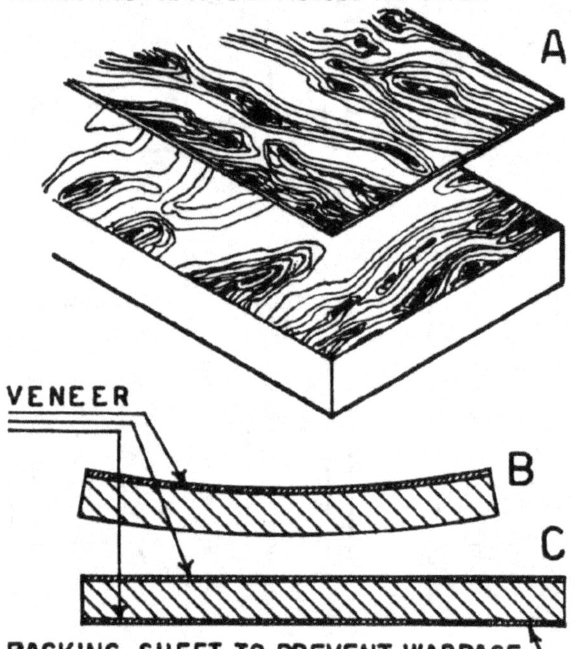

IF VENEER IS APPLIED TO ONE SIDE OF THE WOOD IT WILL BEND THE WOOD. TO OBTAIN A STRAIGHT PANEL APPLY VENEER TO BOTH SIDES.

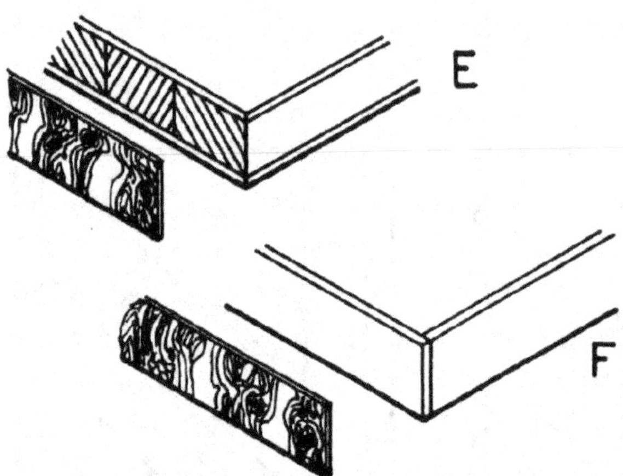

VENEER APPLIED TO BORDERS OF PLYWOOD PANELS WILL TEND TO SHOW JOINT MARKS. TO OBTAIN THE BEST WORK IT IS ADVISABLE TO BORDER THE PANEL WITH HARDWOOD.

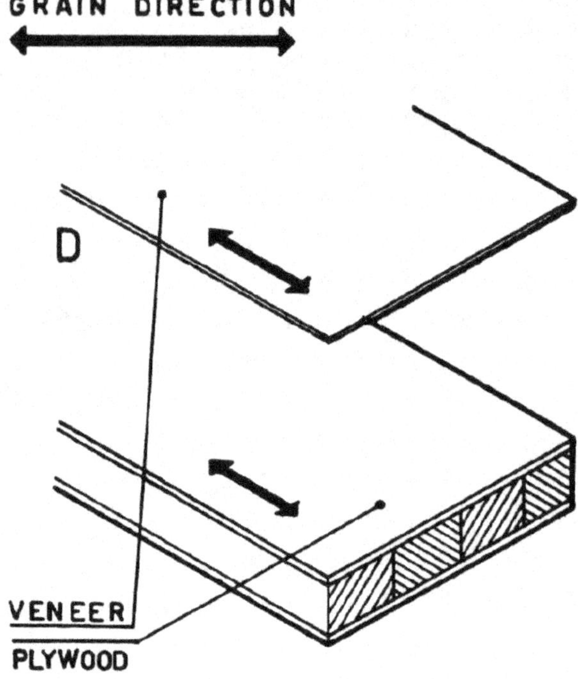

APPLYING VENEER TO OTHER PIECES SO THAT THE GRAINS RUN PARALLEL MAY CAUSE SMALL CRACKS IN TIME.

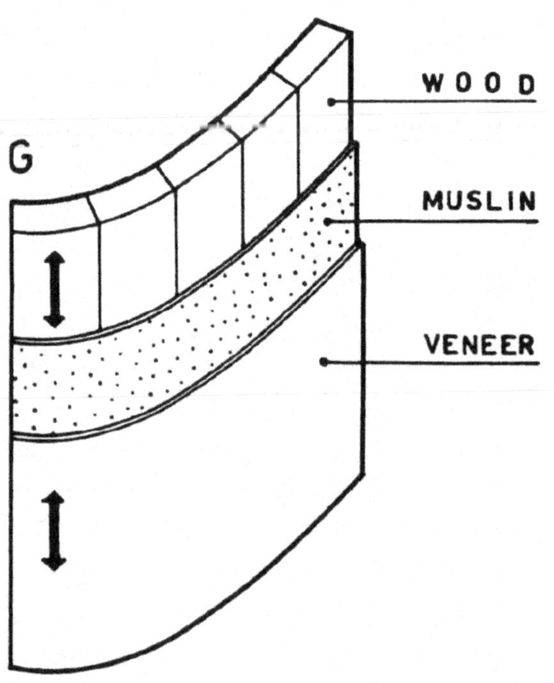

CURVED PANEL MADE WITH VENEER-COVERED SEGMENT. TO AVOID MARKS IT IS BEST TO PLACE MUSLIN BETWEEN THE VENEER AND THE WOOD.

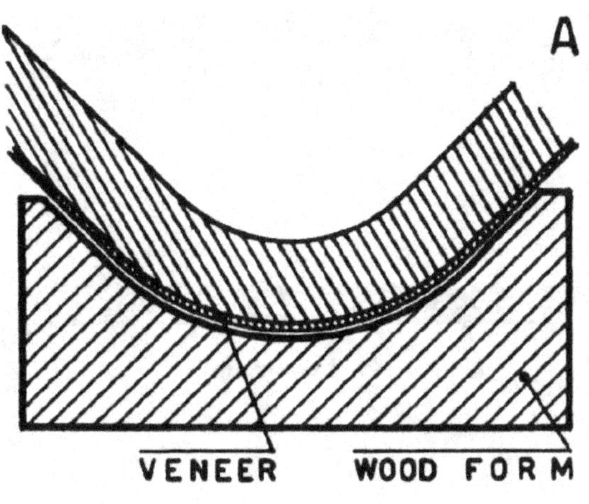

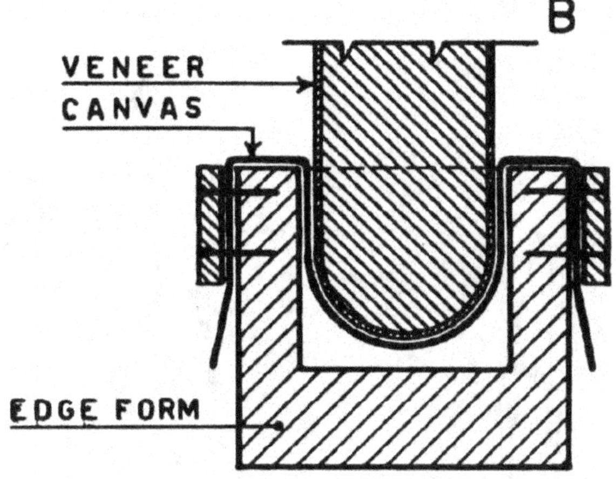

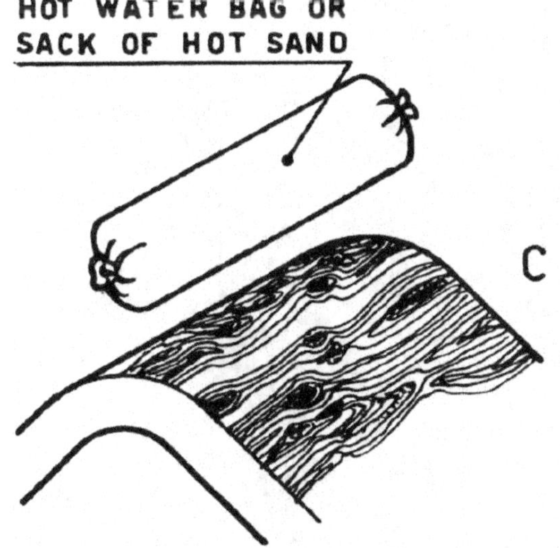

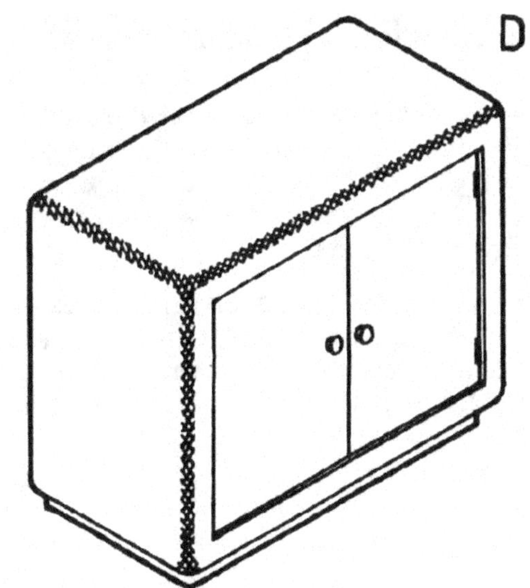

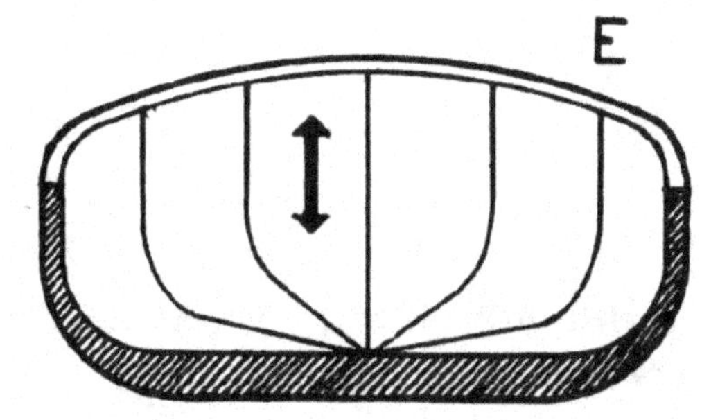

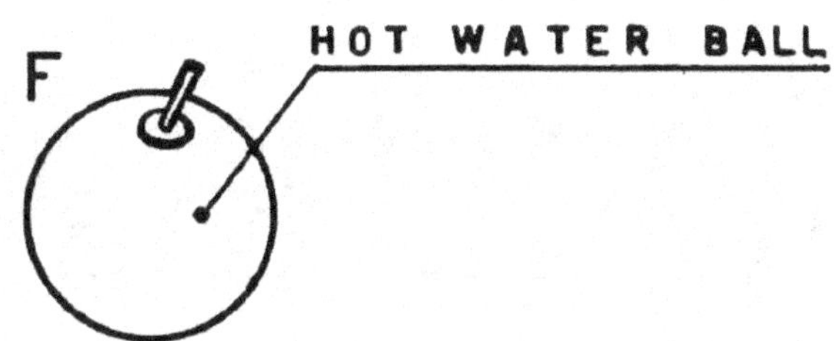

THREE DIFFERENT SYSTEMS TO KEEP VENEER BENT UNTIL THE GLUE HAS DRIED. SHOULD THE VENEER BE APPLIED TO SPECIFIC SURFACES, EITHER CONCAVE OR CONVEX, IT IS BEST TO USE A HOT WATER BALL, OR A SMALL SACK OF HOT SAND TO MAKE THE VENEER ADHERE TIGHTLY TO THE WOOD.

GRAIN DIRECTION IN CURVED PIECES

VARIOUS TYPES OF CURVES APPEAR IN FURNITURE DESIGN. ONE FINDS BOTH INTERNAL AND EXTERNAL ANGLES, AND COMPLETE CURVATURE IN CYLINDRICAL SHAPES IS OBTAINED BY PRESSING MORE THAN ONE LAYER OF WOOD TOGETHER.

THERE ARE MANY WAYS OF CONSTRUCTING THESE CURVES. I SHALL EXPLAIN THE PROPERTIES OF THE DIFFERENT CURVES, DESCRIBE SEVERAL WAYS TO BUILD THEM, AND RECOMMEND THE BEST ONES TO USE IN SPECIFIC TYPES OF WORK.

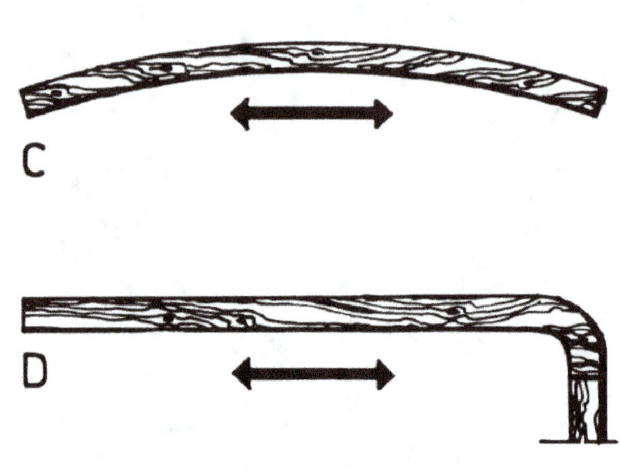

GRAIN DIRECTION

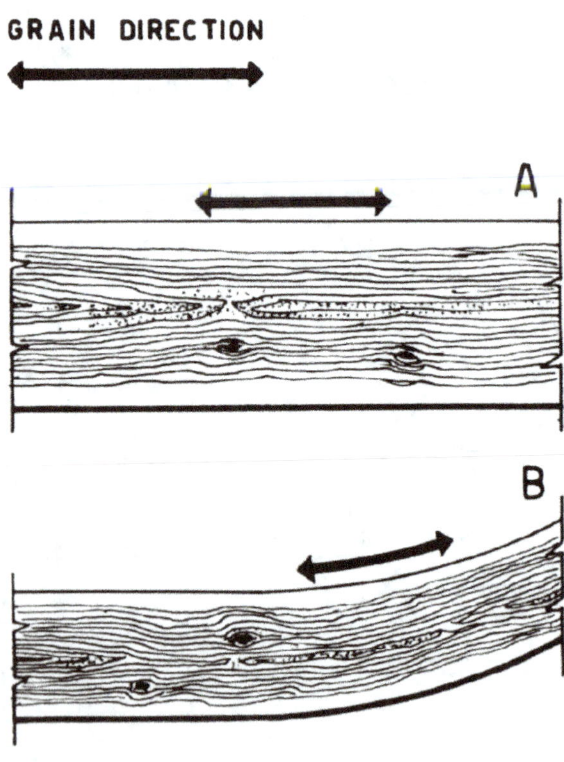

IN "A" THE NATURAL DIRECTION OF THE GRAIN IS STRAIGHT, WHILE THE GRAIN IN "B" IS NATURALLY CURVED.

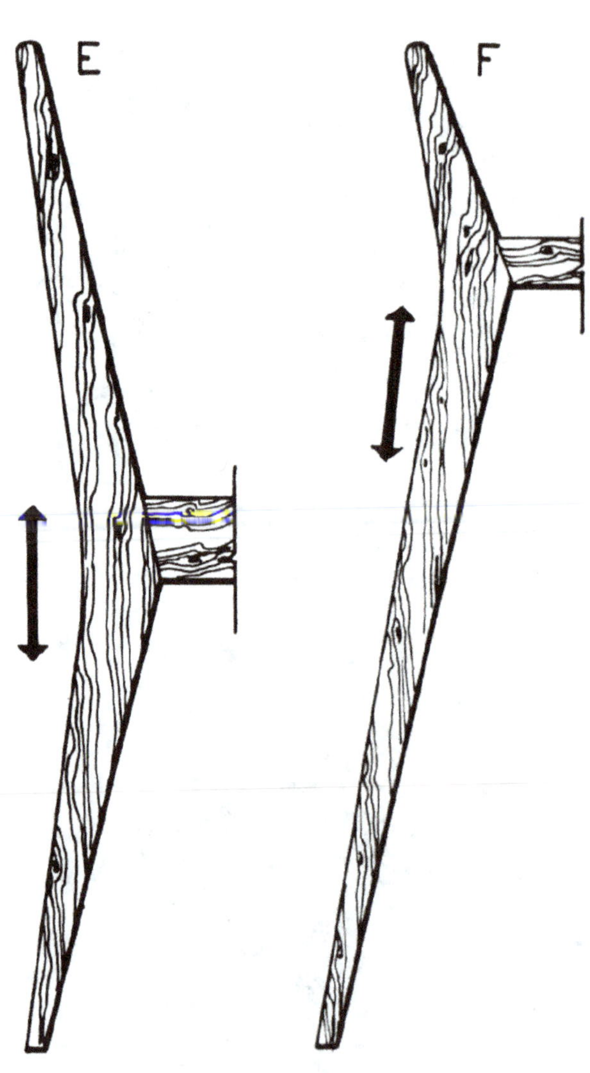

FOUR DIFFERENT EXAMPLES OF GRAIN DIRECTION IN CURVED PIECES. NOTE THAT THE FUNDAMENTAL BASE OF THE GRAIN RUNS IN THE DIRECTION IT MUST SUPPORT. THIS IS DONE TO KEEP THE WOOD FROM CRACKING.

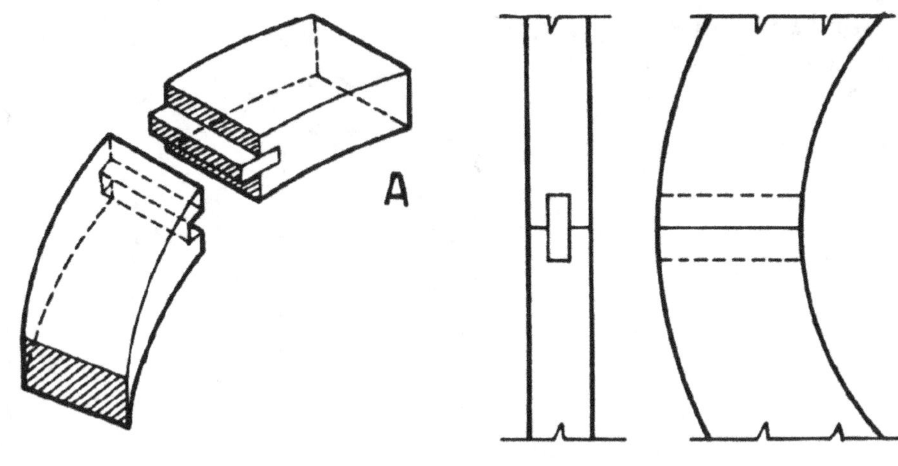

FEATHER JOINT. THIS IS A COM-
MON METHOD OF JOINING
CURVED PIECES.

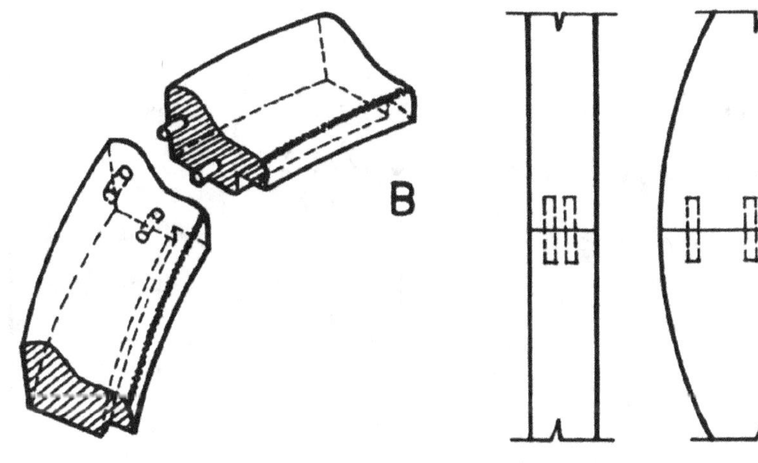

DOWEL JOINT. EASILY MADE AND
USED BY THE AMATEUR CRAFTS-
MAN.

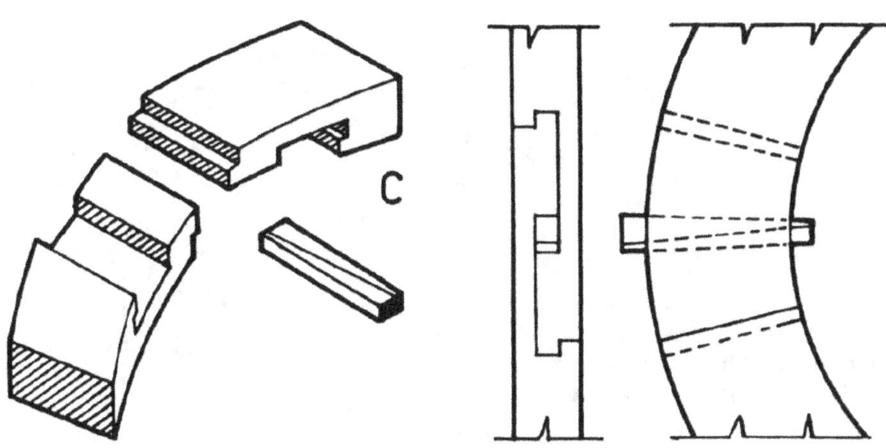

SCARF JOINT WITH WEDGES.
USED IN CARPENTRY WORK.

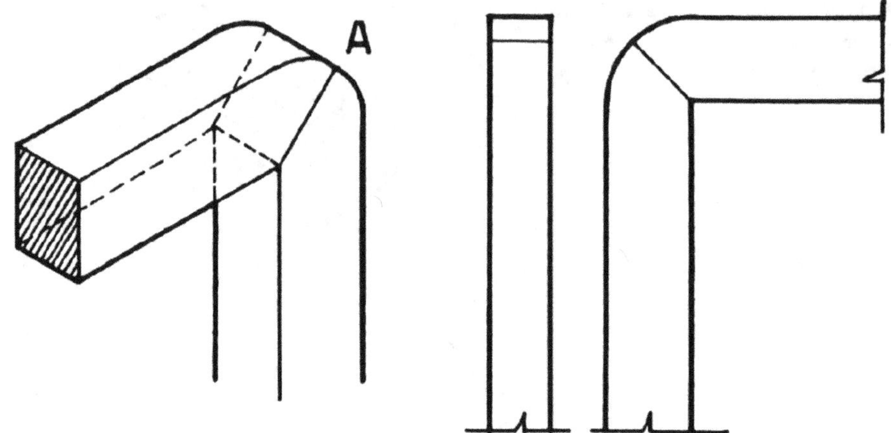

FRAME WITH ROUND CURVE.
COMMON TYPE AND USED EX-
TENSIVELY.

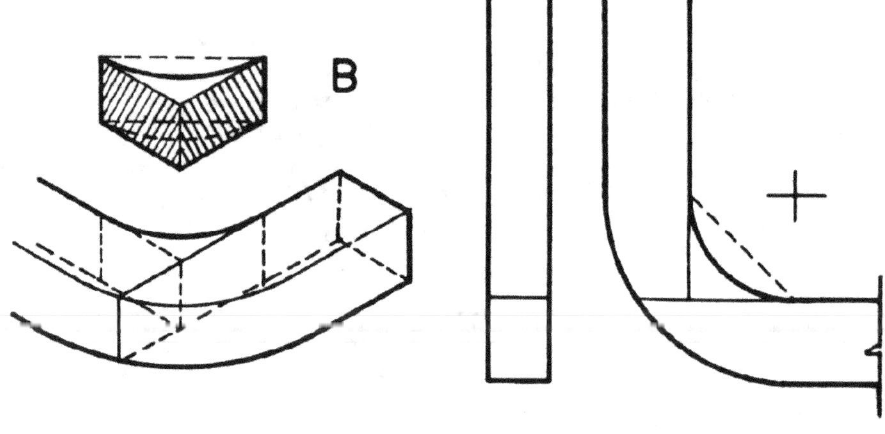

ROUND CORNER FRAME REIN-
FORCED WITH BLOCK. USED
WHEN CURVE HAS WEAKENED
THE JOINT OF THE TWO RAILS.

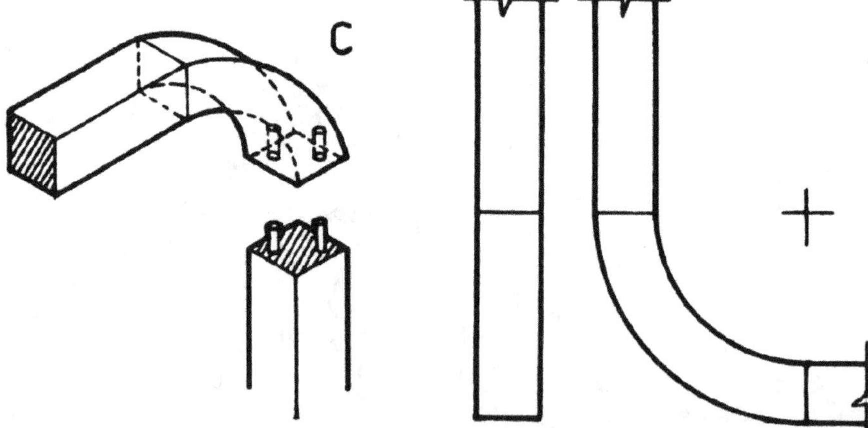

ROUND CORNER WITH DOWEL.
USED WHEN THERE IS A LARGE
CURVE.

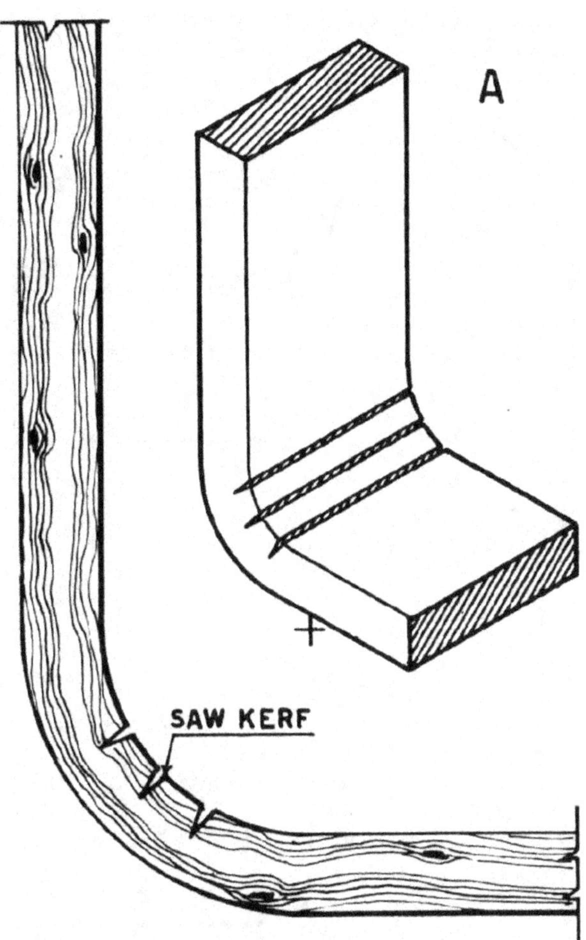

A — CURVE IN A NORMAL TRANSVERSE TO ACHIEVE DESIRED RESULTS A SERIES OF SAW KERFS SHOULD BE MADE IN THE WOOD.

C — CURVE OF A CLOSED BAND WITH A THIN BATTEN.

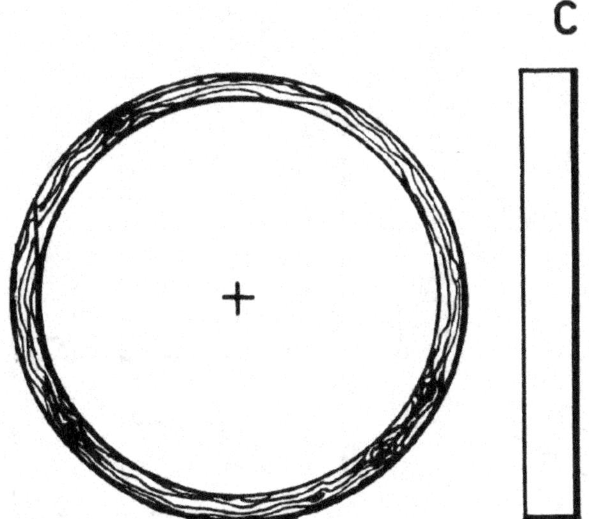

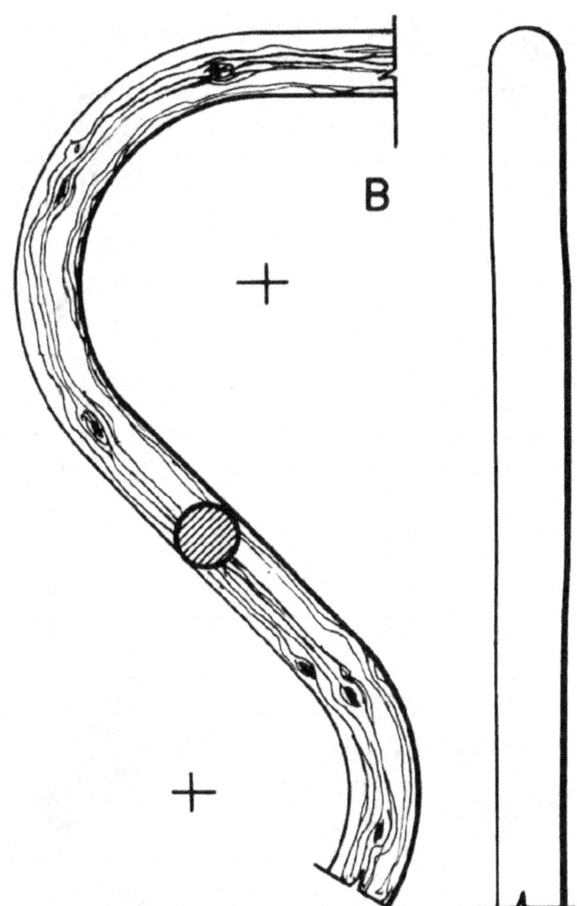

B — CURVE OF A WOOD DOWEL. ALMOST ANY TYPE OF A CURVE CAN BE MADE WITH A DOWEL.

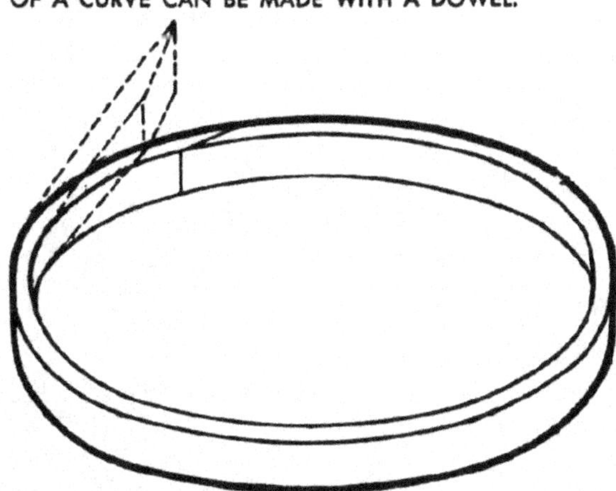

STEAM BENDING. WOOD WHICH IS CURVED WITH STEAM GIVES EXCELLENT RESULTS IN SOME TYPES OF WOOD SUCH AS THE HARD WOODS, OAK, ASH, AND WALNUT. IT IS OF ABSOLUTELY NO USE IN OTHER TYPES.

THE EXAMPLES SHOWN PRESENT THE BASIC TYPES OF CURVES WHICH MAY BE CONSTRUCTED BY THIS METHOD.

GRAIN BANDING ON A PLY-
WOOD BOARD. THIS IS USED IN
STANDARD PRODUCTION.

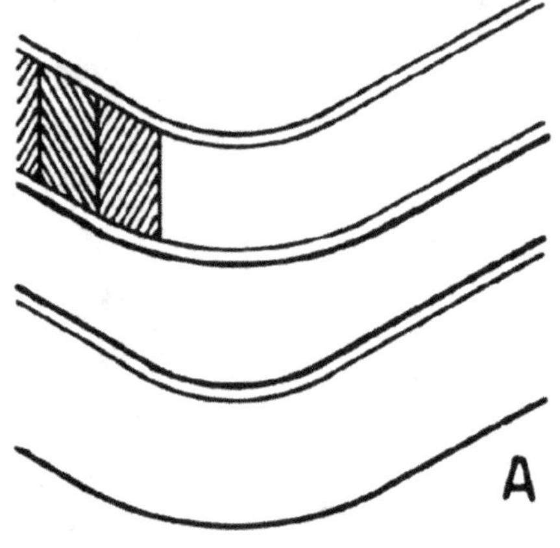

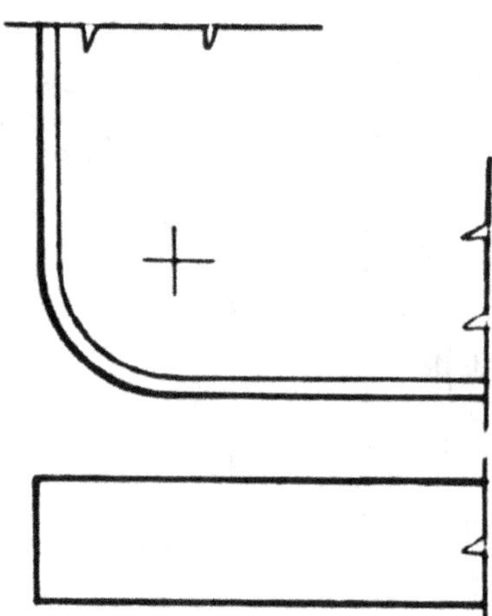

A

ROUND CORNER EDGE AS AP-
PLIED IN GOOD TYPES OF CON-
STRUCTION.

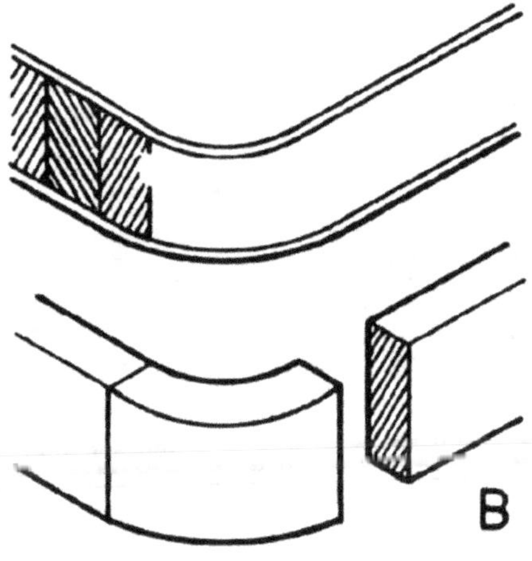

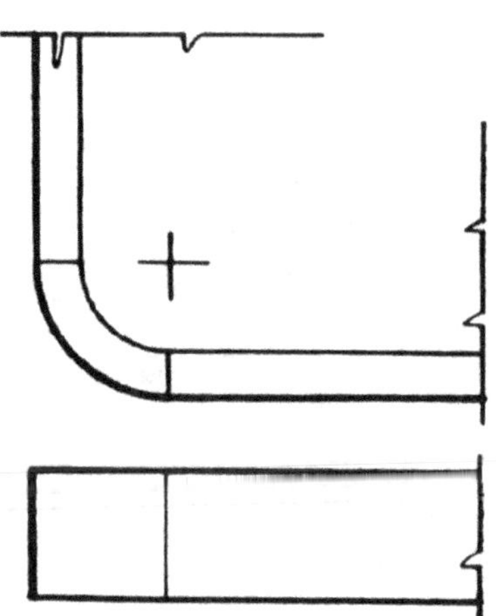

B

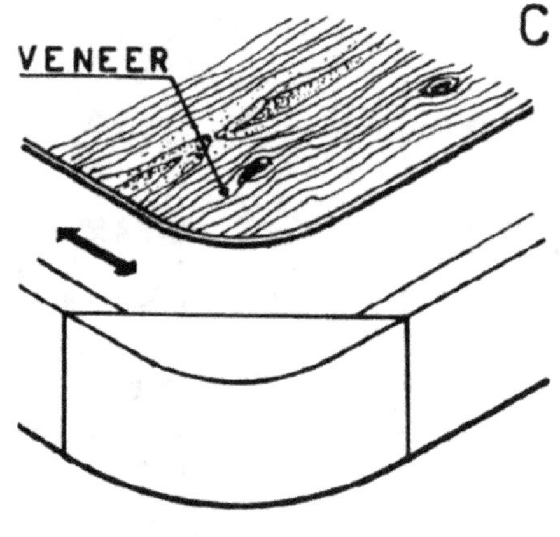

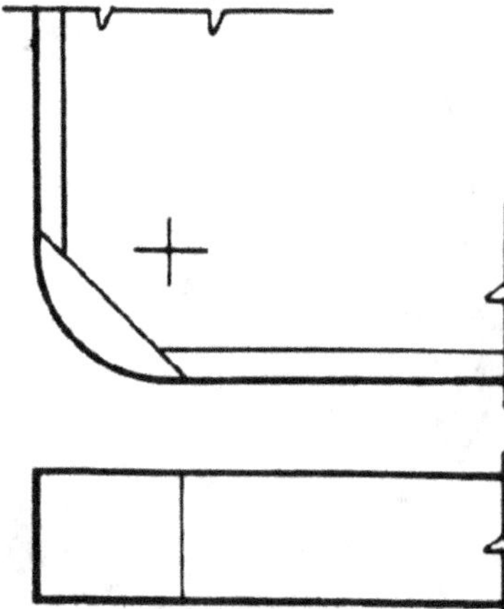

C

CORNER BLOCK, USED WHEN THE
PANEL IS COVERED WITH VENEER. —

JOINING TWO FRAMES WITH CURVED CORNER BLOCK. THIS TYPE OF CONSTRUCTION IS USED IN SMALL CURVED PIECES.

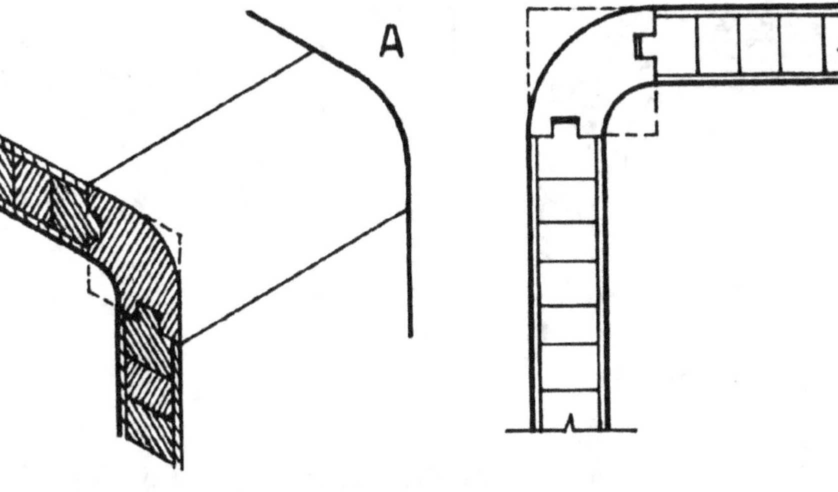

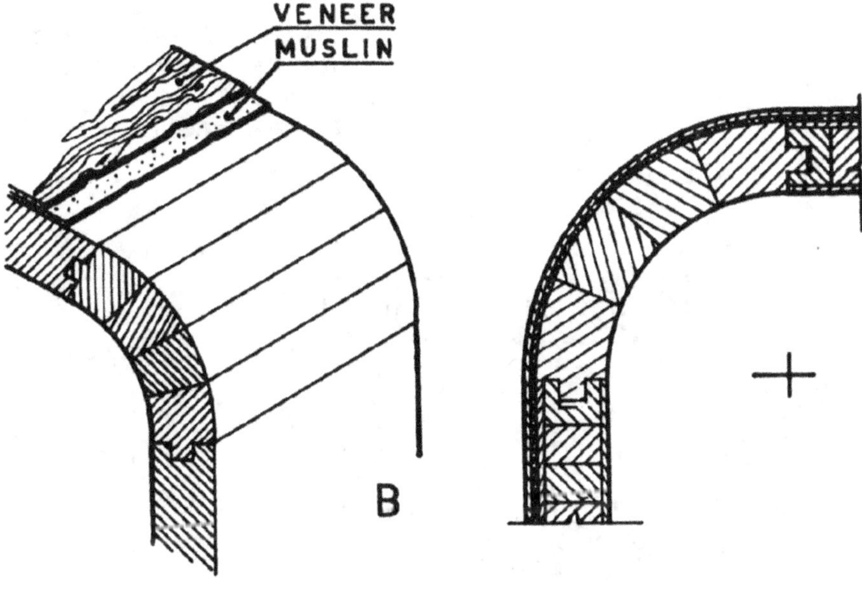

FRAME JOINT USING CURVED SEGMENT. THIS METHOD GIVES MAXIMUM STABILITY TO A CURVE.

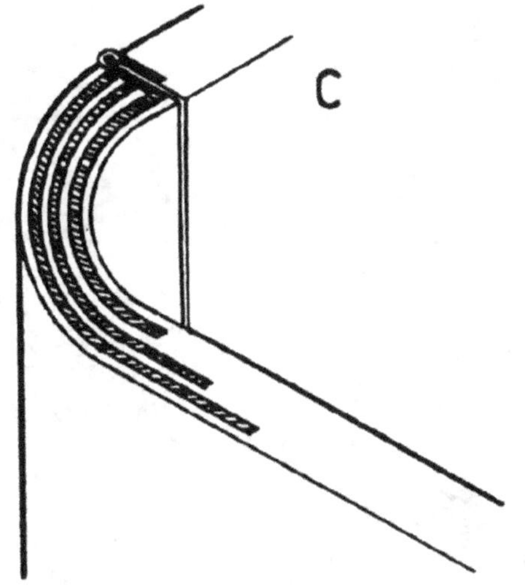

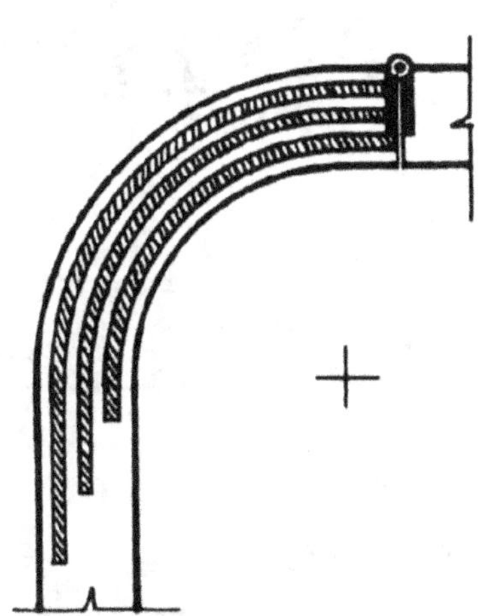

LAMINATED CURVE IN THE CORNER FRAME. THIS MAKES A GOOD STRONG CURVE. IT IS OFTEN USED IN DOOR CONSTRUCTION.

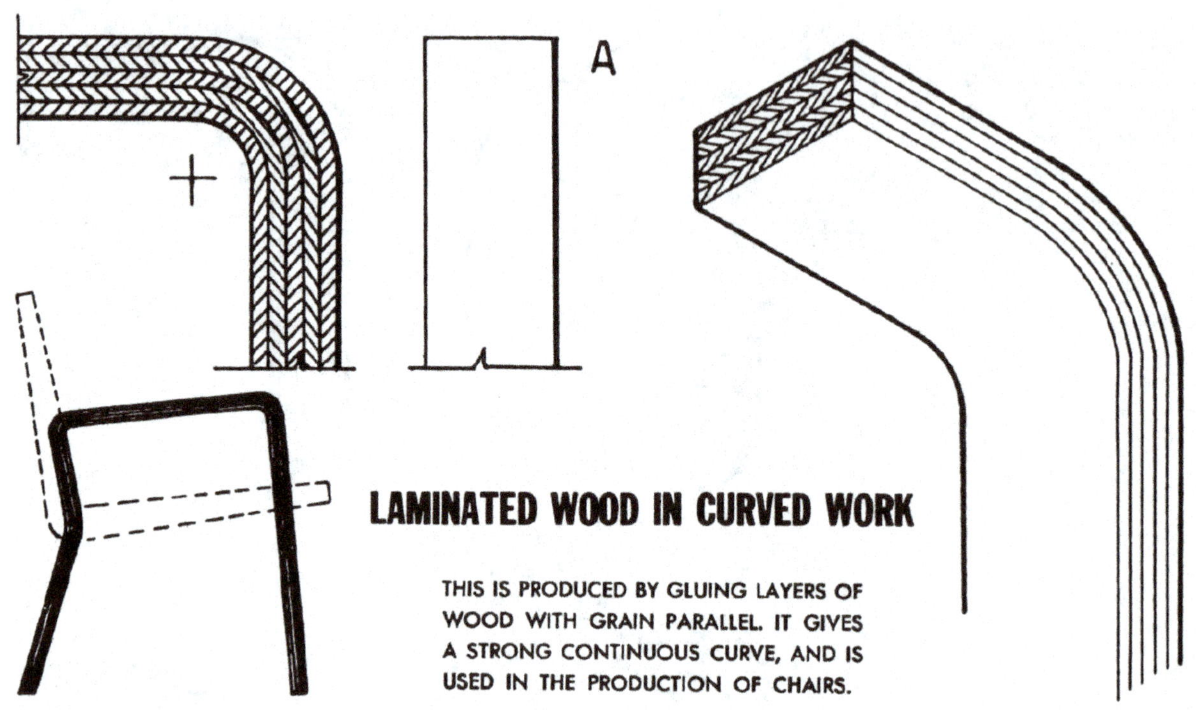

LAMINATED WOOD IN CURVED WORK

THIS IS PRODUCED BY GLUING LAYERS OF WOOD WITH GRAIN PARALLEL. IT GIVES A STRONG CONTINUOUS CURVE, AND IS USED IN THE PRODUCTION OF CHAIRS.

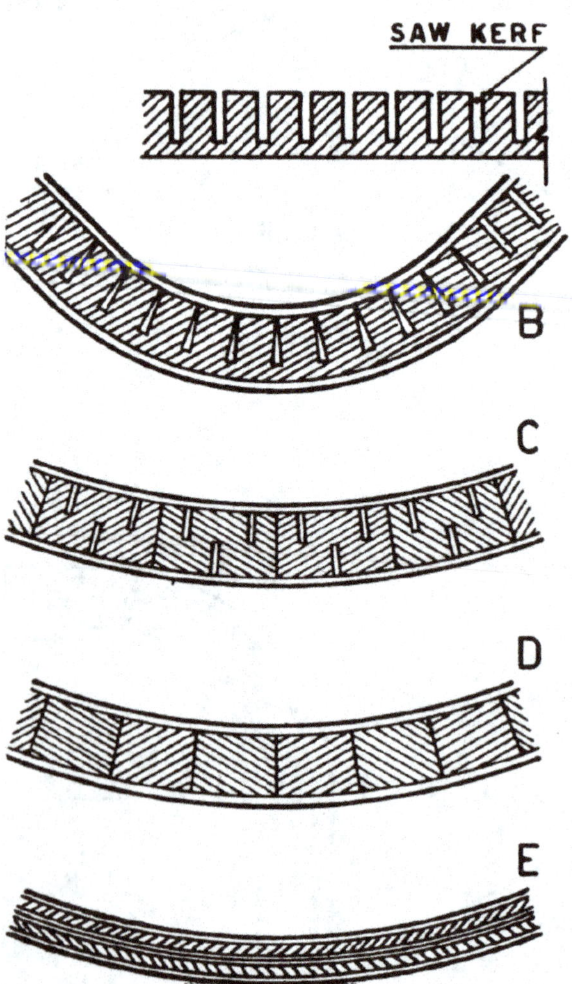

B — LUMBER CORE PLYWOOD: SAW KERFING SHOULD BE DONE ON ONE SIDE OF THE SOLID CORE, THEN GLUED INTO THE FRAME WITH TWO PANELS OF PLYWOOD ON EACH SIDE. THIS MAKES A GOOD PANEL.

C — D — HERE ARE TWO OTHER METHODS.

E — TWO PLYWOOD PANELS ARE GLUED TOGETHER IN A FORM TO OBTAIN ONE PANEL WITH DESIRED CURVATURE.

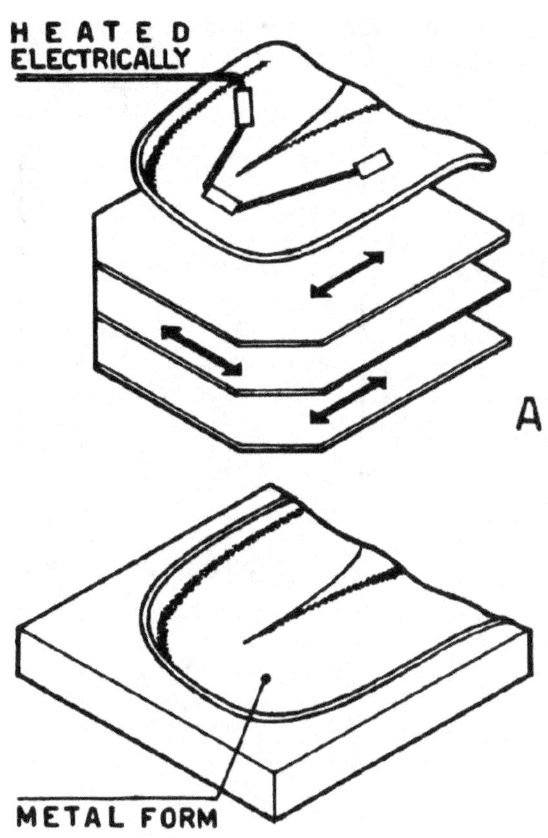

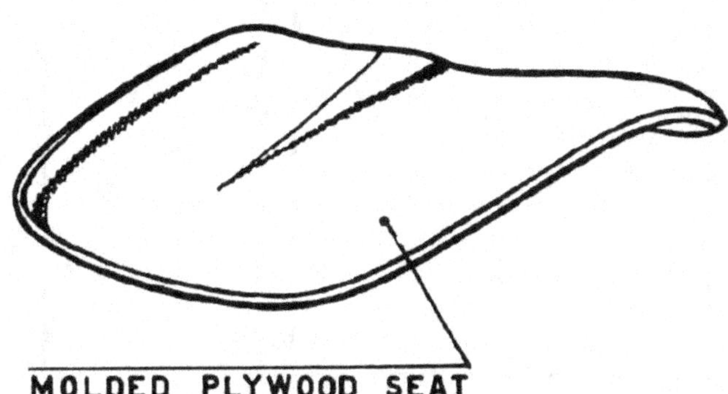

MOLDED PLYWOOD

LIGHT MOLDED PLYWOOD IS OBTAINED BY GLUING LAYERS OF WOOD INTO FORMS OF METAL (MALE AND FEMALE). THE MOLD IS PRESSED TOGETHER WITH CLAMPS. THIS METHOD IS IN WIDE USE IN THE PRODUCTION OF CHAIR SEATS AND BACKS.

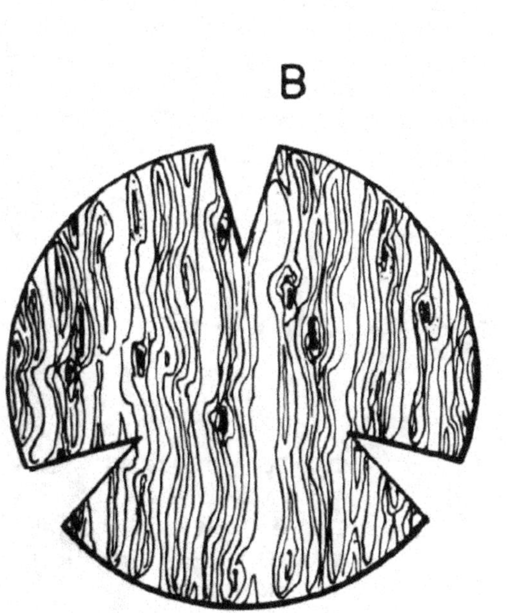

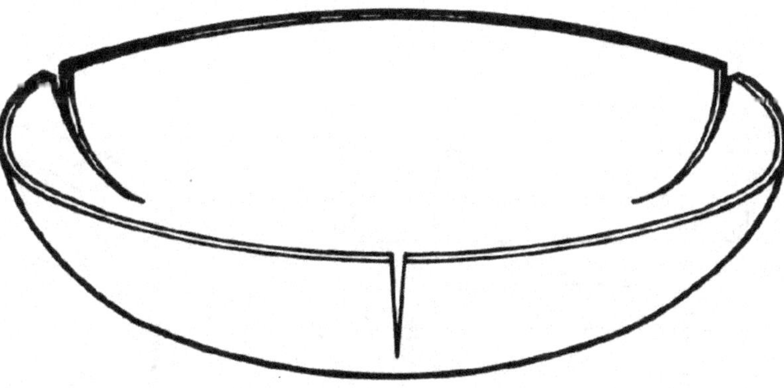

HEAVY MOLDED PLYWOOD. THE WOOD IS DIFFICULT TO MOLD IN A FORM. ITS STRENGTH MAKES IT VERY DIFFICULT TO SHAPE IN OTHER THAN NORMAL CURVES. IF ONE DESIRES TO MAKE OTHER CURVES IT IS NECESSARY TO CUT OR REMOVE SECTORS OF THE WOOD SO THAT THE CURVING WILL FILL IN THE OPEN SECTORS. WITH THIS METHOD YOU CAN MAKE LARGE CURVED SHAPES SUITABLE FOR CHAIRS, ARMCHAIRS, ETC.

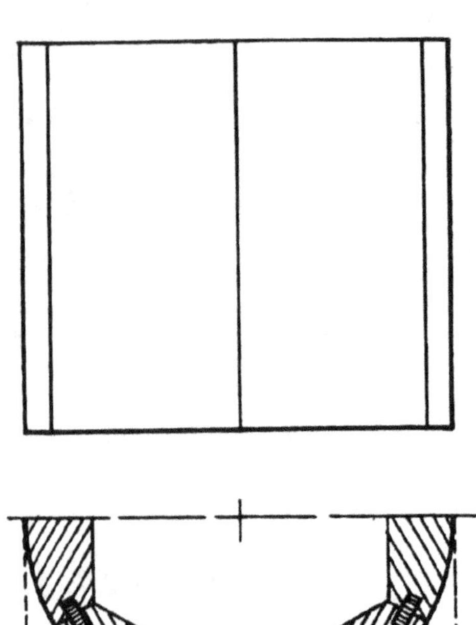

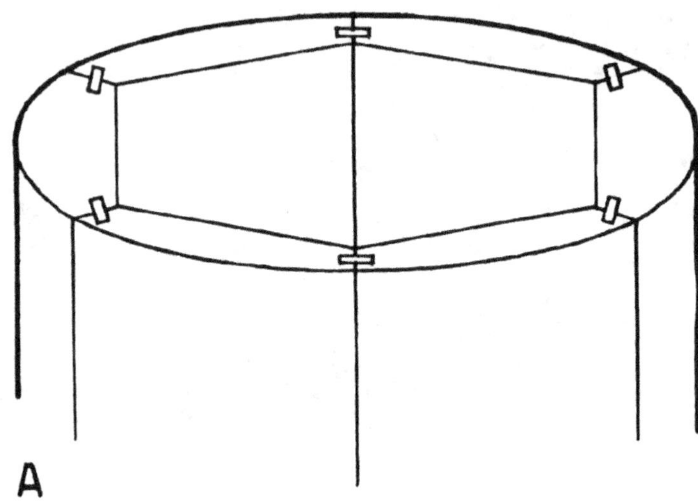

CYLINDER WITH FEATHER.

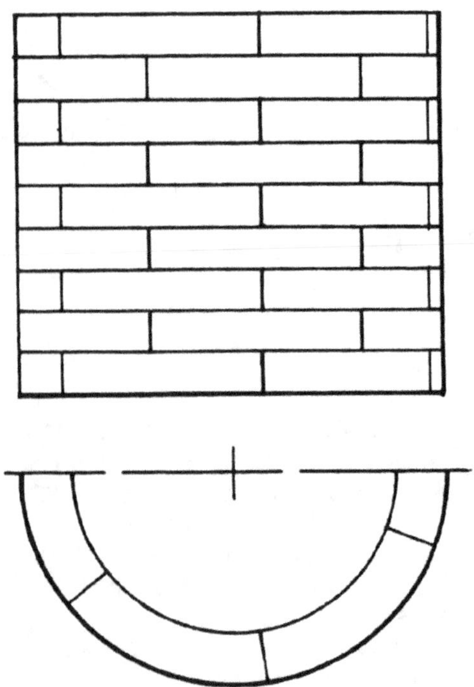

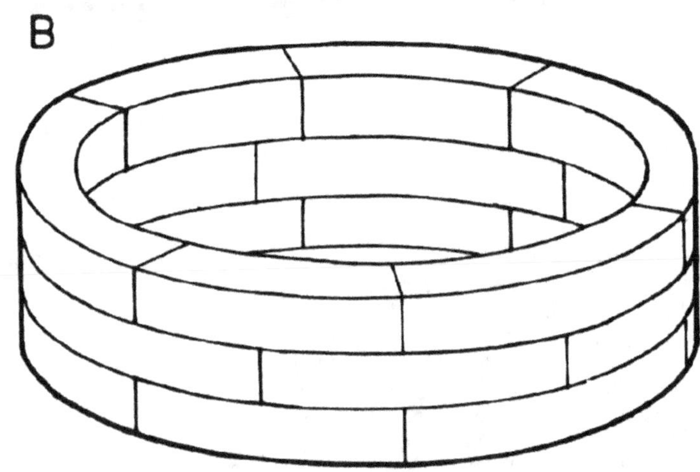

CYLINDER WITH LAP BUTT JOINT. A STRONG TYPE OF JOINT EXCEPT THAT THE GRAIN RUNNING PARALLEL TO THE LENGTH HAS A TENDENCY TO SHRINK.

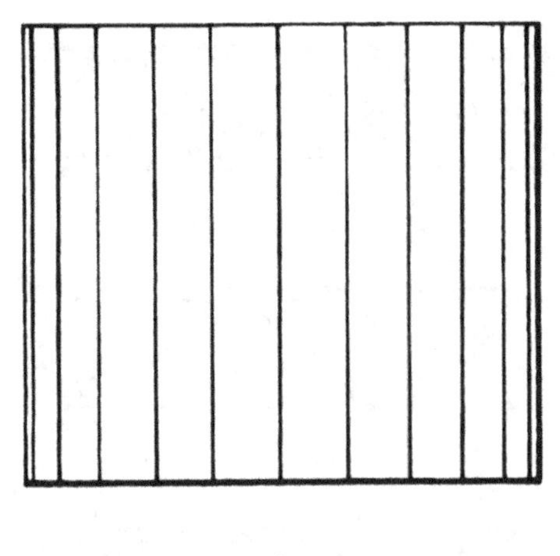
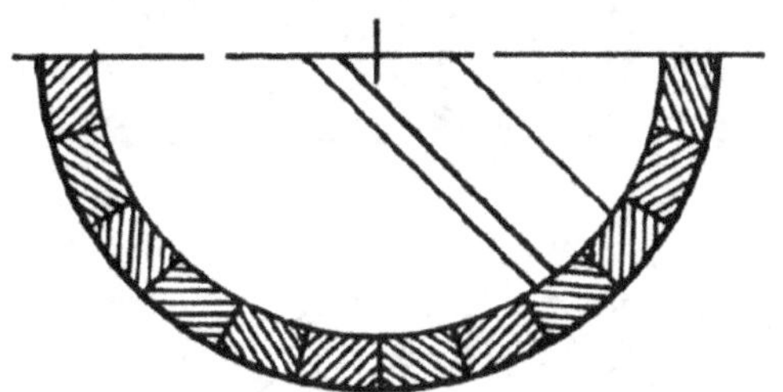
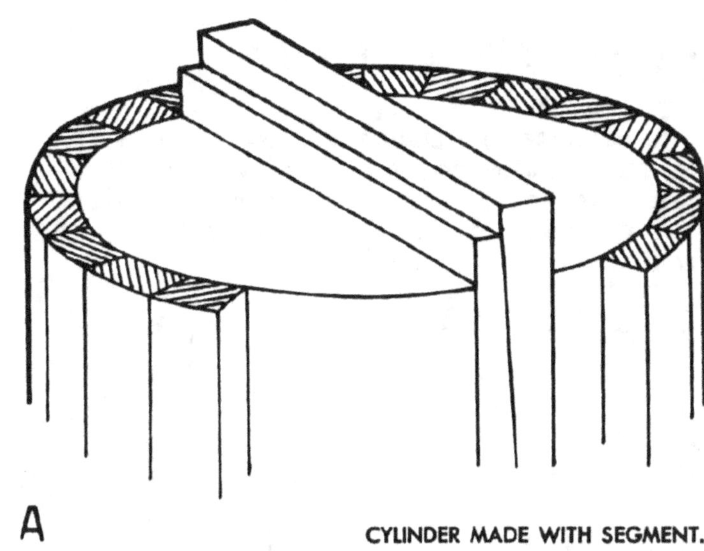

A

CYLINDER MADE WITH SEGMENT. A GOOD SYSTEM OF CONSTRUCTION WHICH CAN BE USED WITH WOOD TURNING MACHINE.

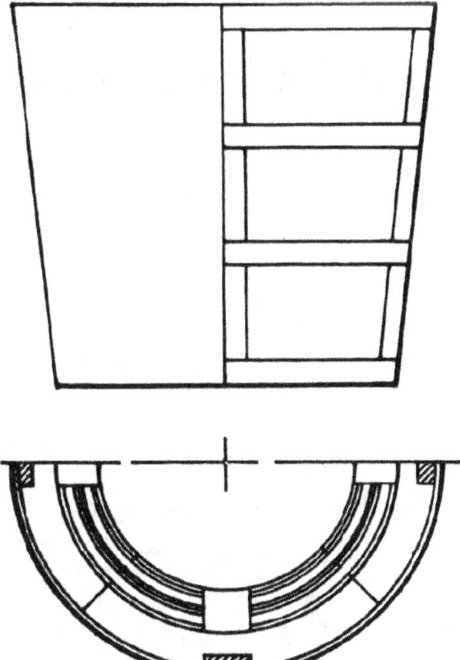
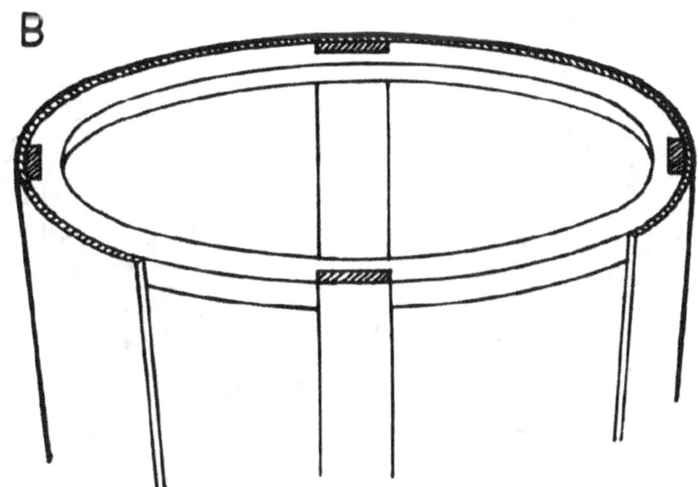

B

CONE WITH EXTERIOR PLYWOOD, IF USED IN CABINET WORK, AND WITH CARDBOARD IF USED IN UPHOLSTERY WORK.

EDGE TREATMENT

IN ORDER TO KEEP THE LAMINATES IN PLYWOOD OR
EDGE OF A LUMBER CORE PANEL FROM VIEW THE
LAYER SURFACES MUST BE COVERED WITH HARDWOOD
EDGES. THE METHODS USED ARE ILLUSTRATED AS
FOLLOWS:

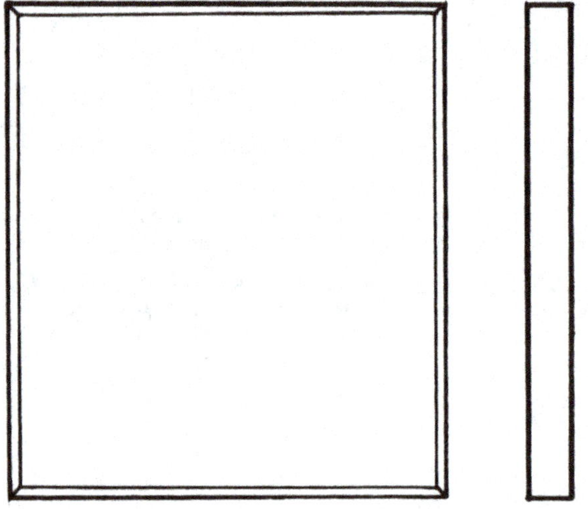

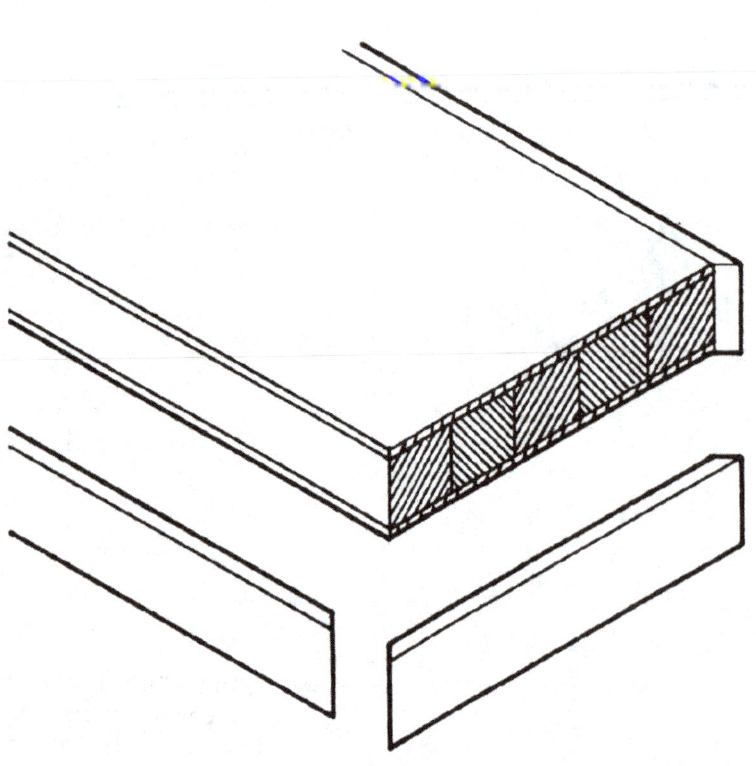

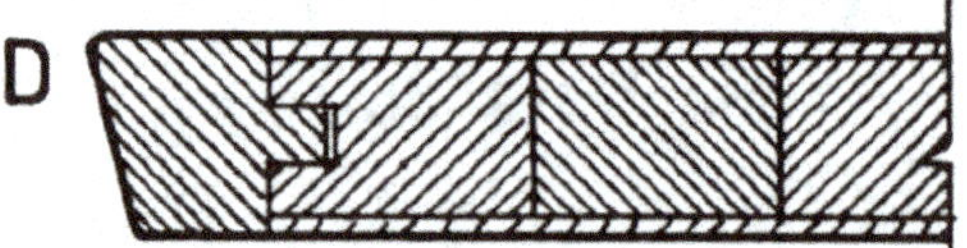

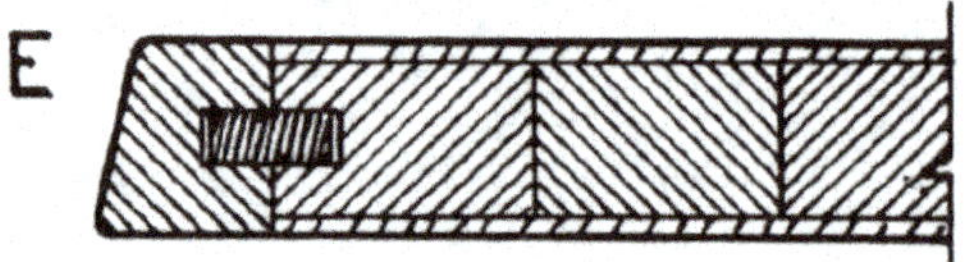

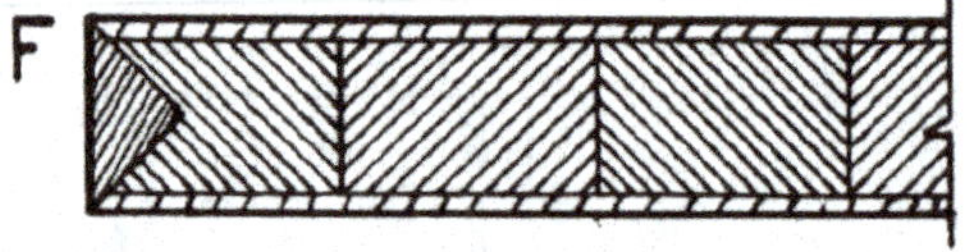

A — VENEER BANDING USED IN STANDARD WORK.

B — WITH SOLID EDGE.

C — TONGUE, FRAME, AND GROOVE EDGE.

D — TONGUE EDGE AND GROOVE FRAME.

E — WITH FEATHER.

F — WITH MITER JOINT USED IN FINE WORK.

FIXED FABRIC ON BOARD

THERE ARE VARIOUS TECHNIQUES WHEREBY THE FABRIC MAY BE ATTACHED TO A PANEL.

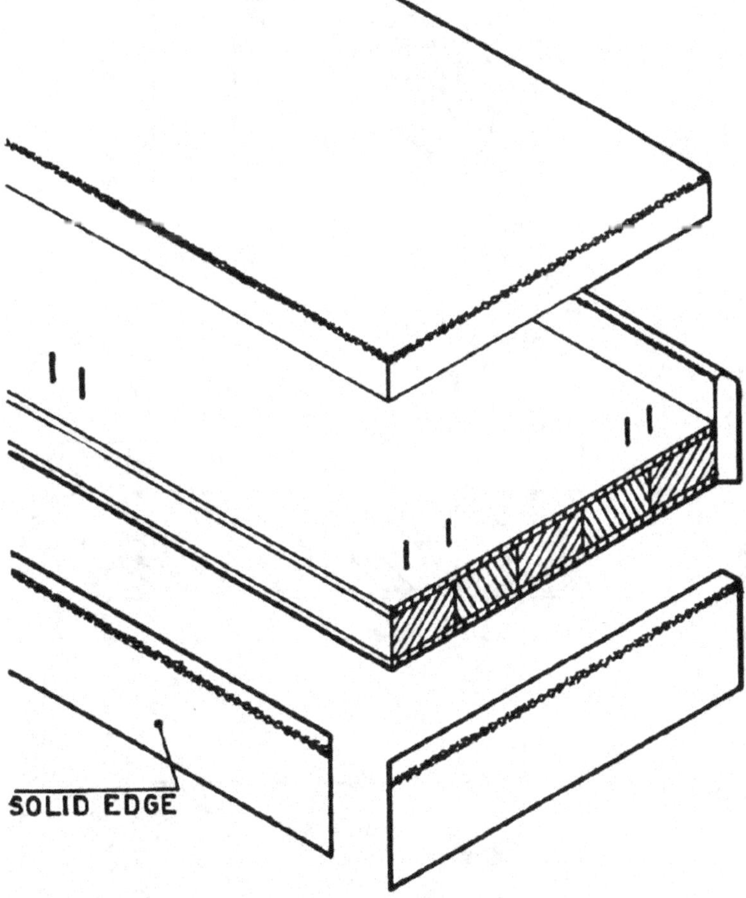

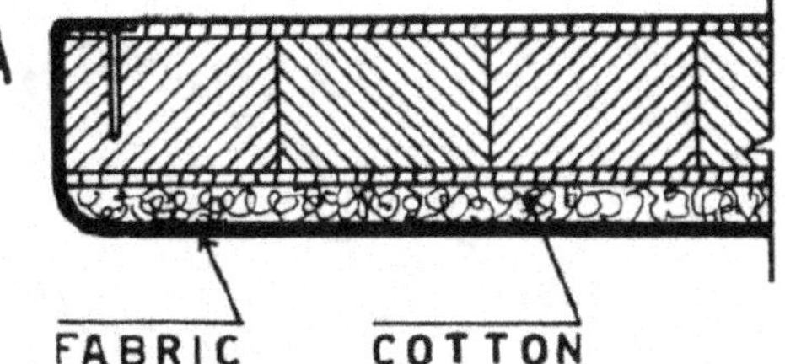

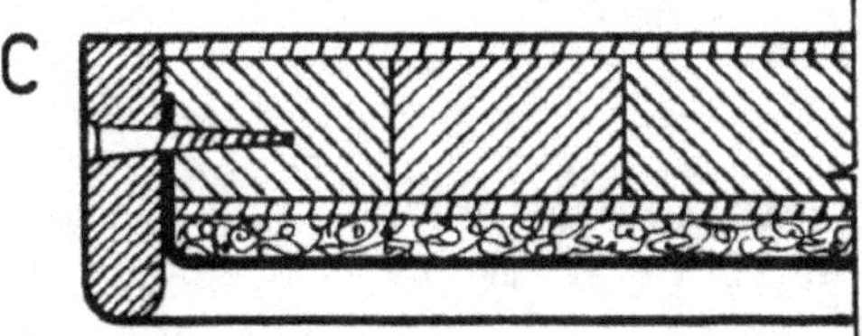

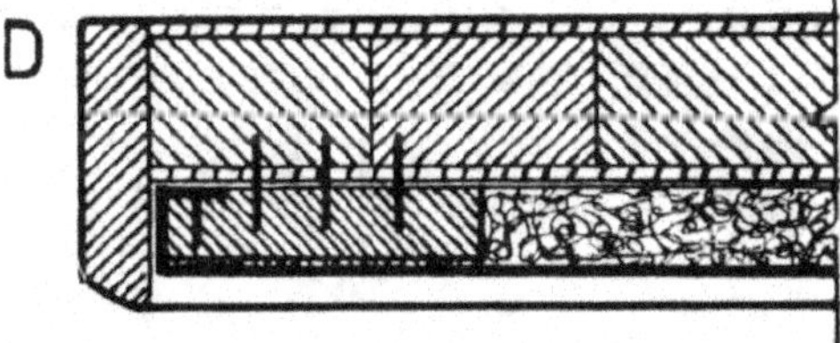

A — FABRIC APPLIED IN THE BACK WITH TACKS.

B — WITH STRIP IN BACK.

C — WITH THE SOLID BOARD EDGE.

D — SOLID EDGE IN THE BOARD OF AN INDEPENDENT PANEL FRONT. EACH OF THESE TYPES GIVES EXCELLENT RESULTS.

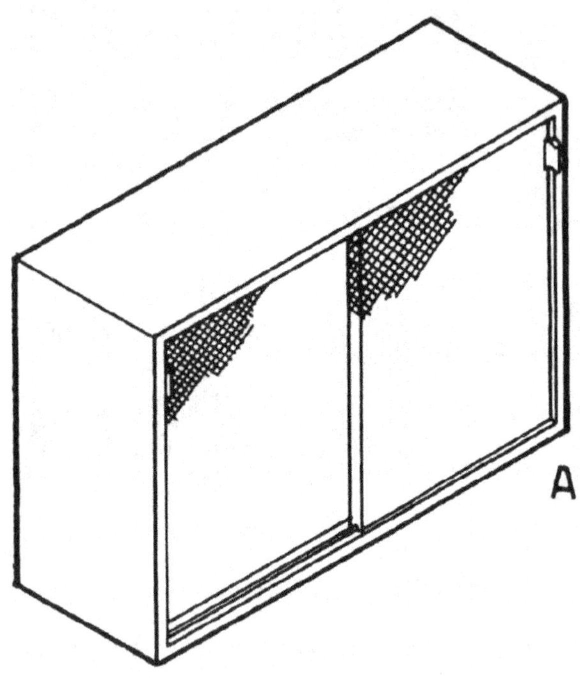

A — PANDANUS APPLICATION IN A SLIDING DOOR WITH FEATHER EDGE.

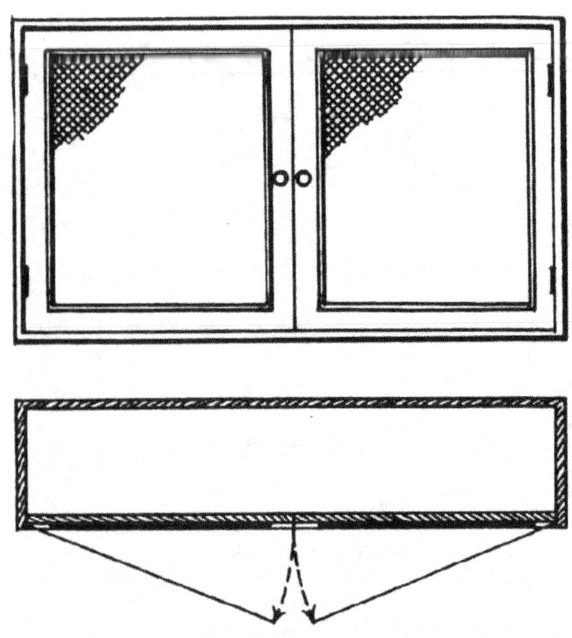

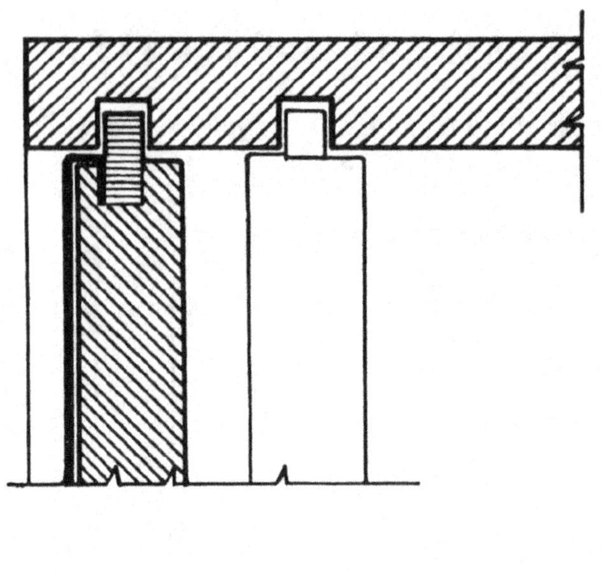

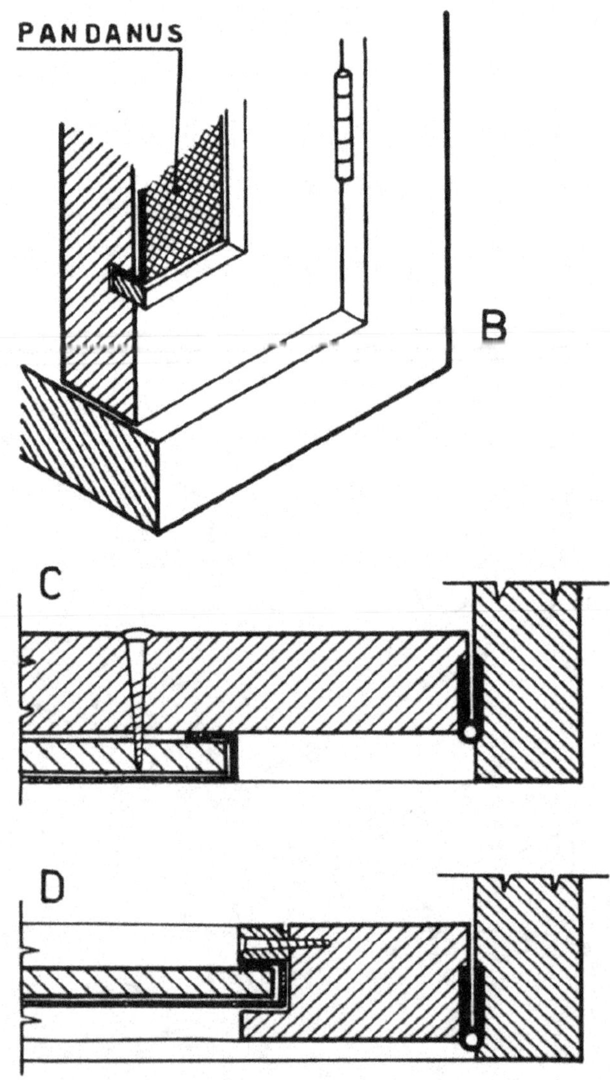

B — PANDANUS APPLICATION ON THE FRONT DOORS.
C, D — TWO DIFFERENT APPLICATIONS OF PANDANUS PANEL ON THE FRAME.

DOOR STOPS

THE BASIC USES OF THE SINGLE OR DOUBLE DOOR
STOPS ARE MAINLY TO SEAL THE FURNITURE PIECE AND
TO PROTECT ITS CONTENTS FROM DUST AND OTHER
DETRIMENTAL OBJECTS. THEY ALSO HELP TO AVOID
ANY SHRINKING WHICH WOULD TAKE PLACE IN THE
WOOD. IN MASS PRODUCTION THESE PRINCIPLES ARE
NOT FOLLOWED. IN ORDER TO EXPEDITE THE WORK
A STRAIGHT BOARD IS USUALLY USED.

THE TYPES PRESENTED GIVE YOU VARIOUS SOLUTIONS
. . . STRAIGHT BOARD, RABBET, TONGUE AND GROOVE.
THIS LAST ONE IS USED WHEN DOORS ARE UPRIGHT
WITH SIMULTANEOUS OPENING.

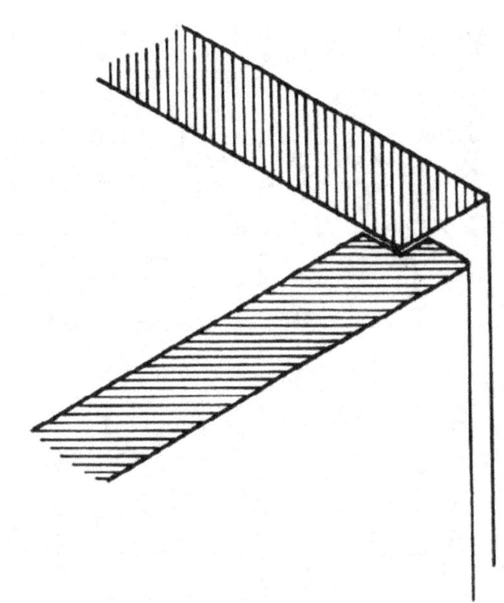

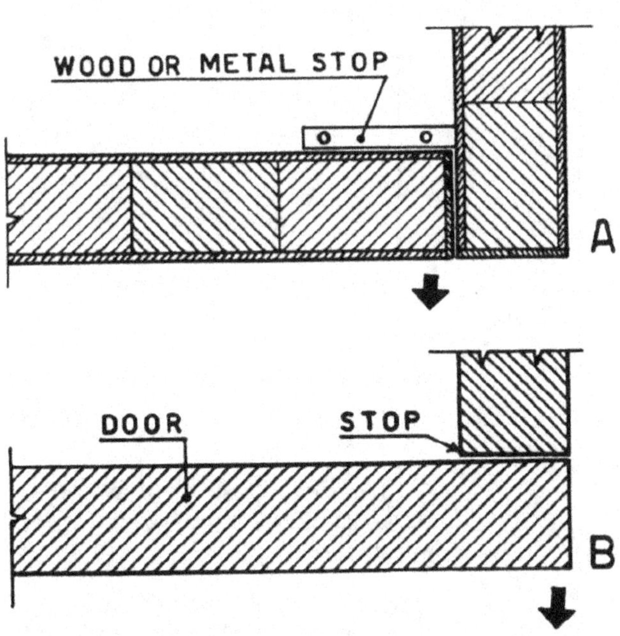

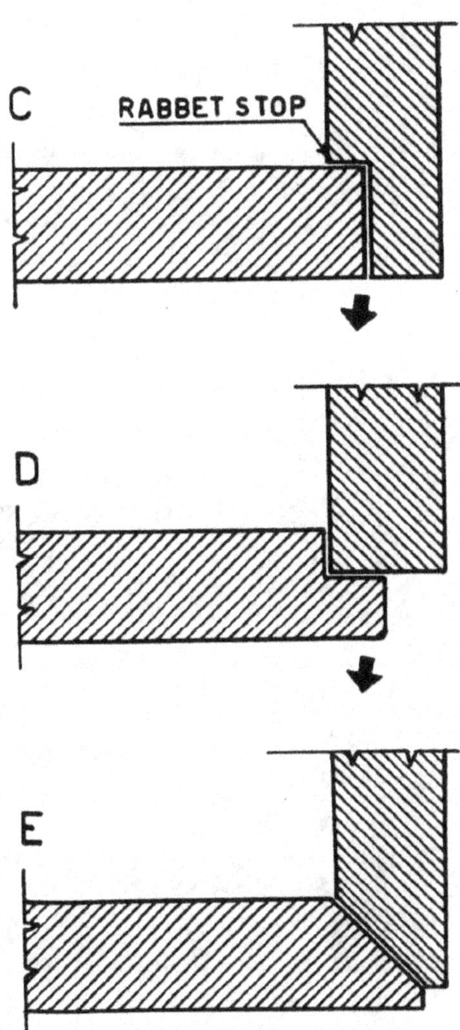

A — STRAIGHT BOARD DOOR WITH WOOD OR METAL
STOPS. NORMAL METHOD USED IN STANDARD PRO-
DUCTION.

B — STRAIGHT STOP BOARD. USED FOR SPECIAL SO-
LUTION.

C — RABBET STOP ON SIDE.

D — RABBET STOP ON DOOR. VERY GOOD METHOD.

E — MITER STOP USED IN SPECIAL WORK.

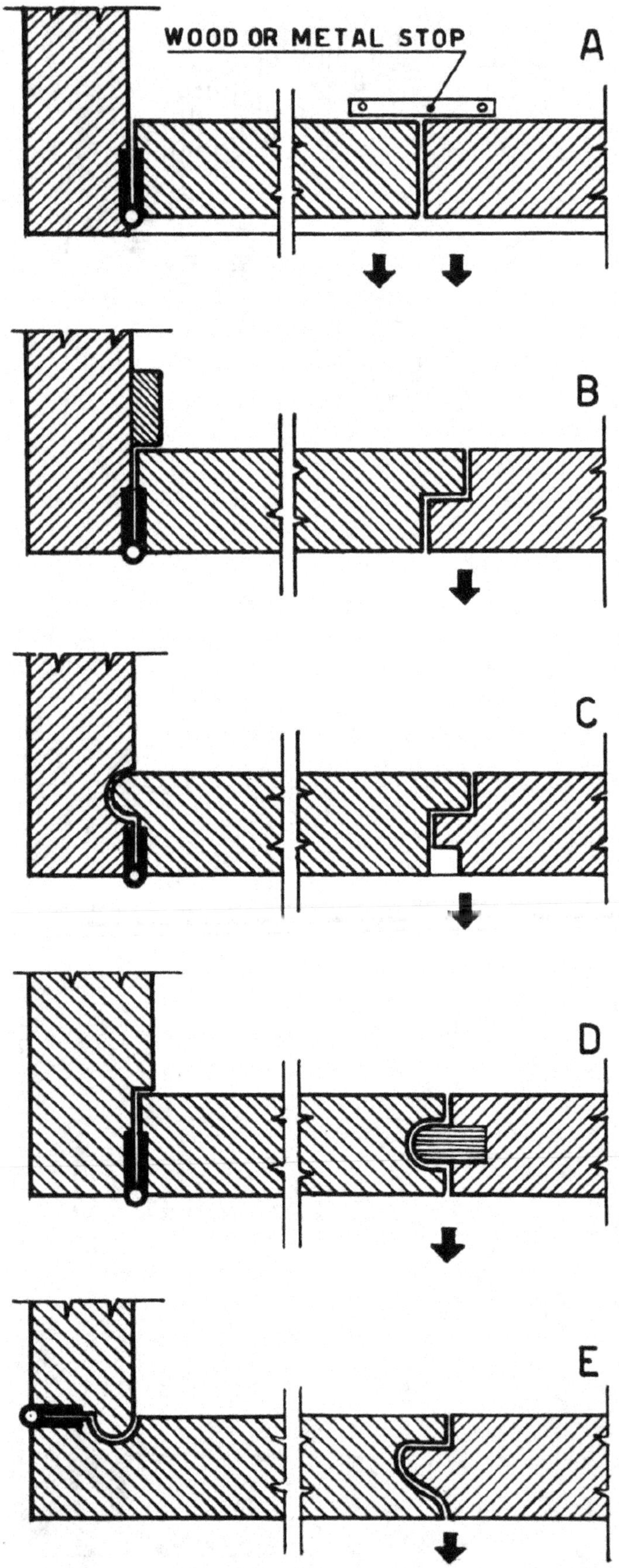

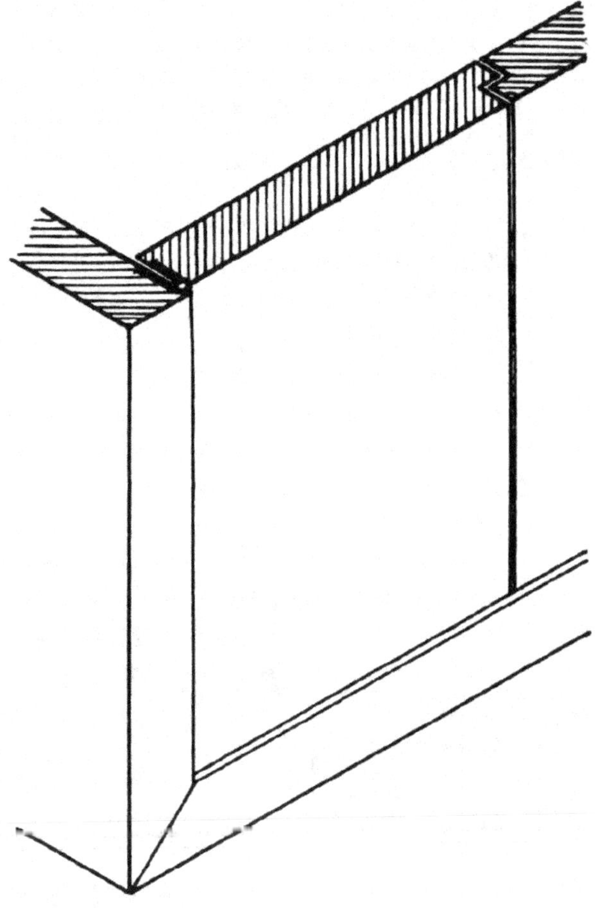

A — STRAIGHT BOARD WITH WOOD OR METAL STOP AS USED IN MASS PRODUCTION.

B — WITH RABBET STOP ON THE BOARD.

C — RABBET STOP SAME AS PRECEDING. THE SCORE IN THE FRONT HIDES ESSENTIAL MOVEMENTS OR SHRINKING OF DOORS.

D — WITH TONGUE AND GROOVE. THIS METHOD ALLOWS SIMULTANEOUS OPENING OF THE DOORS.

E — VARIATION OF THE PRECEDING TYPE.

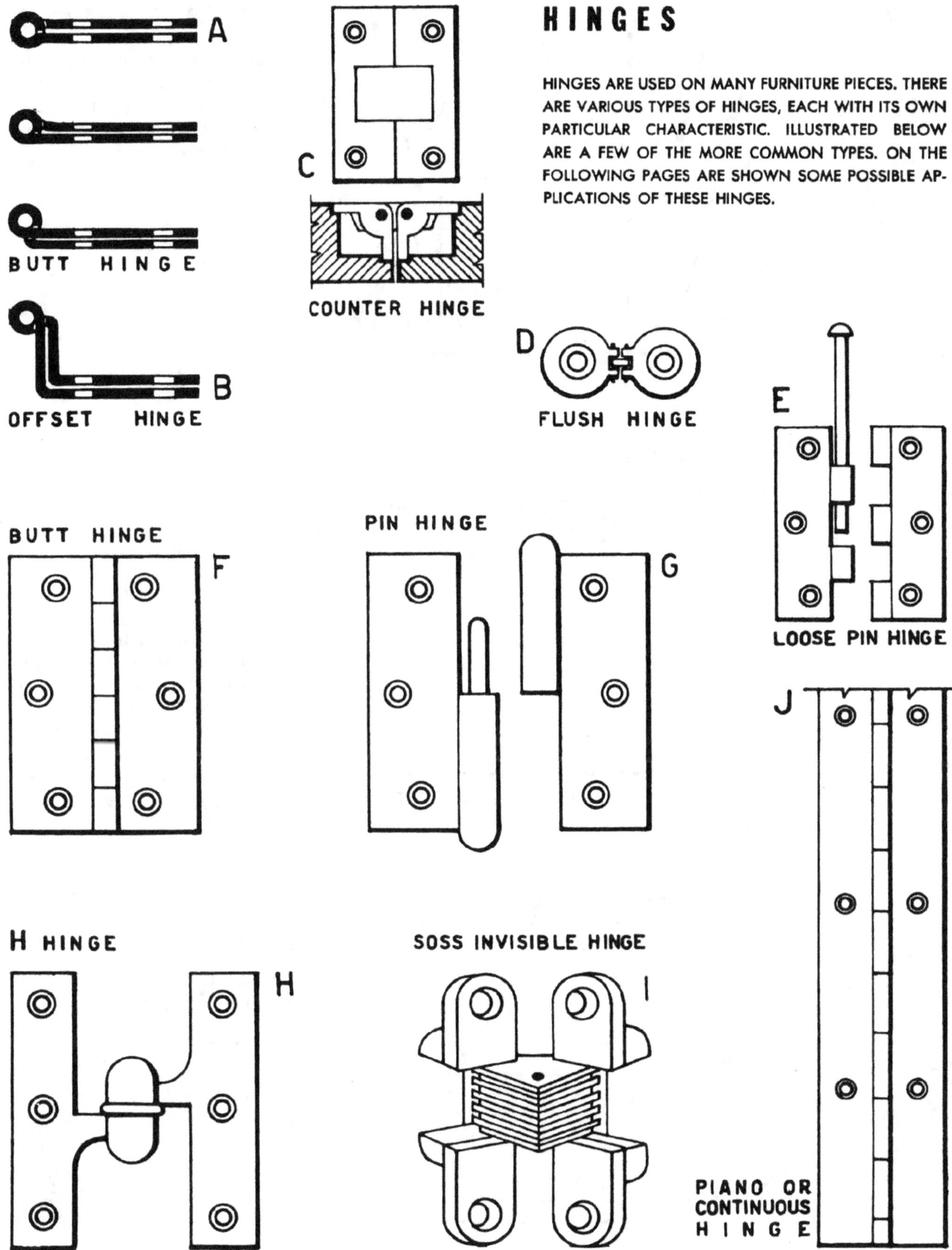

HINGES

HINGES ARE USED ON MANY FURNITURE PIECES. THERE ARE VARIOUS TYPES OF HINGES, EACH WITH ITS OWN PARTICULAR CHARACTERISTIC. ILLUSTRATED BELOW ARE A FEW OF THE MORE COMMON TYPES. ON THE FOLLOWING PAGES ARE SHOWN SOME POSSIBLE APPLICATIONS OF THESE HINGES.

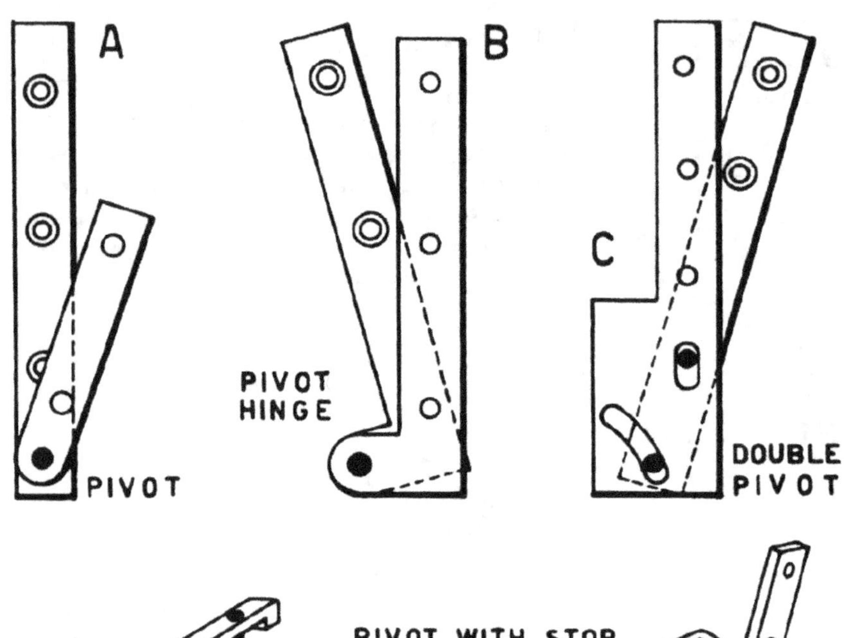

PIVOT HINGES

LIKE THE HINGE, THE PIVOT IS A NECESSARY ACCESSORY IN THE CONSTRUCTION OF FURNITURE. THE ILLUSTRATIONS SHOW THE PRINCIPAL TYPES, WITH METHODS OF APPLICATION.

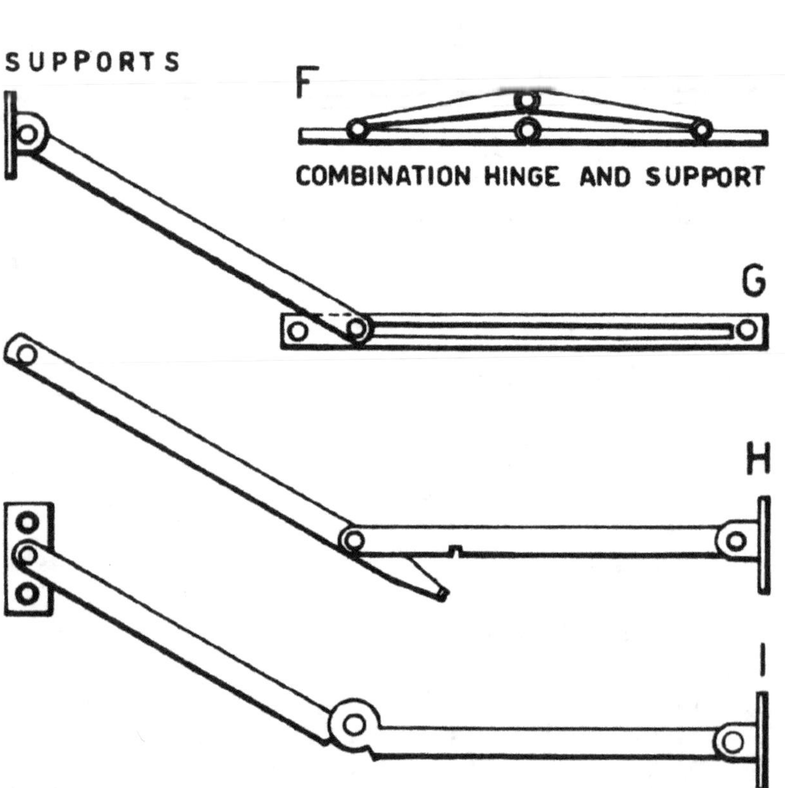

SUPPORTS

ALTHOUGH SUPPORTS ARE NOT SO PRACTICAL AS THE HINGES OR PIVOT, THEY PLAY AN IMPORTANT PART IN THE CONSTRUCTION OF THE FURNITURE PIECES. HERE ARE VARIOUS TYPES WITH THEIR METHODS OF APPLICATION.

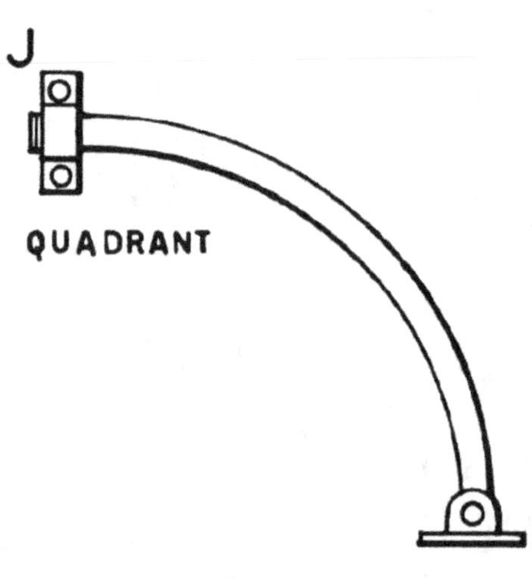

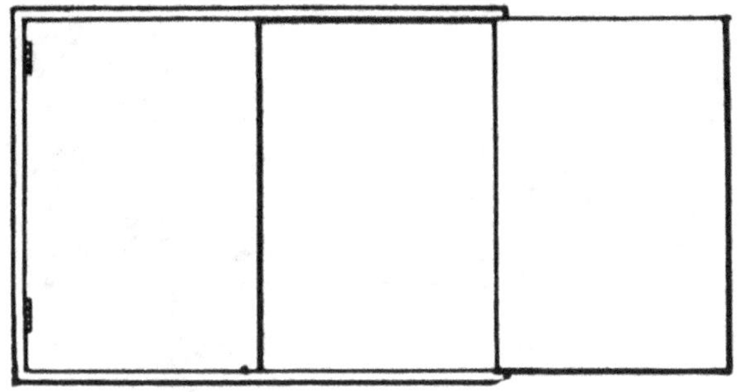

APPLICATION OF DOORS TO FURNITURE

THE APPLICATION OF NORMAL DOORS TO FURNITURE PIECES MAY BE DONE BY VARIOUS METHODS ACCORDING TO THE TYPE OF HINGE USED. SYSTEMS OF APPLICATION MAY VARY. GENERALLY THESE HINGES ARE APPLIED BY MEANS OF SCREWS.
PIANO HINGES MAY ALSO BE USED.

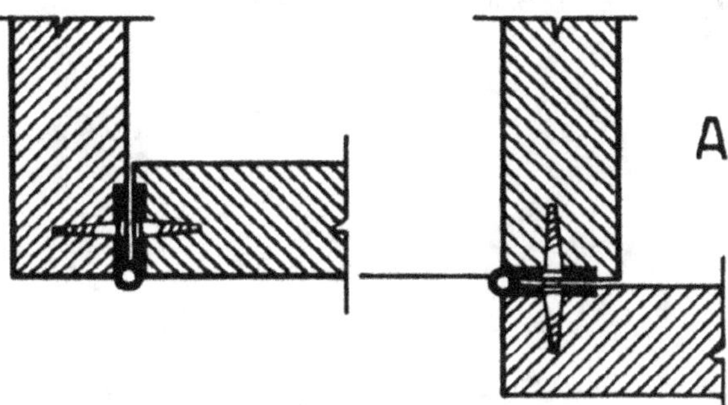

BUTT HINGES ARE USED IN MASS PRODUCTION.

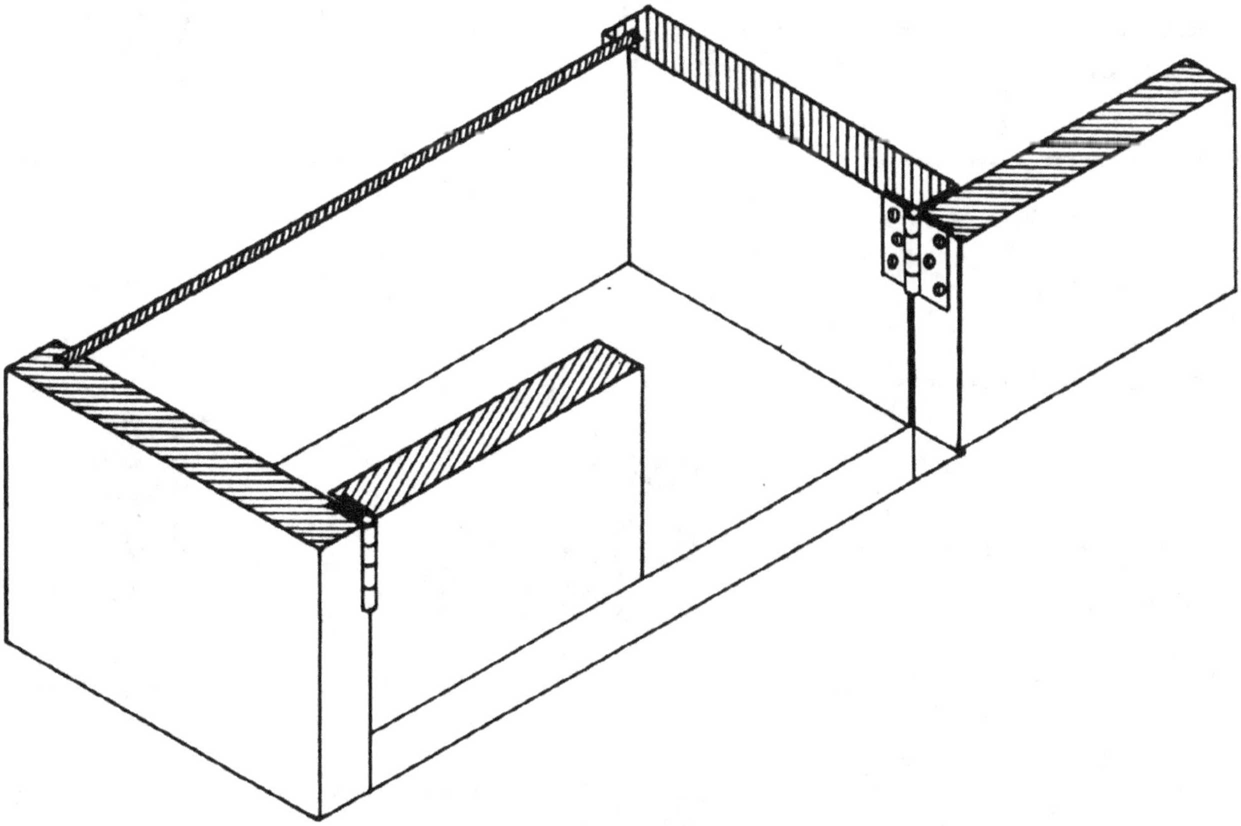

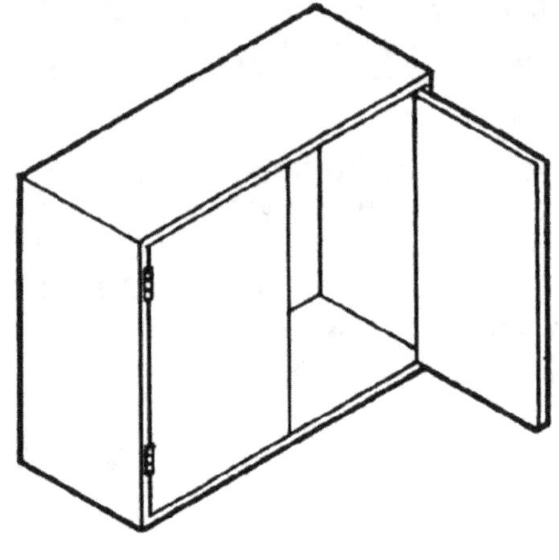

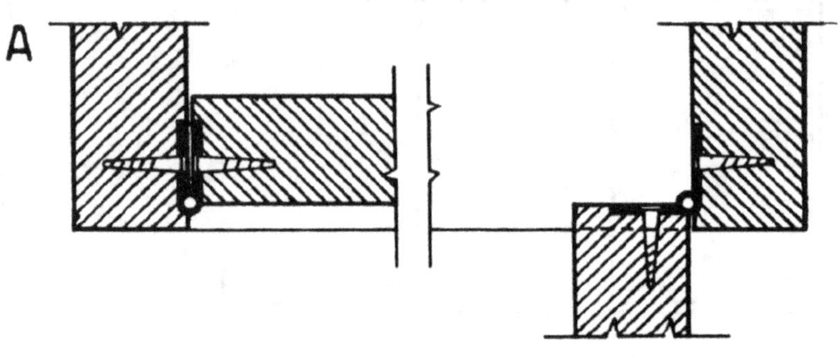

A

RECESS DOORS WITH BUTT HINGES. NOTE THAT SIDE PANEL ACTS AS DOOR STOP.

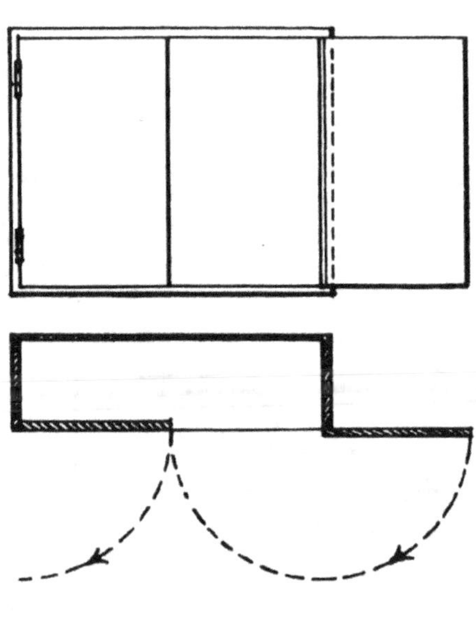

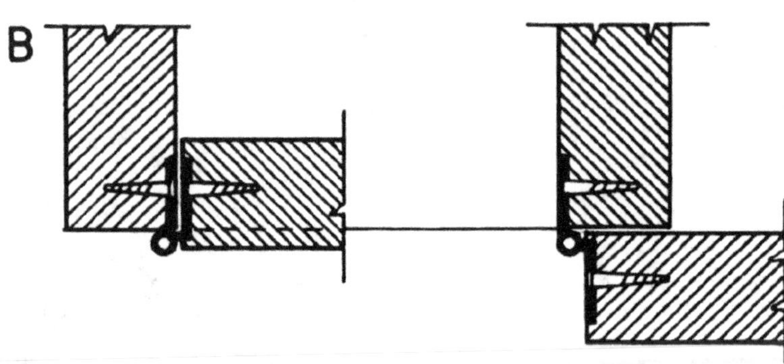

B

EXTERNAL DOORS WITH BUTT HINGES. DOORS USING THIS TYPE OF HINGE OPEN ALL THE WAY.

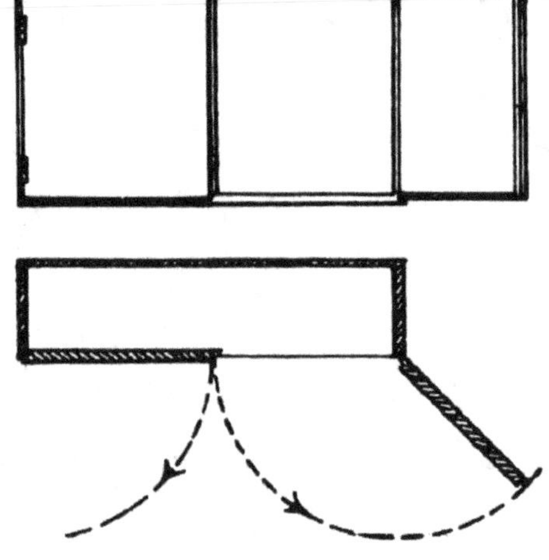

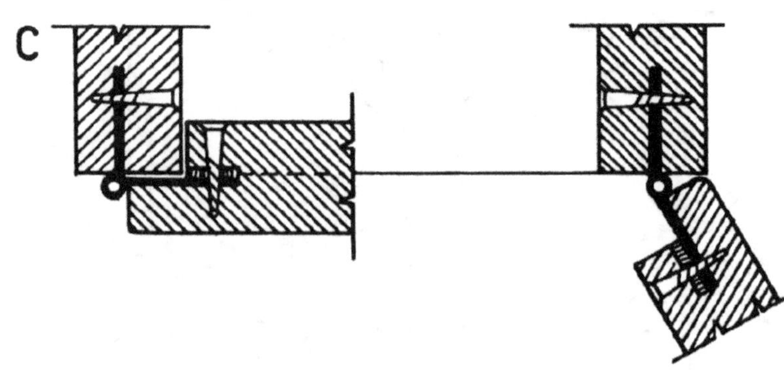

C

RABBET DOORS WITH BUTT HINGES. ALL THESE METHODS ARE USED IN GOOD WORK.

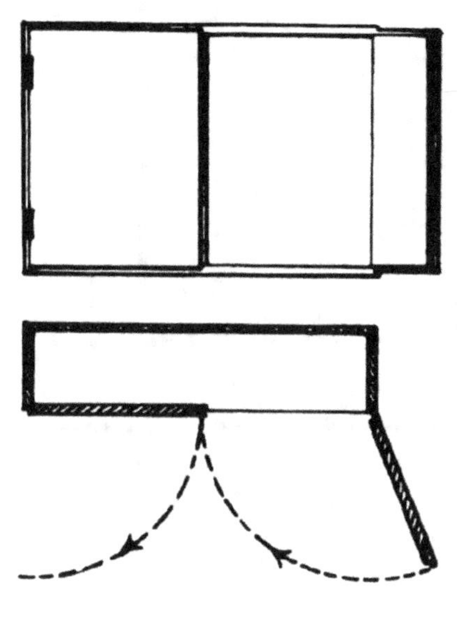

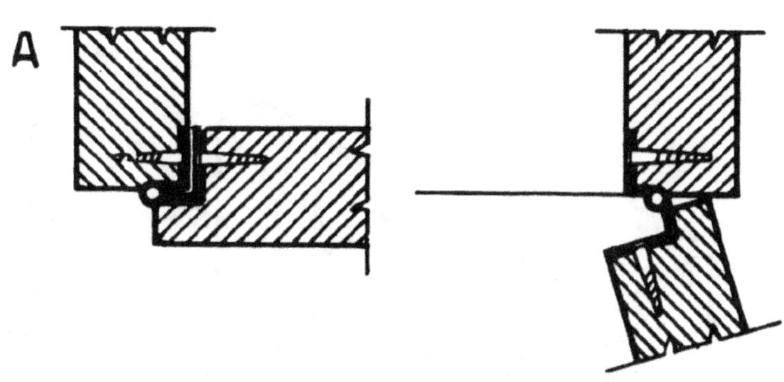

RABBET DOORS WITH OFFSET HINGES.

A

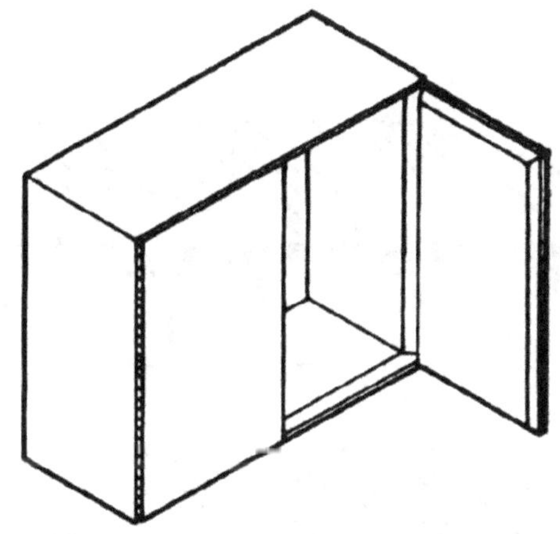

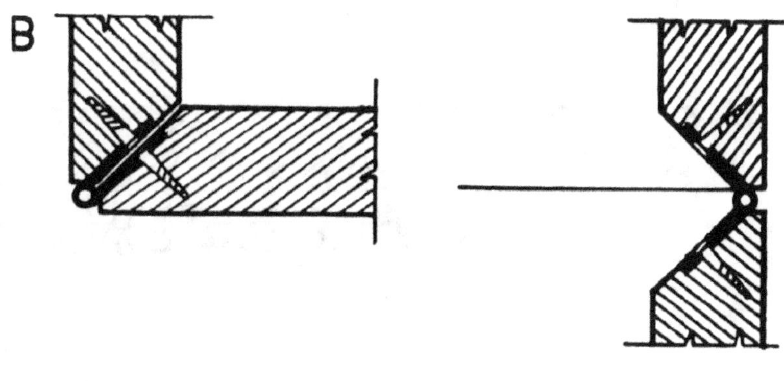

MITER DOORS WITH BUTT HINGES USED FOR SPECIAL WORK.

B

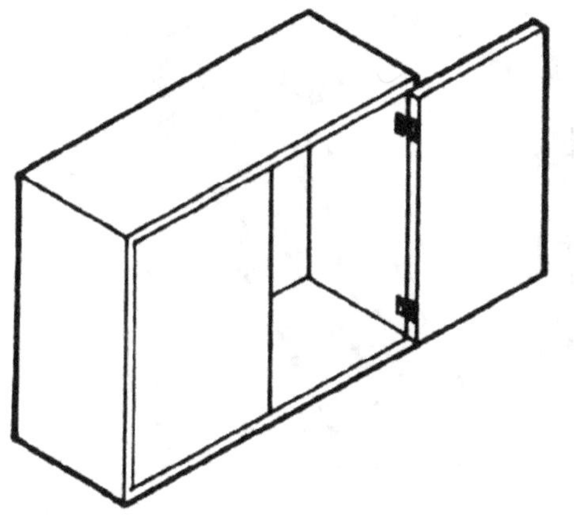

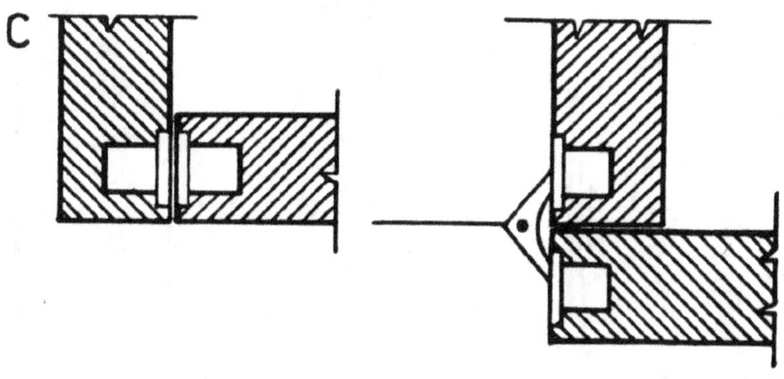

DOOR APPLICATION WITH SOSS INVISIBLE HINGES USED IN FINE FURNITURE.

C

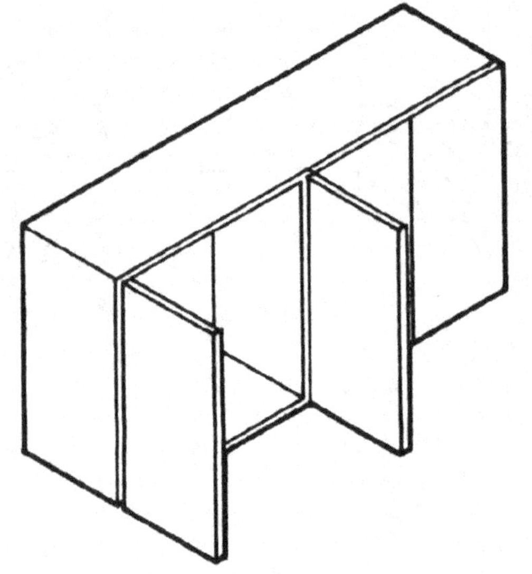

METAL KITCHEN CABINET DOORS OFTEN USE THIS TYPE OF SPECIAL HINGE, WHICH IS BOLTED OR WELDED TO THE SIDE PANEL.

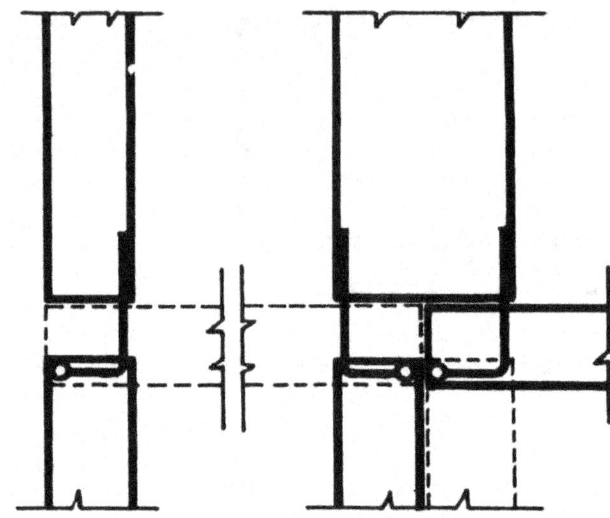

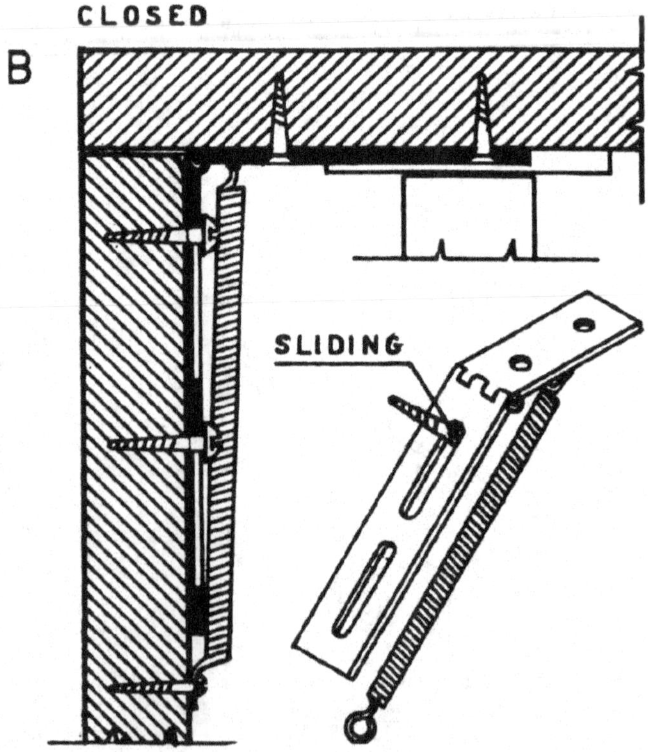

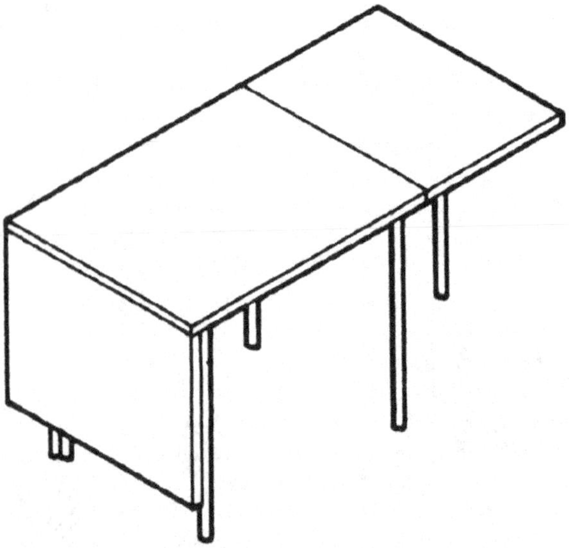

THIS LOOSE SPRING HINGE IS OFTEN USED IN EX-TENSION TABLES AND DESKS. IT IS FAIRLY EASY TO ATTACH.

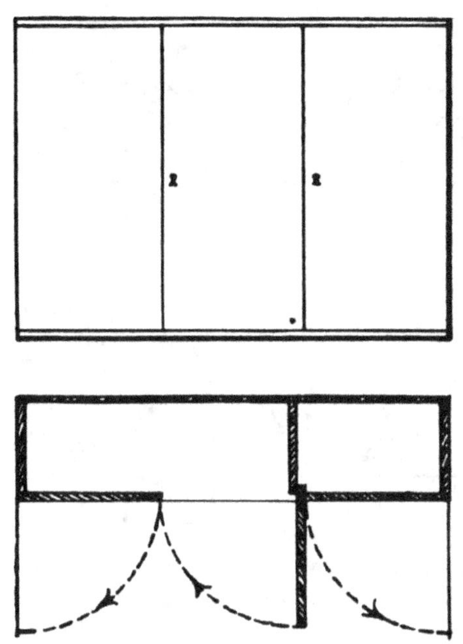

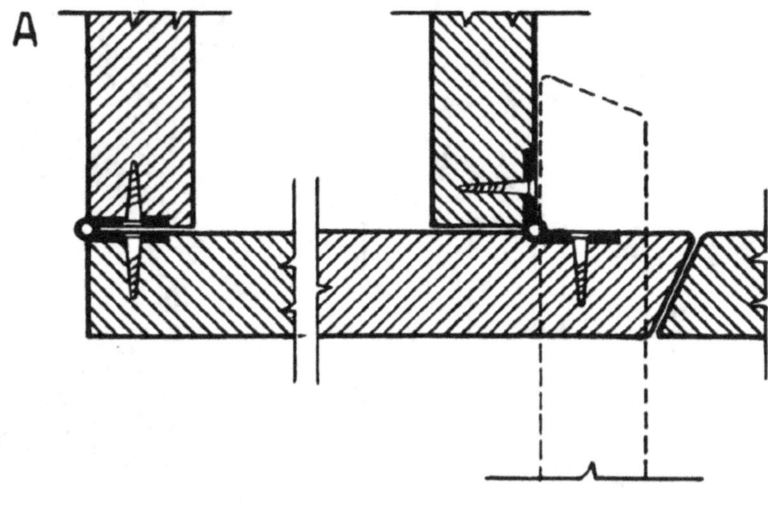

A CABINET WITH THREE DOORS PRESENTS SPECIAL PROBLEMS. HERE IS ONE SOLUTION.

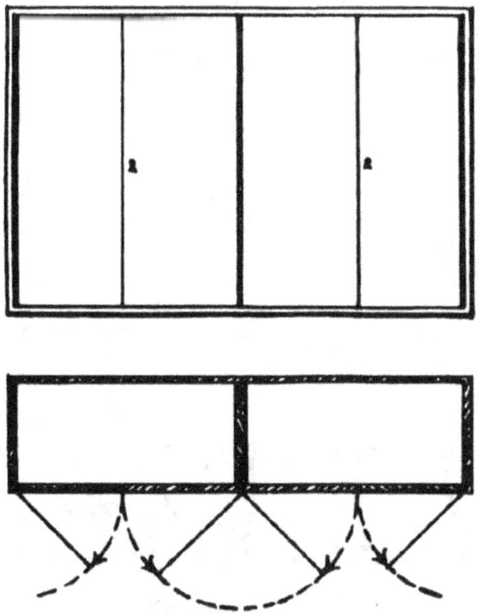

PIANO HINGES MAY BE USED WHEN TWO SETS OF DOORS APPEAR ON THE FRONT. NOTE THAT THE PIANO HINGE HAS BEEN CUT. THIS IS A PRACTICAL METHOD OF HIDING THE CENTRAL DIVIDER.

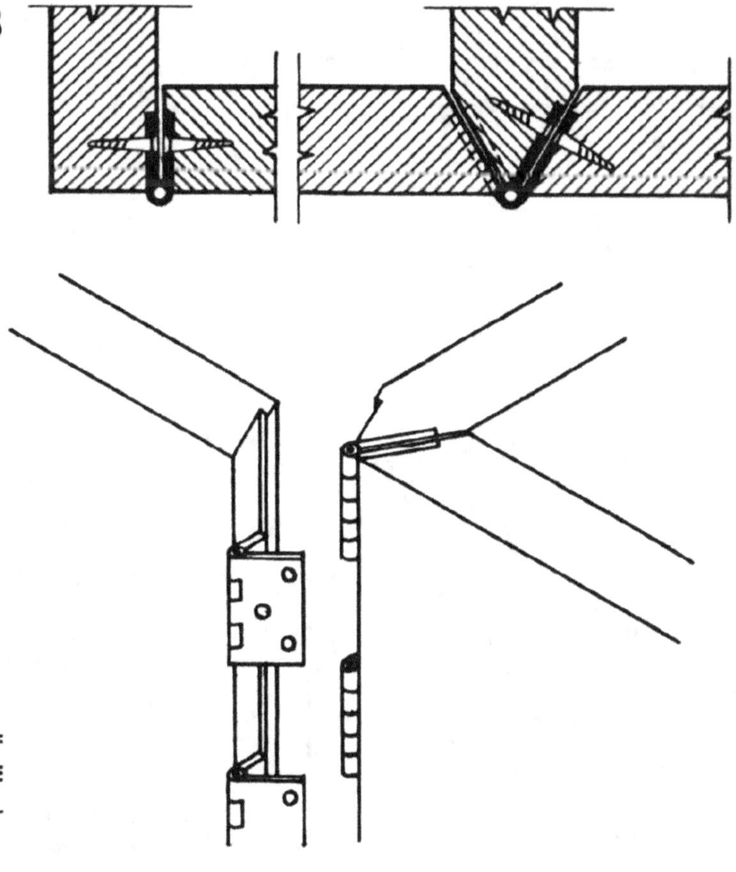

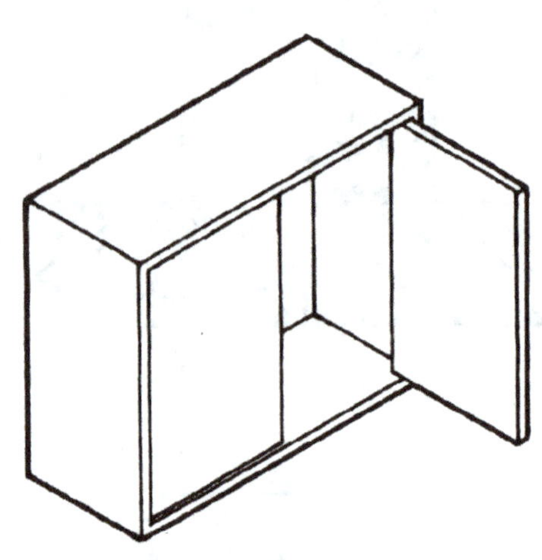

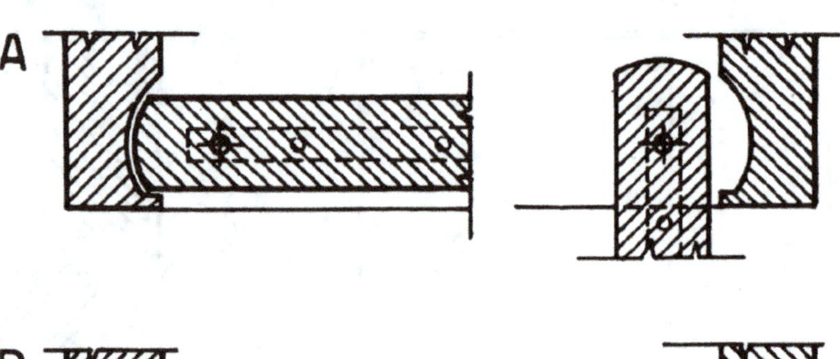

A

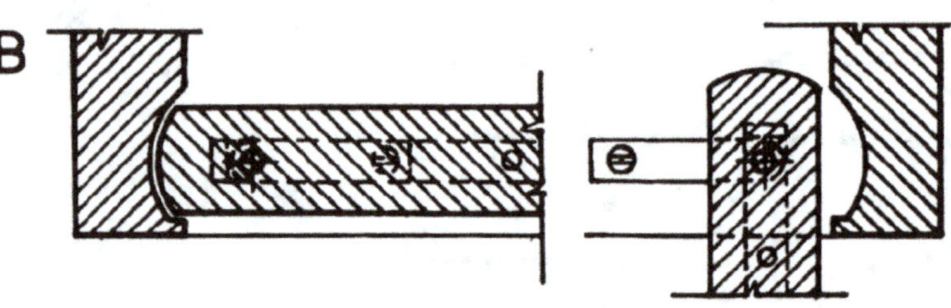

B

THESE DOORS USE INTERNAL PIVOTS AT THE TOP AND BOTTOM. NOTE THAT "B" USES A STOP PIVOT. (SEE PAGE 56, FIG. D).

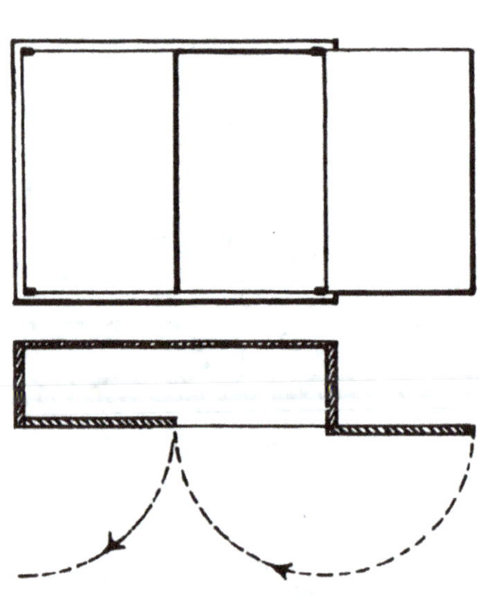

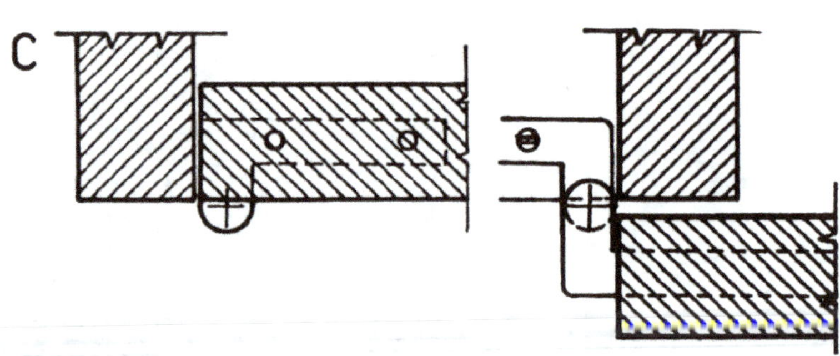

C

THIS SET OF DOORS USES AN EDGE OR EXTERNAL TYPE OF PIVOT HINGE.

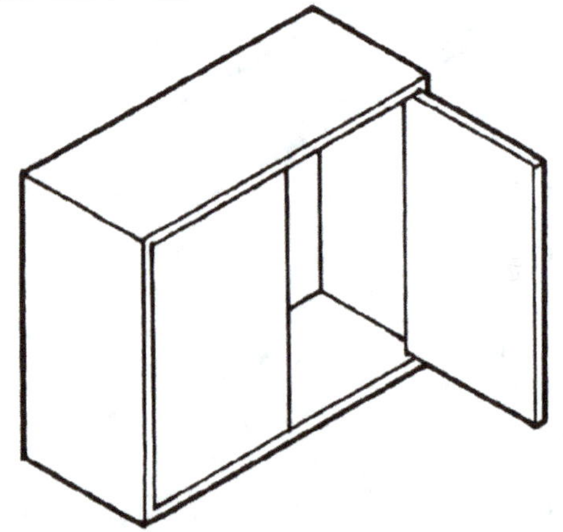

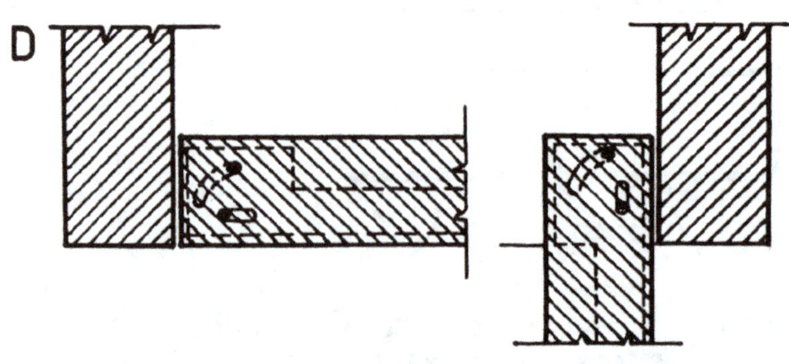

D

A DOUBLE PIVOT HINGE HAS BEEN USED ON THESE DOORS. NOTE HOW THE SIDE PANEL ACTS AS THE DOOR STOP (SEE PAGE 56.)

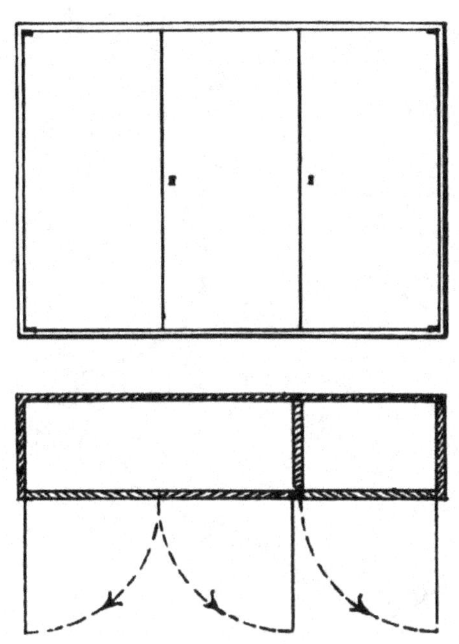

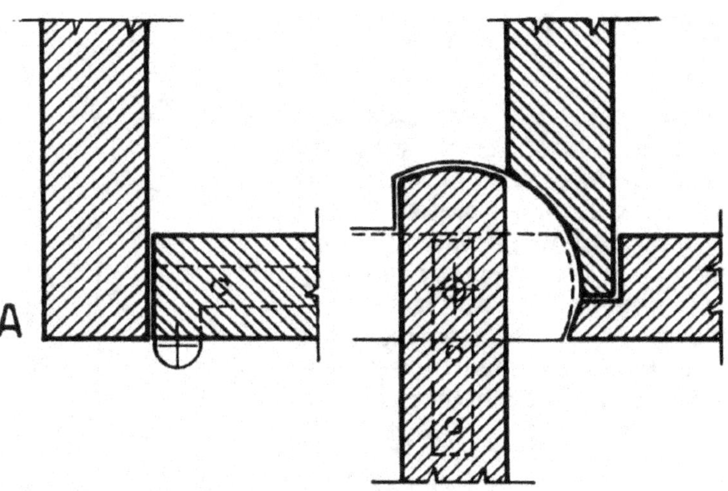

A

THIS THREE-DOOR PROBLEM HAS BEEN SOLVED BY USING AN EXTERNAL PIVOT HINGE ON TWO DOORS AND AN INTERNAL ONE ON THE MIDDLE PANEL.

COMMON PIVOT HINGE ON A FOUR-DOOR CABINET ALLOWS HIDING OF THE CENTER DIVIDER.

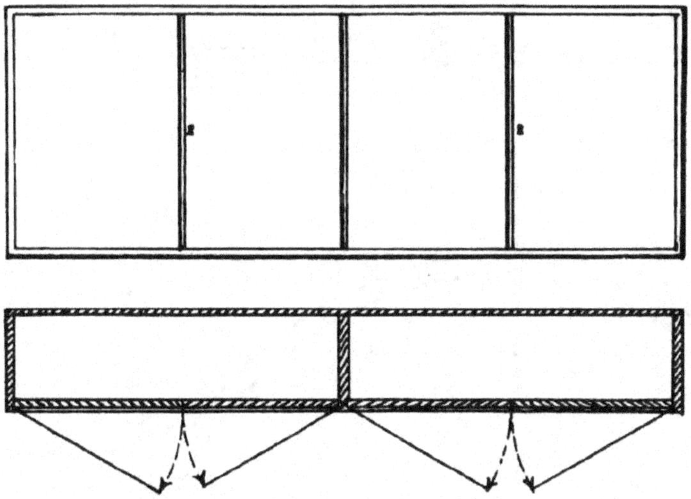

B

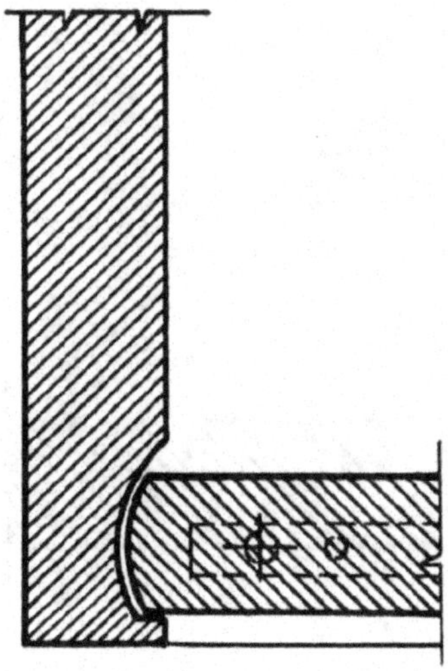

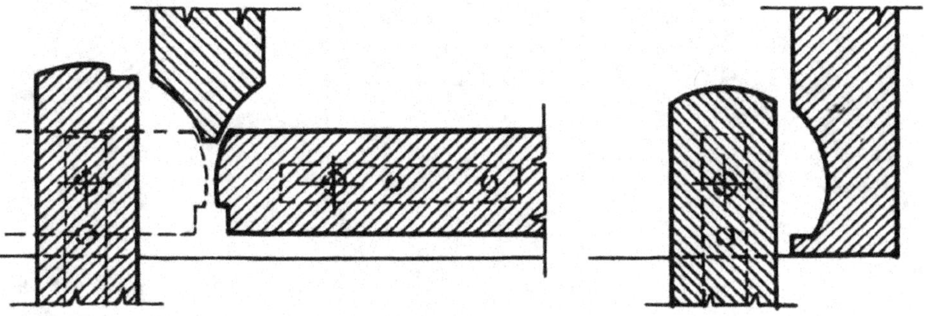

DROP DOORS

A DROP DOOR MAY USE ALMOST ANY TYPE OF HINGE ALONG ITS BOTTOM EDGE. A CHARACTERISTIC OF THIS TYPE OF DOOR IS THAT IT CAN BE USED IN A NUMBER OF WAYS. WHEN OPEN, THE DOOR MAY ACT AS A DESK OR SUPPORT. IT IS THEREFORE ESSENTIAL TO HAVE THE DOOR HELD IN A RIGID POSITION. THIS CAN BE DONE BY USING METAL SUPPORTS ALONG THE OUTER EDGE.

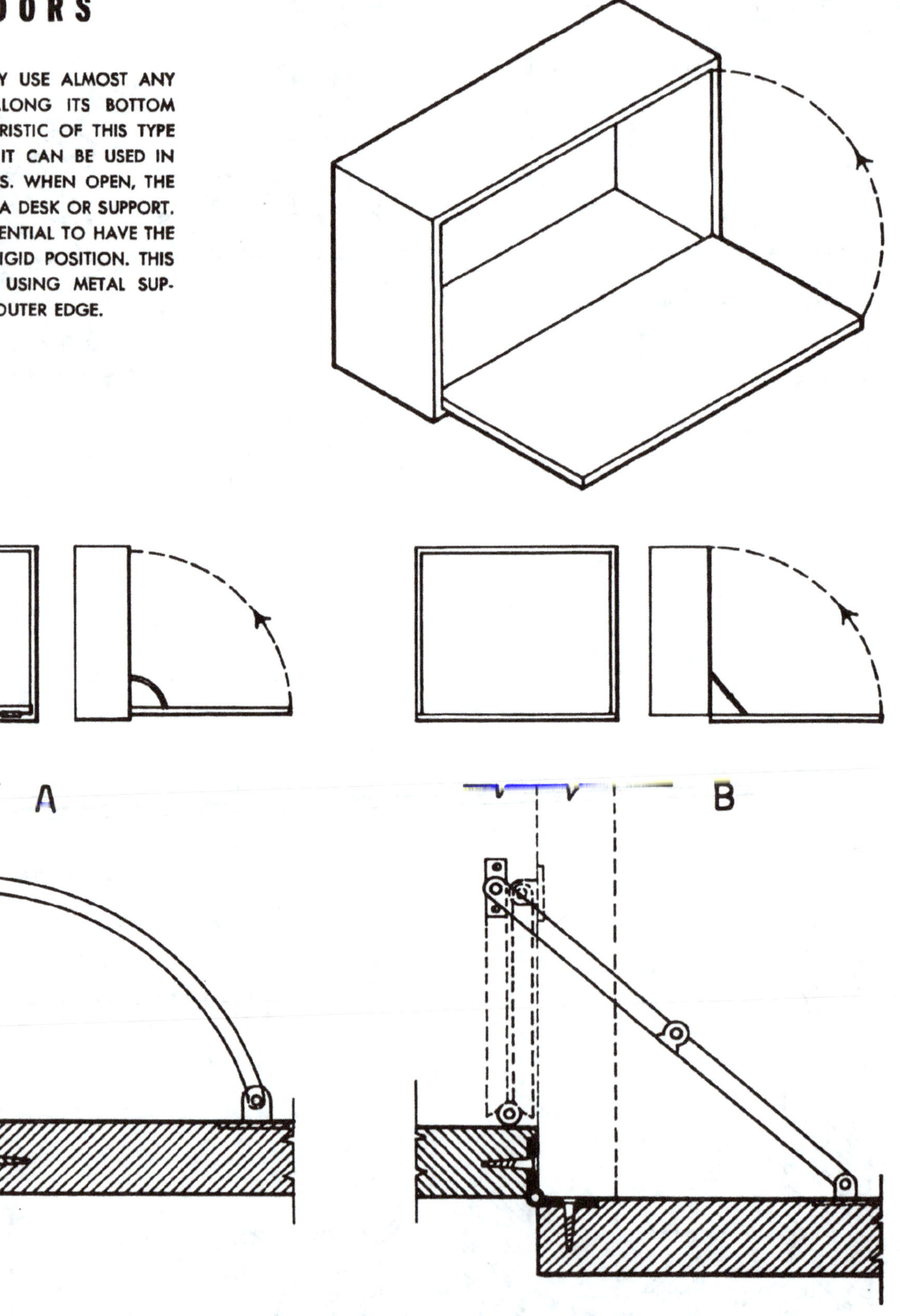

TWO WAYS OF USING A BUTT HINGE. BOTH TYPES OF SUPPORTS ARE VERY PRACTICAL.

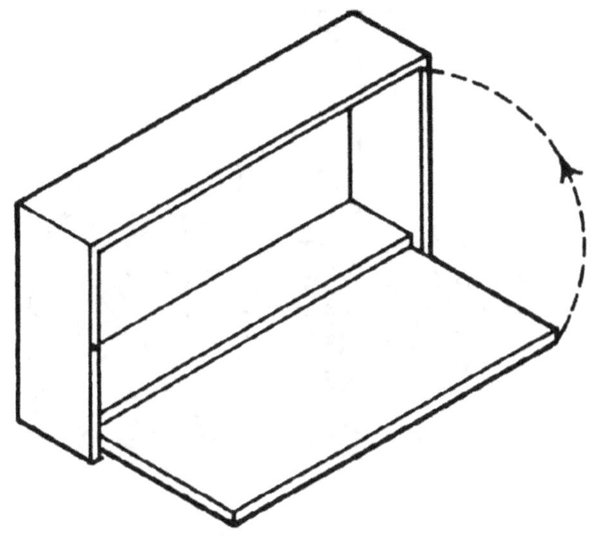

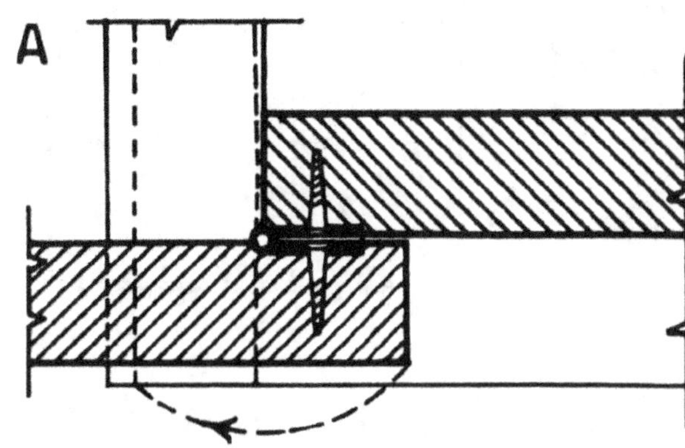

THIS SIMPLE METHOD USES A BUTT HINGE. THE DOOR OVERHANG ACTS AS ITS OWN STOP.

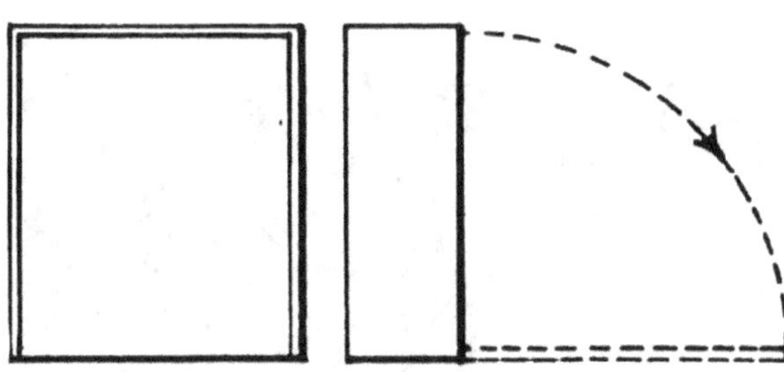

A COMBINATION HINGE AND SUPPORT IS USED WITH THIS DROP DOOR. IT IS A SATISFACTORY METHOD SO LONG AS THE DOOR IS SMALL.

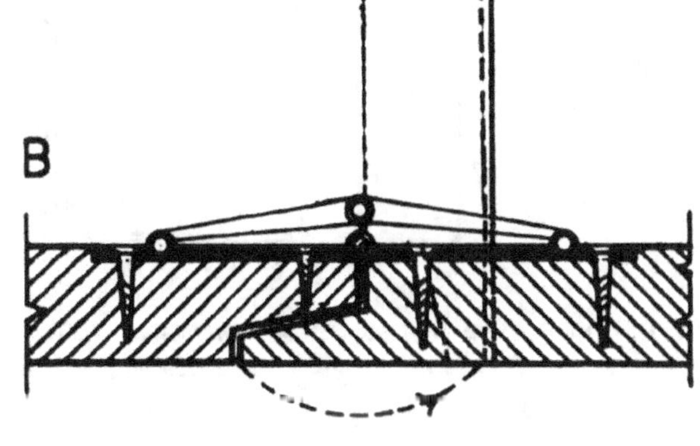

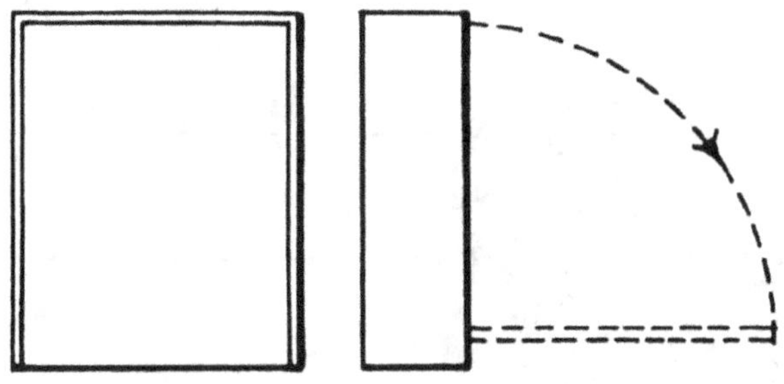

OFFSET HINGES ARE USED IN THIS SCHEME.

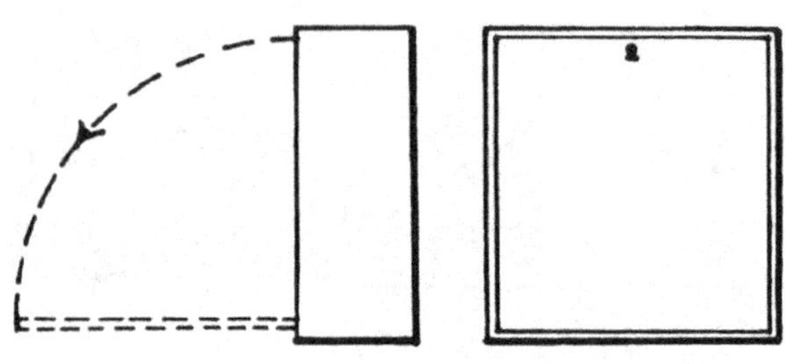

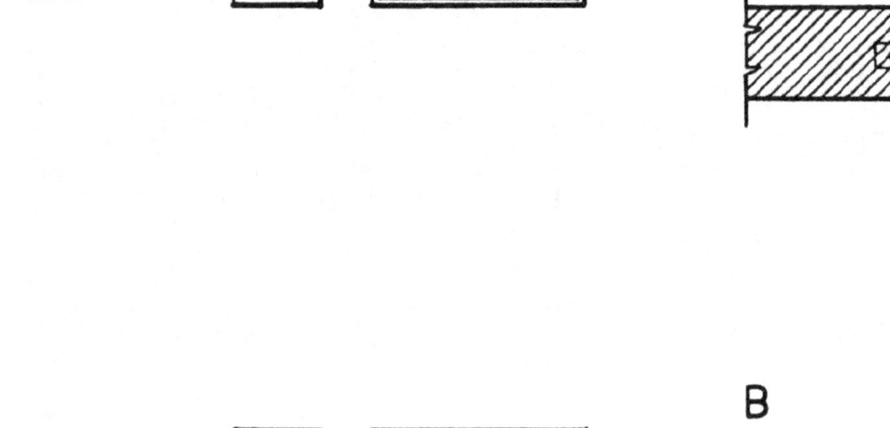

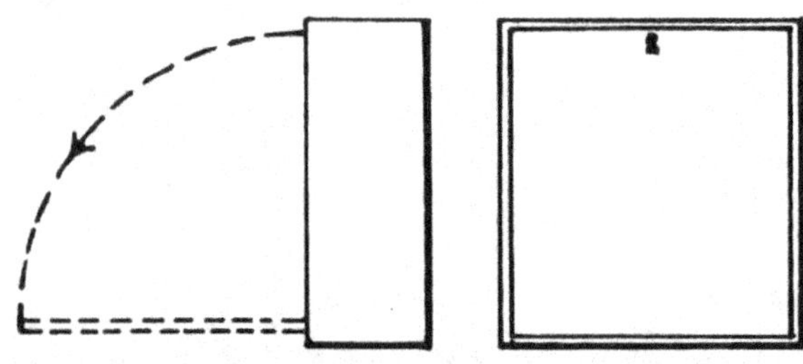

A, C — THESE TWO DOORS USE A COMMON PIVOT. NOTE THE METHODS OF STOPPING THE DOOR.

B — THIS DOOR USES A SPECIAL STOP PIVOT (SEE PAGE 56, FIG. E).

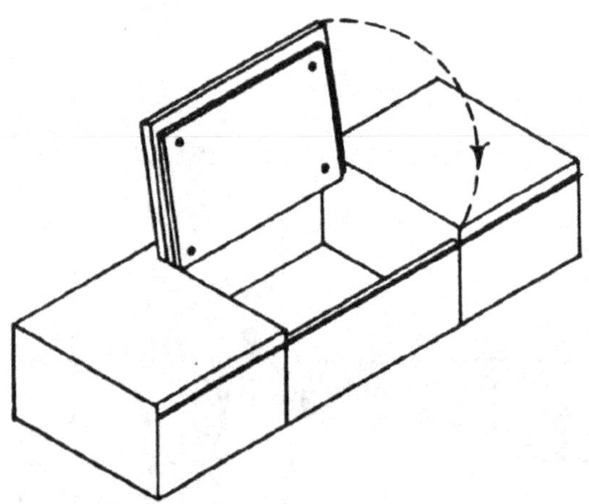

D — PIVOT DROP DOOR SUITABLE FOR VANITIES. VERTICAL AND HORIZONTAL METHOD OF HINGING FOLDED DOORS.

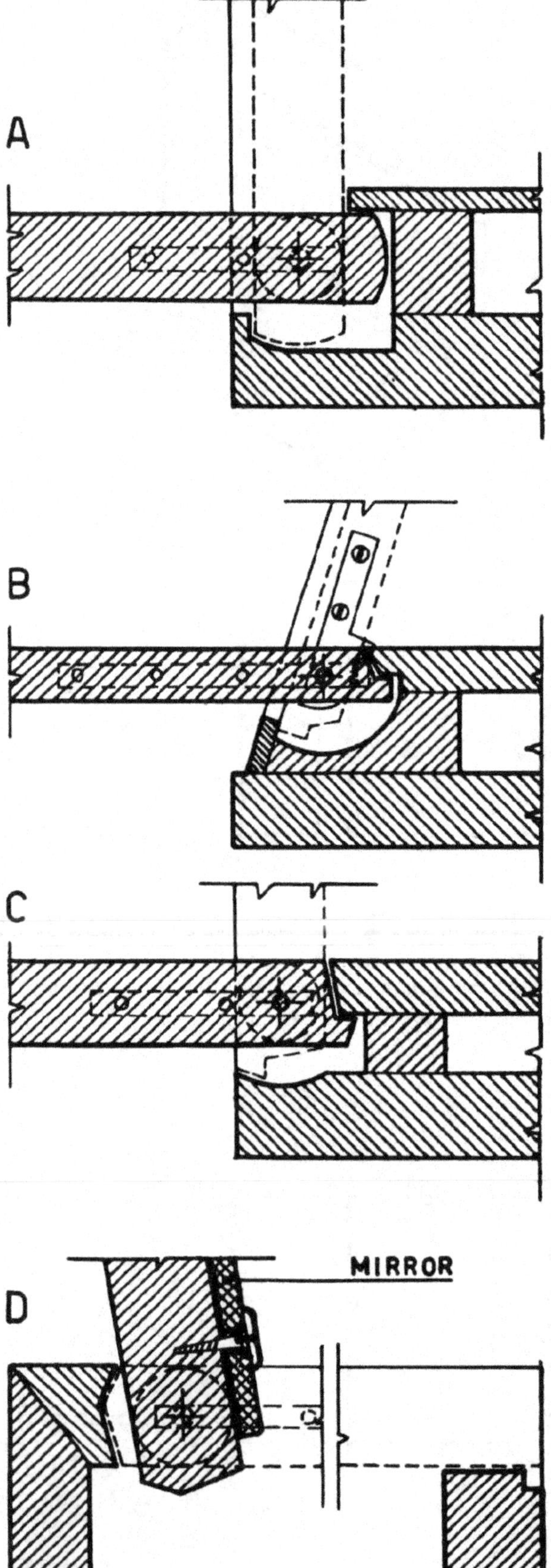

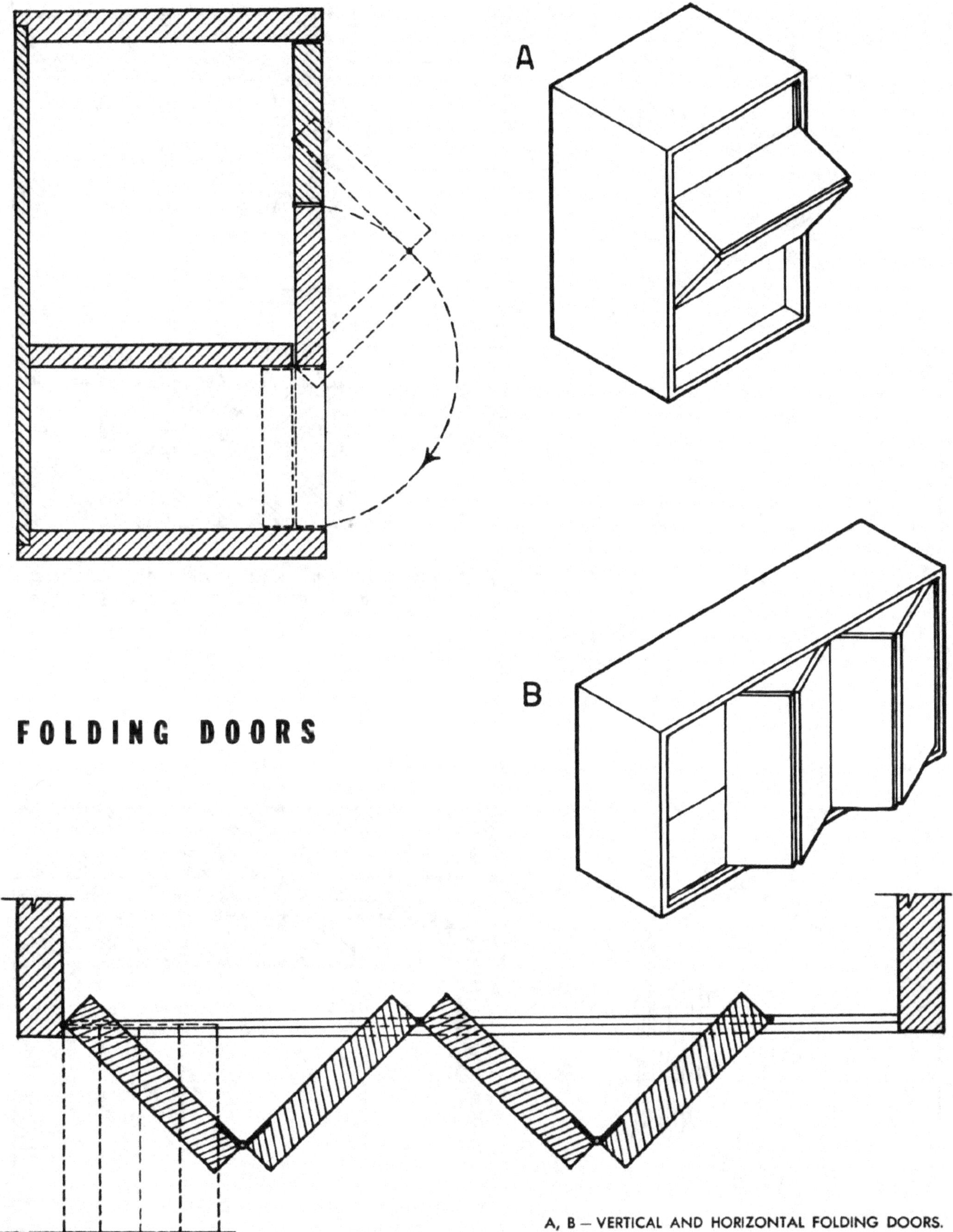

A, B — VERTICAL AND HORIZONTAL FOLDING DOORS.

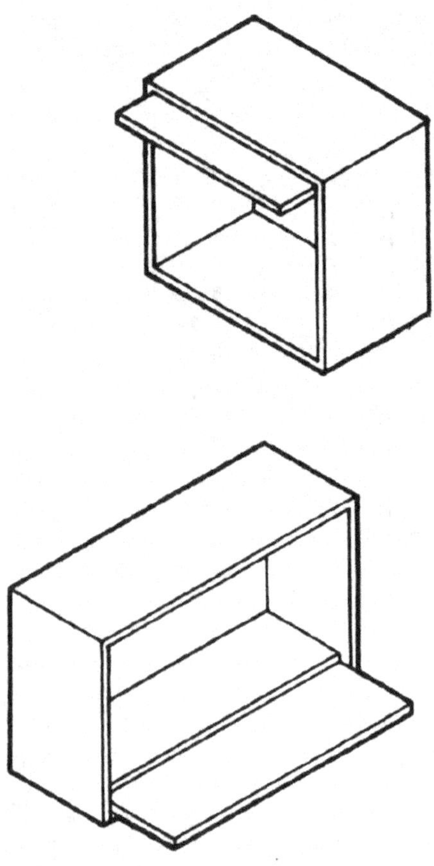

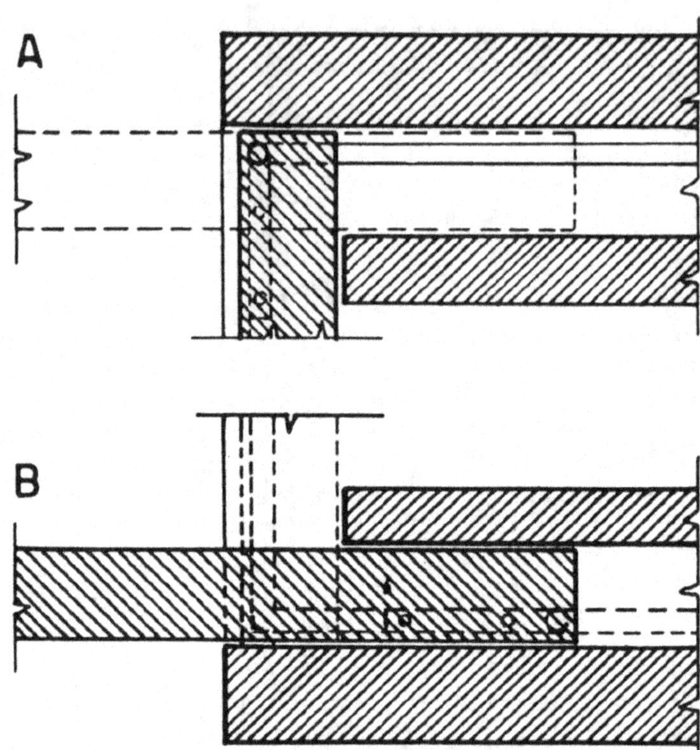

COMBINATION DROP AND SLIDING DOOR SHOWN HERE USES A COMMON PIVOT AND ROUTED TRACK TO PERFORM ITS FUNCTION.

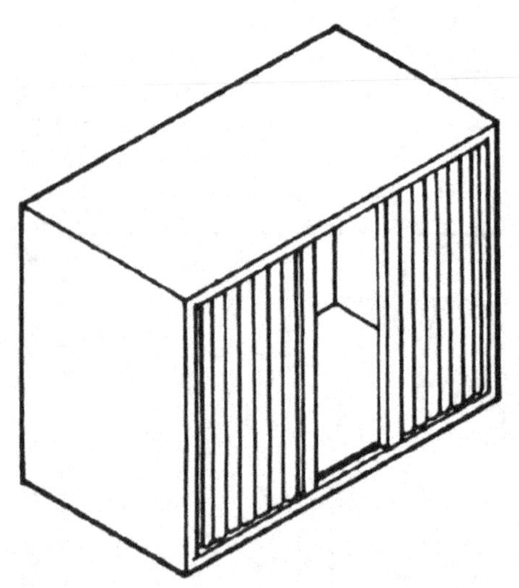

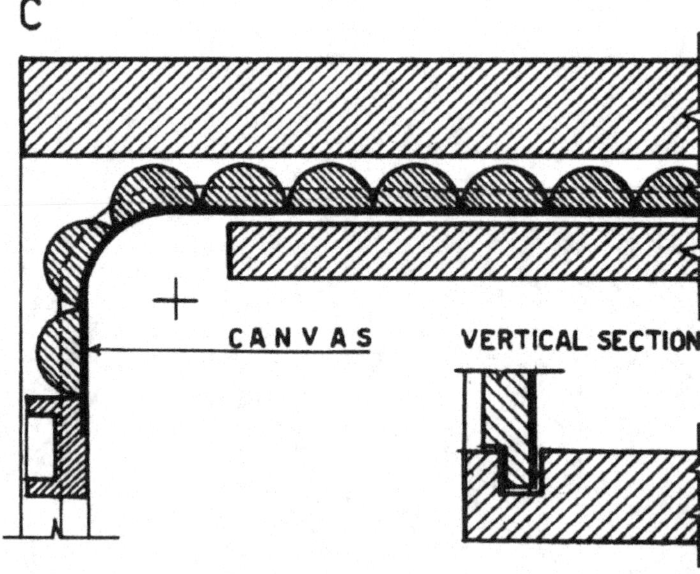

TAMBOUR DOOR AS USED IN OFFICE FURNITURE. THIS IS NOT DIFFICULT TO MAKE.

SLIDING DOORS

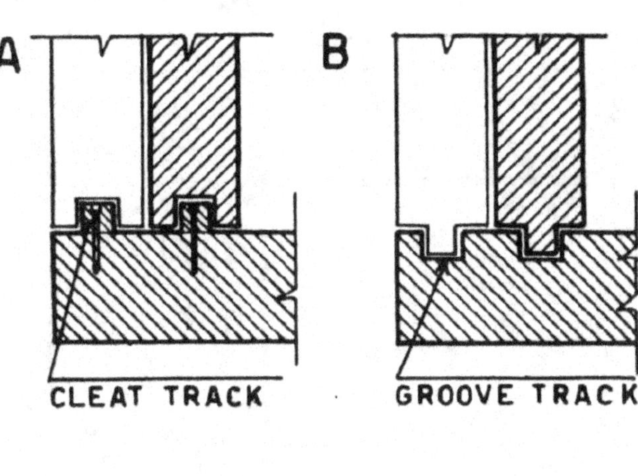

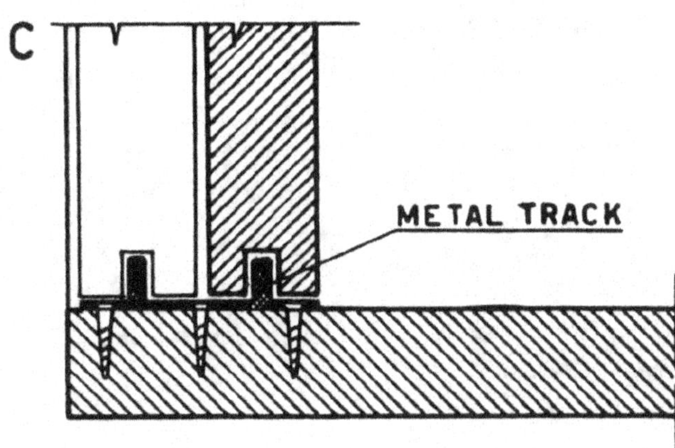

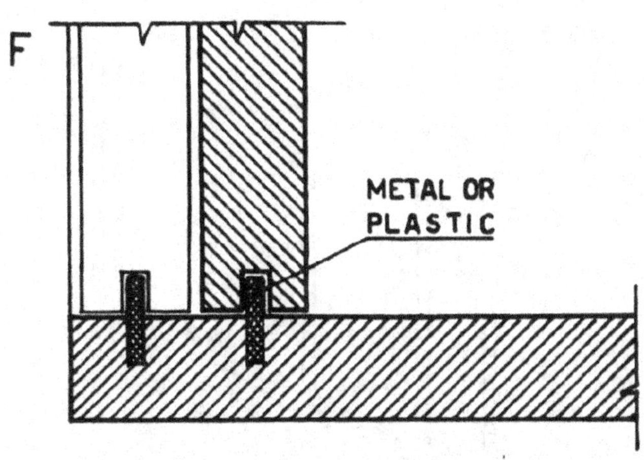

DOORS MAY BE MADE TO SLIDE IN A NUMBER OF
DIFFERENT WAYS. HERE ARE SEVERAL METHODS.

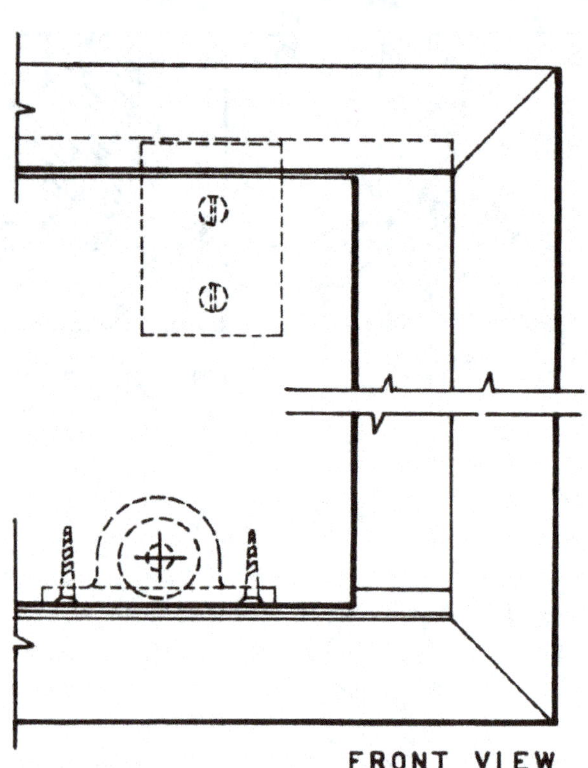

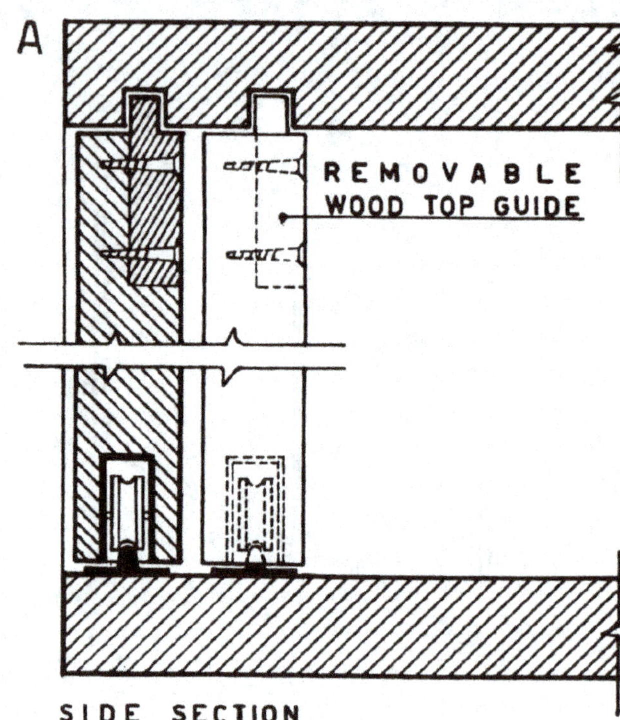

DOORS WILL MOVE MORE EASILY IF WHEELS ARE USED. THESE TWO METHODS WILL GIVE VERY SATISFACTORY RESULTS.

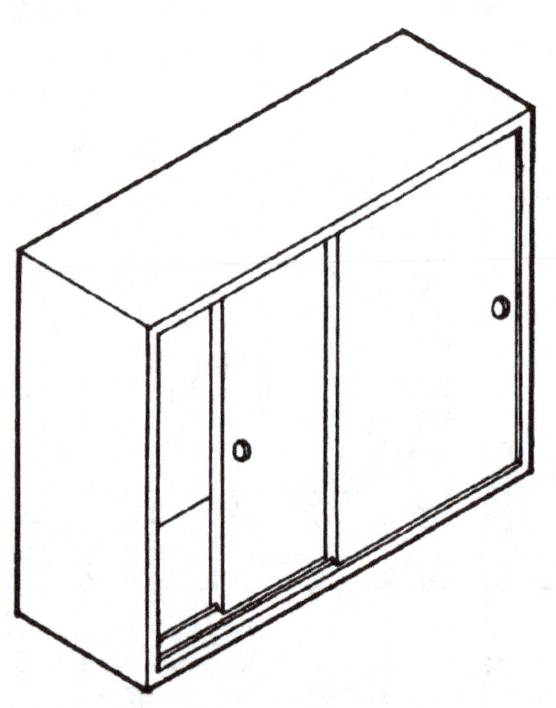

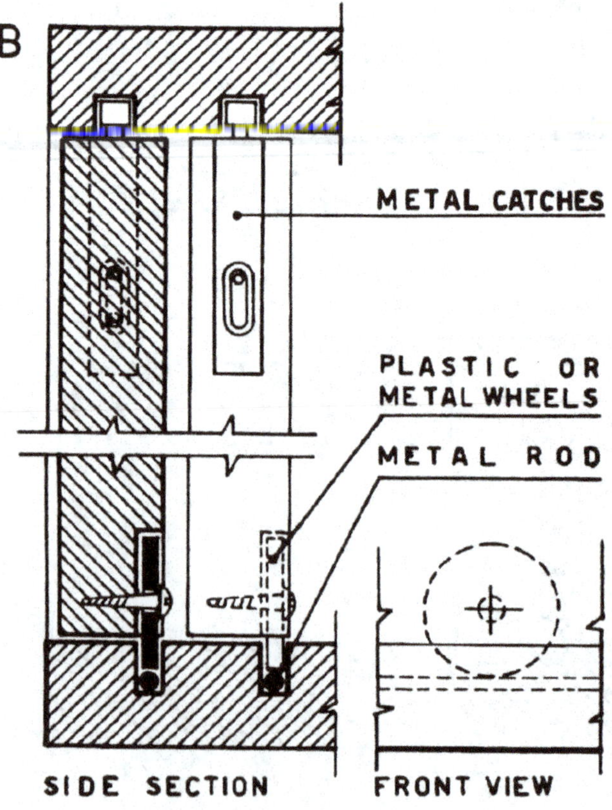

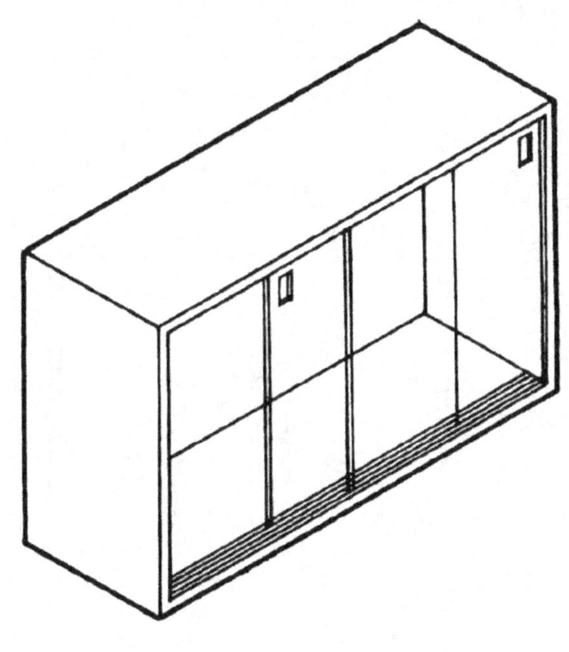

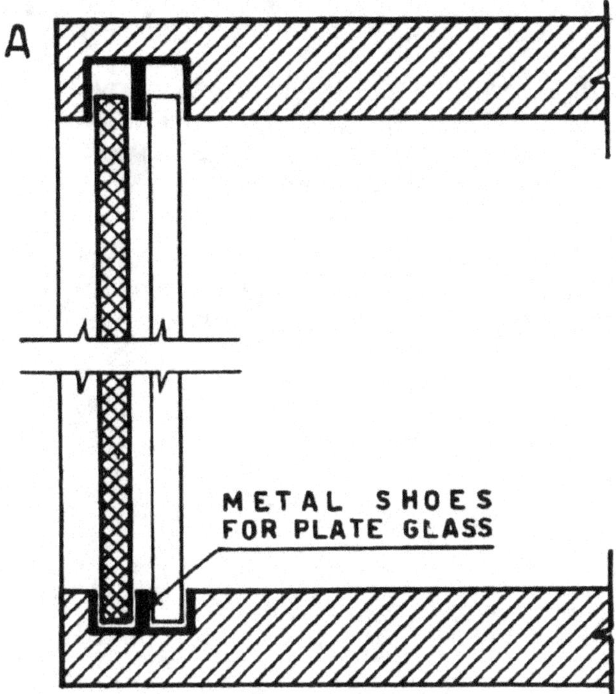

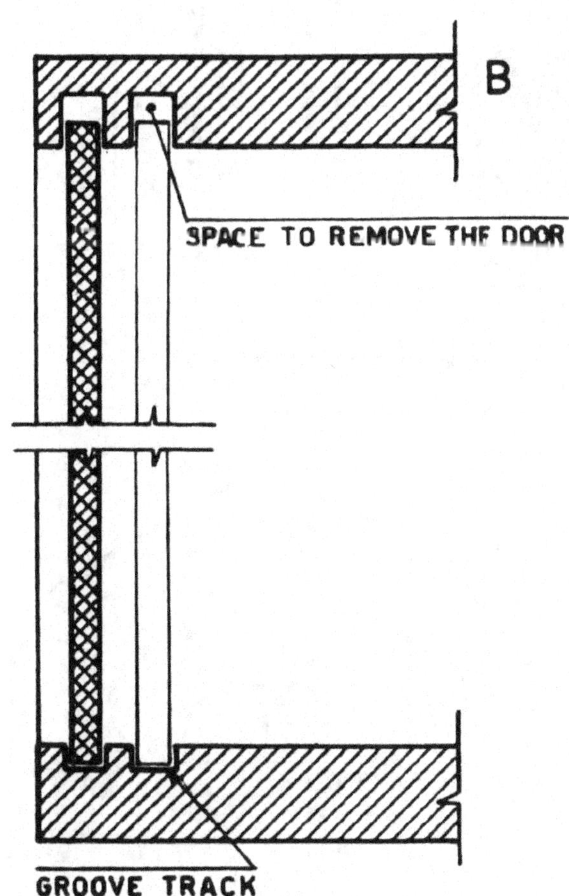

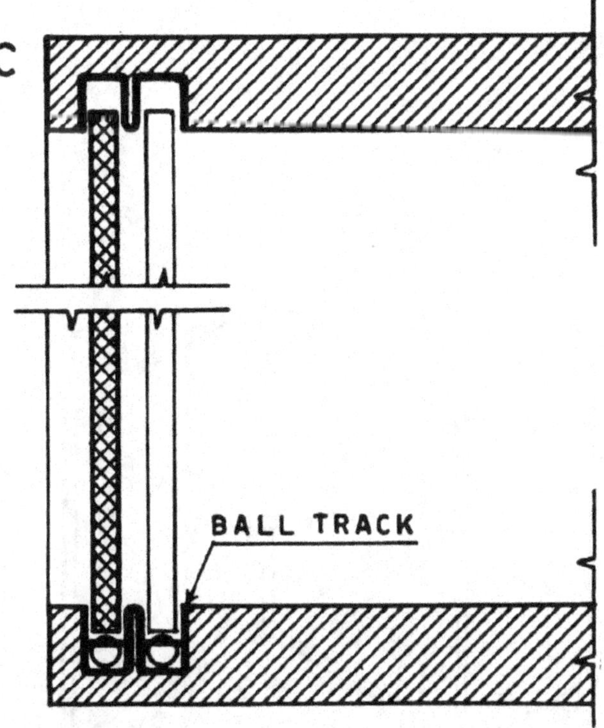

SLIDING DOORS OF PLATE GLASS MAY USE ANY OF
THESE THREE METHODS. "C" WOULD PROBABLY GIVE
THE BEST RESULTS.

CATCHES AND LOCKS FOR DOORS

DOOR HOLDING DEVICES ARE DIVIDED INTO TWO GROUPS: CATCHES AND LOCKS. THE CATCH IS INTENDED TO HOLD THE DOOR IN CLOSED POSITION. IT IS COMMONLY USED IN FURNITURE.

DOOR LOCKS DIFFER FROM CATCHES IN THAT THEY REQUIRE KEYS. IN THIS SECTION I HAVE ILLUSTRATED A FEW COMMON TYPES OF LOCKS AND CATCHES.

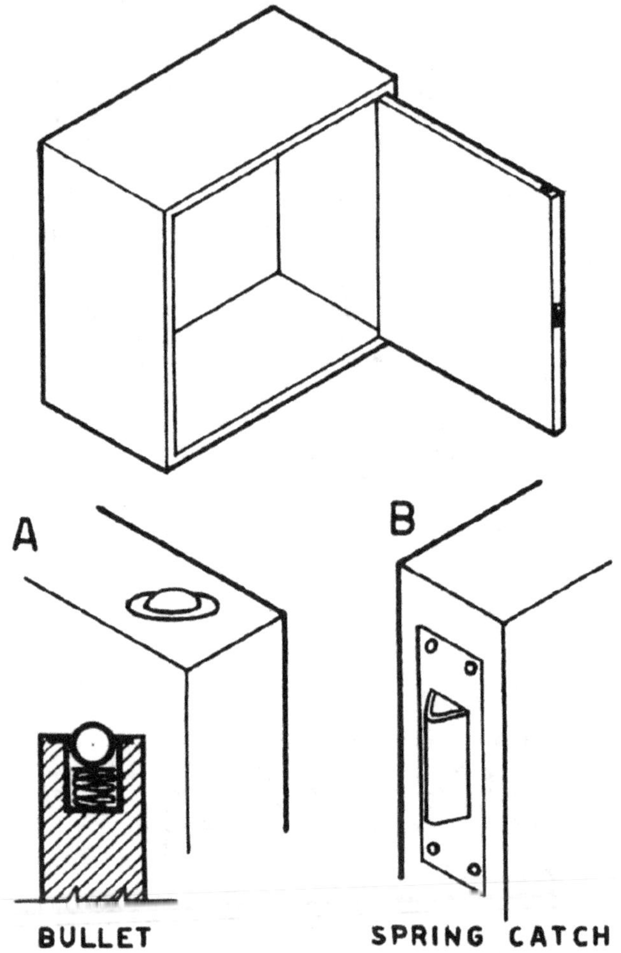

VARIOUS TYPES OF CATCHES.

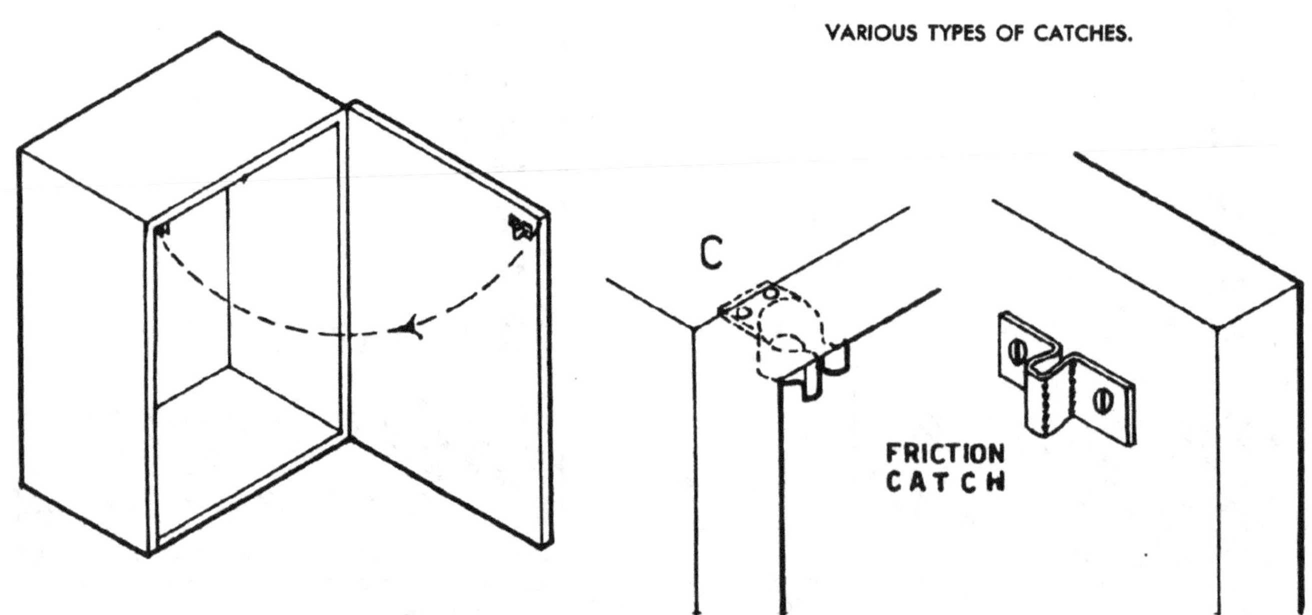

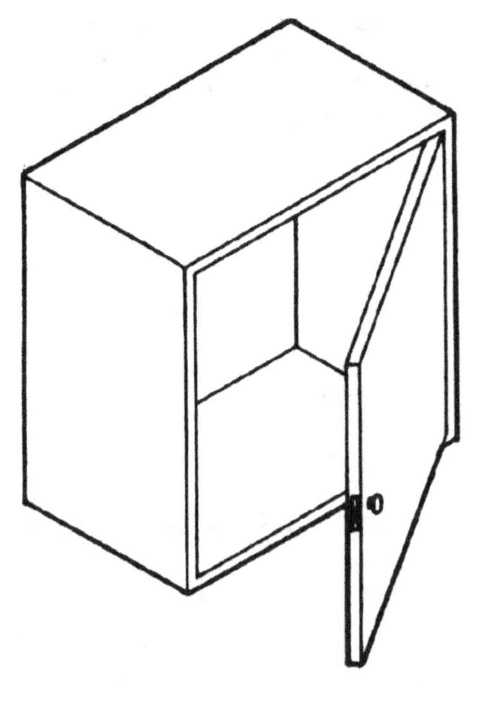

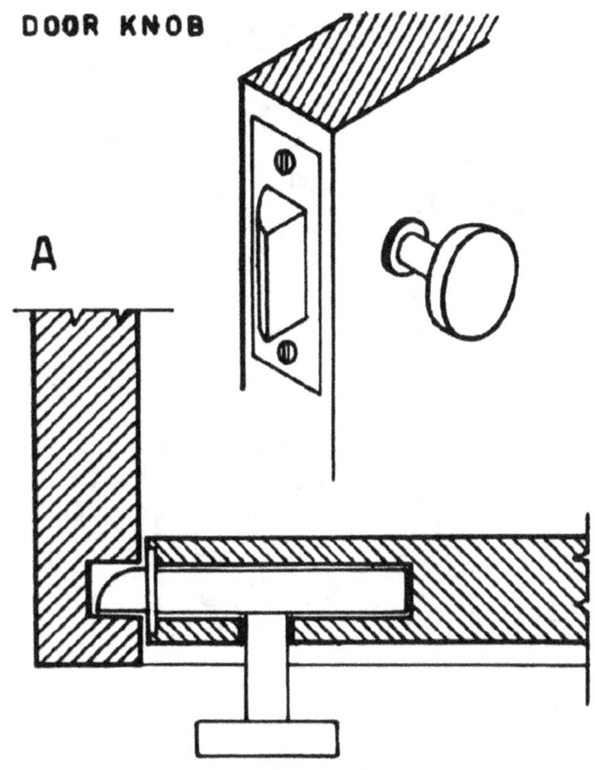

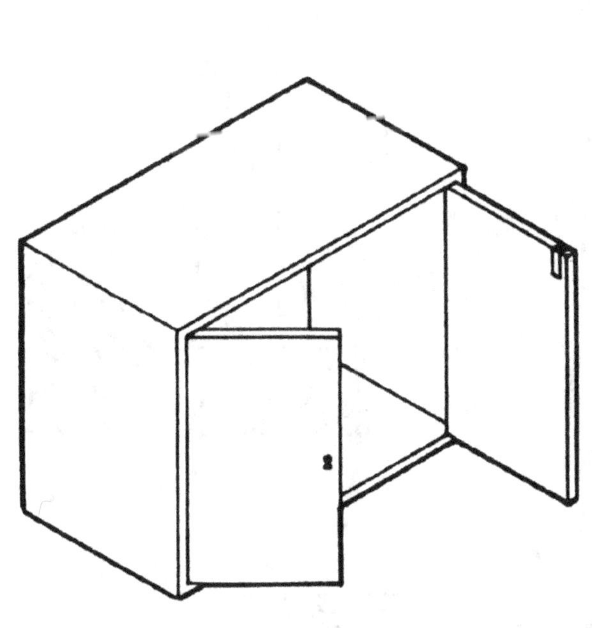

APPLICATION OF FLUSH AND NECK BOLTS
TO DOOR BACK.

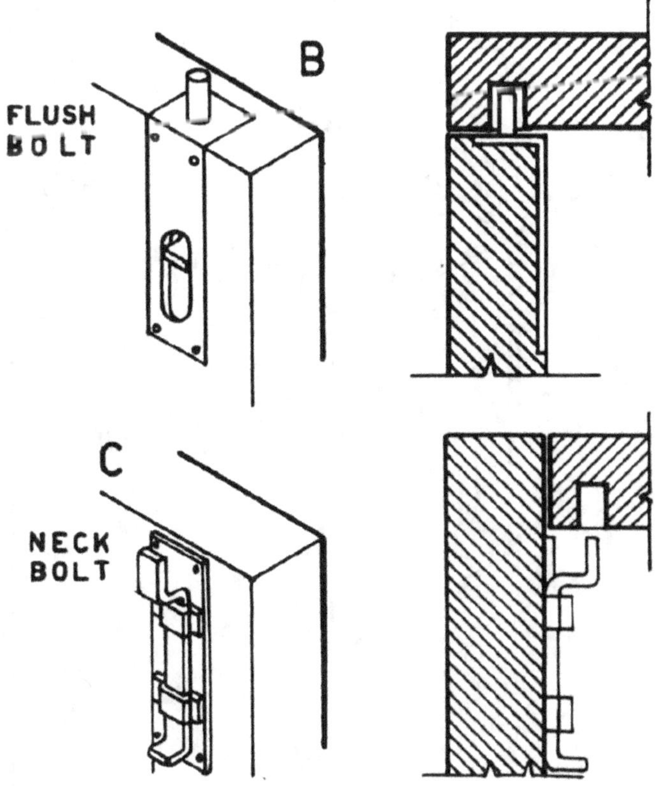

A

MORTISE LOCK

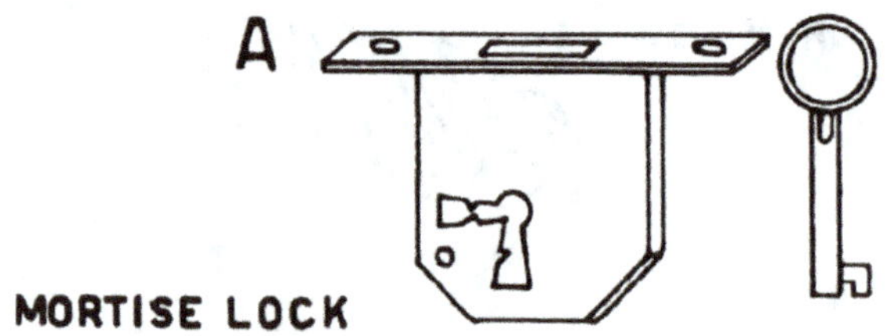

A – MORTISE LOCK IS A COMMON TYPE FOUND IN FURNITURE WORK. IT CAN BE USED WITH SINGLE OR DOUBLE DOORS - AND WITH DRAWERS.

B

SIDE LOCK

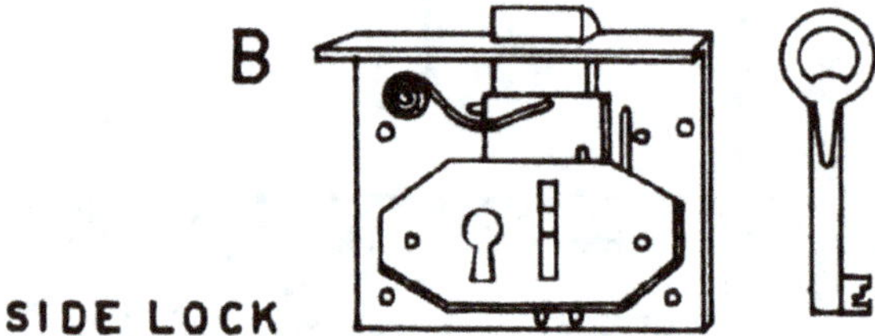

SIDE LOCK, WHICH IS SELDOM USED TODAY.

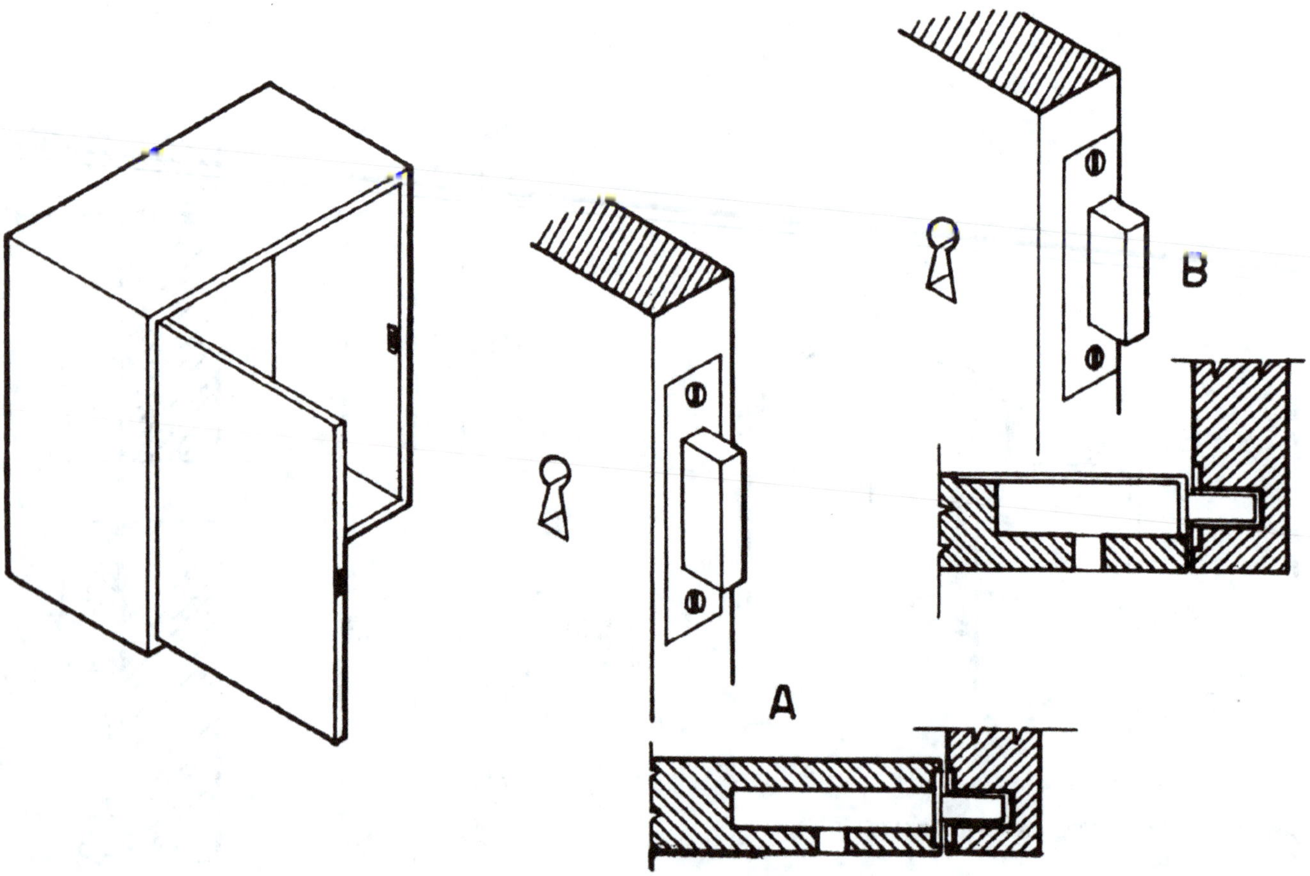

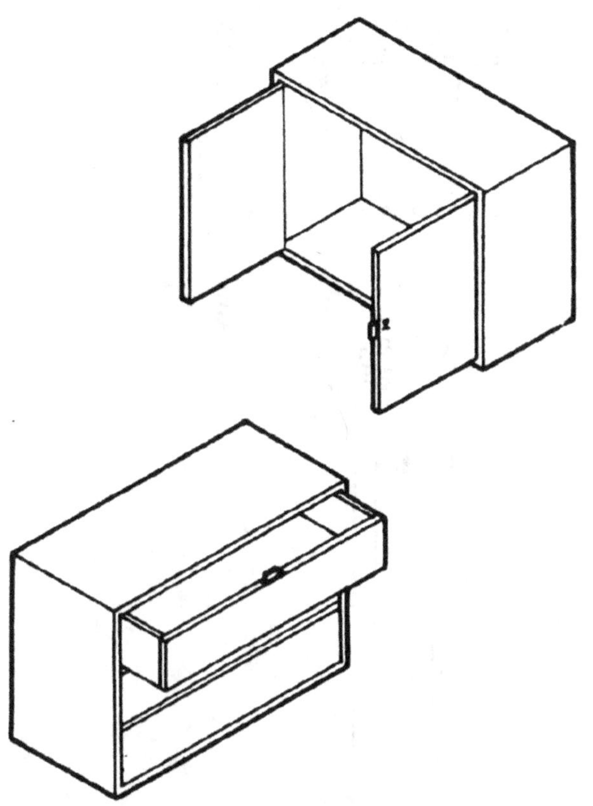

MORTISE AND SIDE LOCK THAT MAY BE APPLIED TO
EITHER DOORS OR DRAWERS.

C

CYLINDER LOCK

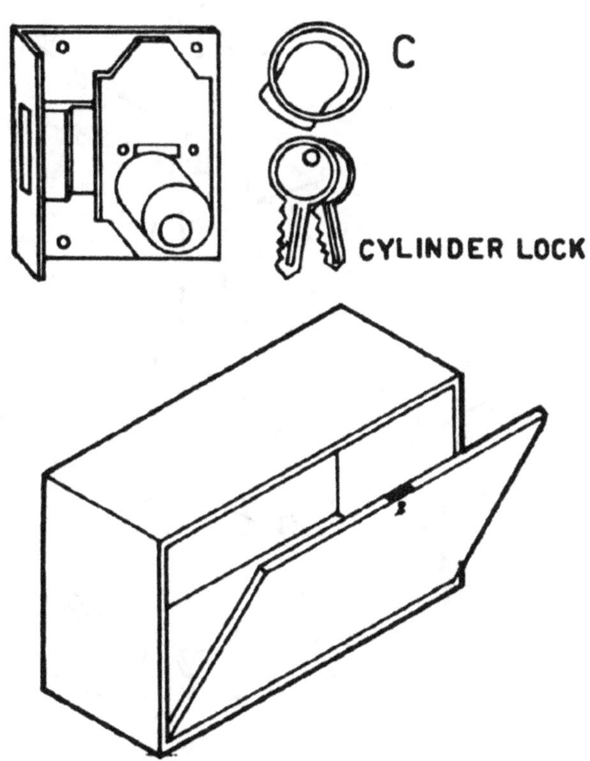

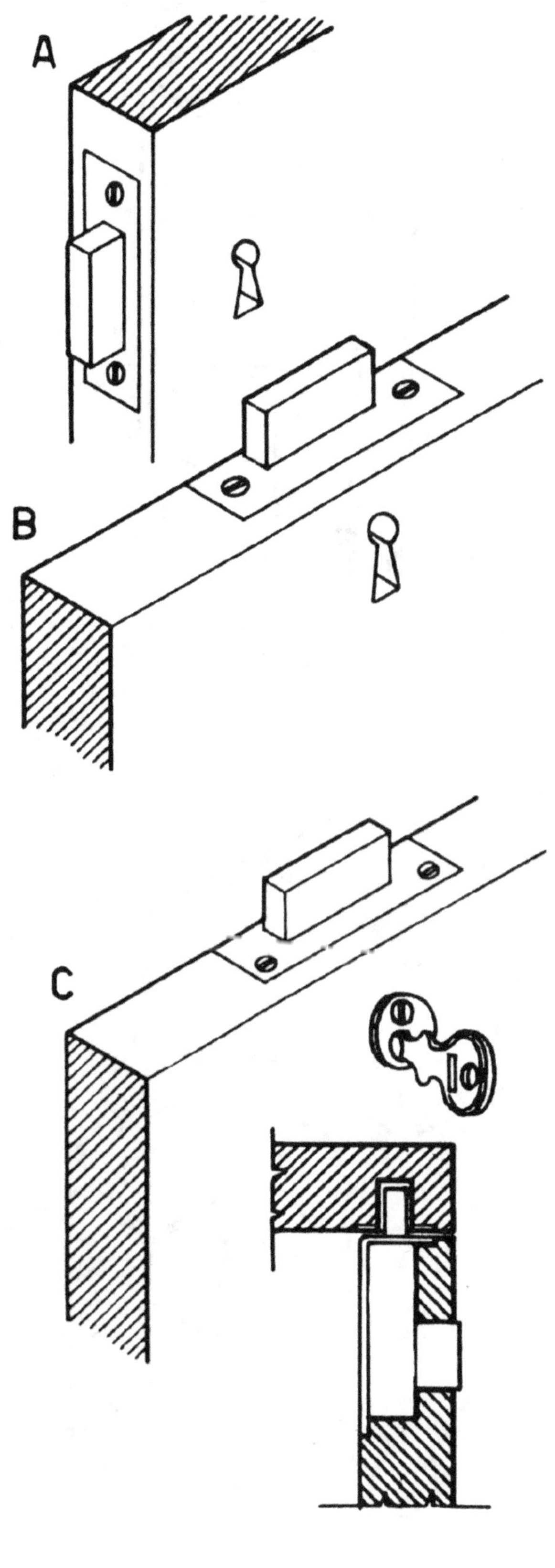

CYLINDER TYPE LOCK WHICH MAY BE USED ON ANY
TYPE OF DOOR.

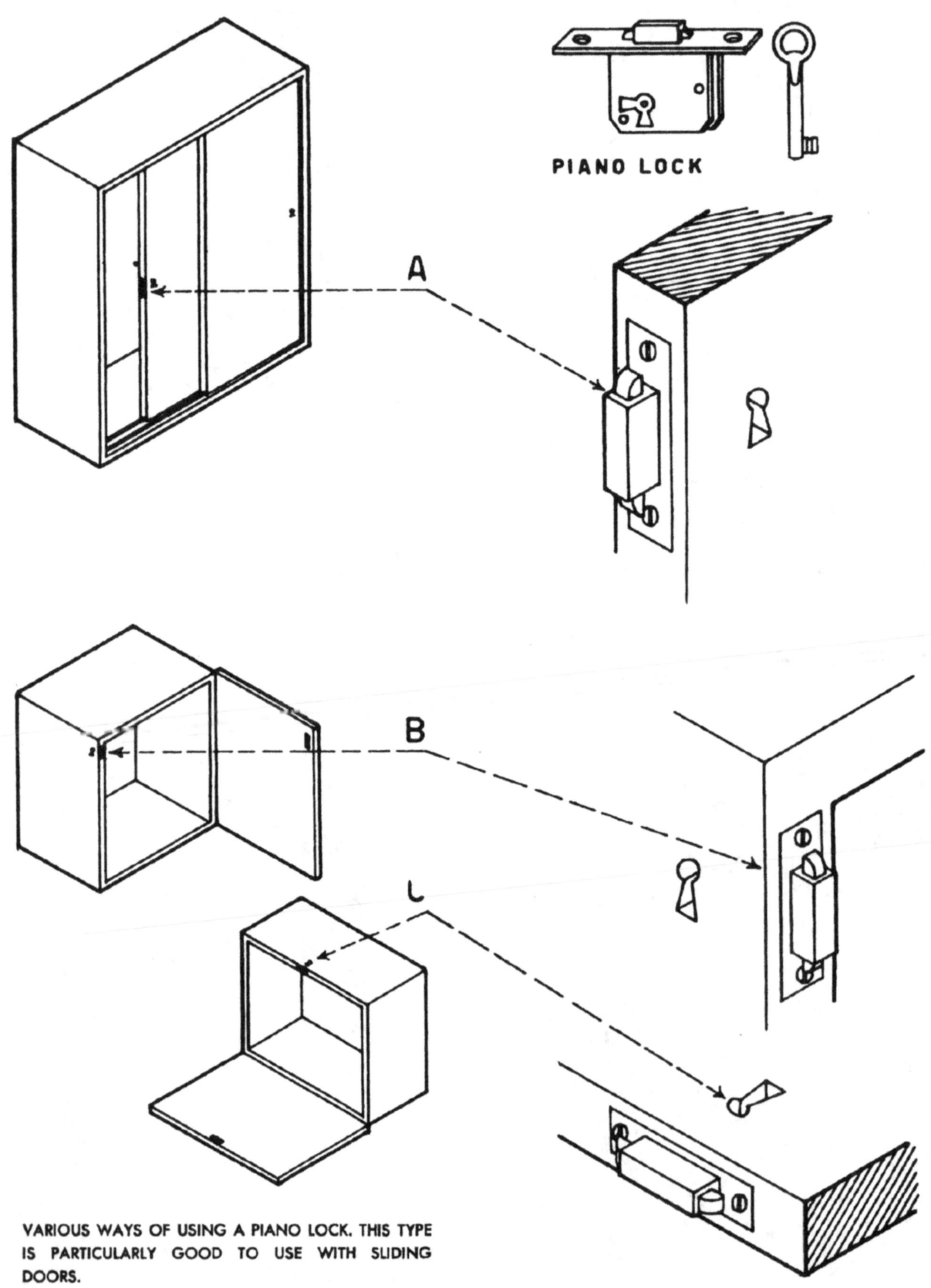

VARIOUS WAYS OF USING A PIANO LOCK. THIS TYPE
IS PARTICULARLY GOOD TO USE WITH SLIDING
DOORS.

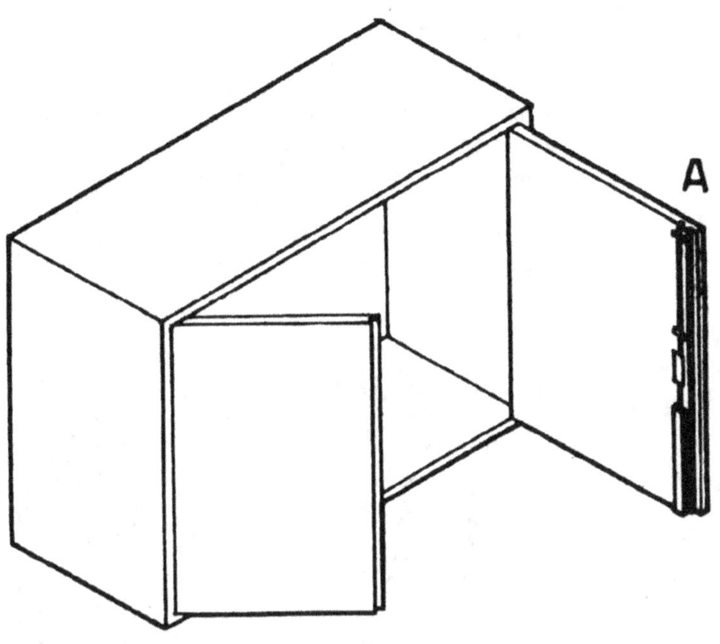

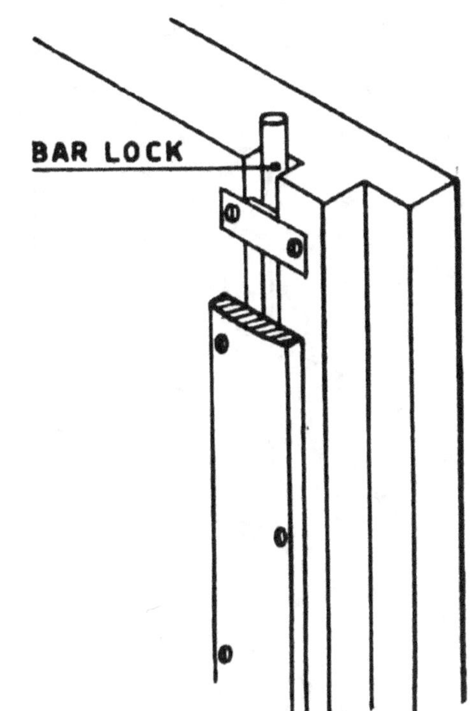

THIS BAR LOCK METHOD CLOSES BOTH DOORS AT THE SAME TIME.

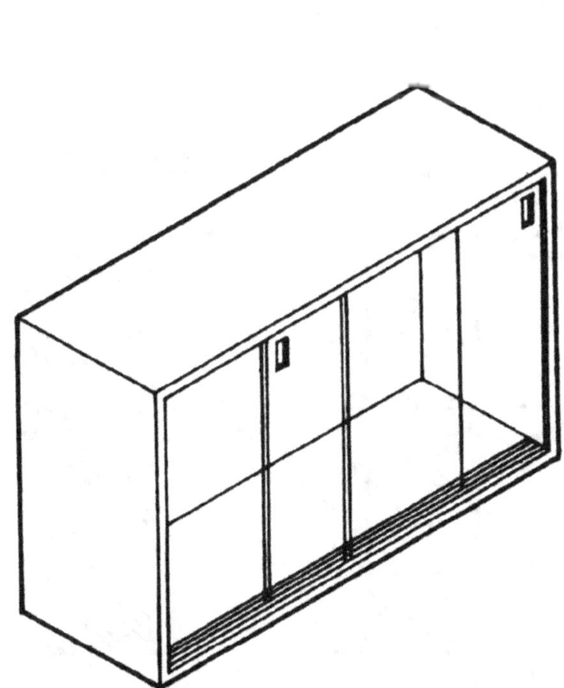

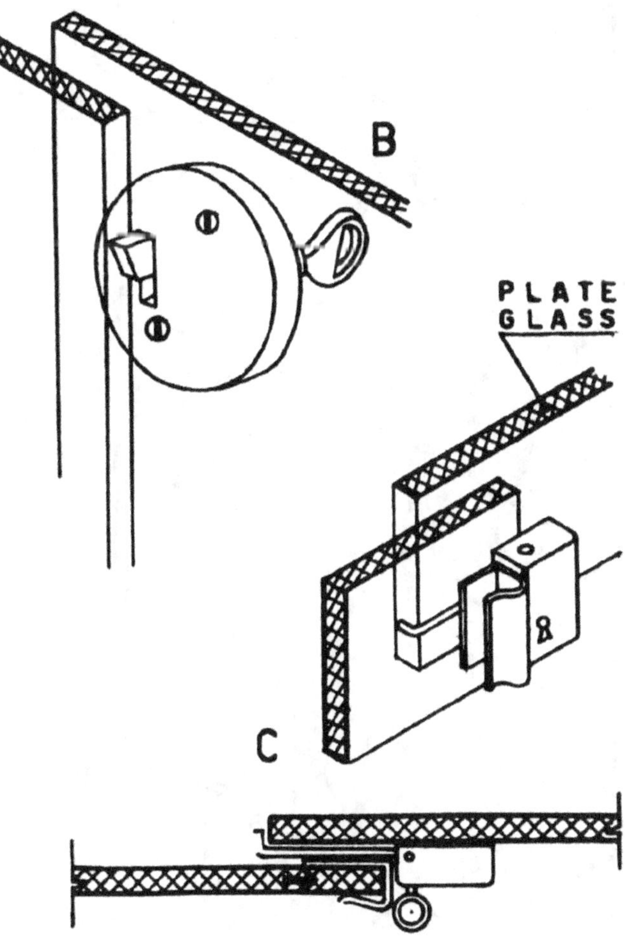

PLATE GLASS LOCKING DEVICES WHICH ARE PARTICULARLY USEFUL. "B" IS SECURED WITH SCREWS; "C" IS APPLIED TO THE BASE OF THE PLATE GLASS.

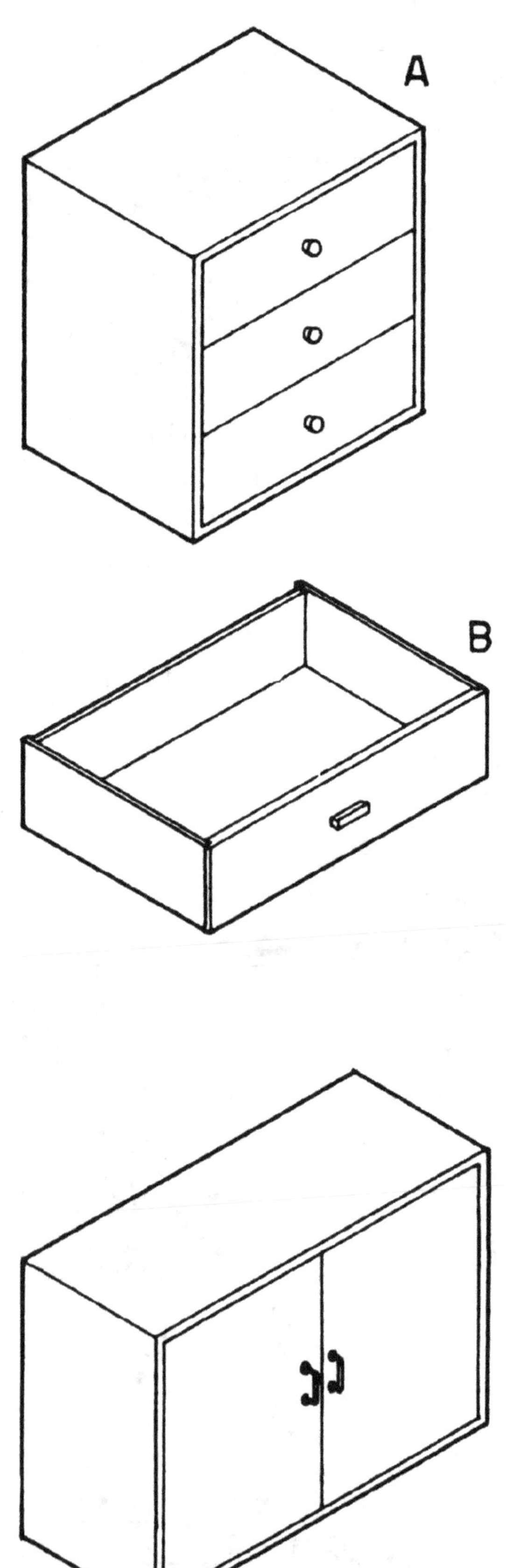

PULLS

THERE ARE MANY TYPES OF PULLS OR KNOBS MADE OF WOOD OR METAL. THESE MAY BE APPLIED TO THE FURNITURE OR BUILT INTO THE ACTUAL DESIGN. IN SOME CASES THE PULLS ARE USED DECORATIVELY, BUT IT IS USUALLY BEST TO BUILD THEM INTO THE ACTUAL FURNITURE AS SHOWN ON PAGE 79.

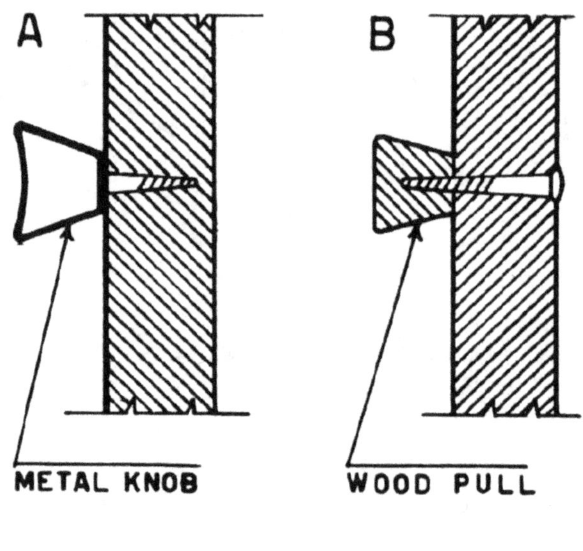

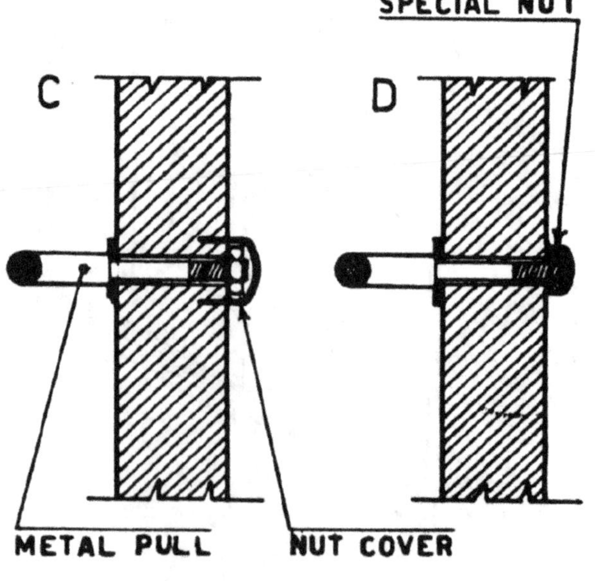

VARIOUS TYPES OF KNOBS AND PULLS WHICH ARE ATTACHED TO THE DOORS OR DRAWERS.

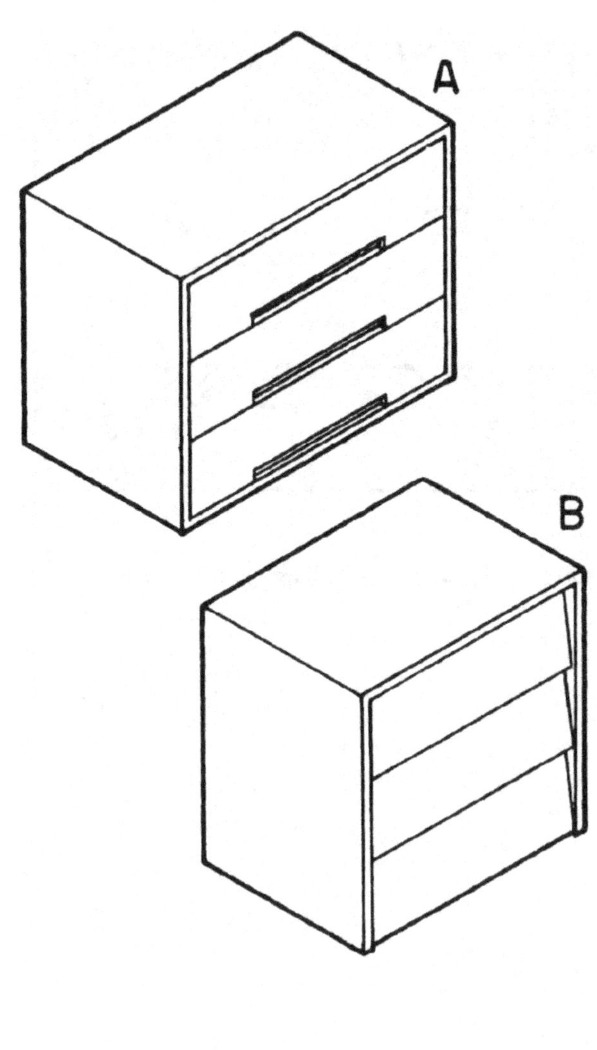

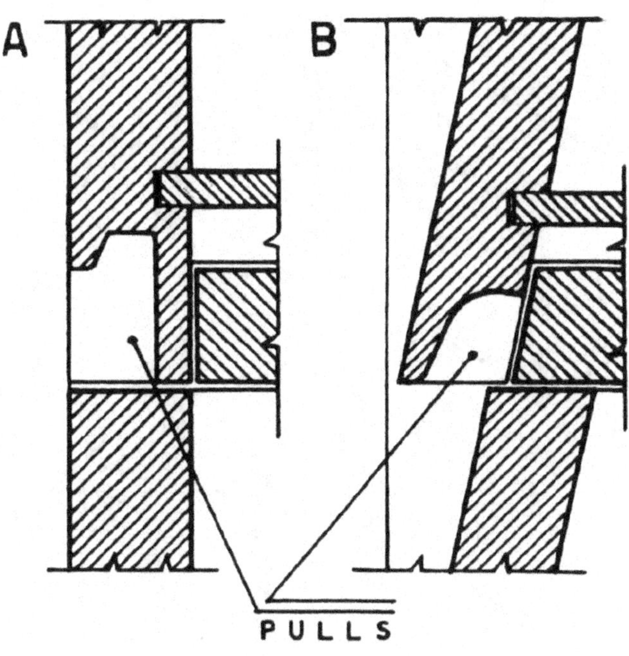

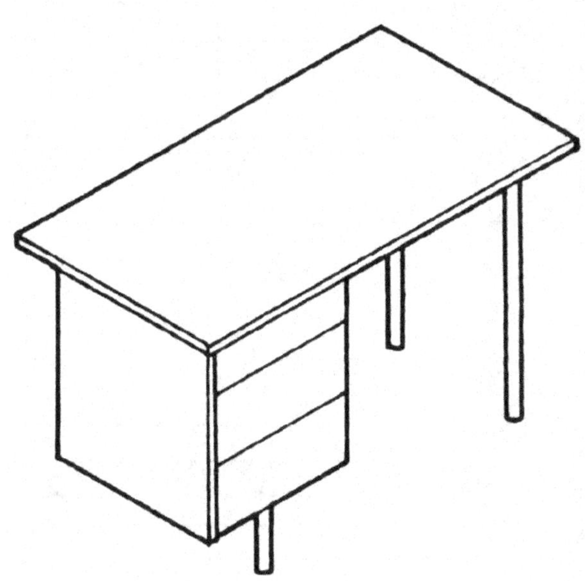

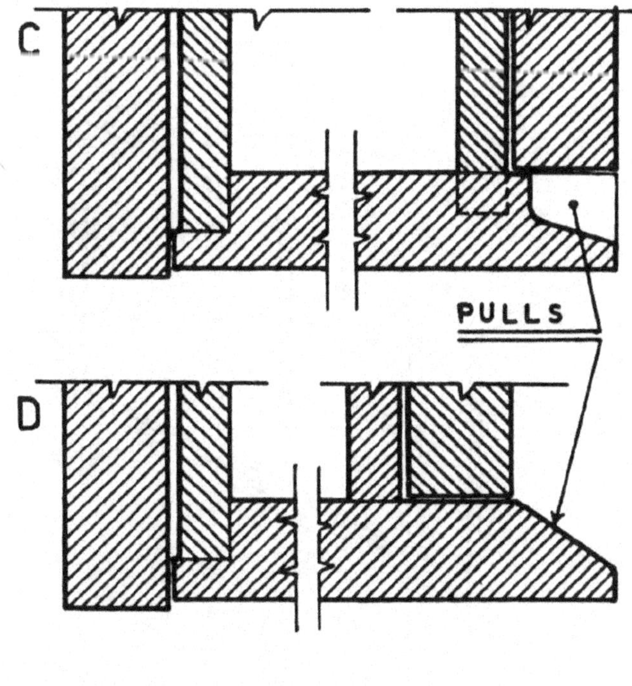

DRAWER AND DOOR PULLS WHICH ARE BUILT INTO
THE FURNITURE.

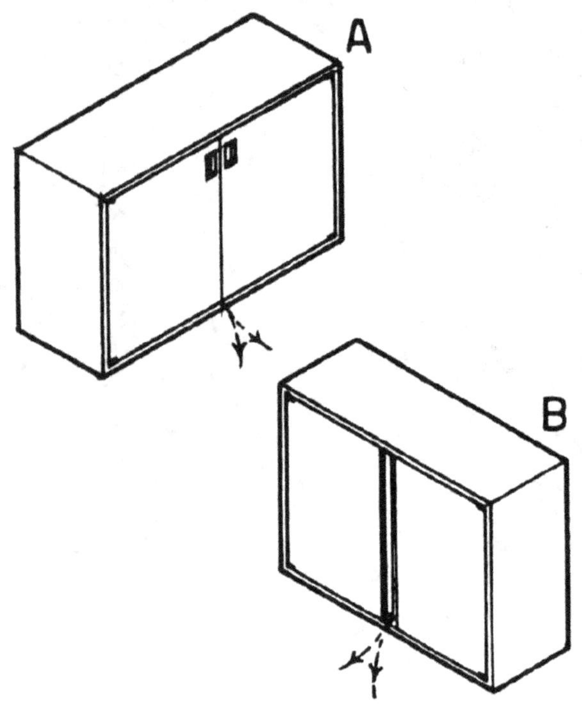

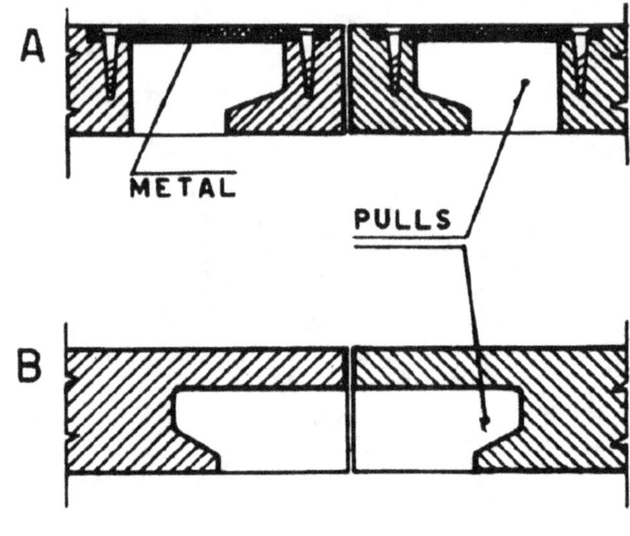

PULLS WHICH ARE MADE A PART OF THE DOOR.

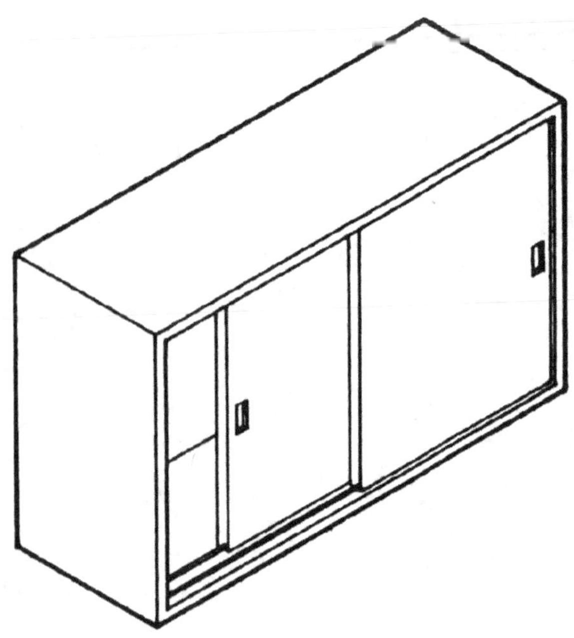

SLIDING DOOR PULLS CUT INTO THE WOOD OR PLATE GLASS.

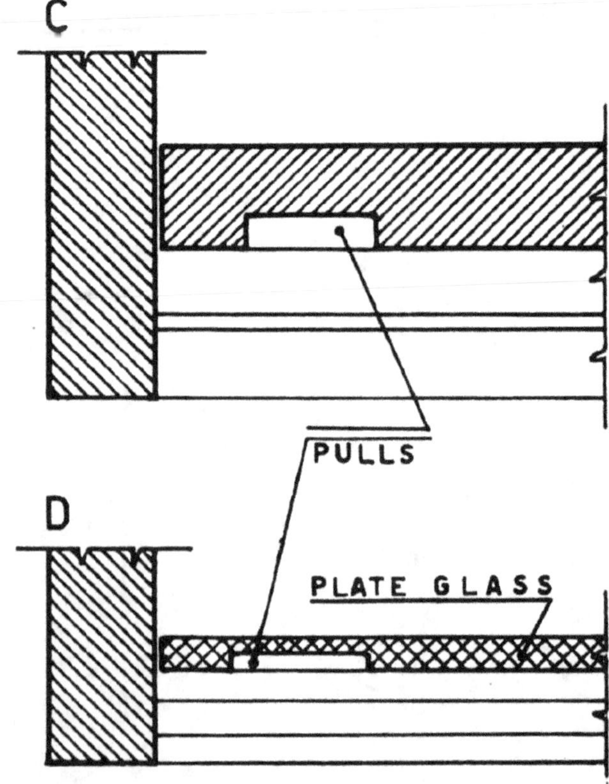

ADJUSTABLE SHELVES

AN ADJUSTABLE SHELF HAS SEVERAL ADVANTAGES. CHIEF OF THESE IS THAT THE SPACING OF THE SHELVES MAY BE VARIED IN ACCORDANCE WITH THE OBJECT TO BE DISPLAYED. THESE SHELVES ARE OFTEN USED IN BOOK STORES, EQUIPMENT, KITCHEN CABINETS AND OTHER FURNITURE. HERE ARE SEVERAL TYPES.

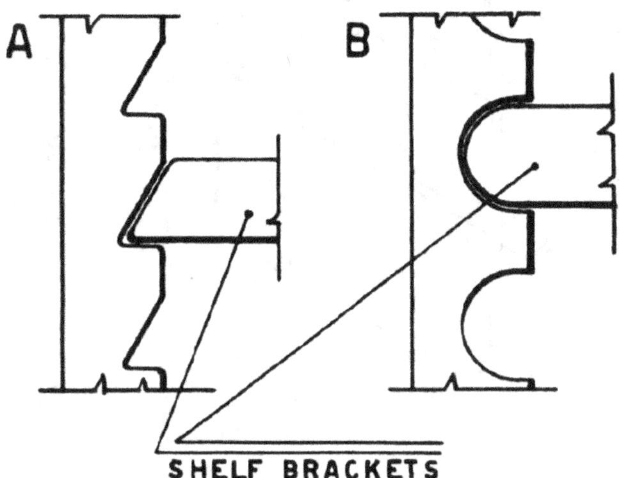

ADJUSTABLE SHELF PINS

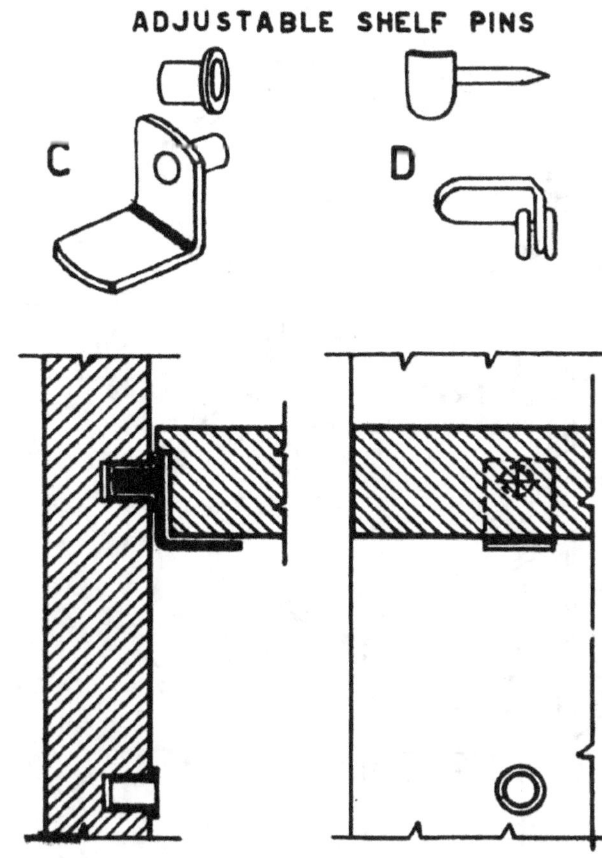

VARIOUS EXAMPLES OF ADJUSTABLE SHELVES. TYPE "C" IS ONE OF THE BEST ARRANGEMENTS.

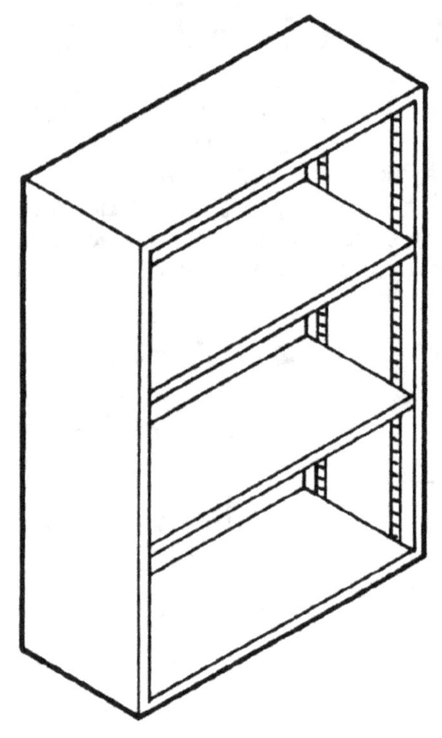

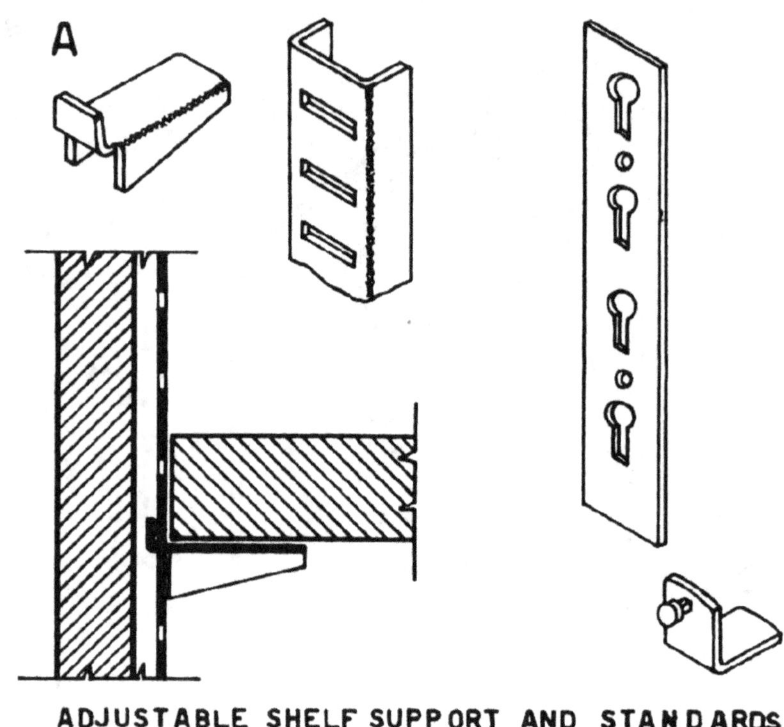

ADJUSTABLE SHELF SUPPORT AND STANDARDS

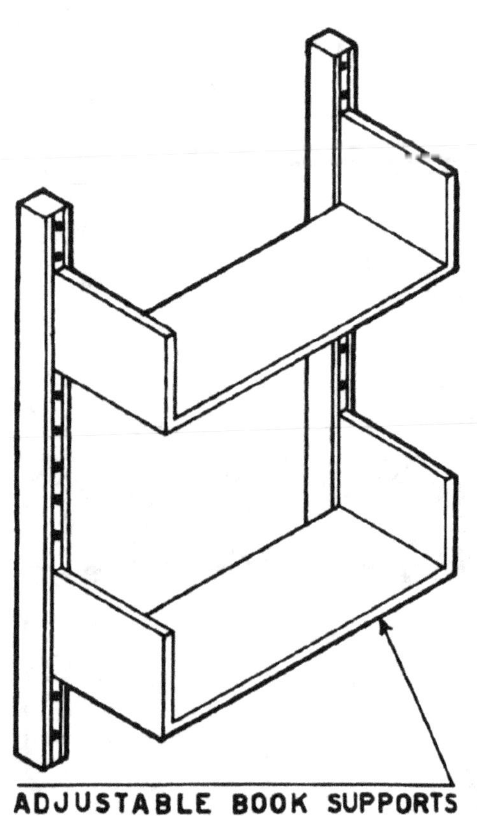

ADJUSTABLE BOOK SUPPORTS

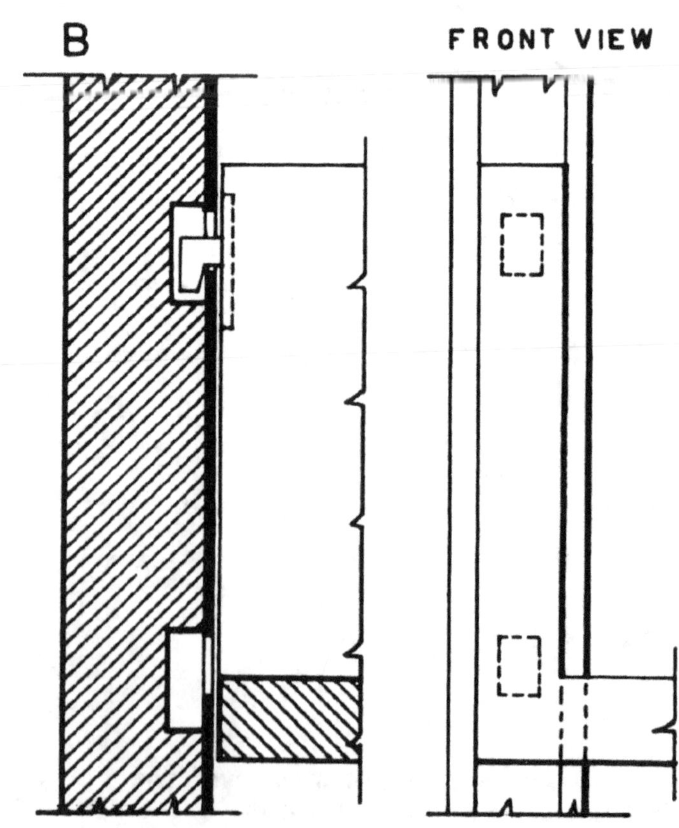

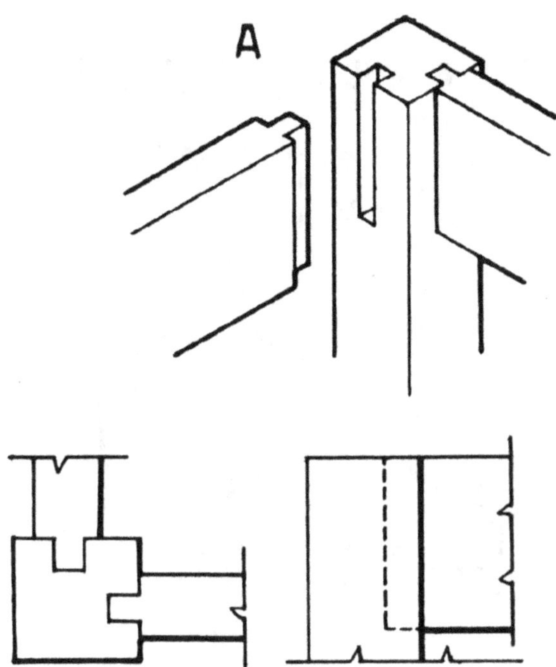

OPEN MORTISE AND TENON JOINT.

LEGS

THERE ARE MANY WAYS OF JOINING LEGS TO TRANSVERSE RAILS AND ATTACHING LEGS AND RAILS TO THE BODY OF THE PIECE OF FURNITURE. GREAT CARE SHOULD BE TAKEN IN THE SELECTION AND EXECUTION OF SUCH JOINTS SO THAT THEY WILL BE ABLE TO WITHSTAND THE STRAIN WHICH MAY BE PUT UPON THEM. IN ADDITION TO THESE JOINTS, THE BUILDER MUST CONSIDER HOW THE LEG IS TO BE PROTECTED WHERE IT IS IN CONTACT WITH THE FLOOR.

JOINING RAILS TO LEGS

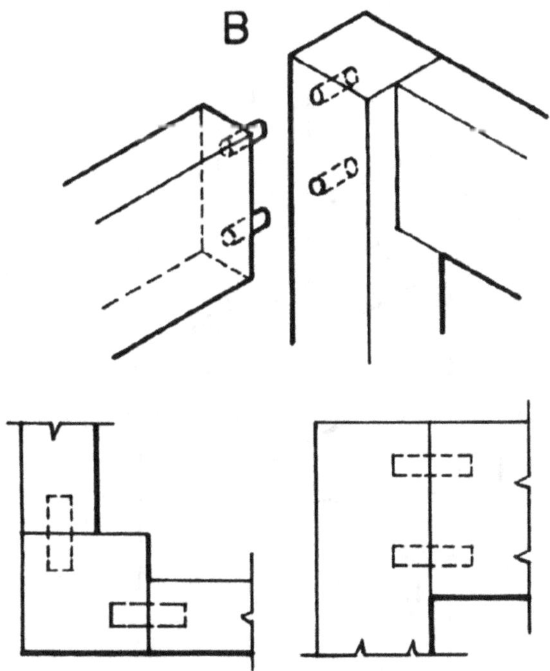

DOWEL JOINT THAT MIGHT BE USED BY THE AMATEUR CRAFTSMAN.

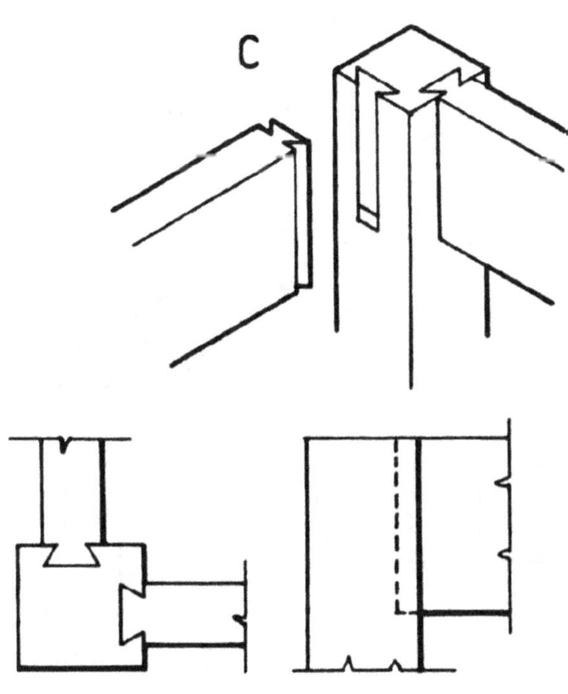

DOVETAIL JOINT: A VERY STRONG METHOD OF JOINING THE PIECES.

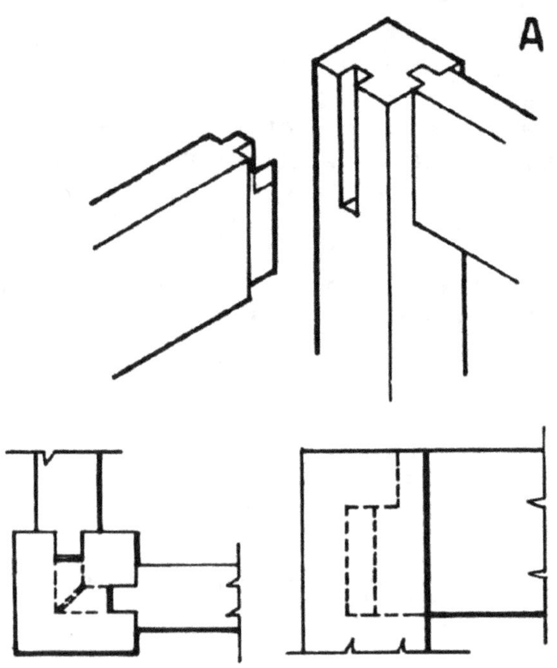

JOINING A LEG TO A RAIL WITH A RABBET MORTISE AND TENON IS AN EXCELLENT METHOD.

JOINING LEGS TO FURNITURE

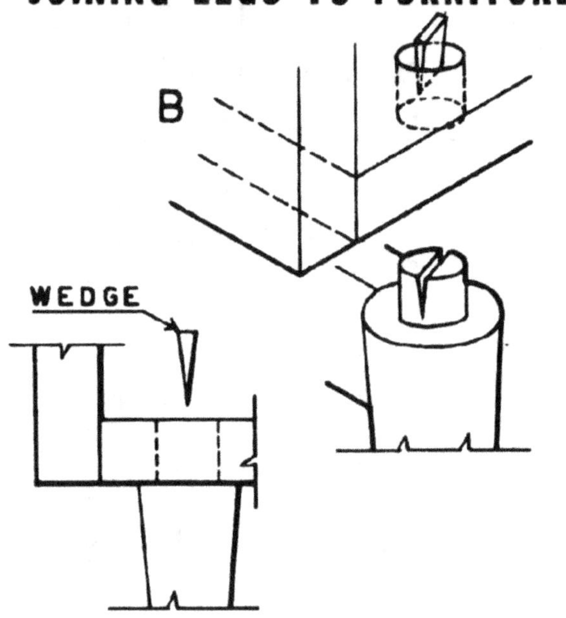

WEDGE AND DOWEL JOINT THAT MAY BE USED. AFTER INSTALLATION THE WEDGE IS CUT FLUSH WITH THE TOP.

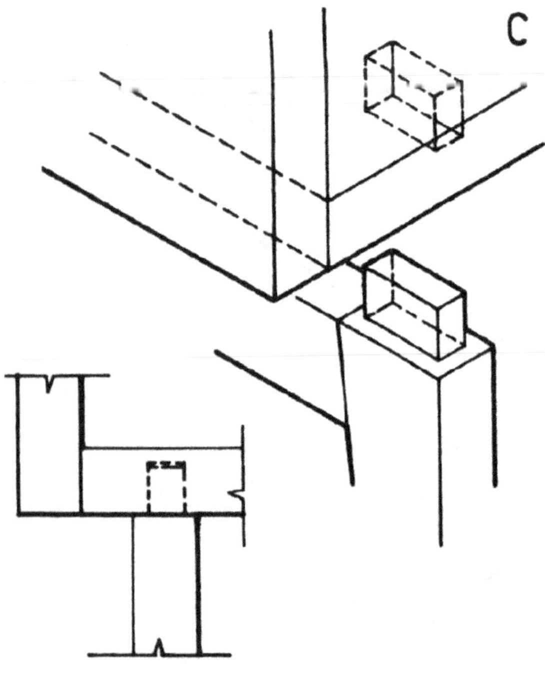

STUB MORTISE AND TENON JOINT WHICH IS GLUED TO THE BODY PIECE.

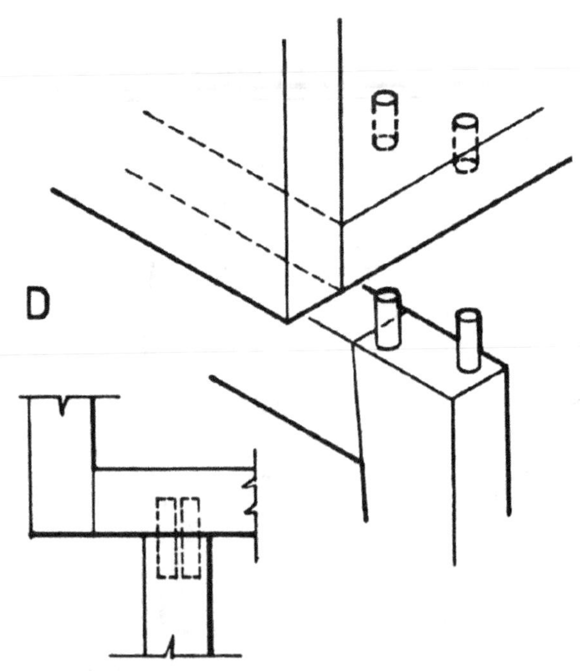

DOWEL JOINT THAT IS IDEAL FOR HOME CRAFTSMEN.

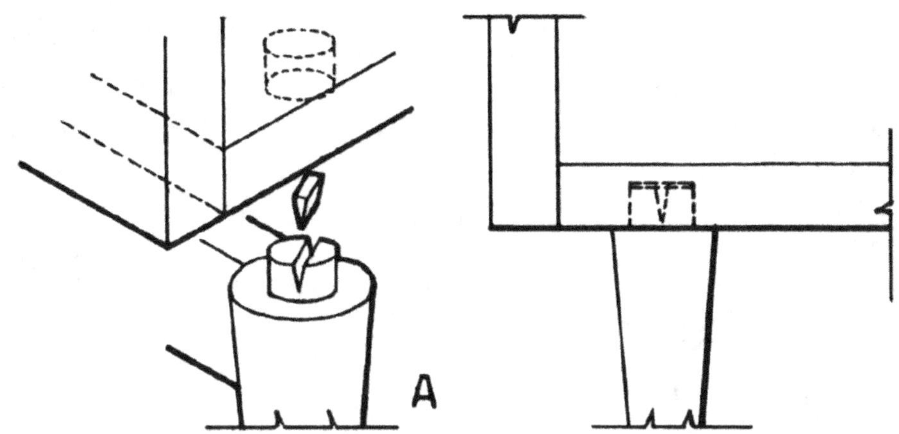

WEDGE IN STUB DOWEL. NOTE THAT HOLE DOES NOT RUN THROUGH.

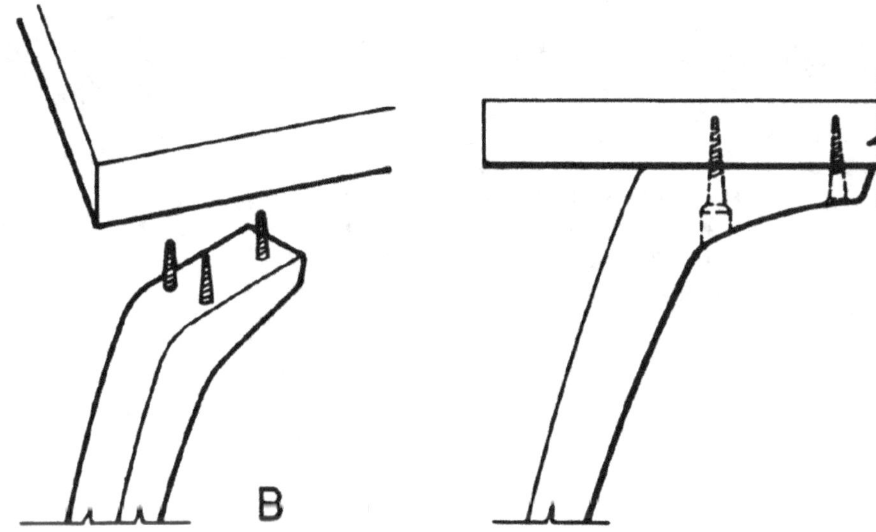

SCREW JOINT THAT IS EASY TO MAKE.

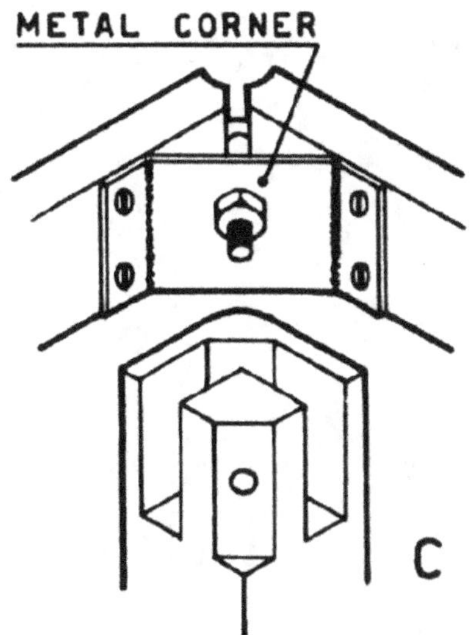

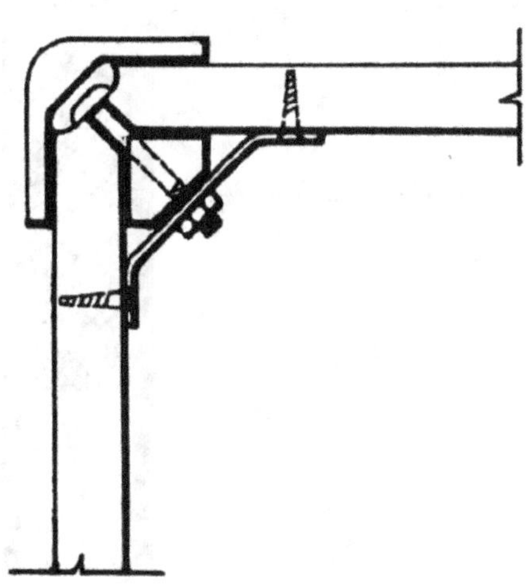

DEMOUNTABLE LEG WITH METAL CORNER. THIS METHOD IS OFTEN USED ON KITCHEN TABLES.

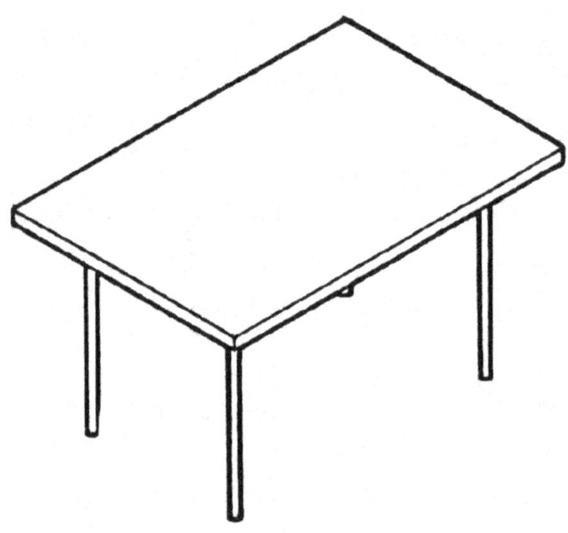

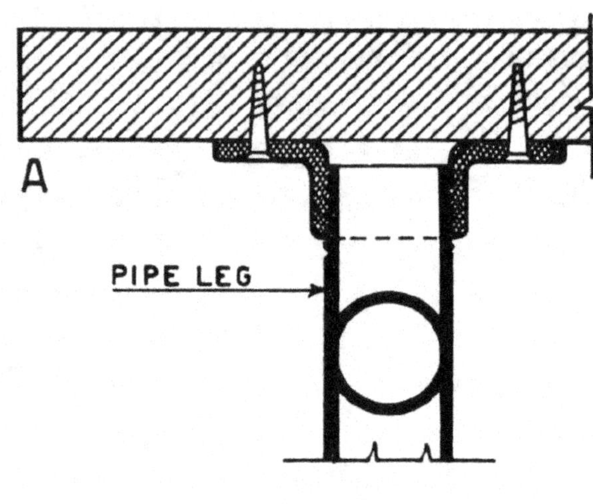

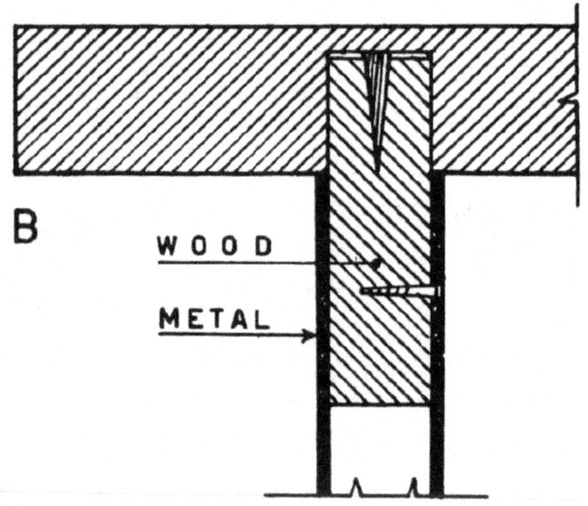

JOINING METAL LEGS TO WOOD TOP

VARIOUS METHODS OF JOINING METAL LEGS TO A WOOD TOP. EACH EXAMPLE ASSURES GOOD RESULTS. "A" USES A METAL PIPE SCREWED TO A PLATE, "B" IS MADE WITH A WOOD STUB TO WHICH A METAL TUBE IS SCREWED. "C" USES A METAL STUB INSTEAD OF A WOODEN ONE. "D" IS SCREWED DIRECTLY TO THE TABLE TOP.

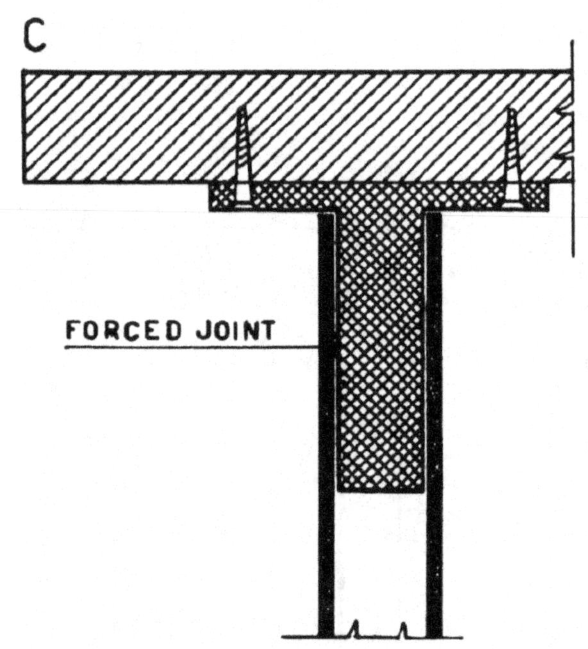

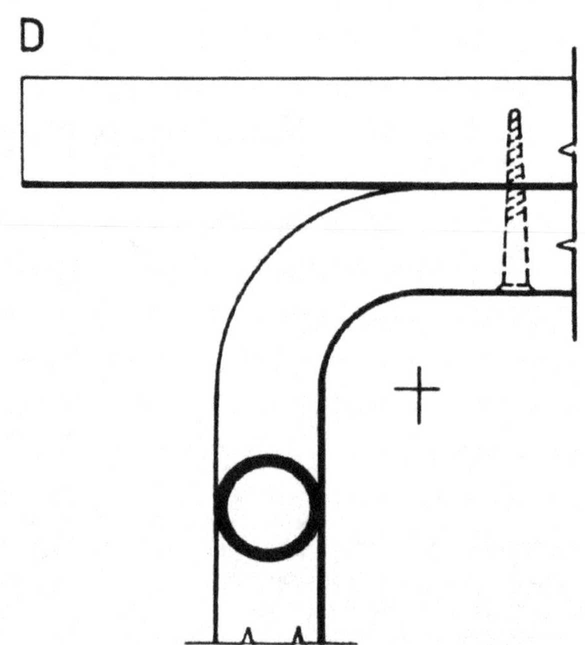

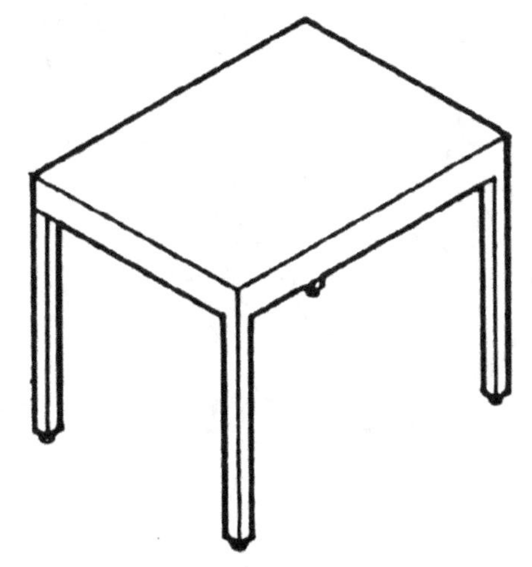

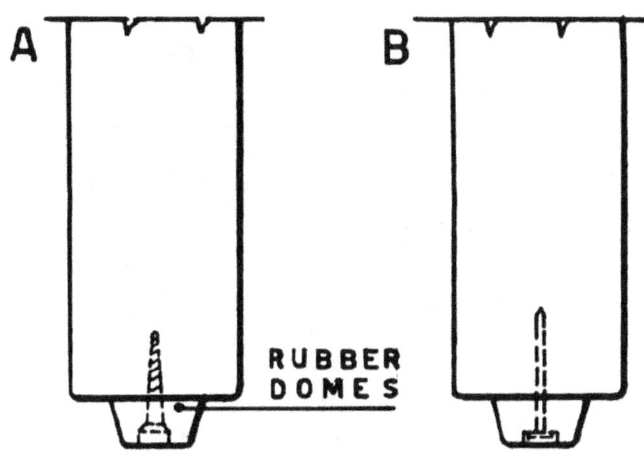

LEG END FITTINGS

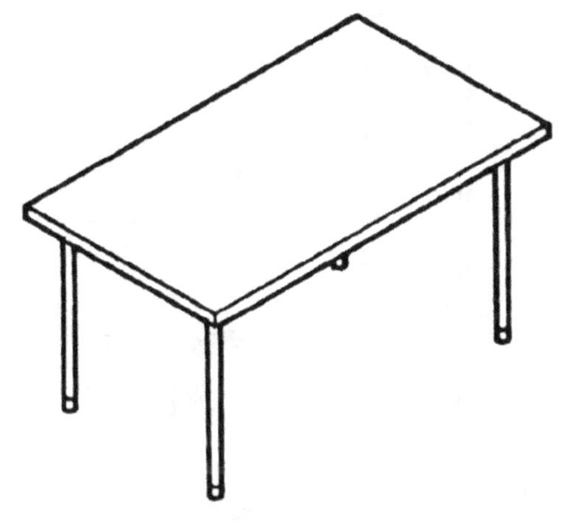

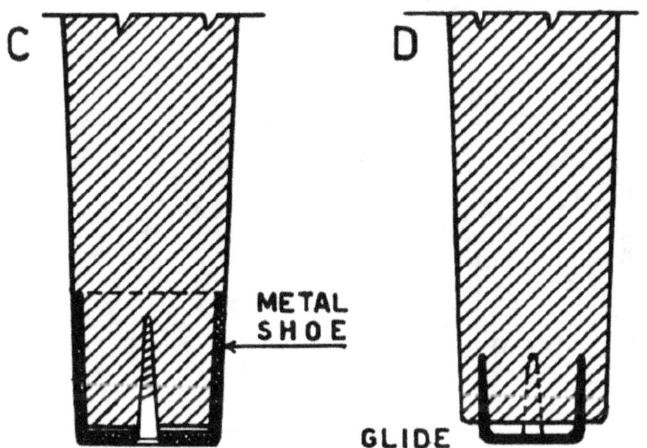

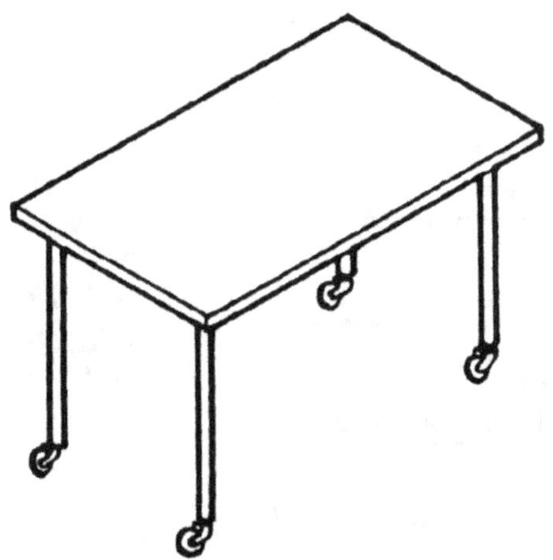

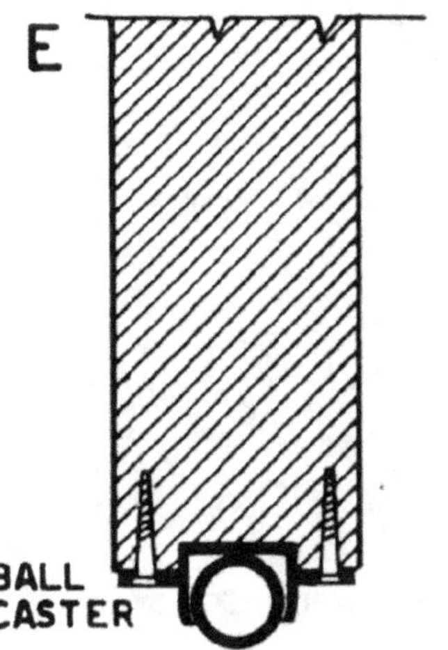

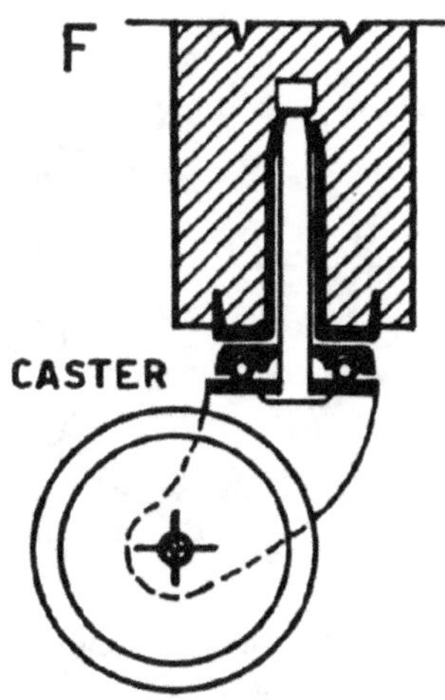

DIFFERENT WAYS OF PROTECTING THE BOTTOM OF THE WOODEN LEG.

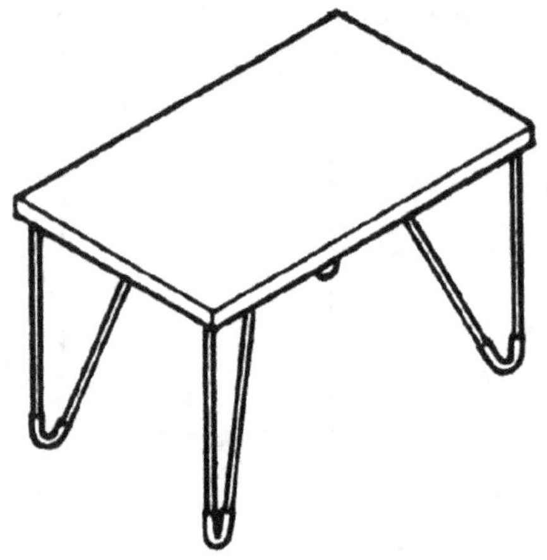

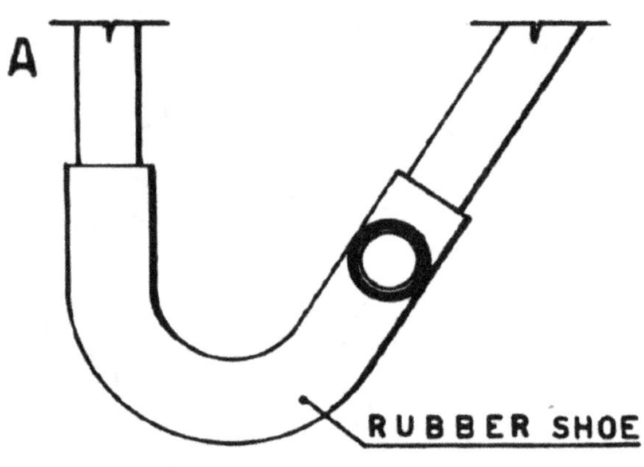

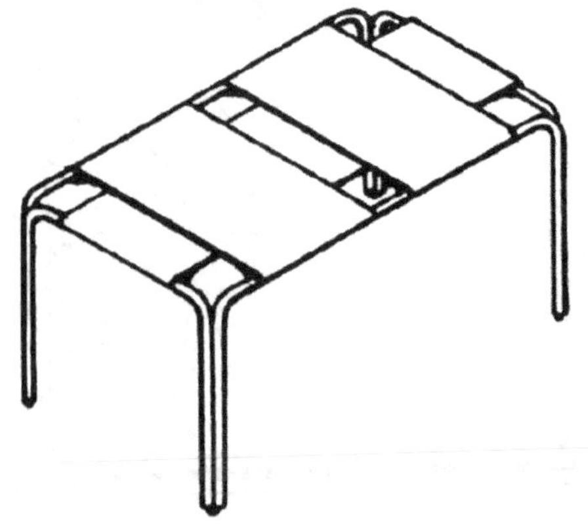

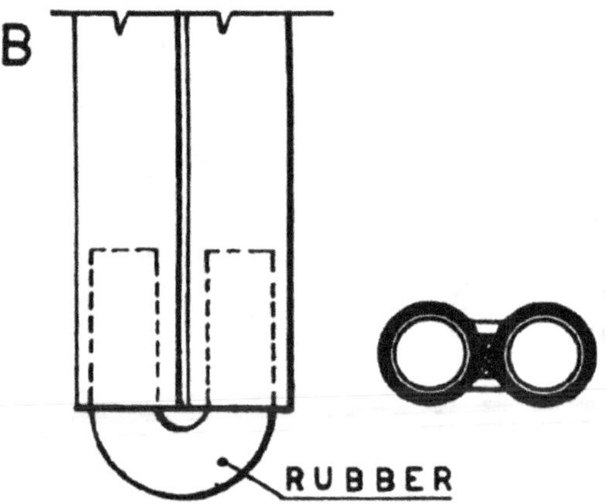

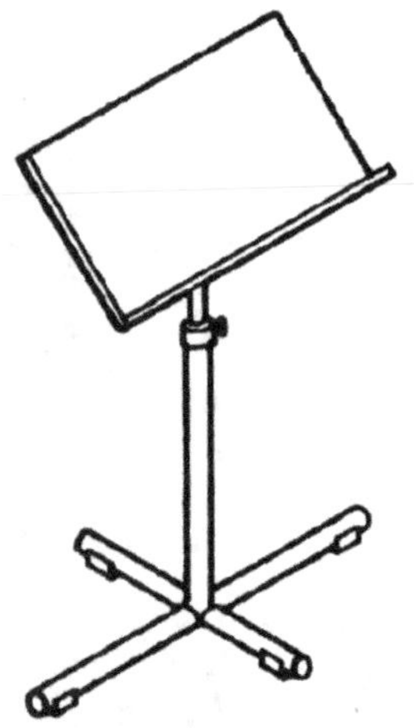

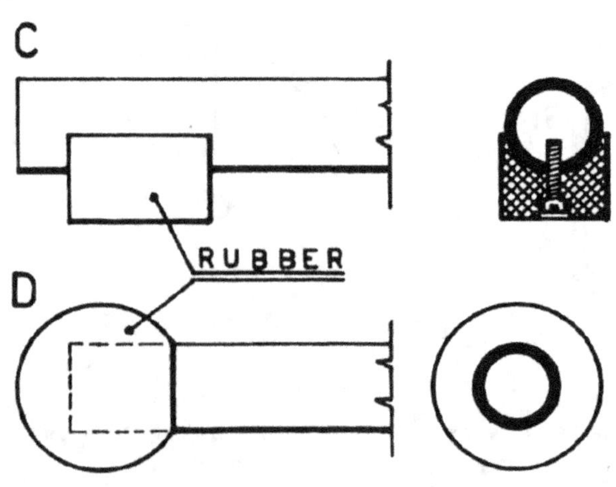

VARIOUS METHODS OF PROTECTING METAL LEGS BY USING RUBBER.

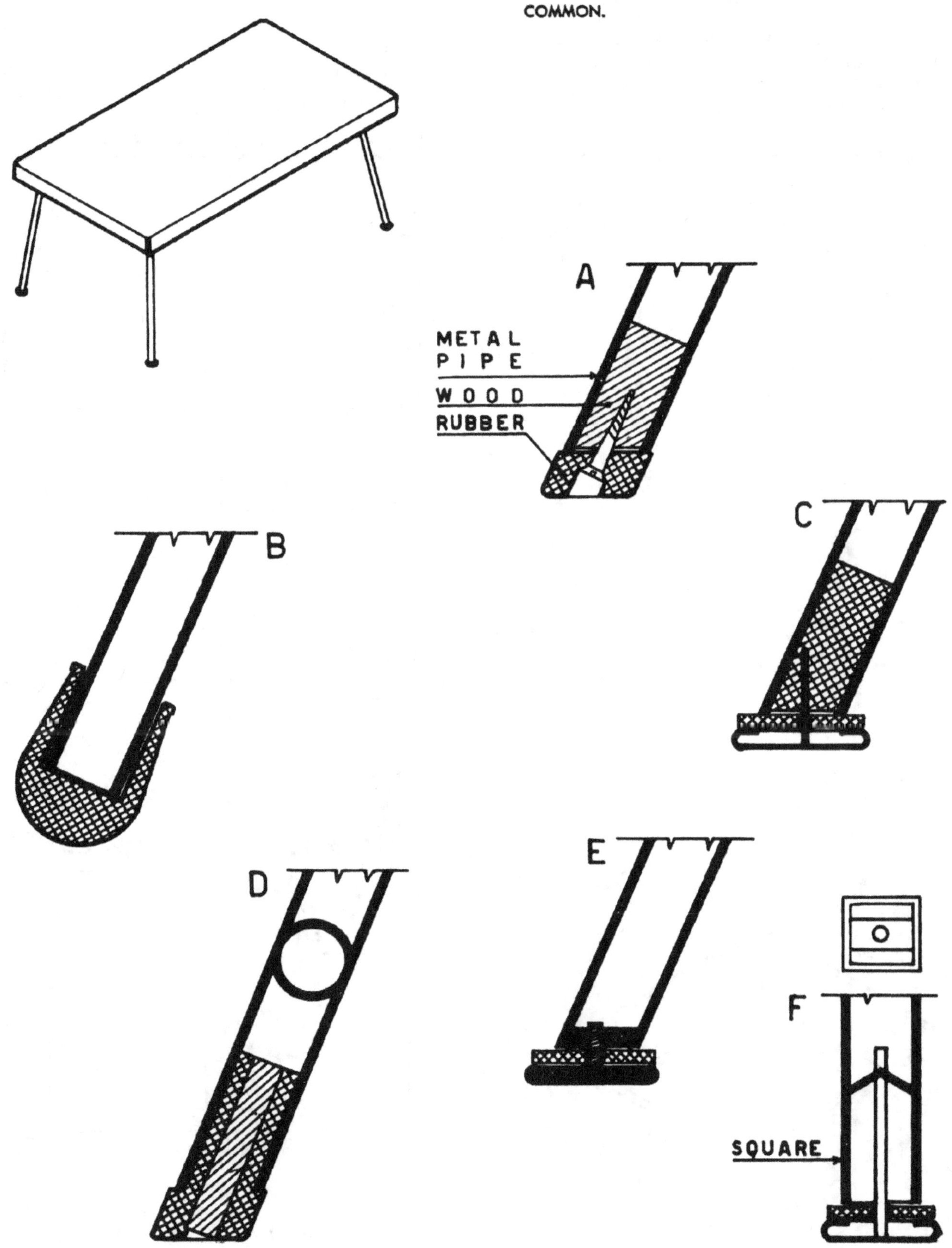

RUBBER CAPS AND GLIDES WHICH MAY BE USED WITH
METAL LEGS. ALL METHODS SHOWN ARE FAIRLY
COMMON.
A
METAL
PIPE
WOOD
RUBBER
B
C
D
E
F
SQUARE

DRAWERS

A DRAWER IS ONE OF THE MOST USEFUL AND IM-PORTANT PARTS OF FURNITURE CONSTRUCTION. THE SMOOTH OPERATION OF THE DRAWER DEPENDS UPON THE PERFECT ASSEMBLY AND DESIGN OF THE FUR-NITURE PIECE.

DRAWERS MAY BE HIDDEN BY DOORS OR THEY MAY BE EXPOSED. MANY SOLUTIONS ARE POSSIBLE UNDER EITHER CONDITION. THE TYPES SHOWN IN THIS SEC-TION GIVE A CLEAR IDEA OF THEIR CONSTRUCTION AND APPLICATION.

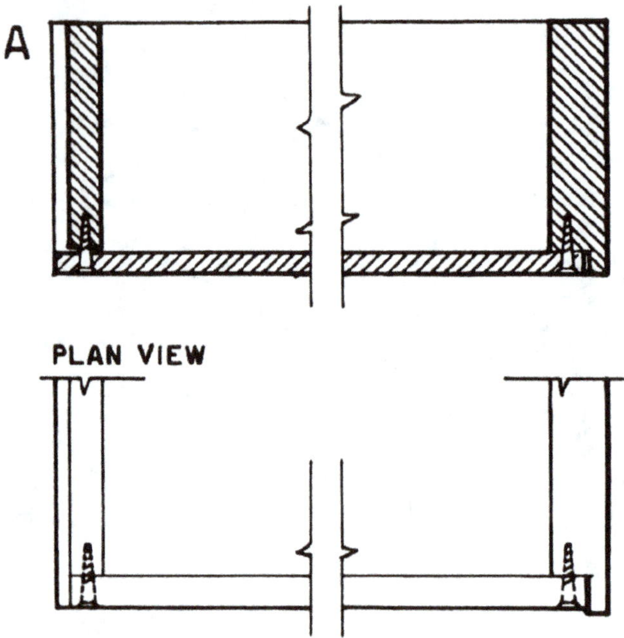

RABBET JOINT USING SCREWS: AN EASY METHOD FOR AMATEUR CRAFTSMEN.

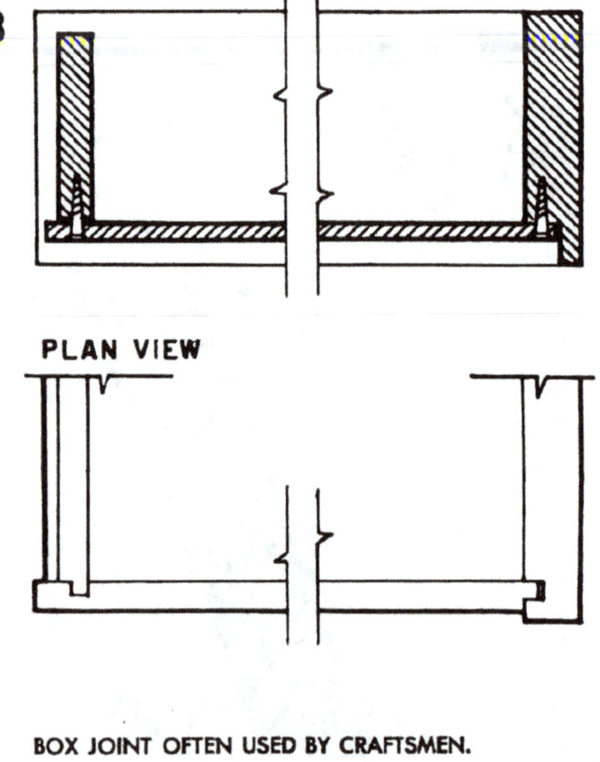

BOX JOINT OFTEN USED BY CRAFTSMEN.

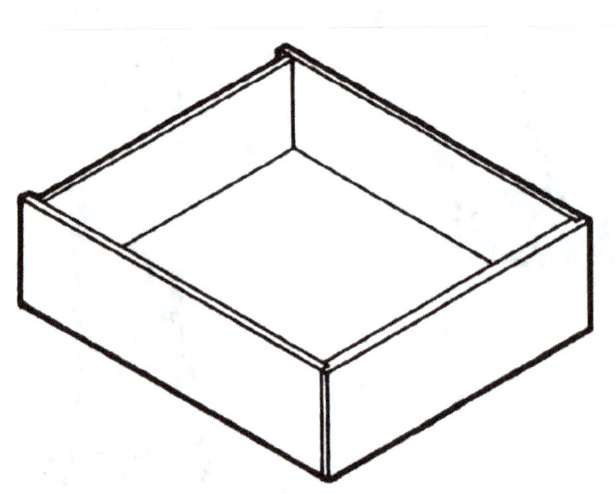

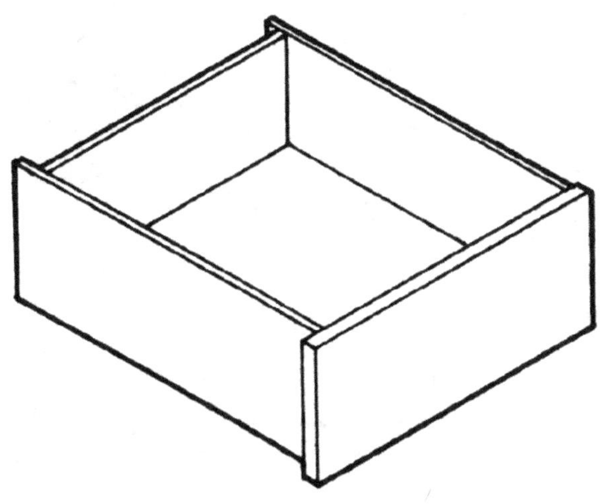

DOVETAIL JOINT WHICH MAY BE USED IN ALL TYPES OF WORK.

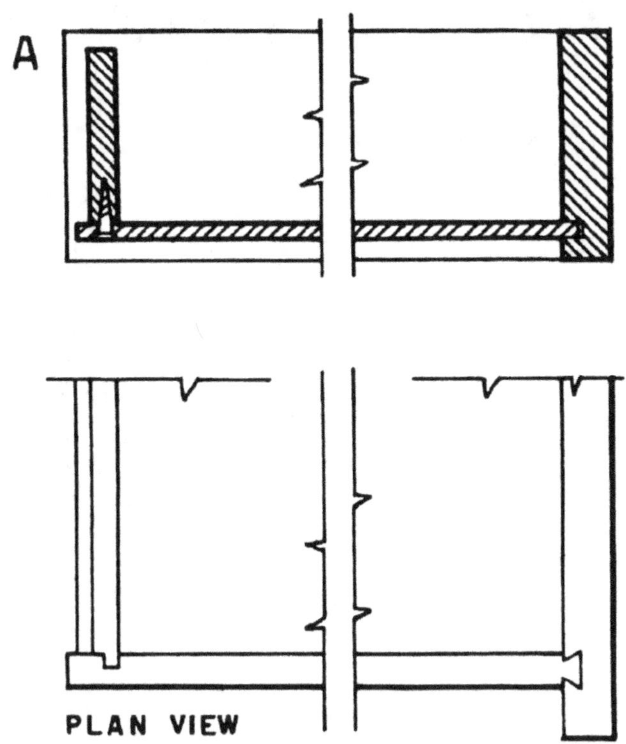

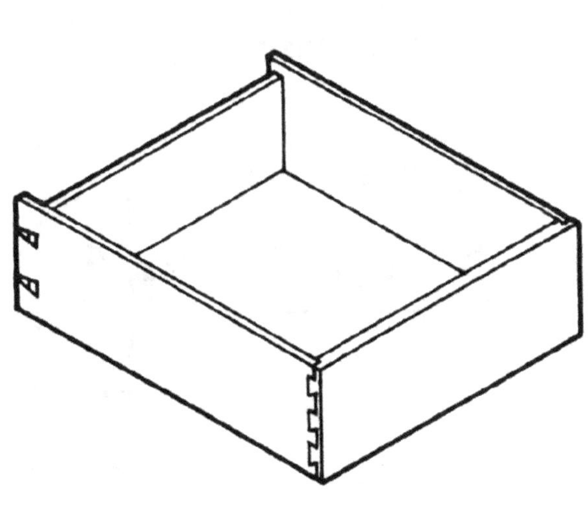

HALF BLIND DOVETAIL OFTEN USED IN FINE WORK.

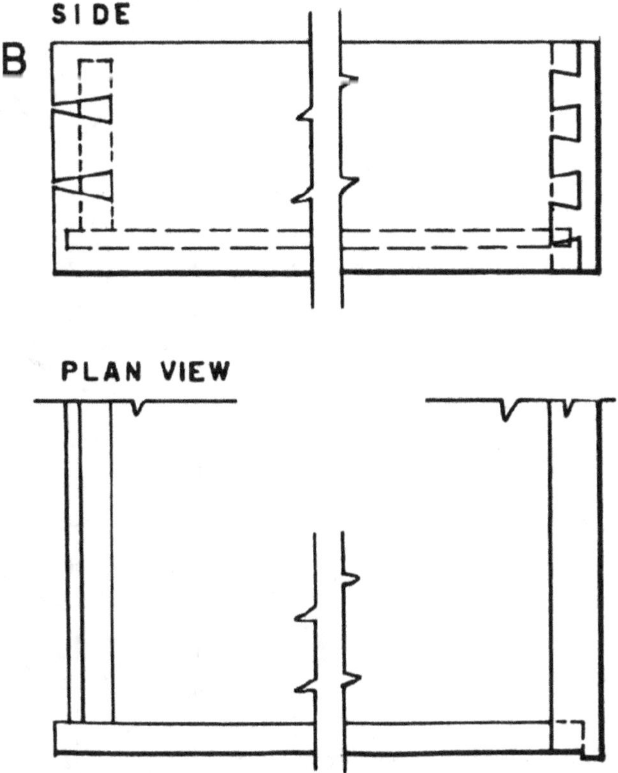

TYPES OF DRAWERS

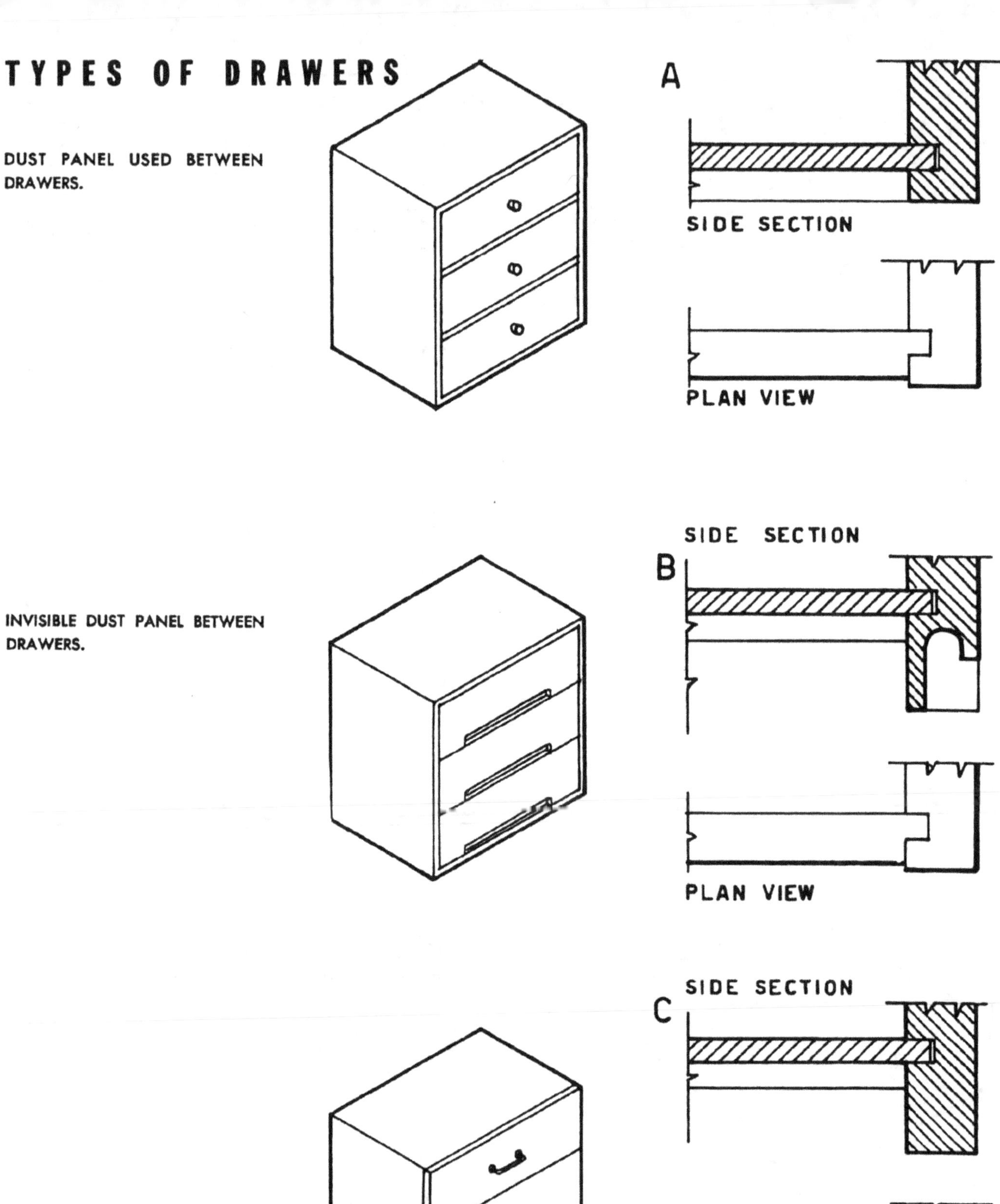

DUST PANEL USED BETWEEN DRAWERS.

INVISIBLE DUST PANEL BETWEEN DRAWERS.

DRAWERS WITH INVISIBLE EDGE.

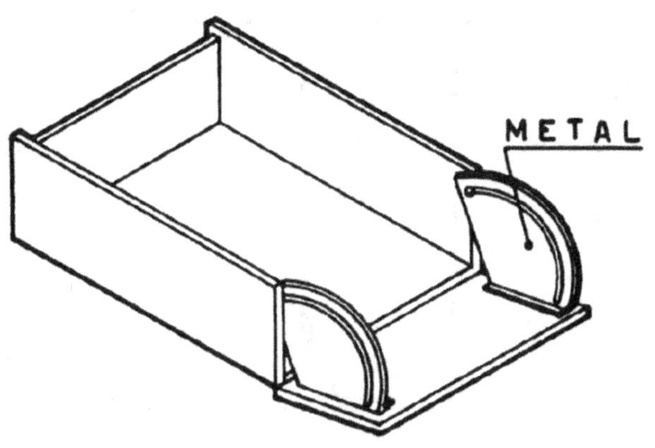

DRAWER WITH DROP FRONT. THIS TYPE IS OFTEN USED IN OFFICE FURNITURE.

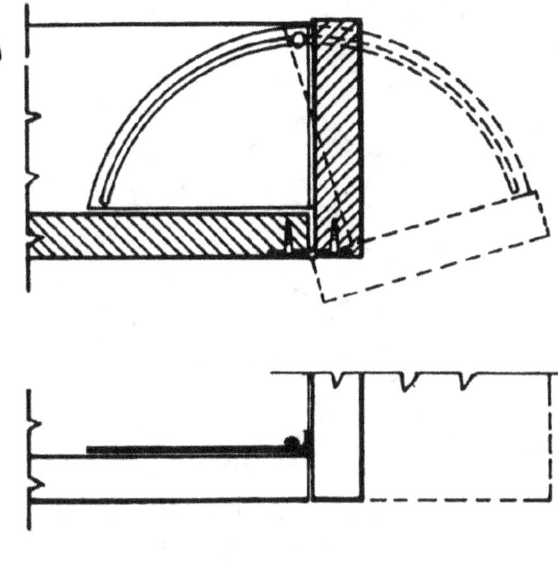

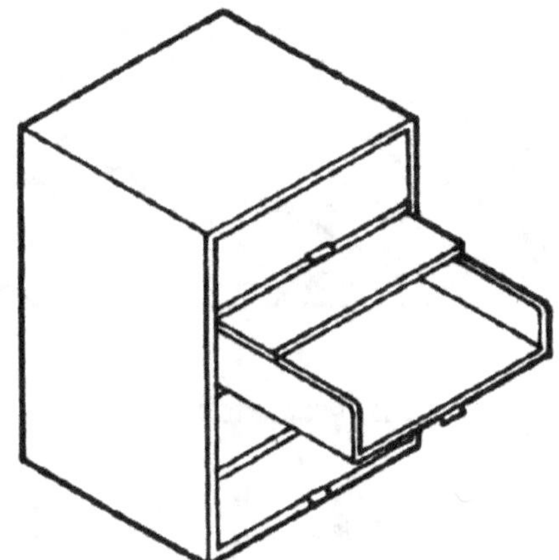

DISAPPEARING DRAWER FRONT. NOTE THE APPLICATION OF THE PIVOT HINGE.

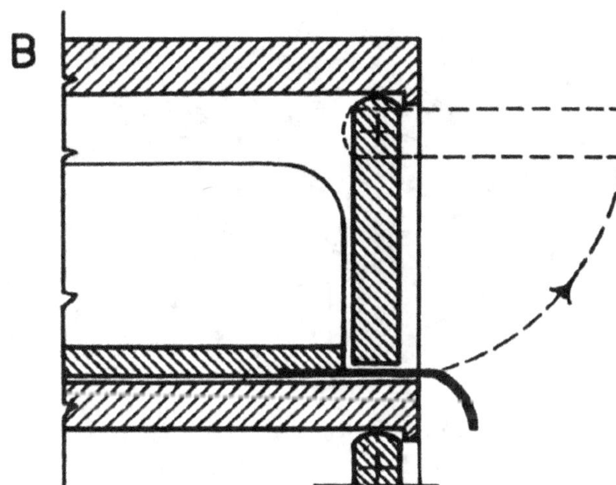

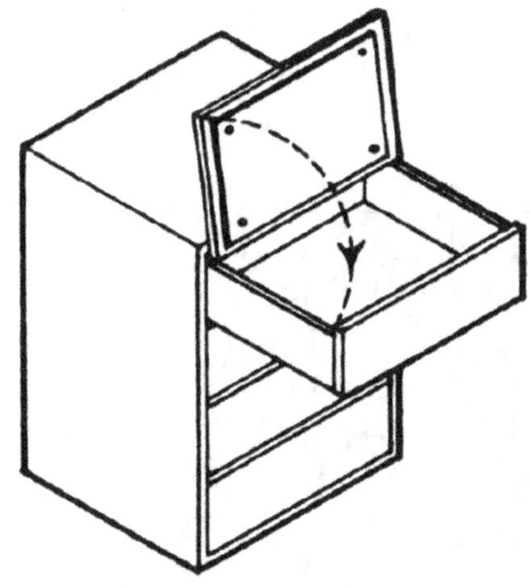

DROP TOP MIRROR USED INSIDE A CHEST DRAWER.

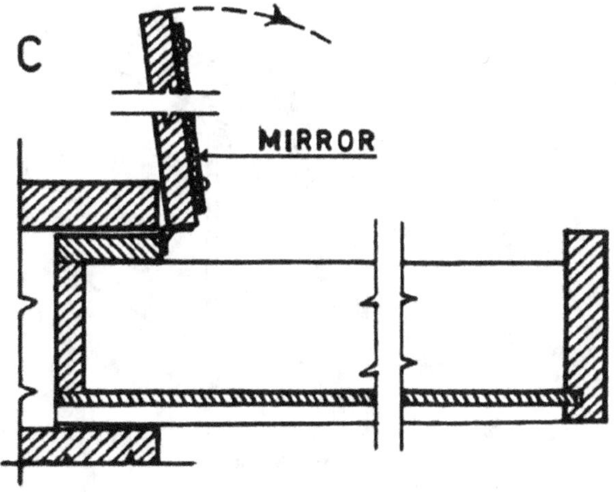

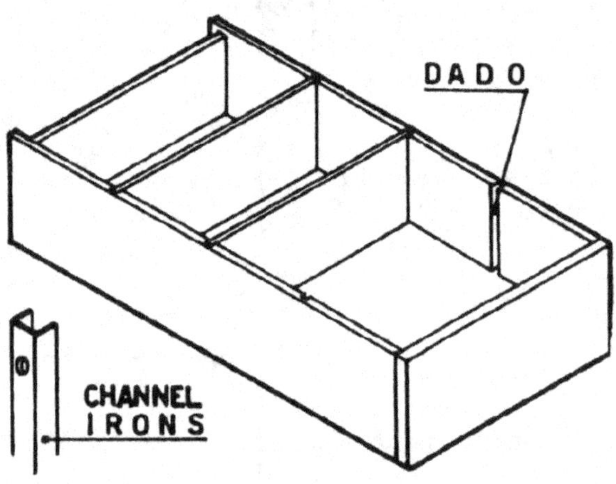

DRAWER WITH REMOVABLE DIVISION STRIPS. THIS METHOD USES A DADO OR A CHANNEL IRON IN THE SIDE OF THE DRAWER.

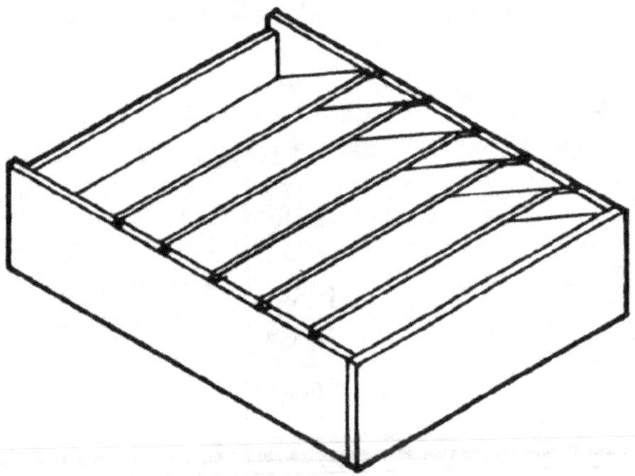

DRAWER WITH OBLIQUE AND REMOVABLE DIVISION STRIPS.

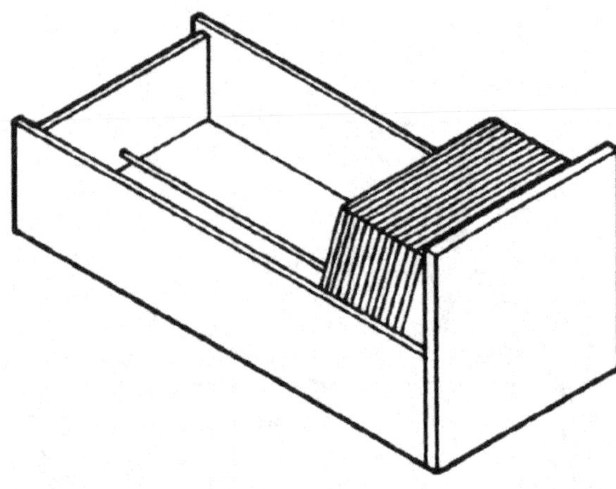

DRAWER FOR FILE INDEX. THESE THREE SYSTEMS ARE USED MAINLY IN OFFICE FURNITURE.

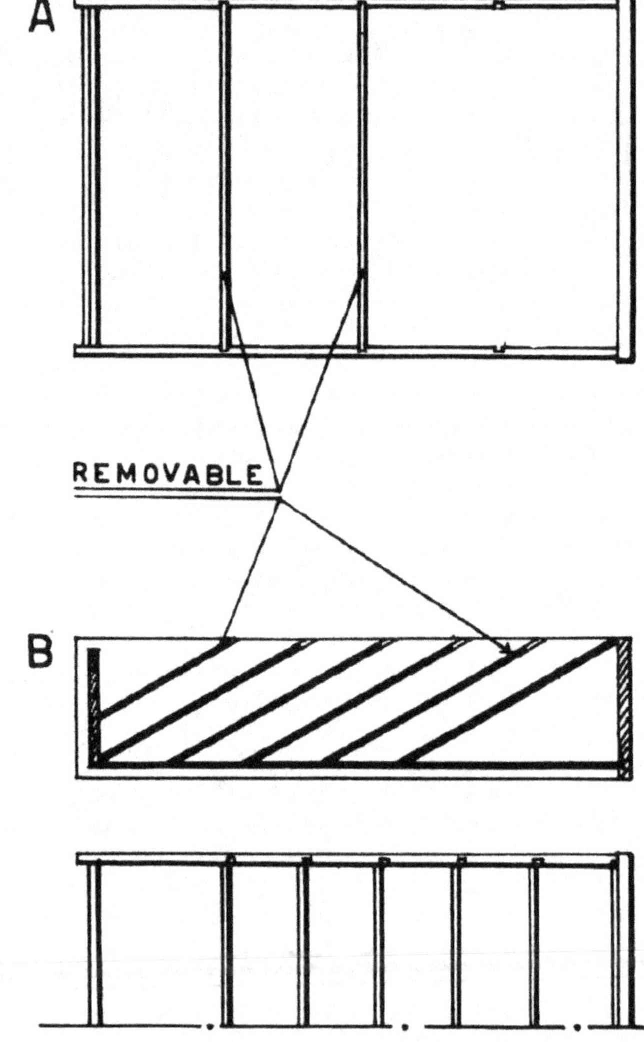

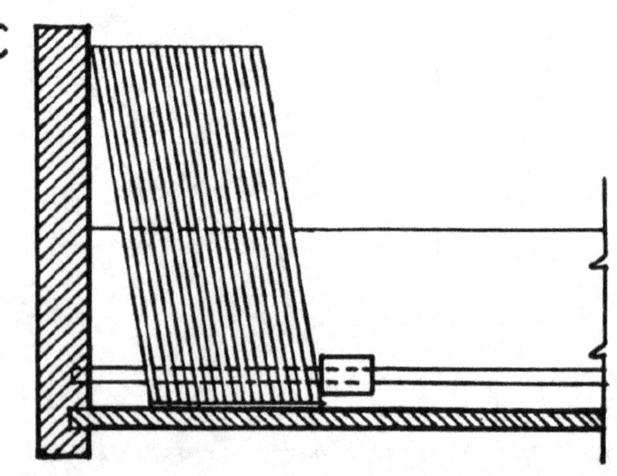

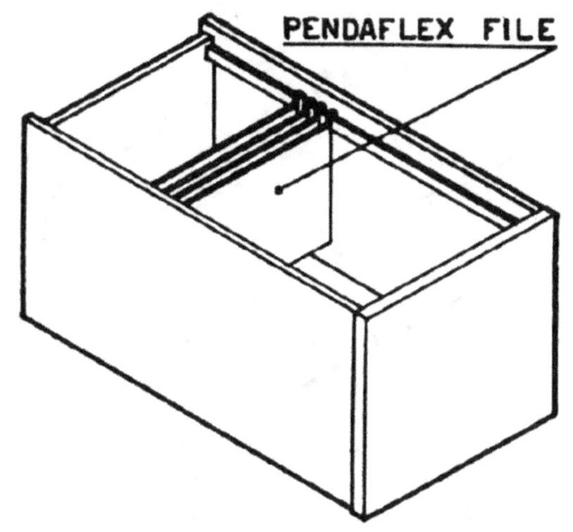

DRAWER FOR CORRESPONDENCE FILE.

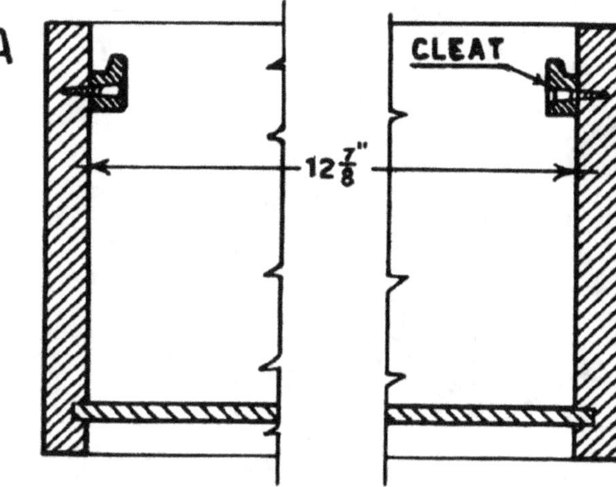

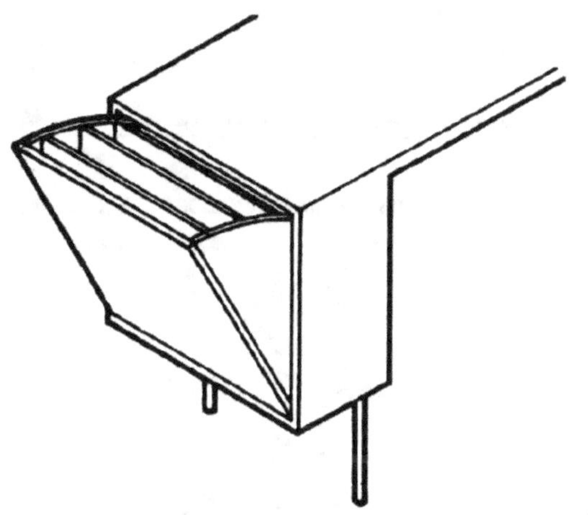

FOLDING DRAWER USED FOR STORAGE OR STA-
TIONERY.

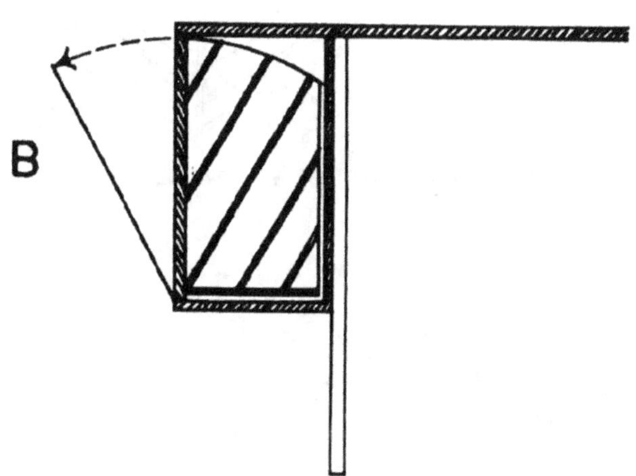

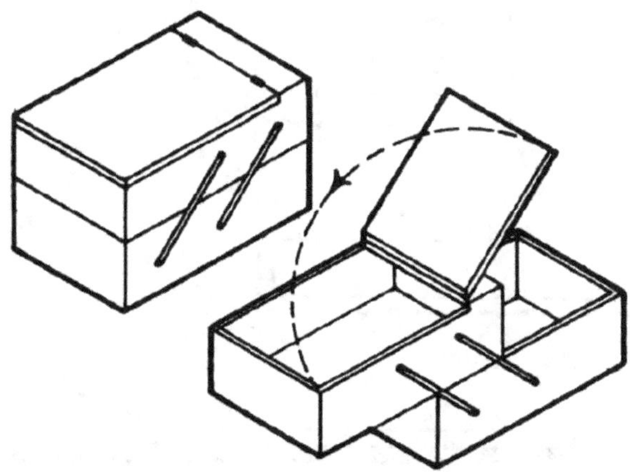

FOLDING DRAWERS USING METAL FLAT STRIPS ON
SIDES.

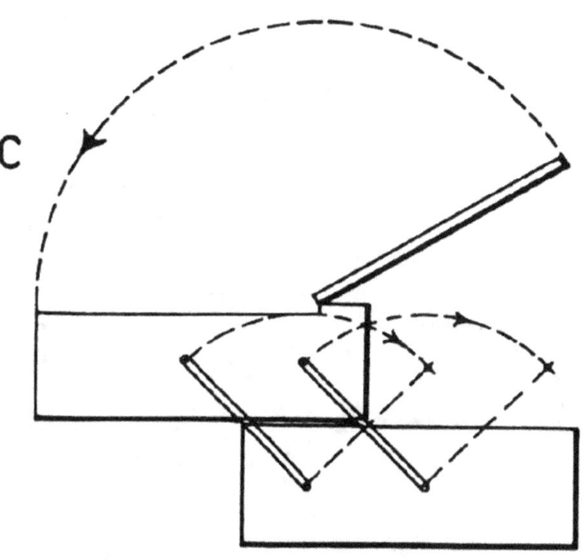

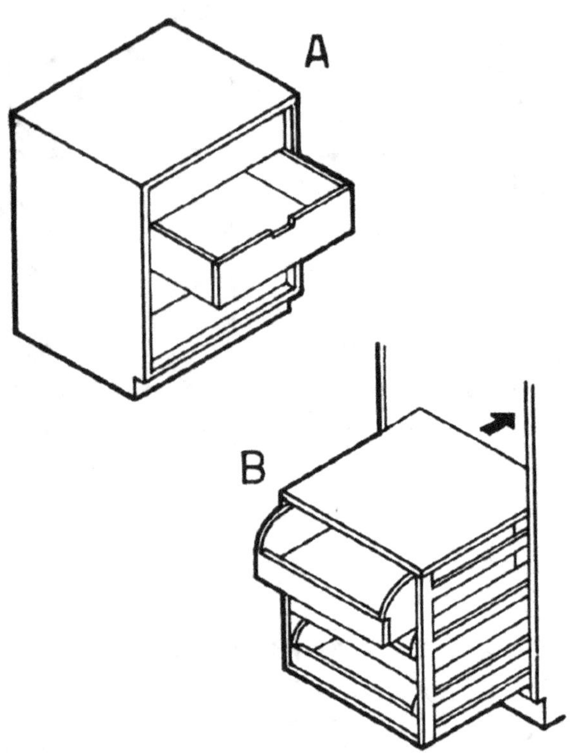

CHEST AND BOX DRAWER FOR WARDROBE.

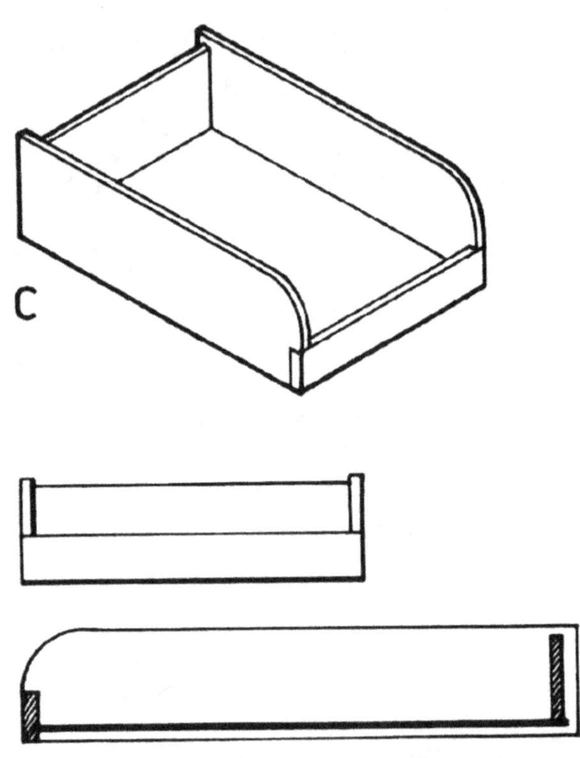

INTERIOR DRAWERS FOR WARDROBE OR CABINET.

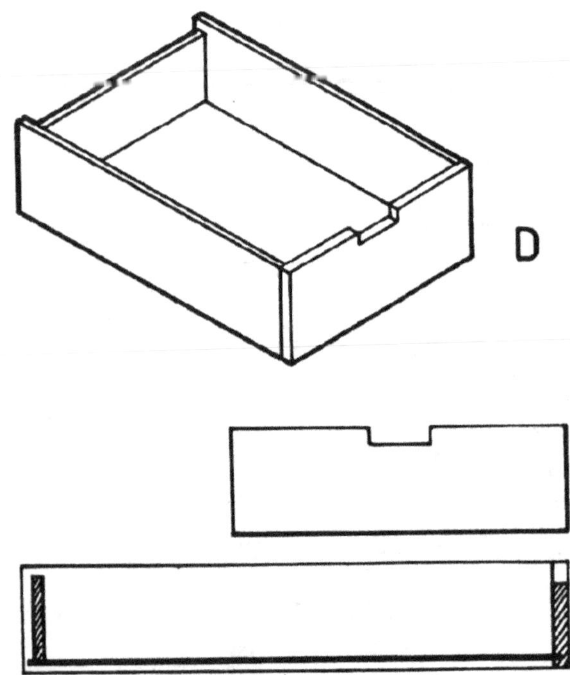

OTHER TYPES OF SIMPLE DRAWERS.

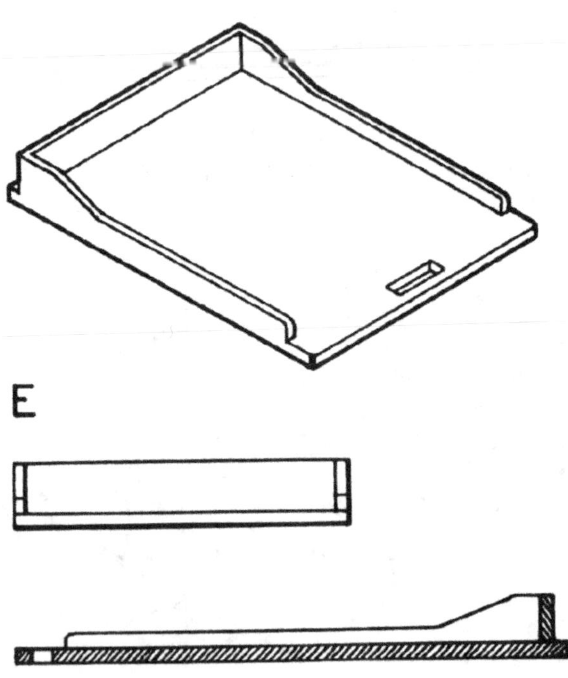

SHIRT DRAWER.

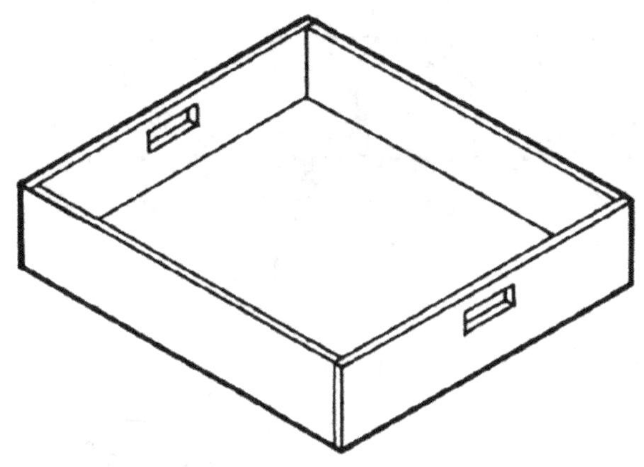
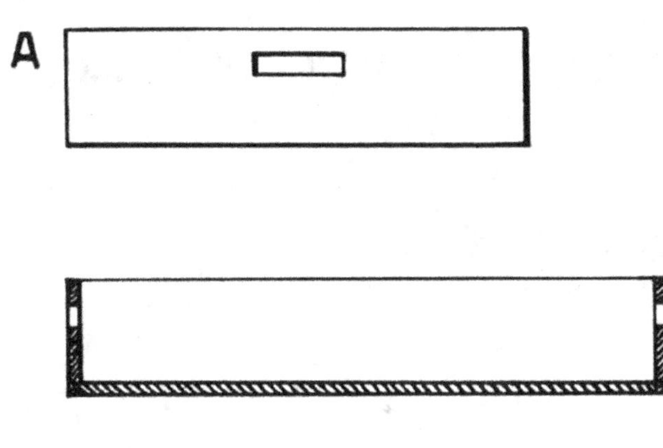

DRAWER WITH PULLS FOR TRAY.

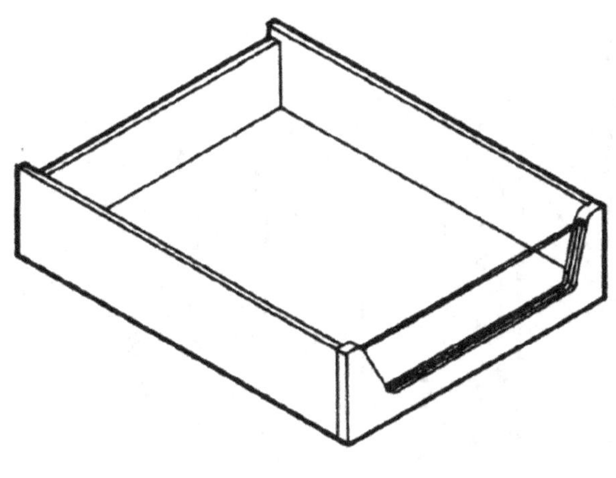
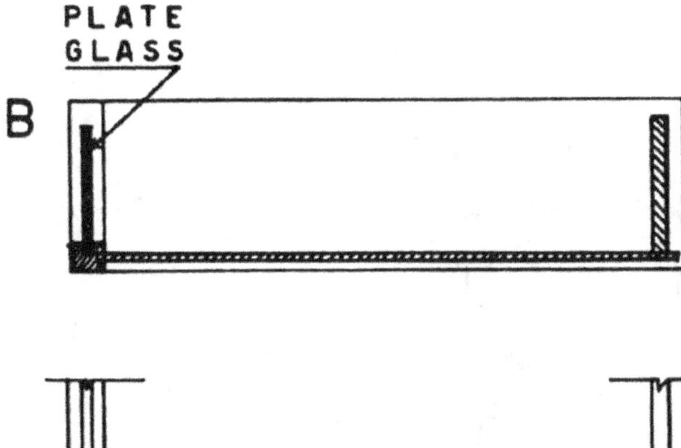

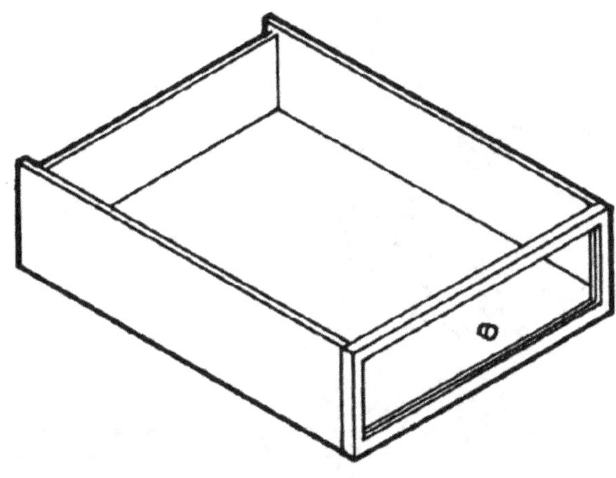
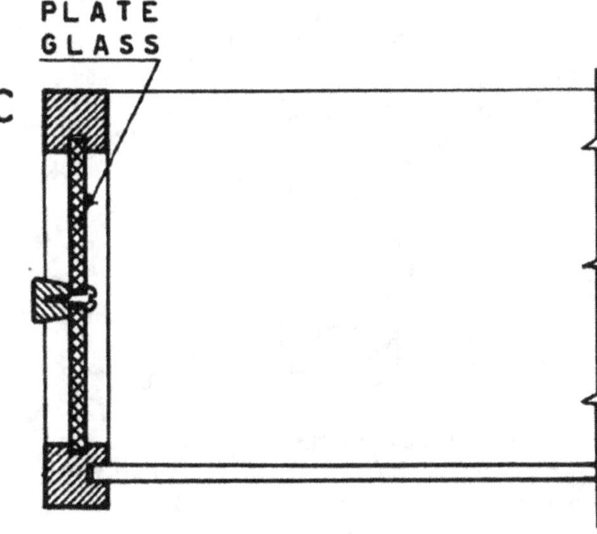

TWO TYPES OF DRAWERS WITH PLATE GLASS FRONT.

SLIDING DRAWER SYSTEMS

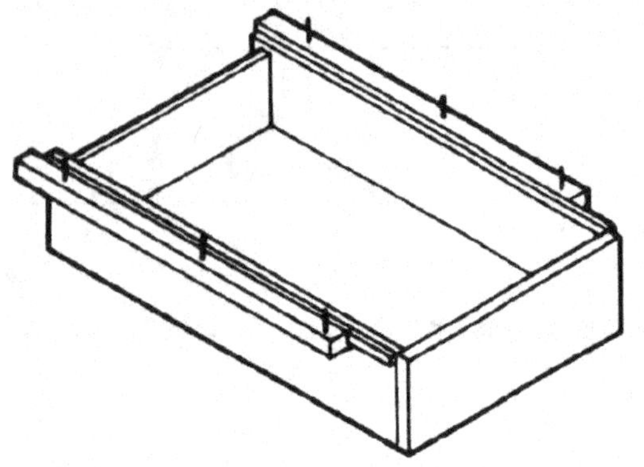

DRAWER WITH SCREWED CLEAT.

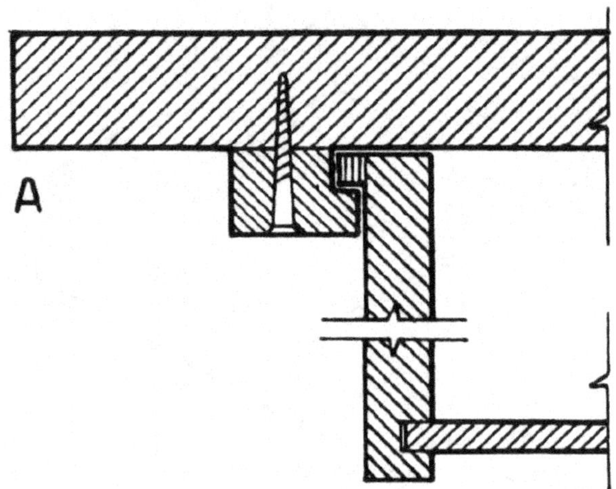

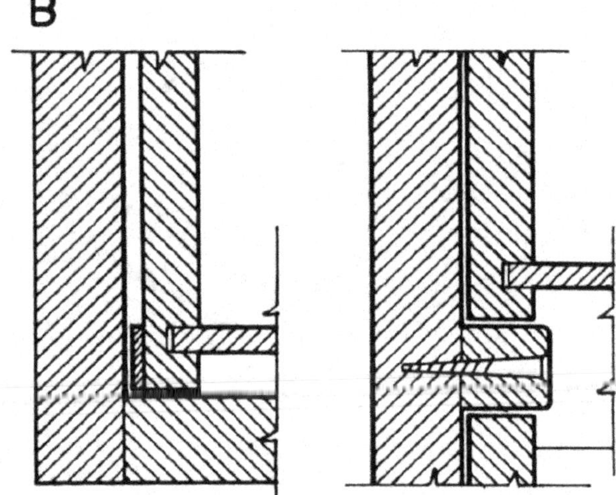

DRAWER WITH BOTTOM RAIL.

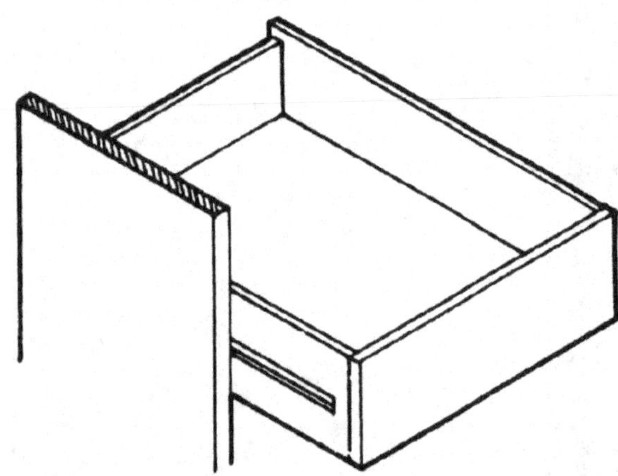

DRAWER WITH RAIL ON THE SIDE. THIS IS AN EASY
AND PRACTICAL SYSTEM WHICH IS USED IN ALL TYPES
OF WORK.

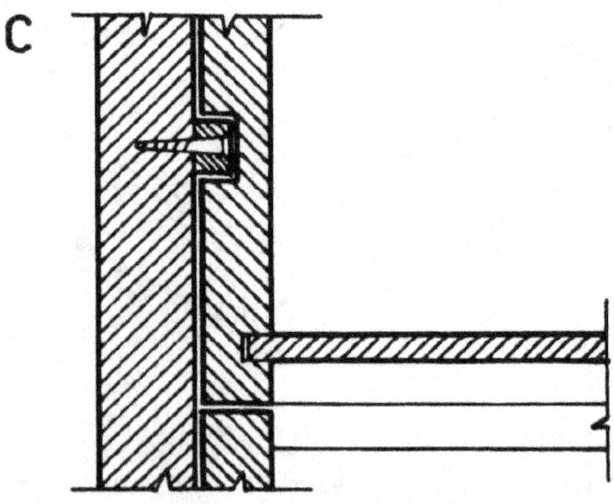

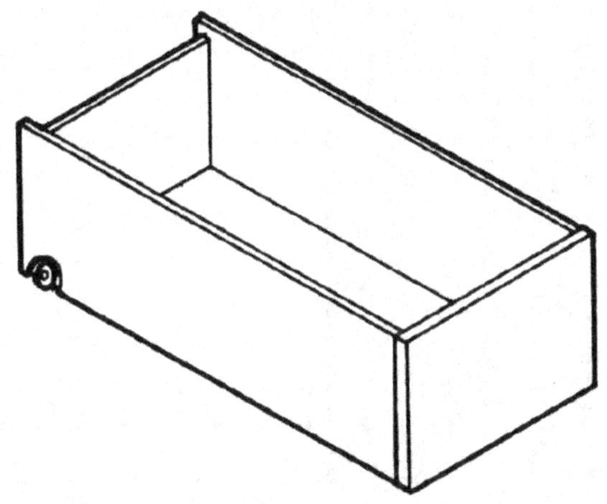

ROLLERS ARE USED WITH HEAVY DRAWERS.

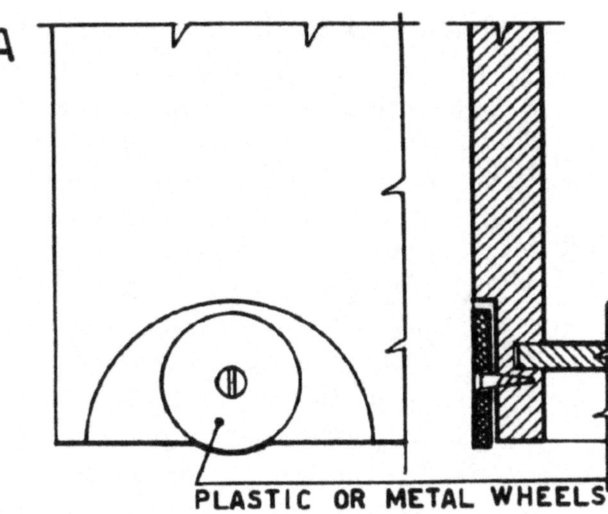

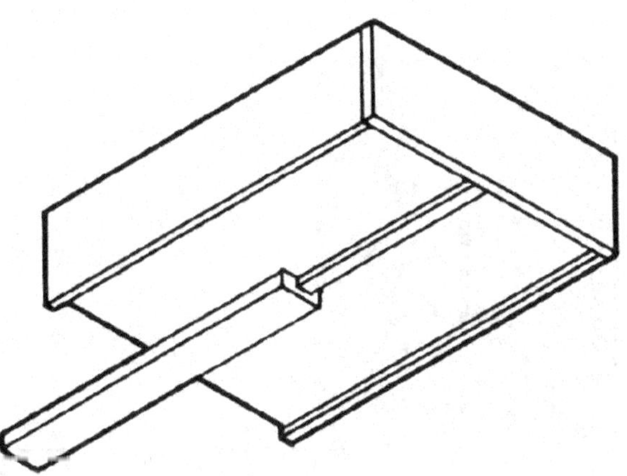

DRAWER WITH CENTER GUIDE. THE GUIDE IS ADVIS-
ABLE AS IT FACILITATES THE MOVEMENT OF THE
DRAWER. IT IS A TYPE USED EXTENSIVELY IN STANDARD
PRODUCTION.

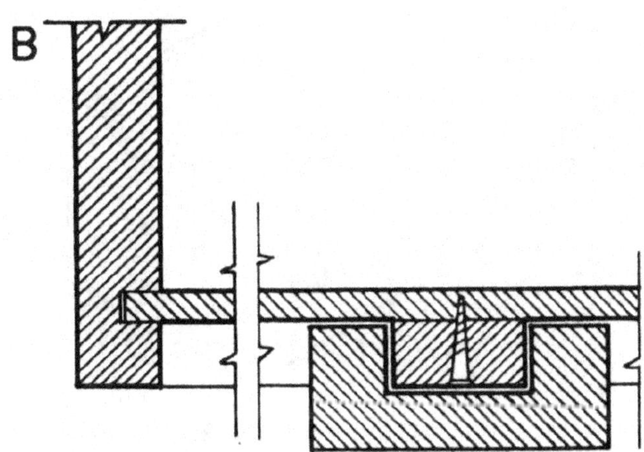

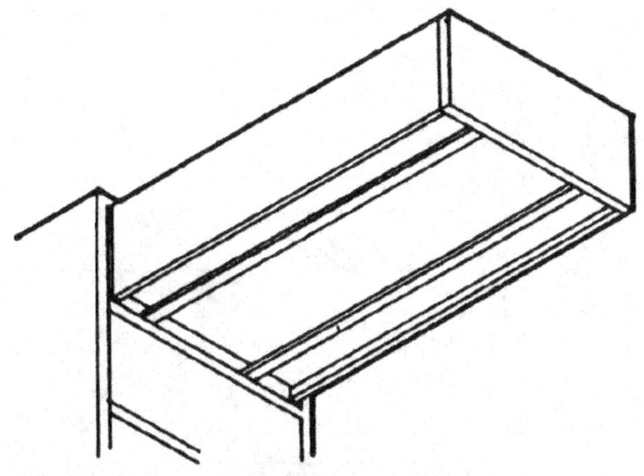

SLIDE DOVETAIL AND SUPPORT. USED WHEN DRAWERS
ARE TAKEN OUT THROUGH THE BACK.

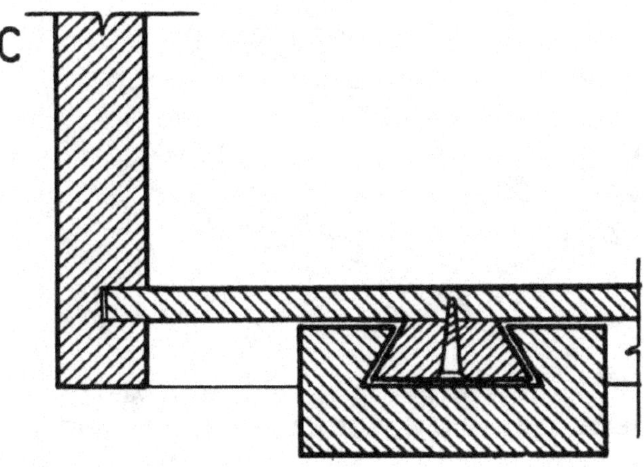

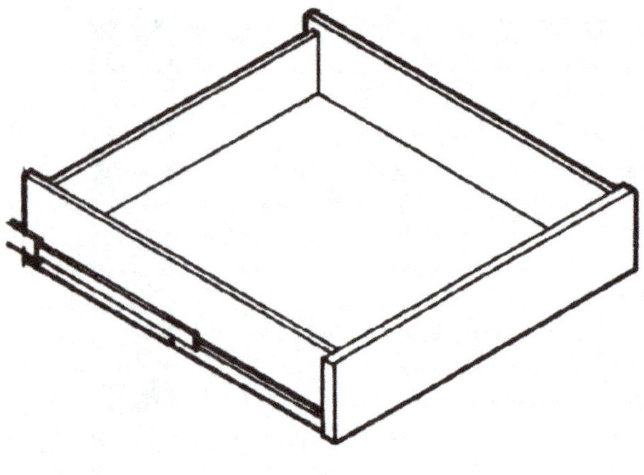

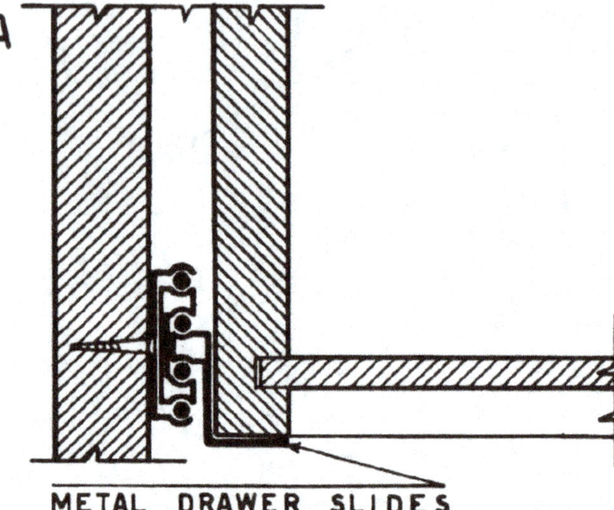

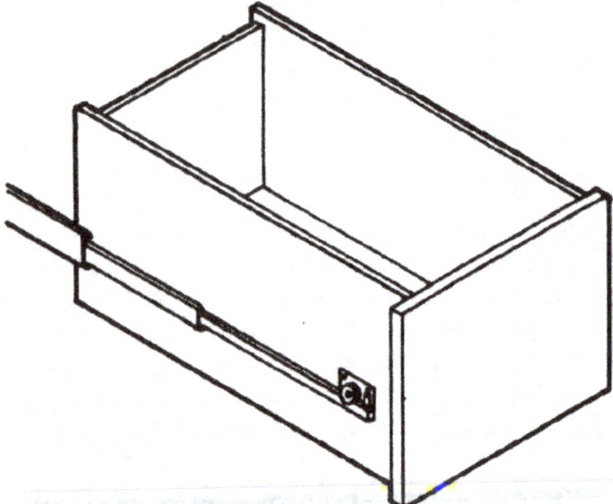

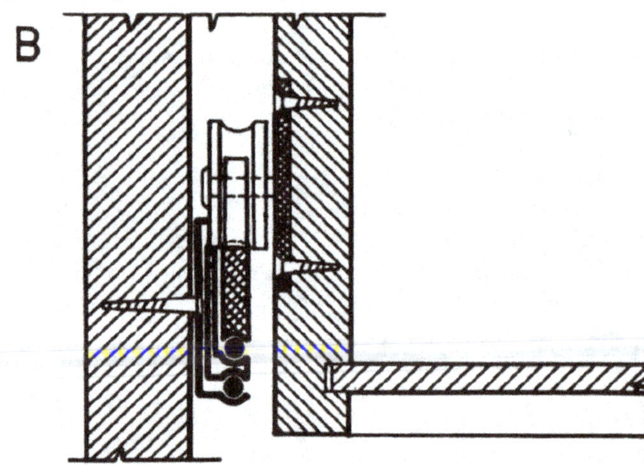

A — DRAWERS HAVING SIDE BALL BEARING. LIGHT TYPE OF CONSTRUCTION WHICH USES NO SCREWS.

B — HEAVY TYPE OF DRAWER WITH SPECIAL BALL BEARING GLIDES.

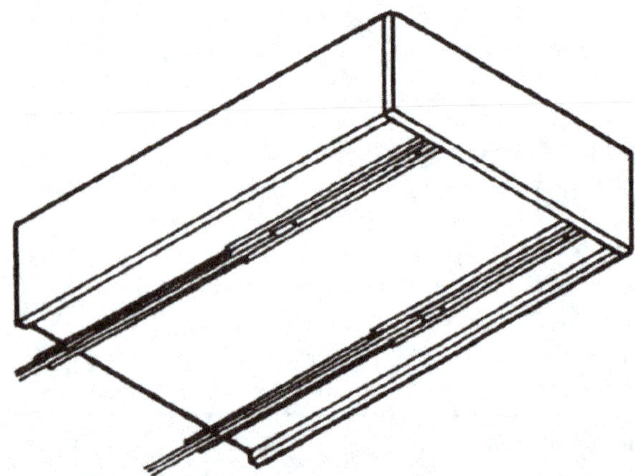

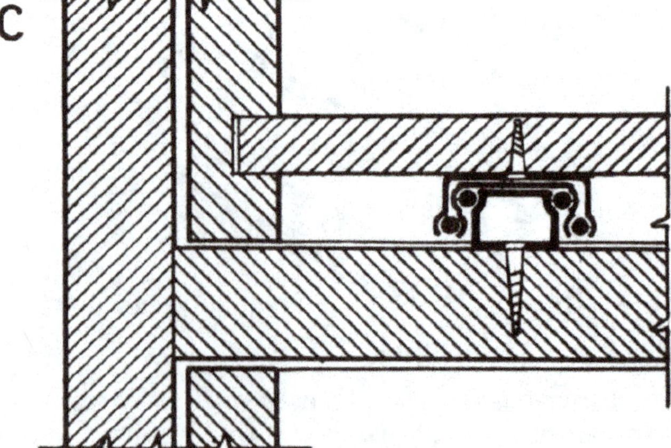

C — BALL BEARING IN BOTTOM OF DRAWER. EACH OF THESE SYSTEMS WILL PRODUCE AN EASILY-GLIDING DRAWER.

DRAWER STOPS

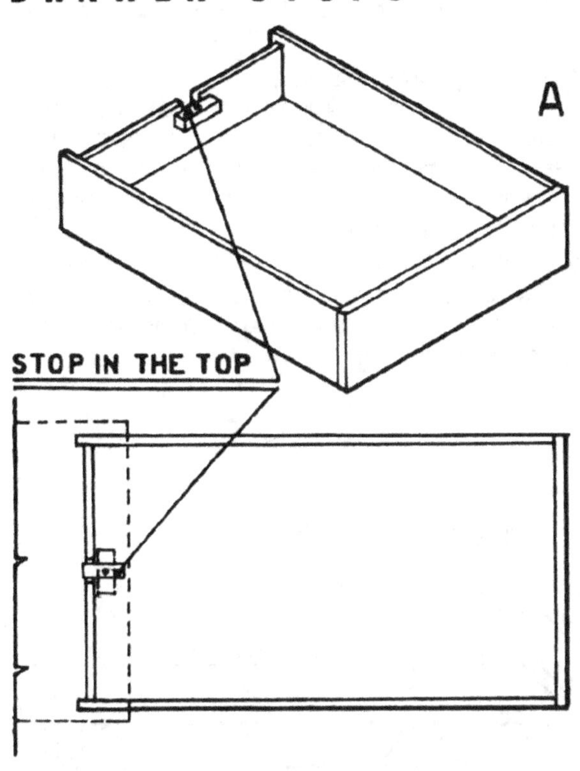

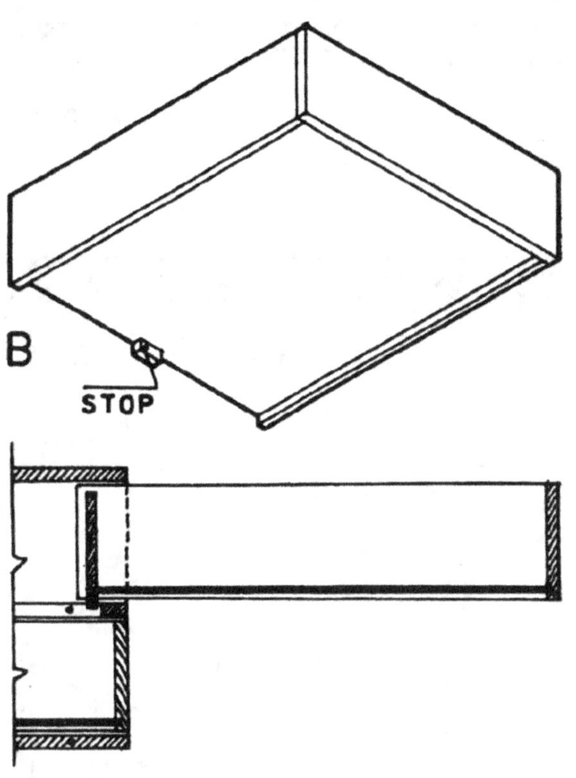

TWO DIFFERENT SOLUTIONS OF STOPS FOR SINGLE DRAWERS.

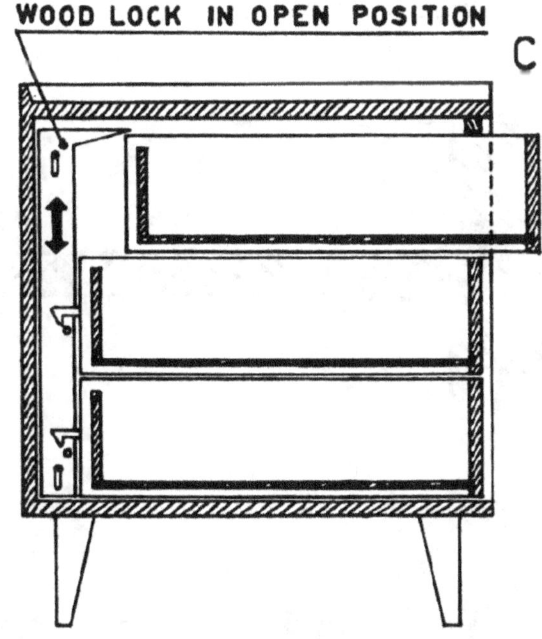

LOCK INSTALLED IN SINGLE PEDESTAL DESK.

LOCK INSTALLED IN DOUBLE PEDESTAL DESK.

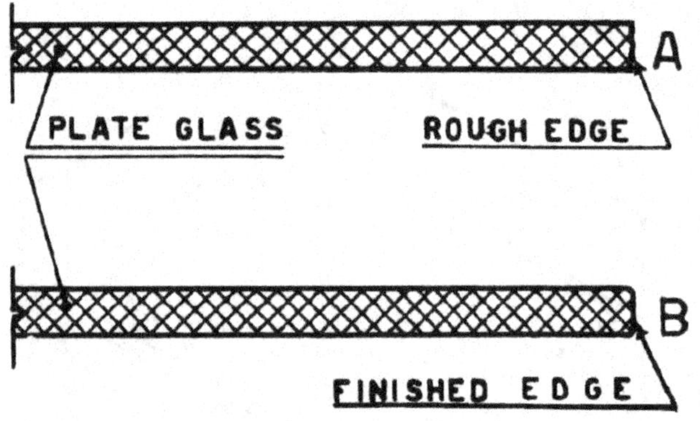

JOINING WOOD AND GLASS

THE APPLICATION OF GLASS, PLATE GLASS OR MIRROR TO THE WOOD IS CONSIDERED ONE OF THE MOST DELICATE TYPES OF WORK IN THE FURNITURE FIELD. THE POSSIBILITY OF BREAKING THE GLASS DURING THE WORKING PROCESS MAKES IT IMPERATIVE THAT GREAT CARE BE TAKEN.

PLATE GLASS OR A MIRROR MAY BE ATTACHED TO THE WOOD IN A HORIZONTAL, VERTICAL OR OBLIQUE POSITION. IT MAY ALSO BE WELDED TO WOOD WITH GLUE OR CEMENT.

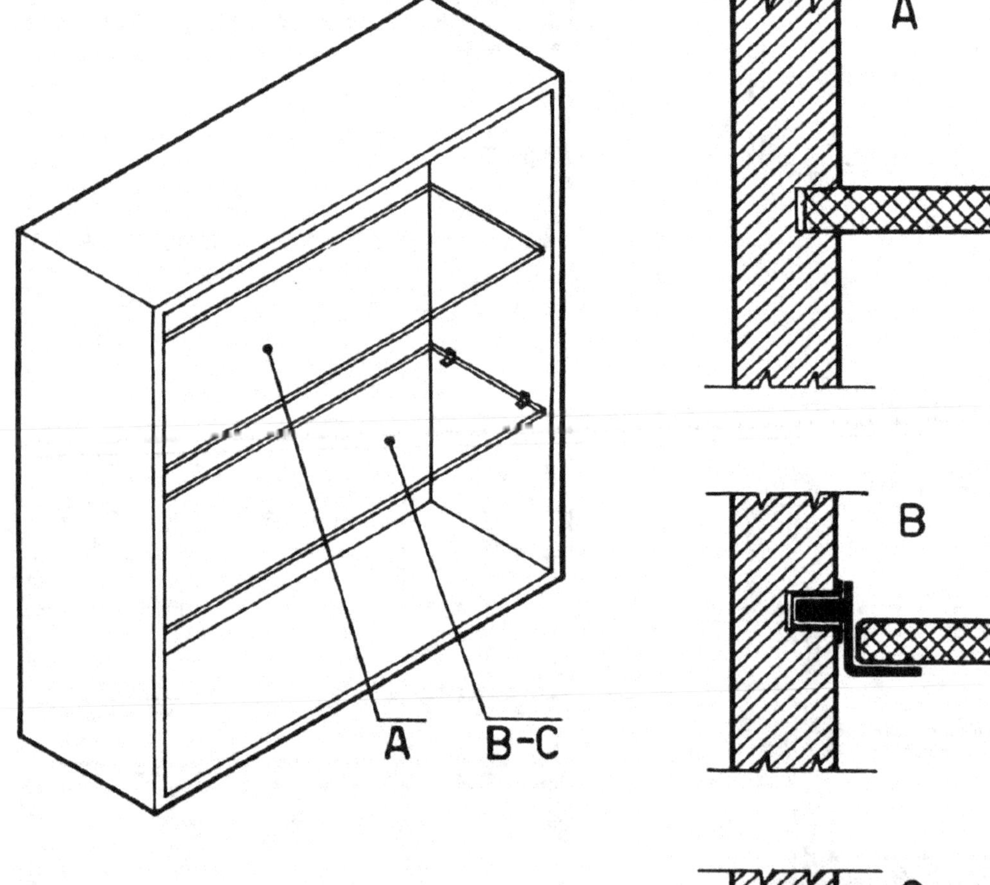

APPLICATION OF PLATE GLASS SHELF "A" SHOWS ROUGH EDGE; "B" AND "C" SHOW METHOD WITH FINISHED EDGE.

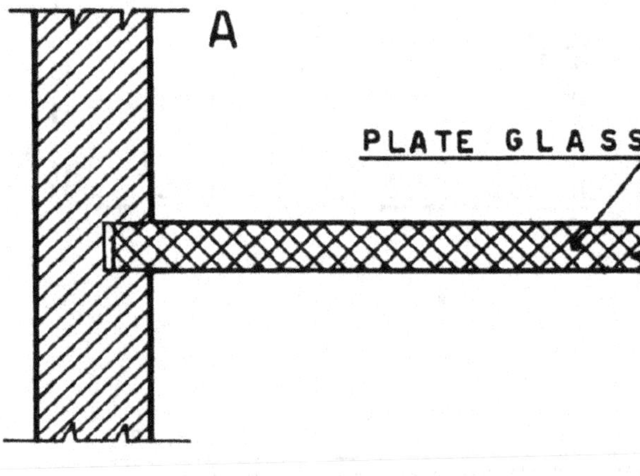

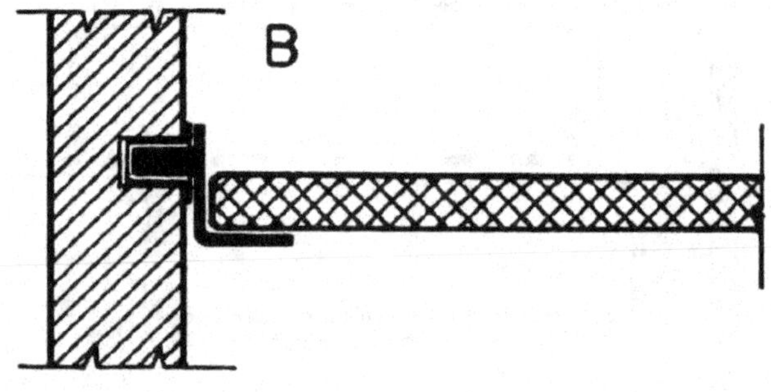

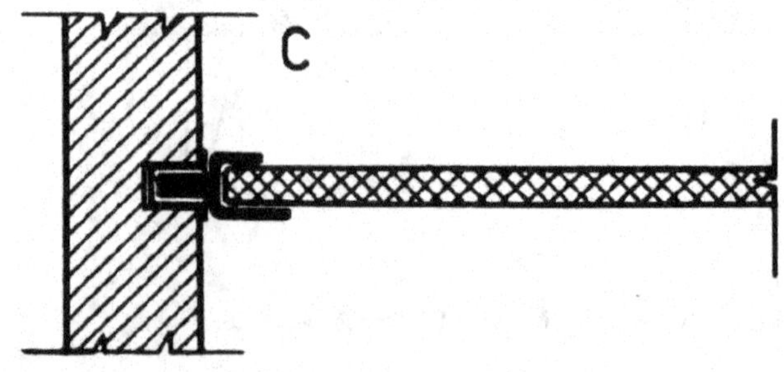

A — APPLICATION OF GLASS IN-
SIDE A PICTURE FRAME.

B — RABBET FRAME SHOWING
PLATE GLASS HELD IN PLACE WITH
PUTTY.
C — PLATE GLASS IN A GROOVE.

D — SLIDING PLATE GLASS IN A
GROOVED TRACK.

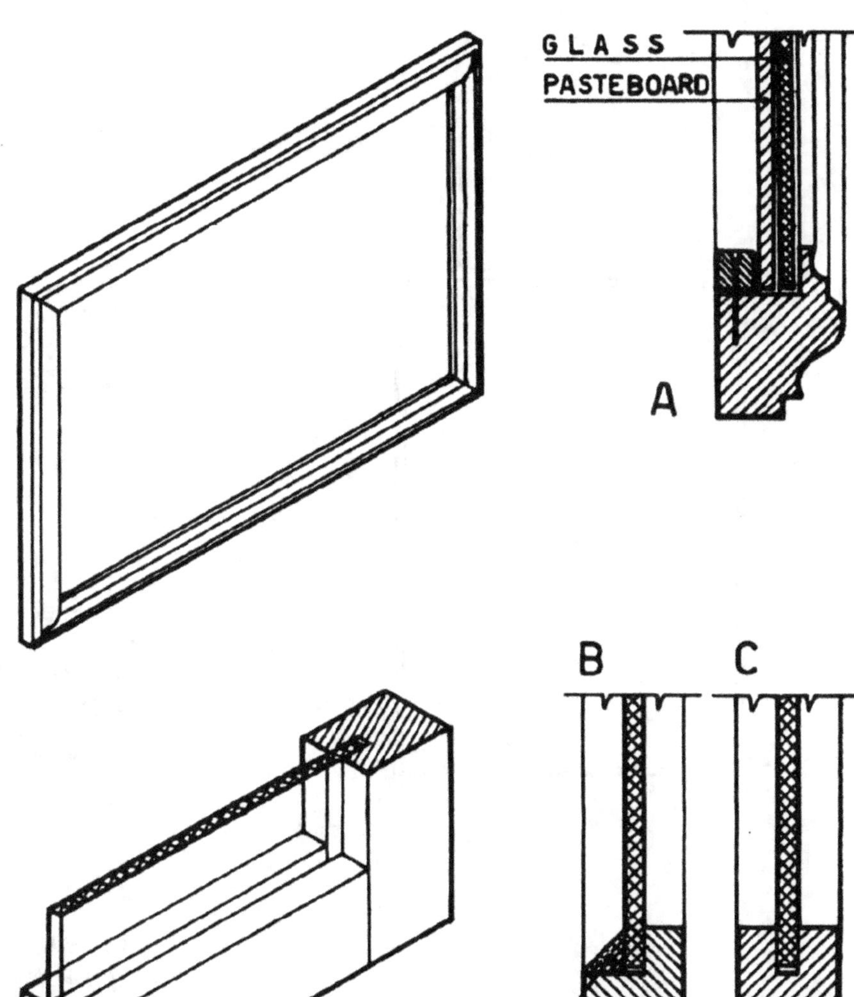
GLASS
PASTEBOARD
A

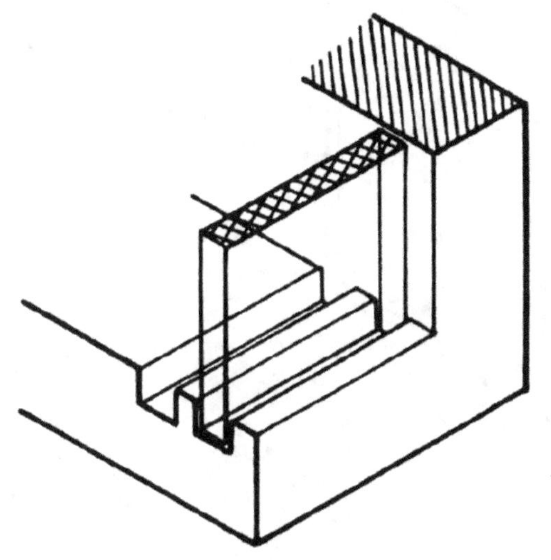
B
C
PUTTY

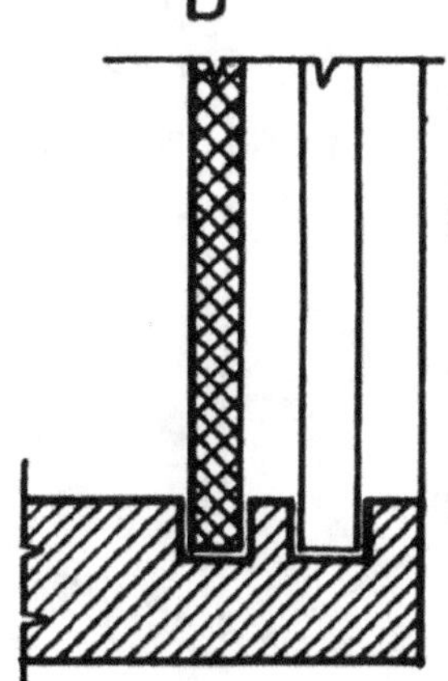
D

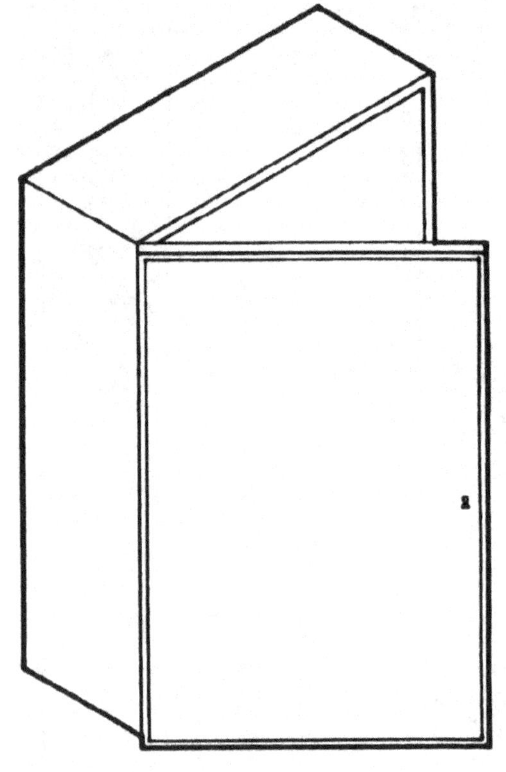

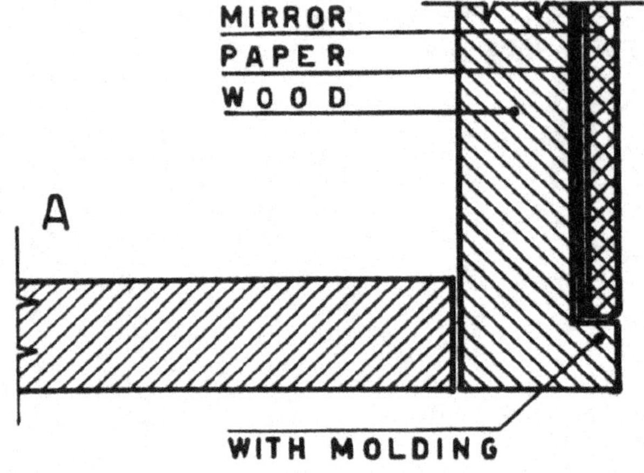

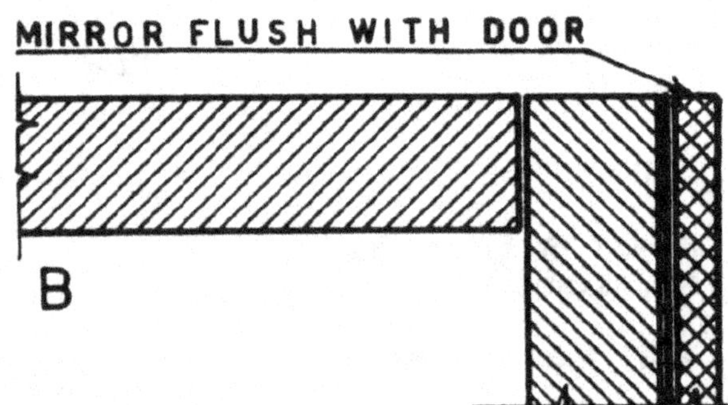

THERE ARE SEVERAL WAYS OF ATTACHING GLASS TO WOOD SURFACES. THE TWO EXAMPLES ABOVE USE PAPER BETWEEN THE MIRROR AND WOOD SURFACE. GLUE IS USED IN BOTH CASES. LARGE GLASS AREAS SHOULD HAVE A MOLDING AROUND THE EDGE. GLASS MAY BE ATTACHED TO WOOD WITH CEMENT WITH-OUT USING A PAPER BACKING.

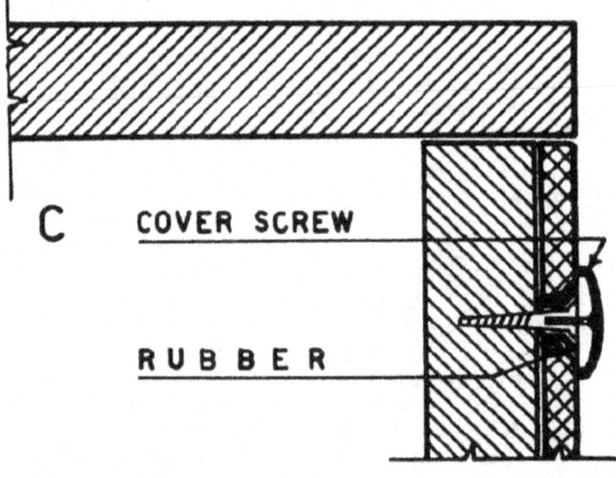

SCREWS ARE USED TO ATTACH THE MIRROR TO THE WOOD IN THIS CASE.

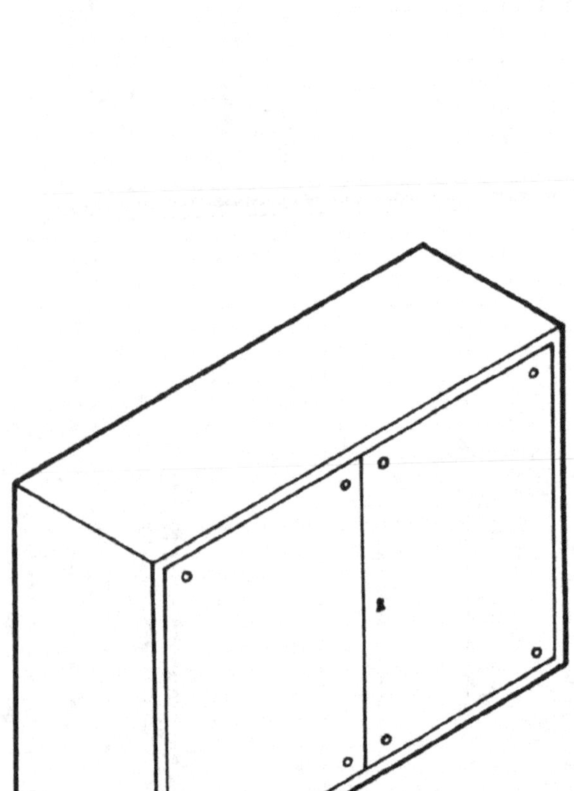

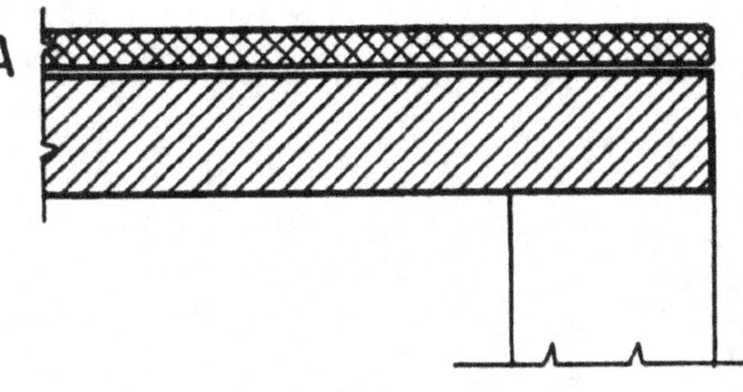

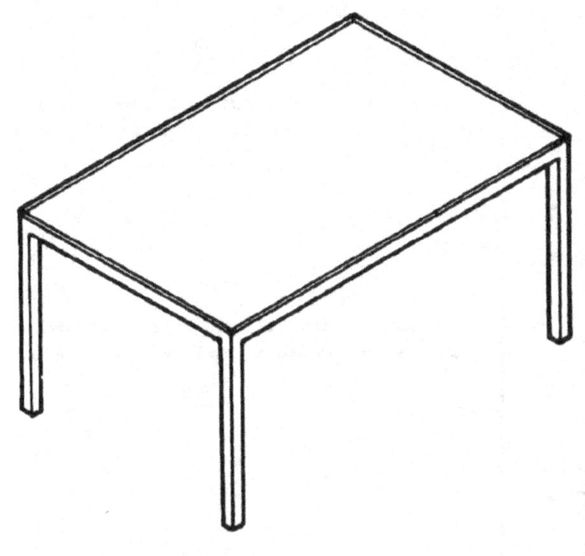

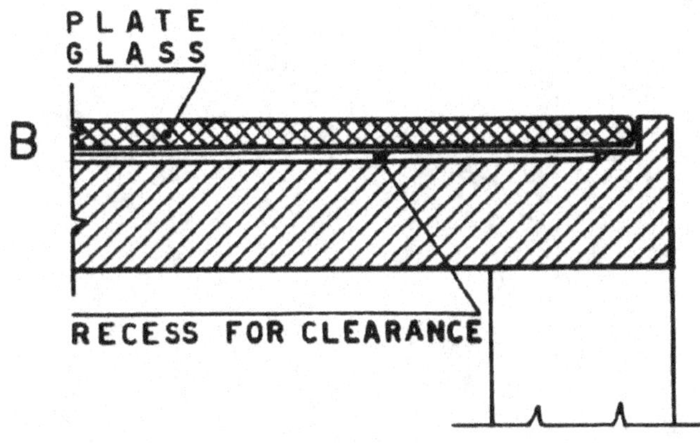

VARIOUS METHODS MAY BE USED TO ATTACH PLATE GLASS TO ANOTHER SURFACE WHEN THE GLASS IS IN A HORIZONTAL POSITION.

A — PLATE GLASS WITHOUT FASTENERS IS ADVISABLE ONLY FOR LARGE TOPS.

B — GLASS WITH MOLDING AND RECESS BENEATH.

C — GLASS OVER SPECIAL LEGS. NOTE RUBBER PROTECTOR.

D — SAME ARRANGEMENT AS ABOVE EXCEPT THAT A SCREW IS ALSO USED.

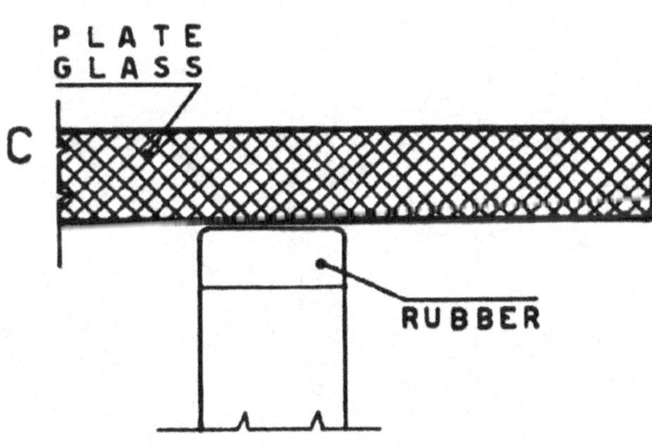

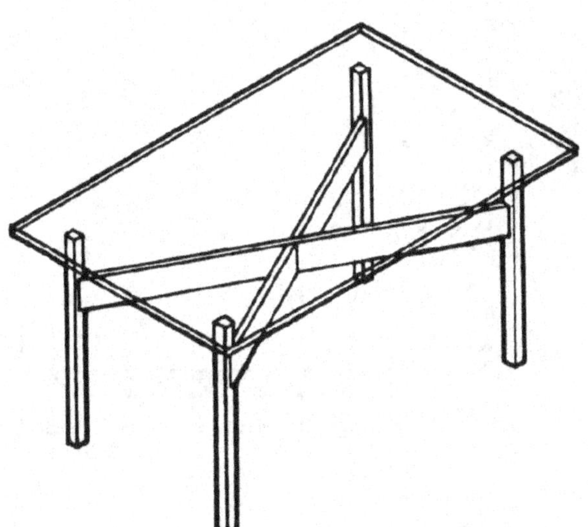

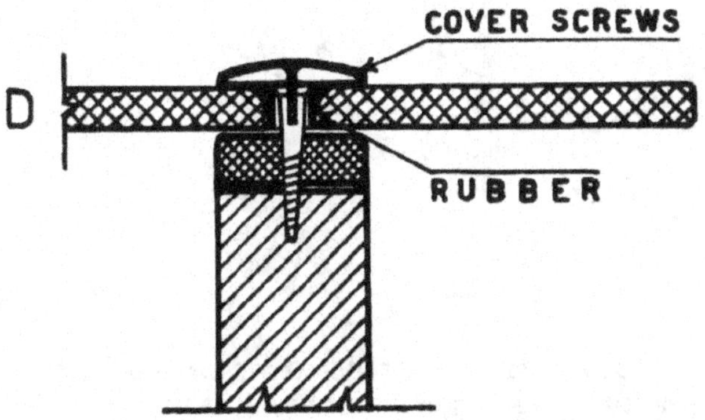

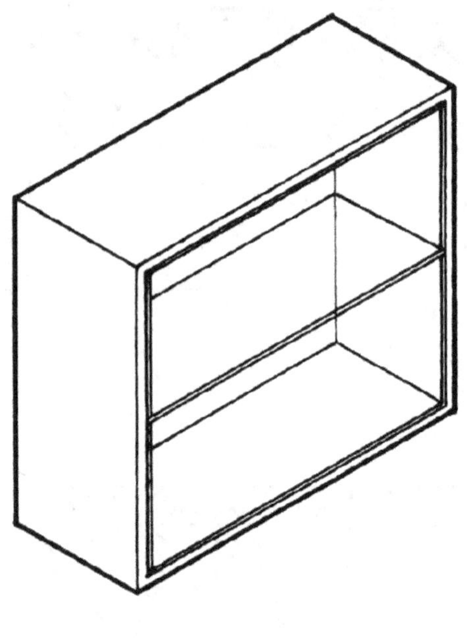

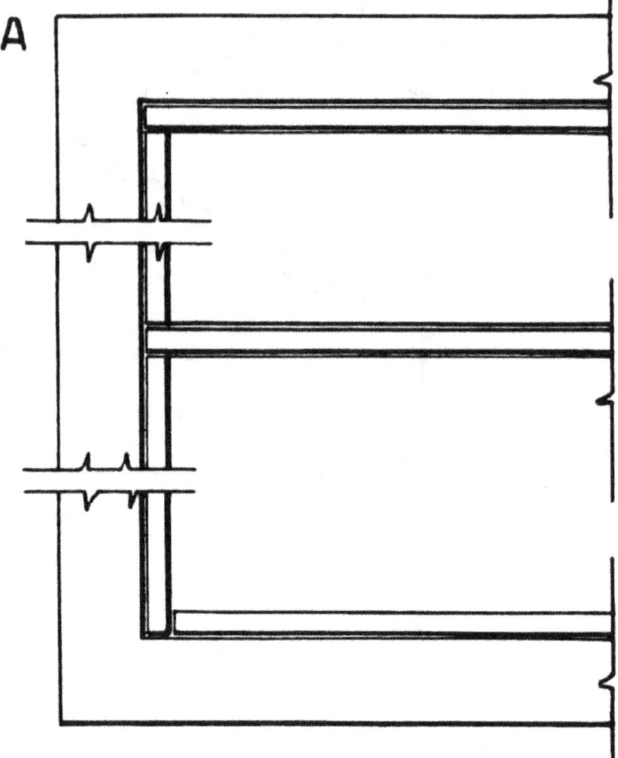

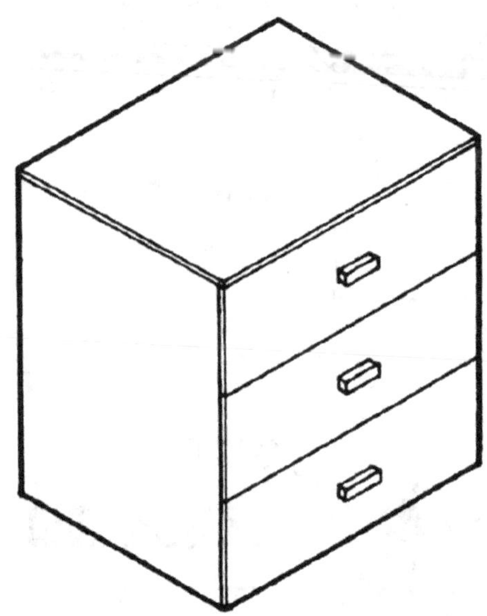

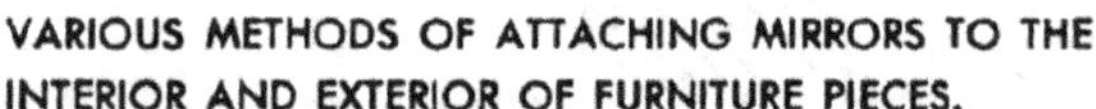

VARIOUS METHODS OF ATTACHING MIRRORS TO THE
INTERIOR AND EXTERIOR OF FURNITURE PIECES.

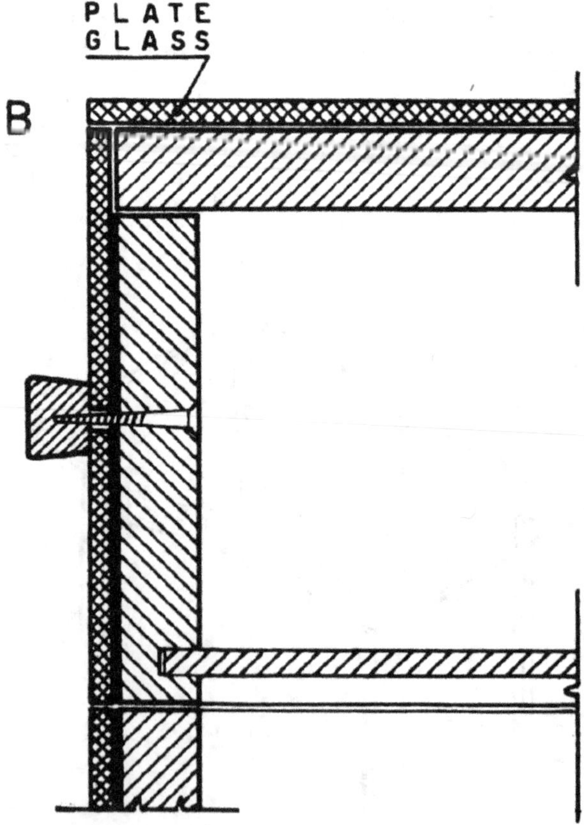

JOINING METAL AND WOOD

IN THE CONSTRUCTION OF FURNITURE PIECES IT IS OFTEN NECESSARY TO JOIN WOOD AND METAL PARTS. WHILE IT IS CUSTOMARY TO JOIN THESE MATERIALS WITH BOLTS OR SCREWS, SPECIAL ADHESIVES MAY BE USED INSTEAD. BY MEANS OF GLUE, METAL SHEETS CAN BE WELDED TO CELLULAR CORES TO FORM LARGE WATERPROOF PANELS.

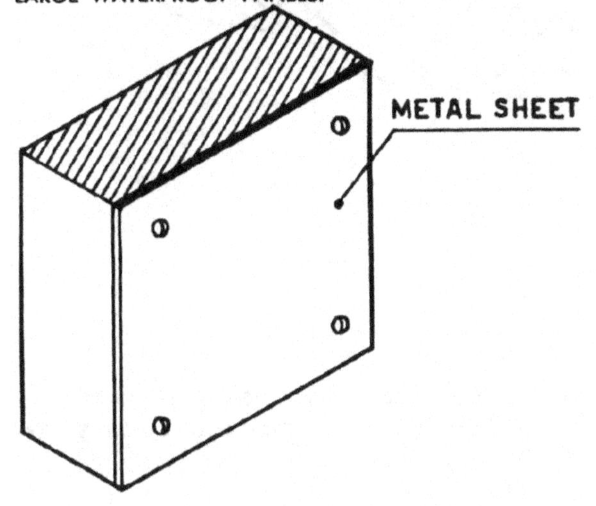

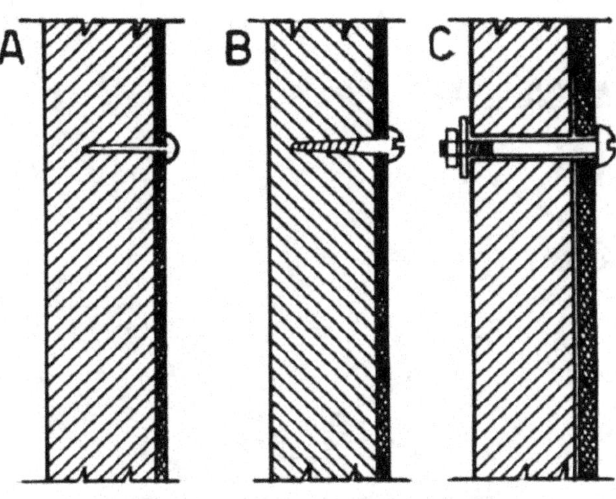

THREE DIFFERENT METHODS OF JOINING METAL SHEETS TO WOOD PANELS.

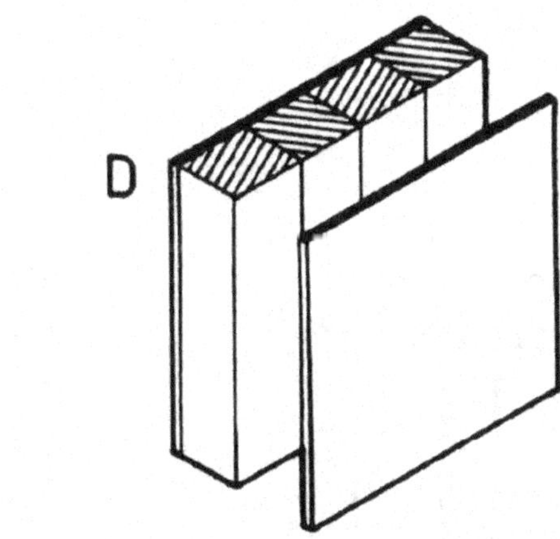

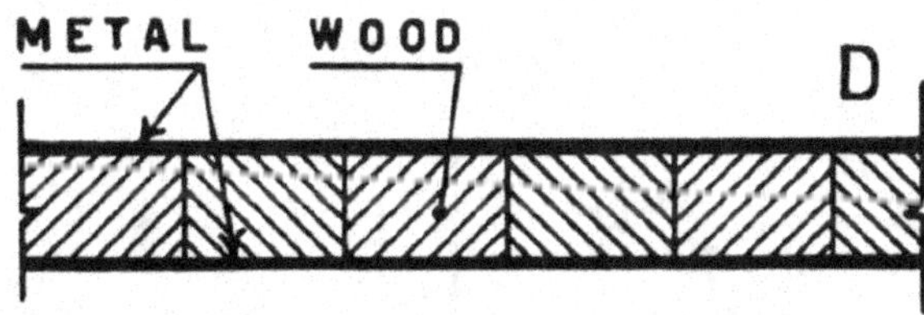

TWO METAL SHEETS HAVE BEEN WELDED TO A WOOD CORE WITH SPECIAL GLUES.

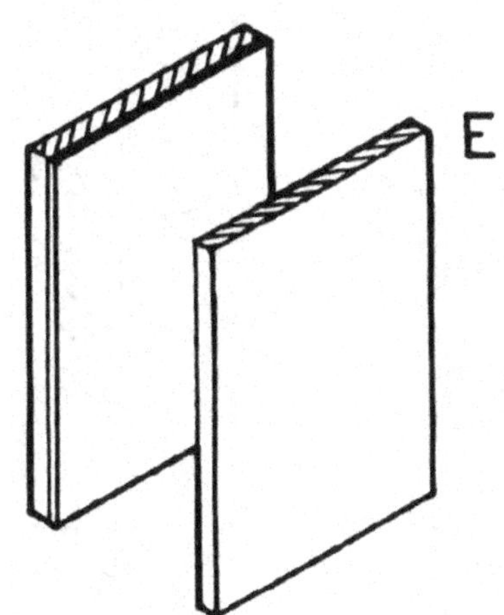

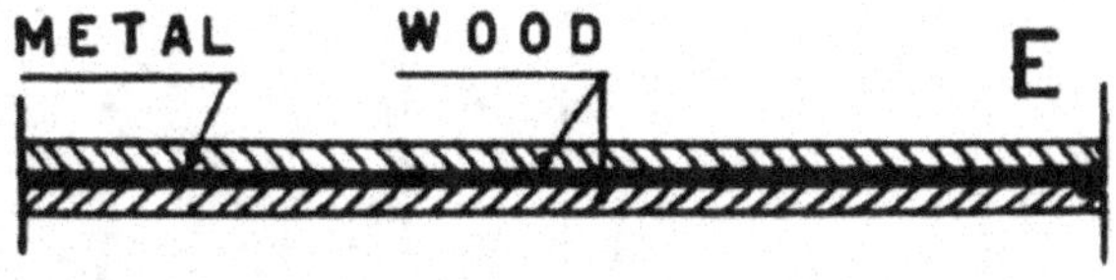

LIGHT METAL SHEET WELDED BETWEEN TWO LAYERS OF WOOD. THIS SHEET WOULD BE WATERPROOF.

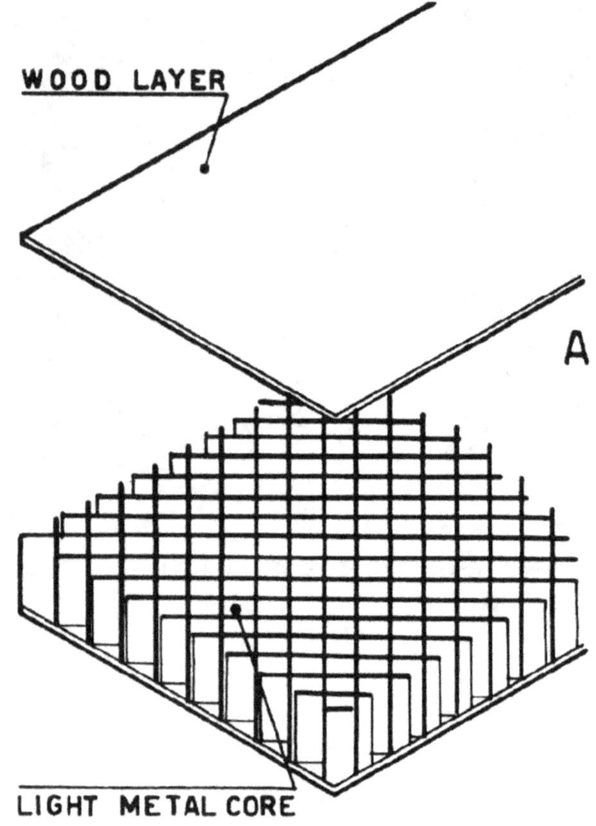

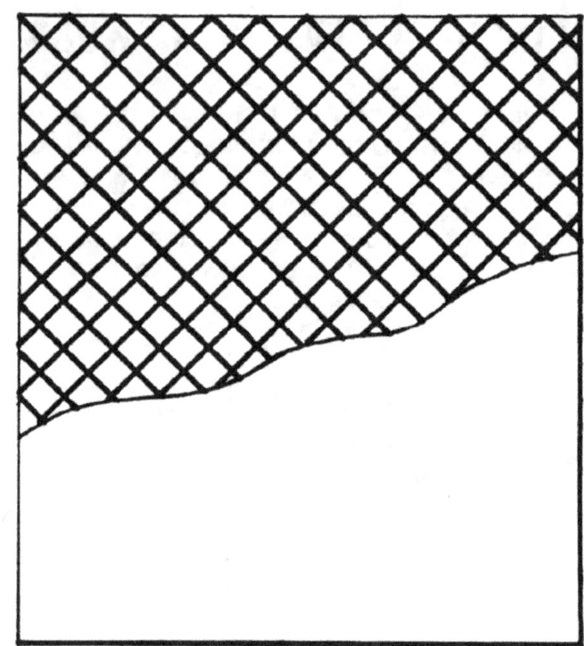

LIGHT METAL HONEYCOMB WELDED BETWEEN TWO WOOD SHEETS. A SPECIAL GLUE MAKES THIS WATER-PROOF.

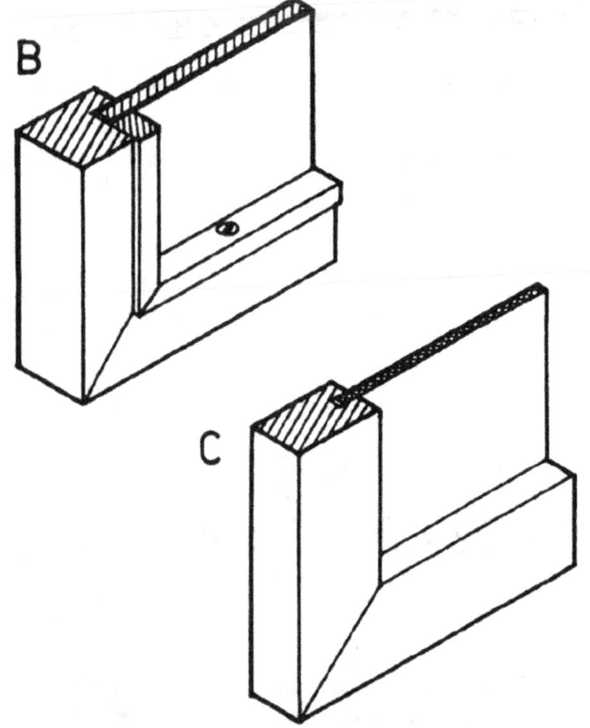

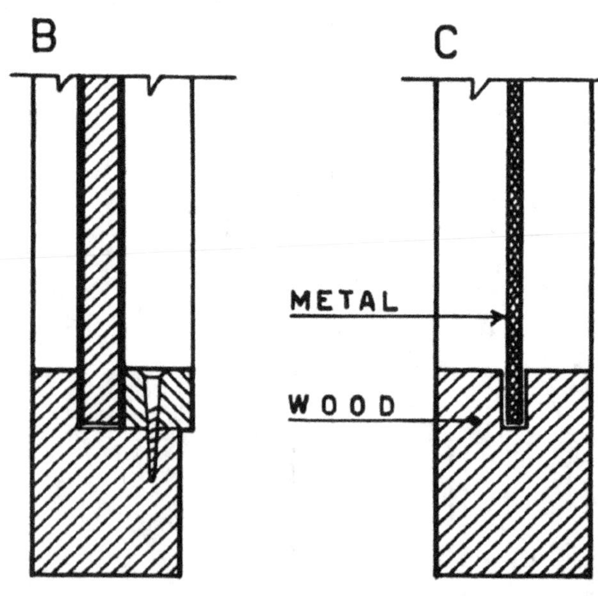

"B" SHOWS A WOOD AND METAL PANEL IN A RABBET FRAME WITH MOLDING. "C" IS A METAL SHEET IN A GROOVED FRAME.

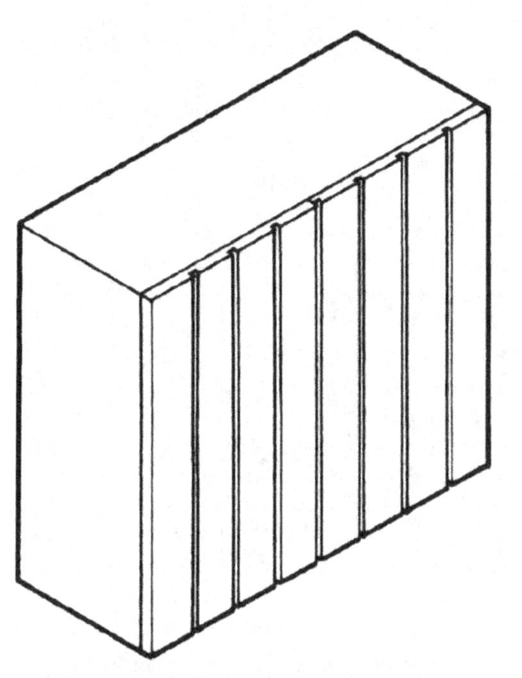

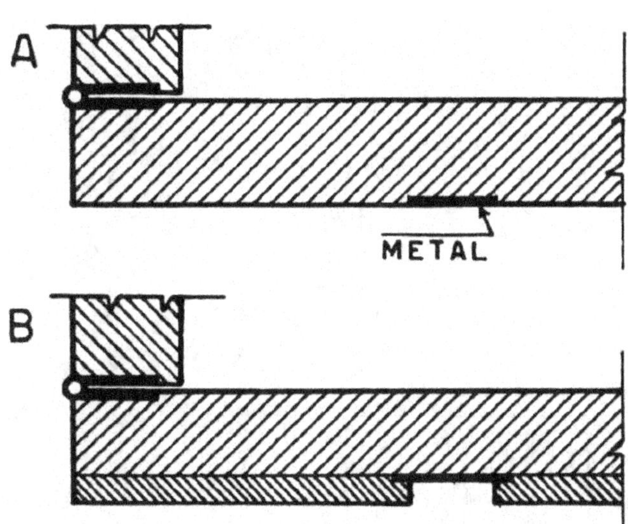

TWO DIFFERENT WAYS OF ATTACHING FLAT METAL TO WOOD SURFACES. TYPE "A" IS EASY TO APPLY BUT HAS A TENDENCY TO PULL OUT IN TIME. TYPE "B" ARRANGEMENT IS PREFERABLE.

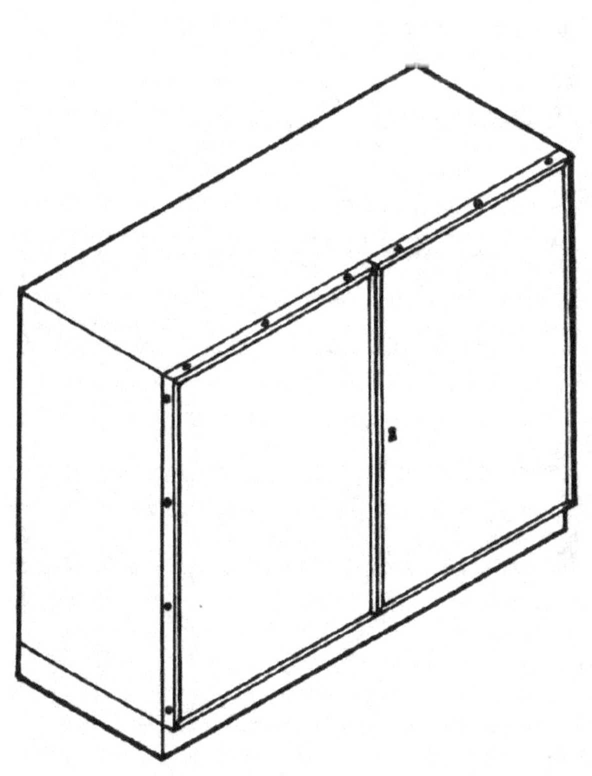

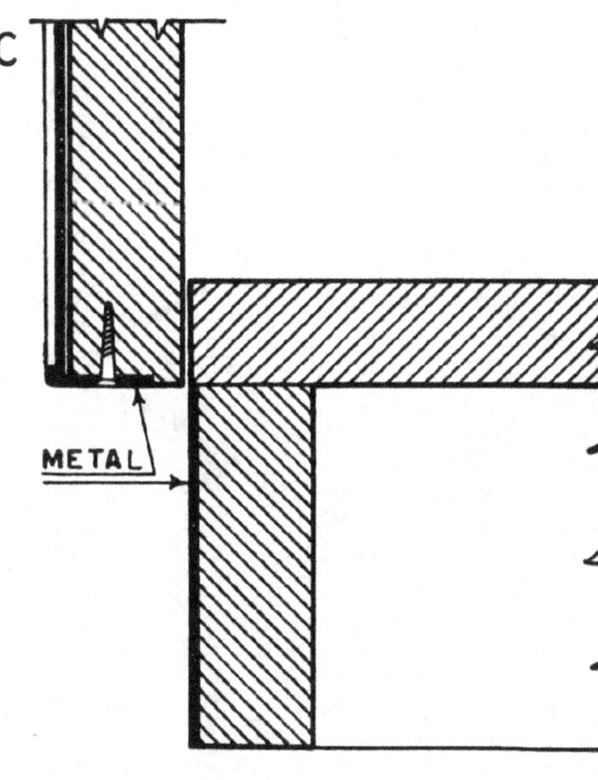

POSSIBLE METHOD OF ATTACHING METAL MOLDING AND A METAL KICK PLATE.

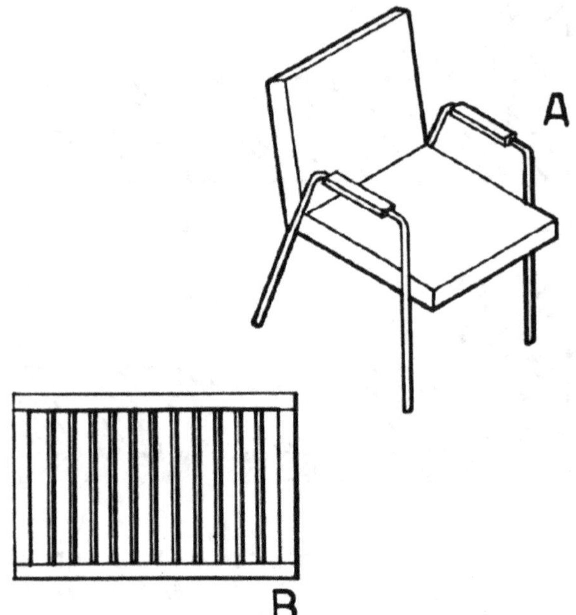

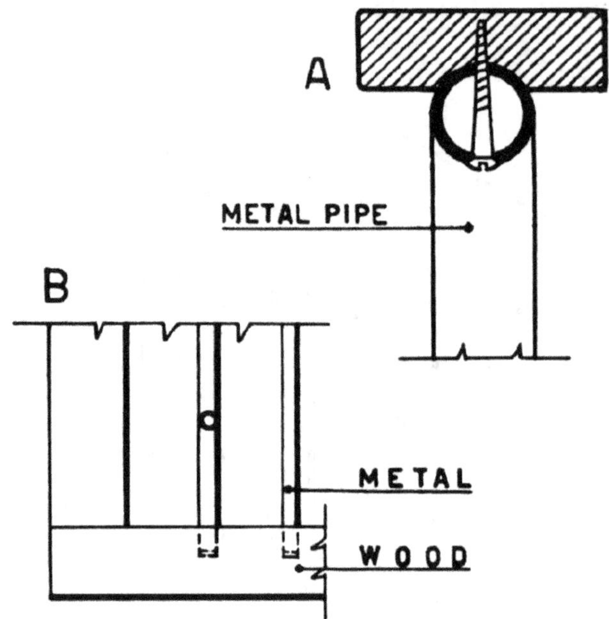

A, B — TWO COMMON WAYS OF JOINING METAL AND WOOD PARTS.

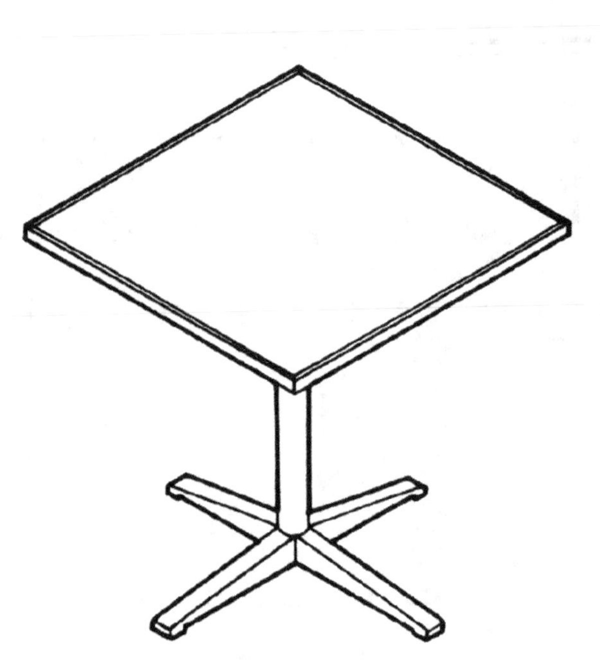

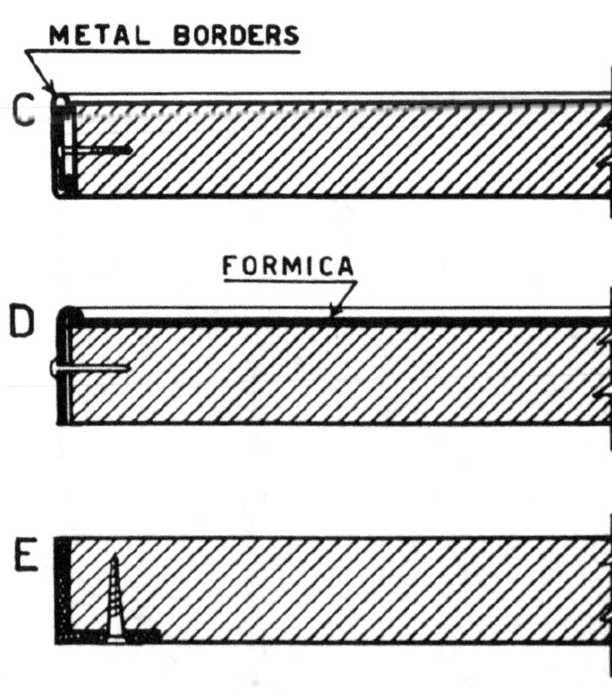

C, D, E—THREE DIFFERENT METHODS OF APPLYING METAL BORDERS.

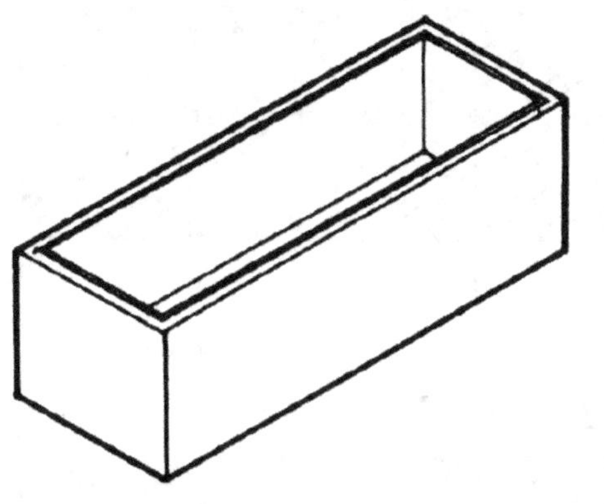

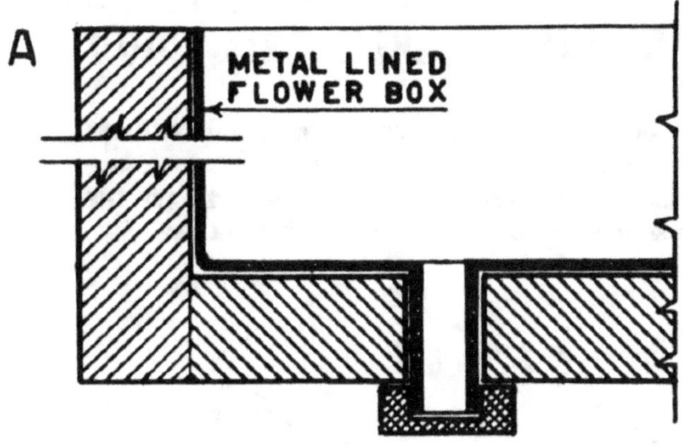

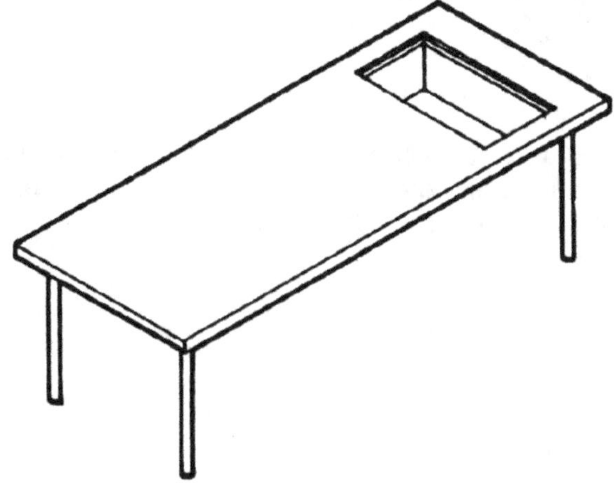

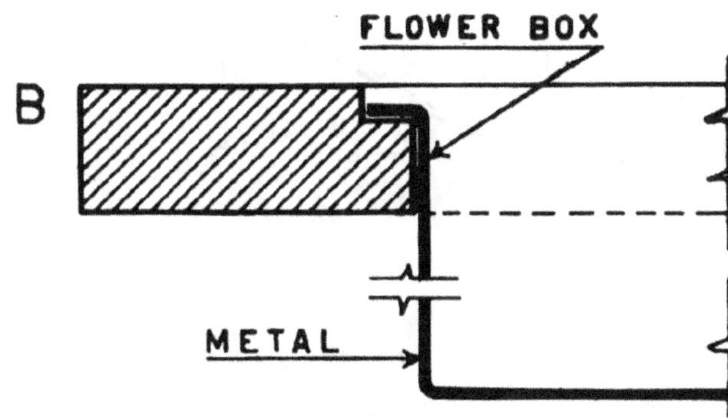

SEVERAL METHODS OF JOINING METAL PANS AND TRAYS TO WOOD. THE METAL DRAWER ARRANGEMENT IS PARTICULARLY SUITABLE FOR KITCHEN CABINET WORK.

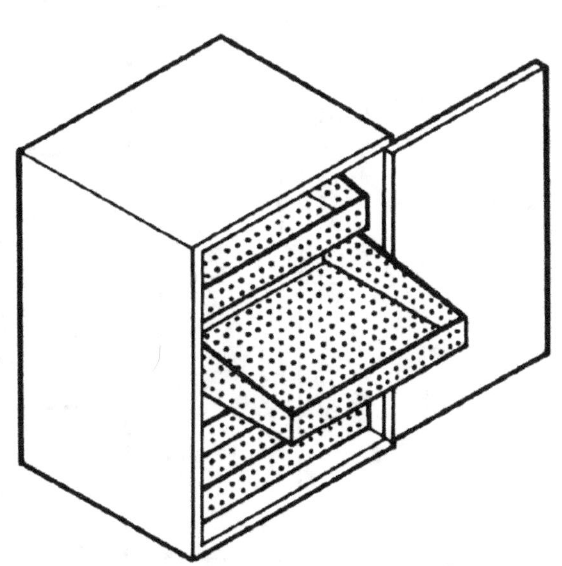

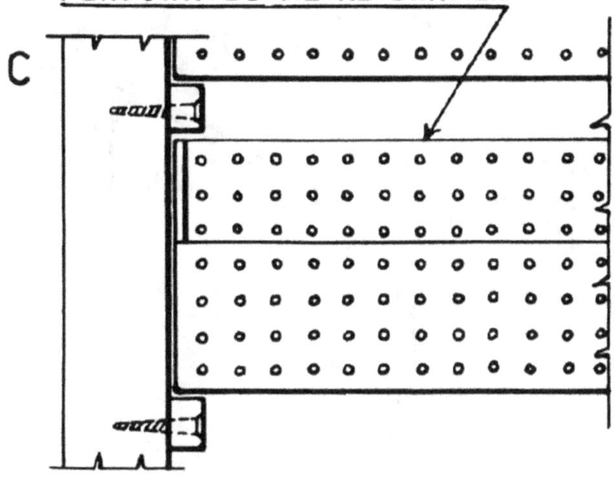

JOINING MARBLE AND WOOD

MARBLE AND WOOD MAY BE JOINED IN A NUMBER OF WAYS. BASICALLY, THE METHODS ARE THE SAME USED WITH GLASS. SHOWN ON THIS PAGE ARE THE USUAL METHODS. SCREWS AND BOLTS MAY BE USED.

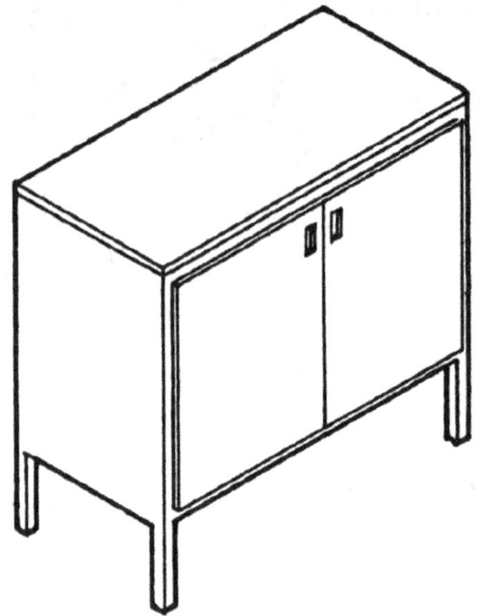

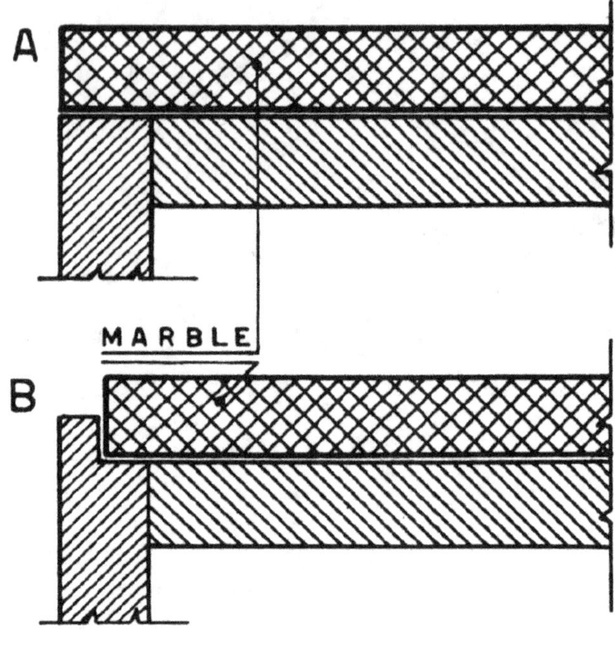

THE TWO EXAMPLES SHOWN ABOVE ARE SIMPLE METHODS. THE EXAMPLE BELOW USES A STUB TENON WITH A MORTISE IN THE MARBLE.

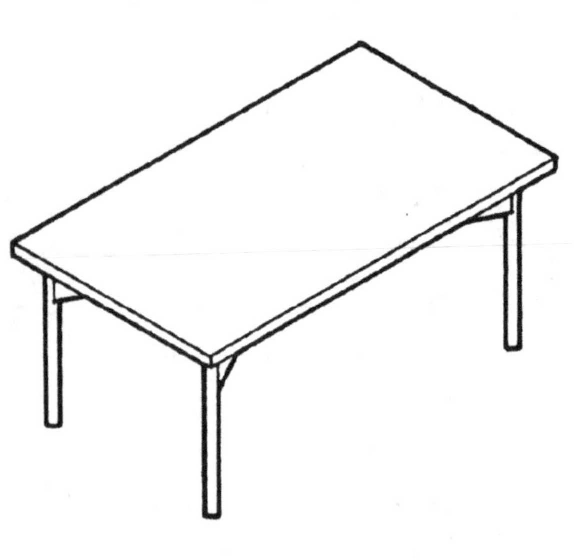

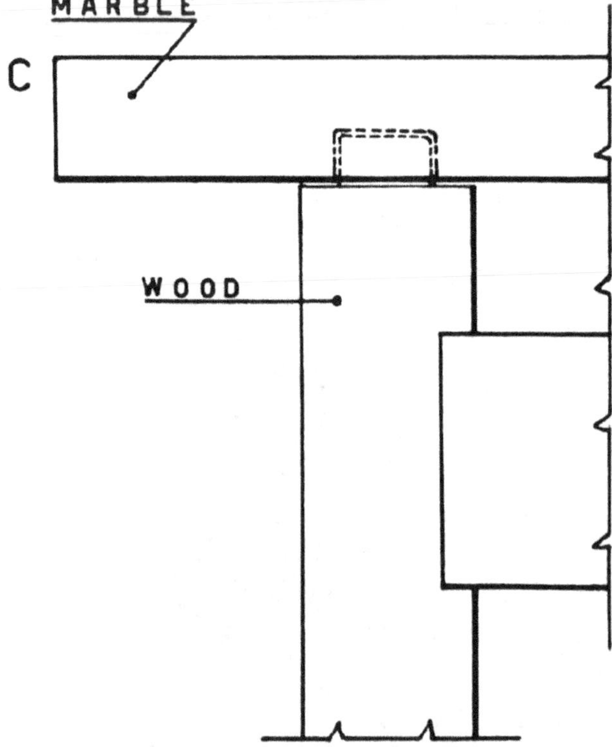

JOINING SPECIAL FACINGS TO WOOD

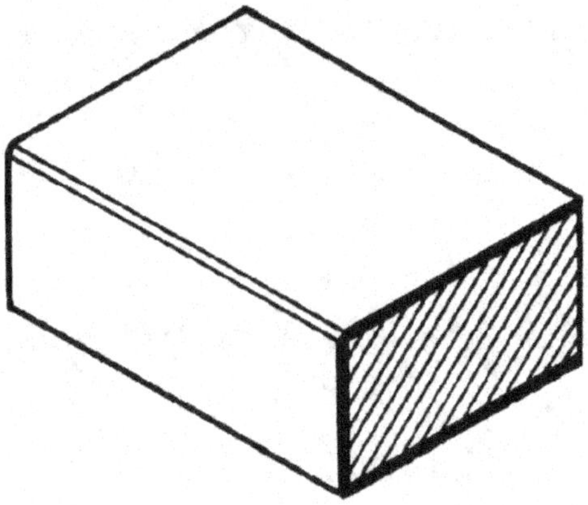

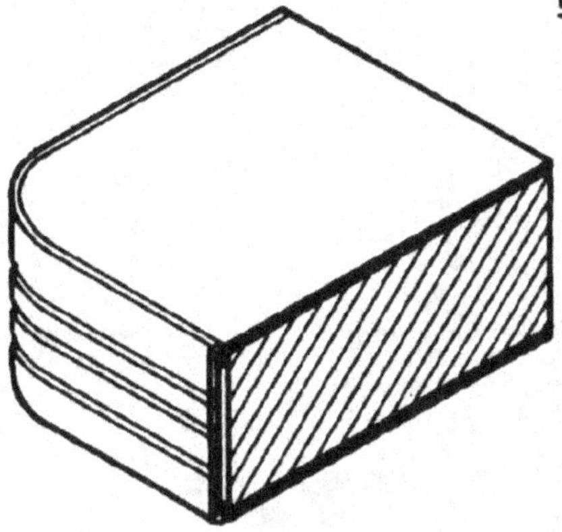

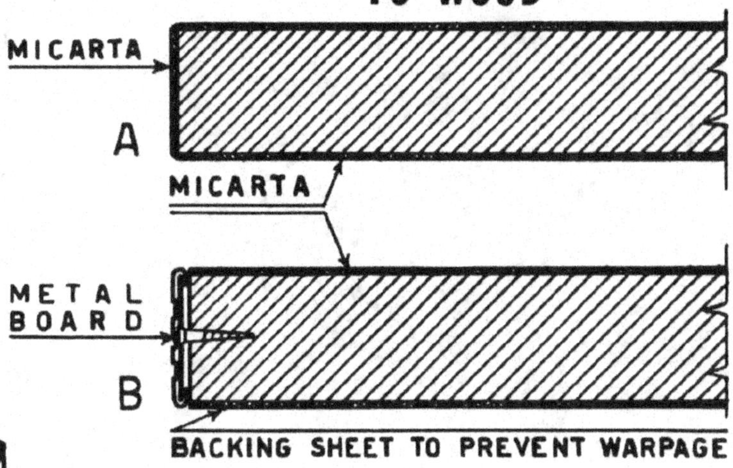

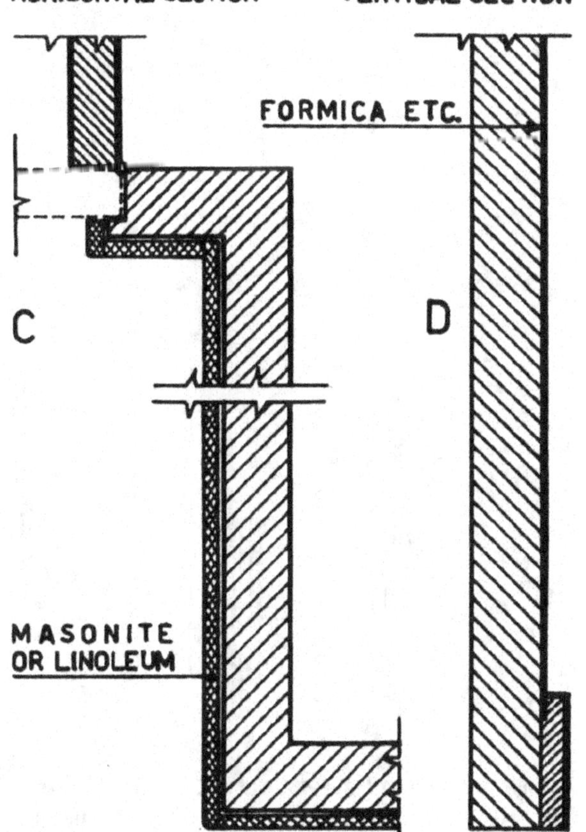

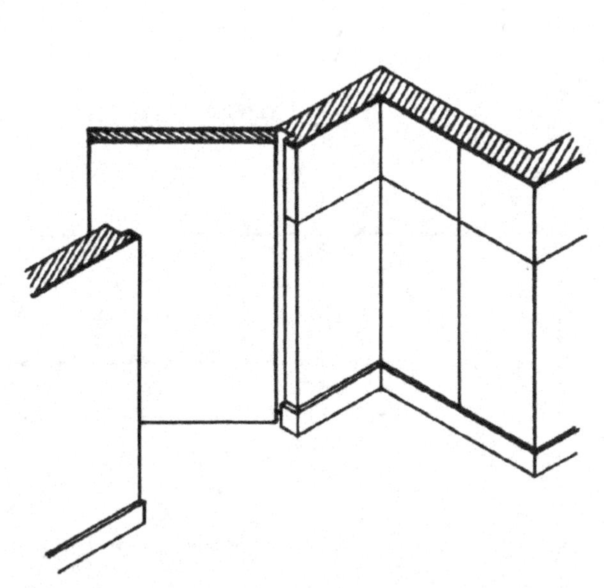

FORMICA, MASONITE AND OTHER MATERIALS CAN BE APPLIED TO ONLY ONE SIDE WHEN THE FRAME IS TOTALLY ENCLOSED.

JOINING RUBBER TO WOOD

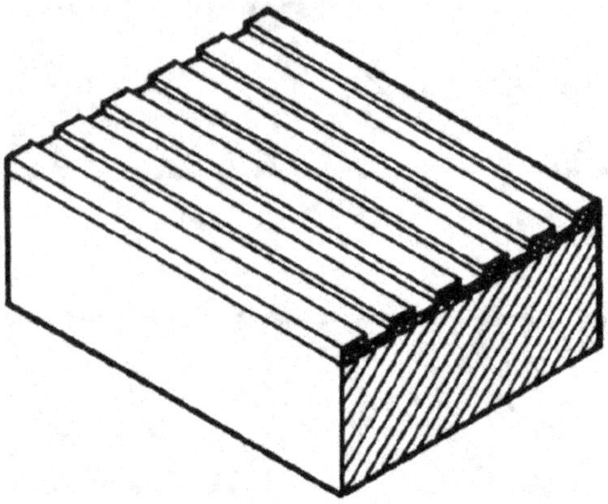

A

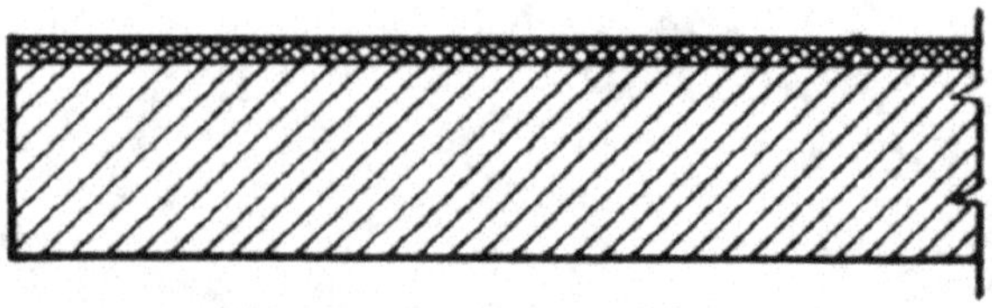

B

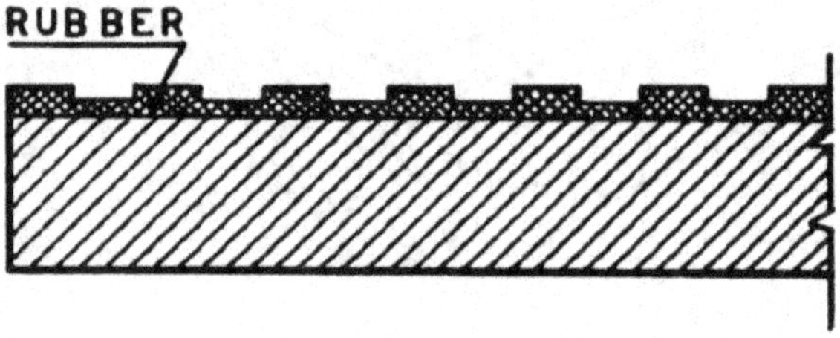

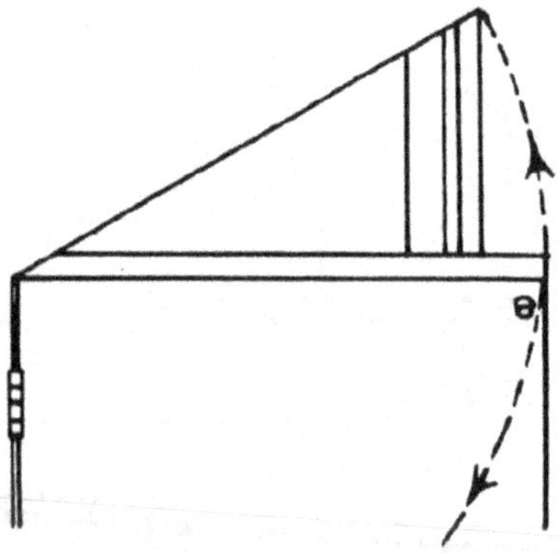

C

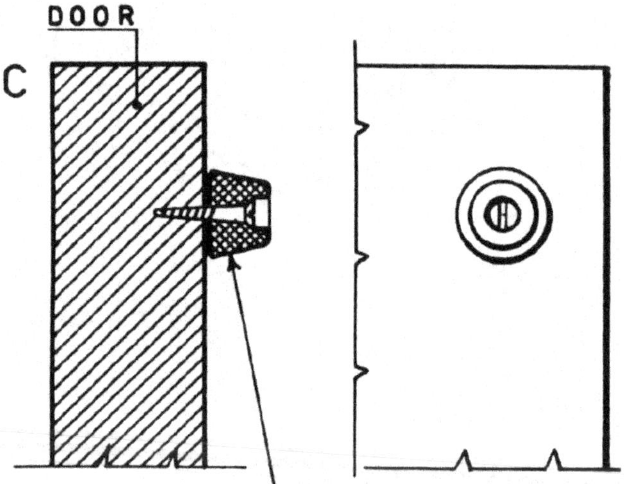

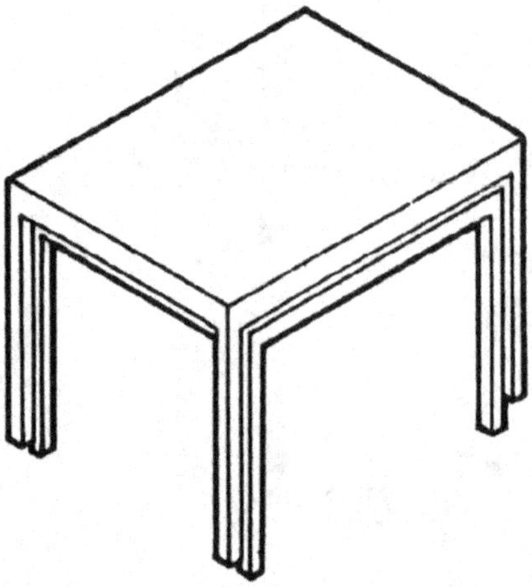

D

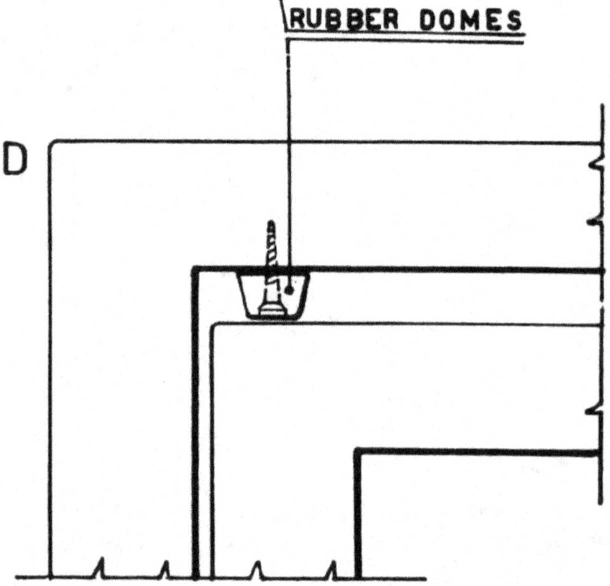

RUBBER IS A GOOD MATERIAL TO USE IN PROTECTING FURNITURE. HERE ARE SOME WAYS IT MAY BE USED.

PERFORATED TRANSITE JOINED TO WOOD

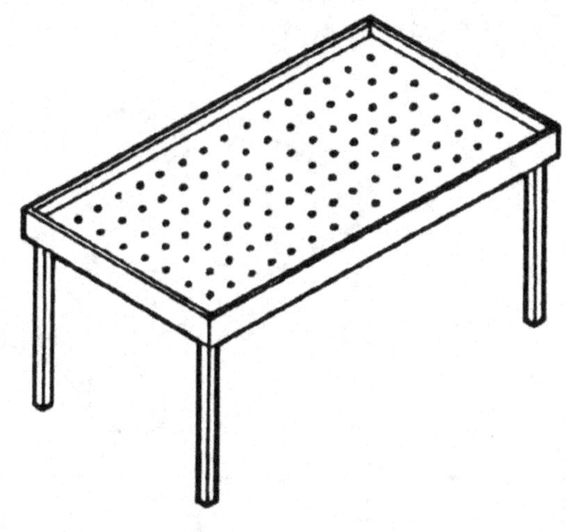

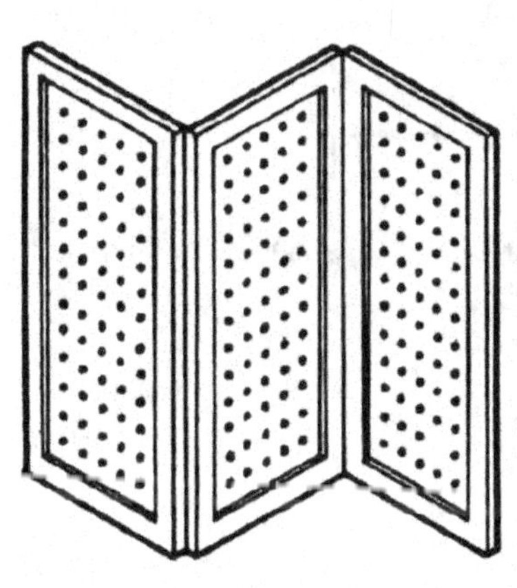

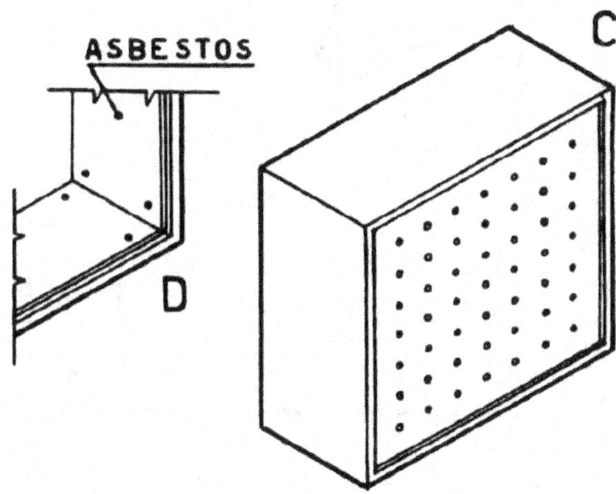

PERFORATED TRANSITE MAY BE ATTACHED IN THE VARIOUS WAYS SHOWN ABOVE. "D" USES ASBESTOS FOR FIRE PROTECTION.

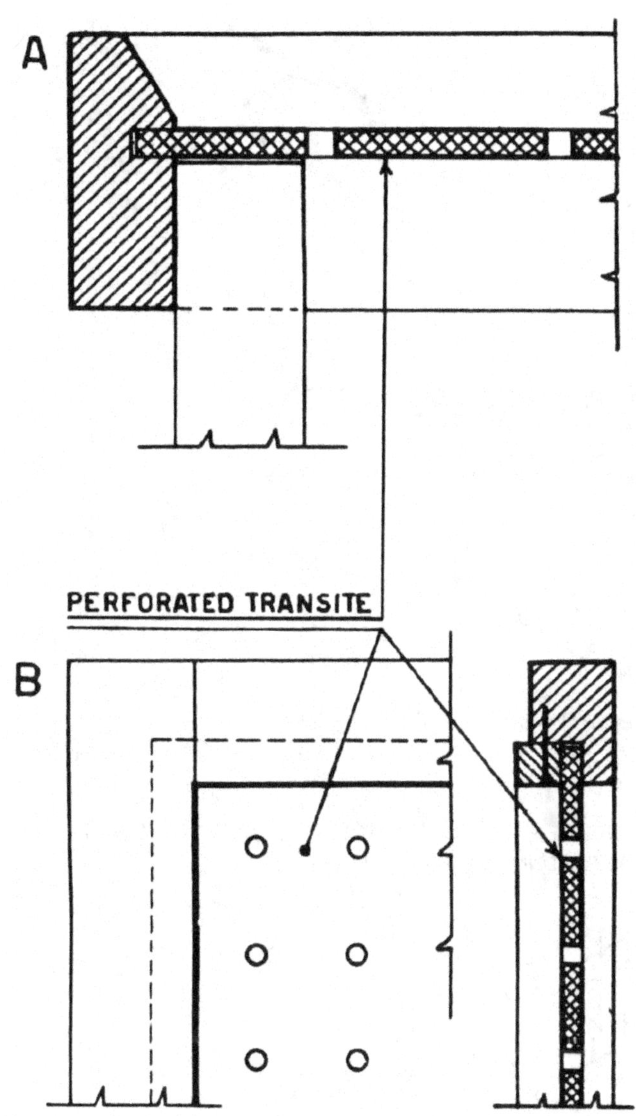

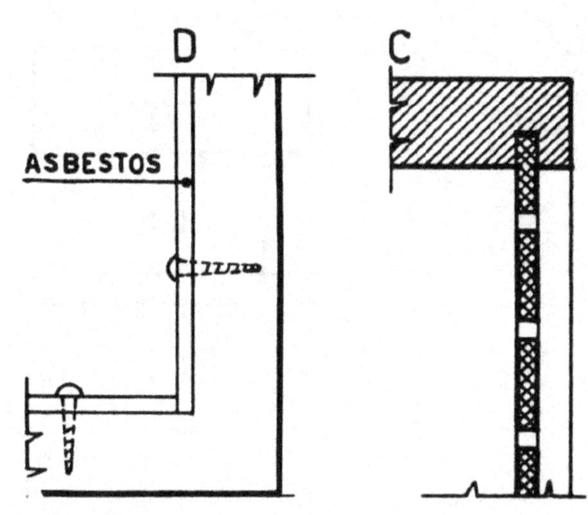

COMMON METAL JOINTS

HERE ARE SEVERAL COMMON METAL JOINTS. METAL MAY BE USED FOR COMPLETE FURNITURE PIECES OR FOR PARTS OF FURNITURE.

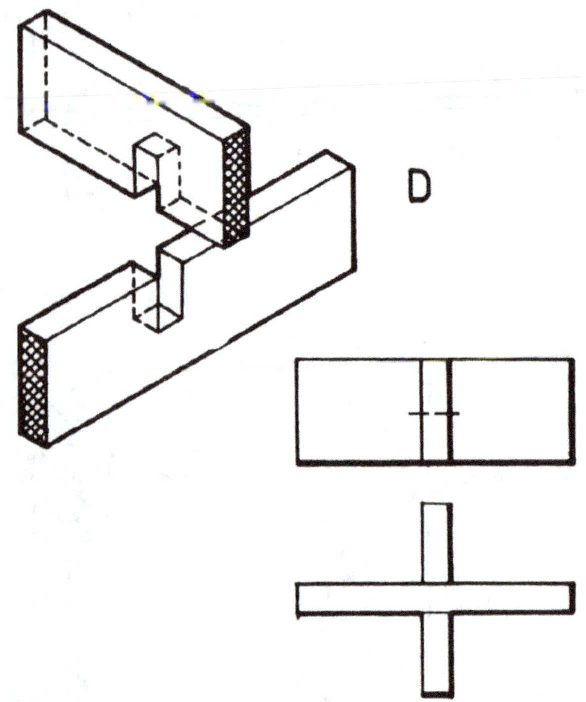

SLIDING METAL JOINTS. NOTE THAT EITHER PIECE MAY BE FIXED IN PLACE WITH SCREWS.

CROSS LAP JOINT USING TWO METAL STRIPS.

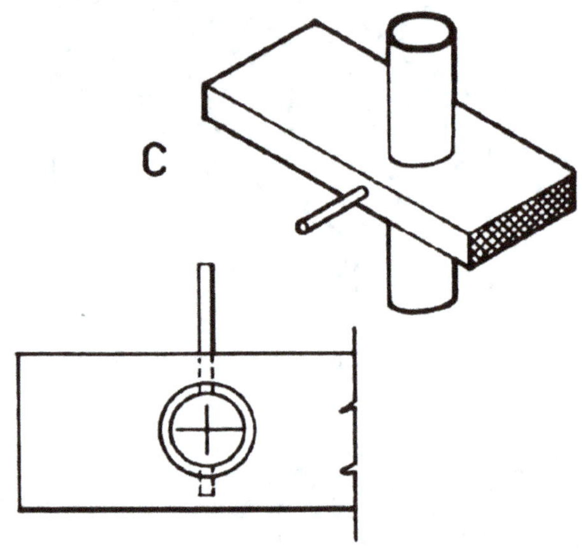

UNION OF PIPE AND METAL STRIP HELD IN PLACE WITH A LOCKING PIN.

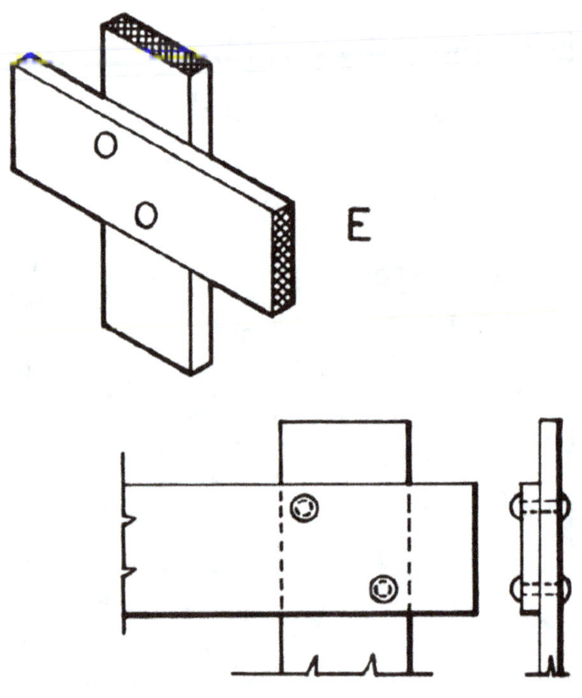

RIVETED JOINING OF TWO METAL STRIPS.

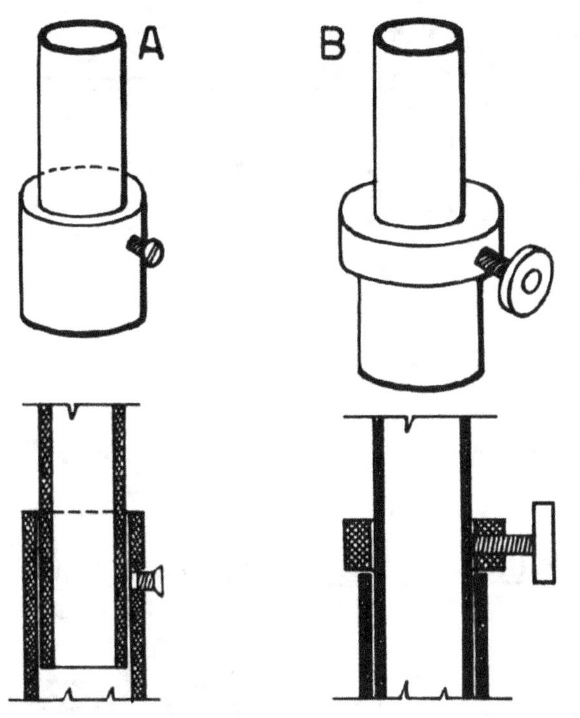

REMOVABLE PIPE JOINTS WHICH ARE HELD IN PLACE WITH SCREWS.

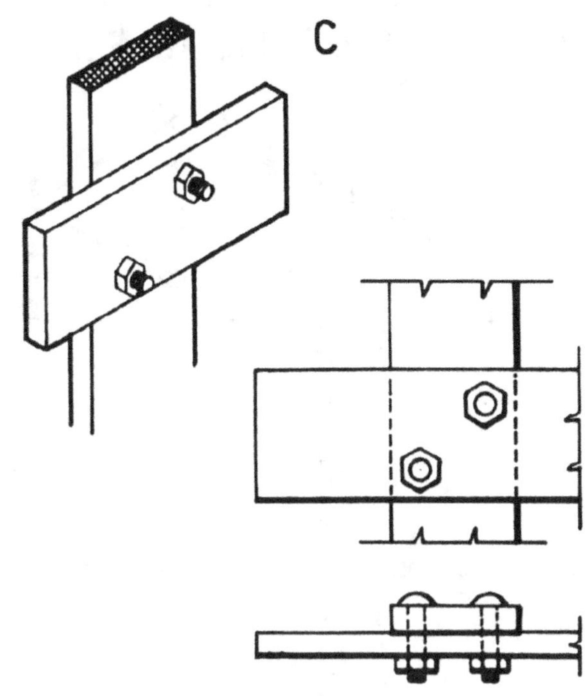

METAL STRIP JOINT HELD IN PLACE WITH BOLTS.

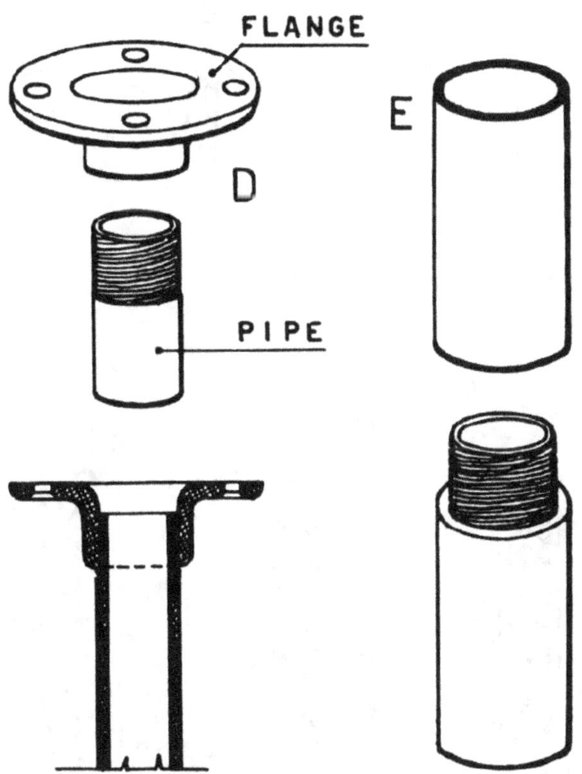

PIPE JOINTS USING SCREWED ENDS.

WELDED PIPE AND STRIP JOINTS.

JOINING PLATE GLASS TO METAL

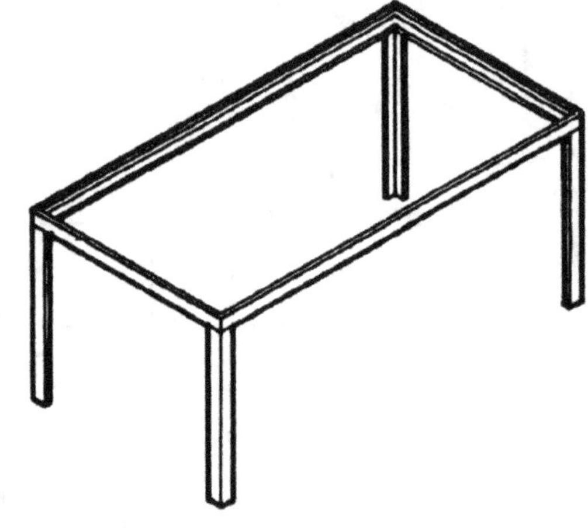

METHOD OF APPLYING PLATE GLASS TO METAL FRAME.

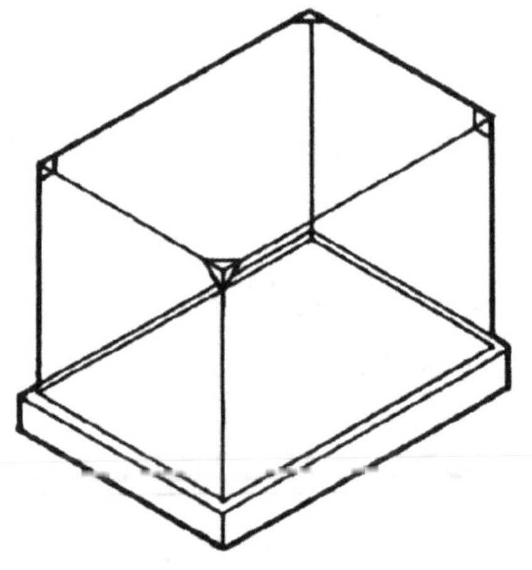

GLASS BOX WITH WOOD BASE USING METAL CORNERS.

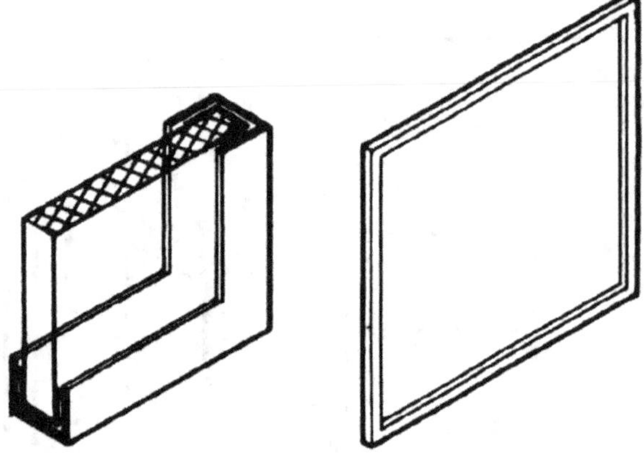

VARIOUS WAYS OF ATTACHING METAL FRAMES TO GLASS.

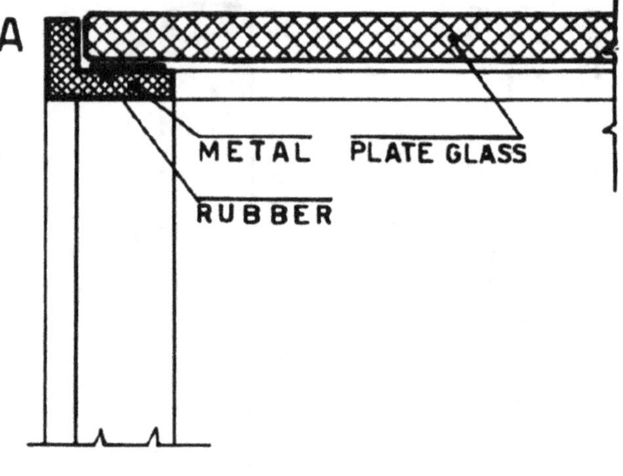

CORNER BRACKETS FOR PLATE GLASS

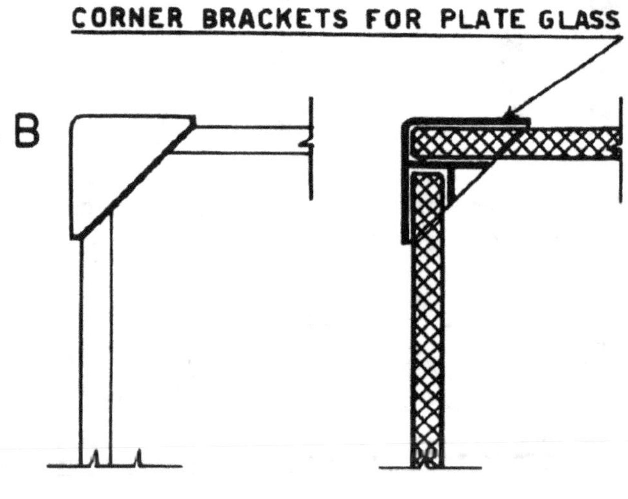

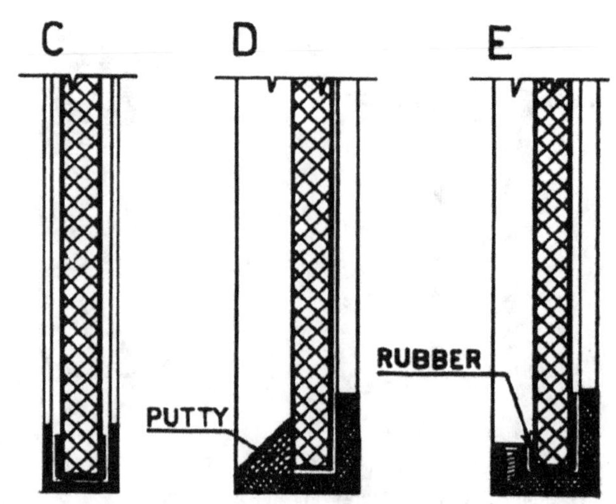

JOINING METAL TO RUBBER

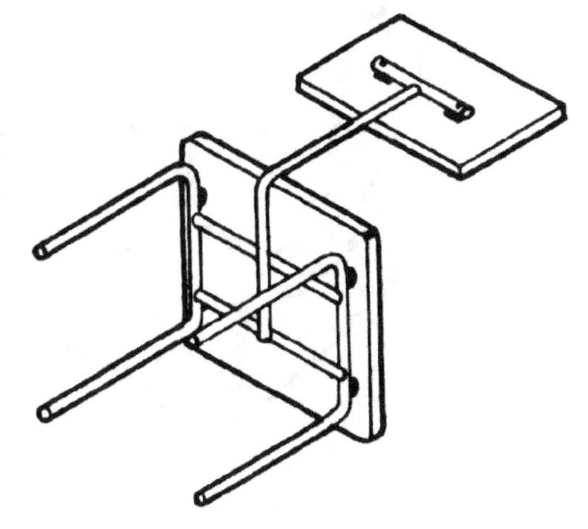

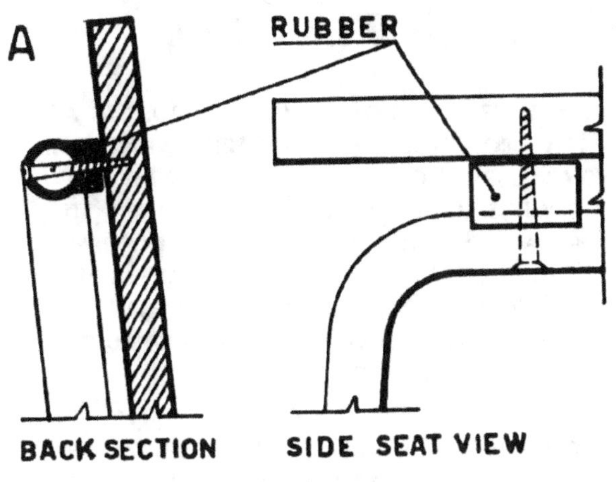

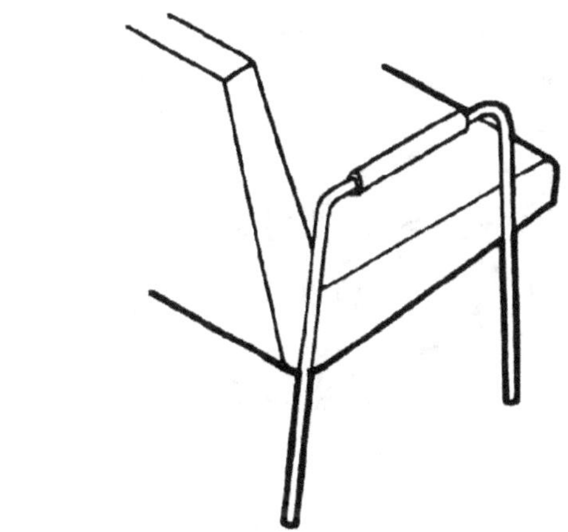

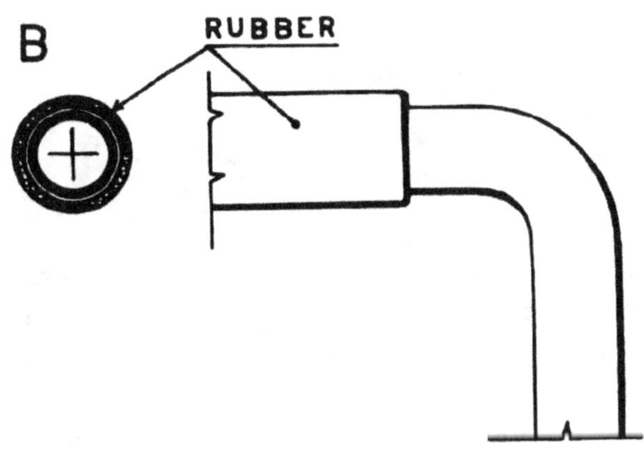

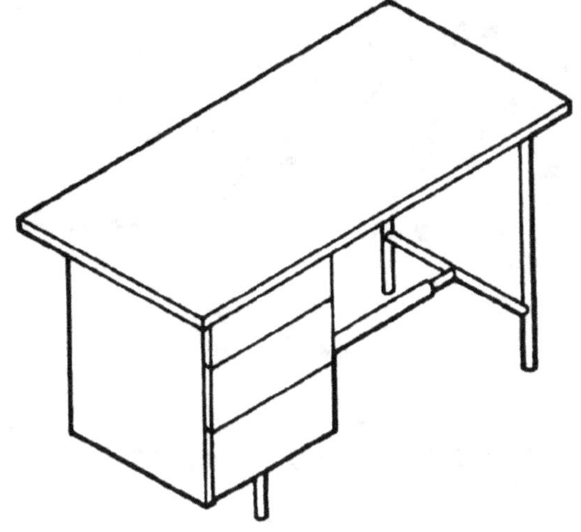

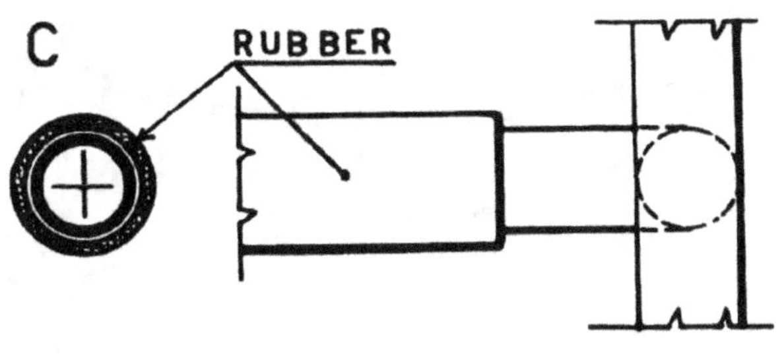

RUBBER AND METAL MAY BE JOINED IN ANY OF THE WAYS SHOWN ABOVE.

MOLDED PLASTIC

WITHIN THEIR OWN DOMAIN, PLASTICS POSSESS AT LEAST AS BROAD A RANGE OF PROPERTIES AS METALS, AND ARE CAPABLE OF AT LEAST AS GREAT A DIVERSITY OF COMPOSITIONS. IN GENERAL, THEY HAVE THE ADVANTAGE THAT THEY CAN BE MOLDED IN FORMS. IT IS ONLY COMPARATIVELY RECENTLY THAT PLASTICS HAVE COME INTO COMMON USE IN THE FURNITURE FIELD. CONTINUOUS RESEARCH IS BEING CONDUCTED TO FURTHER DEVELOP THEIR MANY USES.

WE DO KNOW ENOUGH ABOUT THE CHARACTERISTICS OF PLASTICS TODAY SO THAT THEY MAY BE USED WITH THE ASSURANCE THAT THEY WILL STAND WEAR. HOWEVER, IT IS BEST TO CHECK THE SPECIFIC CHARACTERISTICS OF EACH PLASTIC BEFORE USING IT.

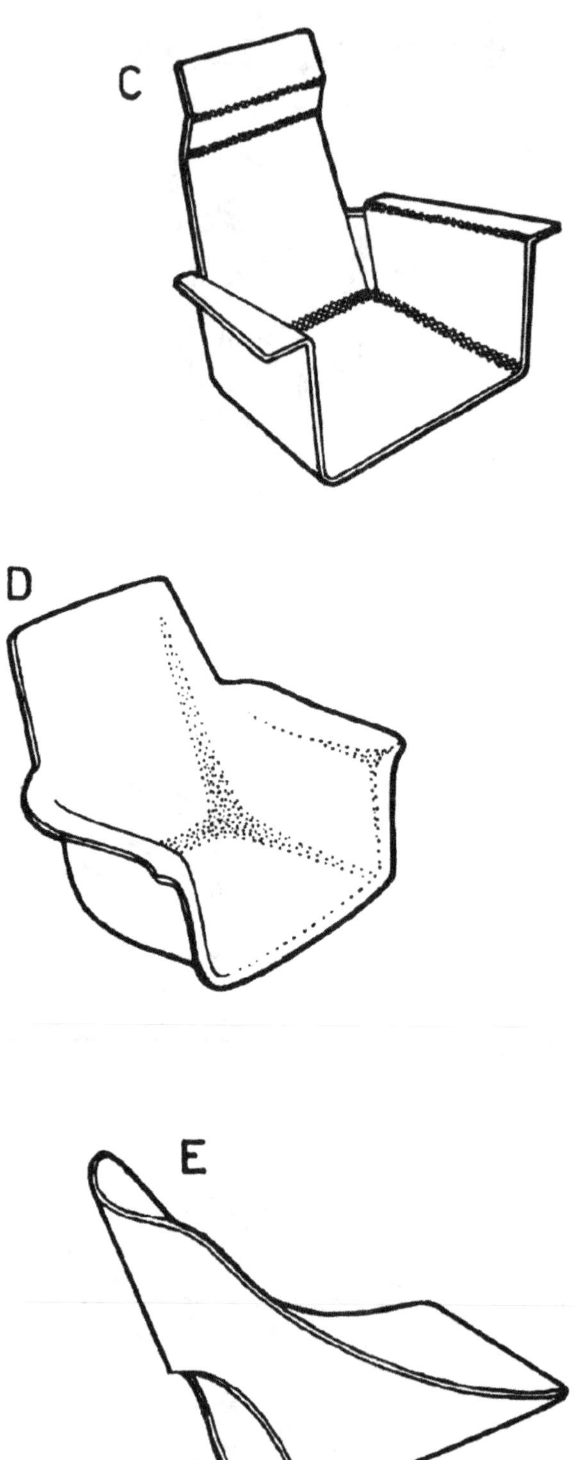

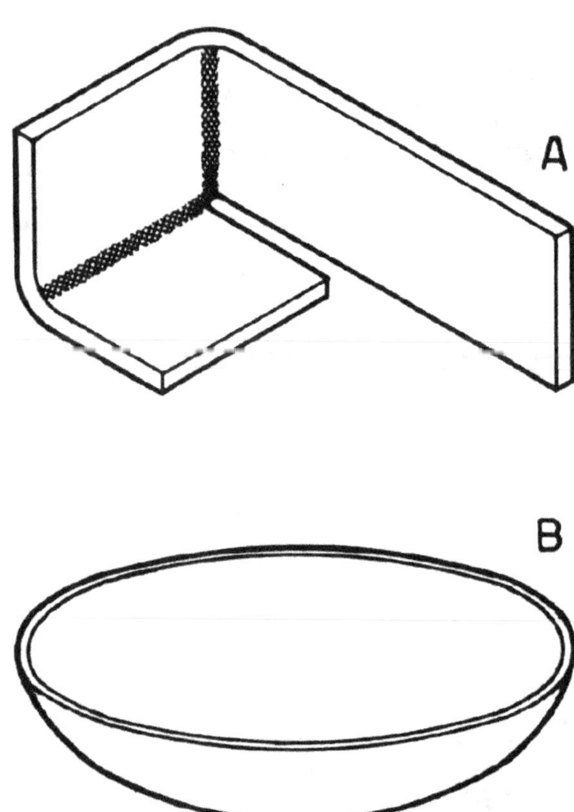

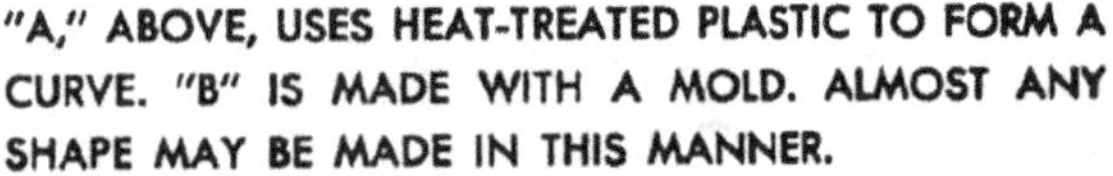

"A," ABOVE, USES HEAT-TREATED PLASTIC TO FORM A CURVE. "B" IS MADE WITH A MOLD. ALMOST ANY SHAPE MAY BE MADE IN THIS MANNER.

THREE PLASTIC CHAIRS

THE METHOD OF MAKING CHAIR "C" IS SIMILAR TO "A." "D" USES A MOLD. "E" IS ALSO MOLDED, BUT HAS A SECTION REMOVED TO TAKE UPHOLSTERING.

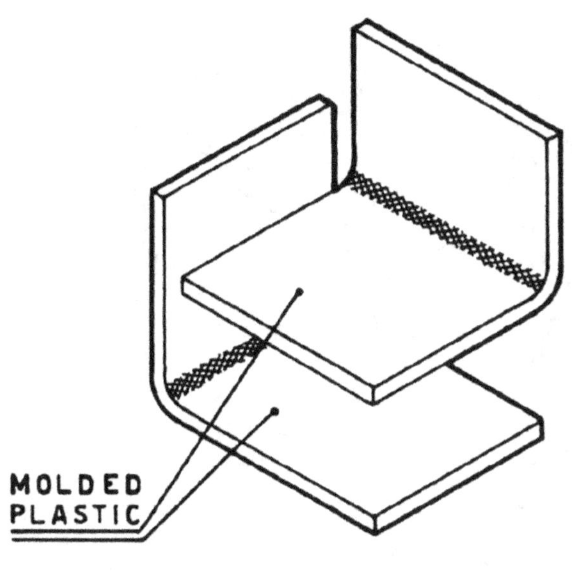

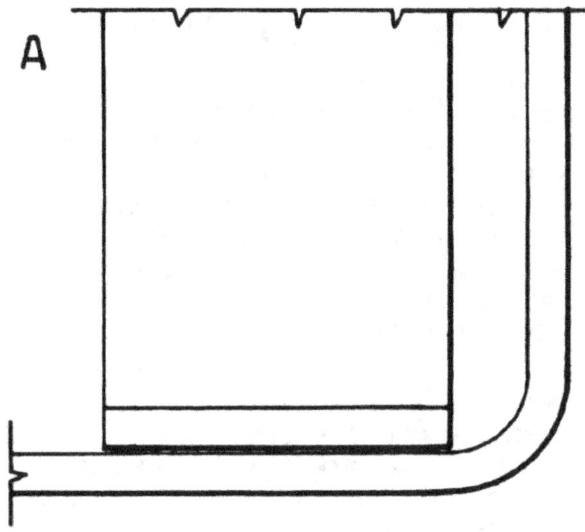

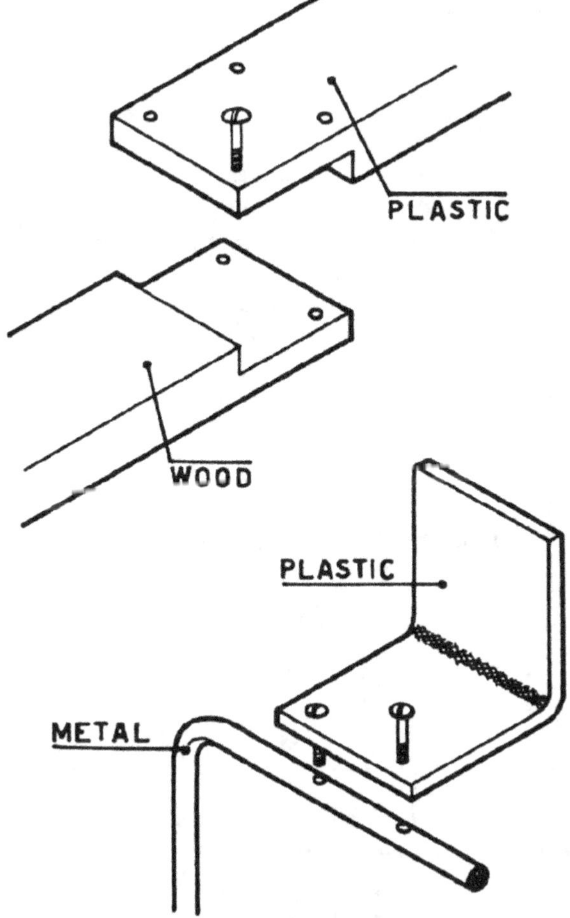

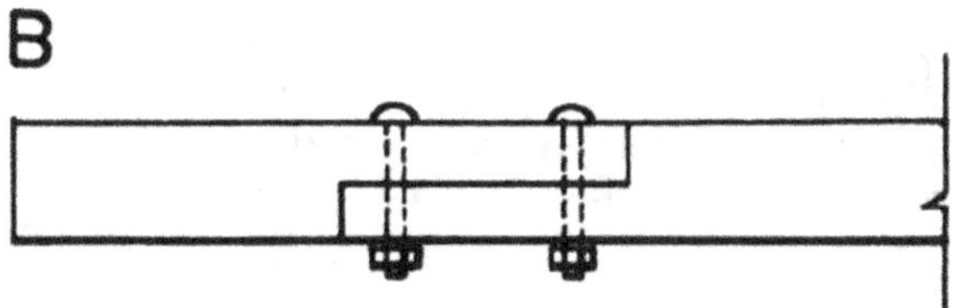

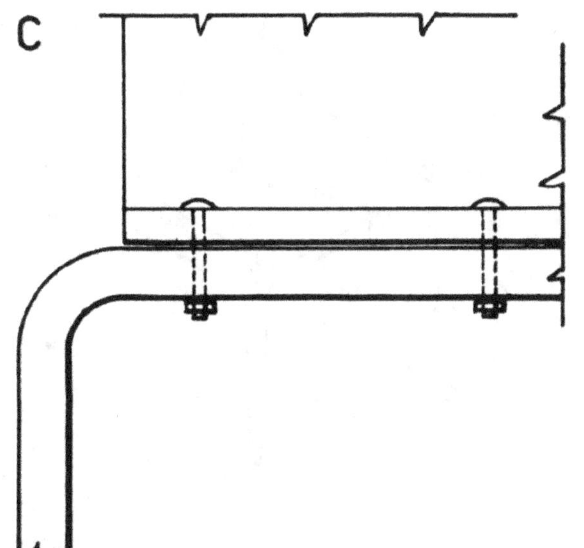

A — PLASTIC PIECES JOINED WITH ADHESIVE. SPECIFIC ADHESIVES HAVE BEEN DEVELOPED FOR USE WITH THE VARIOUS TYPES OF PLASTICS.

B — WOOD AND PLASTIC JOINED WITH GLUE AND BOLTS.

C — PLASTIC AND METAL JOINED WITH BOLTS.

UPHOLSTERY WORK

UPHOLSTERING IS AN ART IN ITSELF AND IT STILL REMAINS A HANDCRAFT SYSTEM OF PRODUCTION. WHILE OTHER PARTS OF FURNITURE CONSTRUCTION ARE MOSTLY DONE BY MACHINE, THE UPHOLSTERY WORK IS STILL DONE BY HAND. EXPERT WORKMEN HAVE USUALLY SERVED A LONG APPRENTICESHIP BEFORE ACQUIRING THE SKILL NECESSARY FOR UPHOLSTERING A CHAIR OR DIVAN.

THERE ARE, HOWEVER, SEVERAL WAYS THAT UPHOLSTERY WORK CAN BE DONE BY APPRENTICES AND AMATEURS. CHAIRS, STOOLS AND OTHER PIECES CAN BE UPHOLSTERED BY SUBSTITUTING FOAM RUBBER FOR THE MATERIALS USED IN NORMAL WORK.

I SHALL NOT GO INTO DETAIL ABOUT UPHOLSTERING, BUT I HAVE ILLUSTRATED THE VARIOUS TYPES OF FRAMES, MATERIALS AND METHODS OF APPLICATION. I HAVE TRIED TO SIMPLIFY THE PRESENTATION TO ENABLE EVEN THE UNSKILLED TO UNDERSTAND EACH METHOD.

FRAME

THE FRAME, IN EITHER WOOD OR METAL, IS THE SKELETON OF THE FURNITURE PIECE. UPON ITS CONSTRUCTION DEPENDS THE COMFORT AND STRENGTH OF THE CHAIR.

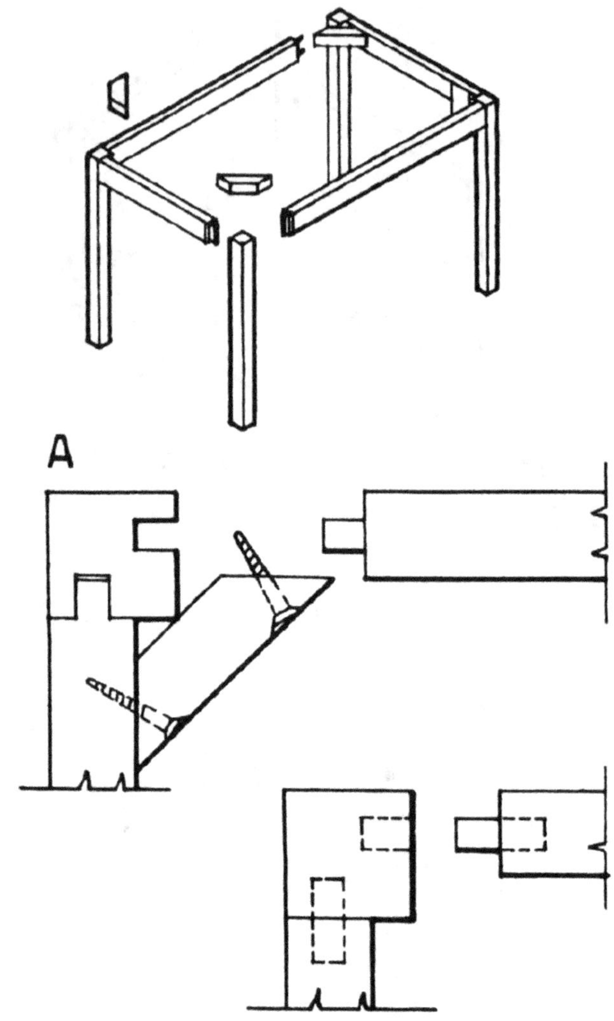

TWO DIFFERENT TYPES OF BENCH FRAMES.

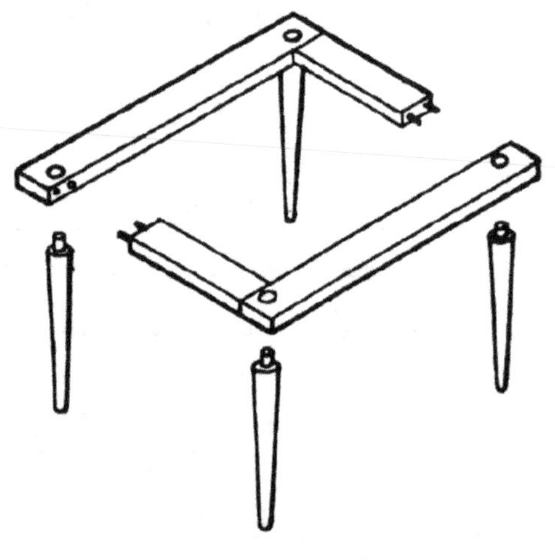

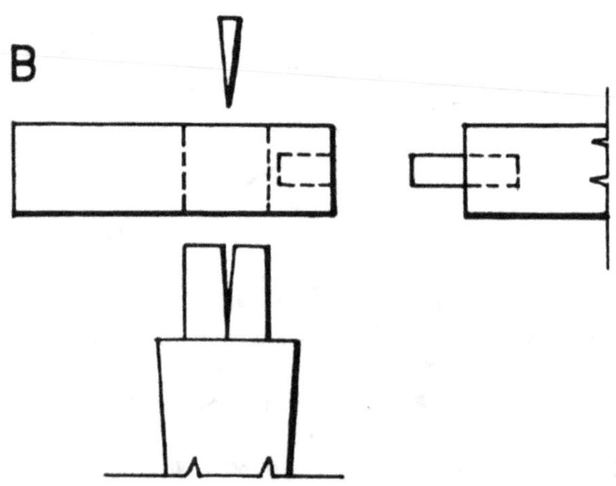

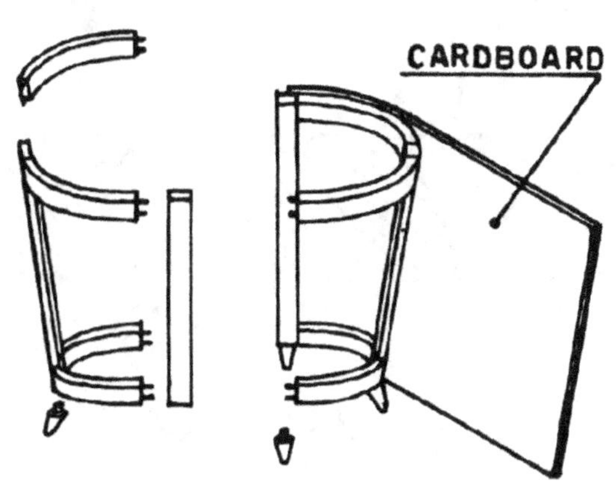

ROUND FRAME THAT IS COVERED WITH CARDBOARD.
THE UPHOLSTERING MATERIAL IS ADDED LATER.

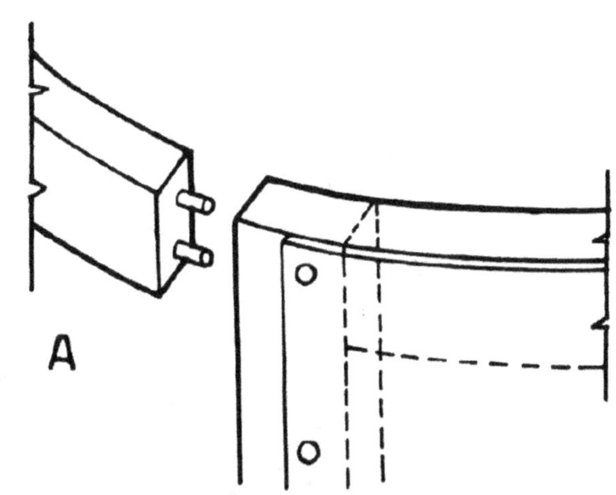

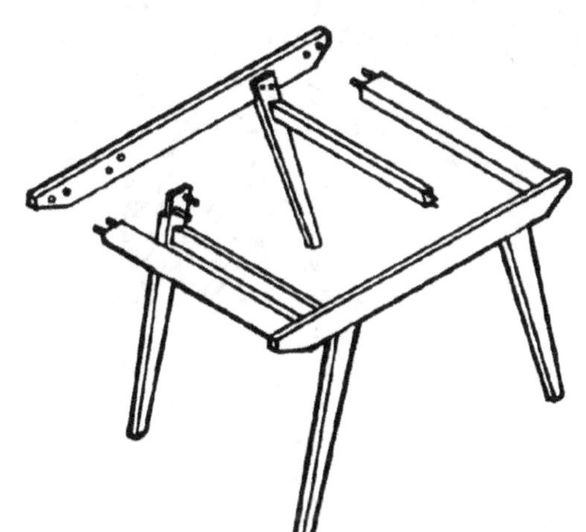

FRAME FOR WEBBING SEAT.

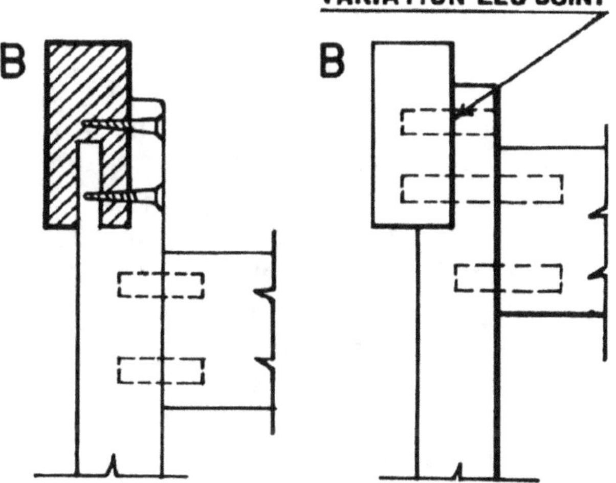

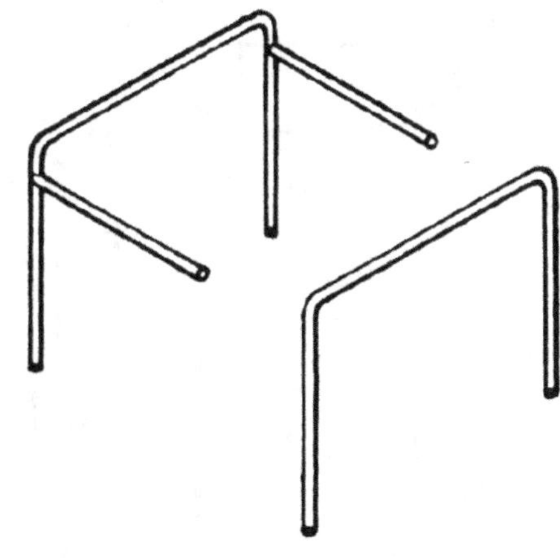

METAL FRAME STOOL FOR CORD OR CANVAS SEAT.

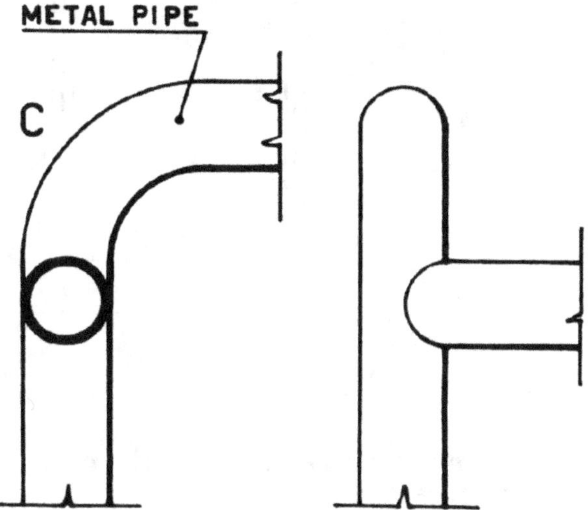

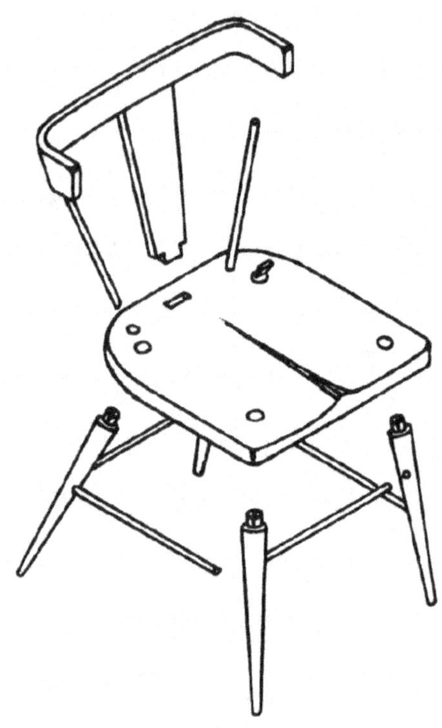

MASS PRODUCED WOODEN CHAIR. NOTE THE TWO
METHODS OF JOINING SEAT AND LEGS.

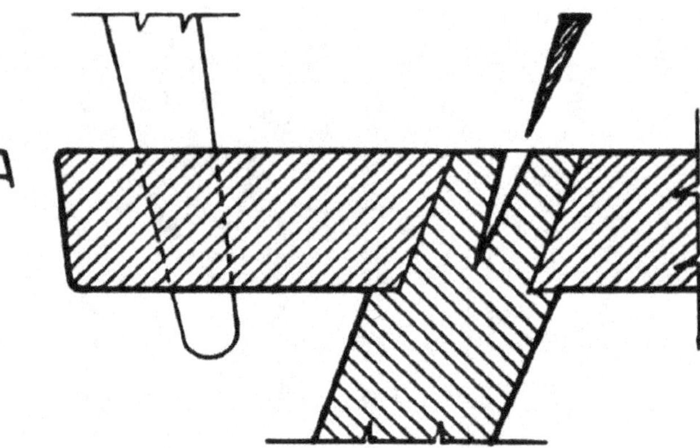

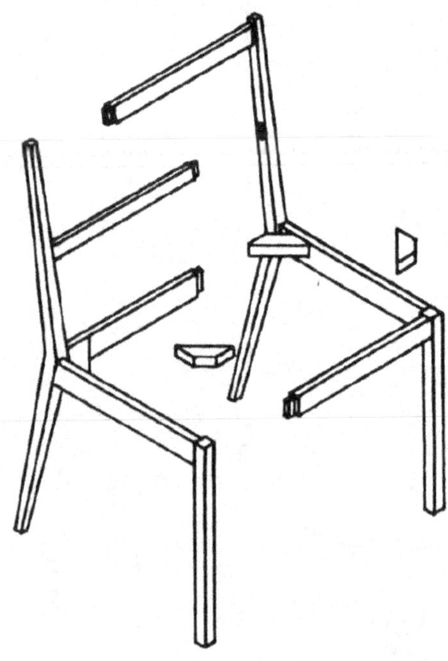

COMMON TYPE OF CHAIR FRAME THAT WILL TAKE AN
UPHOLSTERED SEAT.

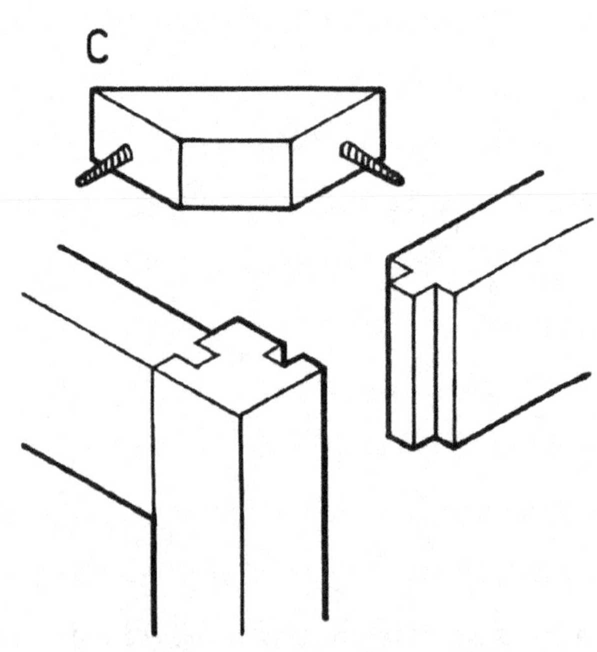

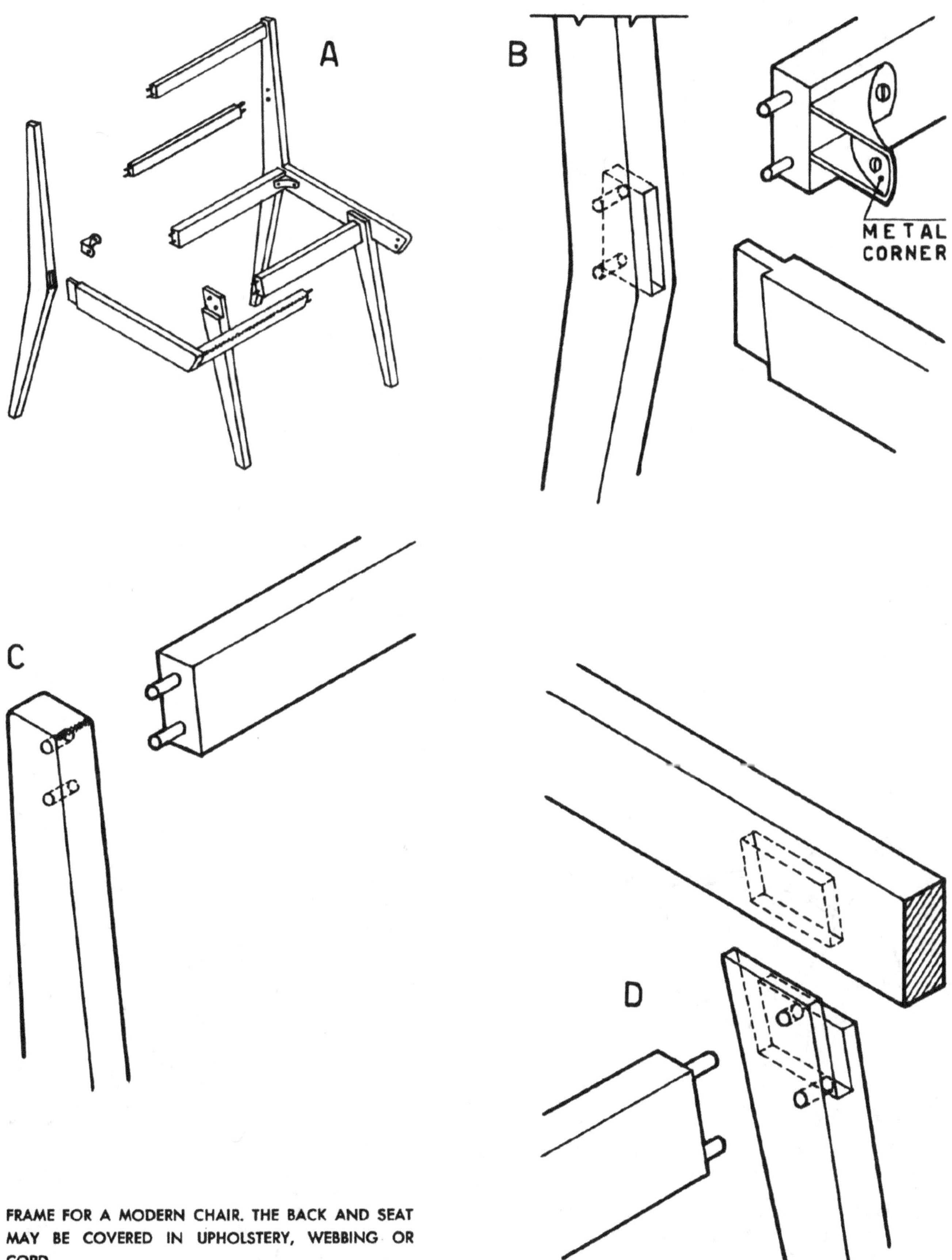

FRAME FOR A MODERN CHAIR. THE BACK AND SEAT MAY BE COVERED IN UPHOLSTERY, WEBBING OR CORD.

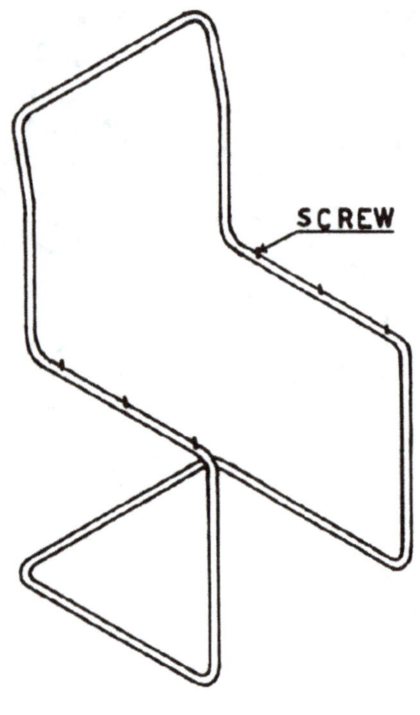

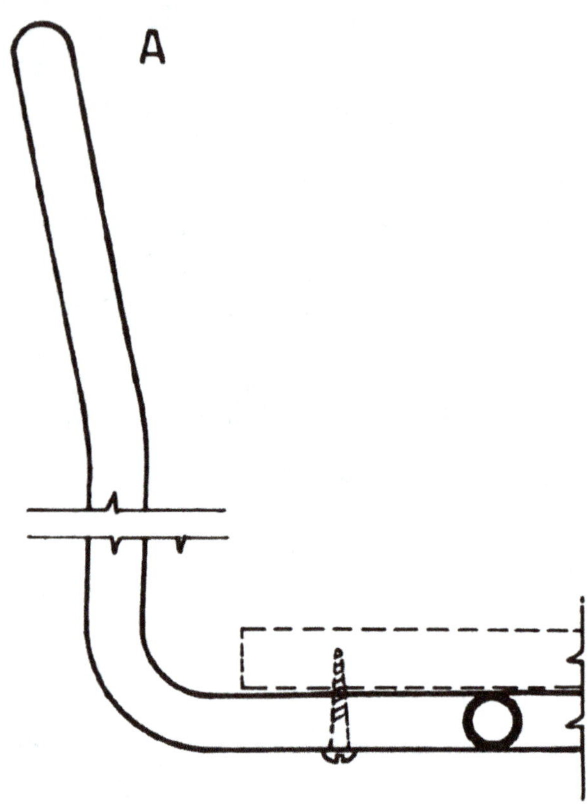

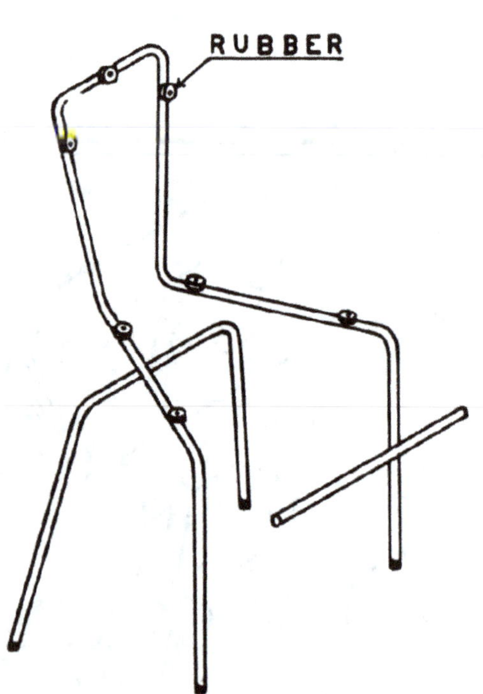

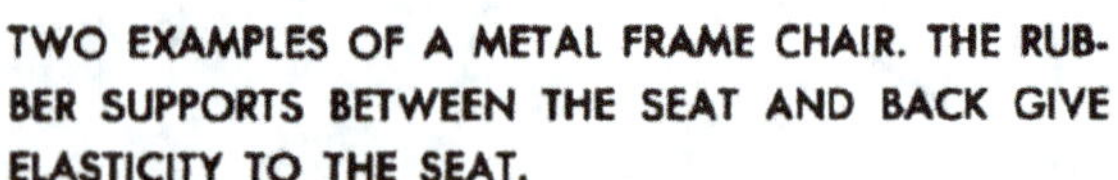

TWO EXAMPLES OF A METAL FRAME CHAIR. THE RUBBER SUPPORTS BETWEEN THE SEAT AND BACK GIVE ELASTICITY TO THE SEAT.

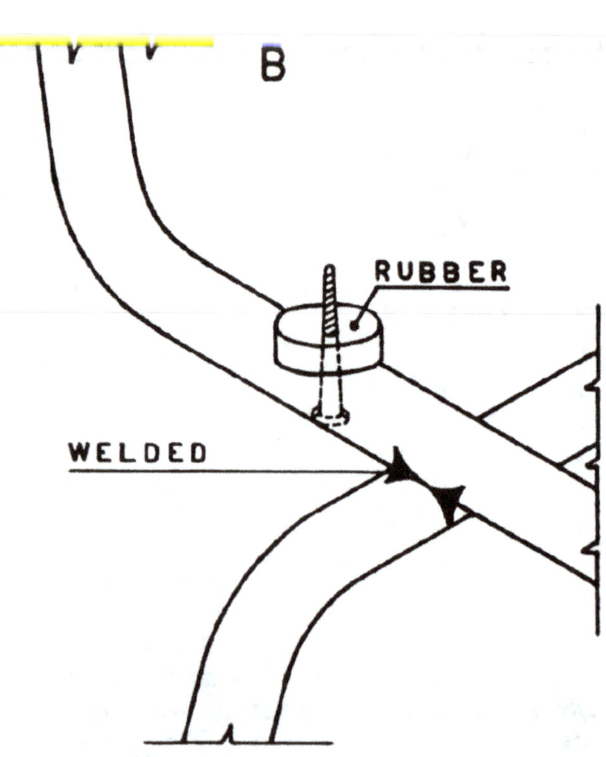

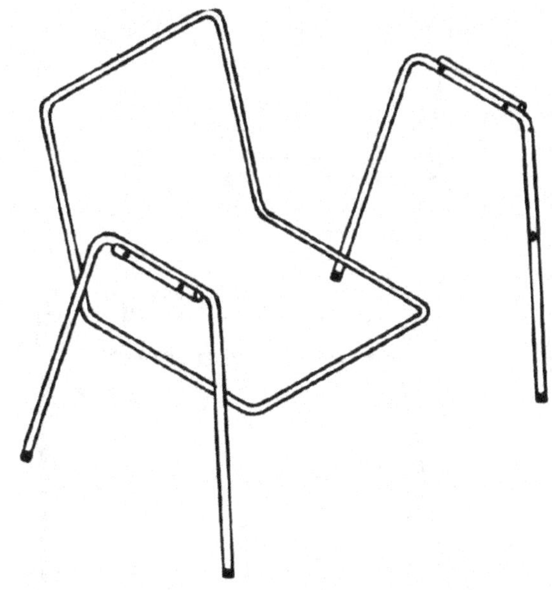

METAL FRAME ARMCHAIR. THE SEAT AND BACK CAN
BE COVERED WITH CANVAS OR CORD.

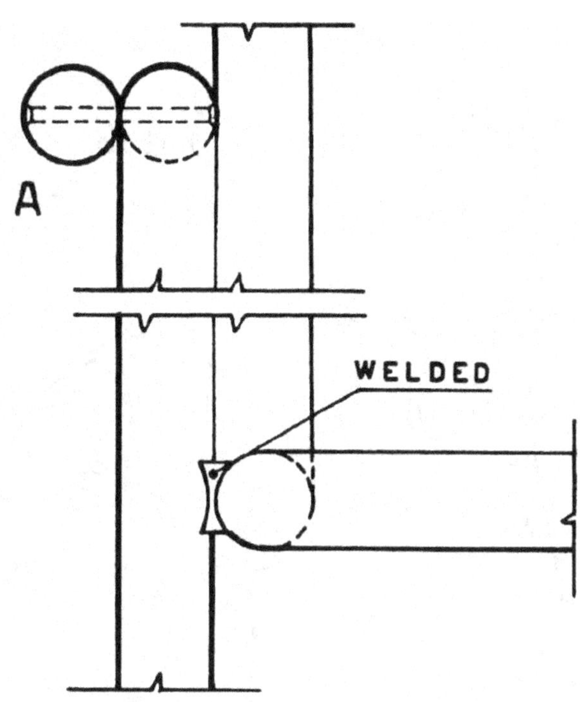

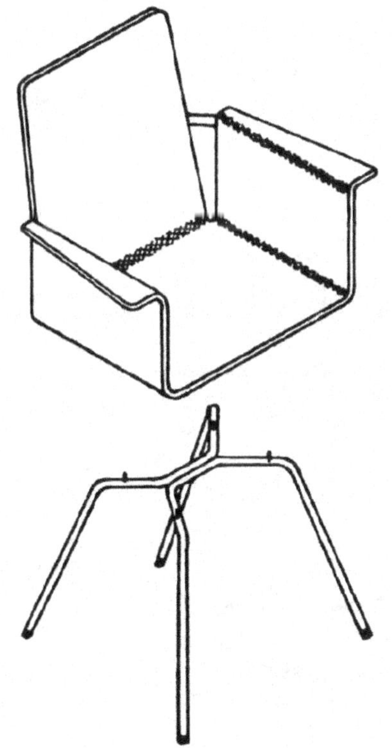

PLASTIC CHAIR THAT CAN BE UPHOLSTERED WITH RUB-
BER. LEGS ARE OF METAL.

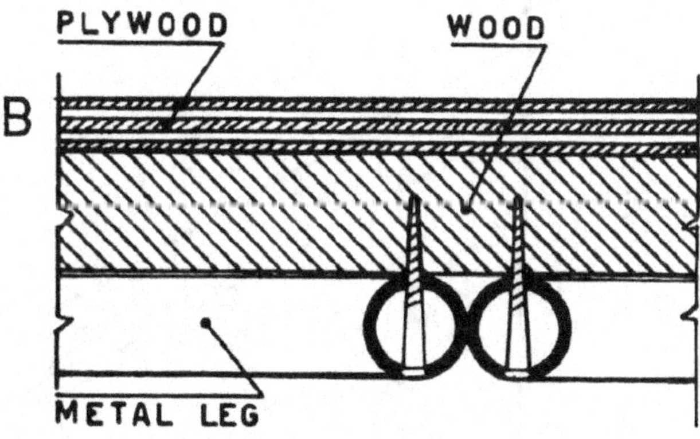

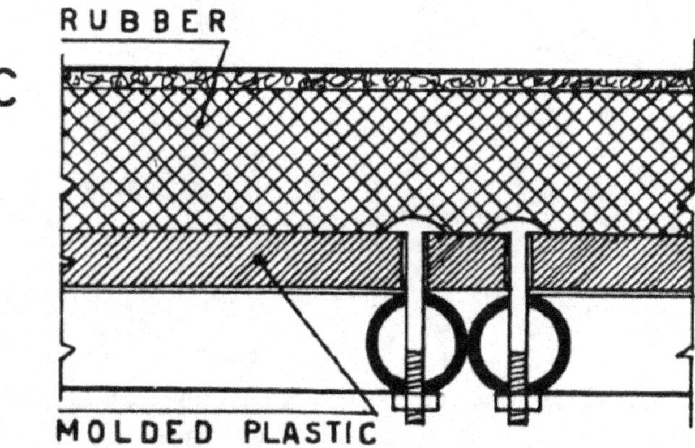

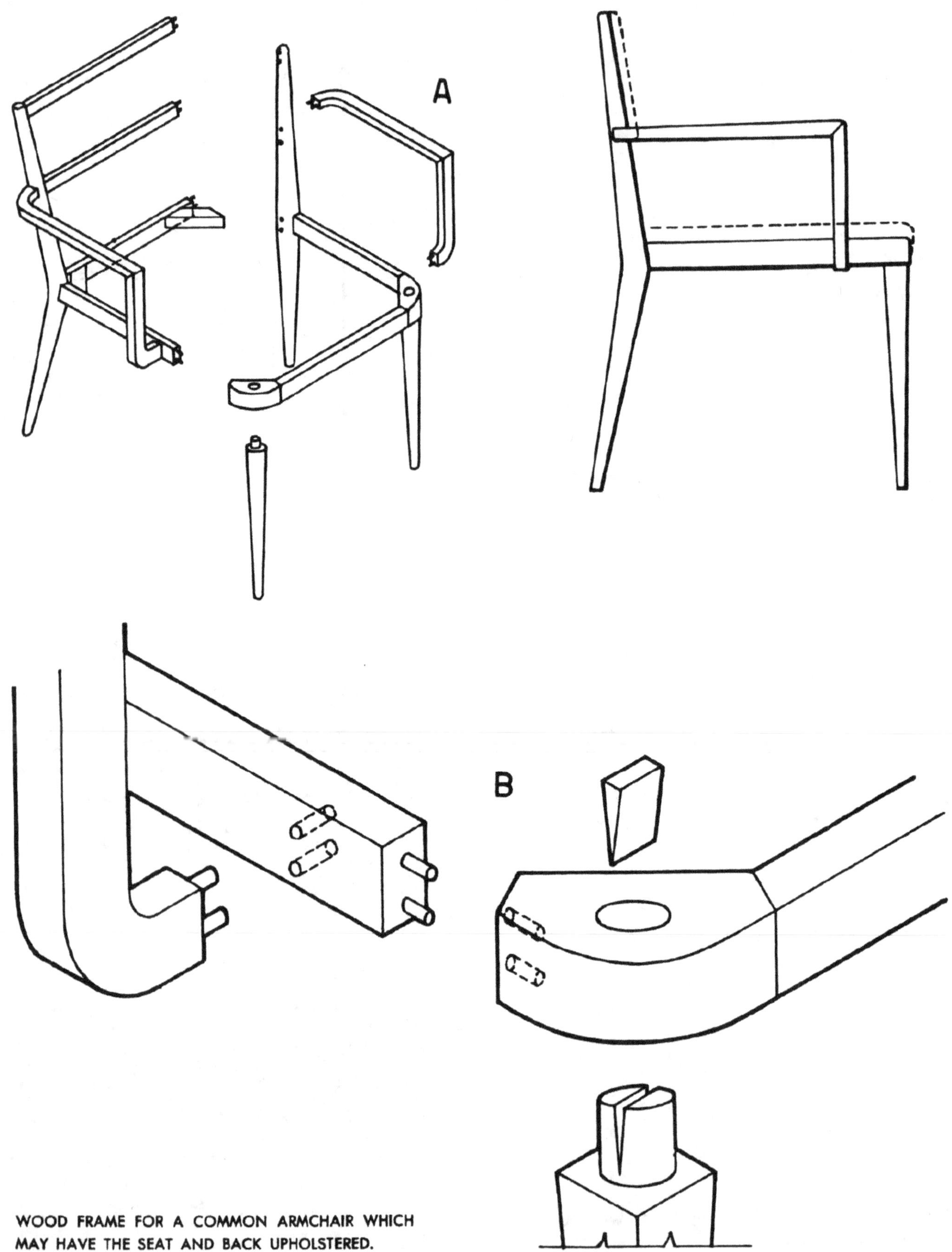

WOOD FRAME FOR A COMMON ARMCHAIR WHICH
MAY HAVE THE SEAT AND BACK UPHOLSTERED.

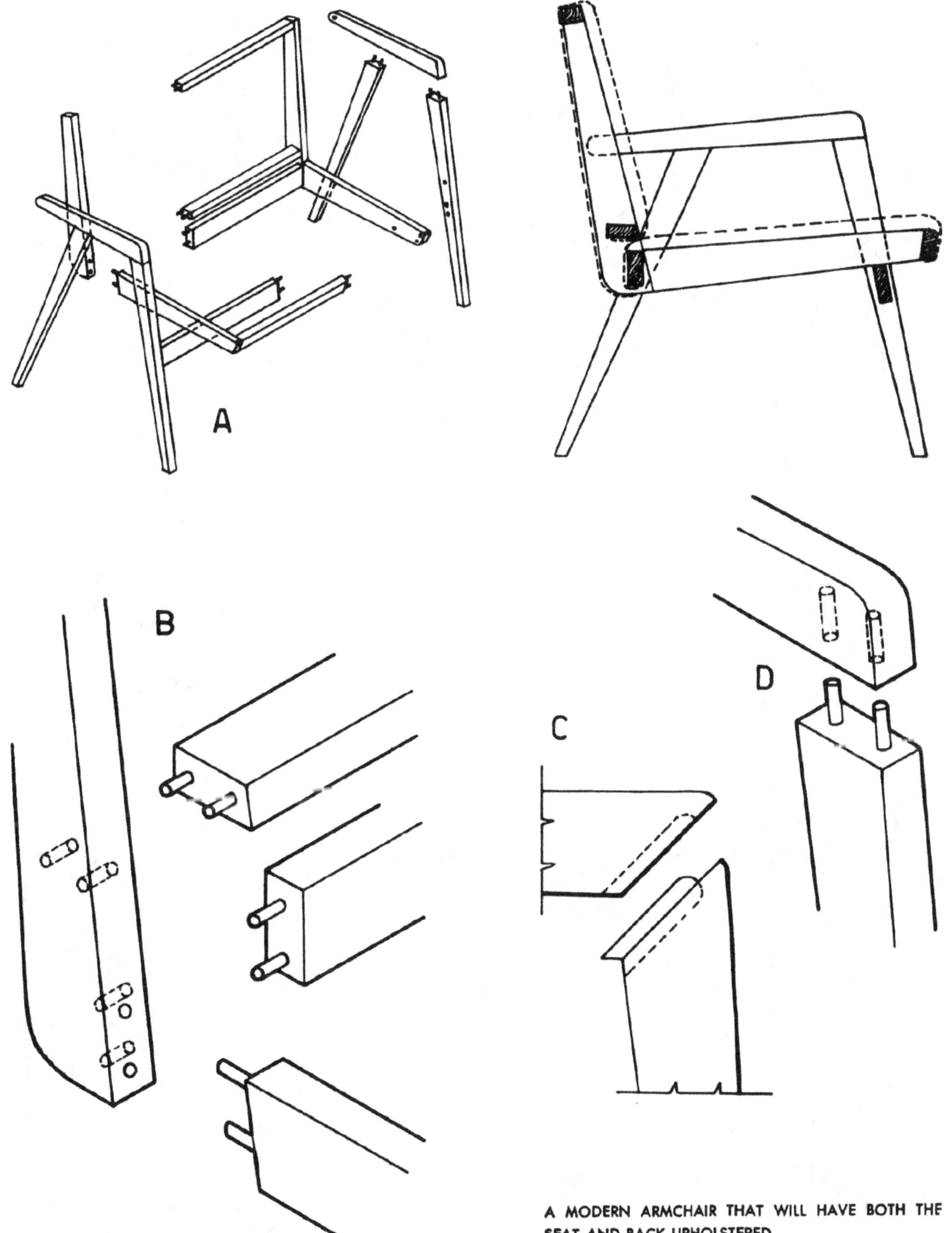

A MODERN ARMCHAIR THAT WILL HAVE BOTH THE SEAT AND BACK UPHOLSTERED.

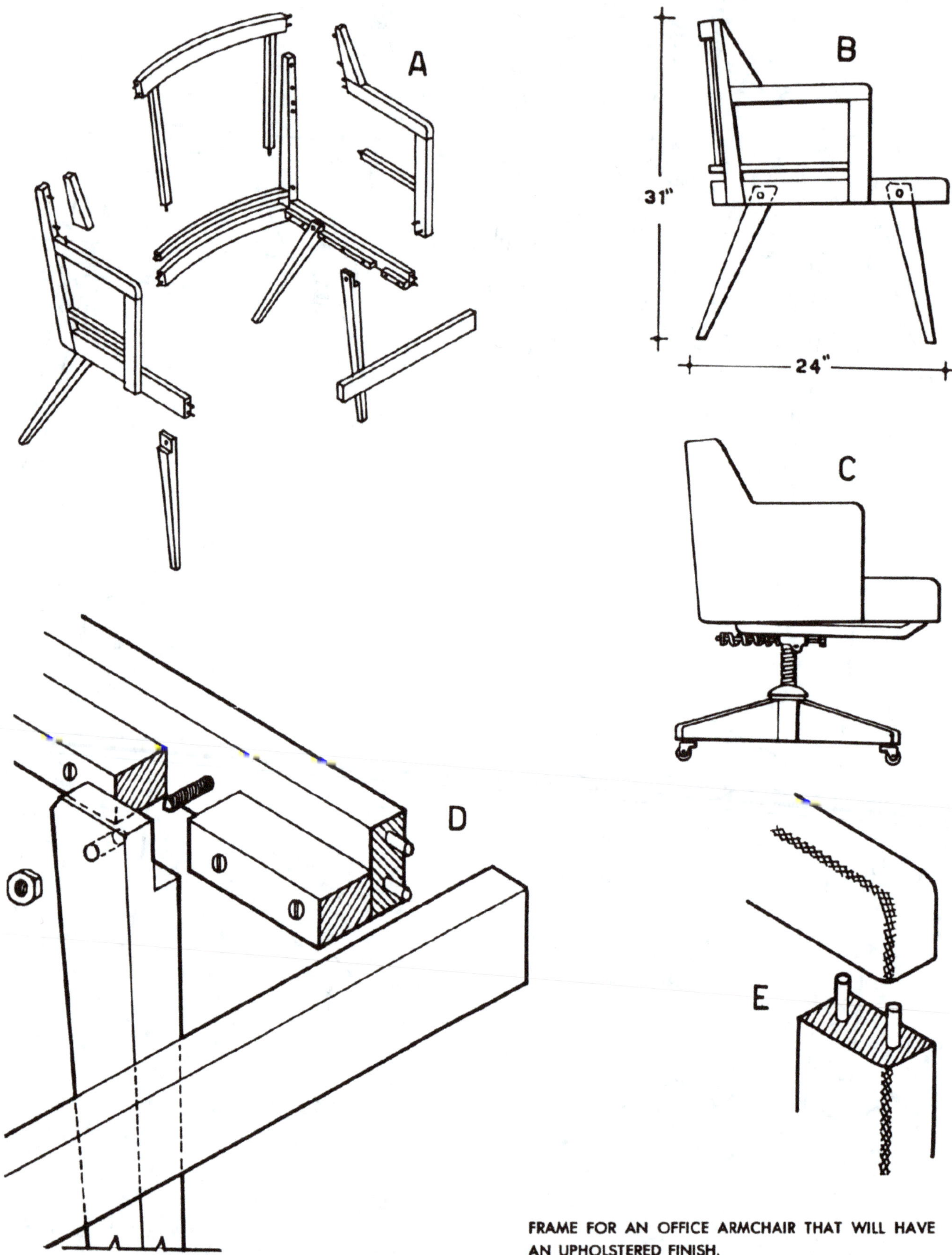

FRAME FOR AN OFFICE ARMCHAIR THAT WILL HAVE AN UPHOLSTERED FINISH.

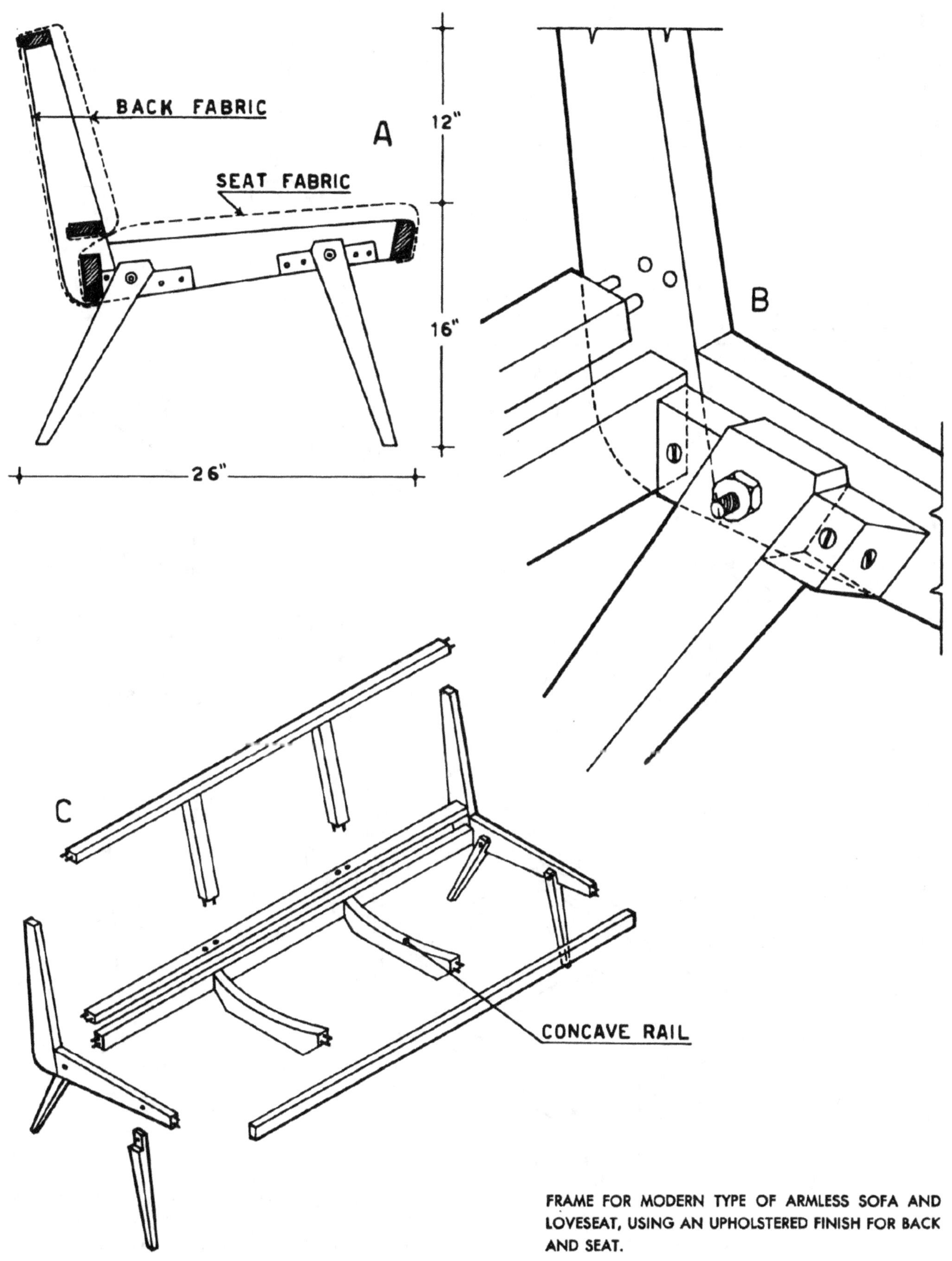

FRAME FOR MODERN TYPE OF ARMLESS SOFA AND LOVESEAT, USING AN UPHOLSTERED FINISH FOR BACK AND SEAT.

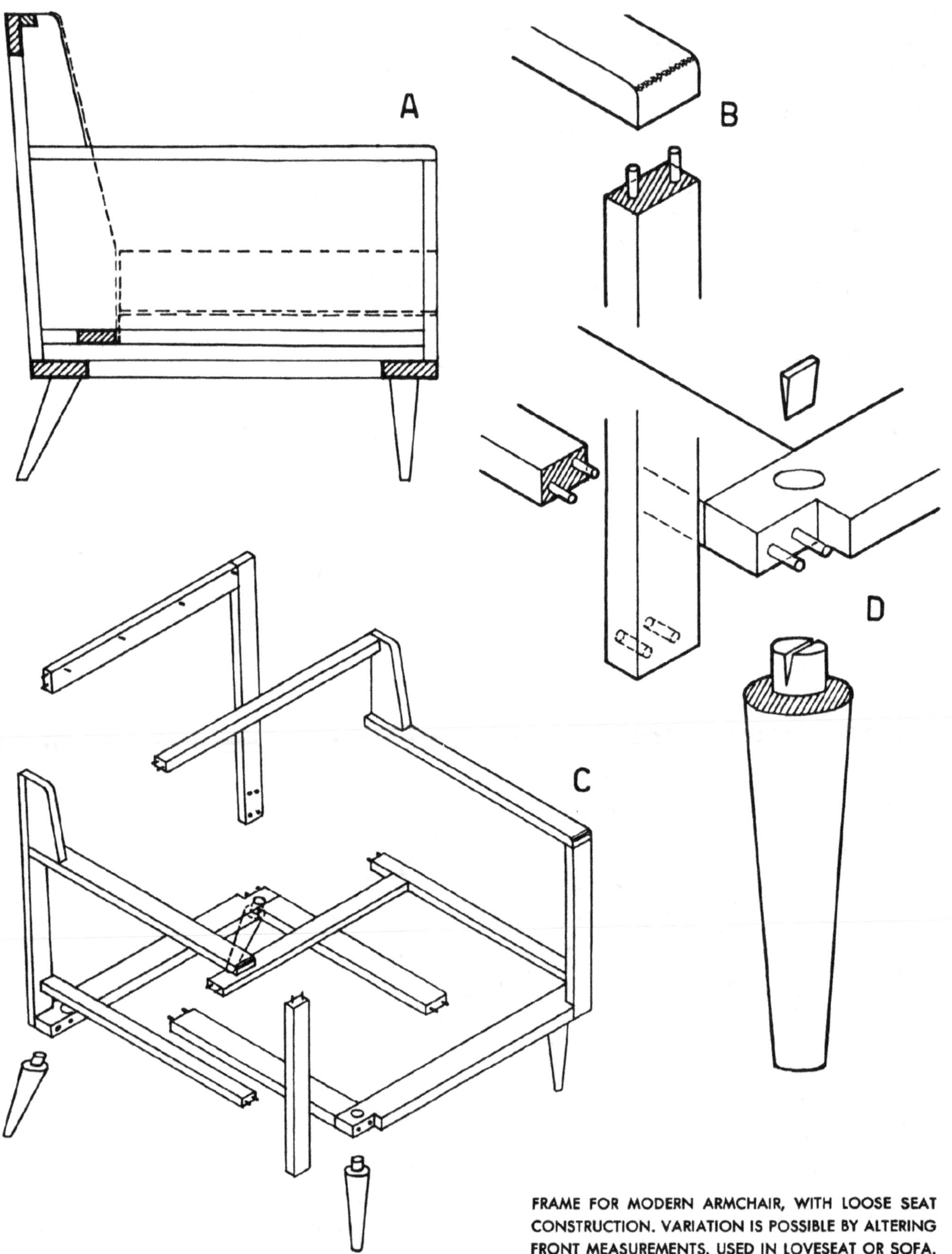

FRAME FOR MODERN ARMCHAIR, WITH LOOSE SEAT
CONSTRUCTION. VARIATION IS POSSIBLE BY ALTERING
FRONT MEASUREMENTS. USED IN LOVESEAT OR SOFA.

UPHOLSTERY MATERIALS

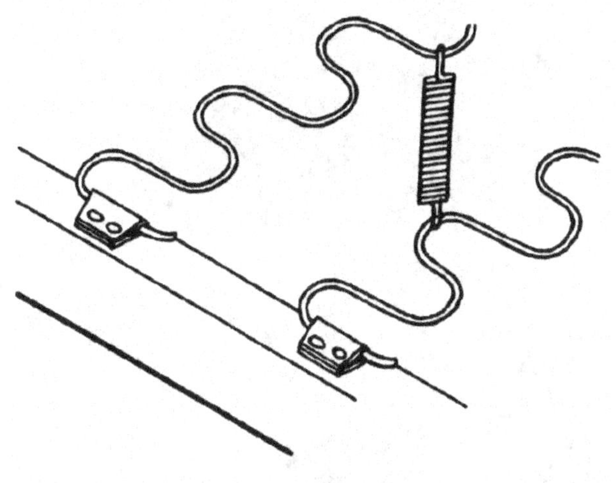

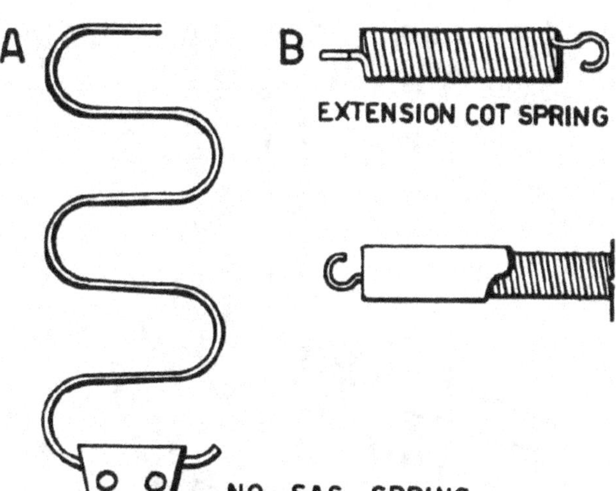

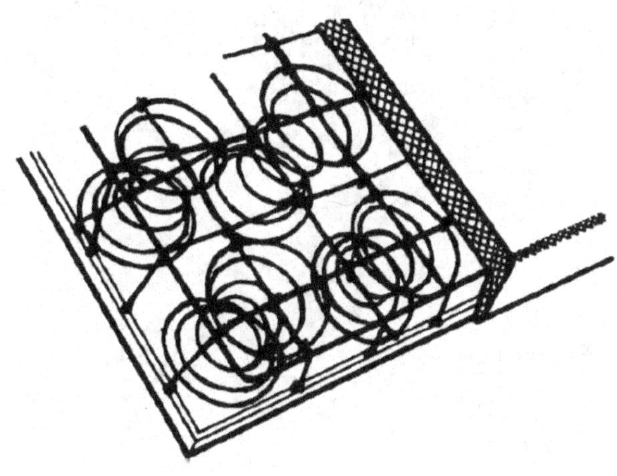

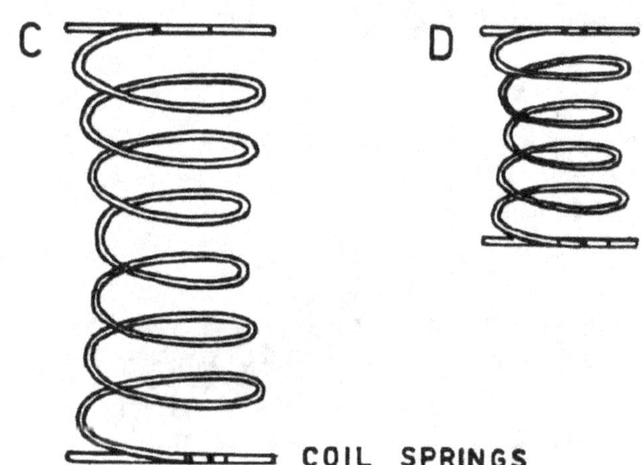

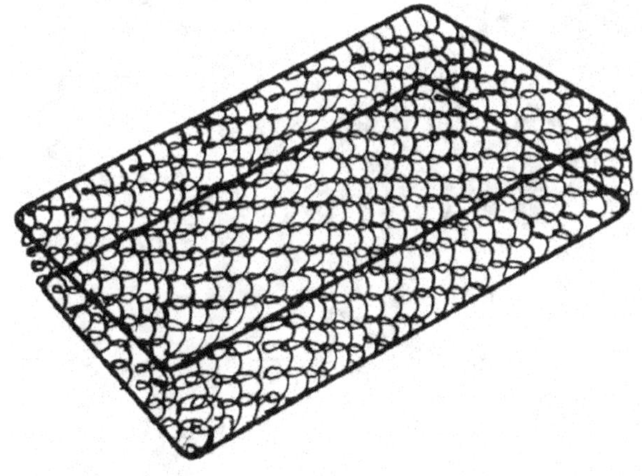

VARIOUS TYPES OF SPRINGS USED IN UPHOLSTERY WORK.

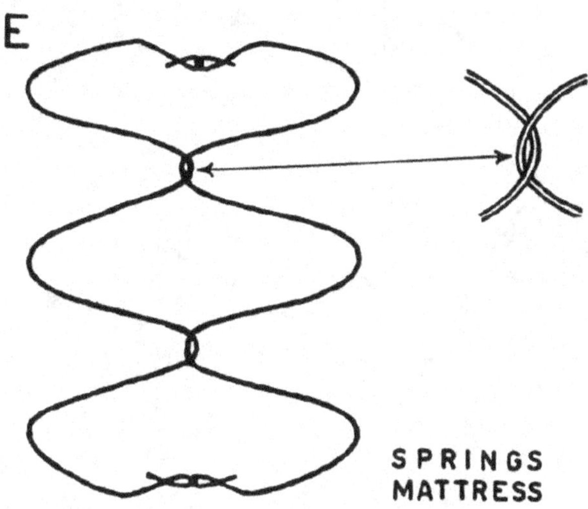

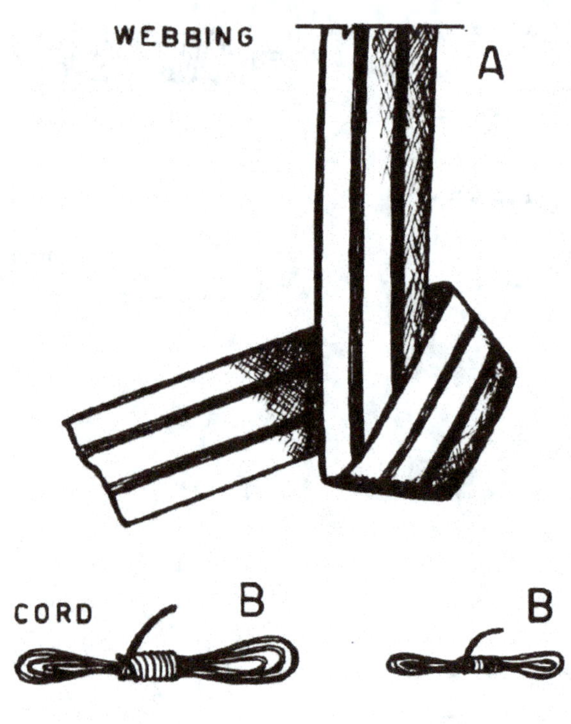

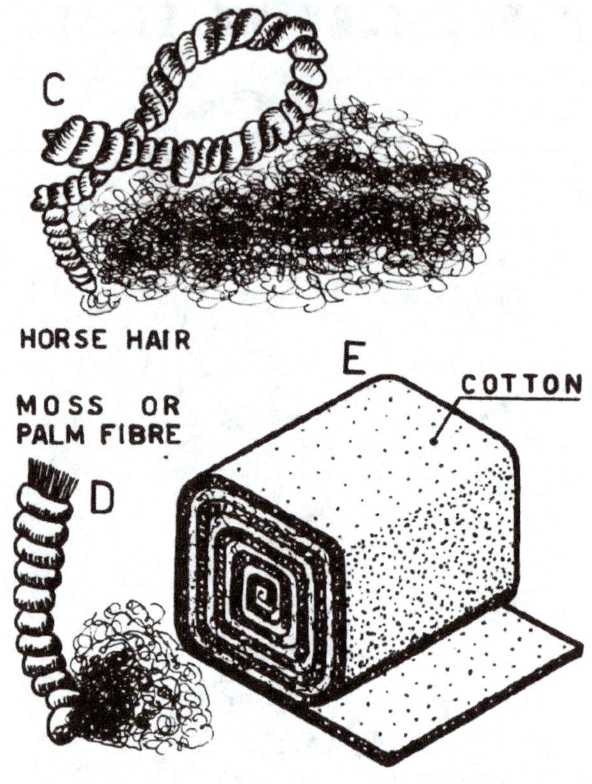

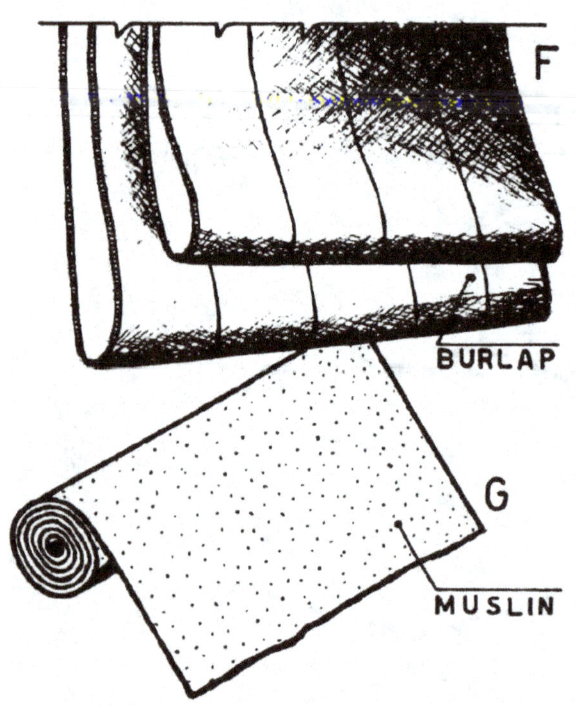

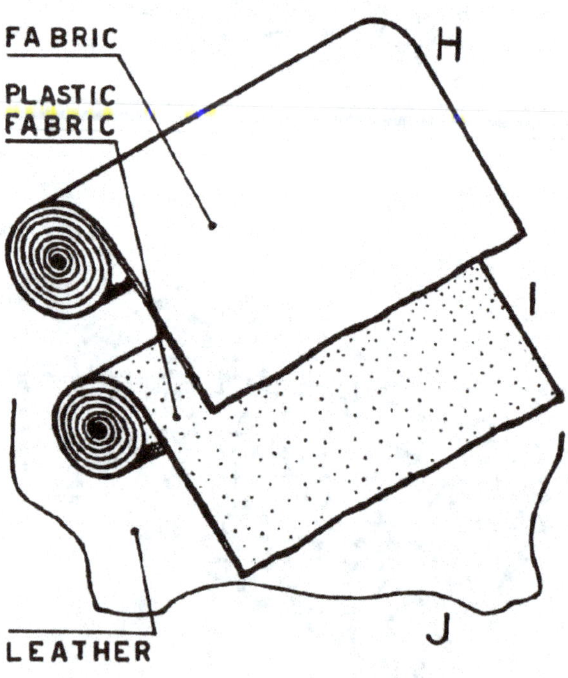

VARIOUS MATERIALS USED IN UPHOLSTERY.

RUBBERIZED HAIR

A LIGHT AND ELASTIC MATERIAL OF RELATIVE LOW COST WHICH IS USED IN MASS PRODUCTION. IT CAN BE EASILY APPLIED USING STAPLES OR TACKS, AND THE SIZE IS THE SAME AS FOAM RUBBER.

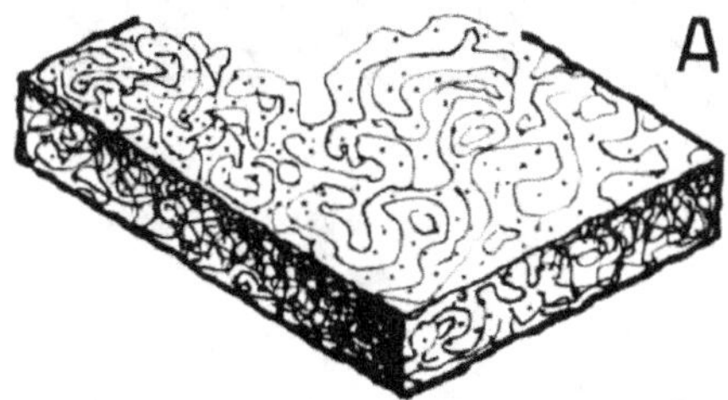

FOAM RUBBER

MADE FROM LIQUID LATEX WHICH FORMS A CREAM-LIKE FOAM AFTER BEING PUT THROUGH AIR PRESSURE. IT IS THEN POURED INTO MOLDS OF DESIRED SIZE. IN UPHOLSTERY WORK IT GIVES BETTER RESULTS THAN STUFFING AND IS QUICKER AND EASIER TO USE.

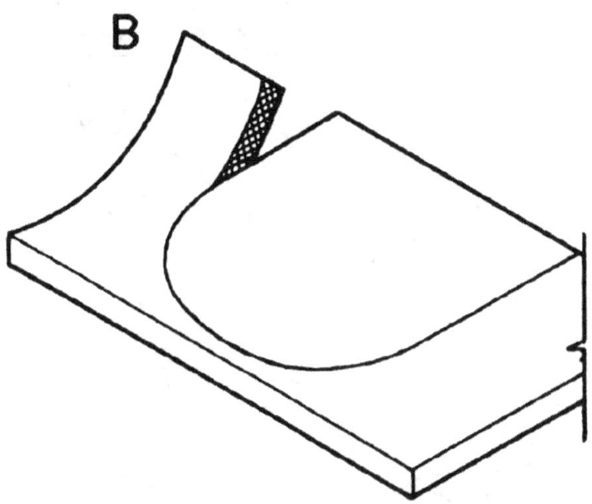

CUT FOAM RUBBER WITH SCISSORS FOR CUSTOM WORK. USE BAND SAW FOR STANDARD PRODUCTION. RUBBER SLABS GLUED TOGETHER WITH CEMENT.

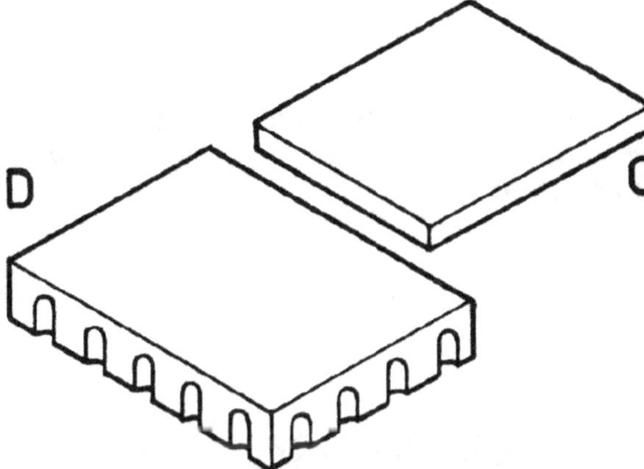

C — SOLID SLAB UTILITY STOCK COMES IN MANY THICKNESSES FROM ¼" TO 1¼".

D — CORED UTILITY STOCK IS DIFFERENT FROM THE SOLID SLAB IN THAT IT HAS A UNIFORM OPEN CORE. ITS THICKNESS VARIES FROM ¾" TO 4½".

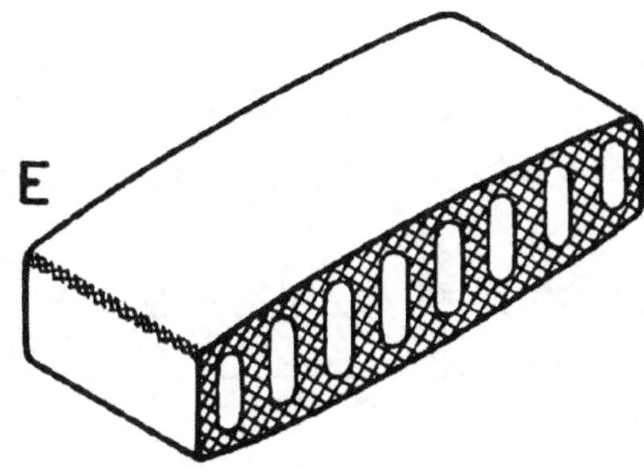

E — FULL MOLDED CUSHION CAN BE MADE IN DIFFERENT SIZES AND SHAPES.

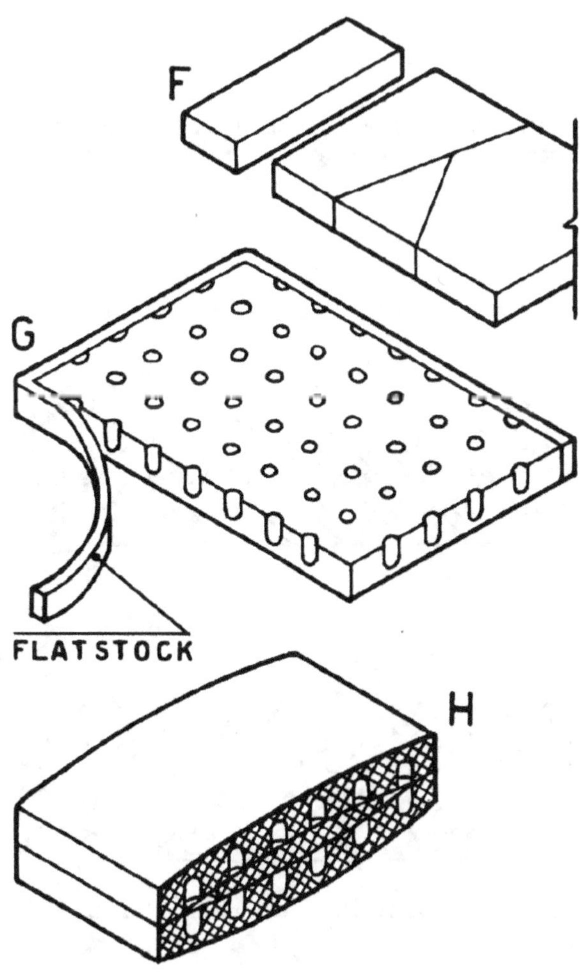

F — SMALL PIECES GLUED TOGETHER TO FORM ONE LARGE PIECE. G — FLATSTOCK GLUED TO A SLAB. H — A FULL CUSHION MADE FROM CORED STOCK.

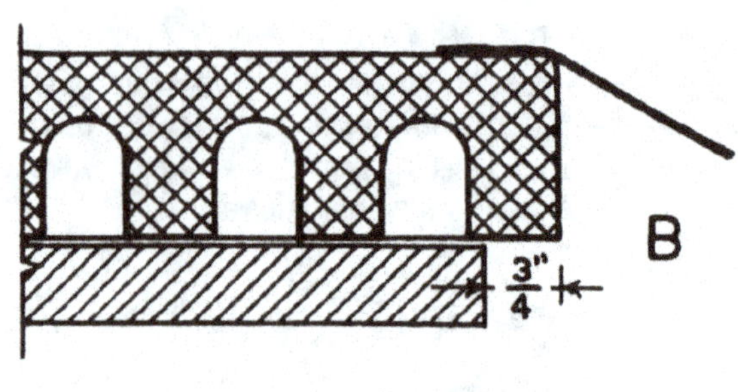

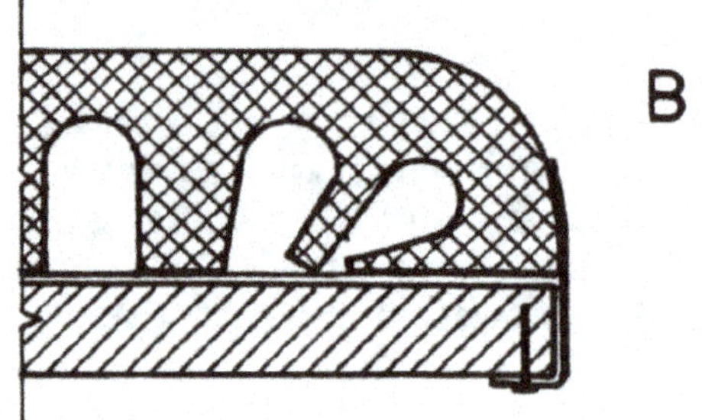

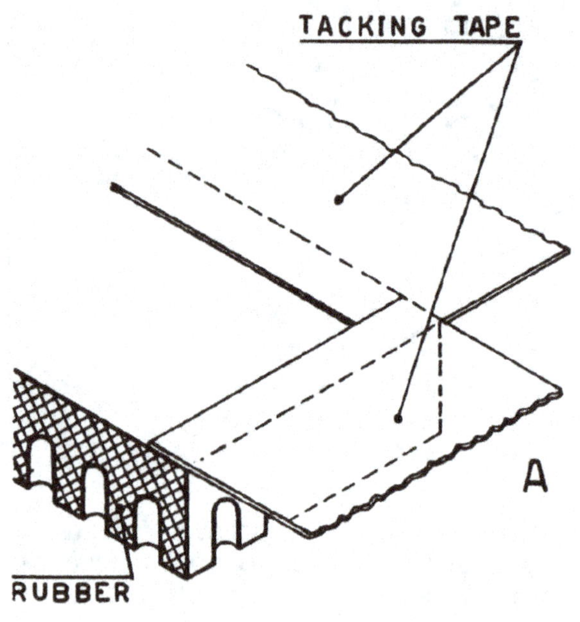

METHOD OF APPLYING TACKING TAPE AROUND THE EDGES OF A FOAM RUBBER SLAB USING CEMENT.

IN MAKING CONTOURED EDGES THE FOAM RUBBER SHOULD BE CUT ¾" LARGER THAN THE PIECE BEING UPHOLSTERED.

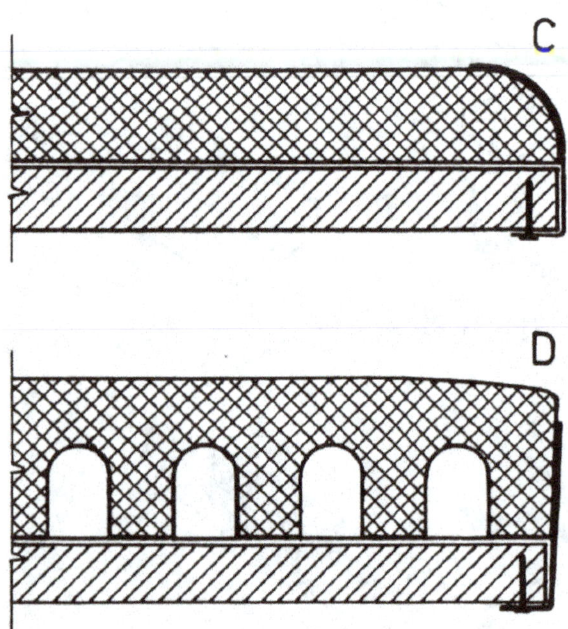

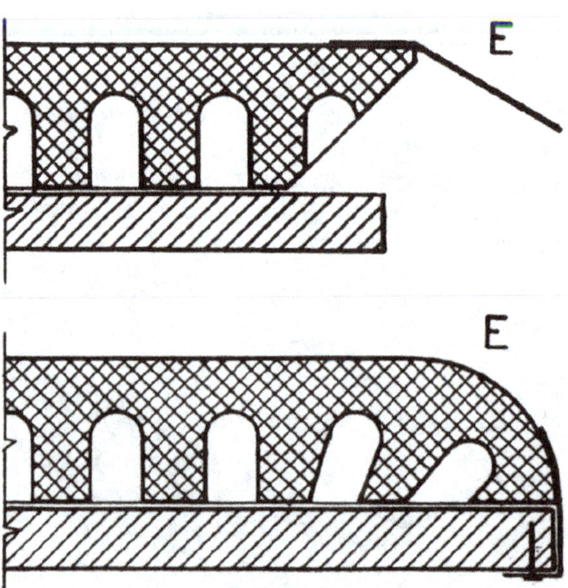

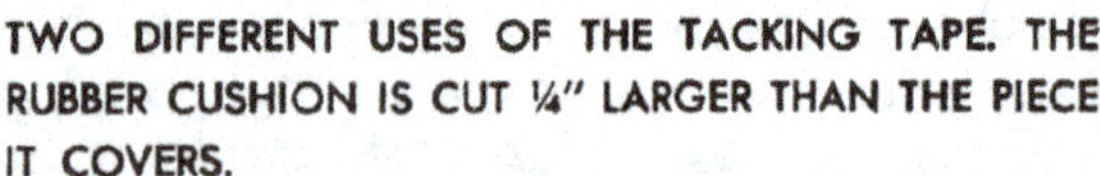

TWO DIFFERENT USES OF THE TACKING TAPE. THE RUBBER CUSHION IS CUT ¼" LARGER THAN THE PIECE IT COVERS.

ANOTHER WAY OF MAKING A CURVED EDGE.

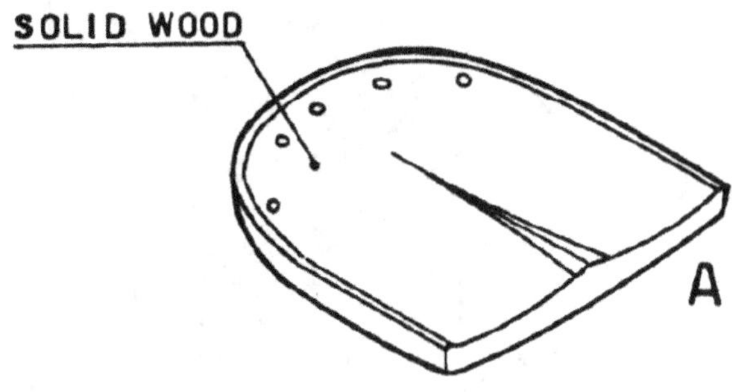

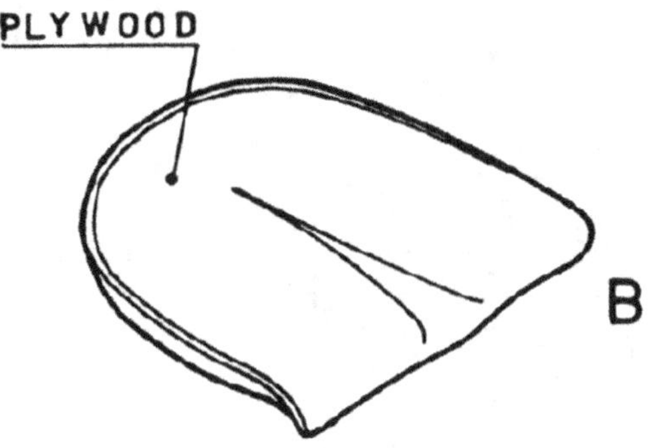

TWO TYPES OF WOOD SEAT THAT MAY BE USED. THE UPPER ONE IS OF SOLID WOOD, THE LOWER OF PLYWOOD.

SEATS

THE SEAT DESIGN IS THE MOST IMPORTANT POINT IN UPHOLSTERY WORK FOR UPON ITS CONSTRUCTION DEPENDS THE USEFULNESS OF THE CHAIR OR DIVAN. EACH SEAT MUST BE MADE IN ACCORDANCE WITH THE TYPE OF FRAME TO WHICH IT IS ATTACHED. IT MAY BE MOVABLE OR FIXED, LIGHT OR HEAVY. A WIDE VARIETY OF MATERIALS MAY BE USED.

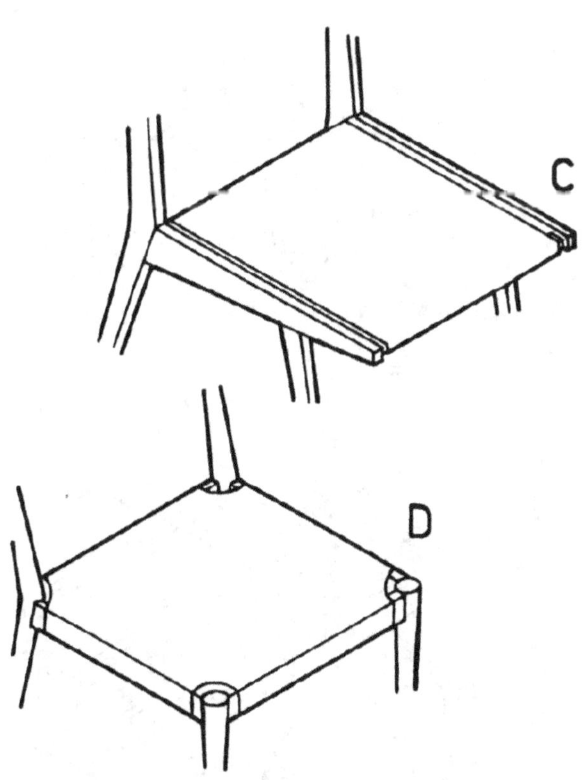

LEATHER SEATS LIKE THESE ARE EASY TO MAKE.

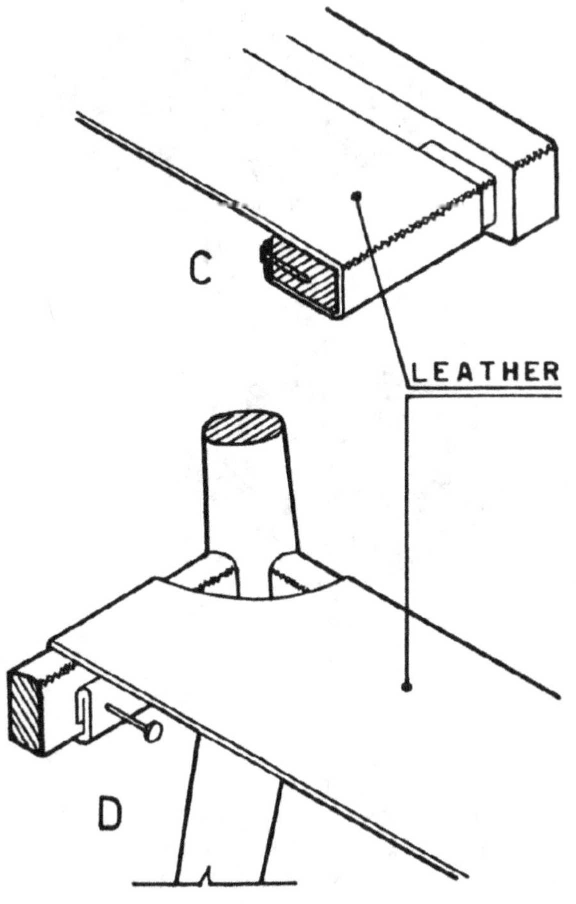

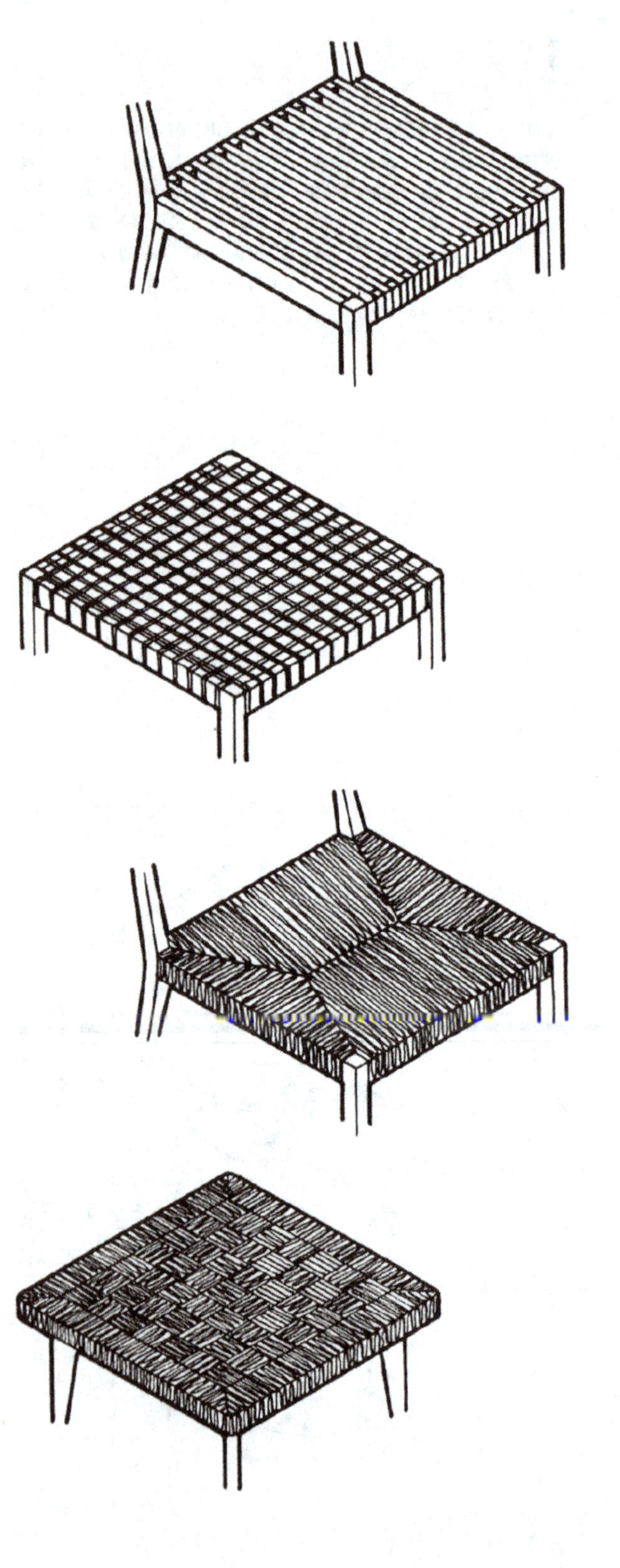

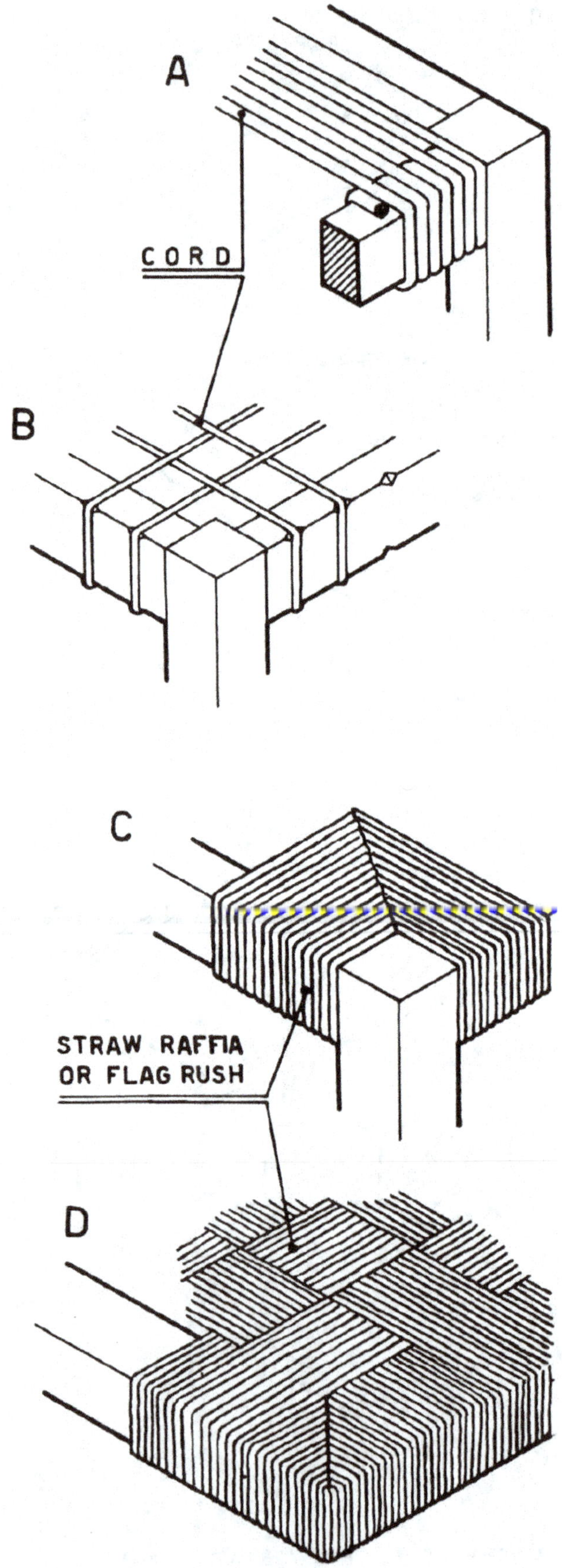

VARIOUS TYPES OF SEATS THAT CAN BE MADE WITH CORD, STRAW, RAFFIA OR FLAG RUSH. IN GENERAL, ANY OF THESE SYSTEMS IS TIME-CONSUMING.

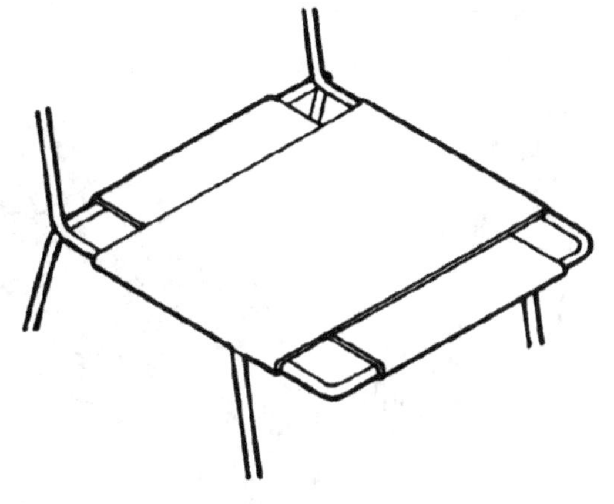

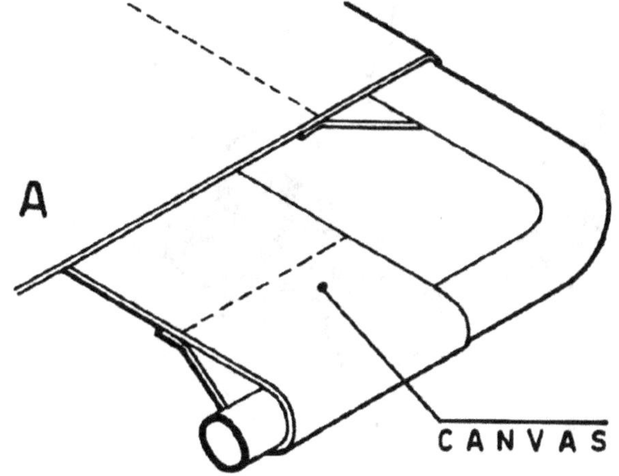

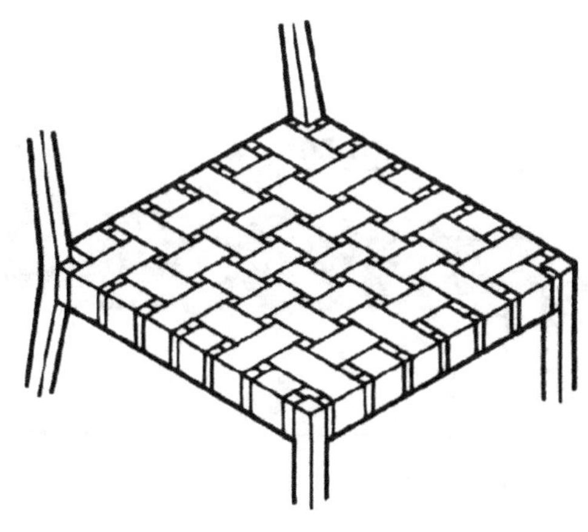

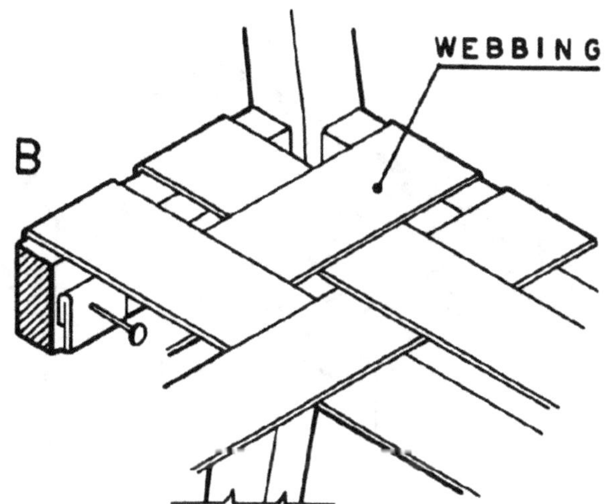

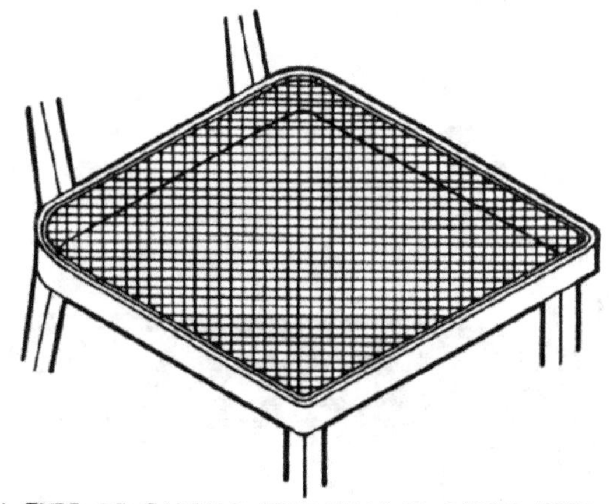

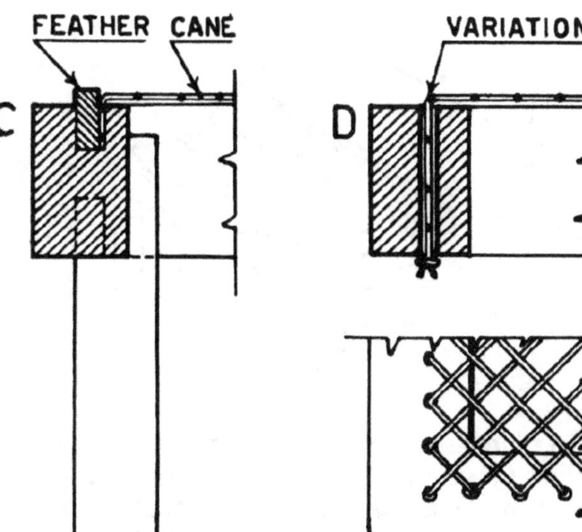

A — A TYPE OF CANVAS SEAT THAT IS OFTEN USED WITH STEEL FRAMES.

B — WEBBING SEAT WHICH IS USED ON MODERN FURNITURE.

C — CANE MAKES A GOOD TYPE OF SEAT. NOTE THE ALTERNATE METHOD OF ATTACHING THE CANE SHOWN IN DIAGRAM D.

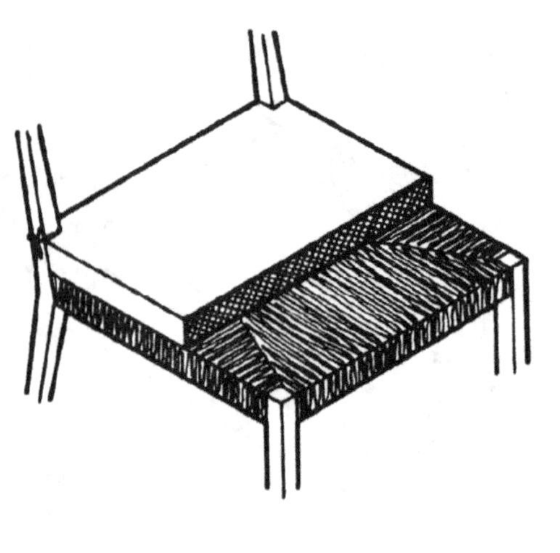
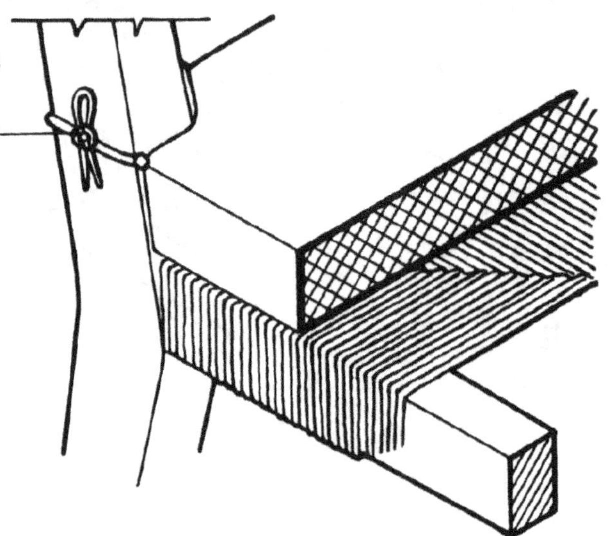

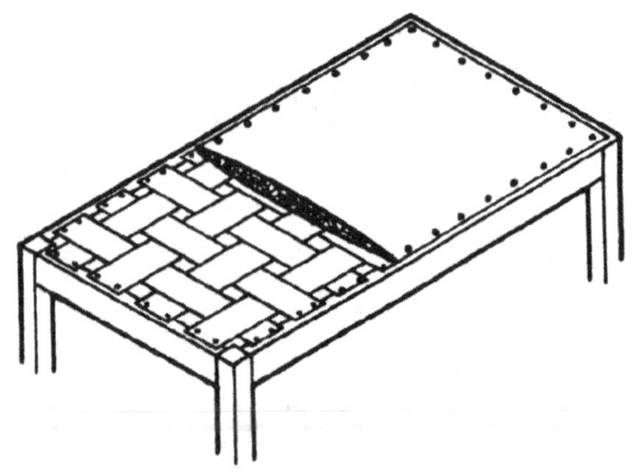
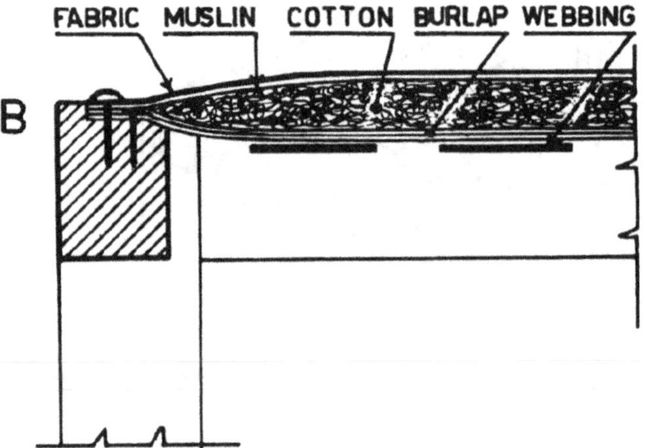

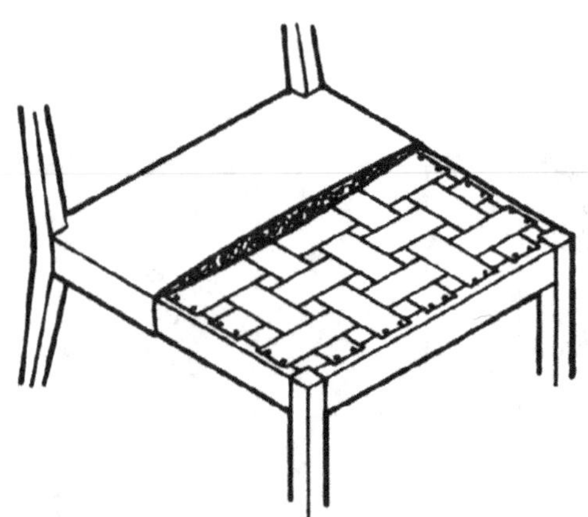
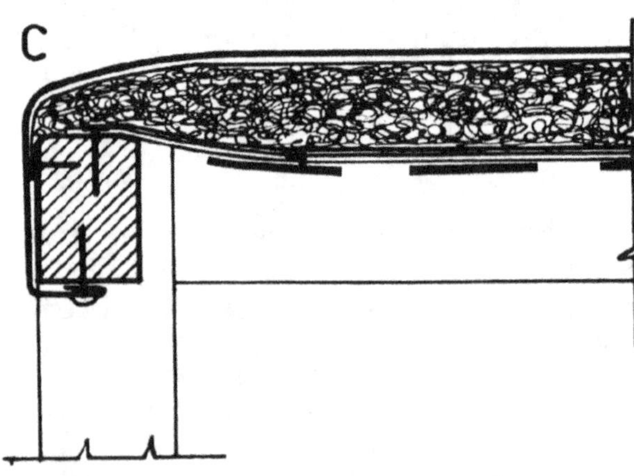

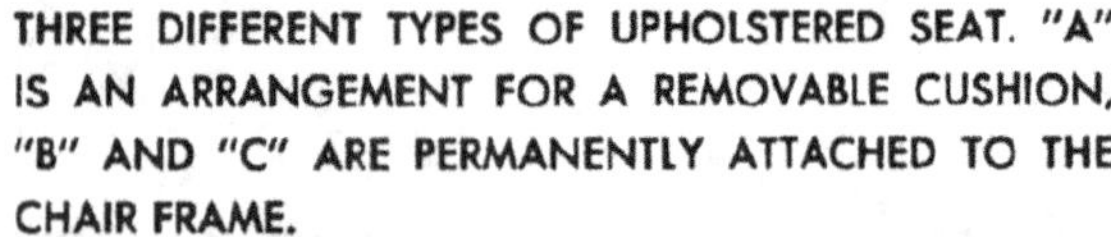

THREE DIFFERENT TYPES OF UPHOLSTERED SEAT. "A" IS AN ARRANGEMENT FOR A REMOVABLE CUSHION, "B" AND "C" ARE PERMANENTLY ATTACHED TO THE CHAIR FRAME.

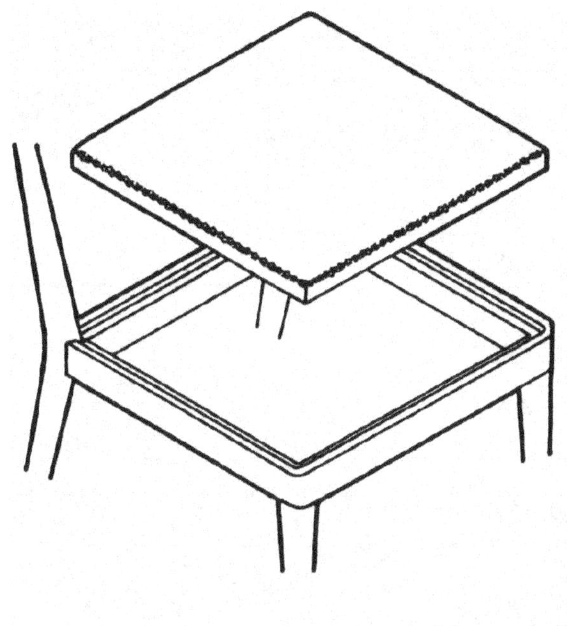

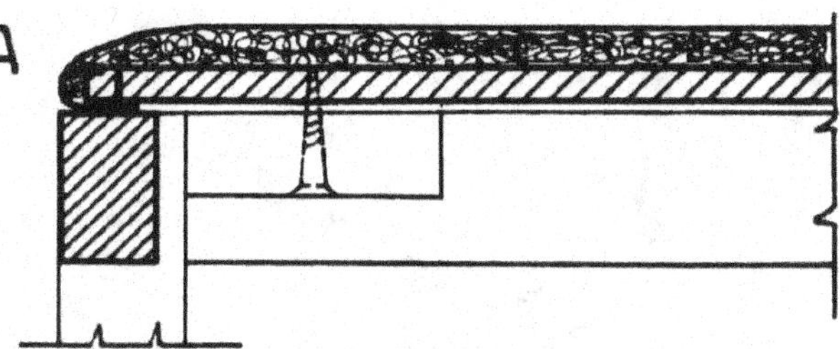

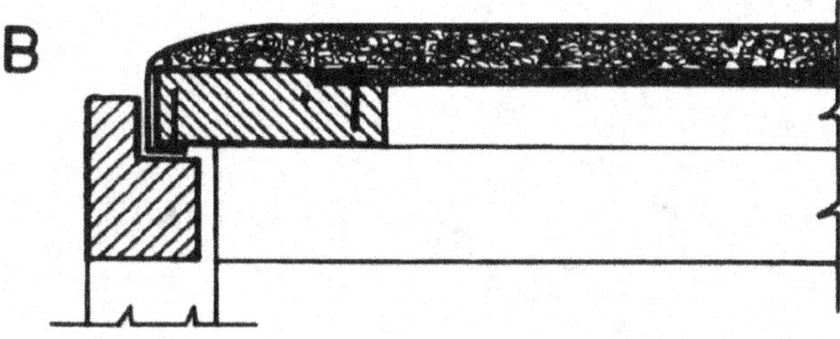

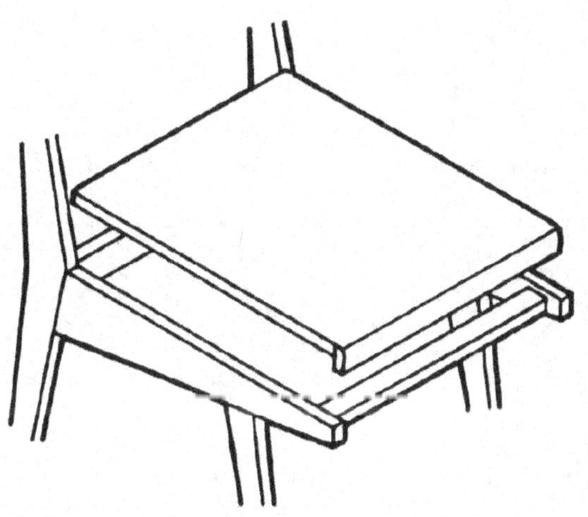

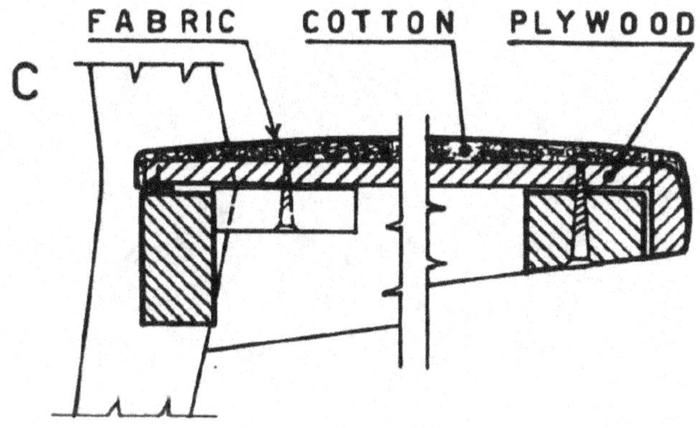

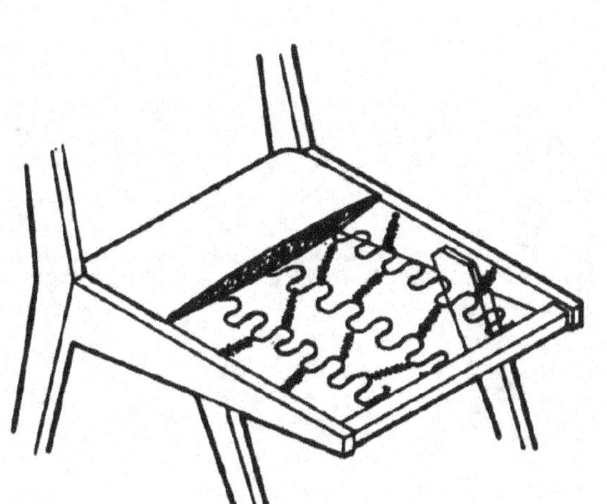

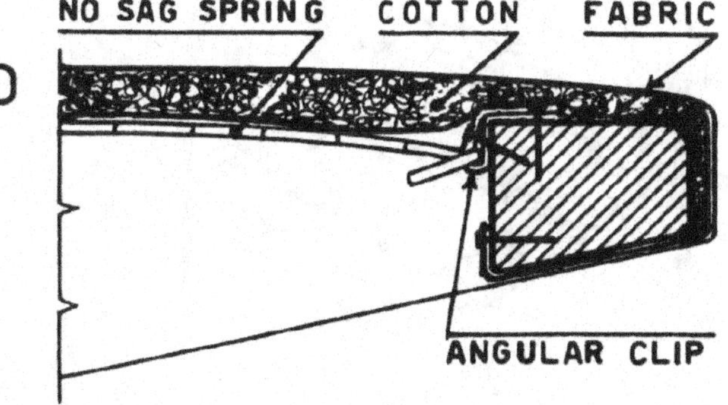

THESE FOUR SEATS ARE MADE INDEPENDENTLY OF THE CHAIR FRAME. IN COMMERCIAL WORK, GREATER SPEED OF ASSEMBLY IS POSSIBLE WHEN THE FRAME AND SEAT CAN BE MADE INDEPENDENTLY.

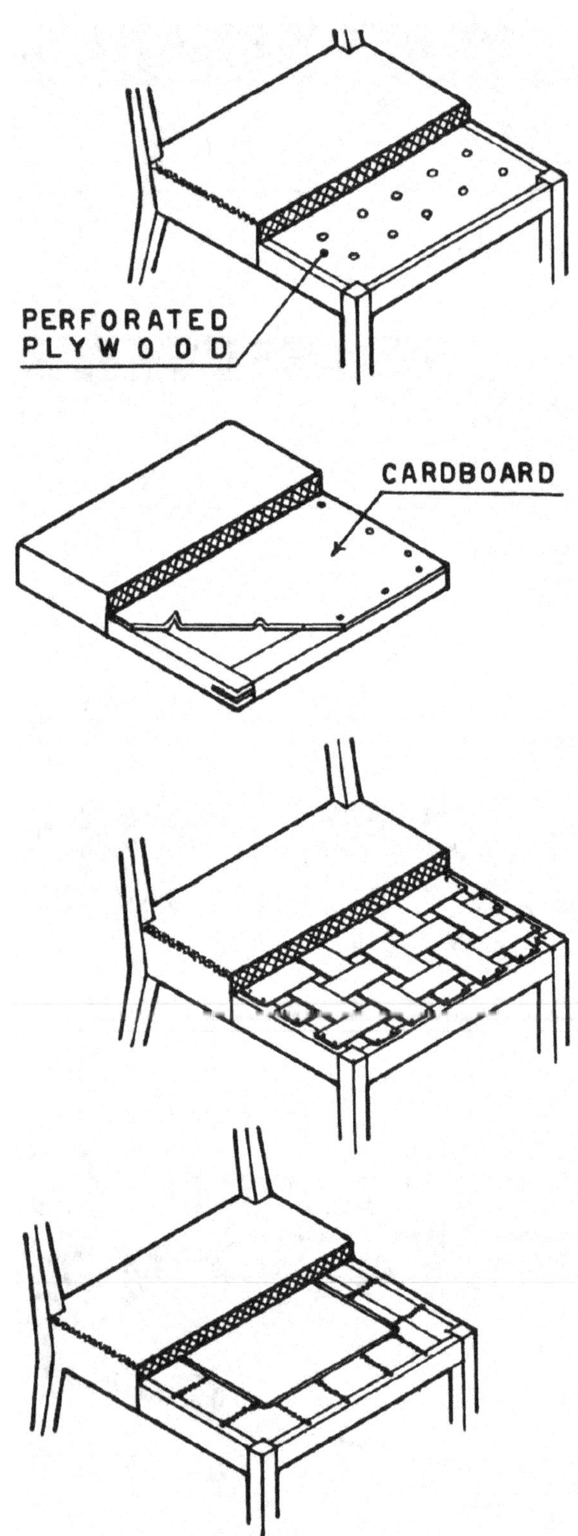

PERFORATED
PLYWOOD
CARDBOARD

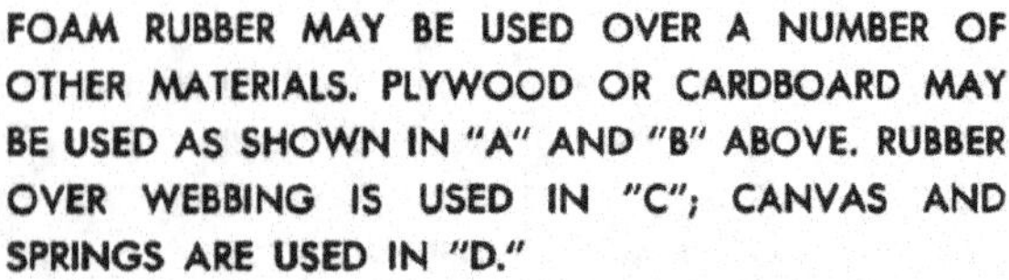

FOAM RUBBER MAY BE USED OVER A NUMBER OF
OTHER MATERIALS. PLYWOOD OR CARDBOARD MAY
BE USED AS SHOWN IN "A" AND "B" ABOVE. RUBBER
OVER WEBBING IS USED IN "C"; CANVAS AND
SPRINGS ARE USED IN "D."

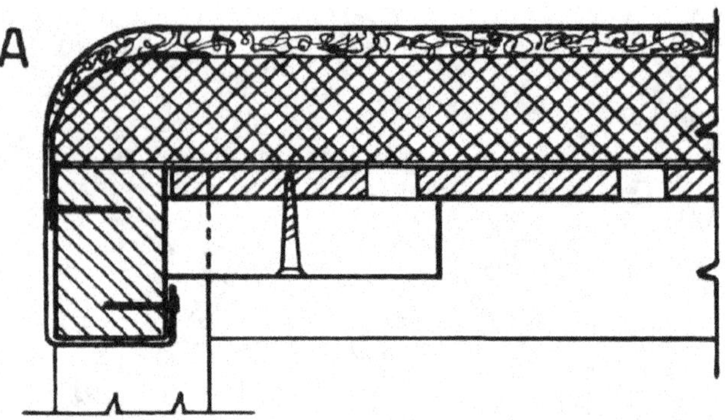

A

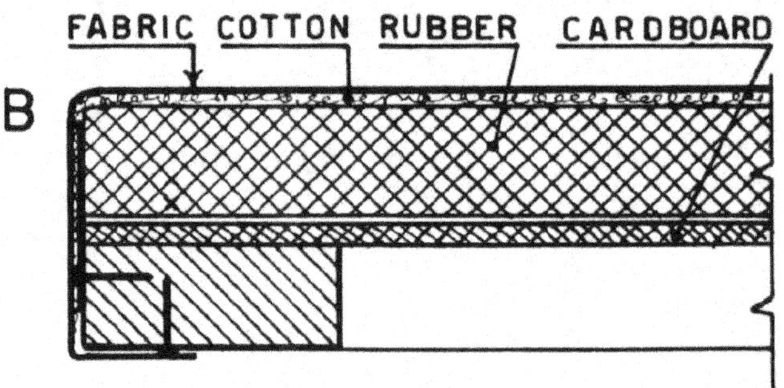

FABRIC COTTON RUBBER CARDBOARD
B

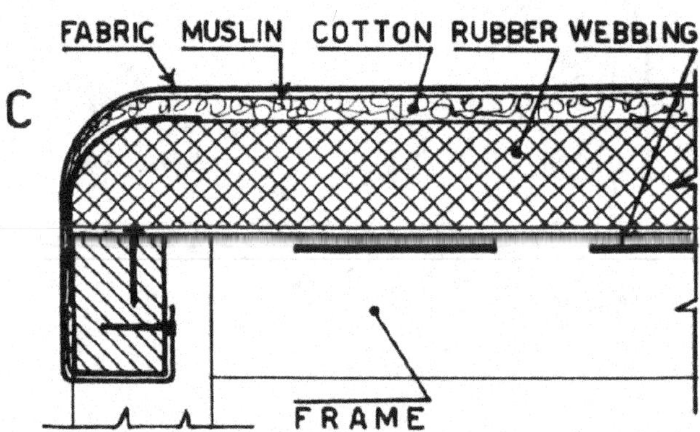

FABRIC MUSLIN COTTON RUBBER WEBBING
C
FRAME

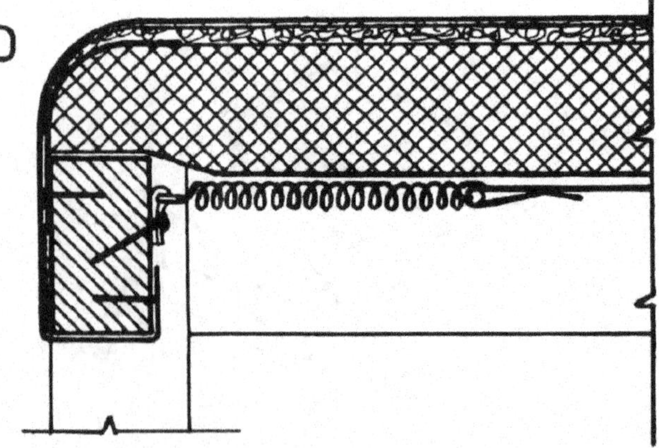

D

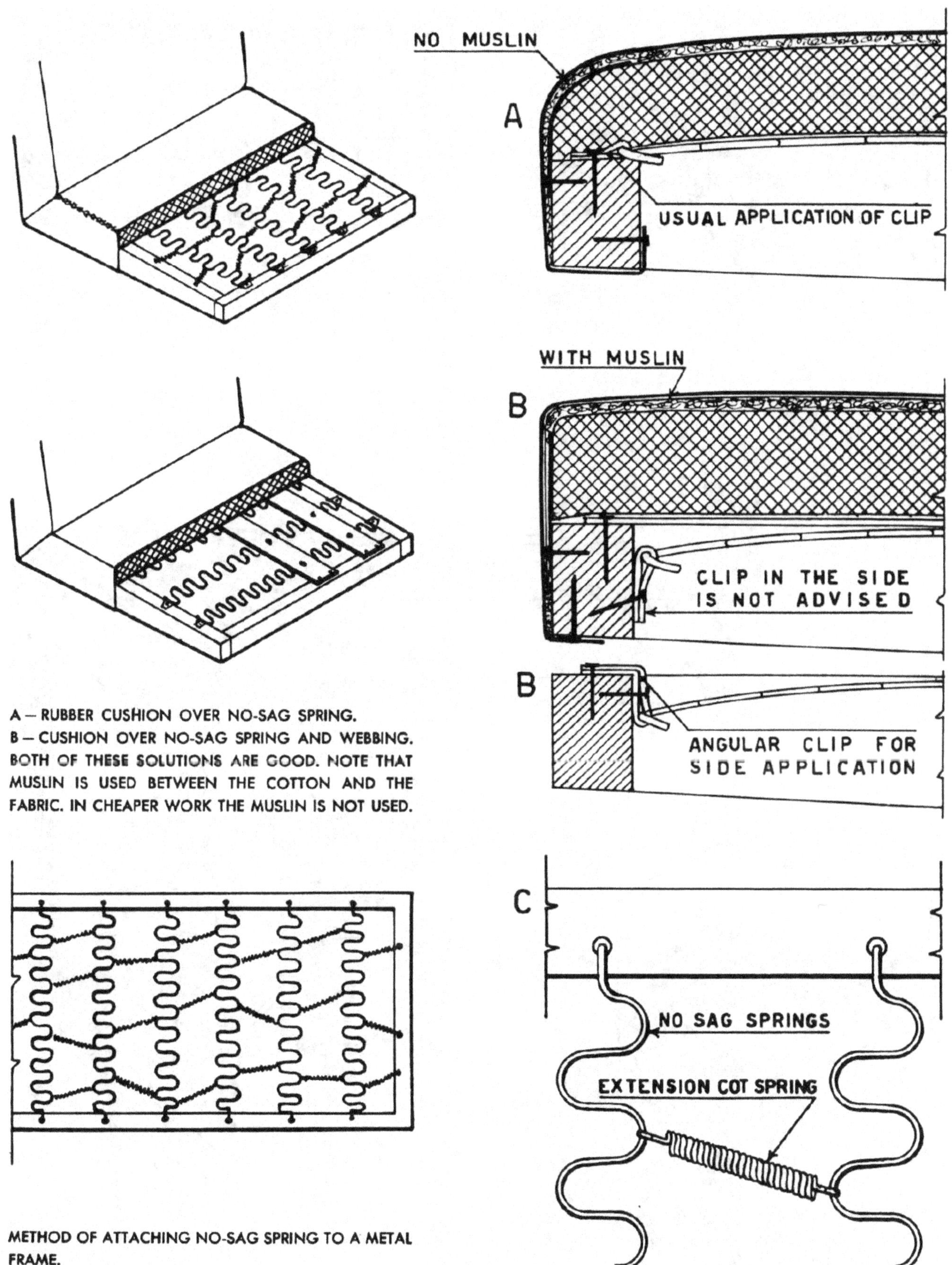

A — RUBBER CUSHION OVER NO-SAG SPRING.
B — CUSHION OVER NO-SAG SPRING AND WEBBING.
BOTH OF THESE SOLUTIONS ARE GOOD. NOTE THAT
MUSLIN IS USED BETWEEN THE COTTON AND THE
FABRIC. IN CHEAPER WORK THE MUSLIN IS NOT USED.

METHOD OF ATTACHING NO-SAG SPRING TO A METAL
FRAME.

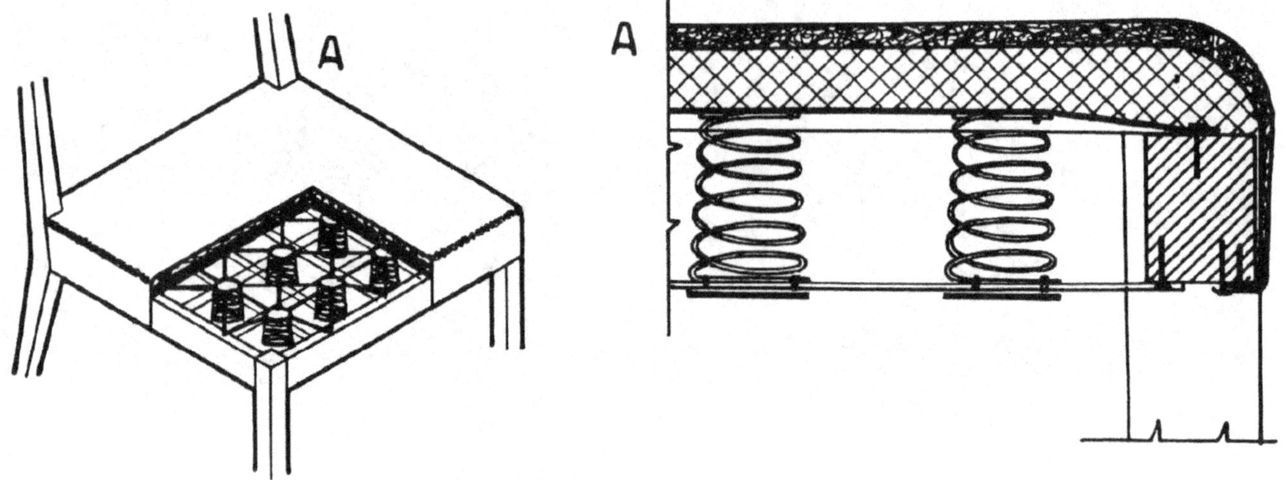

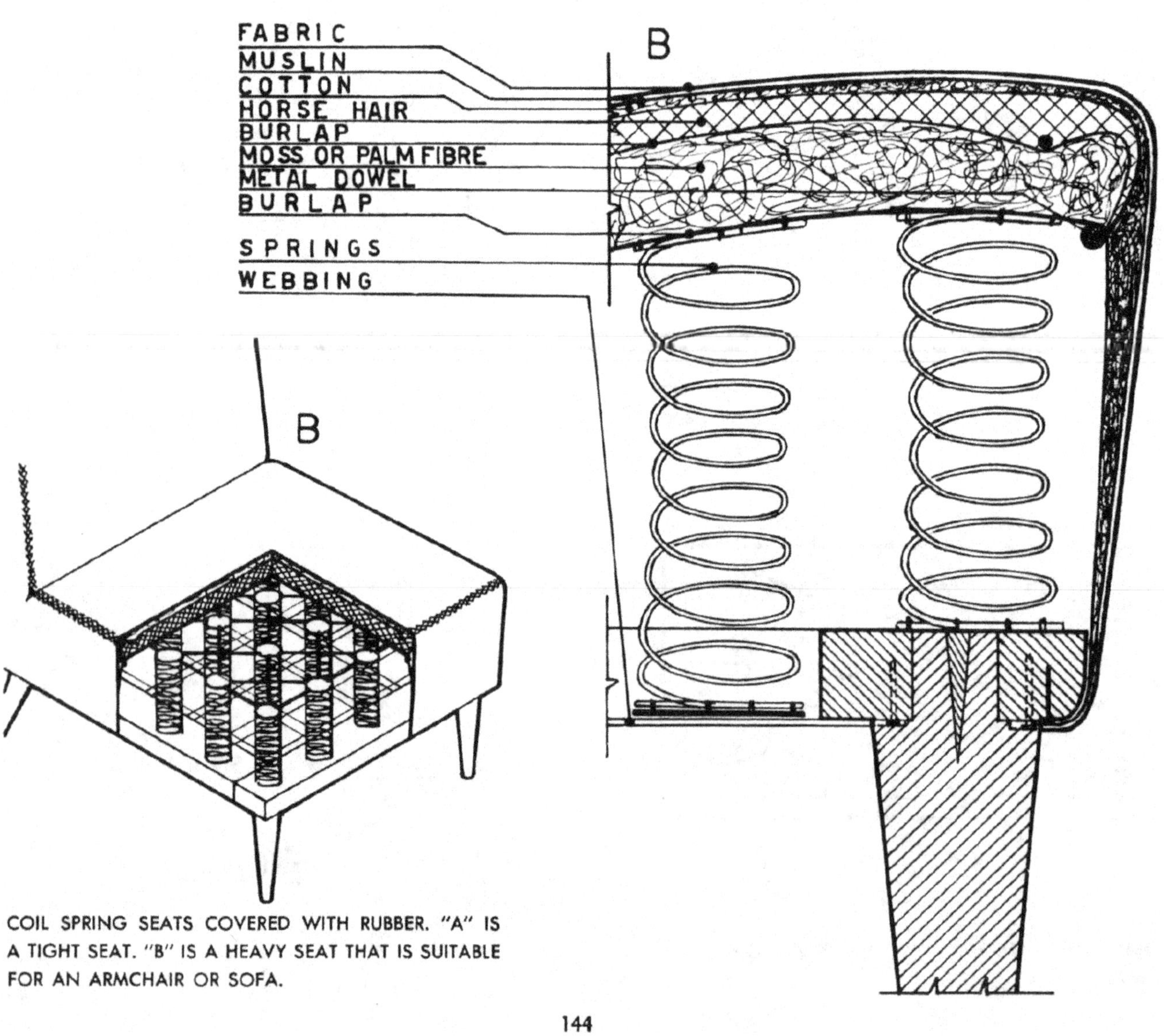

COIL SPRING SEATS COVERED WITH RUBBER. "A" IS
A TIGHT SEAT. "B" IS A HEAVY SEAT THAT IS SUITABLE
FOR AN ARMCHAIR OR SOFA.

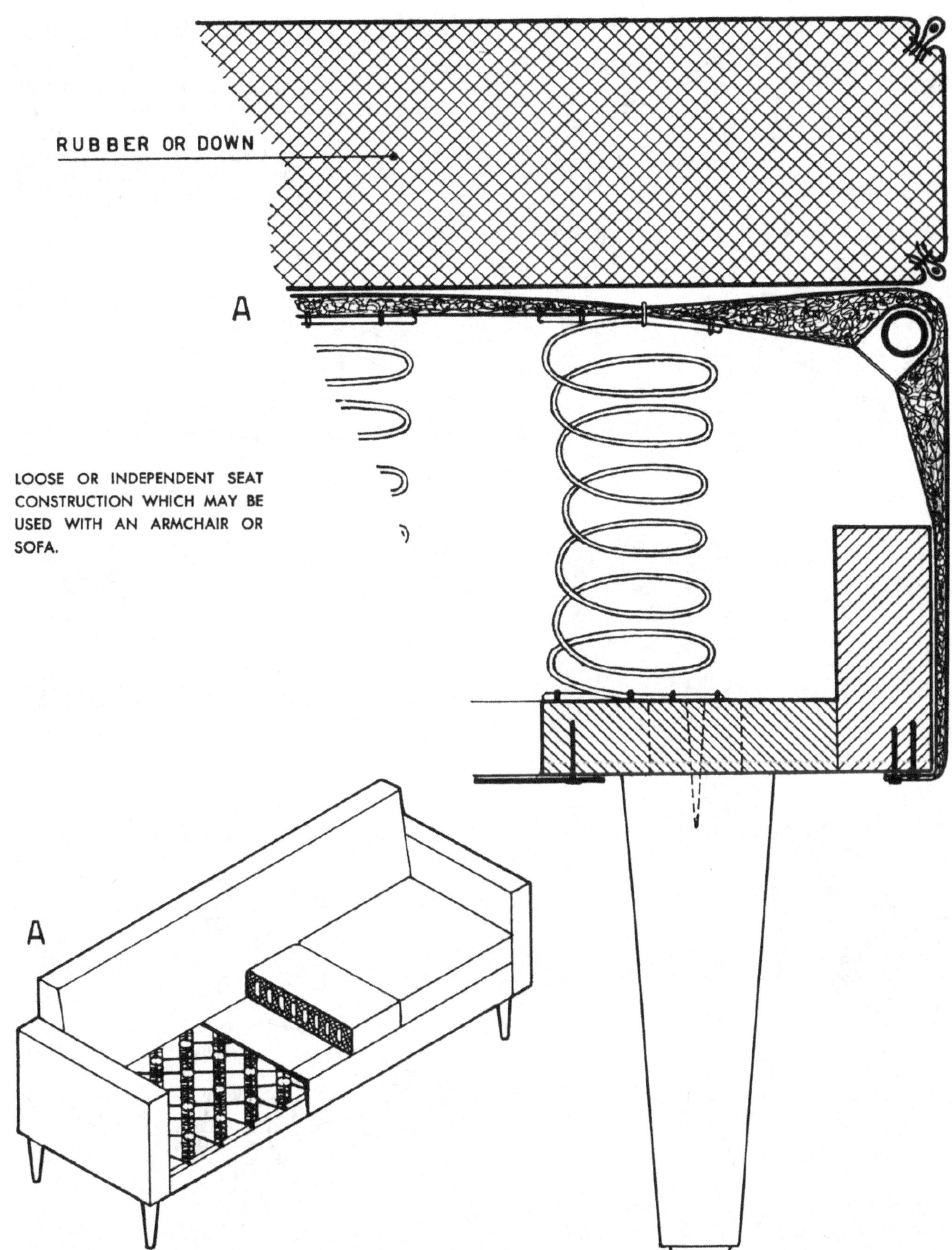

RUBBER OR DOWN
A
LOOSE OR INDEPENDENT SEAT
CONSTRUCTION WHICH MAY BE
USED WITH AN ARMCHAIR OR
SOFA.
A

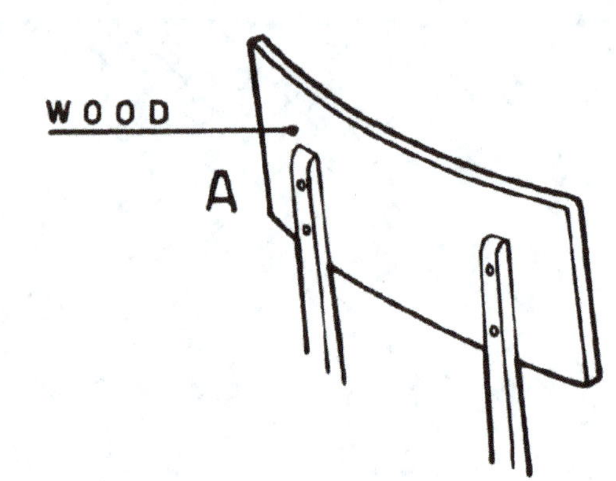

BACKS

THE BACK OF A CHAIR IS USUALLY LIGHTER IN CON-
STRUCTION AND MORE RIGID THAN THE SEAT. THERE
ARE EXCEPTIONS; SOMETIMES THE SEAT IS OF WOOD
AND THE BACK IS UPHOLSTERED. LIKE THE SEAT, THE
BACK MAY BE CONSTRUCTED IN A NUMBER OF WAYS.
I HAVE ILLUSTRATED A FEW OF THE BEST METHODS.

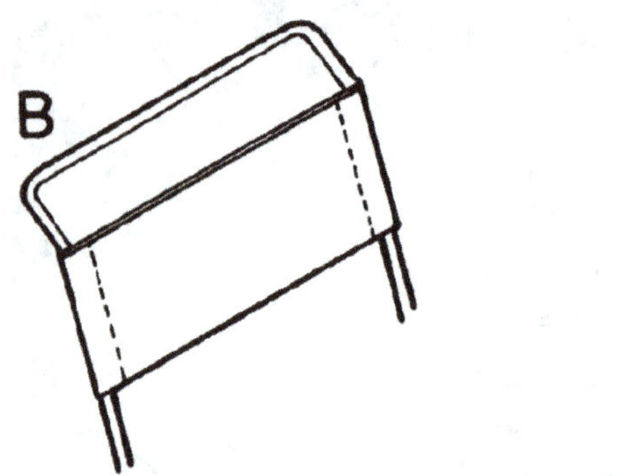

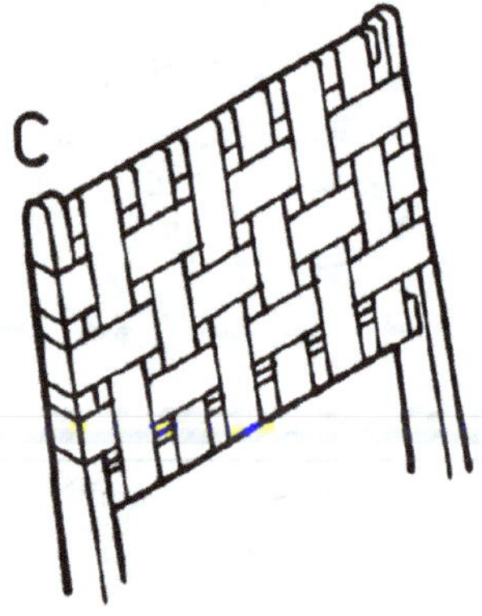

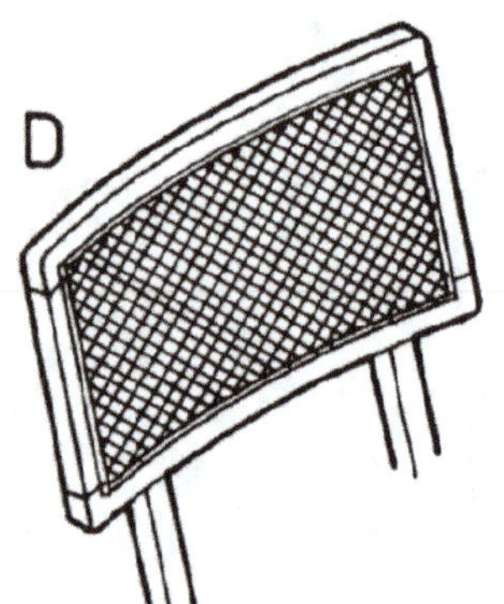

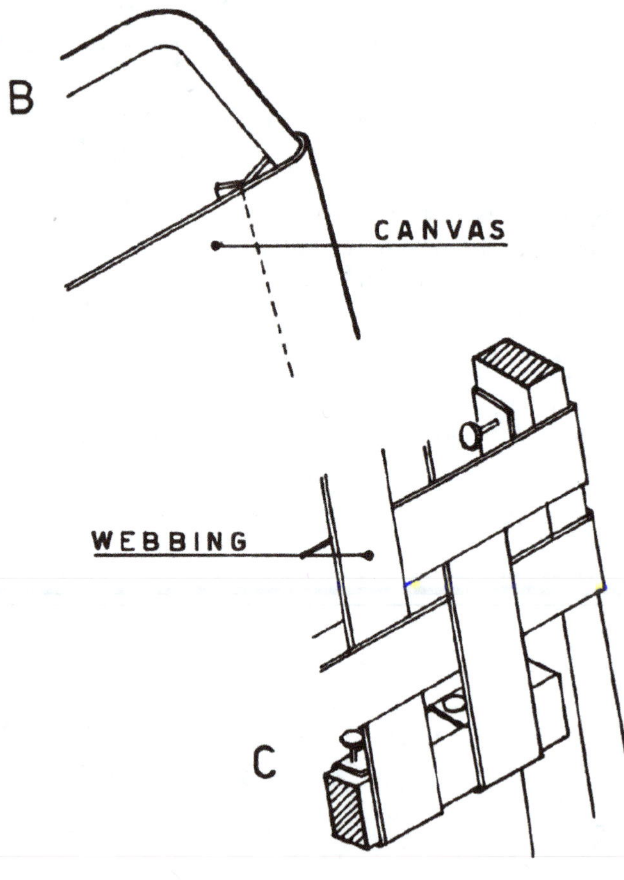

FOUR TYPES OF BACKS THAT CAN BE USED: "A" IS
MADE OF WOOD; "B" IS OF CANVAS; "C" USES WEB-
BING; "D" IS OF CANE.

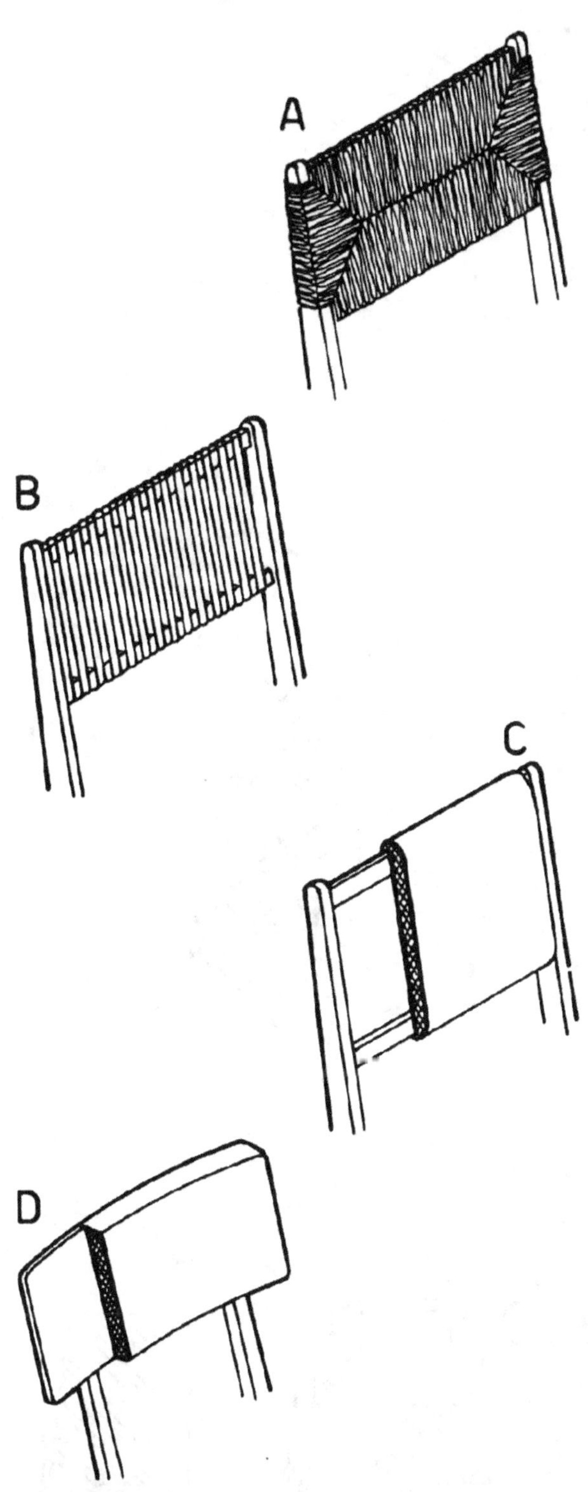

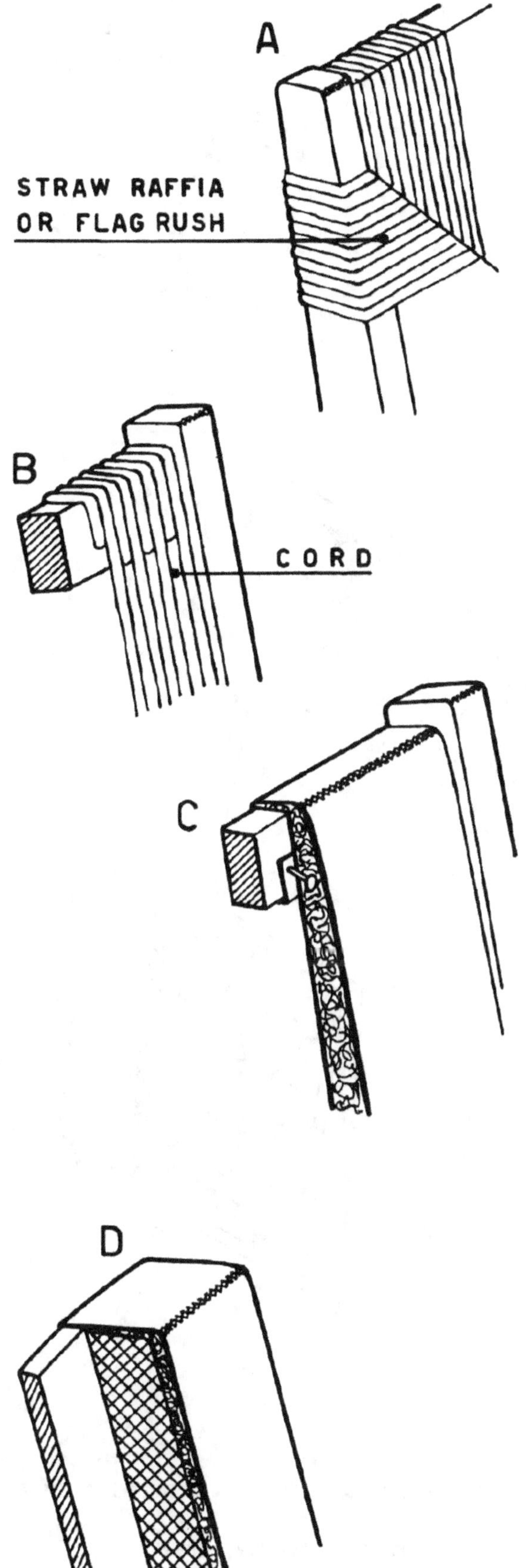

A — STRAW, RAFFIA OR FLAG RUSH USED TO FORM BACK.

B — CORD BACK THAT IS EASY TO MAKE.

C — SIMPLE UPHOLSTERED BACK SUITABLE FOR MODERN FURNITURE.

D — WOOD BACK COVERED WITH FOAM RUBBER AND FABRIC.

A

B

C

D

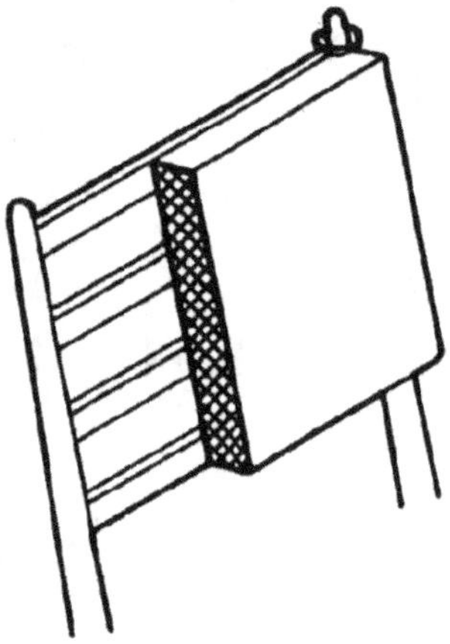

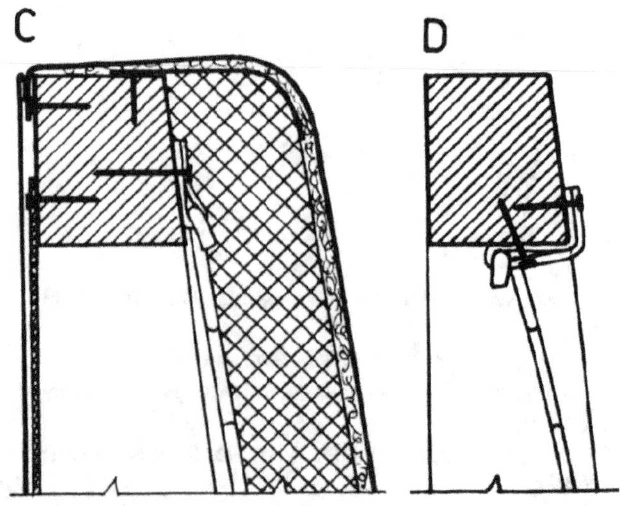

A — REMOVABLE BACK CUSHION ATTACHED WITH A STRING.

B — FOAM RUBBER BACK OVER WEBBING.

C — FOAM RUBBER APPLIED OVER A NO-SAG SPRING.

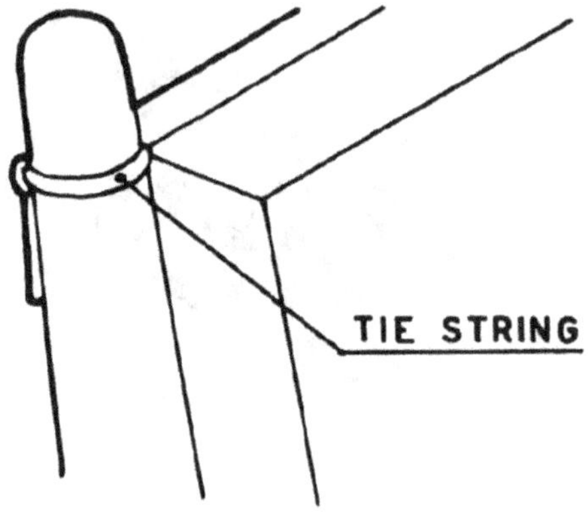

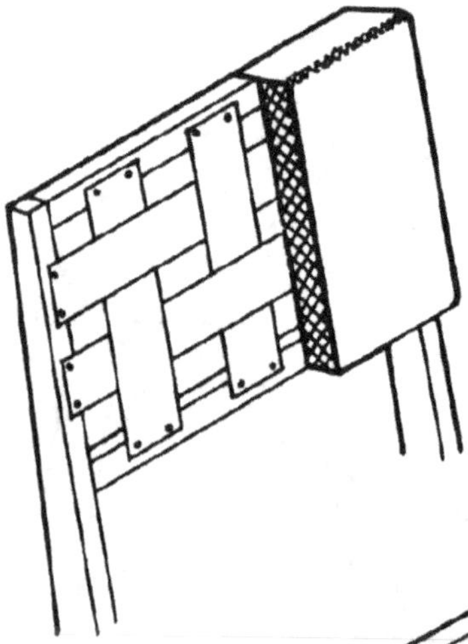

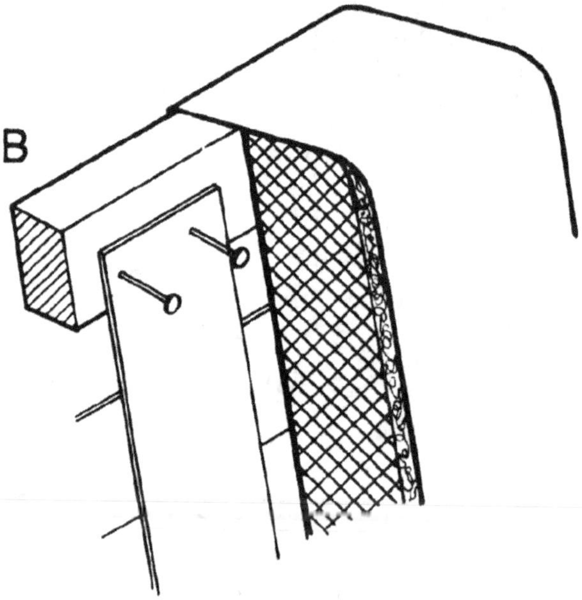

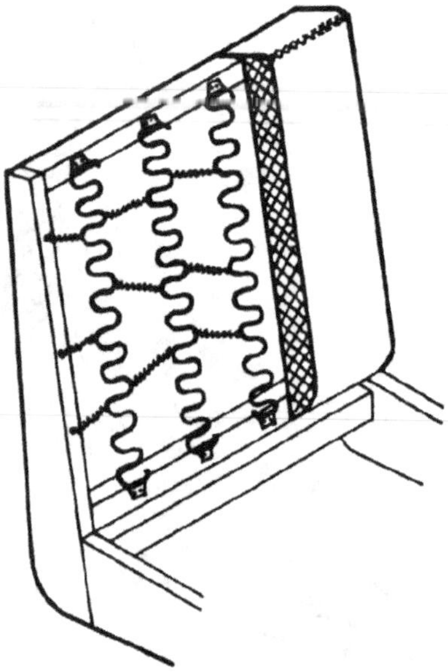

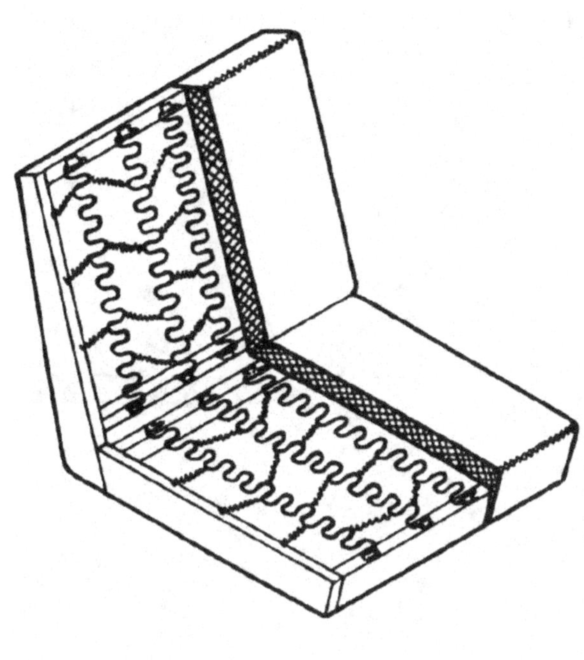
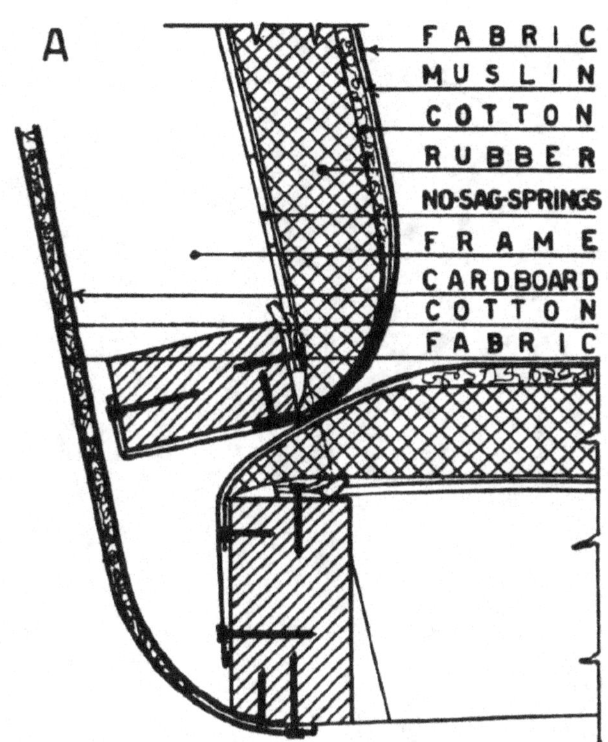

METHOD OF APPLYING UPHOLSTERY MATERIAL IN THE
CORNER FORMED BY THE SEAT AND BACK.

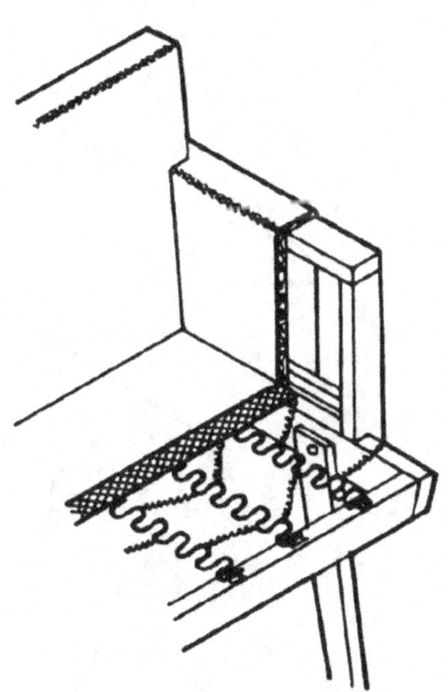
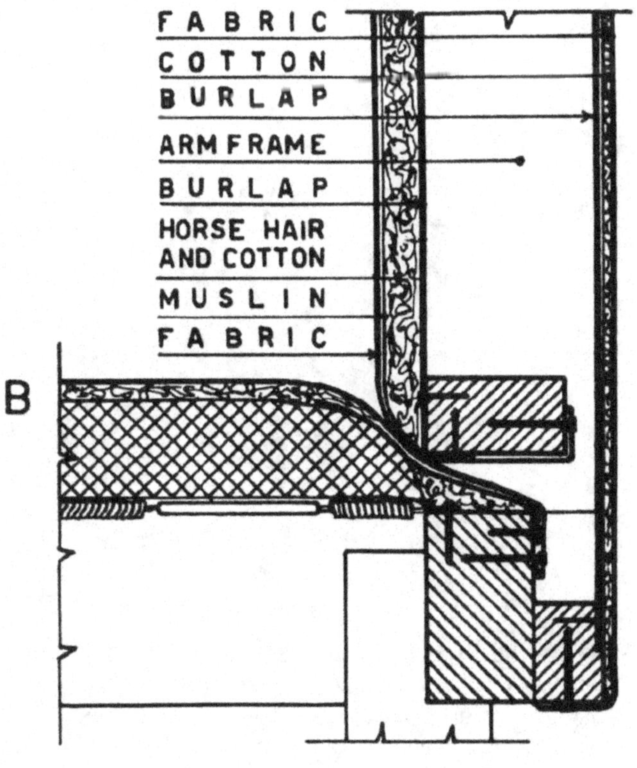

HERE IS ONE WAY OF ATTACHING THE MATERIAL
WHERE THE ARM MEETS THE SEAT.

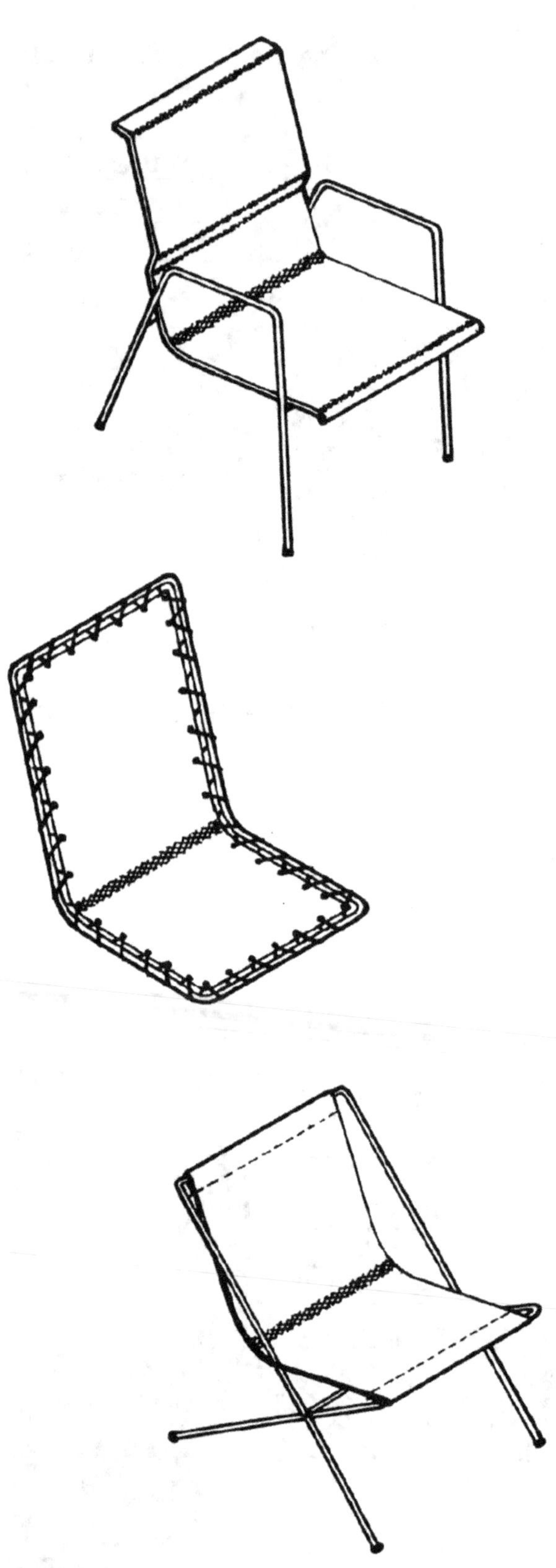

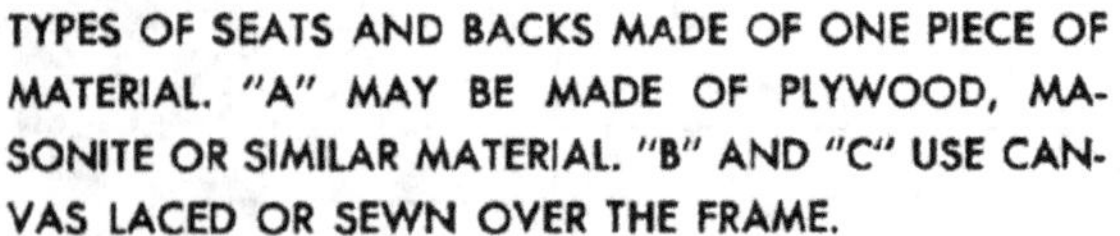
TYPES OF SEATS AND BACKS MADE OF ONE PIECE OF
MATERIAL. "A" MAY BE MADE OF PLYWOOD, MA-
SONITE OR SIMILAR MATERIAL. "B" AND "C" USE CAN-
VAS LACED OR SEWN OVER THE FRAME.

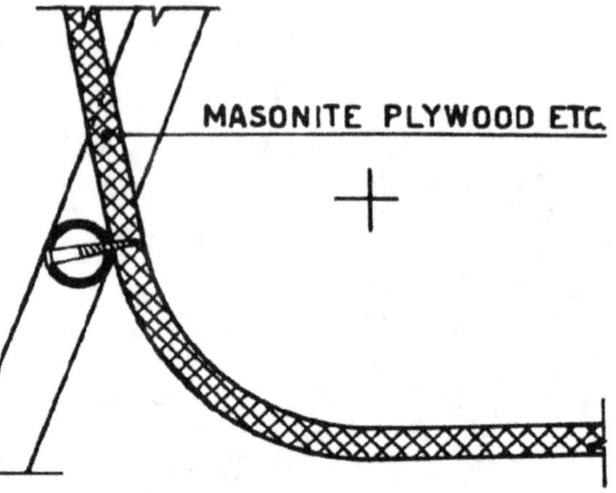

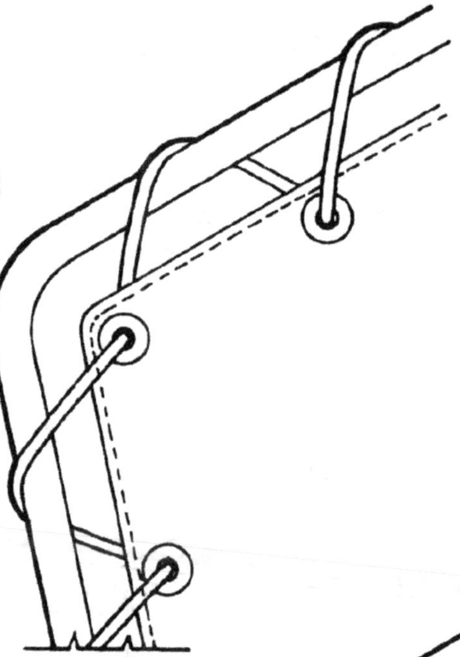

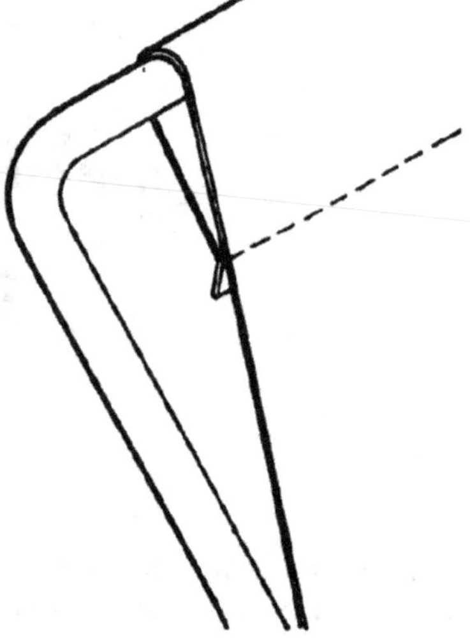

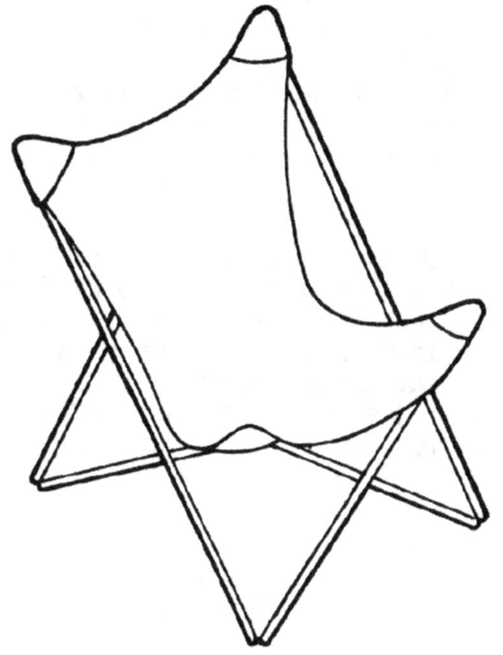

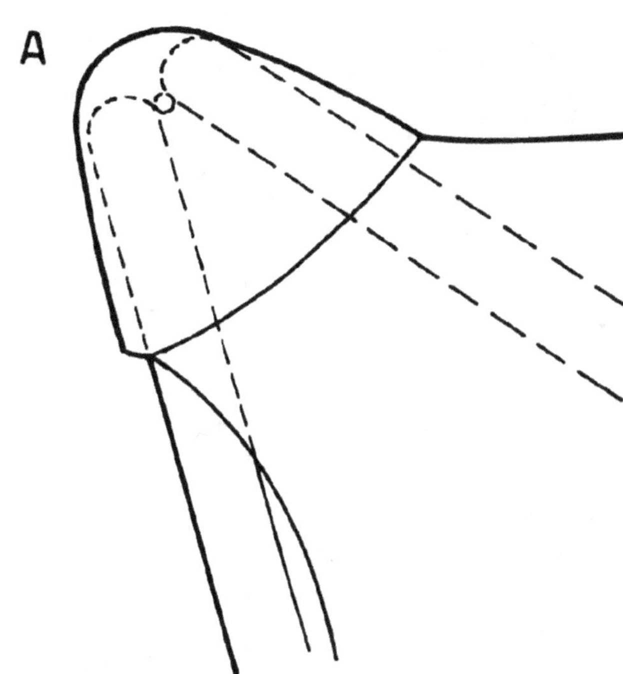

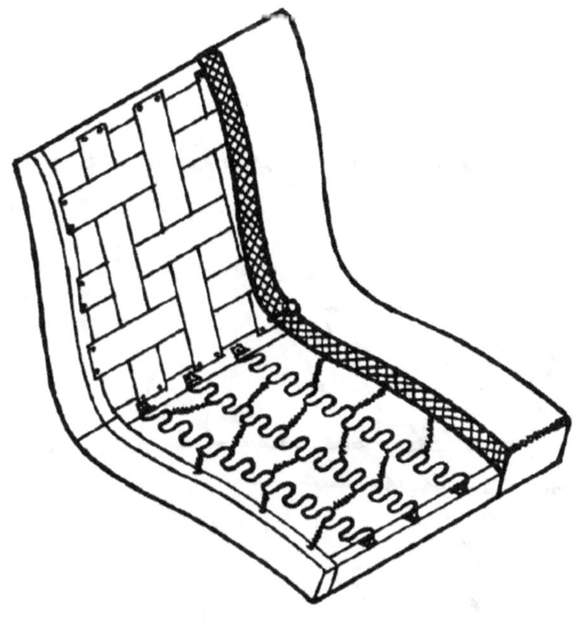

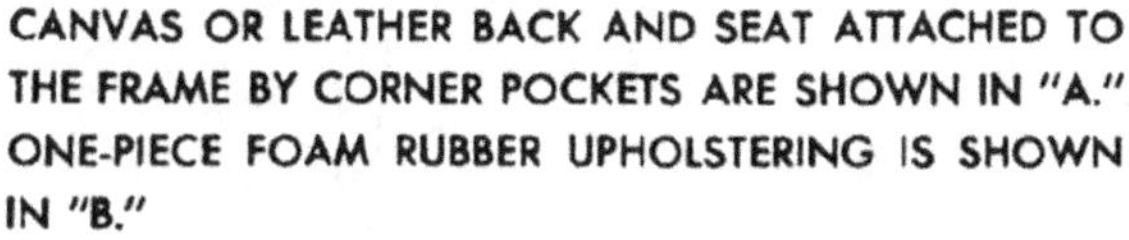
CANVAS OR LEATHER BACK AND SEAT ATTACHED TO
THE FRAME BY CORNER POCKETS ARE SHOWN IN "A."
ONE-PIECE FOAM RUBBER UPHOLSTERING IS SHOWN
IN "B."

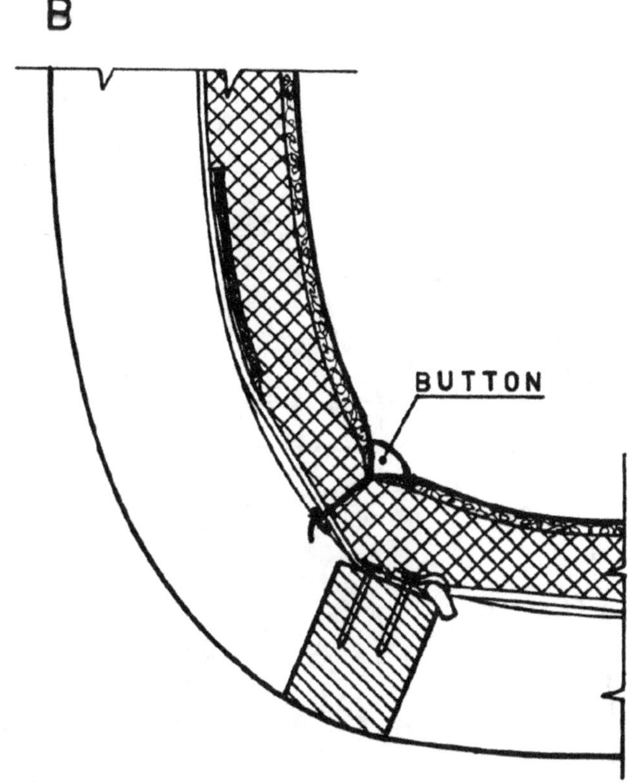

CHAIR ANGLES

MAN SITS TO READ, WORK, REST AND EAT. IN EACH CASE THE FURNITURE MUST BE ADAPTED TO THE COMFORT OF THE INDIVIDUAL. MOST REQUIREMENTS SEEM TO BE FULFILLED BY EITHER THE ARMCHAIR OR THE DIVAN.

WHETHER IT BE A CHAIR, ARMCHAIR OR DIVAN, THE RESPECTIVE ANGLES CANNOT BE CALCULATED MECHANICALLY. THE REAL PROOF OF COMFORT AND APPROVED ANGLE CAN BE CHECKED ONLY FROM A COMPLETED MODEL. IN THE EXAMPLES SHOWN I HAVE GIVEN THE BASIC ANGLES WHICH WILL ASSURE SATISFACTORY RESULTS.

ARMLESS CHAIRS

ARMCHAIRS

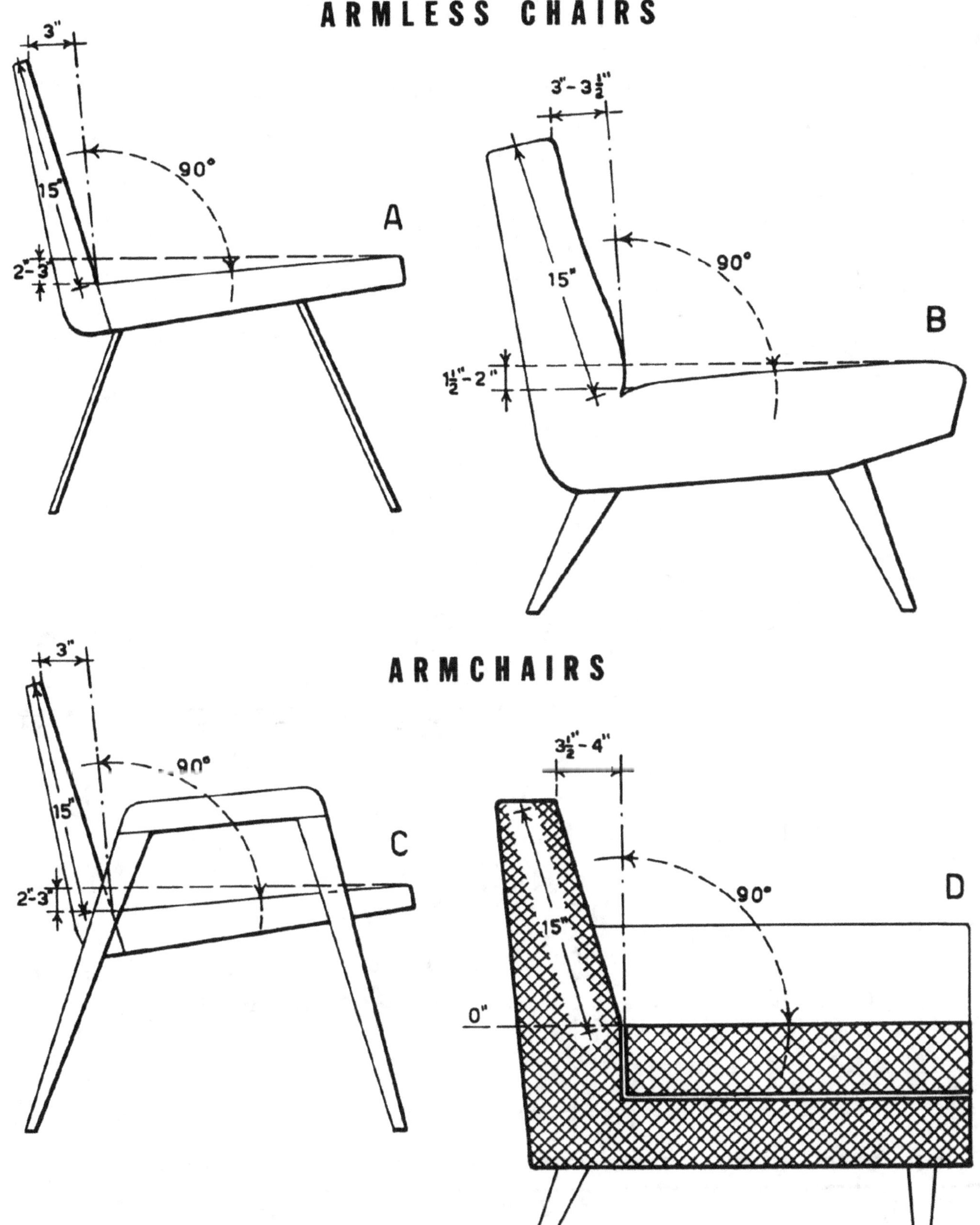

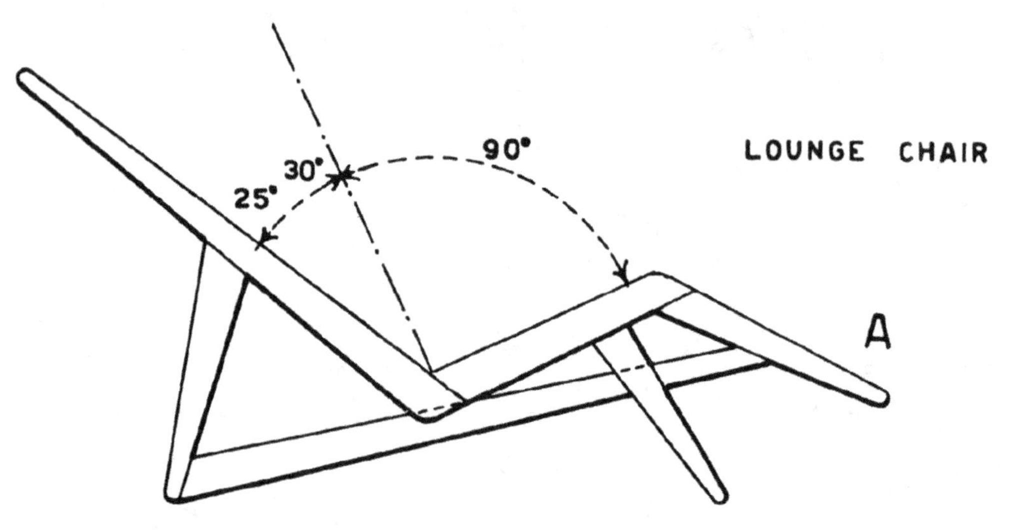

LOUNGE CHAIR
90°
30°
25°
A

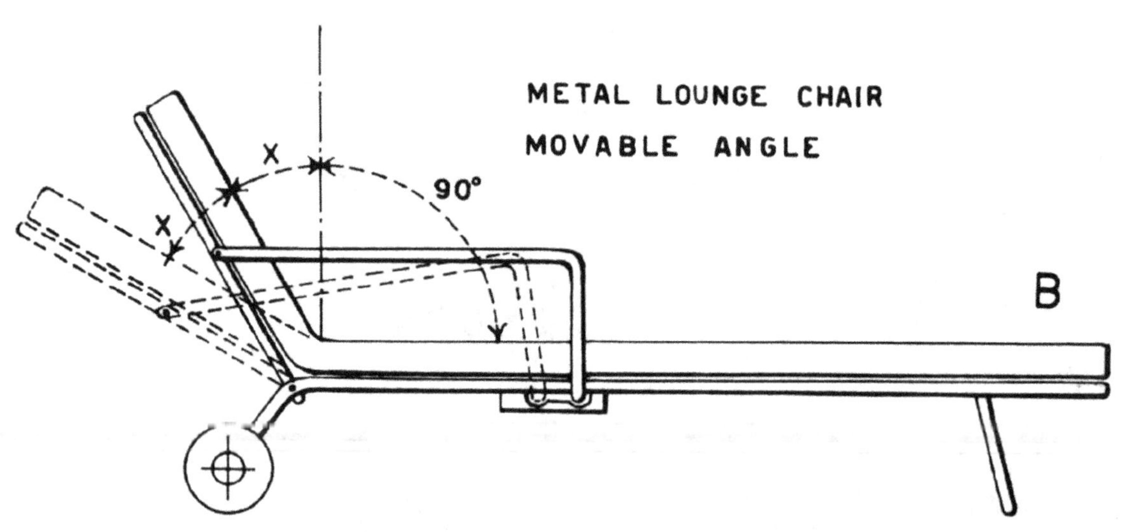

METAL LOUNGE CHAIR
MOVABLE ANGLE
90°
X
X
B

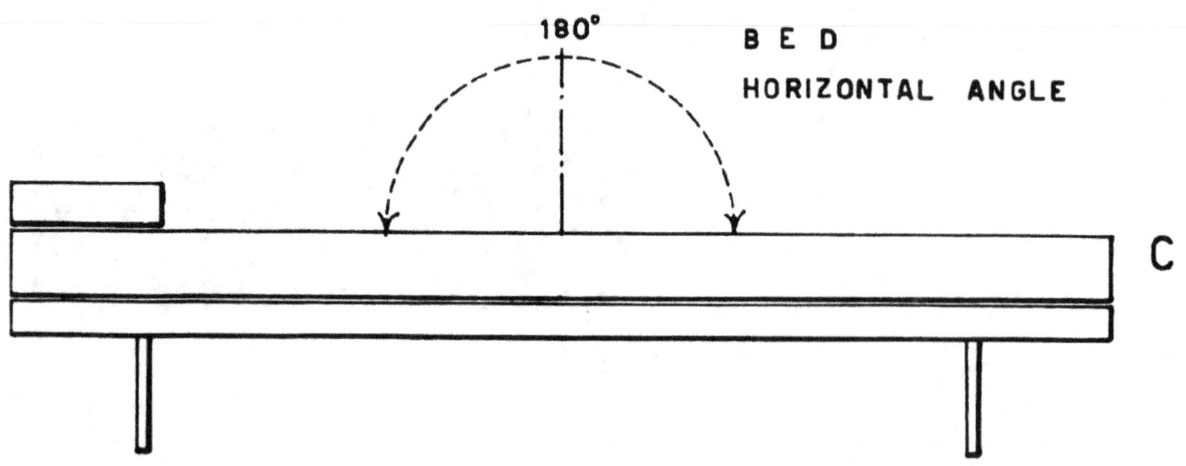

180°
BED
HORIZONTAL ANGLE
C

FURNITURE FOR THE HOME CRAFTSMAN

IN THIS COUNTRY HUNDREDS OF THOUSANDS OF PEOPLE HAVE SMALL WORK-SHOPS IN THEIR HOMES, WITH THE NECESSARY TOOLS TO MAKE REPAIRS AND TO BUILD VARIOUS USEFUL OBJECTS.

THE MAJORITY OF THESE PEOPLE ARE ALSO INTERESTED IN BUILDING VARIOUS PIECES OF FURNITURE. I HAVE DEVOTED THE LAST 15 PAGES OF THIS BOOK TO A SERIES OF EASY FURNITURE PIECES WHICH THEY CAN MAKE.

I HAVE SIMPLIFIED THE METHOD OF PRESENTATION BOTH IN DESIGN AND IN CONSTRUCTION SO THAT THE READERS CAN READILY UNDERSTAND ALL THE PRO-CEDURES. IT IS POSSIBLE TO BUILD THESE PIECES WITH THE ASSURANCE OF SUCCESS.

PROCEDURE

AFTER YOU HAVE SELECTED THE PIECE OF FURNITURE YOU WANT TO BUILD, THE NEXT STEP IS TO ORDER THE LUMBER. ONE WAY IS TO COPY A LIST OF THE MATERIALS REQUIRED AND ASK ANY LUMBER DEALER TO CUT THE PIECES FOR YOU. ANOTHER WAY IS TO USE LUMBER CUT IN STANDARD SIZES.

IF THE MATERIAL IS PURCHASED IN THE SECOND WAY, IT IS ADVISABLE TO DRAW AN OUTLINE OF THE PIECES DIRECTLY ON THE WOOD. CUT OUT WITH A SAW. PLANE THE SAWED PIECES AND USE A FILE ON THE CURVED SURFACES. MARK AND EXECUTE THE JOINTS OF THE VARIOUS PIECES, CHECKING TO SEE THAT EVERYTHING FITS CORRECTLY. THIS DONE, PROCEED WITH THE ASSEMBLING AS SHOWN IN THE DRAWINGS, USING GLUE AND SCREWS. BE SURE TO FOLLOW THE DIRECTIONS INDICATED IN THE LEGEND.

FINISHING

AFTER BUILDING THE PIECE OF FURNITURE, SANDPAPER ALL PARTS FIRST WITH COARSE SANDPAPER AND THEN WITH FINE SANDPAPER, RUBBING IN THE DIREC-TION OF THE GRAIN. APPLY A COAT OF FIRZITE AND ALLOW IT TO DRY FOR ABOUT EIGHT HOURS; THEN SANDPAPER THE SURFACE AGAIN. WITH A CLEAN BRUSH APPLY TWO COATS OF SATIN LAC (ALLOWING FOUR HOURS BETWEEN COATS), AND FINISH WITH FURNITURE POLISH.

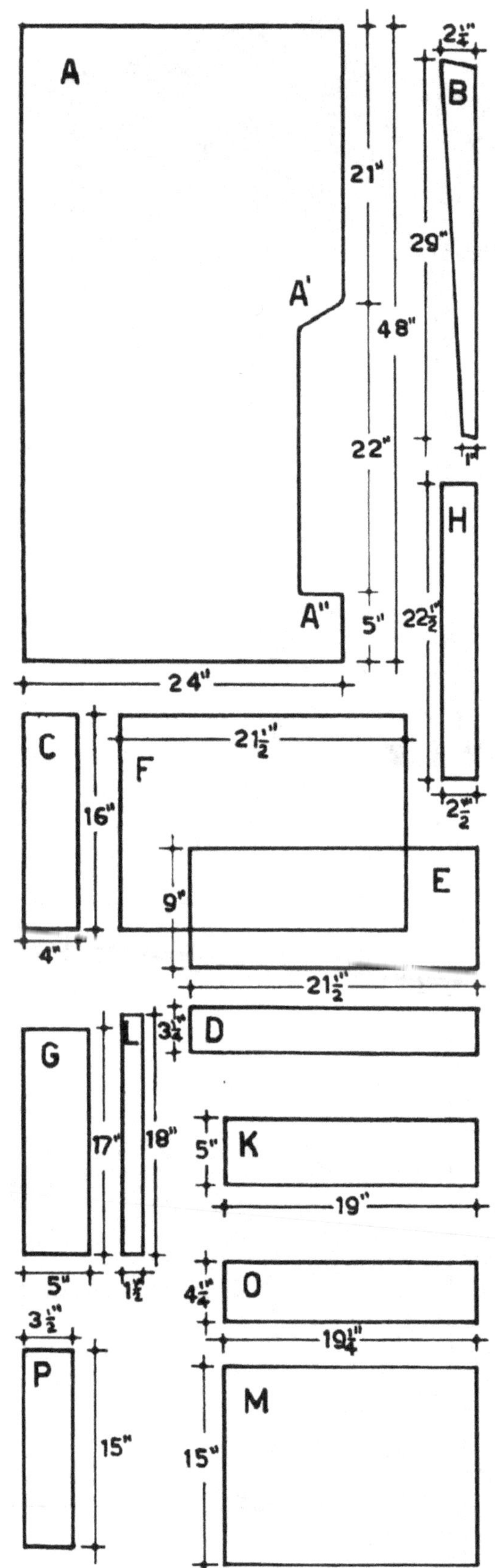

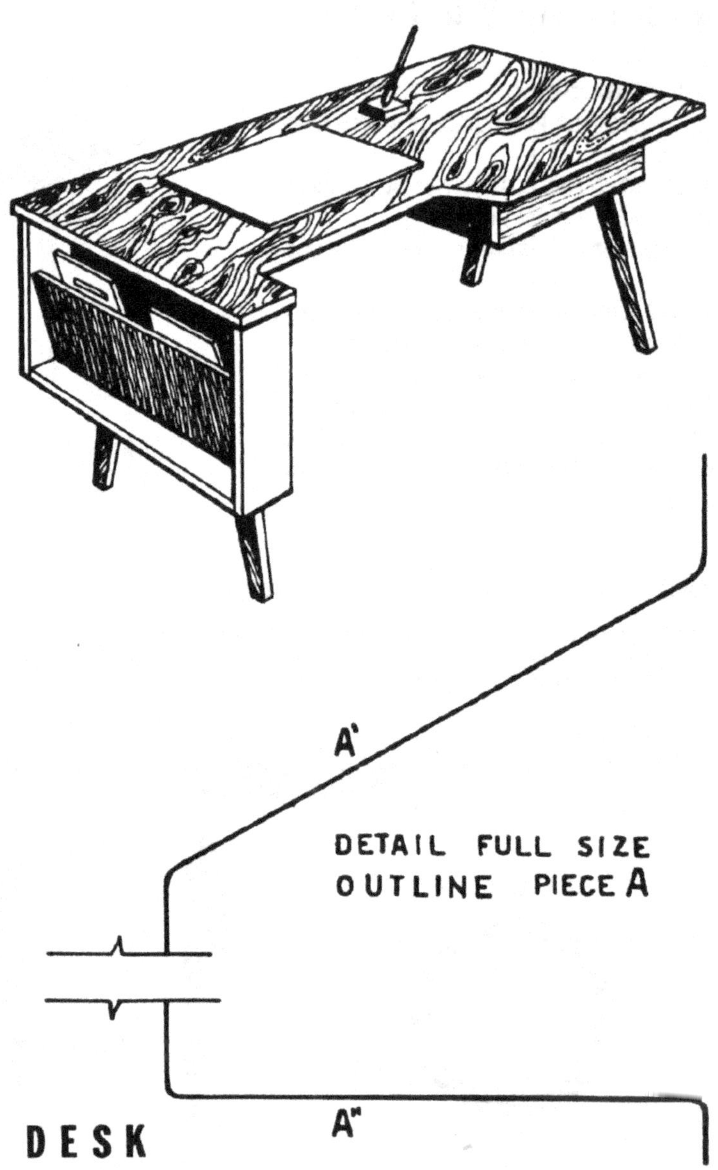

DESK

LIST OF MATERIALS. (USE PLYWOOD OR HARDWOOD).

A — 1 PIECE ¾" THICK AND 48" X 24". B — 4 PIECES 1¼" THICK AND 29" X 2¼". C — 2 PIECES ¾" THICK AND 16" X 4". D — 1 PIECE ¼" THICK AND 21½" X 3¼". E — 1 PIECE ½" THICK AND 21½" X 9". F — 1 PIECE ¾" THICK AND 21½" X 16". G — 2 PIECES ¾" THICK AND 17" X 5". H — 1 PIECE 1¼" THICK AND 22½" X 2½". K — 2 PIECES ¾" THICK AND 19" X 5". L — 3 PIECES ¾" THICK AND 18" X 1½". M — 1 PIECE ¼" THICK AND 19¼" X 15". O — 2 PIECES ½" THICK AND 19¼" X 4¼". P — 1 PIECE ½" THICK AND 15" X 3½". SEE PAGE 155 FOR GENERAL INSTRUCTIONS.

WHEN MATERIAL IS READY FOR ASSEMBLING JOIN THE PIECES AS FOLLOWS:

(1) C WITH DEF; (2) K WITH GL; (3) H WITH FK; (4) APPLY TOP A WITH C, H, G, K; (DETAIL 2, SEE PAGE 84); (5) APPLY LEGS B WITH F AND K; (6) (DRAWER) O WITH G P; (DETAIL 3, SEE PAGE 90). (7) M WITH O G; TO COMPLETE DESK. USE NATURAL FINISH AS INDICATED IN GENERAL INSTRUCTIONS.

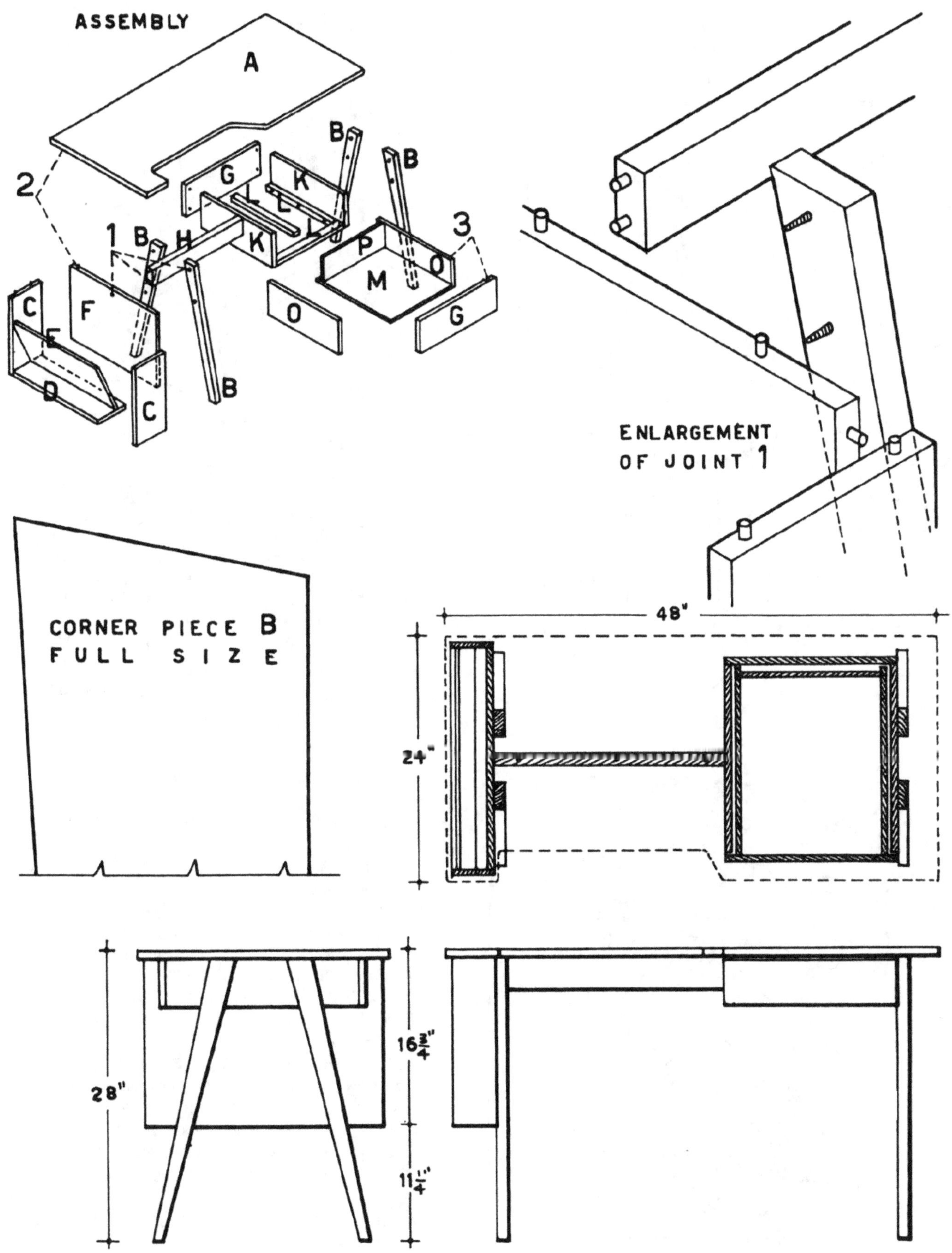

ASSEMBLY
A
2
B
B
G
K
1 B
H
K
P
3
L
C
F
M
O
O
F
G
D
C
B
CORNER PIECE B
FULL SIZE
ENLARGEMENT
OF JOINT 1
48"
24"
28"
16 3/4"
11 1/4"

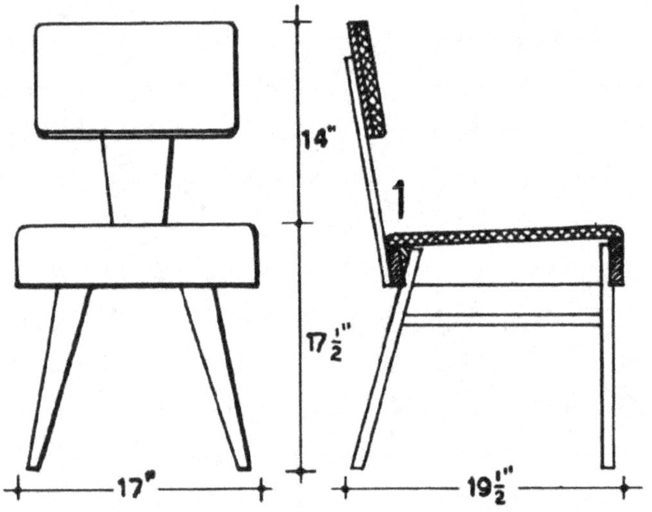

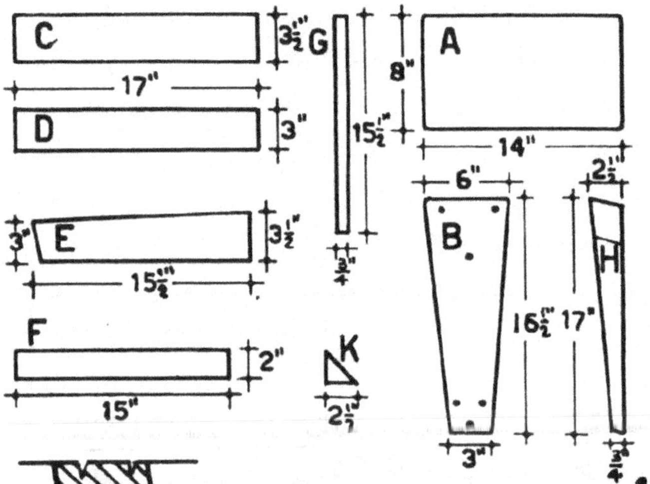

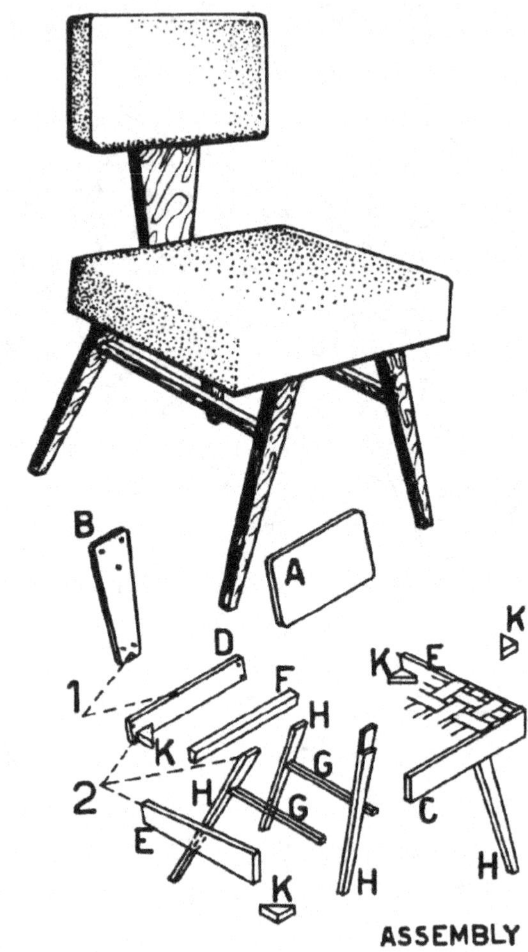

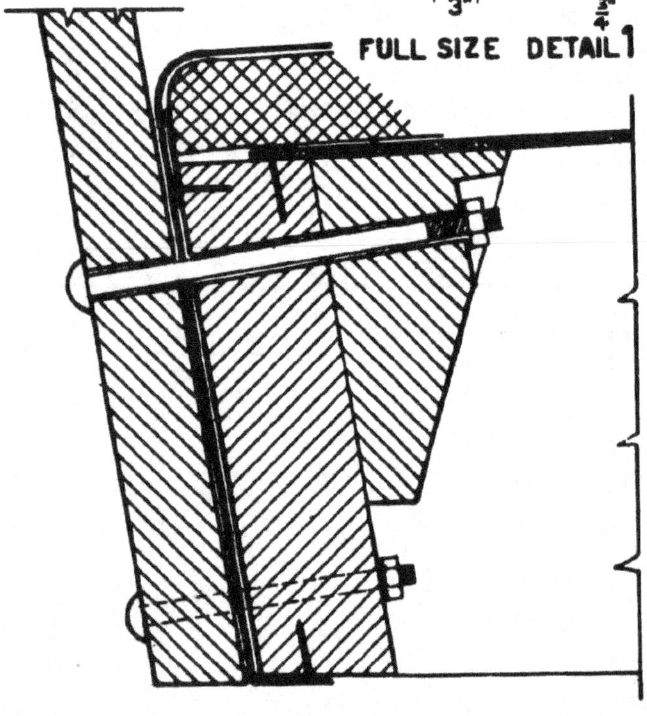

FULL SIZE DETAIL 1

LIST OF MATERIALS. (HARDWOOD).

A — 1 PIECE ½" THICK AND 14" X 8". B — 1 PIECE ½" THICK AND 16½" X 6". C — 1 PIECE ¾" THICK AND 17" X 3½". D — 1 PIECE ¾" THICK AND 17" X 3". E — 2 PIECES ¾" THICK AND 15½" X 3½". F — 1 PIECE 1¼" THICK AND 15" X 2". G — 2 PIECES ¾" THICK AND 15½" X ¾". H — 4 PIECES ⅞" THICK AND 17" X 2½". K — 4 PIECES 1" THICK AND 2½" X 2½" WEBBING 5 YARDS. RUBBER 1 PIECE ¾" THICK AND 27" X 17". FABRIC 1 YARD. 1 BOLT 2¼" LONG AND OTHER 1½". SEE GENERAL INSTRUCTIONS ON PAGE 155.

AFTER MATERIAL IS READY TO BE ASSEMBLED YOU JOIN THEM AS FOLLOWS:

(1) C D WITH "E." (DETAIL 2, SEE PAGE 162 — ENLARGEMENT 2); ATTACH THE CORNER BLOCK "K," JOIN "F" WITH "D", "G" WITH "H." "H" WITH "C, D." UPHOLSTER SEAT AND BACK AS SUGGESTED ON PAGES 142 AND 147. JOIN SEAT AND BACK WITH PIECE MARKED "B" AND YOU HAVE THE COMPLETED CHAIR.

FINISH: COMPLETELY FINISH EXPOSED PARTS BEFORE ASSEMBLING.

ARMLESS CHAIR

LIST OF MATERIALS (HARDWOOD).

A — 1 PIECE ½" THICK AND 11" X 22½". B — 2 PIECES ¾" THICK AND 9" X 2½". C — 1 PIECE ¾" THICK AND 22½" X 1". D — 1 PIECE ¾" THICK 22½" X 2½". E — 2 PIECES ⅝" THICK AND 18" X 2". F — 2 PIECES ¾" THICK AND 24" X 5½". G — 1 PIECE 2" THICK AND 20½" X 2". H — 1 PIECE ¾" THICK AND 22½" X 4½". K — 1 PIECE ¾" THICK AND 22½" X 5½". L — 4 PIECES 1" THICK AND 13" X 3". M — 4 PIECES 1" THICK AND 3½" X 3½". WEBBING 9 YARDS. RUBBER 1 PIECE ¾" THICK AND 38" X 23". FABRIC 1⅔". 4 BOLTS 2¼" LONG. SEE GENERAL INSTRUCTIONS ON PAGE 155.

WHEN MATERIAL IS READY FOR ASSEMBLING JOIN THEM AS FOLLOWS:

F WITH K; ATTACH CORNER BLOCK M; JOIN G WITH H; ATTACH LEGS L. JOIN A WITH B, C, D. APPLY THE UPHOLSTERY WORK AS SHOWN ON PAGES 142 AND 148. ATTACH SEAT AND BACK WITH PIECE E TO COMPLETE ARMLESS CHAIR.

FINISH: COMPLETELY FINISH EXPOSED PARTS BEFORE ASSEMBLING.

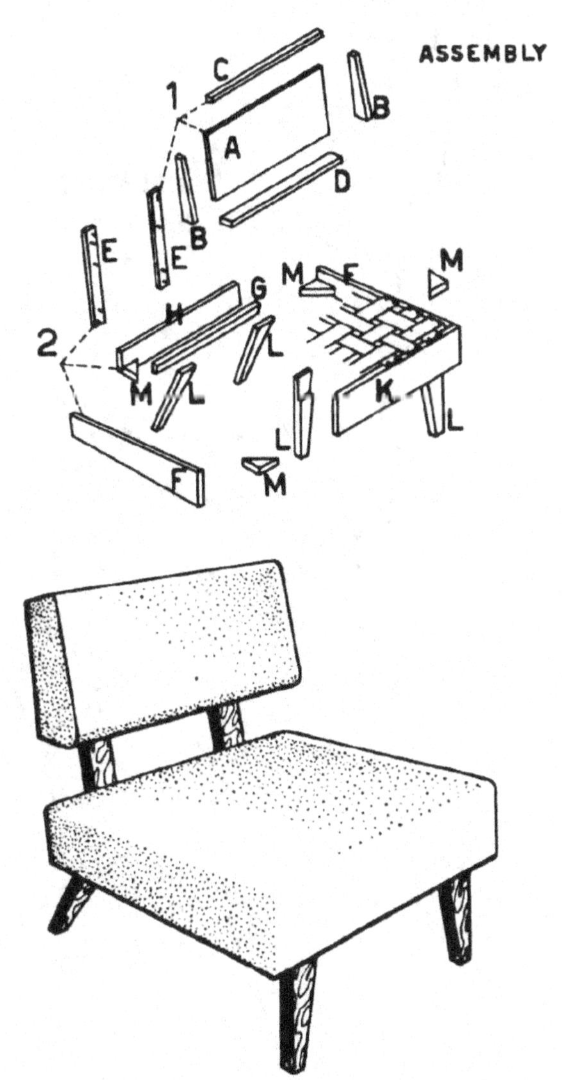

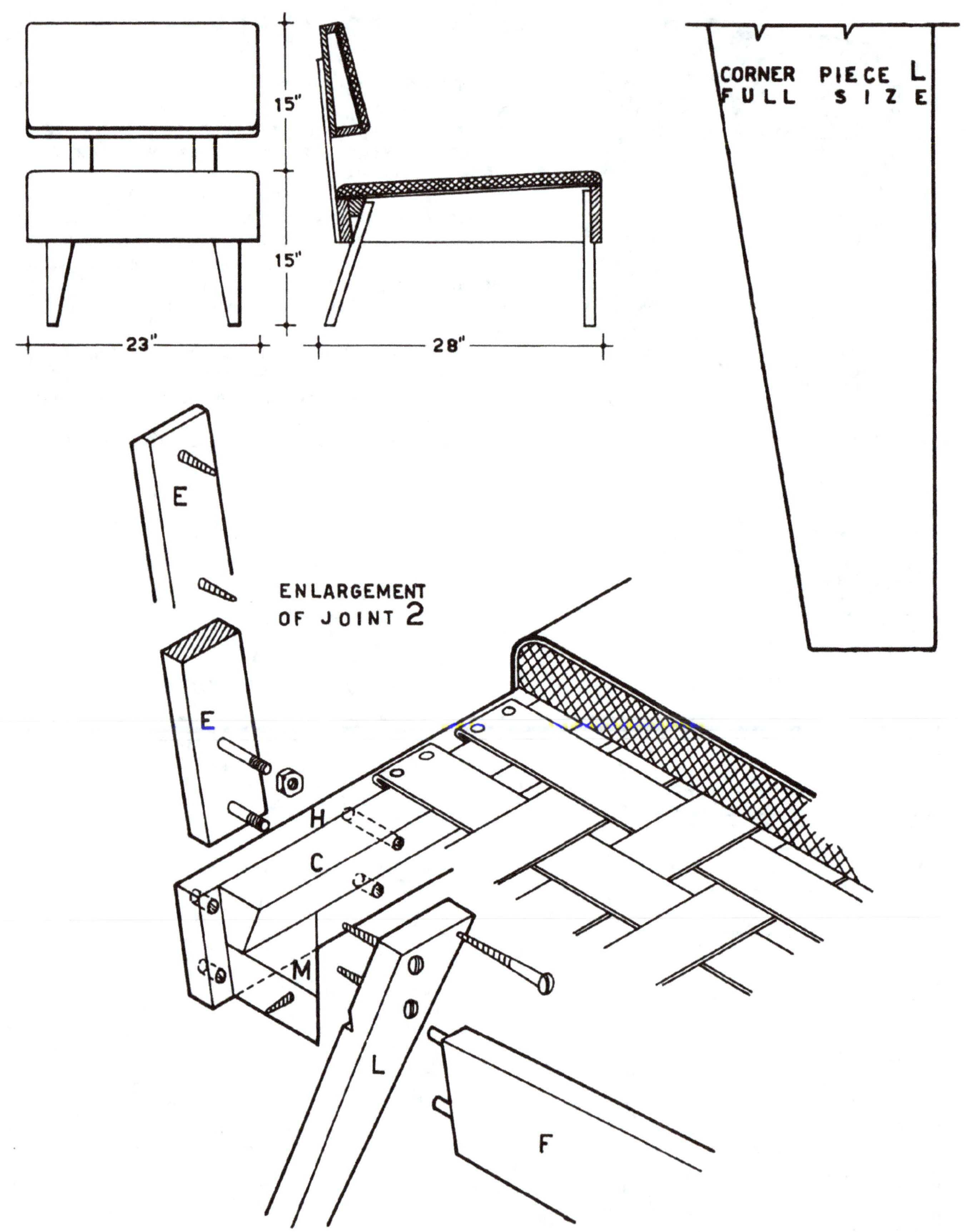

15"
15"
23"
28"
CORNER PIECE L
FULL SIZE
E
E
ENLARGEMENT
OF JOINT 2
H
C
M
L
F

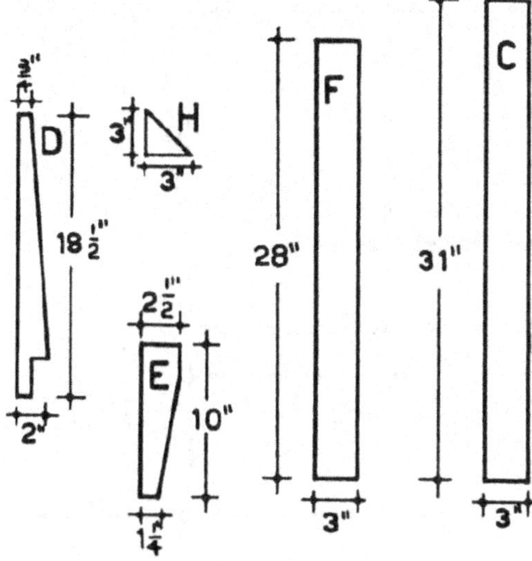

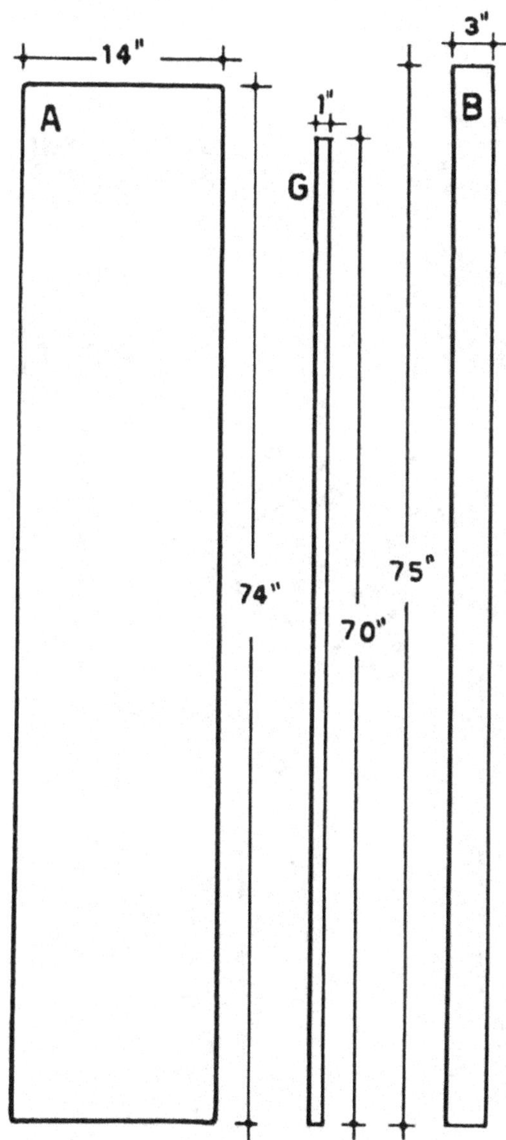

SOFA BED

LIST OF MATERIALS.

A — 1 PIECE ¾" THICK AND 74" X 14". B — 2 PIECES 1½" THICK AND 75" X 3". C — 2 PIECES 1½" THICK AND 31" X 3". D — 2 PIECES 2" THICK AND 18½" X 2". E — 4 PIECES 1¼" THICK AND 10" X 2½". F — 21 PIECES ½" THICK AND 28" X 3". H — 4 PIECES 1½" THICK AND 3" X 3". 1 RUBBER OR NORMAL MATTRESS 4½" THICK AND 75" X 30". THREE RUBBER OR OTHER CUSHIONS 4½" THICK AND 25" X 15". FABRIC 7 YARDS.

FOR GENERAL INSTRUCTION SEE PAGE 155.

AFTER MATERIAL IS READY TO BE ASSEMBLED YOU PROCEED TO JOIN THE PIECES IN THE FOLLOWING MANNER:

B WITH C; ATTACH CORNER BLOCK; ATTACH LEGS E; JOIN G WITH B, C; ATTACH F WITH B AND B TO D; JOIN A TO D; ATTACH MATTRESS AND BACK CUSHIONS TO COMPLETE SOFA.

FINISH THE PART IN VIEW WITH NATURAL FINISH AS INDICATED IN GENERAL INSTRUCTIONS.

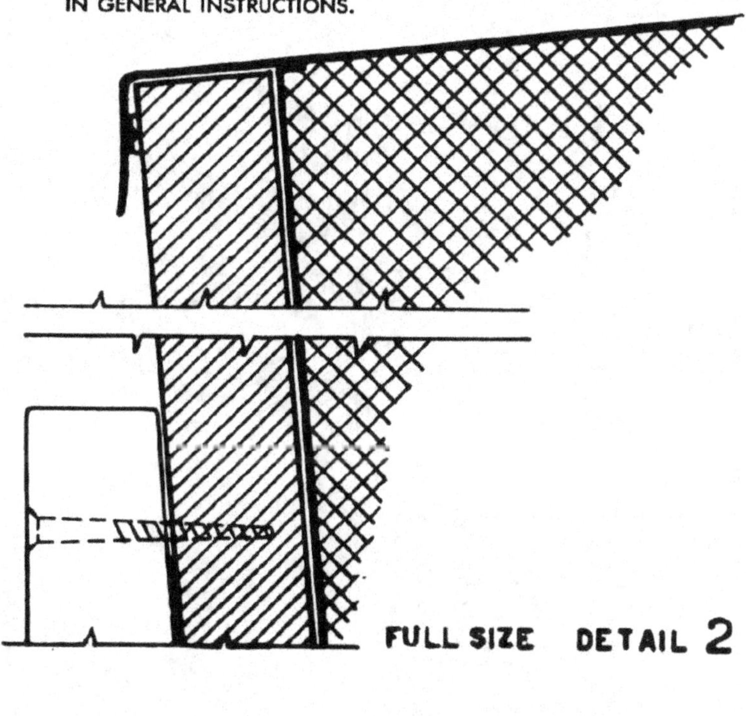

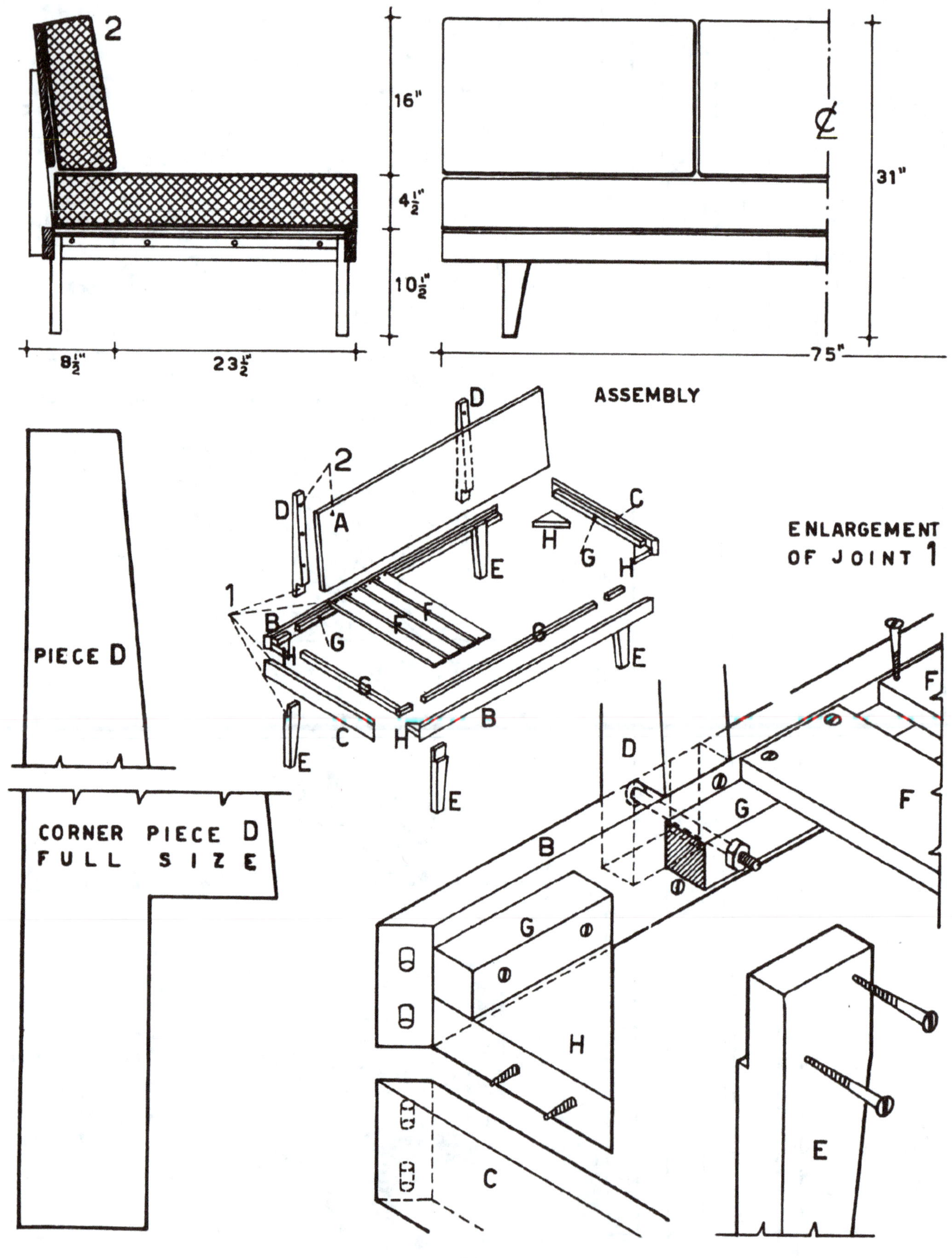

2
16"
4 1/2"
10 1/2"
8 1/2"
23 1/2"
31"
75"
ASSEMBLY
D
D
2
A
D
C
H
G
H
E
ENLARGEMENT
OF JOINT 1
B
G
F
F
1
F
F
G
B
H
E
D
G
PIECE D
C
H
B
E
G
CORNER PIECE D
FULL SIZE
H
C
E

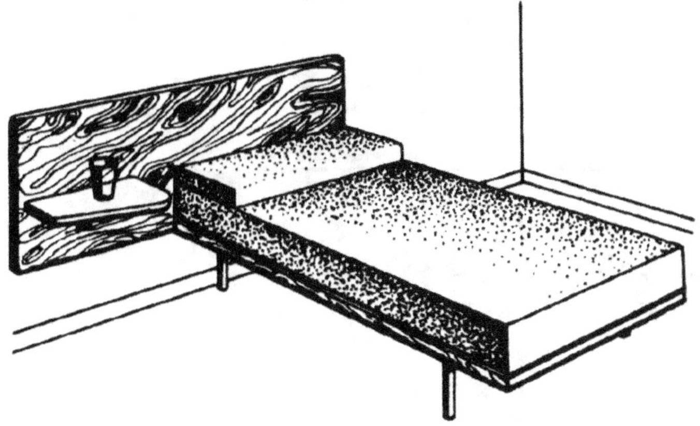

PIECE "A" FIXED ON THE WALL

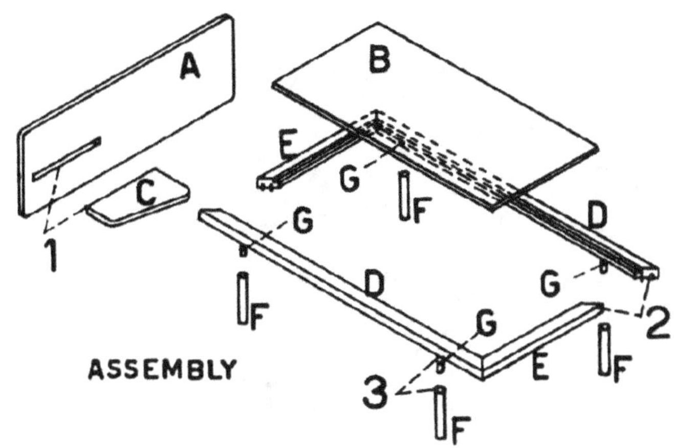

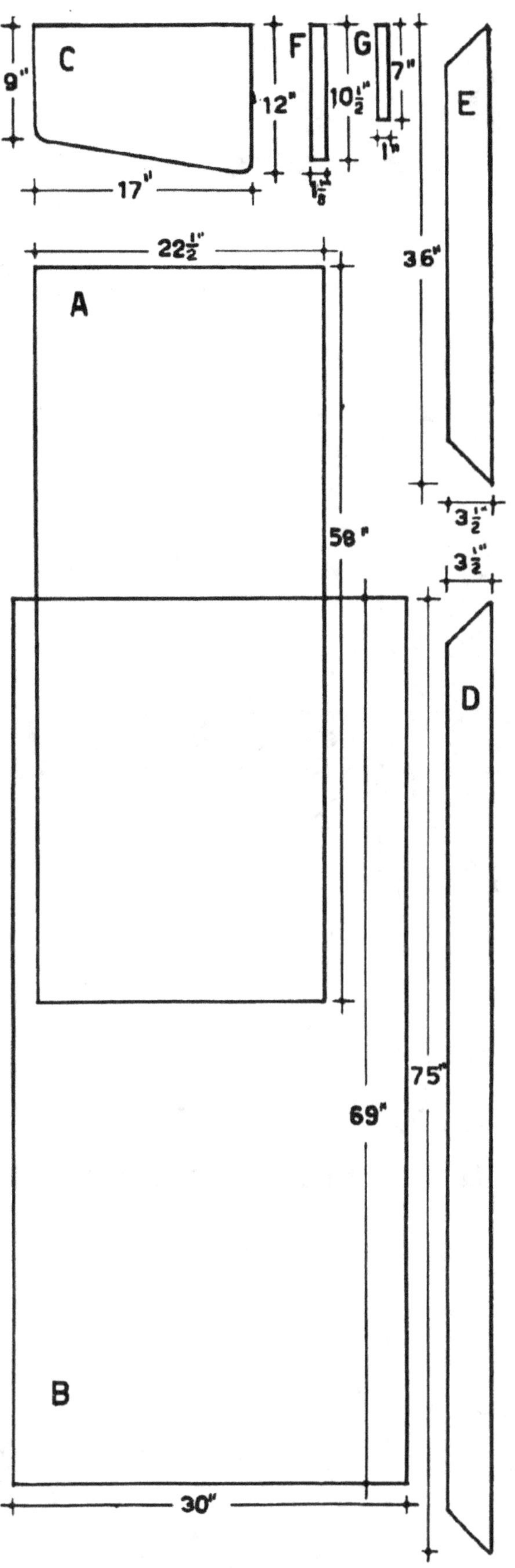

B E D

LIST OF MATERIALS. (PLYWOOD OR HARDWOOD)
A — 1 PIECE ¾" THICK AND 22½" X 58". B — 1 PIECE ½" THICK AND
69" X 30". C — 1 PIECE ¾" THICK AND 17" X 12". D — 2 PIECES
1½" THICK AND 75" X 3½". E — 2 PIECES 1½" THICK AND 36" X
3½". F — 4 PIECES METAL PIPE 10½" LONG AND 1⅛" IN DIAMETER.
G — 4 PIECES 7" LONG AND 1" IN DIAMETER. H — 1 MATTRESS 5"
THICK AND 75" X 36".
SEE PAGE 155 FOR GENERAL INSTRUCTIONS.
AFTER MATERIAL IS READY YOU PROCEED TO JOIN THEM AS
FOLLOWS:
A WITH C; D WITH E; F, G WITH D (SEE PAGE 86, FIG. B); B WITH
D, E. ADD MATTRESS TO COMPLETE THE BED.
FINISH: USE NATURAL FINISH ON EXPOSED PARTS.

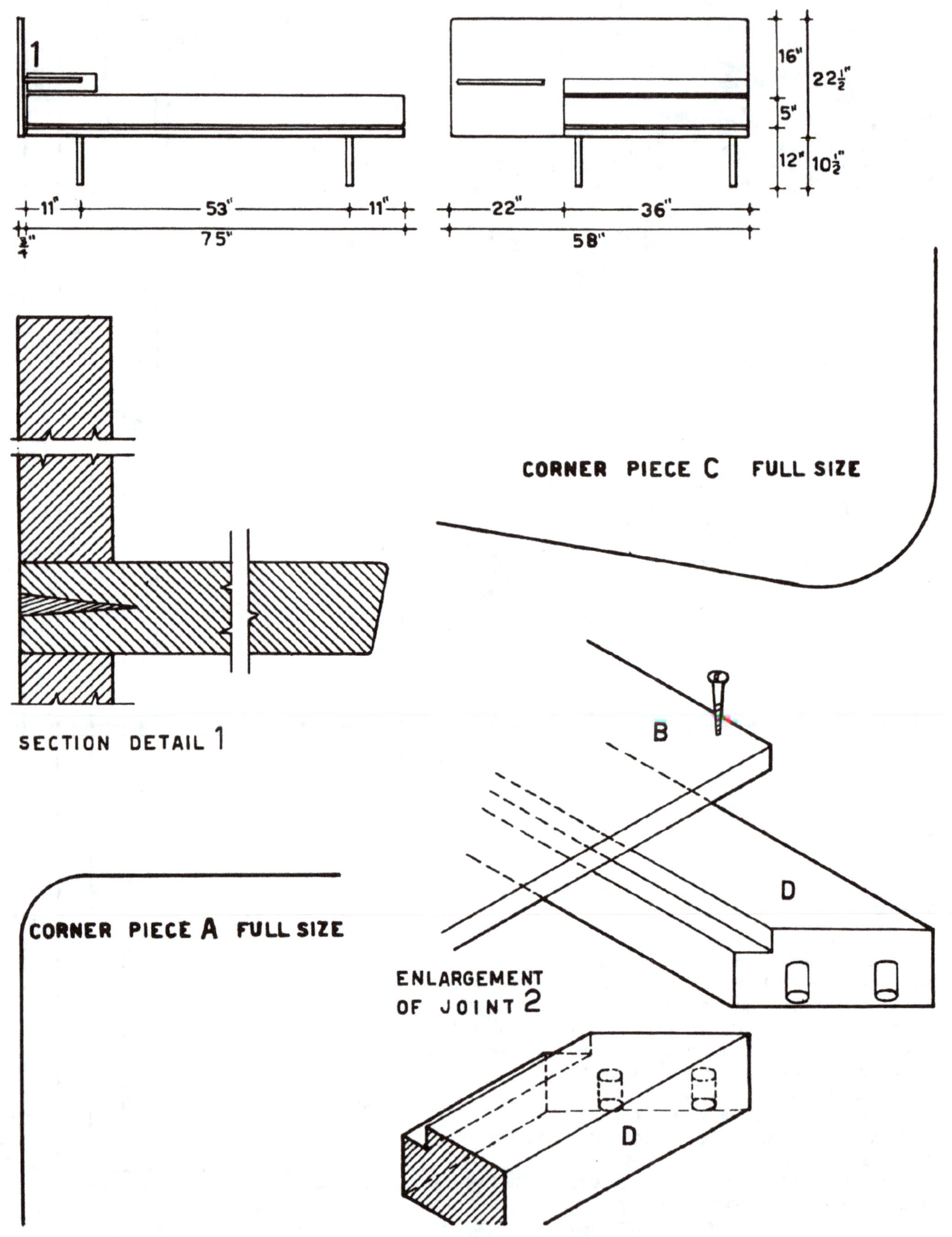

16"
22½"
5"
12"
10½"
11"
53"
11"
¼"
75"
22"
36"
58"
CORNER PIECE C FULL SIZE
SECTION DETAIL 1
B
D
ENLARGEMENT
OF JOINT 2
D
CORNER PIECE A FULL SIZE

BOOKSHELVES

LIST OF MATERIALS.

A — 3 PIECES ¾" THICK AND 34½" X 12". B — 2 PIECES ¾" THICK AND 24" X 12". C — 1 PIECE ¼" THICK AND 35½" X 23½". D — 4 PIECES 1" THICK AND 28" X 1¾".

FOR GENERAL INSTRUCTION SEE PAGE 155.

AFTER MATERIAL IS READY TO BE ASSEMBLED YOU PROCEED AS FOLLOWS:

JOIN "A" WITH "B". (DETAIL 2, SEE PAGE 21, FIG. C AND PAGE 28) "A", "B" WITH "C". (DETAIL 3, SEE PAGE 30). ATTACH LEGS "D" TO COMPLETE YOUR BOOKSHELVES.

FINISH: USE NATURAL FINISH AS DIRECTED IN GENERAL INSTRUCTIONS.

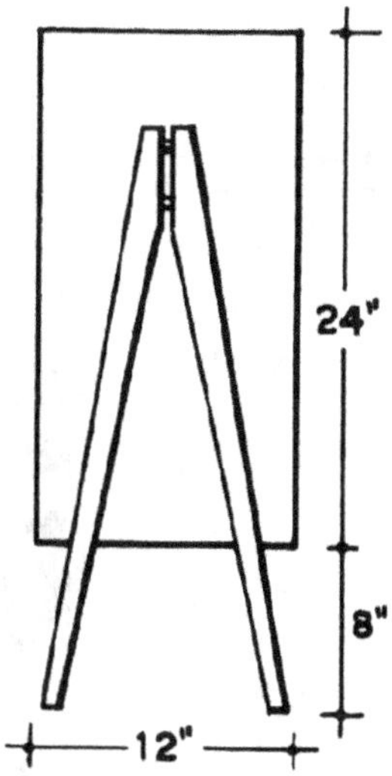

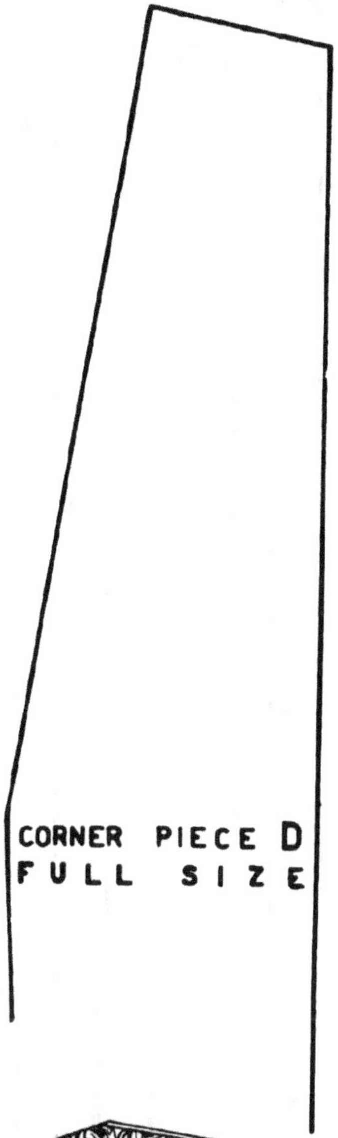

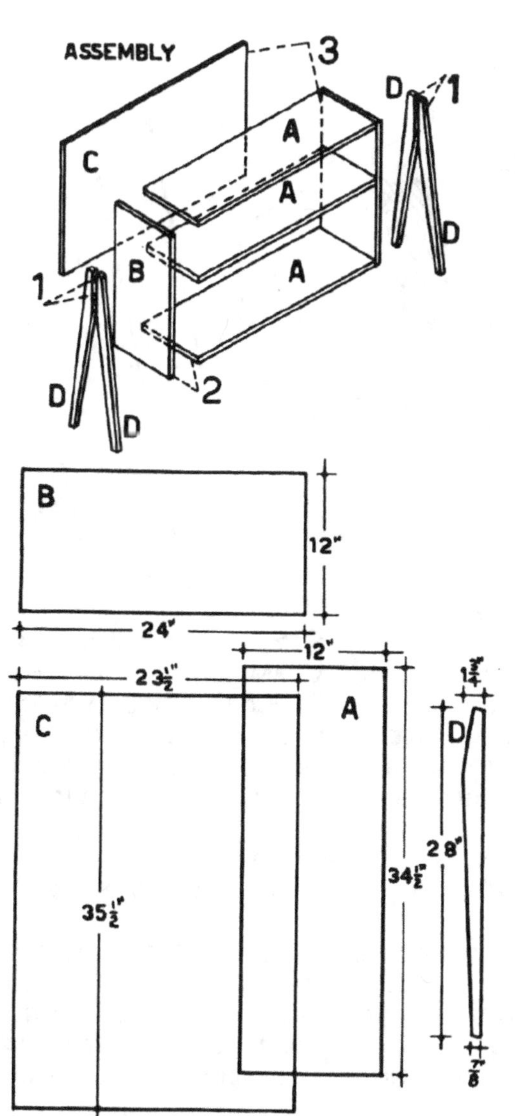

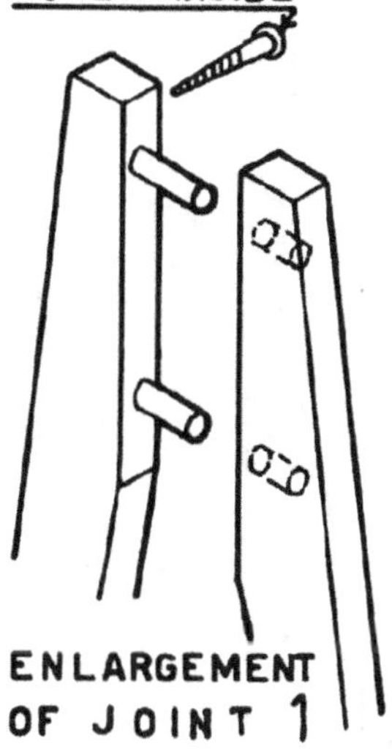

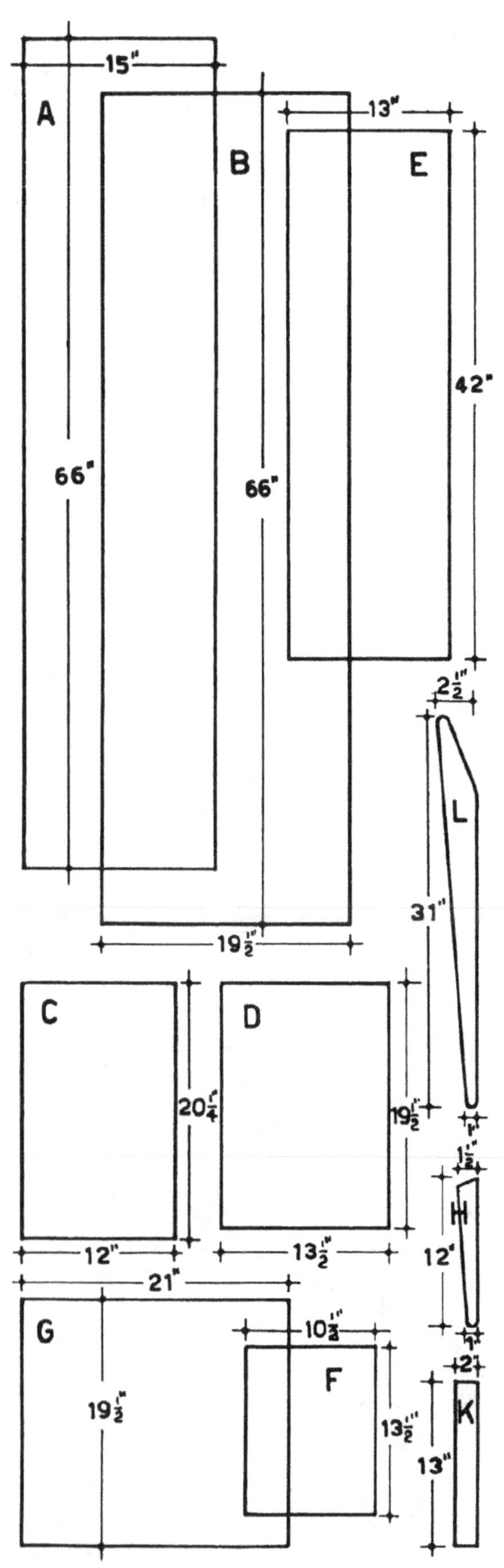

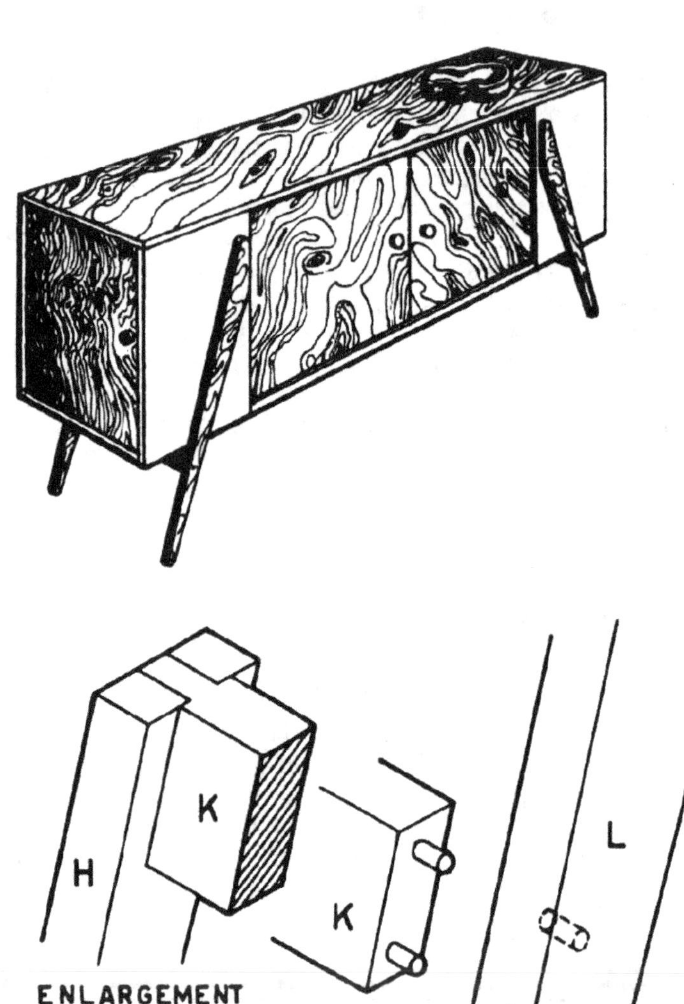

CABINET

LIST OF MATERIALS.

A — 2 PIECES ¾" THICK AND 66" X 15". B — 1 PIECE ¾" THICK AND 66" X 19½". C — 2 PIECES ¾" THICK AND 20¼" X 12". D — 4 PIECES ¾" THICK AND 19½" X 13½". E — 2 PIECES ¾" THICK AND 42" X 13". F — 4 PIECES ¾" THICK AND 13½" X 10½". G — 2 PIECES ¾" THICK AND 19½" X 21". H — 2 PIECES 1" THICK AND 12" X 1½". K — 2 PIECES 1¼" THICK AND 13" X 2". L — 2 PIECES 1" THICK AND 31" X 2½".

FOR GENERAL INSTRUCTIONS SEE PAGE 155.

AFTER MATERIAL IS READY FOR ASSEMBLING YOU PROCEED AS FOLLOWS:

JOIN "A" WITH "B"; (DETAIL 4, SEE PAGE 21, FIG. C); "F" WITH "B", "D"; "C" WITH "A"; "D". ATTACH SHELVES "E" (SEE PAGE 81, FIG. C); ADD DOORS "D" AND "G". (DETAIL 3, SEE PAGE 57, FIG. A). JOIN "H" WITH "H"-"L". ATTACH LEGS TO COMPLETE THE CABINET. FINISH WITH NATURAL FINISH AS INDICATED IN THE GENERAL INSTRUCTIONS.

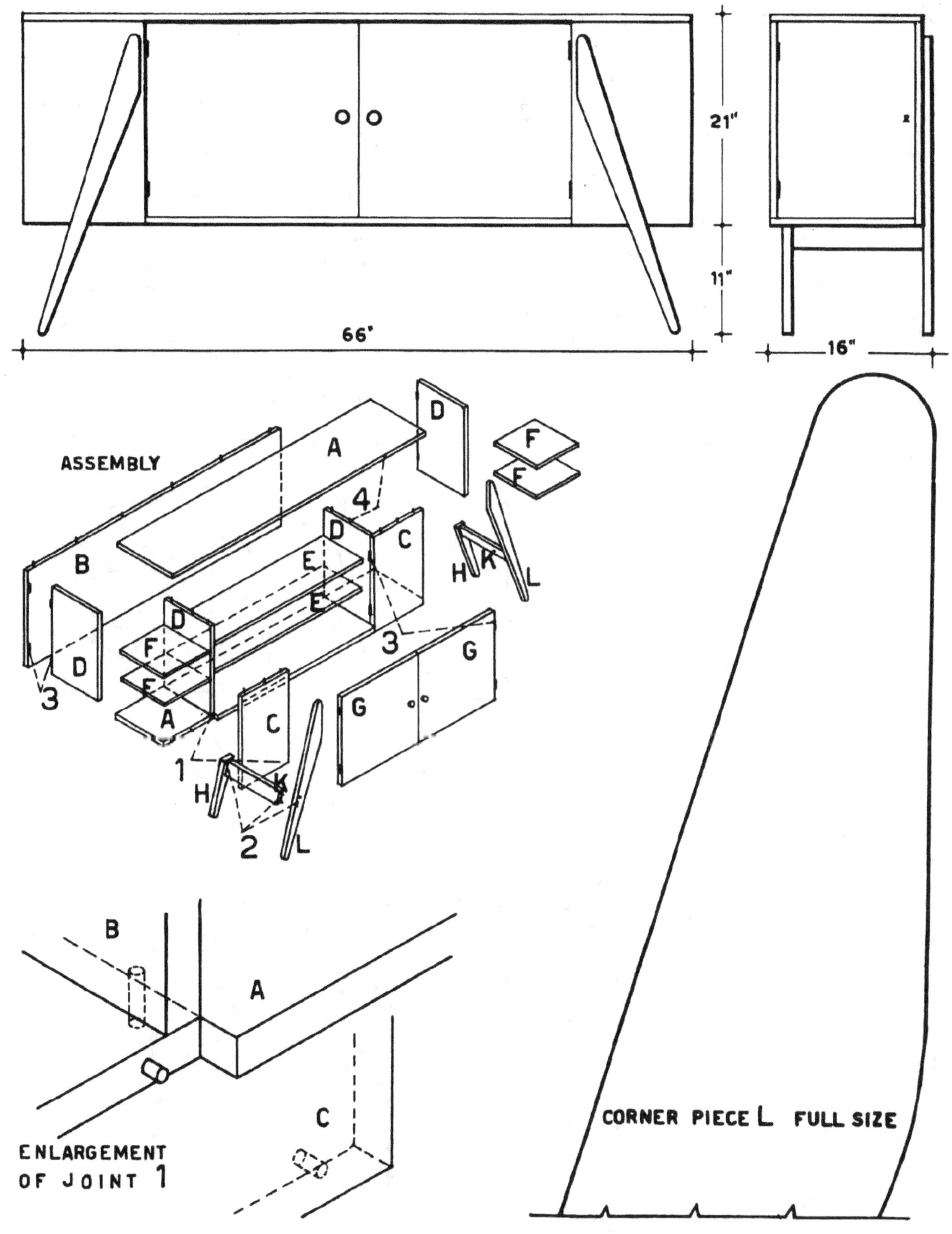

21"
11"
66'
16"
ASSEMBLY
A
B
C
D
D
D
D
E
E
F
F
F
G
G
G
H
K
L
H
K
L
1
2
3
3
3
4
B
A
C
ENLARGEMENT
OF JOINT 1
CORNER PIECE L FULL SIZE

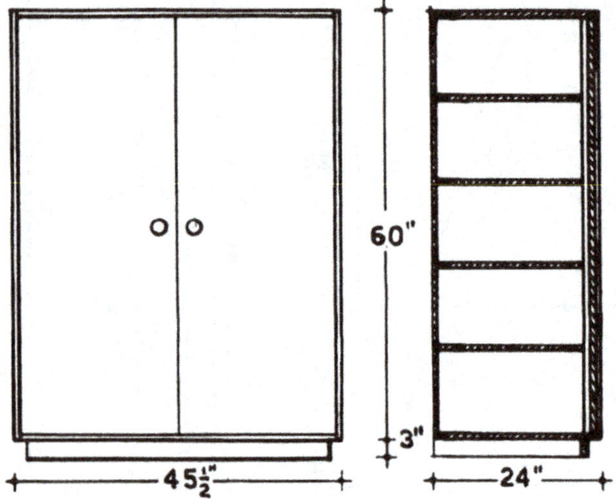

WARDROBE

LIST OF MATERIALS.

A — 2 PIECES ¾" THICK AND 60" X 24". B — 2 PIECES ¾" THICK AND 58½" X 22". C — 2 PIECES ¾" THICK AND 44" X 24". D — 1 PIECE ¼" THICK AND 59½" X 45". E — 4 PIECES ¾" THICK AND 22" X 15". F — 1 PIECE ¾" THICK AND 58½" X 22". G — 1 PIECE 29" LONG AND ¾" IN DIAMETER. H — 1 PIECE 1" THICK AND 41½" X 3". K — 2 PIECES 1" THICK AND 22" X 3".

SEE GENERAL INSTRUCTIONS ON PAGE 155.

AFTER MATERIAL IS READY FOR ASSEMBLING PROCEED AS FOLLOWS:

JOIN "A, C" WITH "A, F, E" (DETAIL 1, SEE PAGE 21, FIG. C AND PAGE 28); ATTACH BACK "D" (SEE PAGE 30); HANG DOORS "B" (SEE PAGE 57, FIG. A); JOIN "C" WITH "H, K" TO COMPLETE THE WARDROBE.

INSTRUCTIONS.

FINISH: USE NATURAL FINISH AS DIRECTED IN GENERAL

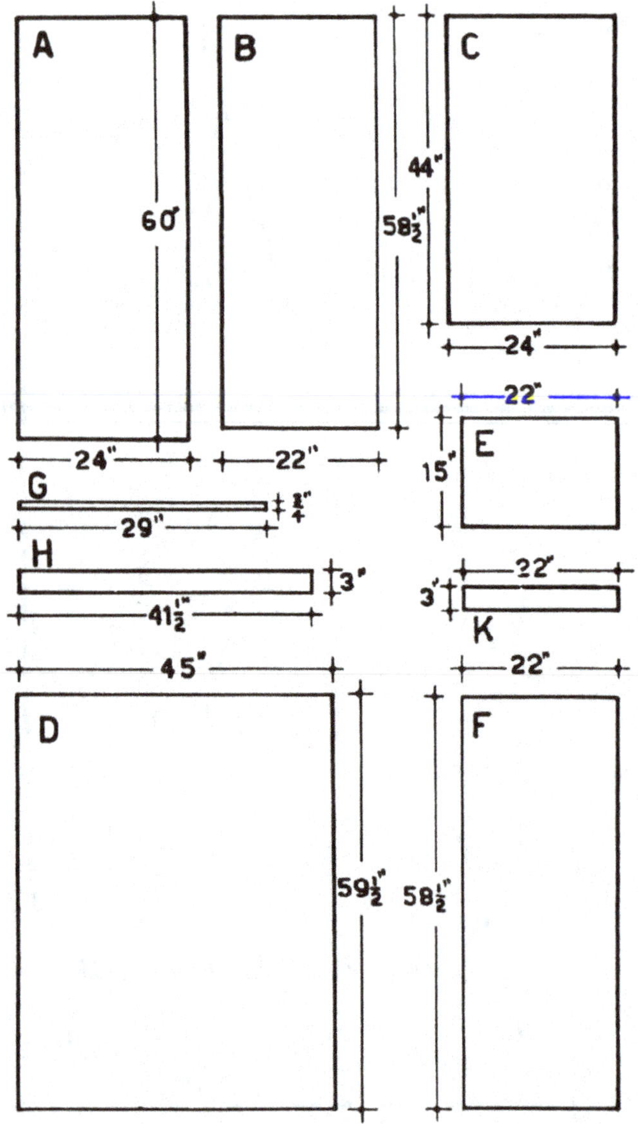

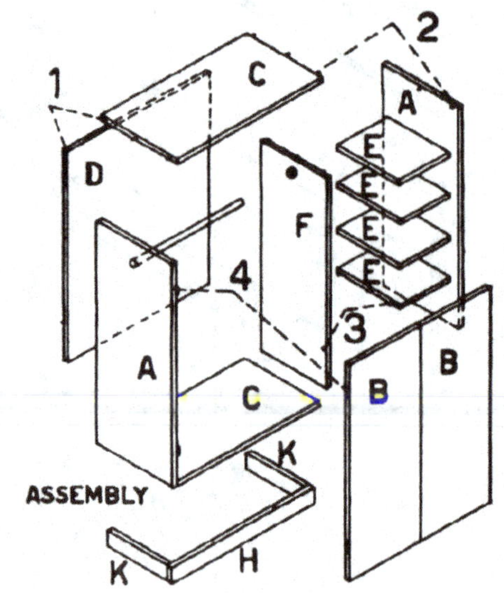

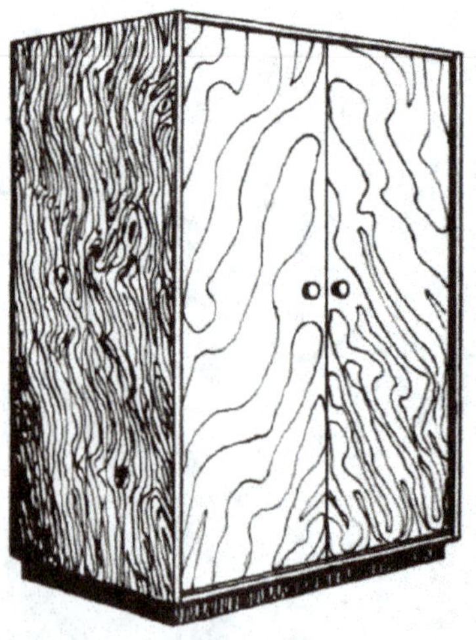

HOW TO BUILD MODERN FURNITURE

MARIO DAL FABBRO

VOL. II   DESIGNS AND ASSEMBLY

PUBLISHED BY F. W. DODGE CORPORATION, NEW YORK

FOREWORD

IN THIS SECOND VOLUME OF **HOW TO BUILD MODERN FURNITURE** I HAVE SHOWN ALL OF THE ESSENTIAL TOOLS AND DESIGN INFORMATION THAT THE AMATEUR CRAFTSMAN WILL NEED TO BUILD BEAUTIFUL MODERN FURNITURE. IN THE FIRST SECTION ARE DESCRIBED THE SIMPLE TOOLS WHICH YOU WILL FIND IN ANY HOME, THE MORE ELABORATE TOOLS WHICH MAY BE ADDED TO THE COLLECTION, WORKBENCHES FOR BEGINNERS AND ADVANCED CRAFTSMEN, AND TWO DIFFERENT WORKSHOP ARRANGEMENTS.

SECTION II, "METHODS OF WOOD WORKING," EXPLAINS THE CORRECT USE OF THE EQUIPMENT DESCRIBED IN THE FIRST SECTION AS WELL AS THE USE OF WOOD-WORKING MACHINERY.

AS A FURTHER AID TO THE CRAFTSMAN I HAVE ILLUSTRATED, IN THE THIRD SECTION OF THE BOOK, THE SIZES OF VARIOUS ARTICLES WHICH MUST BE STORED. I HAVE ALSO INDICATED THE BASIC MEASUREMENTS OF CERTAIN FURNITURE PIECES SUCH AS THE HEIGHTS OF CHAIRS AND TABLES, THE DEPTHS OF CHESTS, AND THE LENGTHS OF SOFAS, BOOKSHELVES AND WARDROBES.

IN THE FOURTH SECTION OF THE BOOK, WHICH DEALS WITH SPECIFIC FURNITURE PIECES, YOU WILL NOTE THAT MOST PIECES CAN BE USED IN SEVERAL DIFFERENT ROOMS. SOME CHAIRS MAY BE IDEAL FOR A LIVING ROOM BUT COULD ALSO BE USED IN A STUDY OR BEDROOM. THE CHESTS COULD ALSO BE USED IN A NUMBER OF ROOMS. THROUGHOUT THE BOOK I HAVE COMBINED VARIOUS PIECES TO MAKE THE ROOM ARRANGEMENTS WHICH BEGIN THE VARIOUS SUB-SECTIONS OF THIS PART OF THE BOOK.

THERE ARE OVER 55 DIFFERENT FURNITURE PIECES SHOWN IN THIS VOLUME. EACH PIECE HAS BEEN DESIGNED SO THAT IT WILL BE EASY TO BUILD AND YET

STRONG IN USE. IT WOULD BE ADVISABLE TO PICK THE PIECES YOU BUILD IN ACCORDANCE WITH YOUR EXPERIENCE AND ABILITY. LEAVE THOSE MORE COMPLICATED PIECES UNTIL LATER — THERE'S NO USE RUSHING IT.

FROM TIME TO TIME YOU MAY FIND IT HELPFUL TO REFER TO *HOW TO BUILD MODERN FURNITURE VOL. I* (PRACTICAL CONSTRUCTION METHODS) FOR DIFFERENT METHODS OF JOINING, FOR UPHOLSTERY PROCEDURES, AND FOR INSTRUCTIONS IN THE USE OF VENEERS, PLYWOODS, GLASS, PLASTICS, AND METALS AND THE APPLICATION OF HARDWARE. THE FIRST VOLUME ALSO INCLUDES NINE MORE FURNITURE DESIGNS FOR THE AMATEUR BUILDER.

I FEEL MOST FORTUNATE IN THE WAY IMPORTANT NEWSPAPERS AND MAGAZINES HAVE RECEIVED MY PREVIOUS BOOKS AND THE INTEREST SHOWN BY THOSE ENGAGED IN FURNITURE DESIGN AND CONSTRUCTION. I WOULD ALSO LIKE TO EXPRESS MY APPRECIATION TO DR. RUDOLPH PAROLA FOR HIS AID IN TRANSLATING THE TEXT AND TO MR. JEFFREY H. LIVINGSTONE, BOOK EDITOR OF THE F. W. DODGE CORPORATION, FOR HIS CONSTANT SUPPORT IN PREPARING BOTH VOLUMES.

Mario Dal Fabbro

TABLE OF CONTENTS

PHOTOGRAPHS

BY

MIDORI, N.Y.

TOOLS
AND
EQUIPMENT

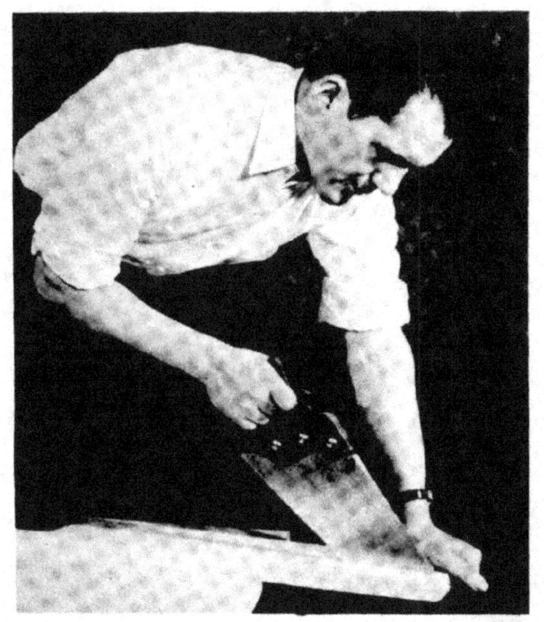

FOUR STEPS IN WOODWORKING

NO ELABORATE TOOLS ARE NEEDED TO CONSTRUCT THE FURNITURE SHOWN IN THIS BOOK. PROBABLY YOU ALREADY OWN THE ESSENTIAL EQUIPMENT: YOU NEED ONLY LEARN TO USE IT.

IN THE PICTURES ON THIS PAGE ARE SHOWN THE FOUR MAJOR STEPS USED IN BUILDING ANY PIECE OF FURNITURE. IN THE PHOTOGRAPH AT THE LEFT I HAVE DEMONSTRATED THE PROPER METHOD OF SAWING. IN THE CENTER ILLUSTRATION IS SHOWN THE BEST METHOD OF HOLDING A PLANE. NOTE THE WOOD BLOCKS USED TO HOLD THE PIECES IN PLACE. DIRECTLY BELOW THE CORRECT METHOD OF HOLDING A BIT AND BRACE IS ILLUSTRATED. IN THE PHOTOGRAPH AT THE BOTTOM OF THE PAGE THE LEGS OF THE TABLE ARE BEING INSTALLED IN THE DRILLED HOLES.

ON THE FOLLOWING PAGES I HAVE DESCRIBED THE USES OF THE MOST COMMON TOOLS, AS WELL AS SOME ADVANCED EQUIPMENT YOU MAY WISH TO ADD TO YOUR COLLECTION.

CUTTING

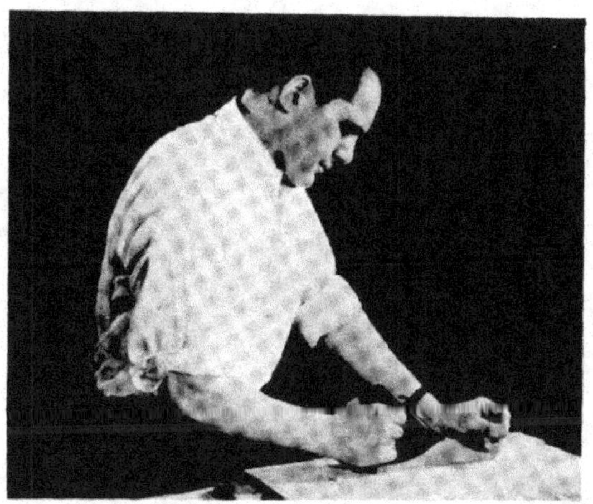

PLANING

DRILLING HOLES

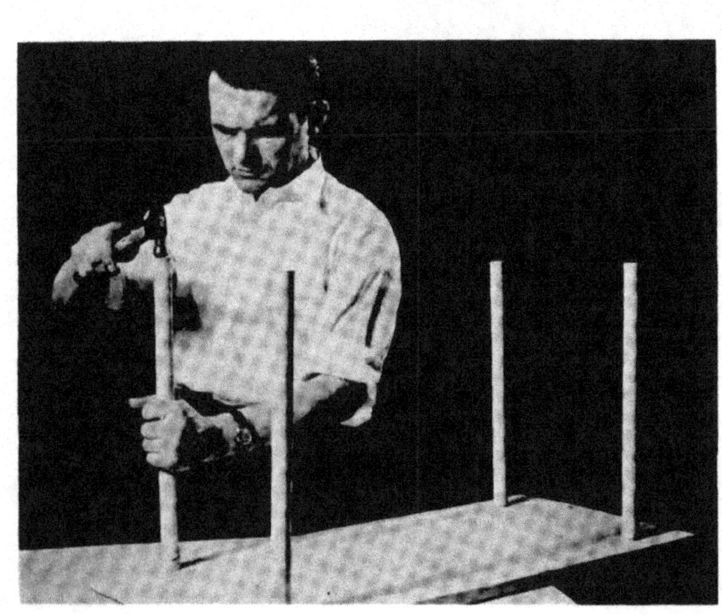

ASSEMBLY

MEASURING DEVICES

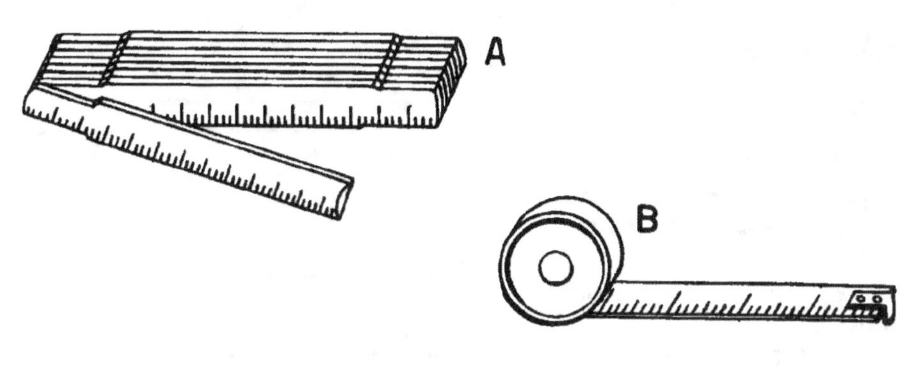

A. THE **FOLDING RULE** IS CON-
STRUCTED OF METAL OR WOOD.

B. THE **PULL-PUSH RULE** IS A FLEX-
IBLE STEEL TAPE. BOTH "A" AND
"B" ARE 6 FEET IN LENGTH.

C. THE **TRY SQUARE** IS A METAL
BLADE FITTED TO FORM A PERFECT
RIGHT ANGLE TO THE STRAIGHT
EDGE OF A HEAVIER PIECE OF
WOOD OR METAL. THE BLADE IS
USUALLY STAMPED IN ONE-INCH
GRADATIONS AND THEIR FRAC-
TIONS, SO THAT THE TOOL CAN
BE USED FOR MEASURING AS
WELL AS SQUARING.

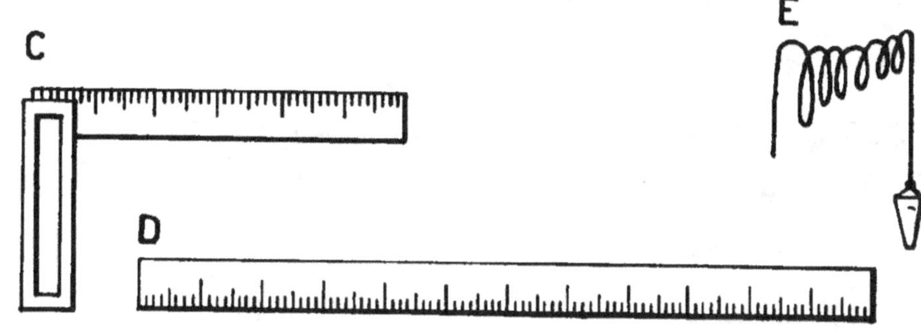

D. **RULES** CAN BE OF WOOD AS
WELL AS OF METAL. THE MOST
COMMON ARE THE YARDSTICK
AND THE FOOT RULER. AN ARCHI-
TECT'S SCALE IS ALSO HELPFUL IN
CONSTRUCTING FULL-SIZE WORK
FROM DRAWINGS.

E. THE **PLUMB BOB** IS A LEAD
WEIGHT ATTACHED TO A LINE
WHICH IS USED TO VERIFY VERTI-
CAL LINES.

SAWS

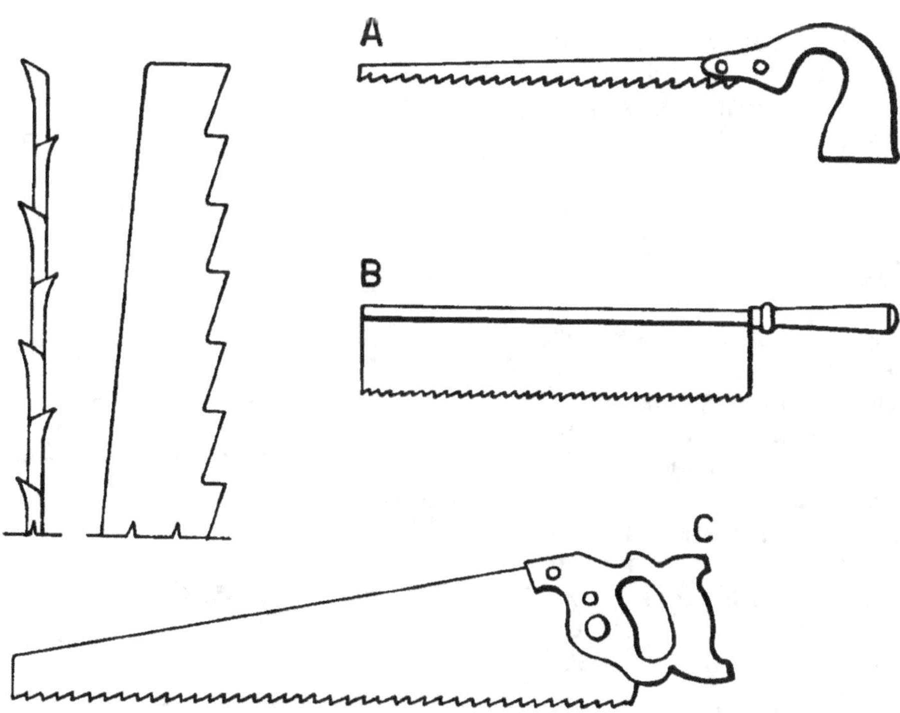

A. THE **COMPASS SAW** IS COM-
MONLY USED TO MAKE CUTOUTS
IN A SECTION OF MATERIAL.

B. THE **BACKSAW** IS REINFORCED
WITH A RIGID STEEL "BACK," HAS
A THIN BLADE AND FINE TEETH,
AND IS USED FOR PRECISION
CUTTING.

C. THE **PANEL SAW** (ALSO CALLED
RIPSAW OR CROSSCUT SAW, AC-
CORDING TO PLACEMENT OF THE
TEETH) IS ONE OF THE MOST
COMMON TYPES AND IS USED
IN ALL PHASES OF CARPENTRY.

HAMMER, NAILS, AND PLIERS

A. CLAW HAMMER
B. TOWER PATTERN PINCHERS
C. ROUND-NOSED PLIERS USED IN UPHOLSTERY WORK
D. TWO TYPES OF FINISHING NAILS
E. UPHOLSTERY TACK

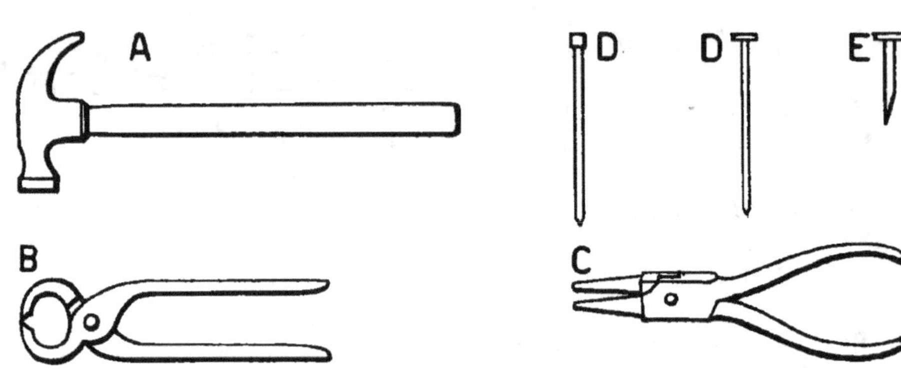

SCREW DRIVER AND SCREWS

A. COMMON TYPE SCREW DRIVER
B. FLAT-HEAD SCREW
C. OVAL-HEAD SCREW
D. ROUND-HEAD SCREW

CHISELS

THESE TOOLS COME IN VARIOUS WIDTHS, FROM ⅛" TO 2", AND ARE USED FOR REMOVING SECTIONS OF WOOD. (SEE PAGE 5 FOR OTHER TYPES)

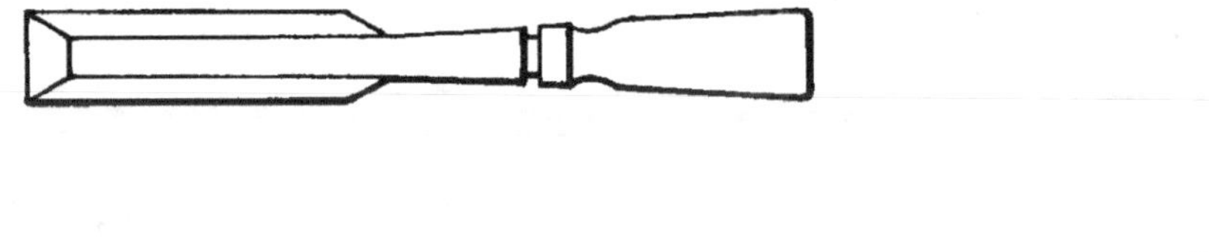

FILES

FILES ARE USUALLY CLASSIFIED BY SHAPE AND THE CUT OF THE TEETH. AT RIGHT ARE THE SQUARE AND ROUND TYPES. THE TEETH MAY BE SINGLE-CUT, DOUBLE-CUT, RASP, OR CURVED. WITH REFERENCE TO COARSENESS OF THE TEETH, THE FILES DESCRIBED ABOVE MAY BE CLASSIFIED AS ROUGH, COARSE, BASTARD, SECOND CUT, SMOOTH, AND DEAD SMOOTH.

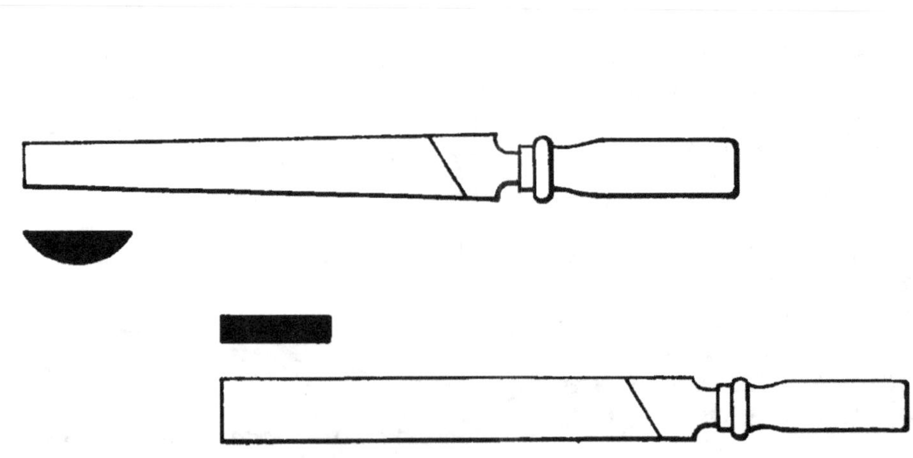

PLANES

THERE ARE MANY TYPES OF PLANES FOR VARIOUS USES. TWO COMMON TYPES ARE SHOWN HERE. THE **JACK PLANE** ("A") IS USED FOR ALL TYPES OF WORK AND IS THE ONE MOST NECESSARY FOR THE HOME WORKSHOP. THE **BLOCK PLANE** ("B") IS USED FOR FINE OR PRECISION WORK.

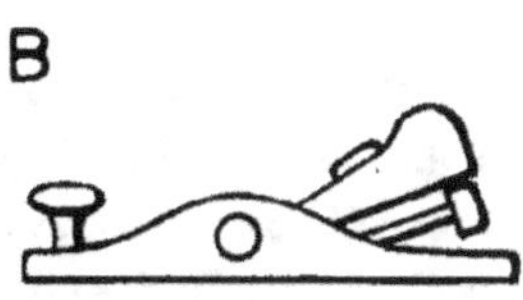

BIT AND BRACE

A. THE **BRACE** IS A CRANK-SHAPED TOOL USED TO HOLD VARIOUS TYPES AND SIZES OF BITS.

B. THE **BIT** IS A SPIRAL-SHAPED TOOL WITH A SCREW POINT. CUTTING ACTION IS PROVIDED BY SHARP NIBS.

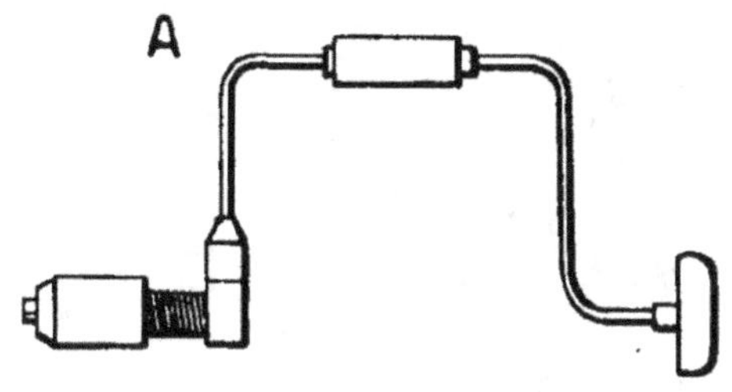

CLAMPS

CLAMPS ARE USED TO MAINTAIN PRESSURE BETWEEN TWO GLUED PIECES OF WOOD UNTIL COMPLETE ADHESION HAS TAKEN PLACE.

A. "C" CLAMP, FOR GENERAL USE, HAS A TIGHTENING DEVICE.

B. **SPRING CLAMP** CONSISTS OF A STEEL WIRE FORMED IN A BROKEN CIRCLE, AND IS USED IN FINER WORK.

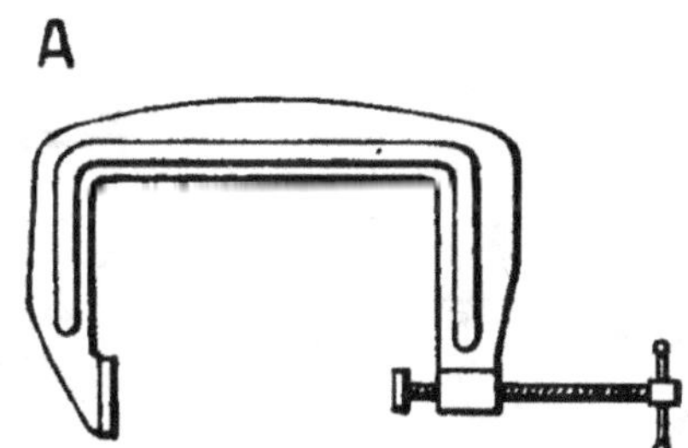
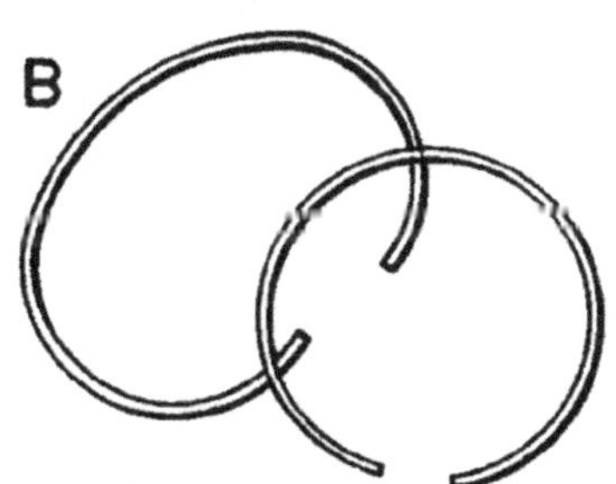

OILSTONE

THE PRINCIPAL USE OF THE **OILSTONE** IS TO SHARPEN HAND TOOLS. THE OILSTONE MUST BE FLAT. OIL IS POURED ON THE SURFACE BY MEANS OF CAN ("B") BEFORE EACH TOOL IS SHARPENED.

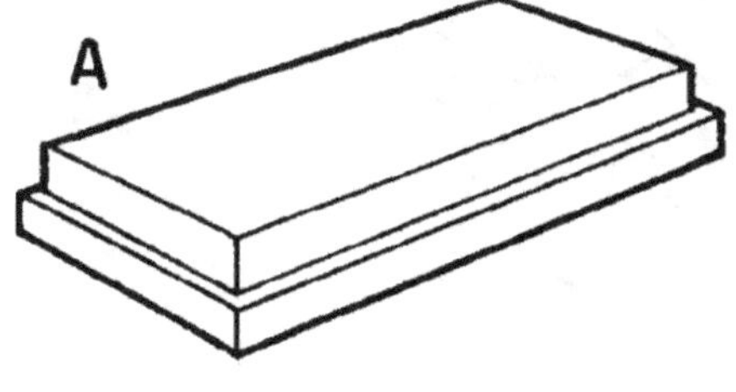
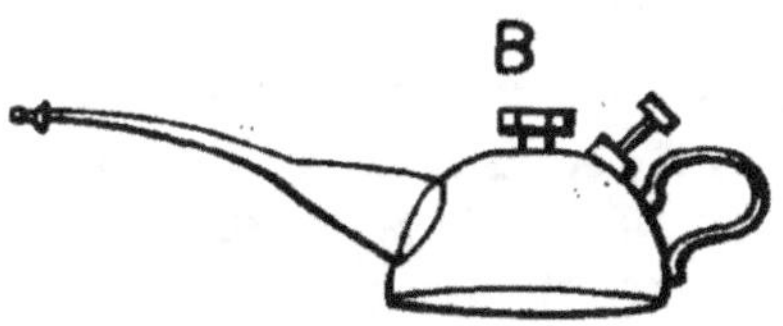

GAUGES

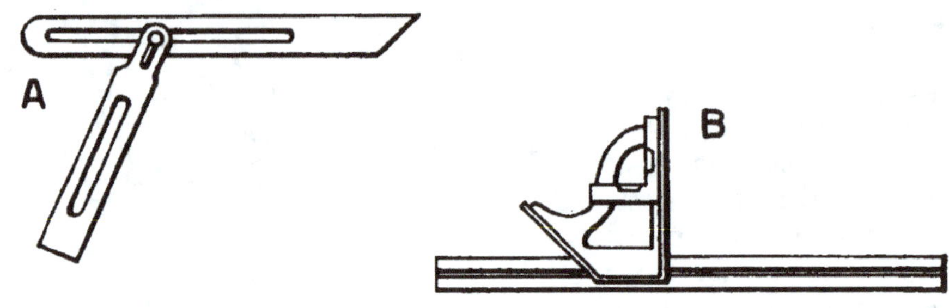

A. THE **BEVEL GAUGE** IS MADE ON THE SAME PRINCIPLE AS THE TRY SQUARE, BUT IS ADJUSTABLE TO ANY DESIRED SLANT. IT IS USED TO MARK AND CHECK ANGLES.

B. THE **COMBINATION SQUARE AND BEVEL GAUGE** IS A VERY PRACTICAL TOOL USED EXTENSIVELY IN CABINET WORK FOR TESTING FOR LEVEL AS WELL AS FOR SQUARE.

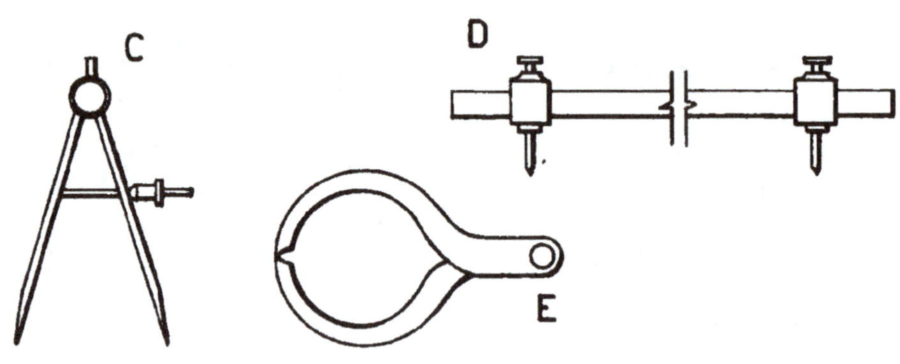

C. THE **COMPASS** IS USED IN THE CABINET MAKER'S SHOP, AS IT IS IN DRAWING, FOR SCRIBING CIRCLES.

D. THE **TRAMMEL POINT** IS USED TO MAKE LARGE CIRCLES ON WOOD.

E. **CALIPERS** ARE USED PARTICULARLY TO CONTROL DIAMETERS IN WOOD TURNING.

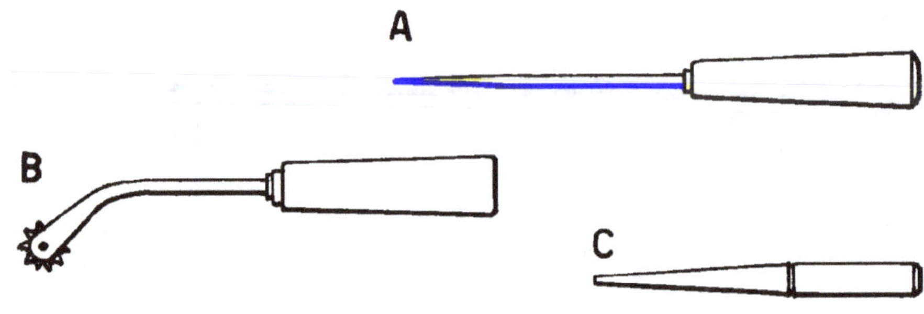

MARKING DEVICES

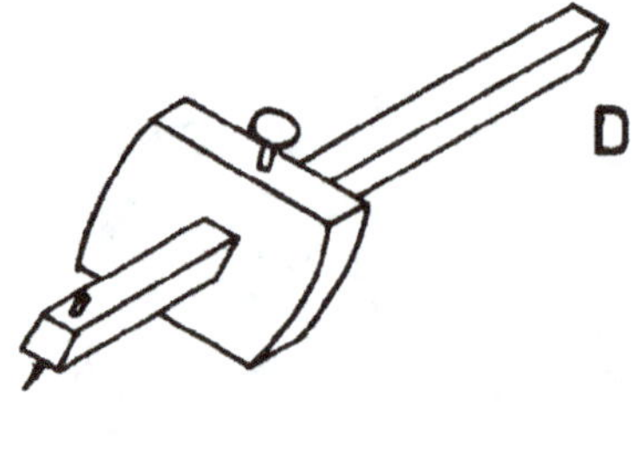

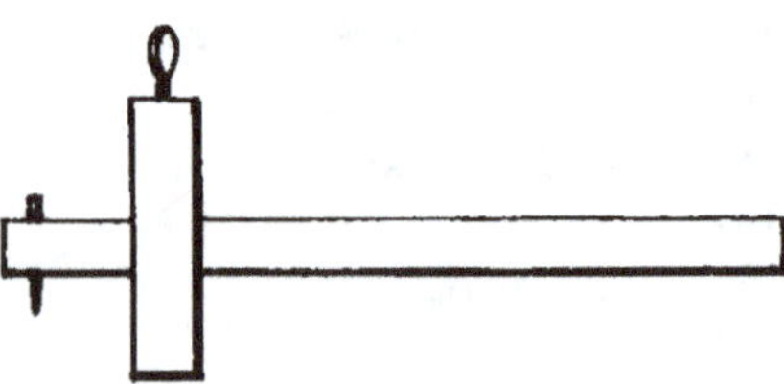

A. THE **SCRIBER** IS USED TO IMPRESS LINES ON SURFACES.

B. THE **TRACER** IS USED TO TRANSFER PAPER PATTERNS TO WOOD SURFACES.

C. THE **NAIL PUNCH**, NORMALLY USED TO DRIVE A FINISHING NAIL BELOW THE SURFACE OF THE WOOD, MAY ALSO BE USED FOR MARKING.

D. THE **MARKING GAUGE** IS USED FOR MARKING LINES A UNIFORM DISTANCE IN FROM THE EDGE OF A PIECE OF WORK.

TOOLS FOR THE ADVANCED HOBBYIST

THE ADVANCED HOBBYIST WILL WANT MANY MORE TOOLS THAN THE MINIMUM EQUIPMENT WHICH HAS BEEN DESCRIBED FOR THE HOME WORKSHOP. WITH THE COMPLETE SET OF TOOLS AND MACHINES FOR WOODWORKING DESCRIBED ON THE FOLLOWING PAGES THE HOBBYIST WILL BE ABLE TO DO HIS WORK FASTER AND MORE ACCURATELY. THIS EQUIPMENT IS EASY TO OBTAIN, SINCE MOST NEIGHBORHOOD STORES HAVE RESPONDED TO THE DEMANDS OF HOBBYISTS.

SAWS

A. THE **TURNING SAW** IS USED FOR CUTTING CURVES, SCROLLS, AND ROUNDINGS. THE THIN BLADE IS REMOVABLE.

B. THE **MITER SAW** IS AN OVER-SIZE BACKSAW NORMALLY USED IN A MITER BOX. IT IS IDEAL FOR MAKING ANGULAR CUTS.

C. THE **DOVETAIL SAW** IS SIMILAR TO THE BACKSAW, BUT HAS A THINNER BLADE AND FINER TEETH. IT IS IDEAL FOR PRECISE AND DELICATE CUTTING.

D. THE **COPING SAW** IS USED FOR CUTTING CURVES AND SPECIAL SHAPES. IT MAY HAVE FINE OR COARSE BLADES.

CHISELS

A. THE **FRAME OR MORTISE CHISEL** IS ADAPTED TO WITHSTAND SEVERE STRAIN. IT COMES IN SIZES FROM ⅛″ TO ⅝″.

B. **GOUGES** ARE CURVED CHISELS USED FOR REMOVING SECTIONS OF WOOD IN DECORATIVE WORK. THEY RANGE FROM ⅛″ TO 1½″.

A. VARIOUS FORMS OF **FILE SECTIONS**.

B. THE **FILE CARD** IS USED TO CLEAN WOOD CHIPS FROM TEETH OF FILES.

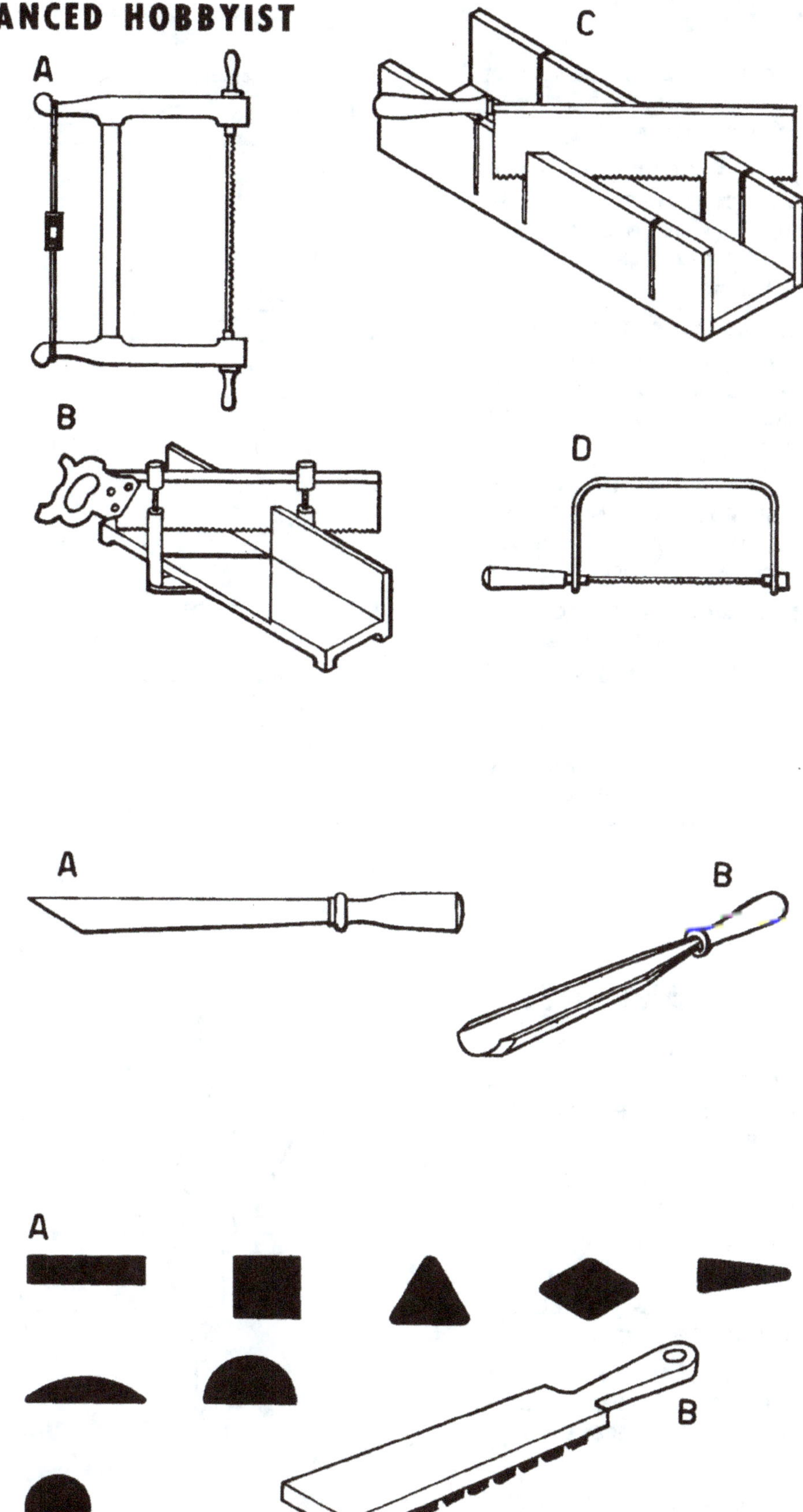

PLANES

A. THE **JOINTER PLANE** IS ABOUT 24" LONG AND USED PRINCIPALLY FOR LONG BOARDS.

B. THE **SMOOTH PLANE** IS USUALLY 10" IN LENGTH. IT IS USEFUL IN PLANING END GRAIN AND CHAMFERS, AND IN OTHER EDGE SHAPING.

C. THE **CIRCULAR PLANE**, FORMED BY CONVEX OR CONCAVE SURFACES, IS ESPECIALLY USEFUL IN SHAPING ROUND EDGES.

D. THE **RABBETING PLANE** IS USED FOR EXECUTING RABBETS OF VARIOUS SIZES ON THE SURFACE OF THE WOOD.

E. THE **SHAPE** IS USED TO ERADICATE MARKINGS ON THE SURFACE OF WOOD BEFORE SAND PAPERING.

F. THE **FLAT-FACE SPOKESHAVE** IS USED PRINCIPALLY ON OVAL SURFACES, OR FOR SHAPING AND SMOOTHING EDGES.

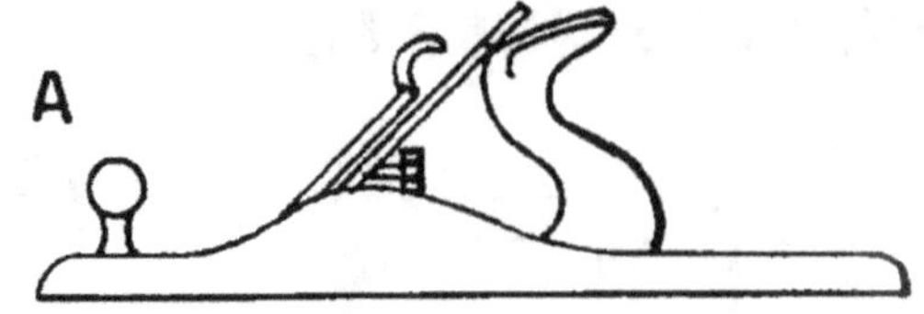

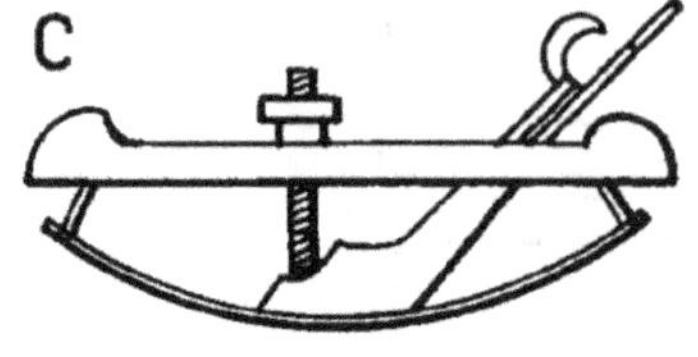
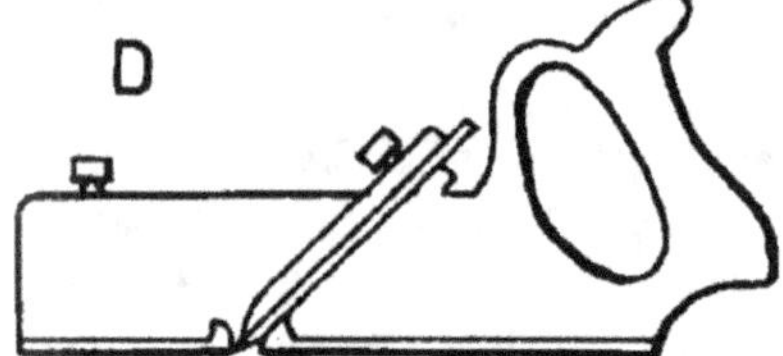
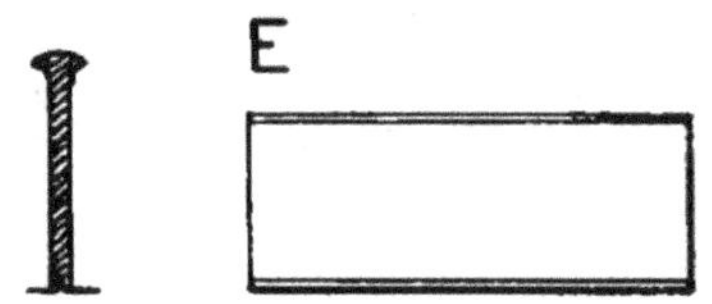
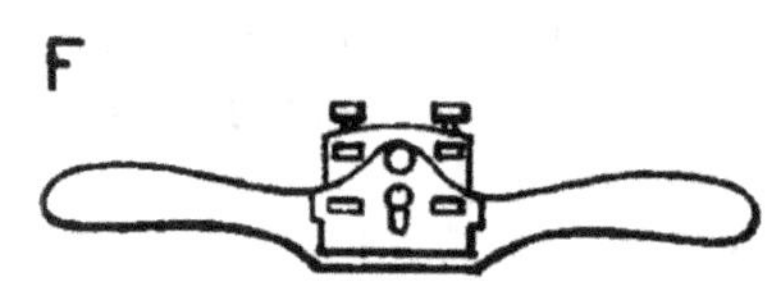

DRILL AND BITS

A. THE **DRILL** HOLDS BITS OF VARIOUS TYPES FOR MAKING HOLES OF DIFFERENT SIZES AND SHAPES.

B. THE **AUGER BIT** IS SPIRAL-SHAPED AND HAS A SCREW POINT.

C. THE **EXPANSIVE BIT** CAN BE ADJUSTED TO BORE A HOLE OF ANY DESIRED SIZE.

D. THE **COUNTERSINK BIT** SPREADS THE SURFACE OF A SMALL HOLE TO RECEIVE A SCREW HEAD.

E. THE **GIMLET BIT** IS USED TO MAKE A SERIES OF SMALL HOLES.

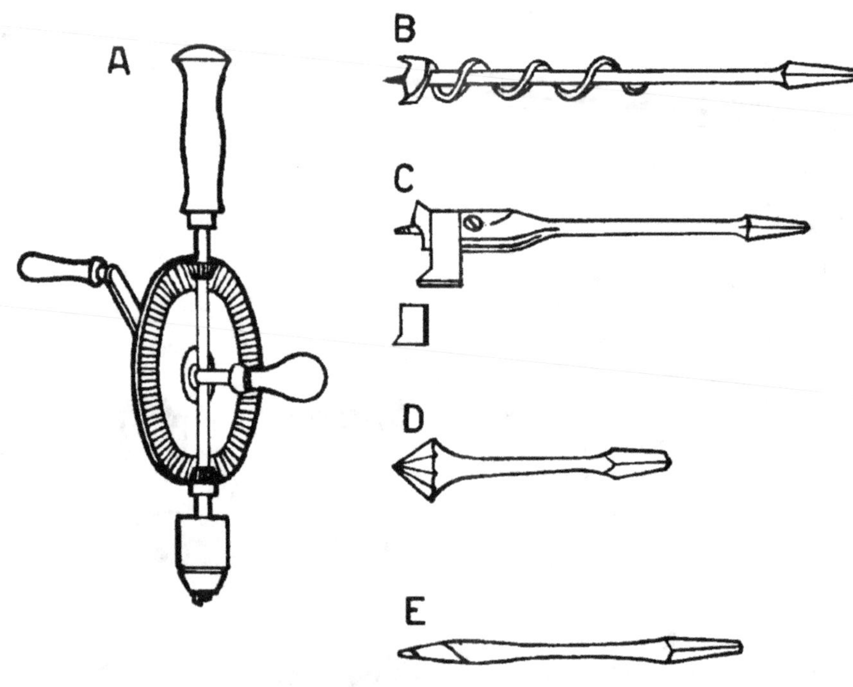

CLAMPS

MANY TYPES OF CLAMPS ARE USED IN THE WOODWORKING SHOP.

A. THE **ADJUSTABLE BAR CLAMP** IS USED TO JOIN BOARDS TO-GETHER. ITS SPREAD IS 2' TO 8'.

B. THE **PARALLEL CLAMP** IS MADE OF WOOD AND USED FOR LIGHT WORK. THE PARTS MUST BE KEPT PARALLEL AS THEY ARE SCREWED TOGETHER.

C. THE **DOUBLE BAR CLAMP** IS USED TO PRESS TOGETHER THIN SECTIONS OF WOOD, AS IN VENEER.

D. THE **CARRIAGE CLAMP** IS THE MOST COMMON TYPE USED IN WOOD WORK, AND COMES IN VARIOUS SIZES.

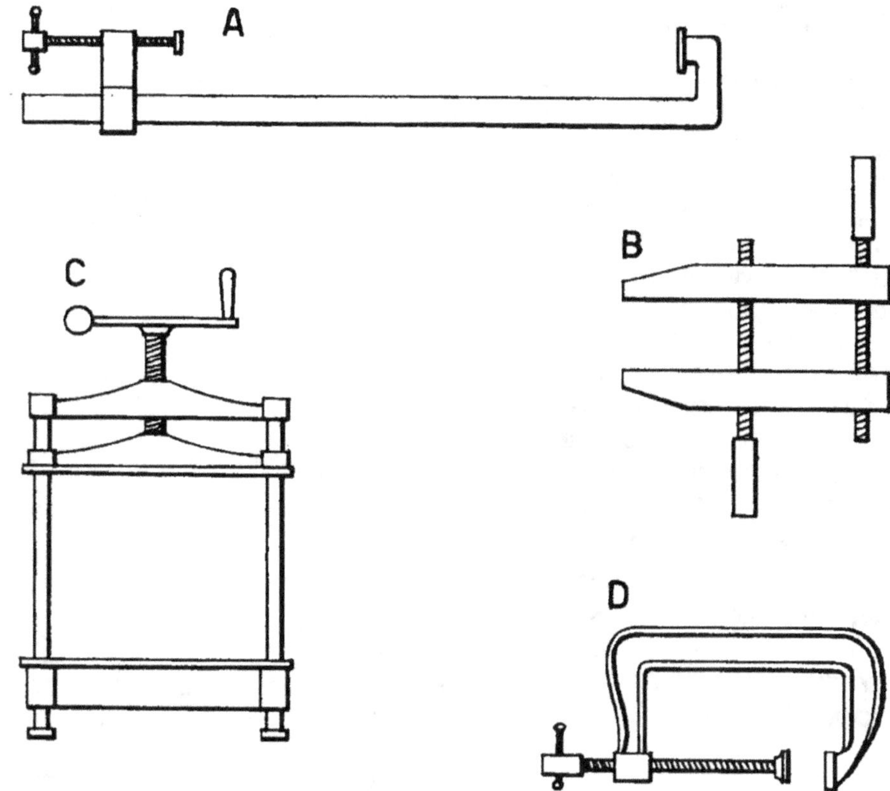

VISE

THE VISE IS AN IMPORTANT PIECE OF WOODWORKING EQUIPMENT. ITS FUNCTION IS TO HOLD A PIECE OF MATERIAL FIRMLY IN PLACE WHILE IT IS BEING WORKED.

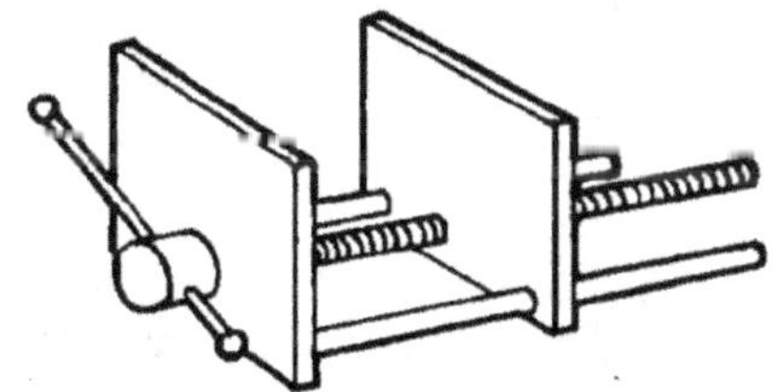

GRINDSTONE

A. THE **WET GRINDSTONE** IS USED FOR PRELIMINARY GRINDING OF PLANE BLADES, CHISELS, AND OTHER TOOLS BEFORE FINAL SHARPENING ON THE OILSTONE.

B. **GOUGE SLIP STONES** ARE PIECES OF OILSTONE IN VARIOUS SHAPES USED FOR SHARPENING SUCH TOOLS AS THE GOUGE AND CHISEL.

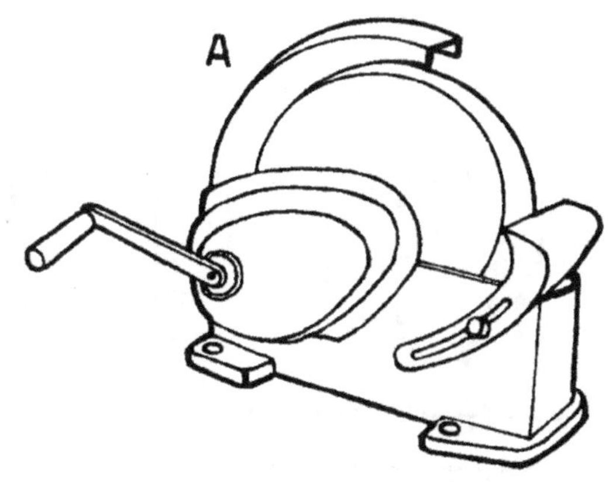

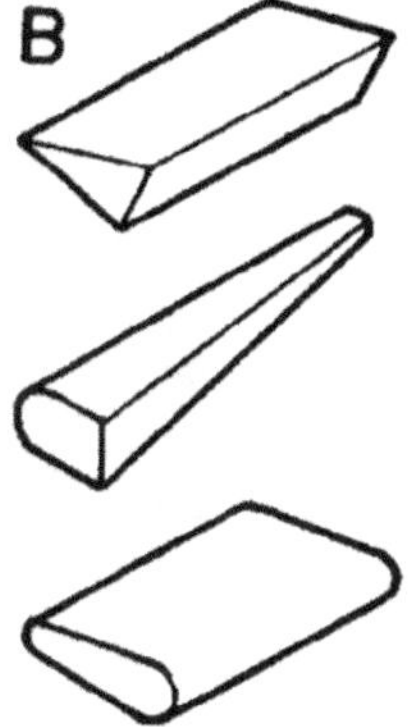

WORKBENCH

A FAMILY WORKBENCH CAN BE ANY SOLID TABLE, WITH A VISE ADDED TO HOLD VARIOUS LENGTHS OF WOOD WHILE THEY ARE BEING WORKED. READY-MADE BENCHES ARE ALSO AVAILABLE; HOWEVER, IF YOU WISH TO MAKE YOUR OWN, THE ILLUSTRATION AT RIGHT SHOWS ONE THAT·IS SIMPLE AND PRACTICAL. IT WILL HOLD ALL OF A HOBBYIST'S TOOLS AND WHEN CLOSED WILL LOOK LIKE A CABINET, SO THAT IT CAN BE PLACED IN ANY PART OF THE HOME.

THE DIAGRAMS GIVE THE IMPORTANT DIMENSIONS, AND ON THE FOLLOWING PAGE IS AN ASSEMBLY SCHEME SHOWING HOW THE WORKBENCH FITS TOGETHER.

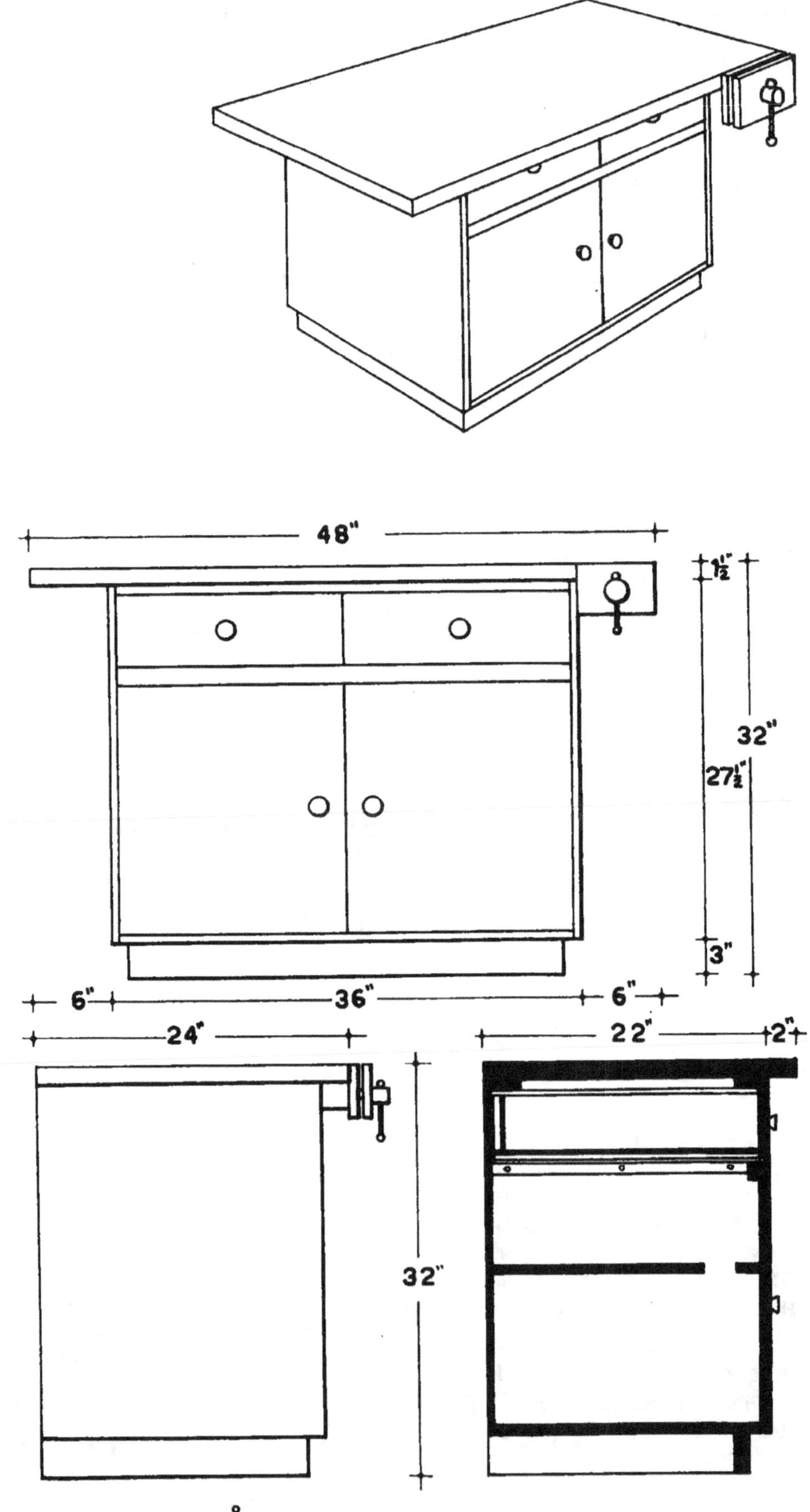

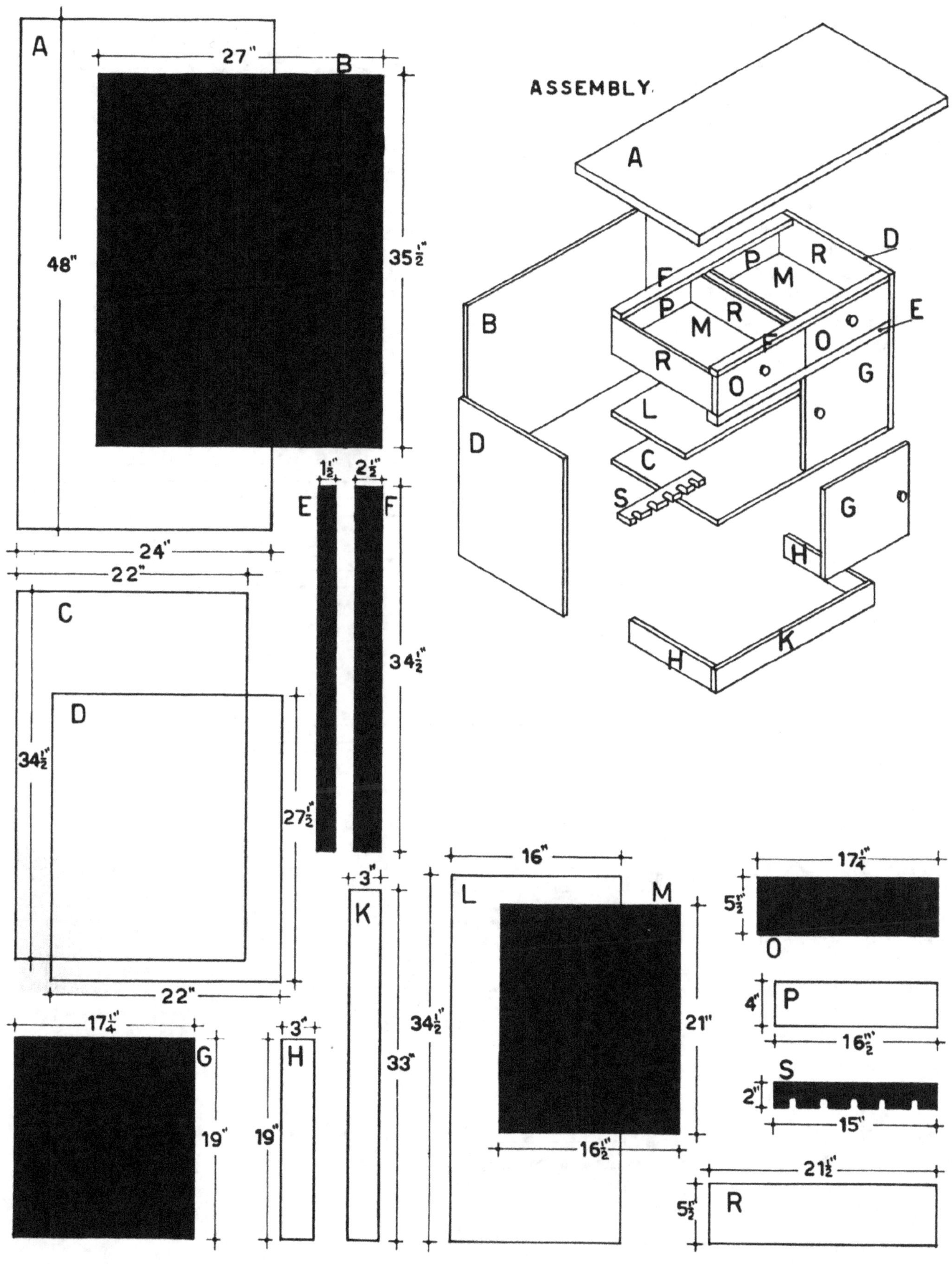

A
B
27"
48"
35½"
ASSEMBLY.
A
D
F
P
M
R
B
P
M
R
E
R
O
G
L
C
S
G
H
K
H
E
F
1½"
2½"
34½"
24"
22"
C
D
34½"
27½"
3"
K
L
M
16"
34½"
21"
33"
16½"
17¼"
5½"
O
4"
P
16½"
S
2"
15"
17¼"
G
3"
H
19"
19"
21½"
5½"
R
9

PROFESSIONAL WORKBENCH

THIS TYPE OF BENCH IS A SOLID
WOOD STRUCTURE WHICH CAN
SUPPORT A STRONG BASE FOR
HEAVY WORK. THE VISE IS PER-
MANENTLY ATTACHED TO THE
END OF THE BENCH TO FACILI-
TATE THE HANDLING OF LONGER
PIECES OF LUMBER. THESE
BENCHES ARE IN STANDARD PRO-
DUCTION FOR PURCHASE BY THE
HOBBYIST, BUT THE EXPERIENCED
CABINETMAKER CAN EASILY BUILD
HIS OWN.

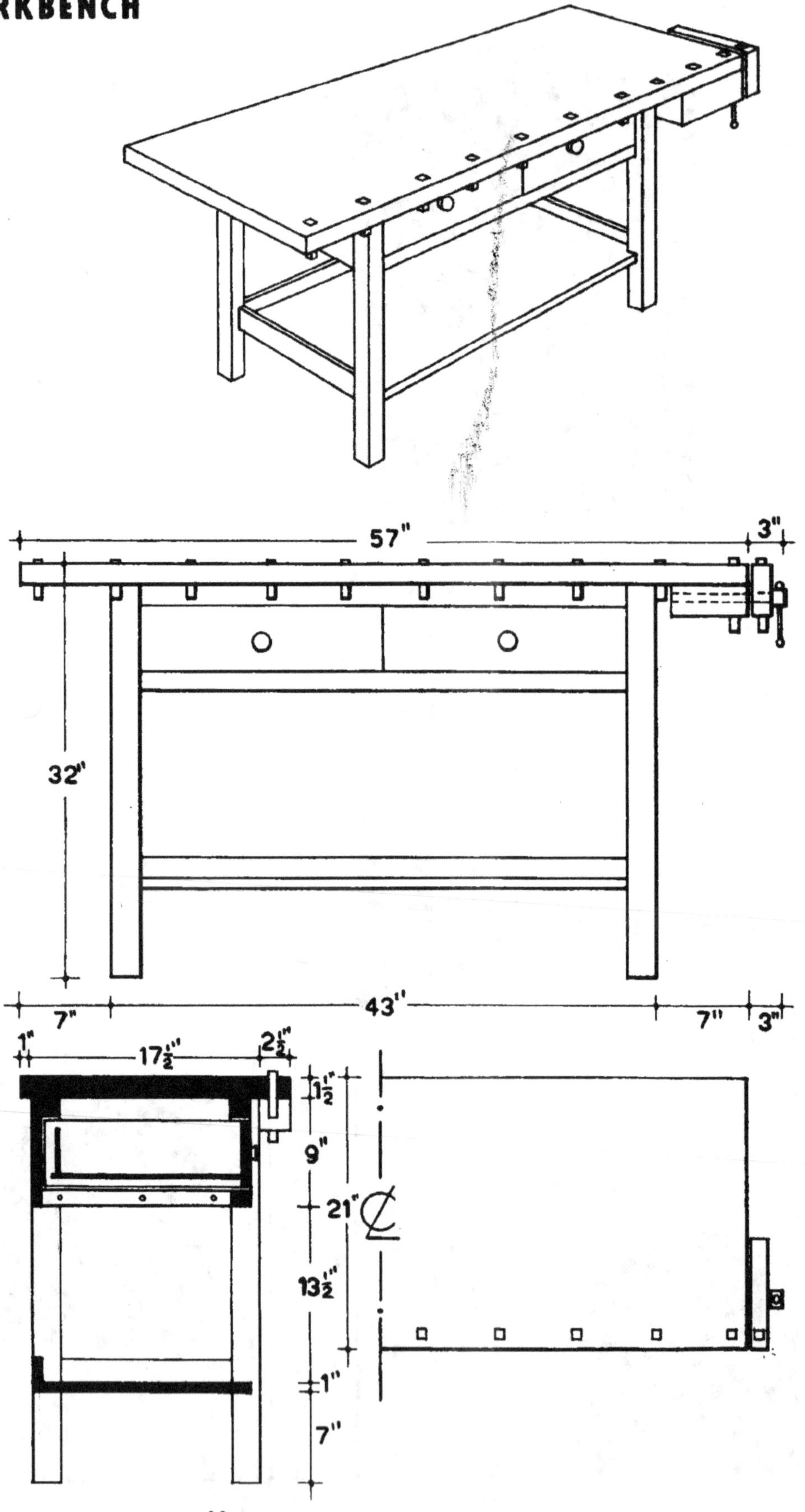

TOOL STORAGE

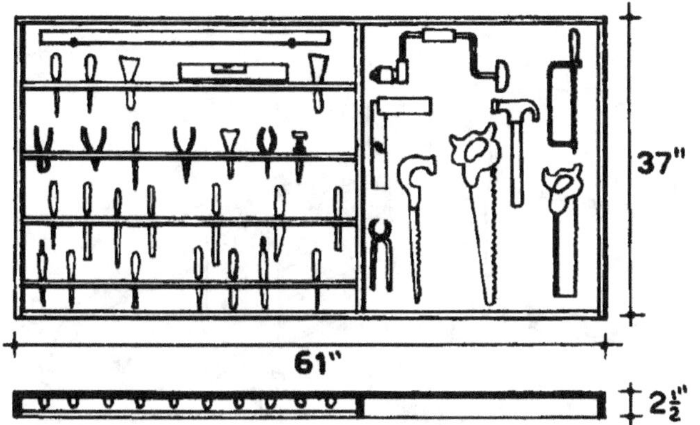

A. TOOL BOARD

61"

37"

2½"

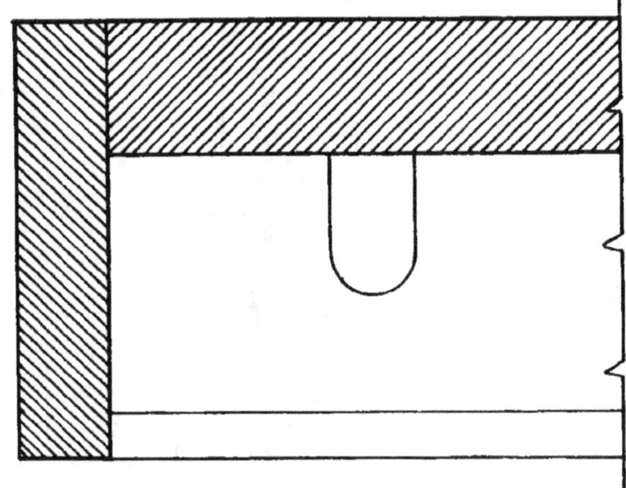

FULL-SIZE DETAIL OF TOOL BOARD ("A")

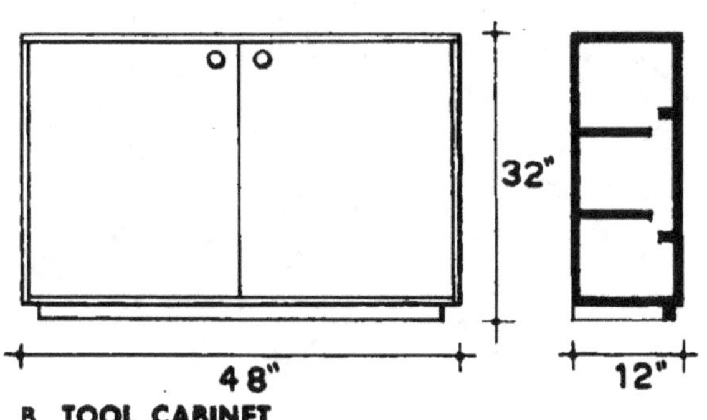

B. TOOL CABINET

48"

32"

12"

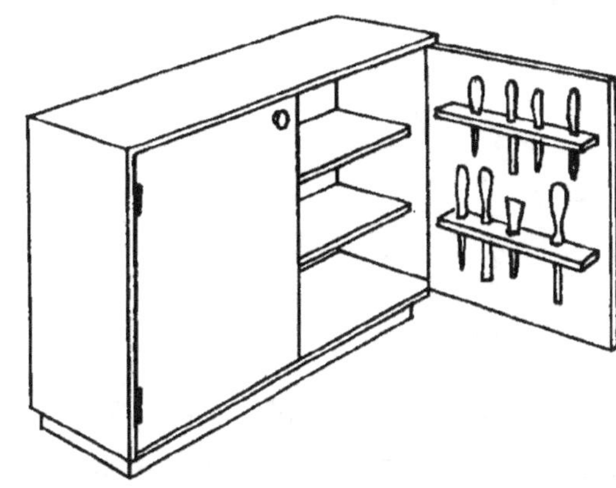

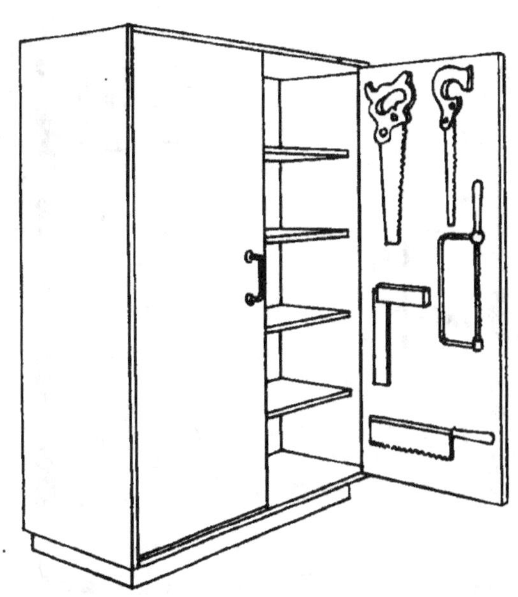

48"

74"

15"

C. TOOL CLOSET WITH REMOVABLE SHELVES

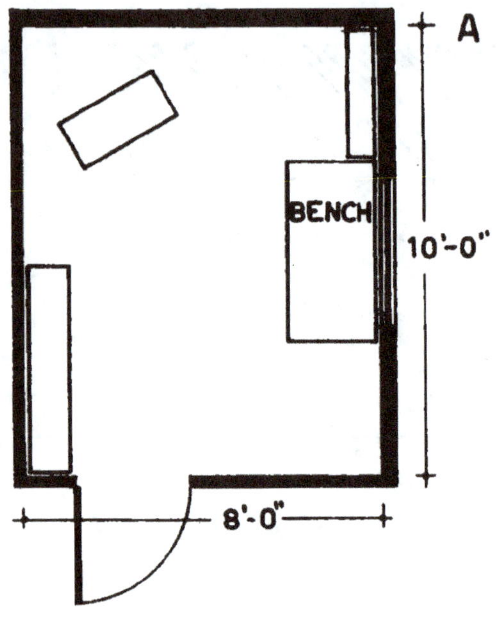

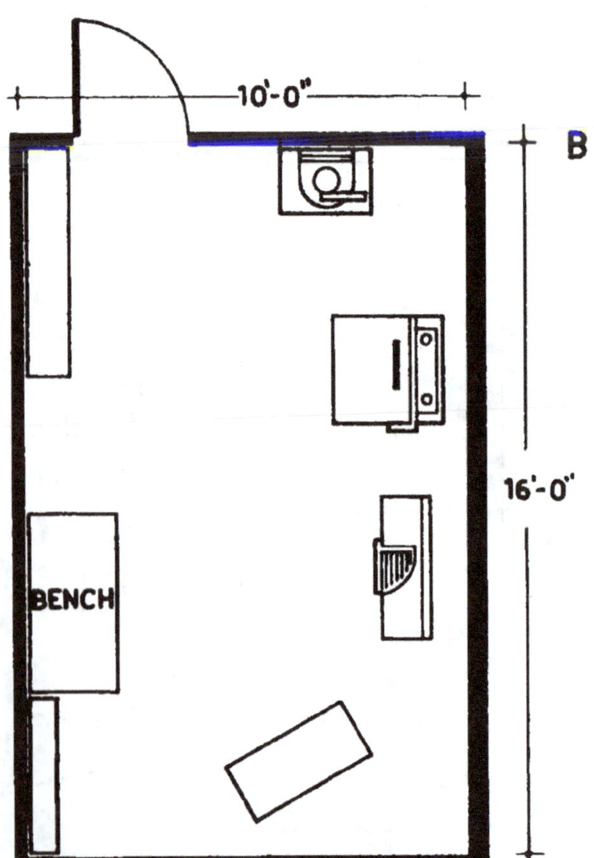

WORKSHOP

THE WORKSHOP CAN BE BUILT IN ANY ROOM OF THE HOUSE, ALTHOUGH THE BASEMENT AND GARAGE ARE CUSTOMARY LOCATIONS. PLENTY OF SUNLIGHT IS IMPORTANT, AND THE WORKBENCH SHOULD BE PLACED NEAR A WINDOW. BOTH PLANS SHOWN ON THIS PAGE ASSURE GOOD NATURAL LIGHT FOR THE CRAFTSMAN'S WORK. THE SIZE OF THE SHOP MAY BE DETERMINED BY THE KIND OF EQUIPMENT TO BE INSTALLED. SCHEME "A" SHOWS ONE WHERE ONLY HAND TOOLS ARE TO BE USED; SCHEME "B" IS A LARGER SHOP WHICH PERMITS THE INSTALLATION OF ADDITIONAL POWER-DRIVEN EQUIPMENT, SUCH AS CIRCULAR SAW, JOINTER PLANE, DRILL PRESS OR ELECTRIC DRILL, BELT AND DISC SANDER, GRINDER, JIG SAW, BAND SAW, SHAPER, AND THICKNESS PLANES.

METHODS OF WOODWORKING

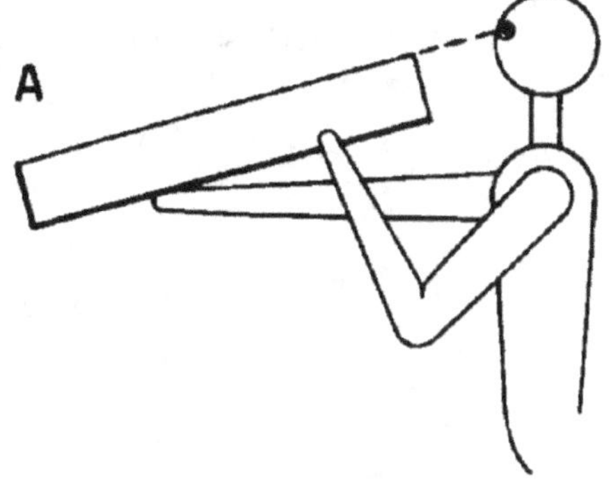

WOOD WORKING

WHETHER WOOD IS SHAPED BY HAND OR BY USE OF WOODWORKING MACHINES, THE PROCESS CONSISTS OF REMOVING SMALL PARTS OF WOOD BY PLANING, SAWING, OR CHISELING IN ACCORDANCE WITH THE SELECTED DESIGN. PROFESSIONAL WORKERS NORMALLY ENLARGE THE DESIGN TO FULL-SIZE SECTIONS IN SCALE WITH MEASUREMENTS AND RELATIVE DETAILS. FOR HOBBYISTS THE PRESENTATION OF THE DESIGN IS SIMPLIFIED. EXAMPLES OF BOTH TYPES OF DRAWINGS ARE SHOWN ON PAGE 16.

AFTER THE DESIGN HAS BEEN STUDIED AND SUITABLE WOOD SELECTED, THE VARIOUS PIECES CAN BE TRACED DIRECTLY ON THE WOOD FOR CUTTING. IN THE CUTTING PROCESS, ALLOWANCE SHOULD BE MADE FOR REDUCTION IN SIZE IN THE FINAL FINISHING. PLANING WILL SMOOTH THE SURFACES AND BRING THE CUT PIECES TO EXACT DIMENSIONS. THE PIECES ARE THEN MARKED TO INDICATE THEIR RELATIONSHIPS FOR JOINING, AND GUIDES FOR THE CUTTING OF THE JOINTS ARE TRACED. FINAL CONSTRUCTION OPERATIONS INCLUDE REPLANING THE SURFACE IN THE JOINT PARTS, RETOUCHING THE VARIOUS UNIONS, APPLYING PLASTIC WOOD AS NEEDED, AND SANDPAPERING WITH VARIOUS GRADES OF SANDPAPER. FINISHING INSTRUCTIONS ARE GIVEN BELOW.

WOOD FINISHES

STAIN

IF IT IS DESIRABLE TO CHANGE THE COLOR OF A PIECE OF FURNITURE TO IMITATE OTHER TYPES OF WOOD, A STAIN MAY BE APPLIED TO THE PLANED AND SANDED SURFACE WITH A BRUSH. SUCH AN APPLICATION MUST BE MADE WITH CARE. THE

STAIN MUST BE EVENLY DISTRIBUTED TO OBTAIN GOOD RESULTS. MAHOGANY, WALNUT, AND OAK STAINS ARE AVAILABLE READY-MIXED IN BASES OF WATER, ALCOHOL, AND OIL.

NATURAL FINISH

NATURAL FINISH MAY BE ACHIEVED BY USE OF VARNISH, SHELLAC, FIRZITE, AND OTHER PLASTIC FINISHES. ONE OF THE MOST COMMON MATERIALS IS READY-MIXED SHELLAC, WHICH IS ALSO APPLIED WITH A BRUSH. WHEN THE PIECE IS READY FOR GLOSS FINISH, IT SHOULD BE GIVEN A FIRST COATING OF SHELLAC. THIS COAT IS ALLOWED TO DRY AND THEN SANDED DOWN WITH FINE SANDPAPER. A SECOND COAT OF SHELLAC IS THEN APPLIED, AND THE FINISH IS COMPLETED WITH FURNITURE POLISH, RUBBED ON WITH A WOOL CLOTH TO OBTAIN A GLOSSY APPEARANCE. ANOTHER METHOD OF NATURAL FINISH, EMPLOYED BY PROFESSIONALS, IS THE USE OF A LACQUER BASE. LACQUER CAN BE APPLIED IN THIN LAYERS WITH A SPRAY, AND A PREPARED COMPOUND RUBBED ON BY HAND OR WITH A BUFFING WHEEL. FOR QUALITY FURNITURE, ONE METHOD OF OBTAINING A GOOD FINISH IS WITH FRENCH POLISH, WHICH CONSISTS OF RUBBING THE SURFACE IN A CIRCULAR MOTION WITH A MIXTURE OF ONE PART SHELLAC WITH THREE PARTS ALCOHOL, APPLIED ON A RUBBER BLOCK. EVERY TYPE OF FINISHING COMPOUND IS SOLD READY-MIXED, IN CANS, WITH COMPLETE INSTRUCTIONS.

PAINT

PAINT IS THE SIMPLEST FINISH TO APPLY. IT IS IMPORTANT TO SELECT THE PROPER TYPE (EXTERIOR OR INTERIOR) AND TO FOLLOW THE MANUFACTURER'S INSTRUCTIONS. COLORS SHOULD BE CAREFULLY CHOSEN IN RELATION TO THE ROOM IN WHICH THE FURNITURE IS TO BE USED.

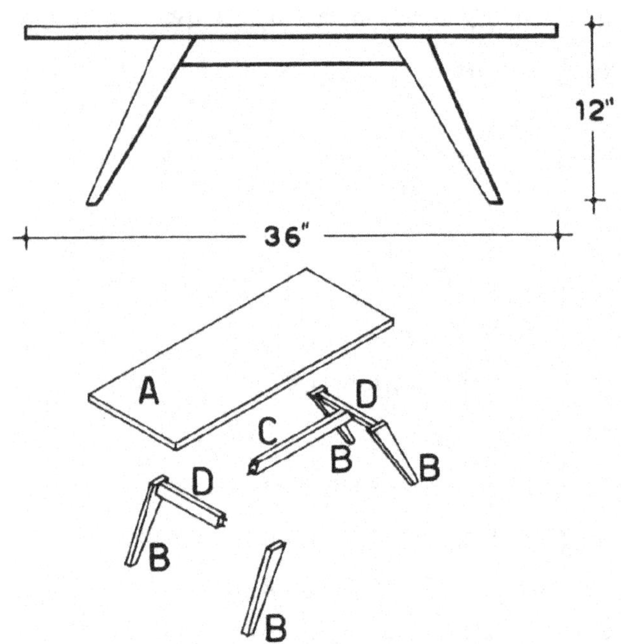

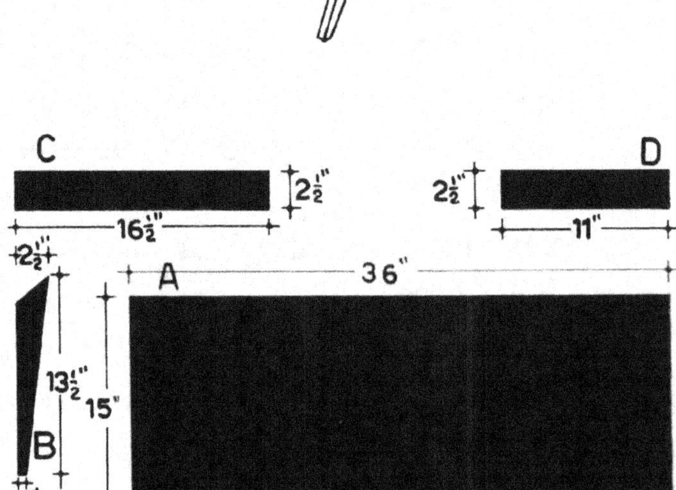

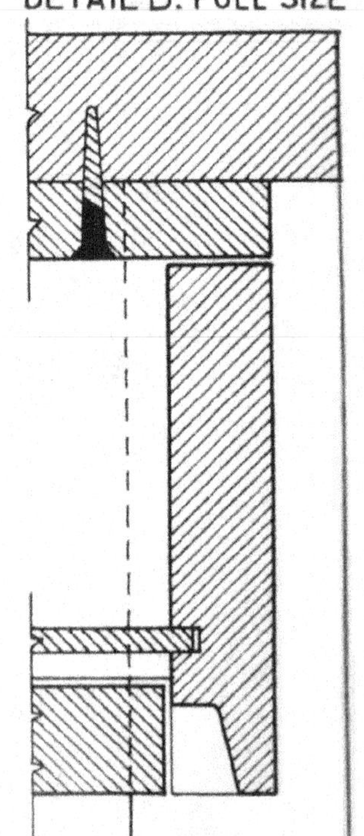

SIMPLIFIED CONSTRUCTION DRAWINGS FOR THE HOBBYIST

ABOVE AND AT THE RIGHT ARE SHOWN CON-
STRUCTION DRAWINGS OF THE TYPE WHICH WILL
BE PRESENTED IN THIS BOOK. THESE DRAWINGS
ARE SIMPLIFIED, WITH PARTS LAID OUT FOR ORDER-
ING AND CUTTING. THE METHOD OF ASSEMBLY
IS SHOWN IN THE EXPLODED VIEW.

PROFESSIONAL CONSTRUCTION DRAWINGS

SIMPLE ELEVATION, SECTION, AND DETAILS ARE
THE ONLY DRAWINGS REQUIRED BY THE PRO-
FESSIONAL CABINET MAKER.

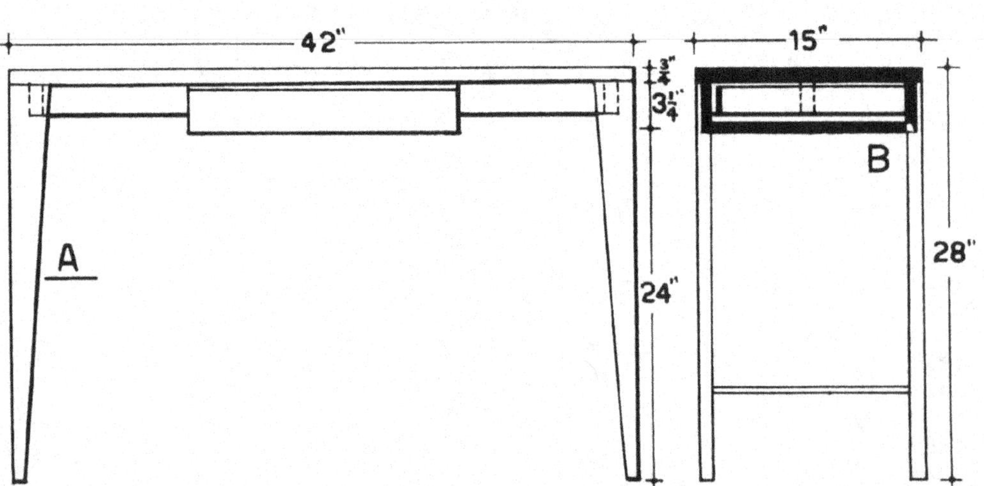

MARKING THE MATERIAL FOR CUTTING

AFTER OBTAINING THE ROUGH WOOD FROM THE LUMBERYARD, MARK OUT THE VARIOUS PIECES ON THE WOOD USING THE STRAIGHT YARD RULE ("A"), THE TRY SQUARE ("B"), OR THE BEVEL GAUGE ("C"). IF YOU USE THE TWO LATTER DEVICES, REMEMBER THAT ONE EDGE OF THE MATERIAL SHOULD BE STRAIGHT.

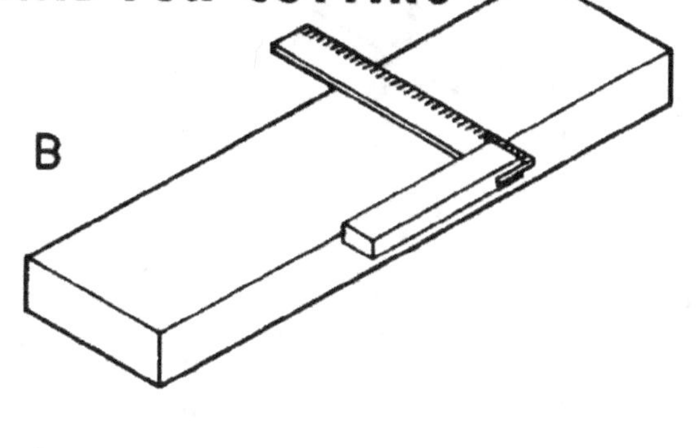

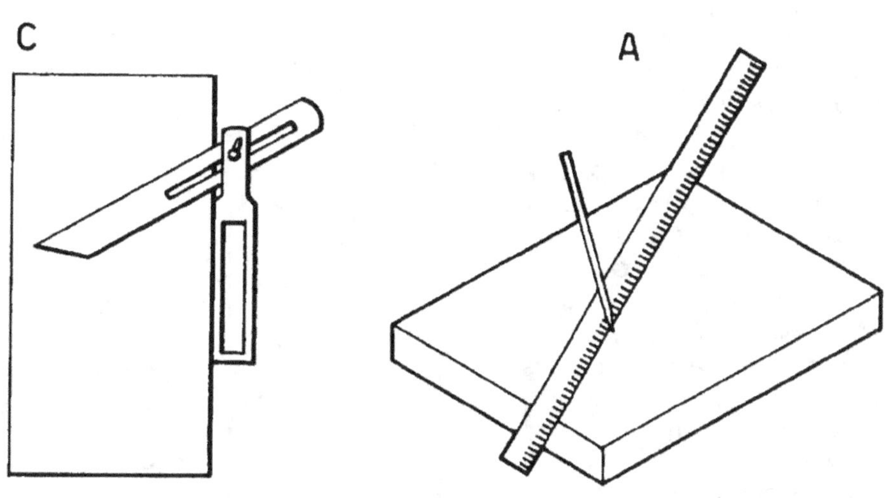

THE MARKING GAUGE ("D") IS USED TO TRACE LINES PARALLEL TO A STRAIGHT BORDER OR EDGE. THE MARKER CAN BE ADJUSTED TO VARY THE DISTANCE FROM THE EDGE.

THE FUNCTION OF THE COMPASS ("E") IS THE SCRIBING OF CIRCLES OR PARTIAL CURVES.

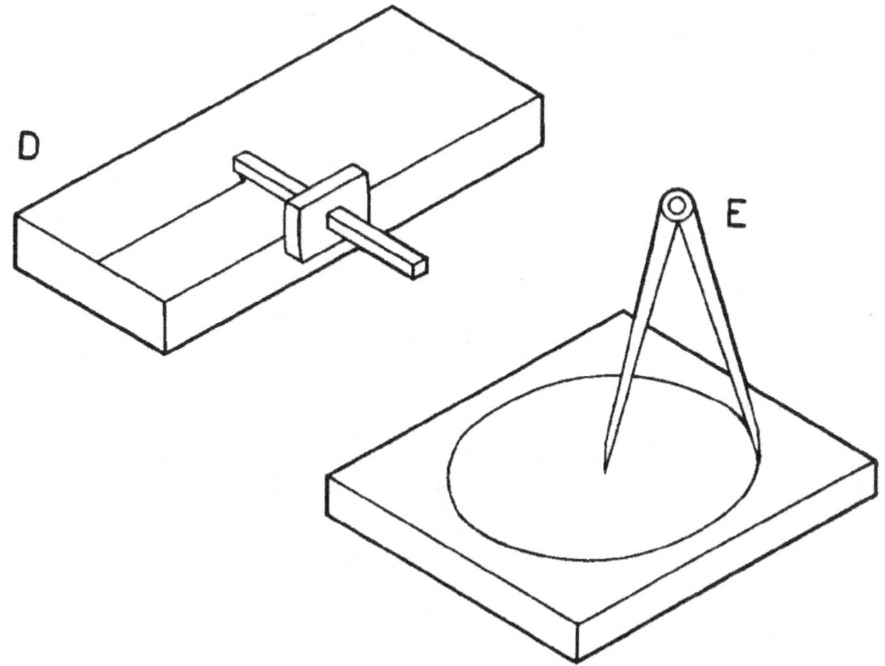

SAWING

THESE DIAGRAMS SHOW THE PROPER USE OF THE SAWS SHOWN ON PAGES 1 AND 5. EACH IS INTENDED FOR A PARTICULAR TYPE OF WORK. TO OBTAIN BEST RESULTS IT IS RECOMMENDED THAT THE SAW BE KEPT PERPENDICULAR TO THE PIECE BEING CUT. NO DOWNWARD PRESSURE SHOULD BE EXERTED ON THE SAW, BUT A STEADY PUSH AND PULL MOTION SHOULD BE MAINTAINED. IT IS IMPORTANT TO USE THE RIGHT TYPE OF SAW FOR THE JOB AT HAND. FOR EXAMPLE, IN SAWING HEAVY BOARDS (WHETHER IN GRAIN DIRECTION OR ACROSS GRAIN) IT IS BEST TO USE A PANEL SAW ("A" AND "B"). FOR CURVED LINE CUTS A NARROW BLADE IS USED, SUCH AS THE TURNING SAW ("C") OR THE COMPASS SAW ("D"). FOR SAWING THIN BOARDS A COPING SAW ("E") IS USED. THE BACK SAW ("F"), USED FOR PRECISION CUTS, SHOULD BE HELD LOOSELY.

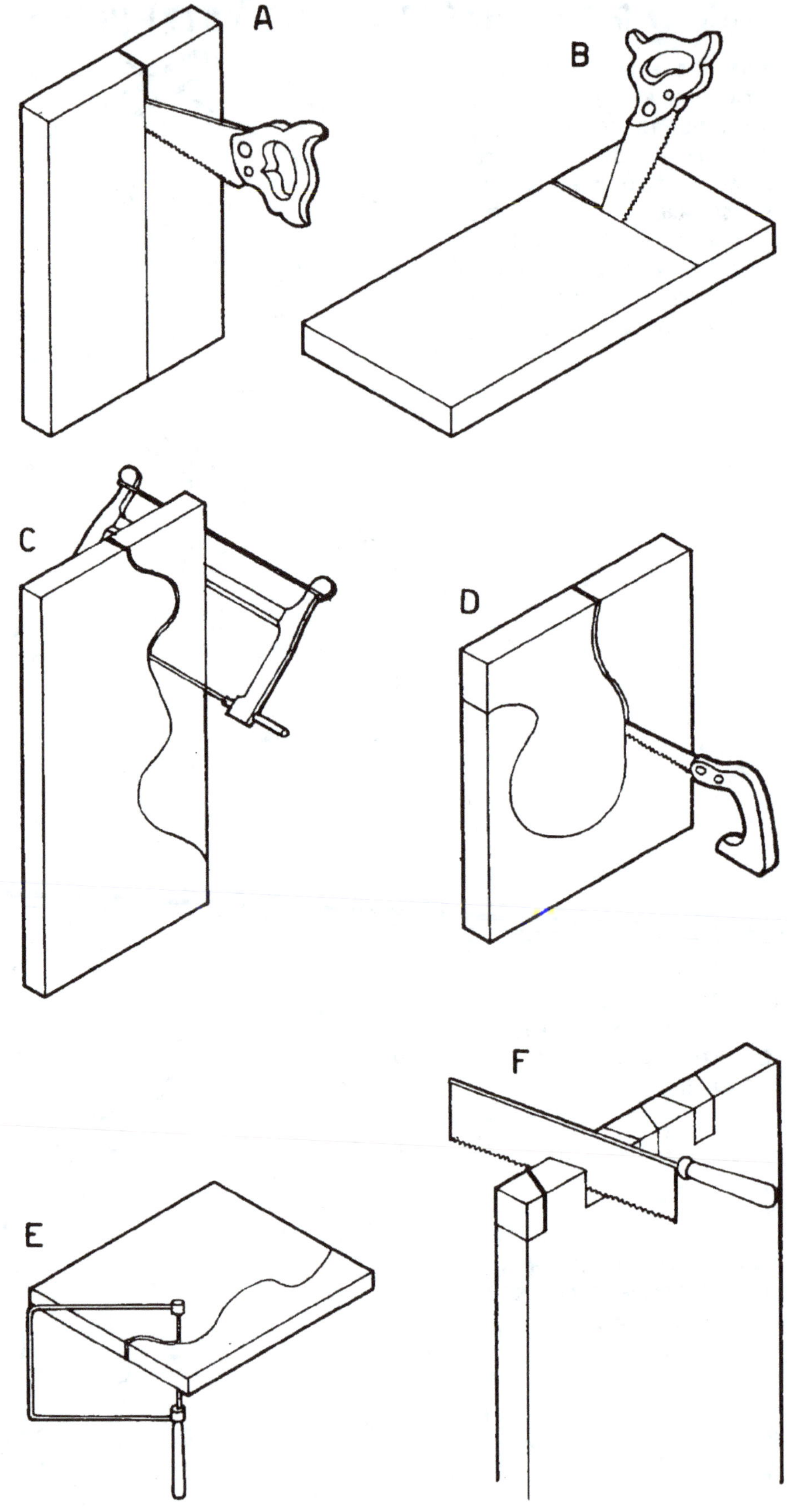

PLANING

THERE ARE VARIOUS TYPES OF PLANES AS SHOWN ON PAGES 3 AND 6. EACH ONE IS ADAPTED TO ITS OWN PARTICULAR TYPE OF WORK. AS AN EXAMPLE, THE JACK PLANE IS USED FOR FIRST PLANING AND COMMON FINISHING. THE SMOOTH PLANE IS USED FOR MORE DELICATE FINISHING. THE JOINER PLANE IS USED FOR STRAIGHT BORDERS. IN GENERAL, THE FUNCTION OF THE PLANE IS TO SMOOTH THE SURFACES AND ADJUST THICKNESSES. IF THE PLANE IS TO FUNCTION PERFECTLY, IT MUST BE HELD FIRMLY IN THE HAND AND APPLIED WITH STEADY PRESSURE ON THE SURFACE OF THE WOOD, AS SHOWN IN "A." IT IS TO BE NOTED THAT THE BLADE OF THE PLANE MUST ALWAYS BE KEPT IN A LEVEL POSITION, AS IN "B." FAILURE TO FOLLOW THIS PRINCIPLE HAS A TENDENCY TO MAKE THE PIECE CONCAVE, AS IN "C." IN CUTTING END GRAIN PLANING SHOULD BE DONE INWARD FROM THE EDGES, AS SHOWN IN "D," TO PREVENT SPLITTING THE WOOD. IN PLANING A SURFACE RUNNING DIAGONAL TO THE GRAIN "E," THE PLANE SHOULD BE RUN STRAIGHT THROUGH IN ONE DIRECTION. THE SAME METHOD IS USED IF THE SURFACE IS OF NORMAL GRAIN, AS IN "F." WHEN A KNOTTY FORMATION EXISTS, AS IN "G," PLANING IS DONE IN TWO DIRECTIONS.

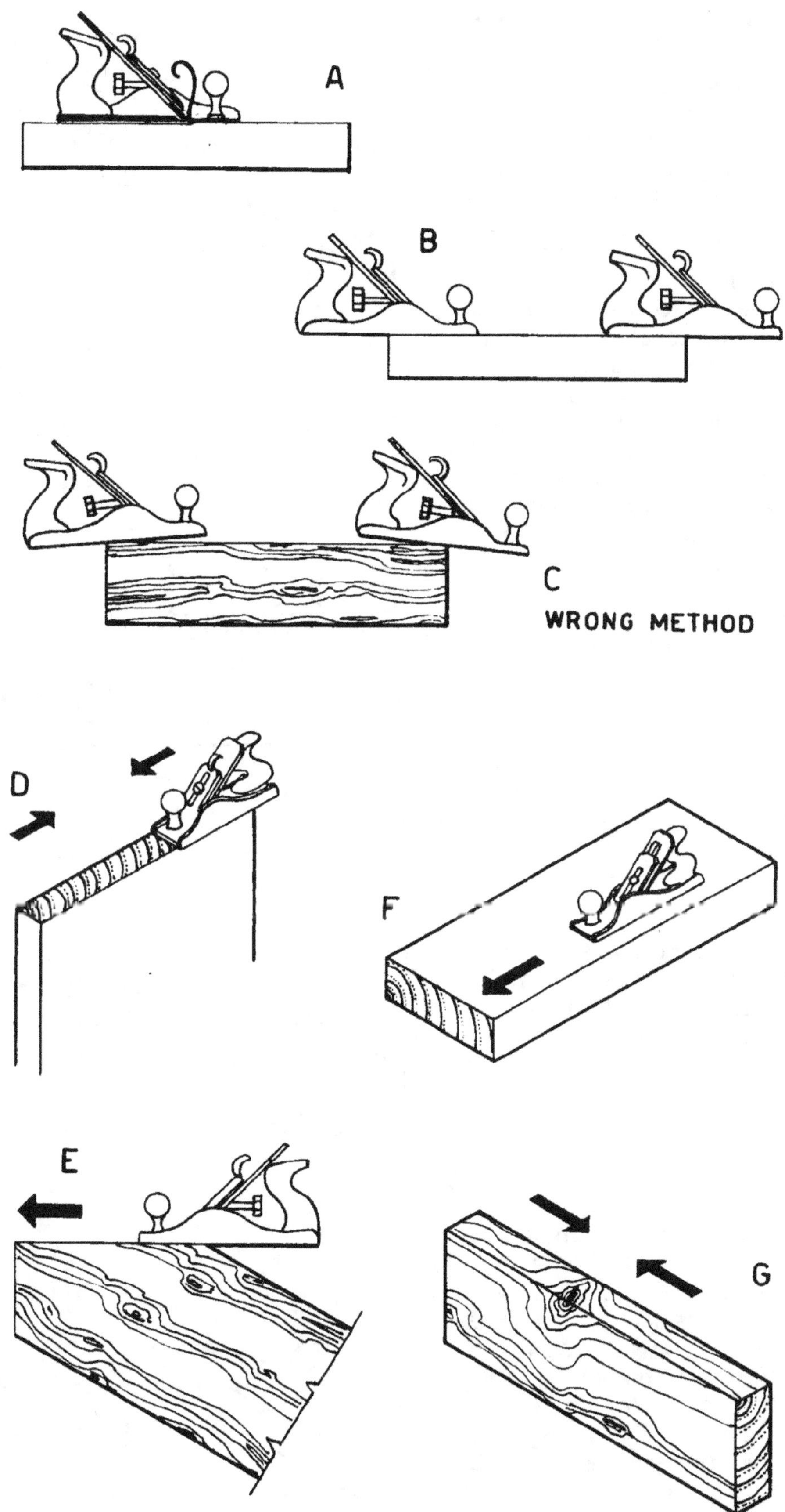

PLANING OF EDGES

A. THE GUIDE SHOWN AT THE RIGHT PROVIDES A SIMPLE METHOD OF SQUARING THE EDGE OF A BOARD FOR GLUING. B. EVEN WITH A GUIDE, EDGES MAY DEVIATE FROM A PERFECT RIGHT ANGLE. THEREFORE, TO INSURE A TIGHT FIT, IT IS CUSTOMARY TO REVERSE ONE OF THE PIECES BEING JOINED, SO THAT THE ANGULAR CUTS WILL FIT SNUGLY TOGETHER, AS ILLUSTRATED IN FIGURE "B." FIGURES "C" AND "D" ILLUSTRATE HOW, WITH THE USE OF A FLEXIBLE PLANE, YOU CAN SMOOTH OUT THE PLANE SURFACES, WHETHER CONCAVE OR CONVEX.

E. RABBETING PLANE. TO RABBET A BOARD A SPECIAL PLANE IS USED TO CUT THE NECESSARY GROOVE OR SLOT.

F. IN MAKING A CYLINDRICAL PART FROM A SQUARE PIECE OF WOOD, THE GENERAL PROCEDURE IS TO TRIM THE PIECE FIRST TO AN OCTAGON AND THEN TO A CYLINDER. THE TOOLS USED FOR THIS PURPOSE ARE THE SPOKE SHAVE "F," THE PLANE "G," THE SCRAPER "H," AND SANDPAPER "K."

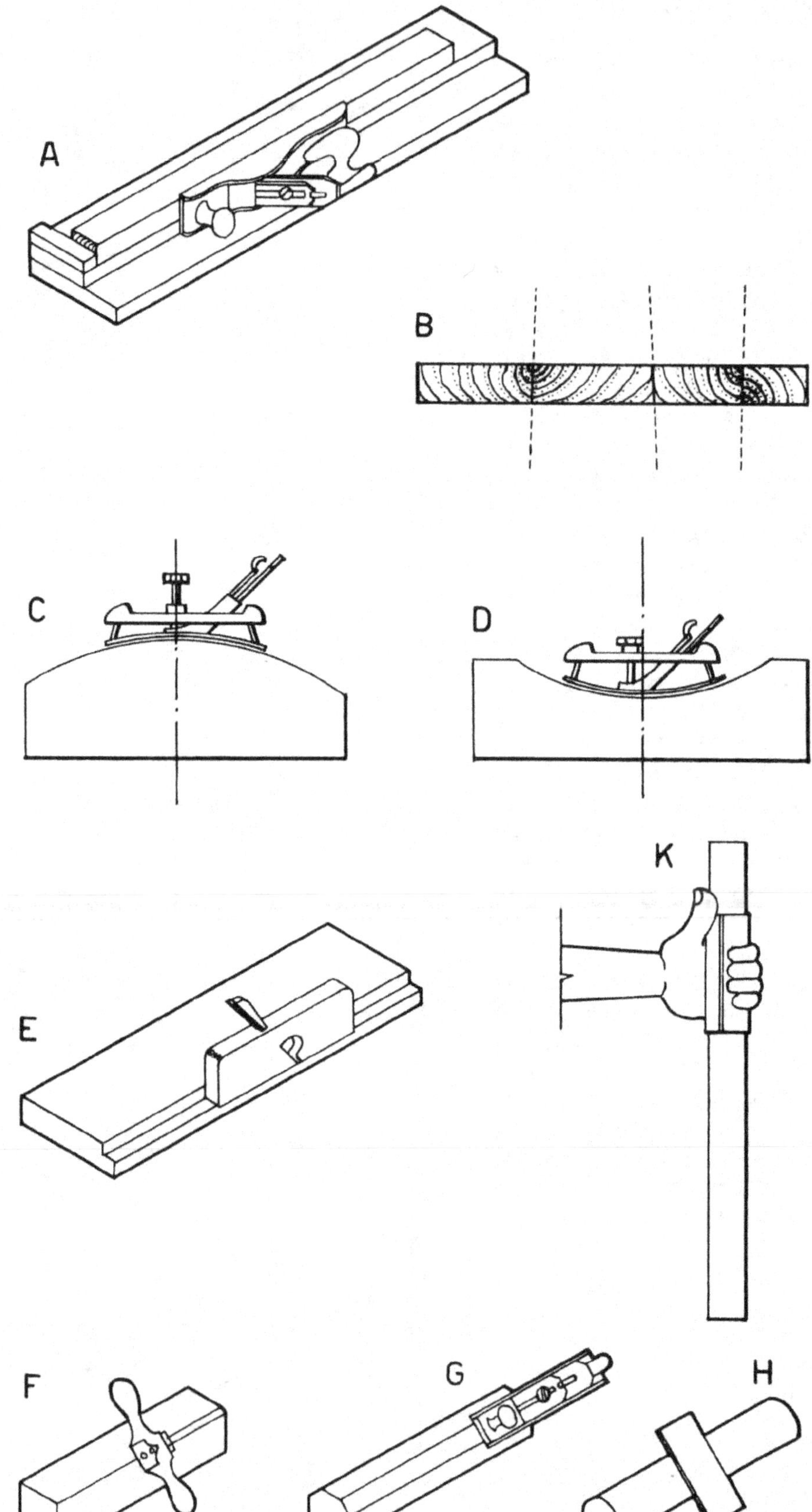

CHECKING ACCURACY OF PLANED BOARDS

AN EXPERT CABINET MAKER CAN PROBABLY TELL WHETHER A SMALL BOARD IS STRAIGHT OR HAS A TWIST BY MERELY LOOKING AT IT. THE LESS EXPERIENCED CRAFTSMAN WILL WANT TO USE ONE OR MORE OF THE METHODS OF CHECKING OUTLINED BELOW.

A RULE ("B") IS LAID ACROSS A PIECE OF WORK, AND IF LIGHT SHOWS UNDER THE STRAIGHT EDGE IT IS AN INDICATION OF AN UNEVENNESS THAT MUST BE CORRECTED. A FURTHER CHECK MAY BE MADE BY PLACING THE RULE DIAGONALLY ACROSS THE BOARD. THIS WILL INDICATE TWIST. A TRY SQUARE ("C" AND "D") AND LEVEL GAUGE ("E") ARE OTHER METHODS OF TESTING SQUARENESS. THEY MAY ALSO BE USED TO CHECK ANGLES.

PARALLEL EDGES MAY BE CHECKED BY USING THE PUSH-PULL RULE AS SHOWN IN "F." THE MARKING GAUGE ("G") CAN BE USED TO CHECK BOARD THICKNESSES IN PRECISION WORK.

USE OF THE CHISEL

THE CHISEL IS VERY IMPORTANT IN CABINET WORKING. IT IS USED IN MORTISE WORK, IN ROUTING FOR THE APPLICATION OF HINGES, AND FOR REVISION AND RETOUCHING OF WORK DONE BY MACHINE. VARIOUS TYPES OF CHISELS ARE USED, ACCORDING TO THE TYPE OF WORK TO BE DONE. IN WORK WHERE THE TOOL UNDERGOES PRESSURE, OR STRAIN, A FLAT CHISEL IS GENERALLY SELECTED. DRAWINGS "B" TO "D" ILLUSTRATE THE PROPER USE OF A LIGHT CHISEL IN RECESSING A DOOR HINGE. THE HINGE IS LAID ON THE DOOR AND THE EDGES MARKED WITH A PENCIL ("A"). A LIGHT CHISEL IS USED TO SCORE THE BOARD ("B"). WITH A SLIDING ACTION AND BY INVERTING THE EDGE OF THE CHISEL ("C") LARGE PIECES OF WOOD ARE REMOVED.
FINISHING IS DONE WITH A SERIES OF SHORT STROKES WORKING IN FROM THE OUTER EDGES.

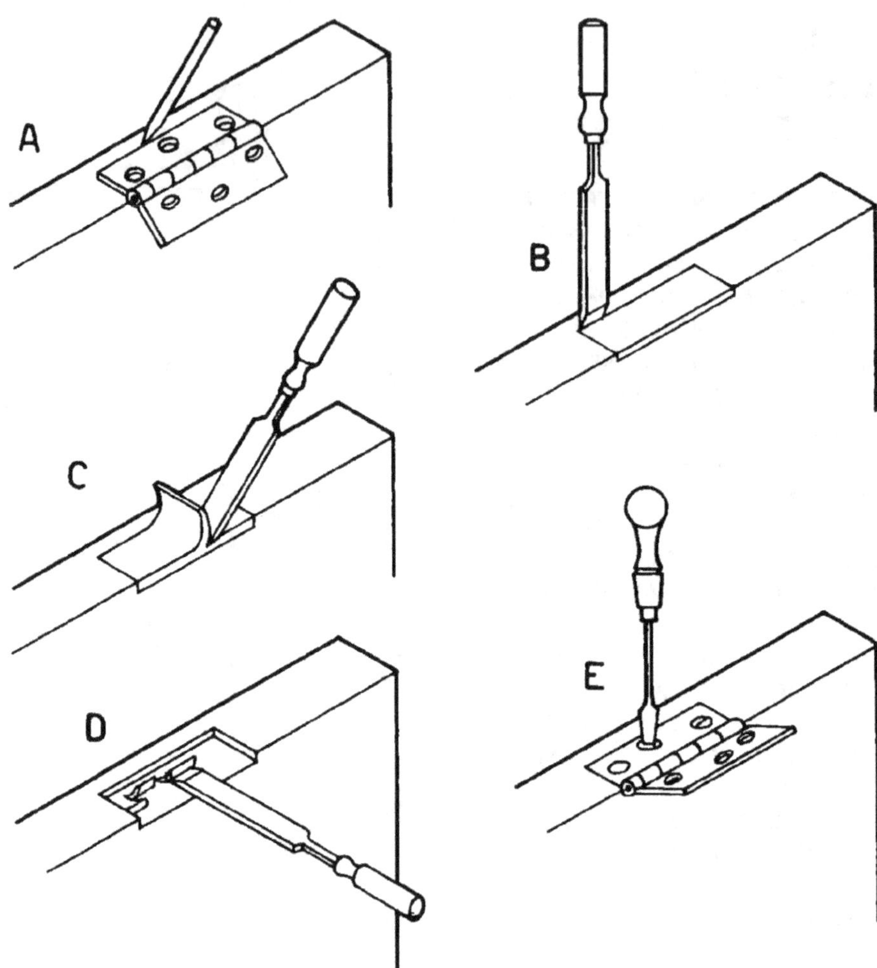

"F" AND "G" ILLUSTRATE USE OF A HEAVY CHISEL FOR A DEEP MORTISE. "B," "C," AND "D" DEMONSTRATE THE THREE BASIC POSITIONS IN WHICH A CHISEL SHOULD BE USED FOR OBTAINING BEST RESULTS.

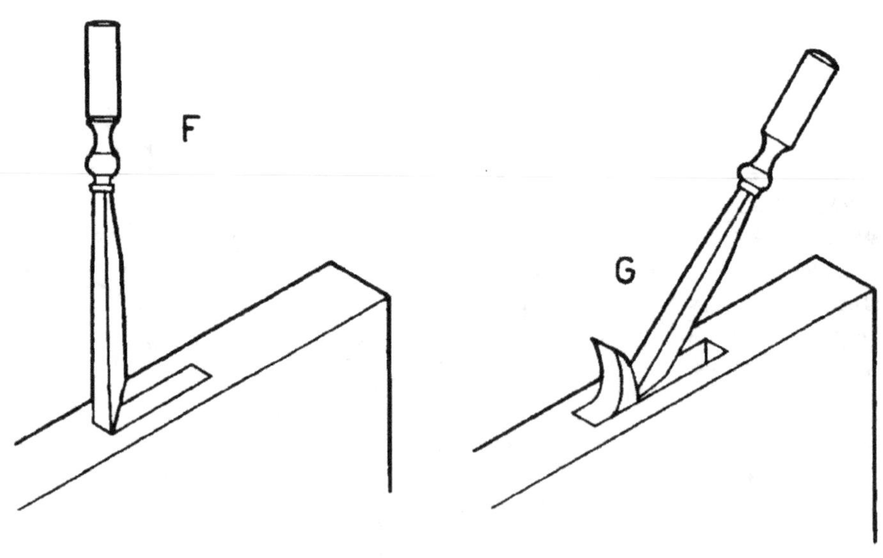

USE OF THE BRACE AND BIT, DRILL, AND GIMLET

THESE TOOLS ARE USED TO PRE-PARE HOLES OF VARIOUS SIZES IN THE WOOD. IT IS IMPORTANT TO SELECT THE PROPER SIZE BIT OR GIMLET FOR THE HOLE TO BE BORED.

AS SHOWN IN "A" AND "B," THE MATERIAL MAY BE PLACED IN A HORIZONTAL POSITION, BUT THE TOOL MUST BE HELD PERPENDICU-LAR TO IT. FOR LARGER HOLES, USE THE COMPASS SAW AS ILLUS-TRATED IN "D."

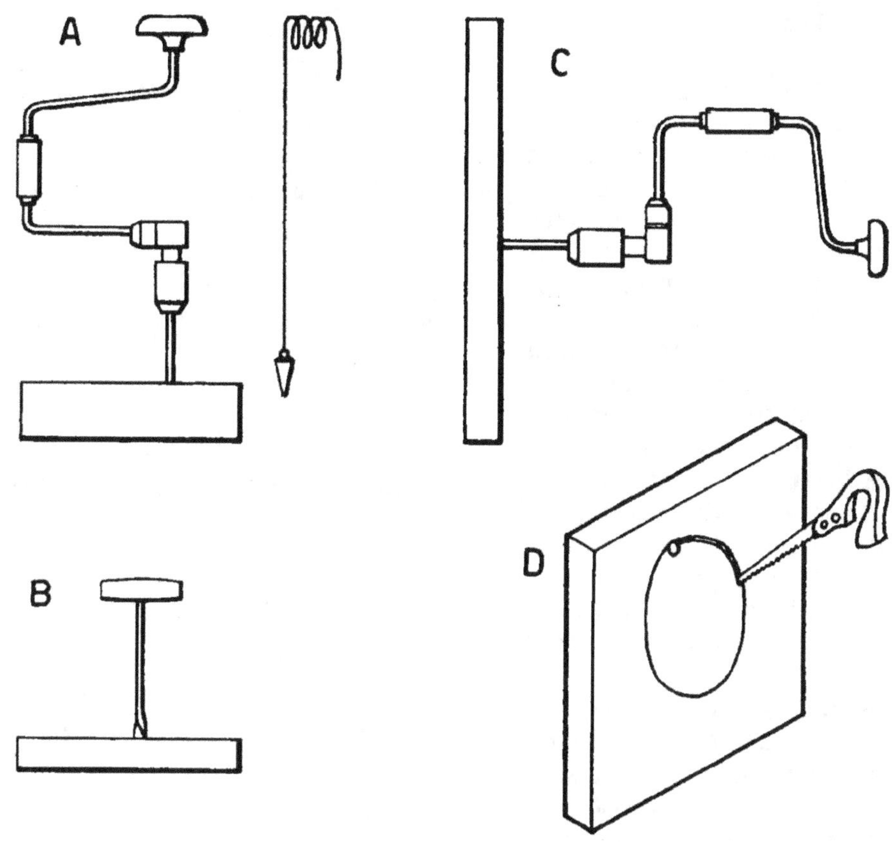

FILES

THE FILE MAY BE USED IN MANY PLACES WHERE A PLANE IS IM-PRACTICAL. AT RIGHT IS SHOWN A ROUNDING ACTION WHICH COULD BE THE FORMATION OF AN ARM OF A CHAIR.

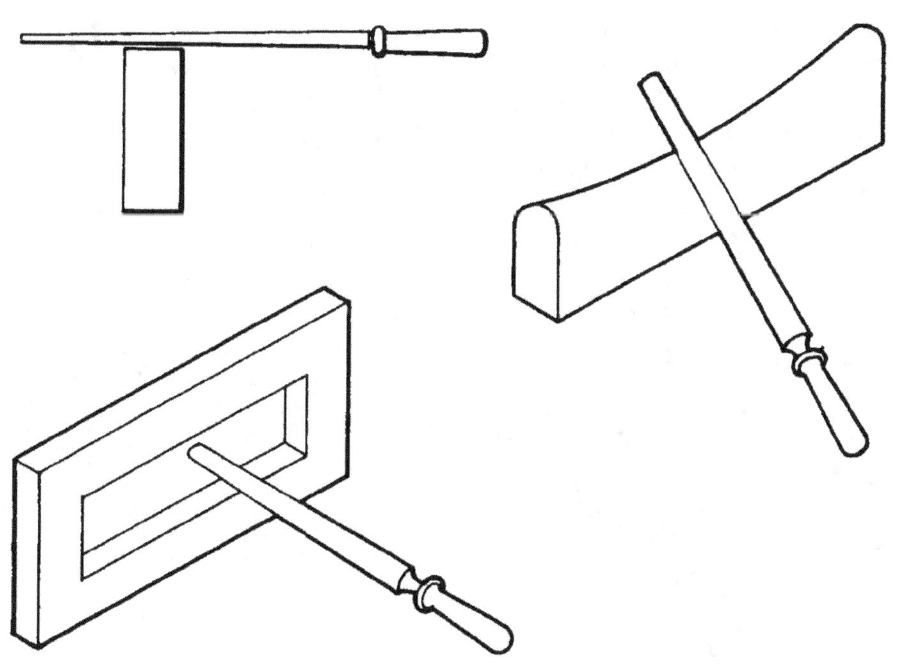

GLUING WOOD

EITHER HOT OR COLD GLUE MAY BE USED IN JOINING WOOD PIECES. AFTER PREPARING THE PIECES TO BE GLUED AND MAKING SURE THAT THE SURFACES ARE SMOOTH, SPREAD THE GLUE ON BOTH OF THE FACES TO BE JOINED. THE GLUED PIECES SHOULD BE PRESSED TOGETHER FOR FOUR TO EIGHT HOURS, DEPENDING ON THE TYPE OF GLUE USED. THE PRESSURE IS USUALLY MAINTAINED BY THE USE OF CLAMPS ("D" AND "E"). BECAUSE OF THE INHERENT STRUCTURE OF WOOD GRAIN IT IS IMPOSSIBLE TO JOIN THE ENDS OF BOARDS SATISFACTORILY BY GLUING (SEE "B").

IN "C" IS SHOWN A SIMPLE METHOD OF JOINING BOARDS WITHOUT THE USE OF CLAMPS. SHORT PIECES OF WOOD ARE NAILED TO THE ENDS OF TWO RAILS AND PRESSURE IS APPLIED BY INSERTING WEDGES. OTHER METHODS OF CLAMPING INCLUDE THE STEEL SPRING ("F" AND "G"). IN ASSEMBLING FURNITURE, DIRECT PRESSURE CAN BE APPLIED BY THE USE OF A ROPE, AS SHOWN IN "H." SCREWS OR NAILS MAY ALSO BE USED TO HOLD PIECES TOGETHER. THESE MAY BE LEFT IN, OR REMOVED AFTER ADHESION HAS TAKEN PLACE.

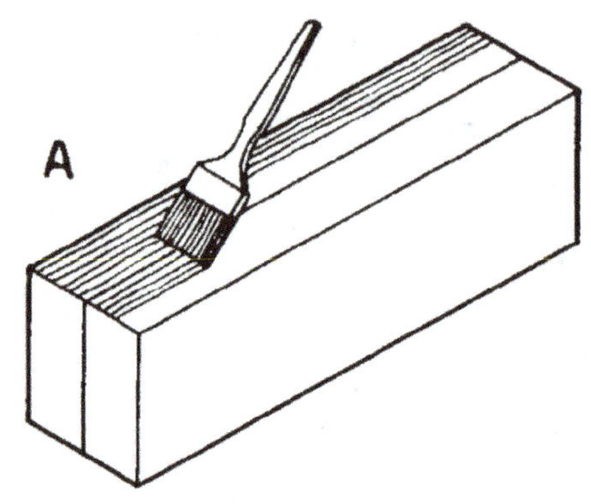

A

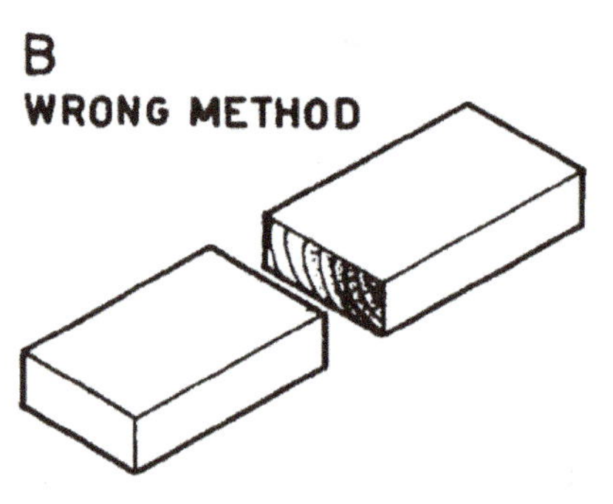

B

WRONG METHOD

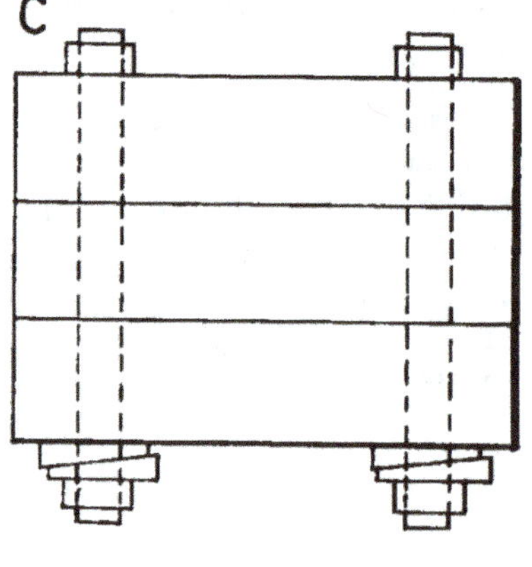

C

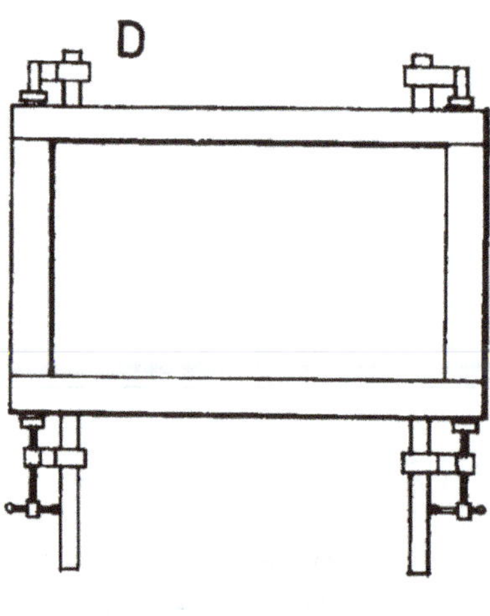

D

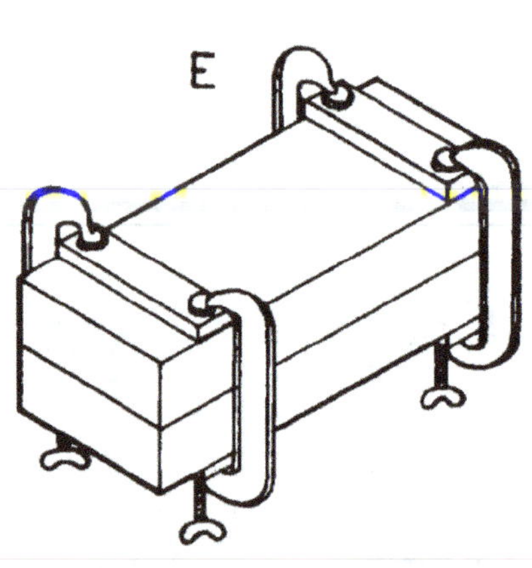

E

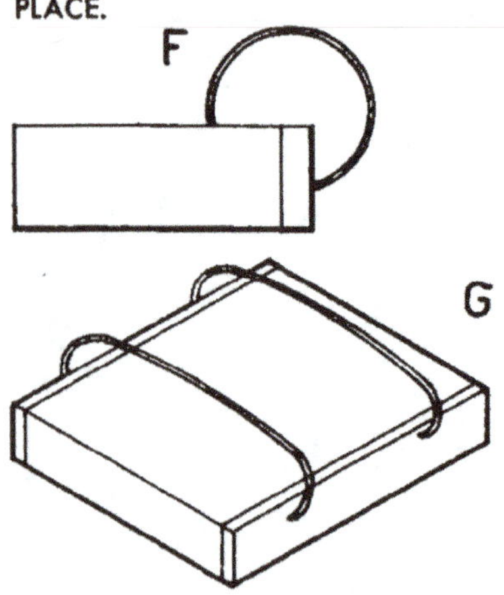

F

G

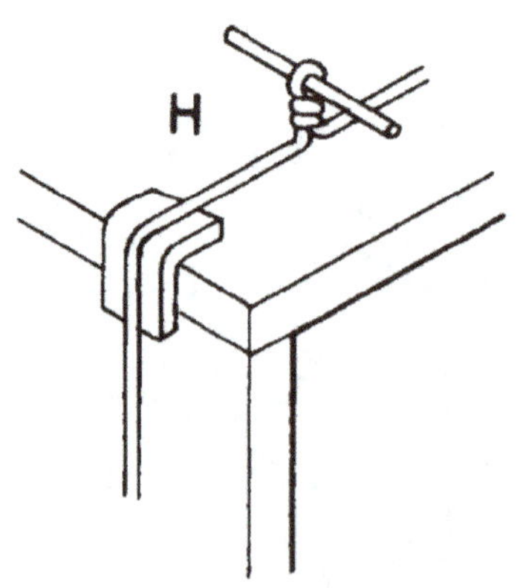

H

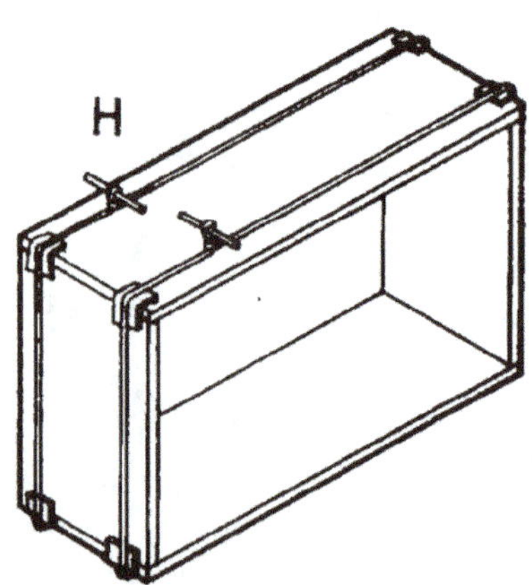

H

USE OF NAILS AND SCREWS

NAILS ARE COMMONLY USED IN WOODWORKING. OBVIOUSLY THE NAIL IS APPLIED WITH A HAMMER. IN ORDER TO MAKE SURE THAT THE NAIL IS DRIVEN AT THE PROPER ANGLE, IT SHOULD BE TAPPED LIGHTLY UNTIL THE DIRECTION IS ESTABLISHED. IF THE NAIL BENDS, IT MUST BE PULLED OUT AND REPLACED. THE CLAW HAMMER OR PLIERS MAY BE USED. IN ORDER TO PREVENT MARRING THE WORK, IT IS IMPORTANT TO PLACE A PIECE OF WOOD BETWEEN THE WORKING SURFACE AND THE TOOL AS IN "C" AND "D." SCREWS, APPLIED WITH A SCREWDRIVER, ARE OFTEN USED TO HOLD PIECES OF WOOD TOGETHER. BORING A HOLE FOR THE SCREW IS IMPORTANT IN HARD WOOD, BUT IN WORKING WITH SOFTER WOODS THIS STEP MAY BE OMITTED.

WHEN THE SURFACE OF THE WOOD IS DEFACED BY KNOTS, OR WHEN NAILS ARE SET BELOW THE SURFACE, PLASTIC WOOD MAY BE USED TO COVER DEFECTS. THE PASTE IS PRESSED INTO THE HOLE WITH A SPATULA, AND THE EXCESS REMOVED WITH THE SAME TOOL.
AFTER THE PLASTIC HAS DRIED, THE ENTIRE SURFACE IS SANDPAPERED.

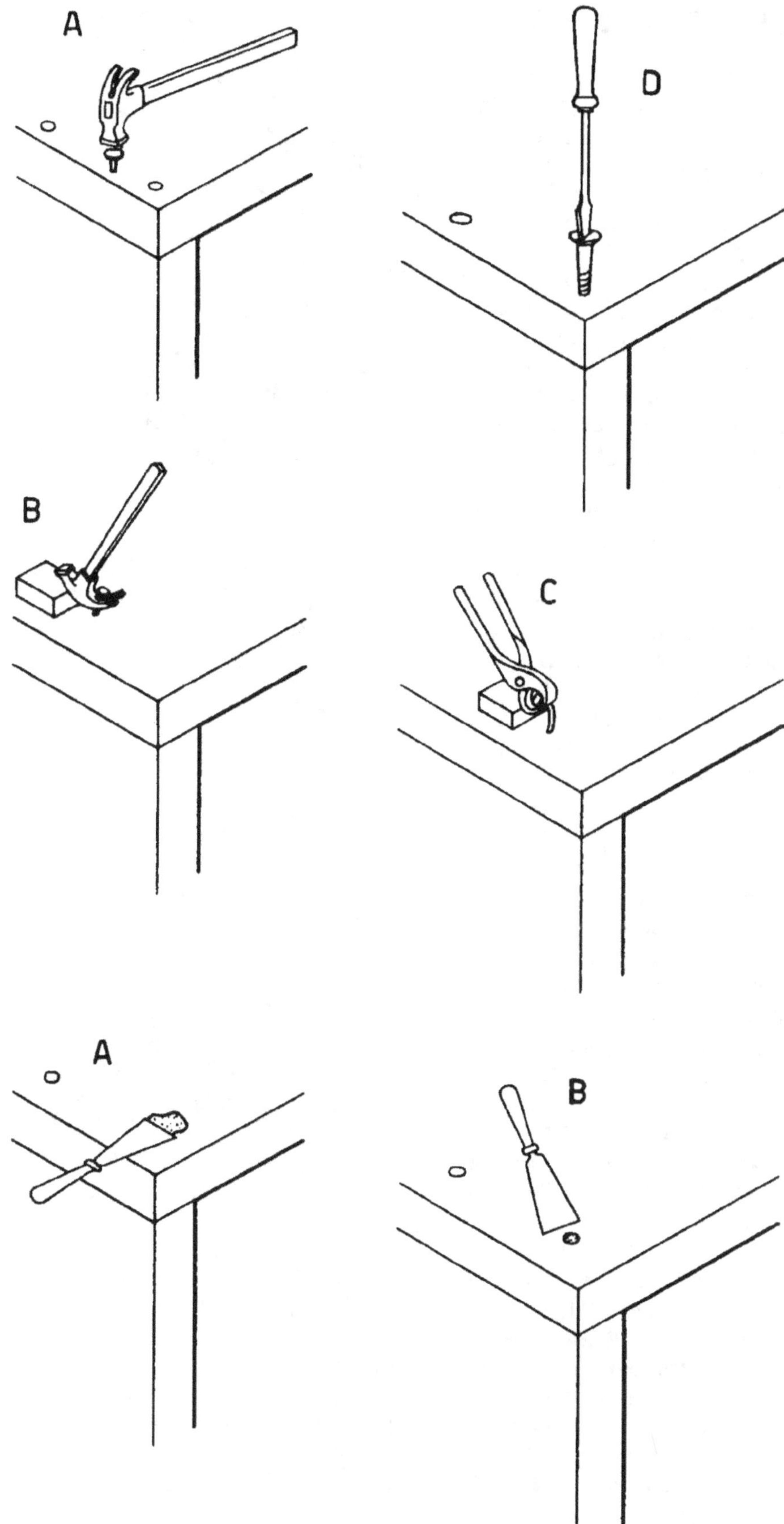

SANDPAPERING

SANDPAPER IS OFTEN USED TO FINISH THE PIECE AFTER THE WOOD HAS BEEN PLANED. IF THE FURNITURE IS TO BE PAINTED, A ROUGH SANDPAPER IS USED, AND CAN BE RUBBED IN ANY DIRECTION. IF A NATURAL FINISH IS TO BE USED, SANDPAPER SHOULD BE USED ONLY IN THE DIRECTION OF THE GRAIN, AS IN "A," NEVER AGAINST THE GRAIN, AS IN "B," SINCE THIS WOULD LEAVE MARKINGS ON THE WOOD EVEN AFTER THE PIECE IS FINISHED FOR THE BEST FINISHING, THE PROCEDURE WOULD BE TO USE TWO OR THREE TYPES OF SANDPAPER (ROUGH, MEDIUM, AND FINE). TO FACILITATE ITS USE, THE SANDPAPER IS WRAPPED AROUND A BLOCK AND APPLIED WITH A STEADY PUSH-PULL MOTION. DRAWINGS "C" AND "D" SHOW THE USE OF SANDPAPER ON EDGES AND CURVED SURFACES.

TOOL SHARPENING

TOOLS WHICH HAVE RECEIVED ESPECIALLY HARD USE MAY HAVE NICKS IN THEIR BLADES: THESE WILL REQUIRE THE USE OF A GRINDER. FOR TOOLS THAT ARE MERELY DULL, AN OILSTONE WILL SUFFICE. THE METHOD OF SHARPENING IS THE SAME FOR ALL TYPES OF TOOLS, BUT IT IS ALWAYS NECESSARY TO KEEP THE ANGLE OF THE BLADE STRAIGHT WITH THE GRINDER, AS IN "A." IN THE USE OF THE OILSTONE, THE BLADES ARE HELD IN THE POSITIONS INDICATED IN "B" AND "C." IN THE SHARPENING OF GOUGES, WHERE THE OILSTONE CANNOT BE USED IN THE CONVEX PART, THE SLIPSTONE CAN BE USED AS SHOWN IN "D." SIZES OF SLIP STONES ARE INDICATED ON PAGE 7.

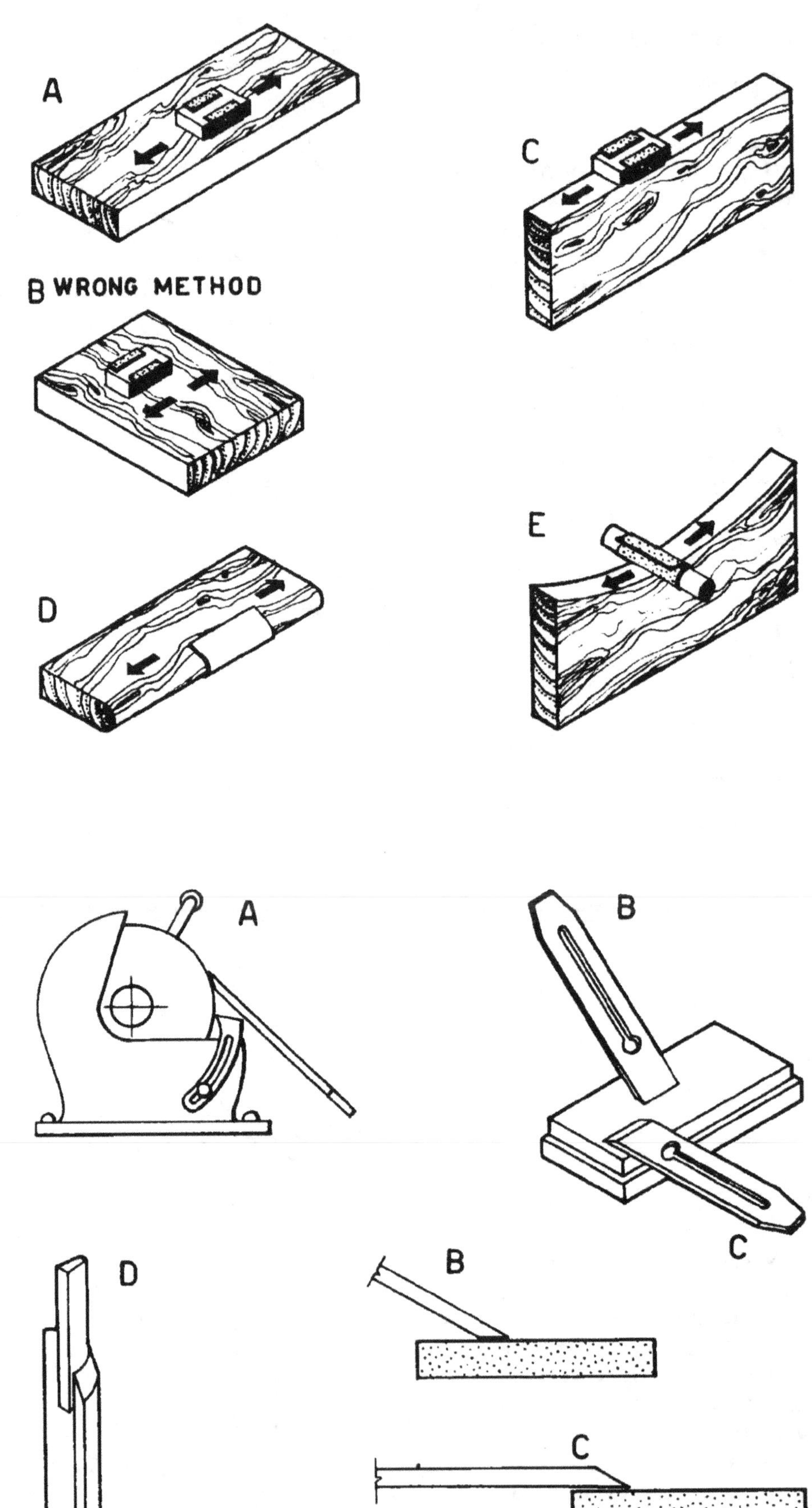

MACHINES FOR WOODWORKING

THESE MACHINES ARE DIVIDED INTO CATEGORIES ACCORDING TO THEIR USE, AND MAY BE CLASSIFIED AS SAWS, PLANES, SHAPERS, DRILLS, LATHES, AND SANDERS. BECAUSE OF POPULAR DEMAND THEY ARE NOW EASILY AVAILABLE TO HOBBYISTS. THEY ARE BEING MADE IN CONVENIENT SIZES FOR THE HOME SHOP, AND MASS PRODUCTION HAS REDUCED PRICES.

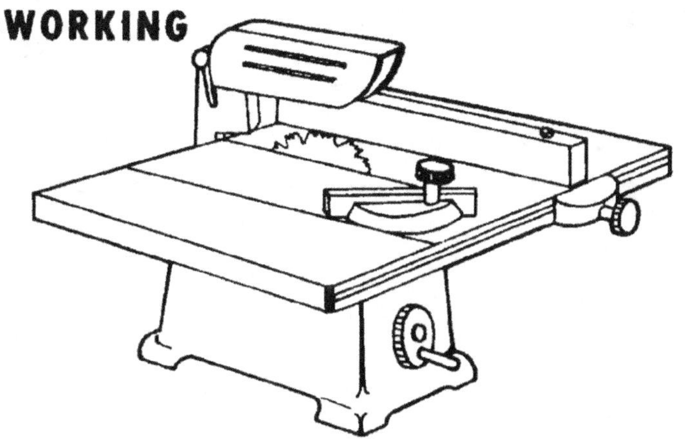

CIRCULAR SAW

THE CIRCULAR SAW ABOVE IS A TYPICAL SMALL TABLE SAW. IT IS USED FOR RIPPING, CROSS-CUTTING, SHAPING AND CUTTING DADOES. IT CONSISTS OF A CIRCULAR BLADE, A FLAT TABLE, A CUTTING FENCE, AND A RIPPING GUIDE.

BAND SAW

THE SAW CONSISTS OF A BLADE IN THE FORM OF AN ENDLESS BELT, REVOLVING AROUND TWO WHEELS. IT IS USUALLY EMPLOYED IN CUTTING CURVED OR IRREGULAR SHAPES. IT CAN ALSO BE USED FOR STRAIGHT CUTS.

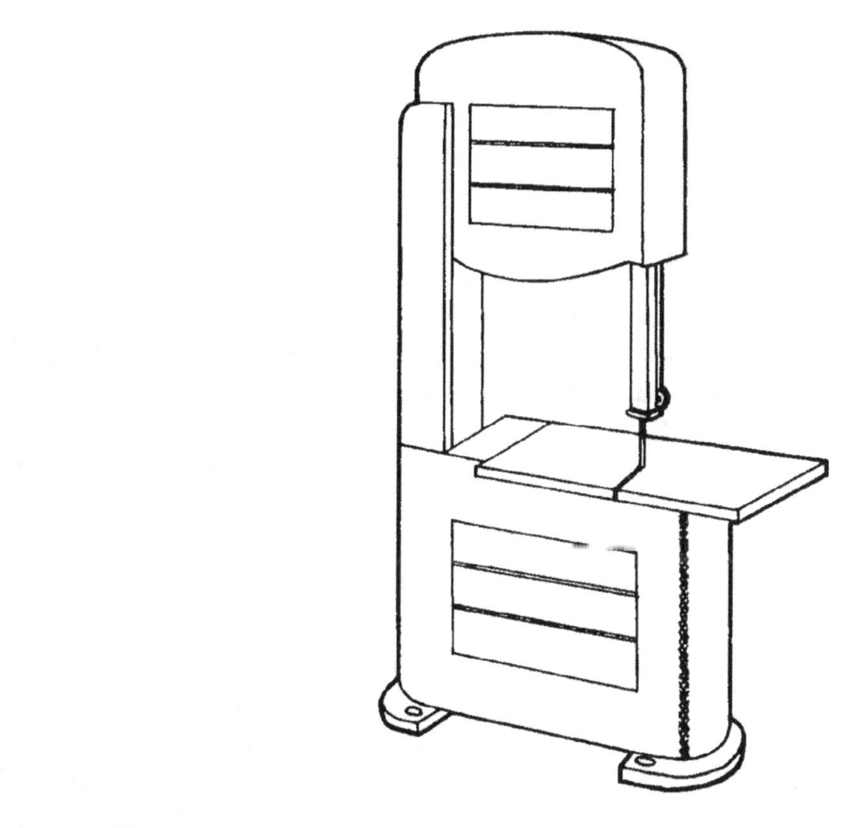

JIG SAW

A THIN STRAIGHT BLADE WHICH IS MOVED UP AND DOWN EITHER BY A WALKING BEAM OR BY VIBRATION IS THE BASIC ELEMENT OF THIS SAW. IT IS USED TO CUT IRREGULAR PIECES FROM LIGHT WOOD.

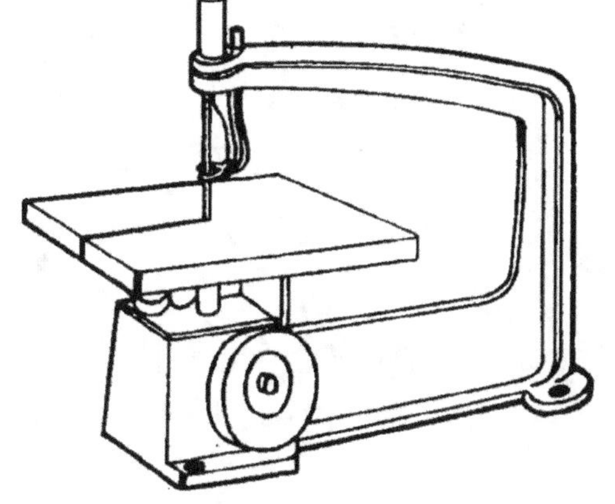

JOINTER-PLANER

LARGE BOARDS ARE EASILY SQUARED WITH THIS MACHINE. IT CONSISTS OF A REVOLVING CUTTER AND AN ADJUSTABLE GUIDE.

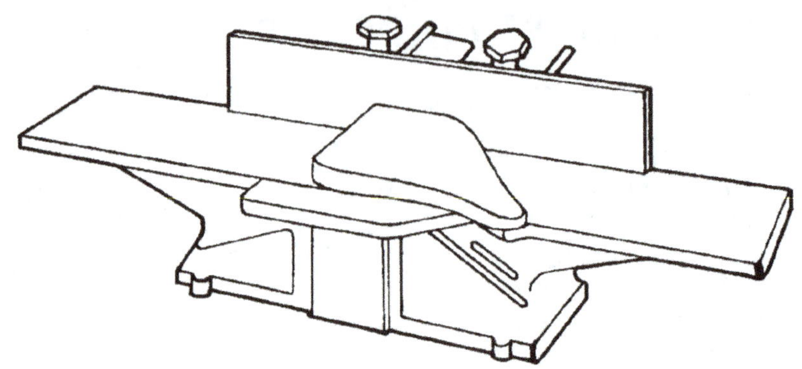

THICKNESS PLANER

THIS MACHINE IS SIMILAR TO THE JOINTER-PLANER, BUT IS USED PRIMARILY TO REDUCE THE THICKNESS OF WOOD.

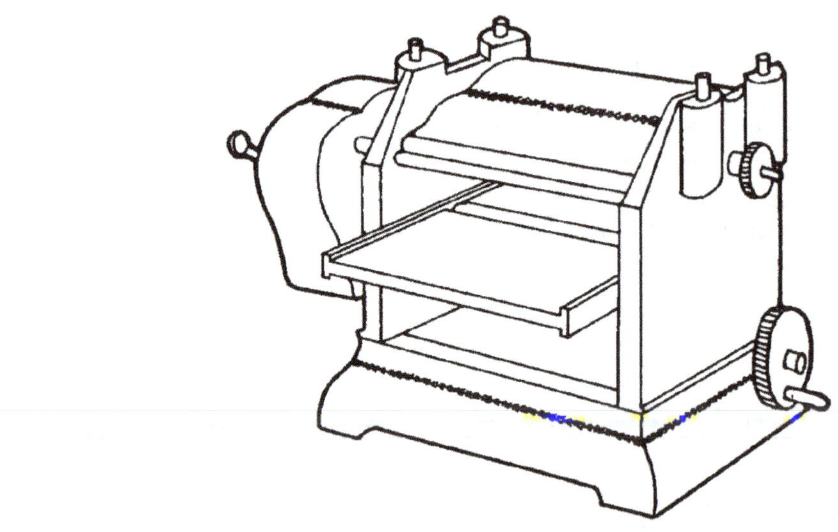

SHAPER

THIS MACHINE IS USED TO SHAPE WOOD INTO DIFFERENT FORMS, AND FOR RABBETING BORDERS. IT CONSISTS OF A VERTICAL ARM IN WHICH CUTTERS OF VARIOUS SIZES MAY BE INSERTED

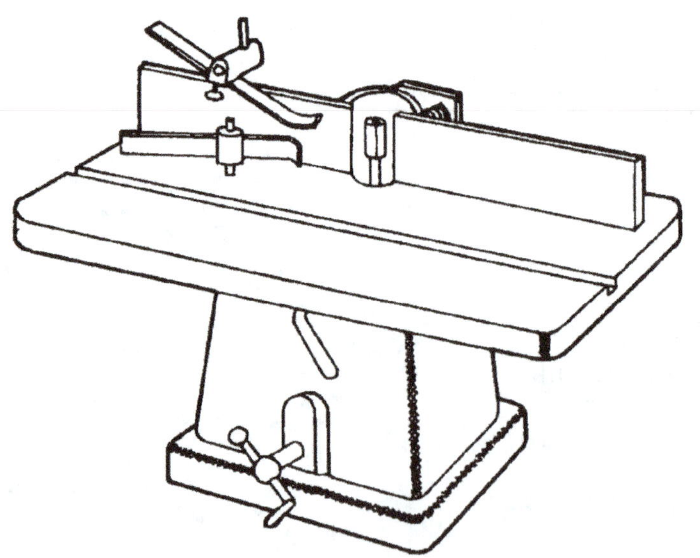

DRILL PRESS

THIS PRESS IS ONE OF THE MOST
POPULAR WOODWORKING
MACHINES FOR BORING HOLES.

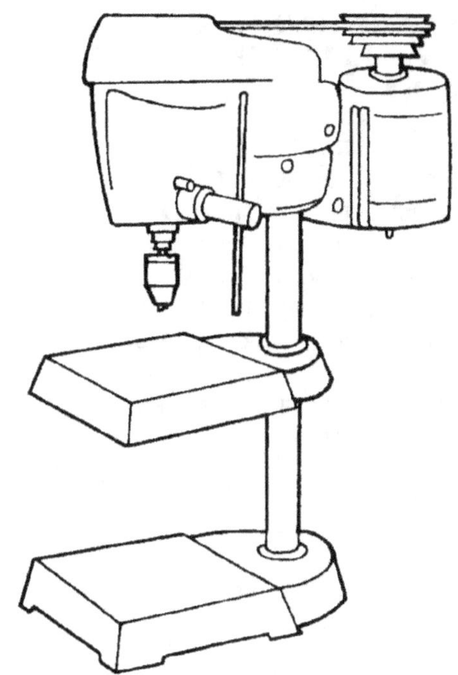

LATHE

THE LATHE IS PARTICULARLY IM-
PORTANT IN SUCH OPERATIONS
AS FINISHING LEGS AND ADDING
DECORATIVE TRIM. ITS USE IS DIF-
FICULT FOR THE BEGINNER BE-
CAUSE OF THE DIFFERENT TYPES
OF CHISELS EMPLOYED, BUT AFTER
SOME PRACTICE THE HOBBYIST
WILL FIND IT FUN TO USE.

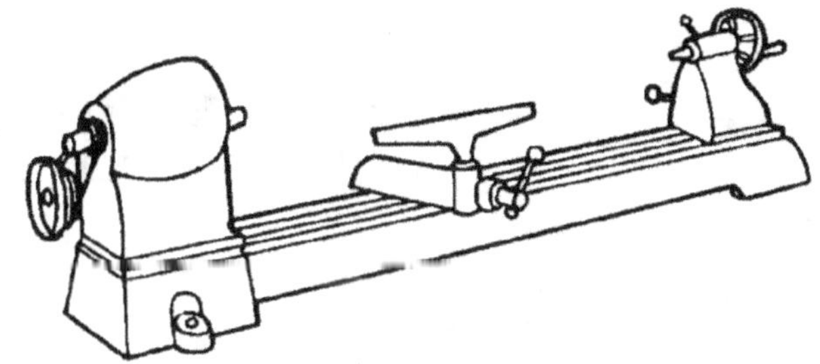

BELT SANDER

THE BELT SANDER IS VERY PRAC-
TICAL FOR FINISHING WORK. IT
IS EASY TO HANDLE; THE ONLY
REQUIREMENT IS TO KEEP THE
PIECES OF WOOD PRESSED ON
THE SANDER.

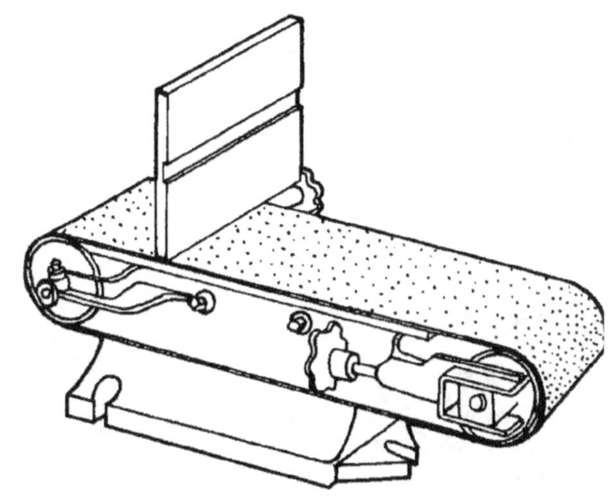

PORTABLE DISC SANDER AND PORTABLE BELT SANDER

EITHER OF THESE SANDERS IS A USEFUL ADDITION TO THE HOBBYIST'S TOOL COLLECTION. THE BELT SANDER HAS THE ADVANTAGE OF MOVING ONLY IN THE DIRECTION OF THE GRAIN. THE DISC SANDER, WHICH WORKS IN A CIRCULAR MOTION, SOMETIMES LEAVES VISIBLE MARKINGS ON THE WOOD.

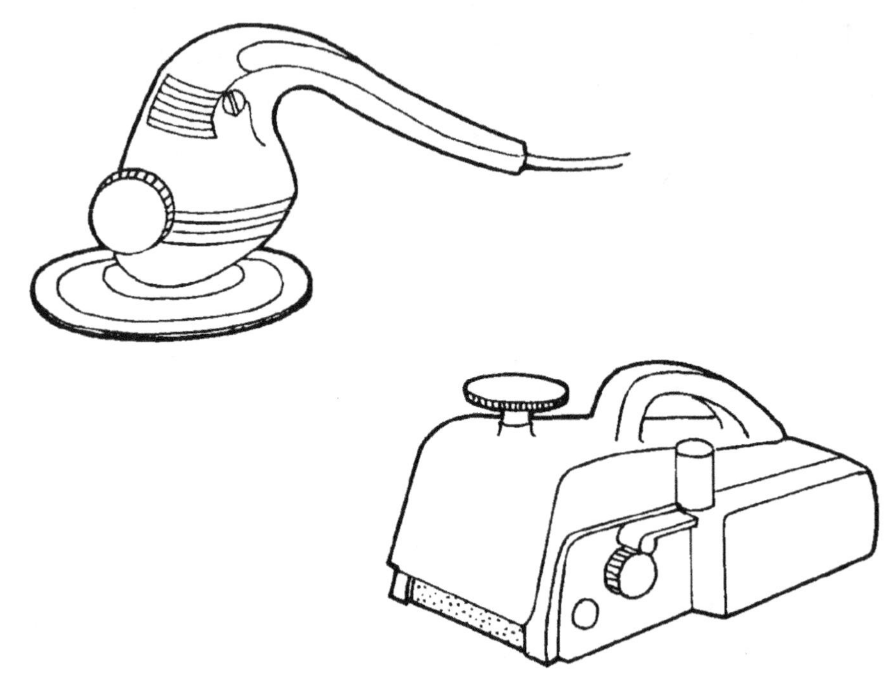

PORTABLE ELECTRIC DRILL

THE PORTABLE ELECTRIC DRILL IS A SIMPLE, PRACTICAL MACHINE FOR BORING HOLES, AND IS VERY POPULAR AMONG HOBBYISTS.

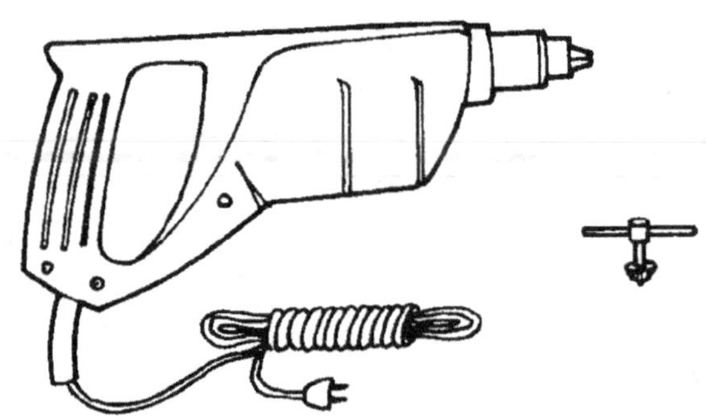

GRINDER

THE GRINDER IS IMPORTANT IN EVERY WOODWORKING SHOP FOR THE SHARPENING OF TOOLS. IT COMES IN VARIOUS SIZES.

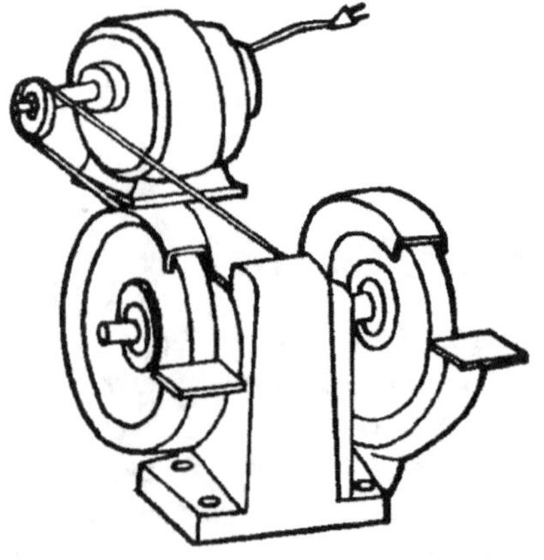

SECTION III

STANDARD
FURNITURE
MEASUREMENTS

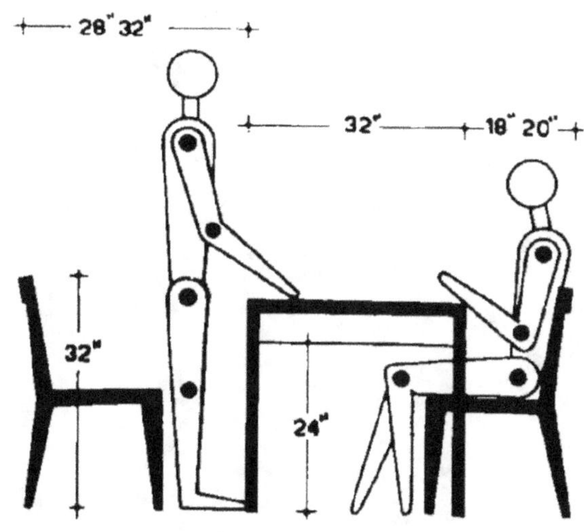

STANDARD FURNITURE MEASUREMENTS

EVERY OBJECT INTENDED FOR HUMAN USE MUST BE PLANNED IN SCALE WITH THE SIZE OF THE HUMAN BODY: THE DIAMETER OF A PENCIL IS CONVENIENT FOR THE FINGERS TO GRASP; STAIR TREADS AND RISERS FIT THE STRIDE; SUBWAY STRAPS ARE WITHIN EASY REACH. FURNITURE IS NO EXCEPTION, AND IF THE PIECES WE BUILD ARE TO BE COMFORTABLE AS WELL AS ATTRACTIVE, HUMAN MEASUREMENTS MUST BE STUDIED AND PROPORTIONS CALCULATED.

THE ILLUSTRATION ON THE OPPOSITE PAGE SHOWS THE RELATIONSHIP OF THE HUMAN BODY TO VARIOUS TYPES OF FURNITURE. NOTICE THAT ALL OF THE MEASUREMENTS GIVEN ARE FOR HEIGHT, THE CRITICAL DIMENSION FOR SITTING, STANDING, AND REACHING. LENGTH AND WIDTH ARE MORE FLEXIBLE, AND ARE OFTEN DETERMINED BY THE PLACE WHERE THE FURNITURE IS TO BE USED, OR THE SIZE OF OBJECTS TO BE STORED.

THE SKETCHES ON THE FOLLOWING PAGES SHOW STANDARD MEASUREMENTS FOR NEARLY EVERY TYPE OF FURNITURE COMMONLY USED IN THE HOME.

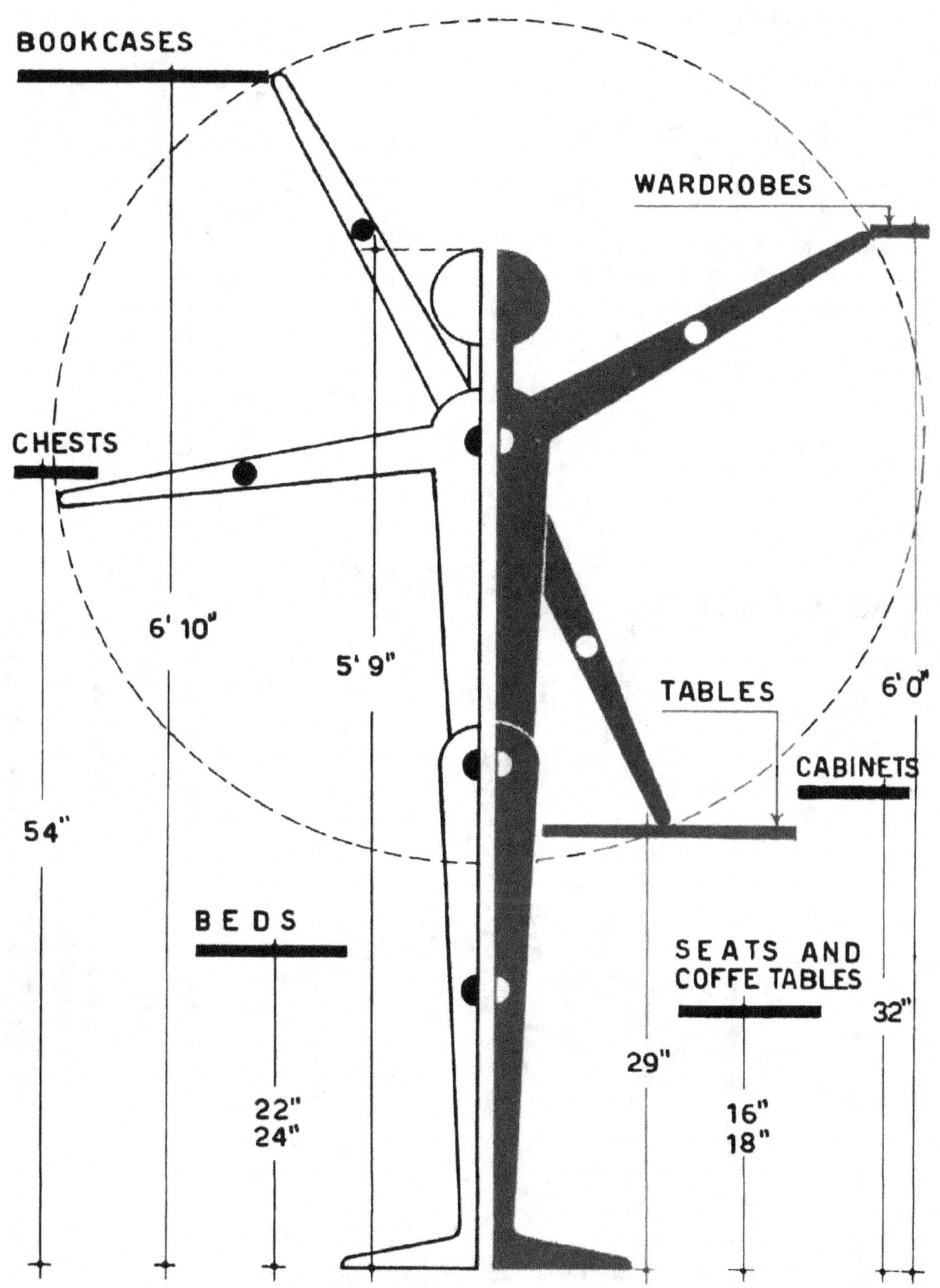

BOOKCASES
WARDROBES
CHESTS
6' 10"
5' 9"
TABLES
6' 0"
CABINETS
54"
BEDS
SEATS AND
COFFE TABLES
32"
29"
22"
24"
16"
18"

STOOL AND BENCH

ILLUSTRATED ARE THE VARIOUS BASIC TYPES OF STOOLS AND BENCHES MADE OF EITHER WOOD OR METAL. THESE DRAWINGS GIVE A CLEAR IDEA OF THE PROPORTIONS AND STANDARD MEASUREMENTS MOST COMMON IN THIS TYPE OF FURNITURE.

THIS EXAMPLE IS OF PRACTICAL USE AS A BASIC UNIT FOR THE CREATION OF NEW DESIGNS. ALSO, ITS MEASUREMENTS CAN BE USED IN PLANNING INTERIORS.

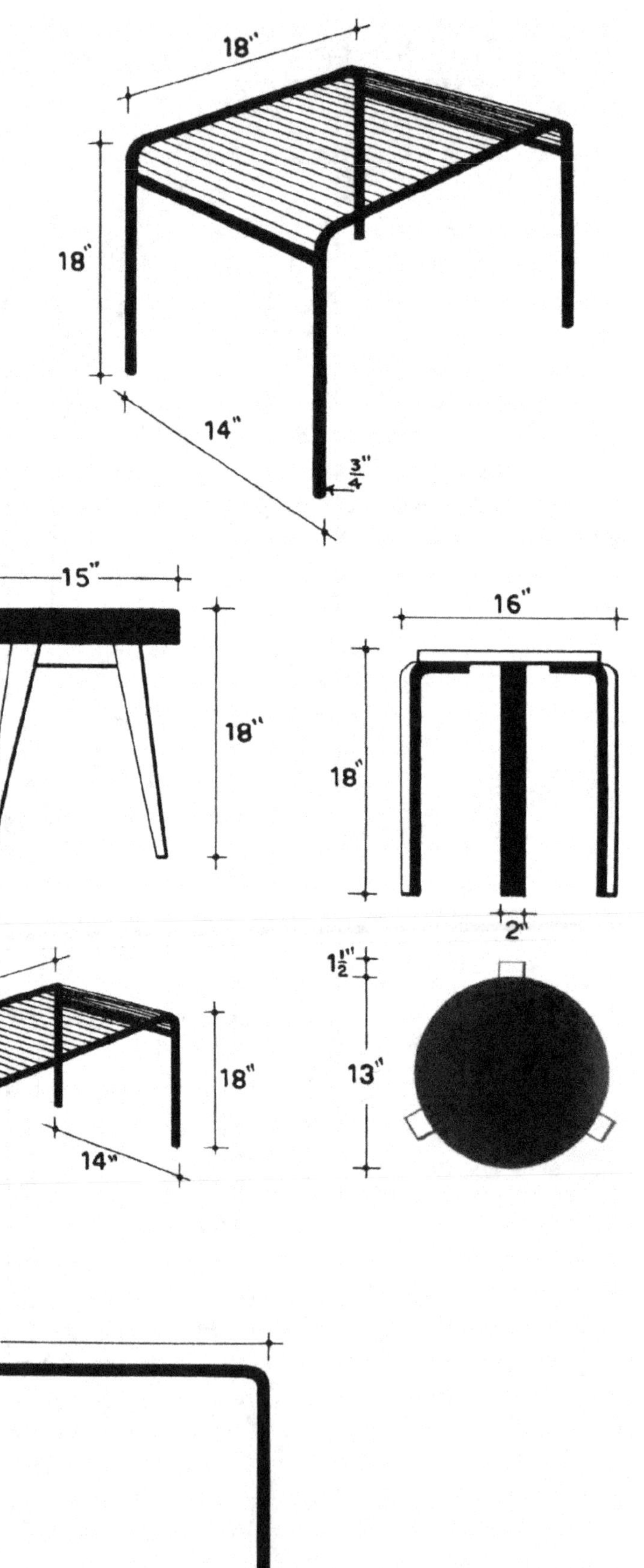

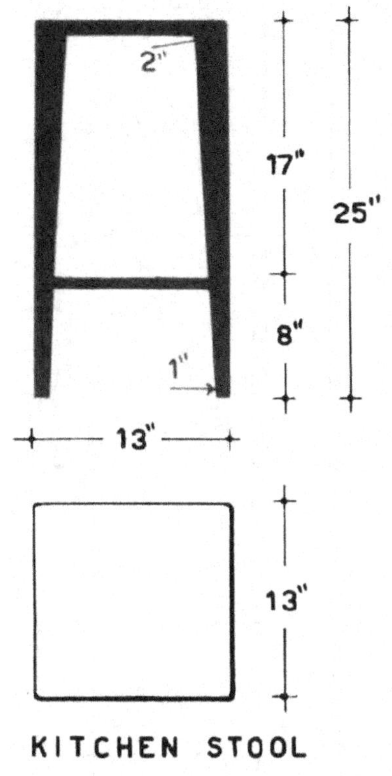

KITCHEN STOOL

BAR STOOL

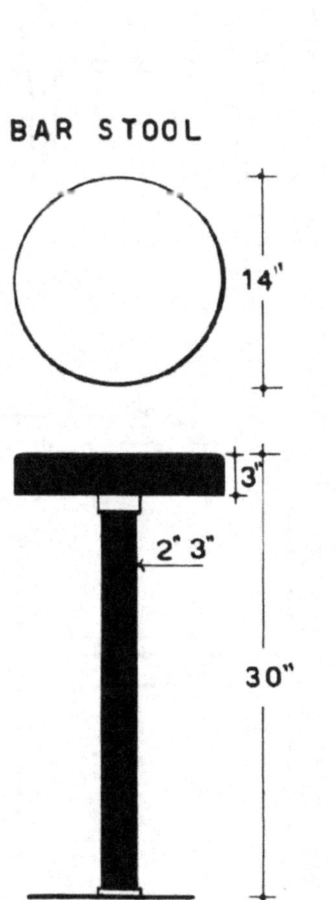

DRAWING STOOL

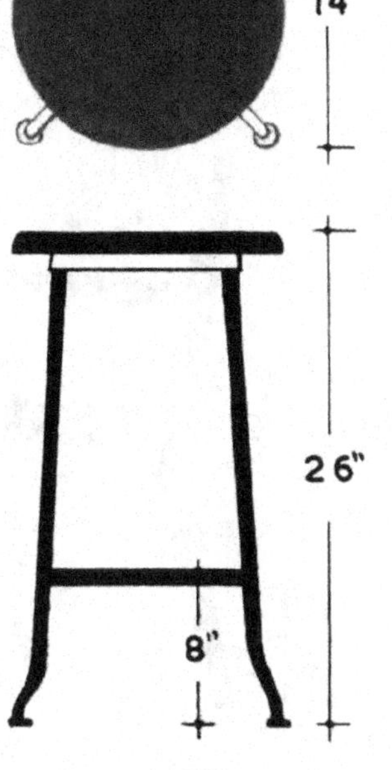

HIGH STOOLS

THESE HIGH STOOLS ARE DIFFERENT FROM THOSE ON THE PRECEDING PAGE. THEY ARE DESIGNED FOR USE IN KITCHENS, BARS AND DRAFTING ROOMS.

CHAIRS

THERE ARE MANY TYPES OF CHAIRS AND SOFAS INCLUDING ARM CHAIRS, LOW ARM CHAIRS, ARMLESS LOUNGE CHAIRS, LOVE SEATS, ETC. THE MEASUREMENTS AND DETAILS ARE CLEARLY ILLUSTRATED. A DESCRIPTION OF EACH PIECE IS UNNECESSARY AS THE ILLUSTRATIONS CLEARLY SHOW THE DESIGN AND RELATIVE MEASUREMENTS.

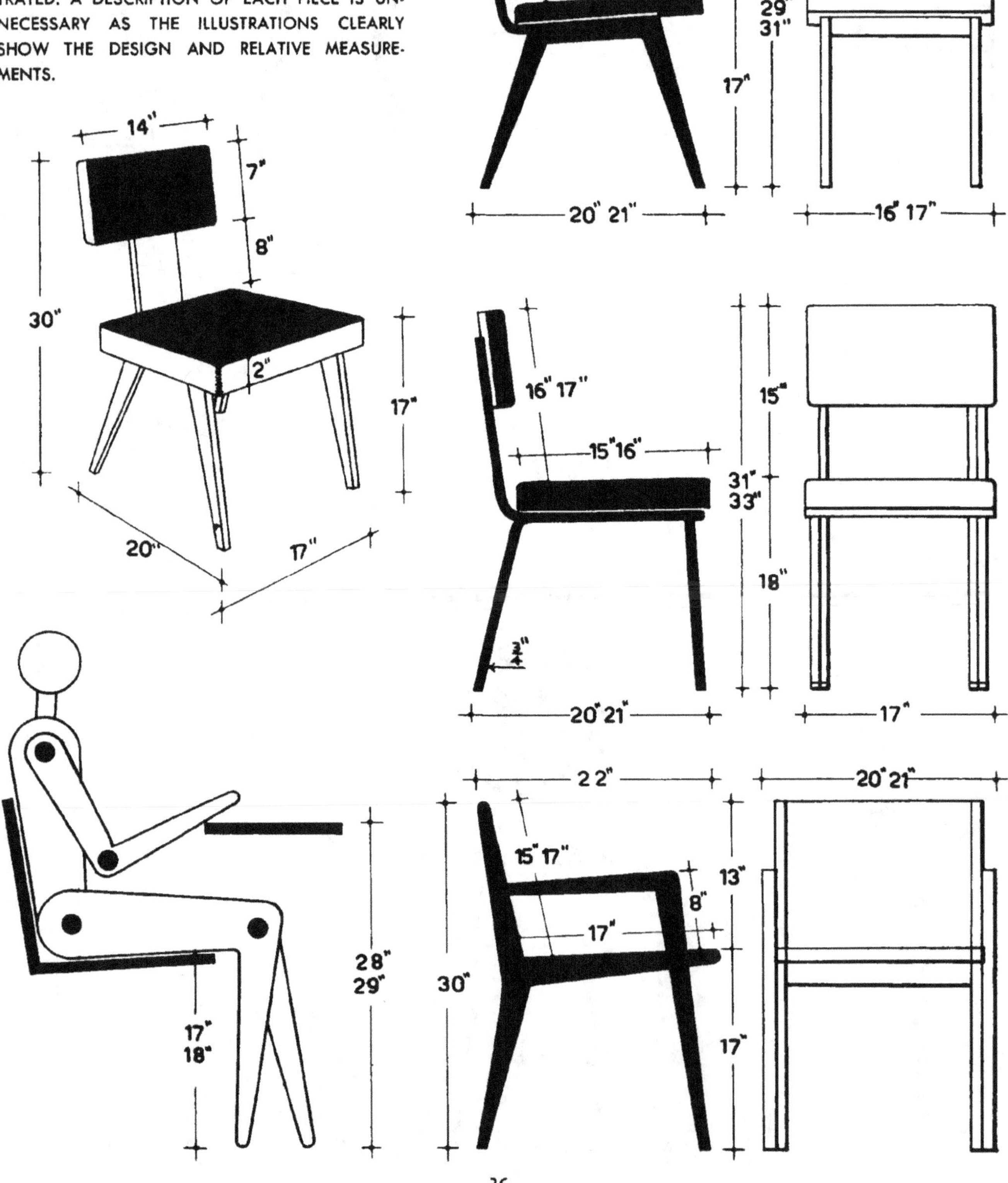

LOW ARM CHAIR AND ARMLESS CHAIR

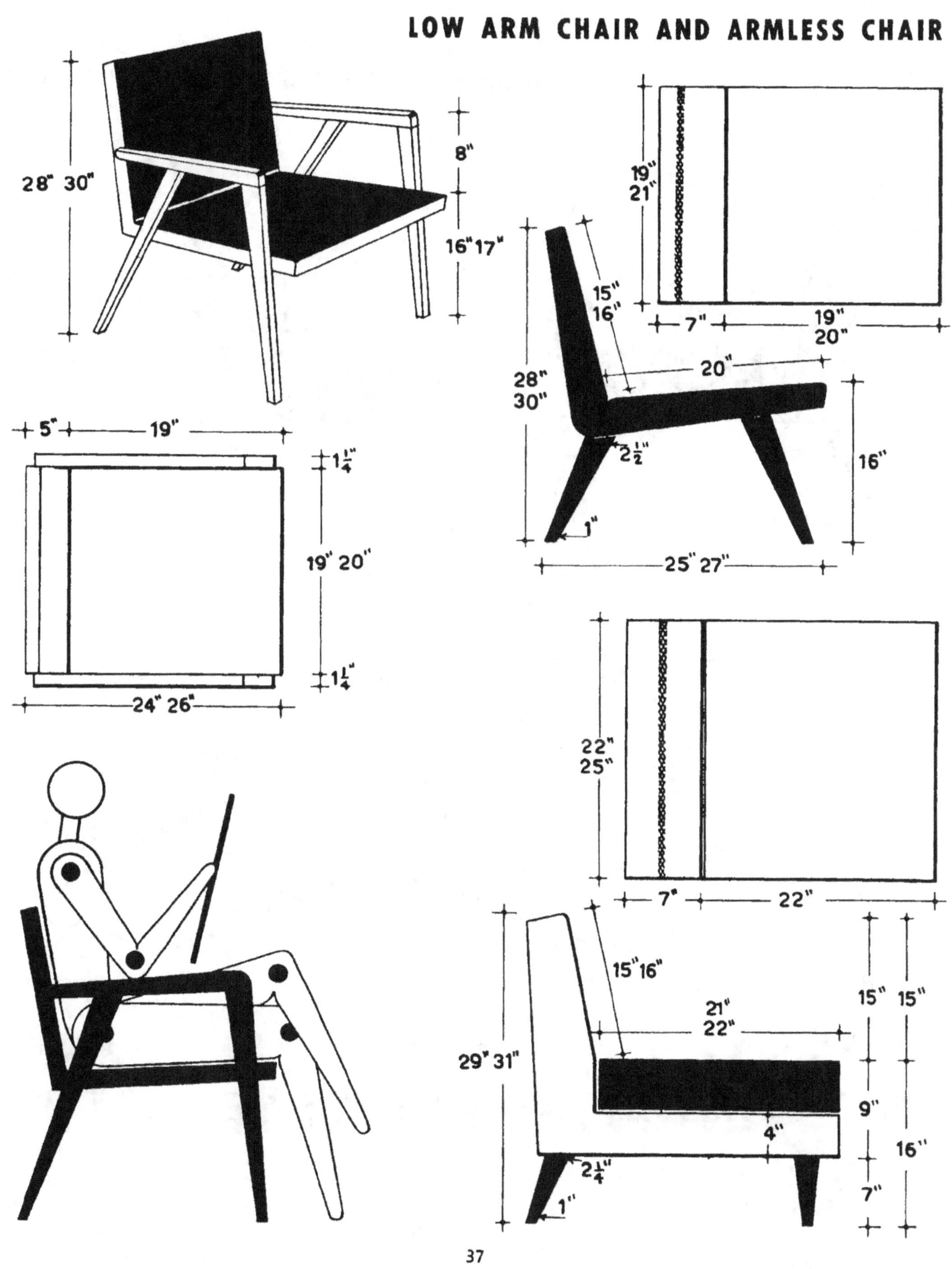

HIGH ARM CHAIR AND LOUNGE CHAIR

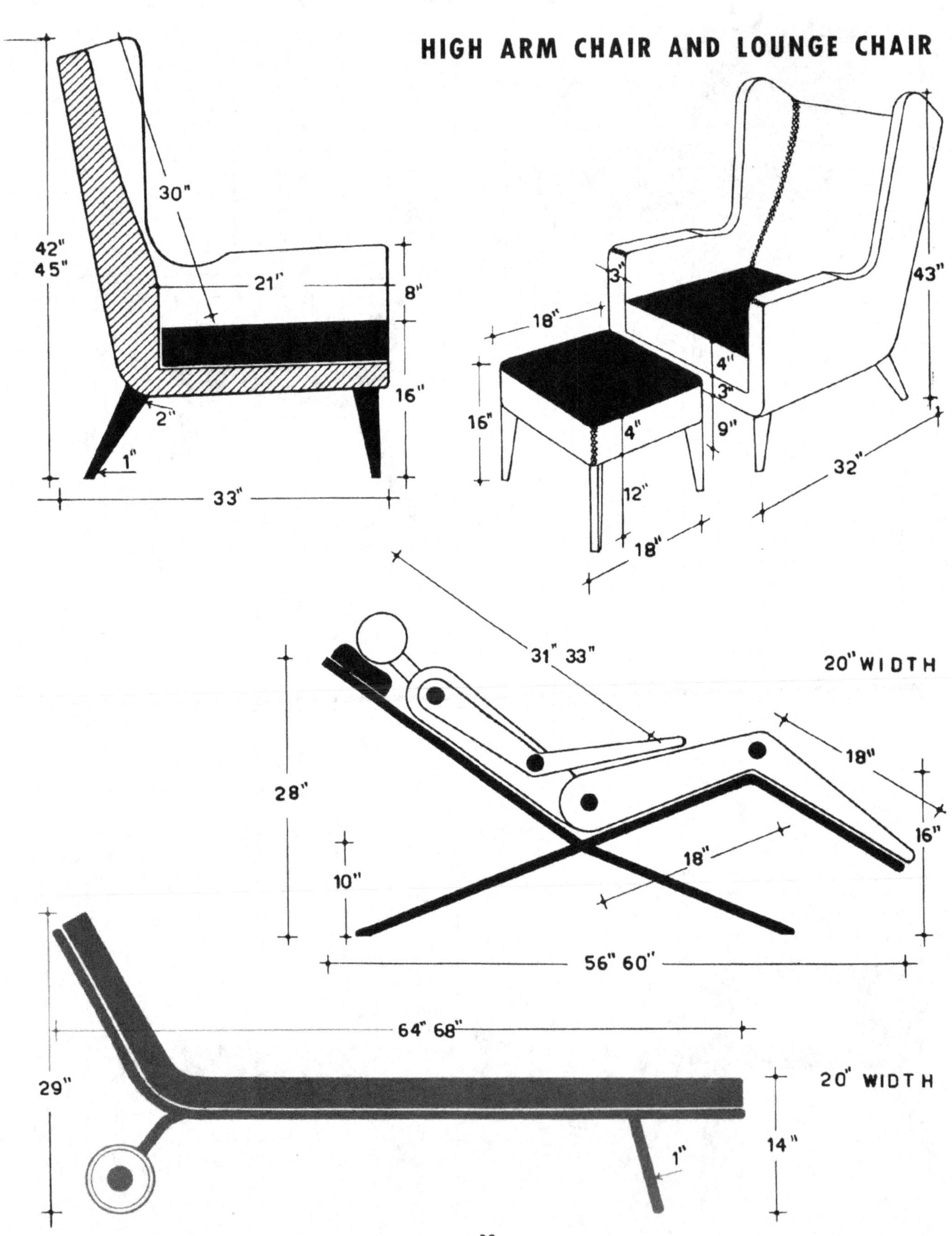

ARM CHAIR, LOVE SEAT, AND SOFA

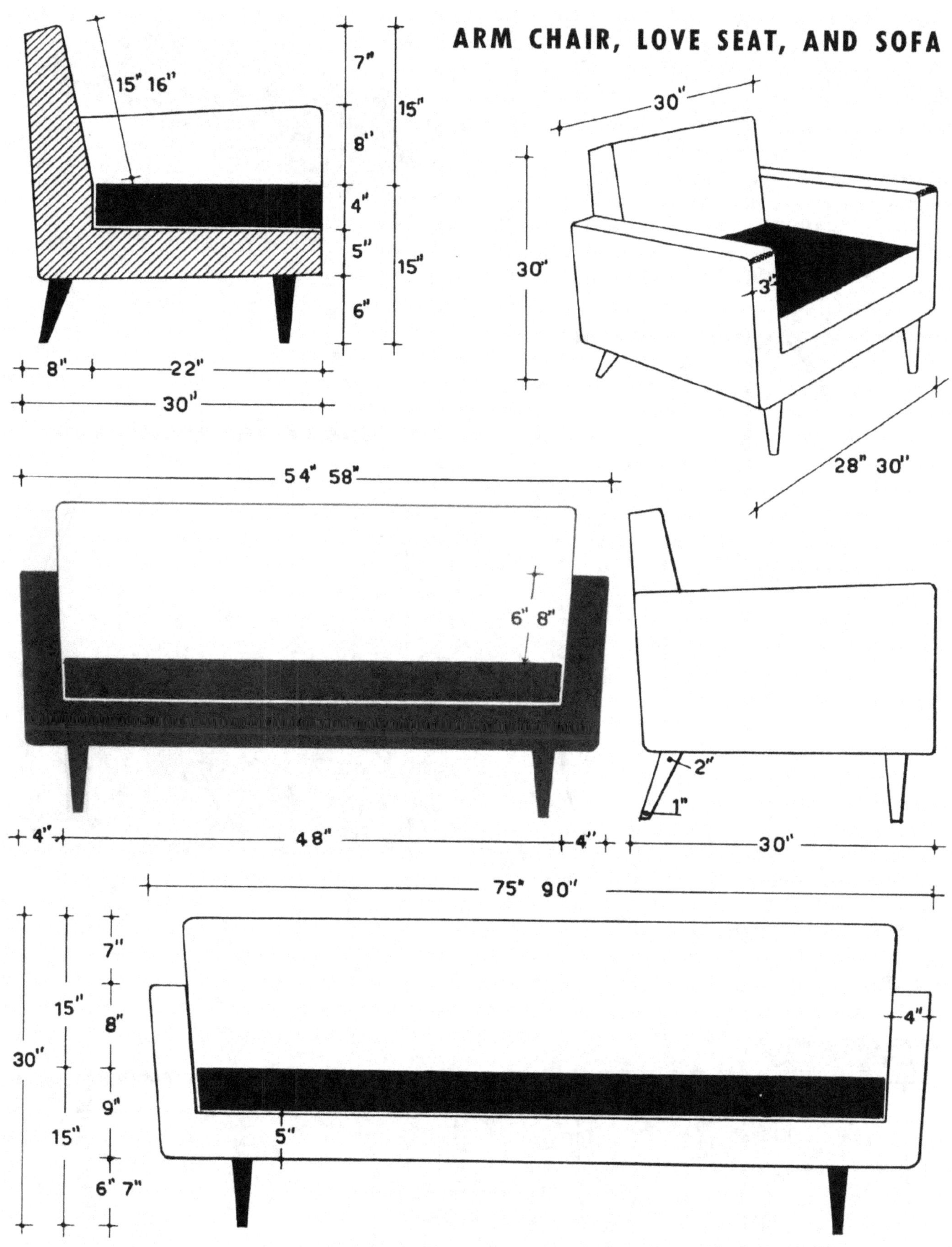

TABLES

THE TABLES ARE DIVIDED INTO VARIOUS CATE-
GORIES SUCH AS COFFEE TABLES, PLAY TABLES,
DINING TABLES, MAGAZINE TABLES, ETC., EACH
HAVING ITS OWN PROPORTIONS AND MEASURE-
MENTS.

PRESENTED ARE A FEW EXAMPLES OF COFFEE
TABLES WHICH MAY BE OBTAINED IN BASIC
STANDARD MEASUREMENTS. NOTICE THAT THE
PROPORTIONS SHOWN FOR THE COFFEE TABLE
AT THE BOTTOM OF THE PAGE MAY ALSO BE
APPLIED TO A BENCH.

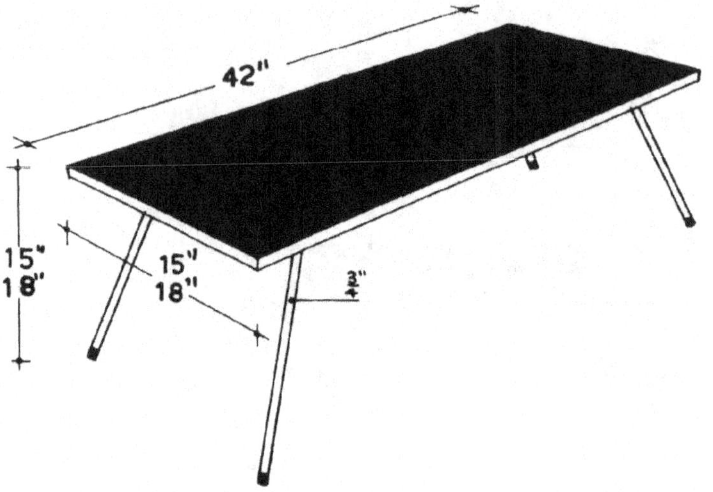

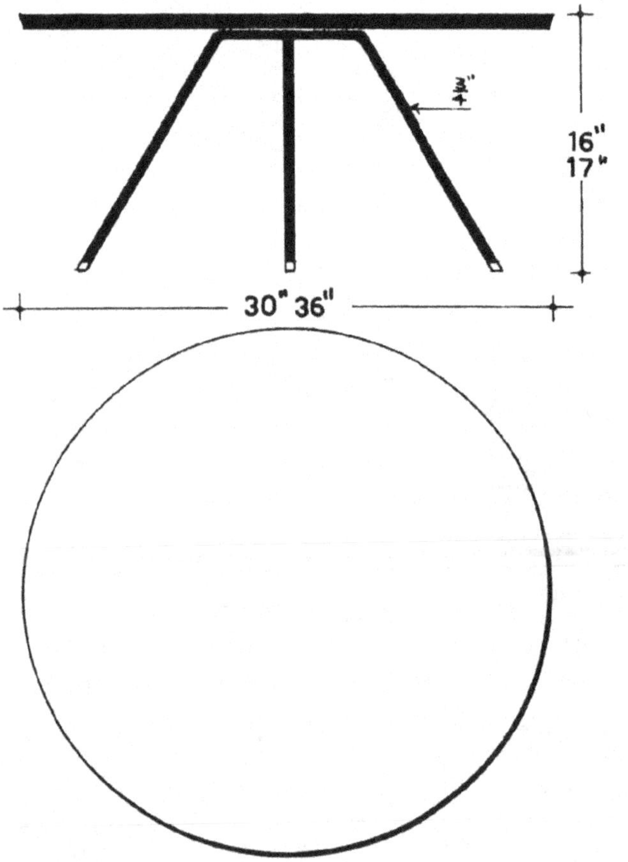

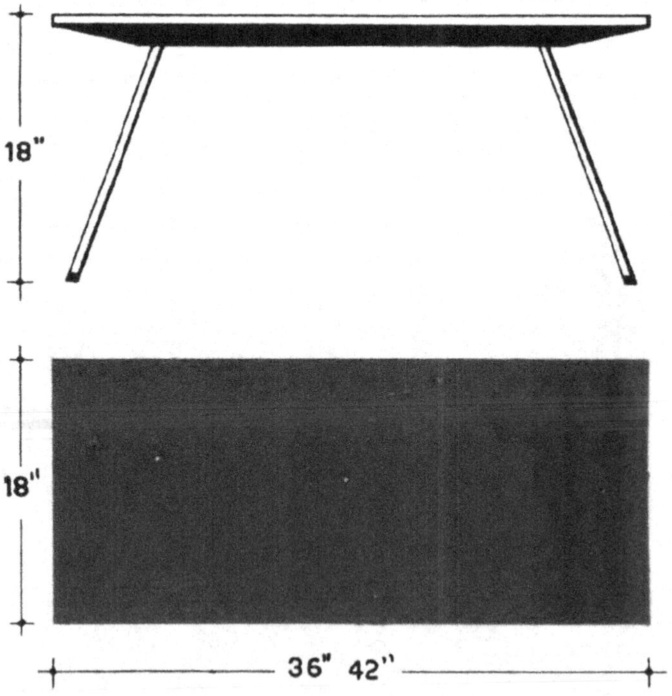

BENCH

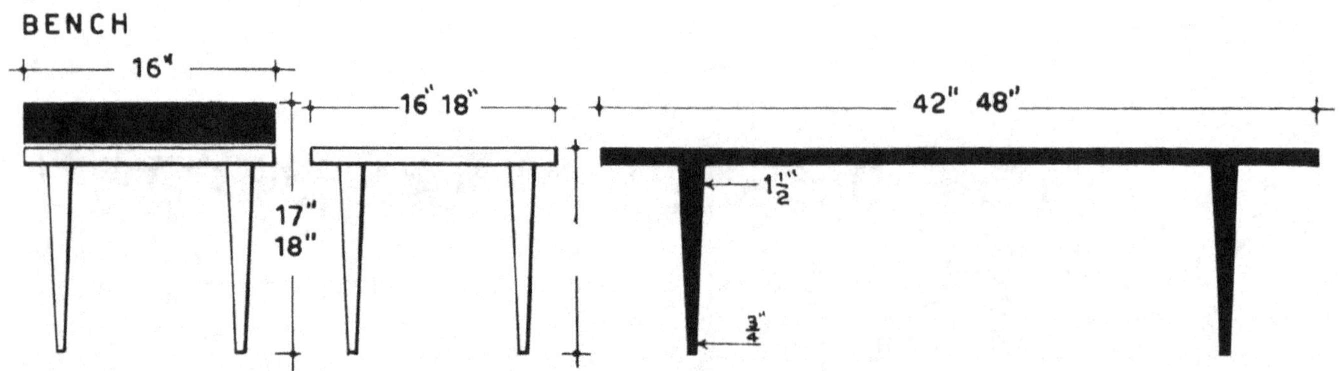

TABLES

SOME TABLES WHICH ARE WIDELY USED IN THE HOME ARE THE ROUND SIDE TABLE, MAGAZINE STORAGE TABLE, END TABLE, AND SERVICE BAR.

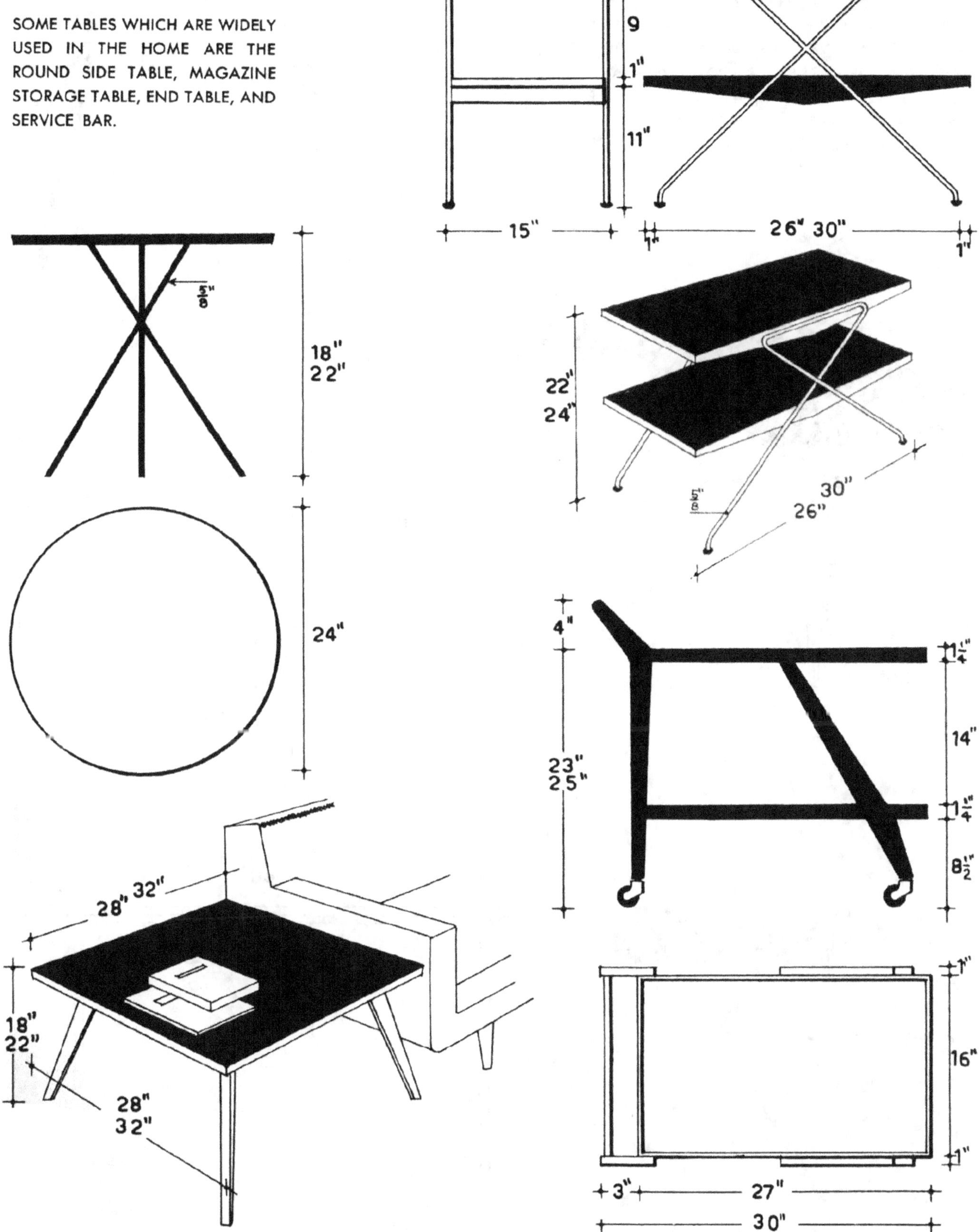

TABLES

PLAY TABLES, KITCHEN TABLES, AND WORK TABLES ARE ALL VERY USEFUL IN THE HOME. ALTHOUGH THESE EXIST IN MANY TYPES AND PROPORTIONS, THOSE SHOWN ILLUSTRATE THE BASIC STANDARD MEASUREMENTS. NOTICE THAT THE STANDARD HEIGHT FOR TABLES OF THIS TYPE IS 29".

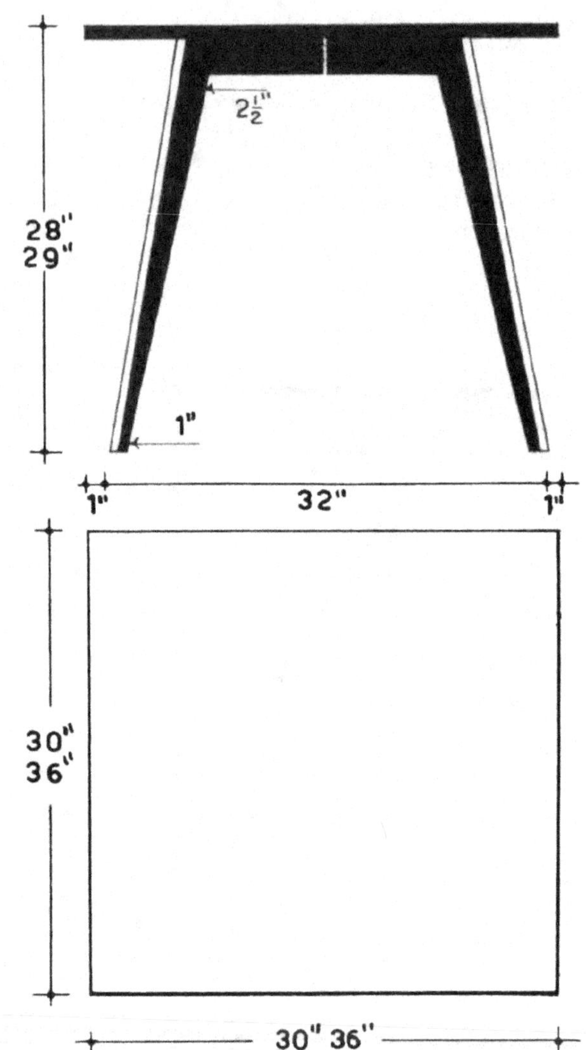

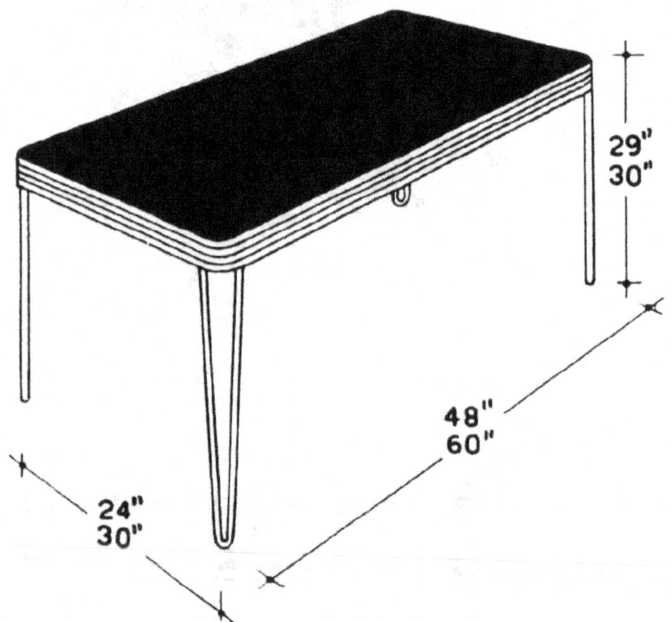

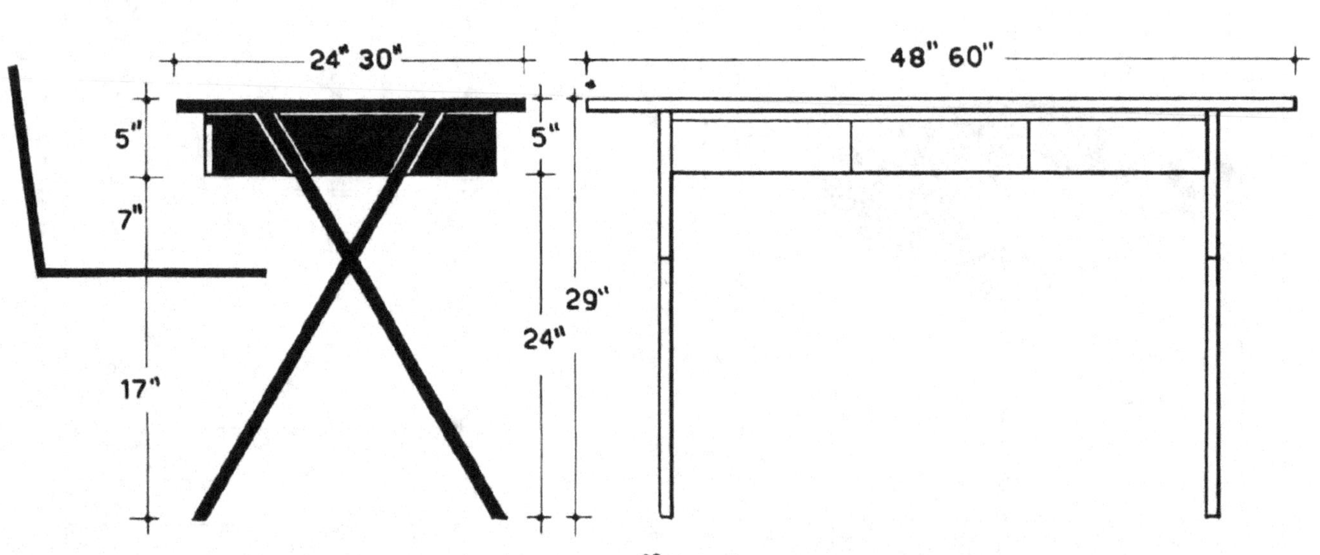

DINING TABLES

THE BASIC STANDARD MEASUREMENTS FOR A DINING TABLE IS 29" IN HEIGHT. IF THE TABLE IS OF CIRCULAR SHAPE, THE DIAMETER IS IN RELATION TO THE NUMBER OF PERSONS TO BE ACCOMMODATED. IN THE RECTANGULAR FORM THE WIDTH VARIES FROM 32" TO 36", WHILE THE LENGTH VARIES ACCORDING TO THE NUMBER OF PERSONS TO BE SEATED, AS INDICATED IN THE ILLUSTRATION BELOW.

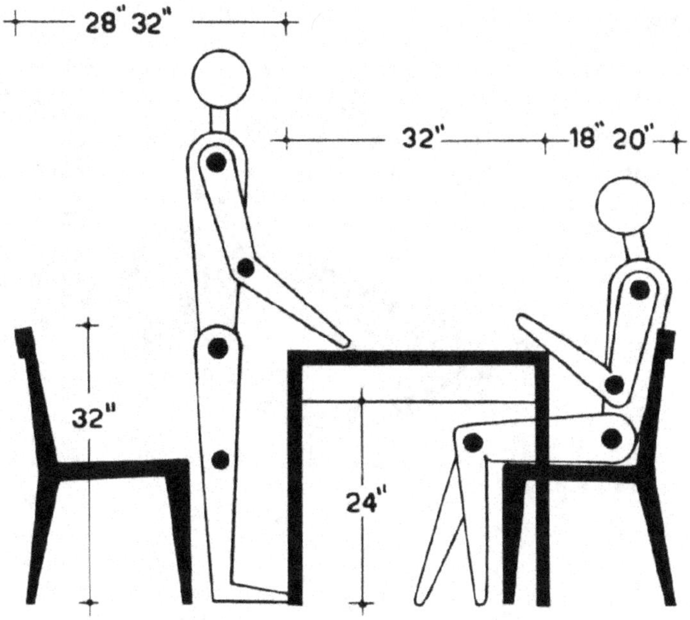

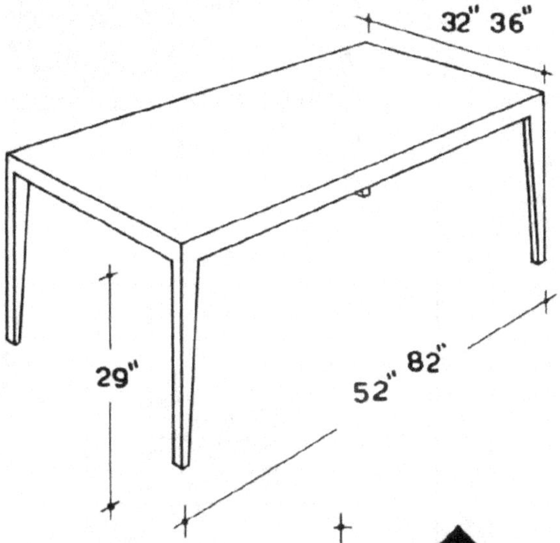

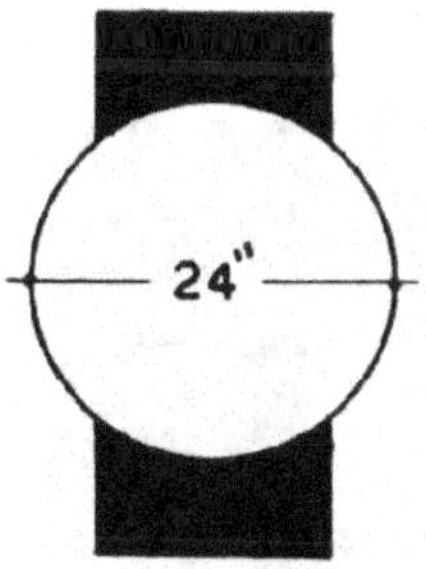

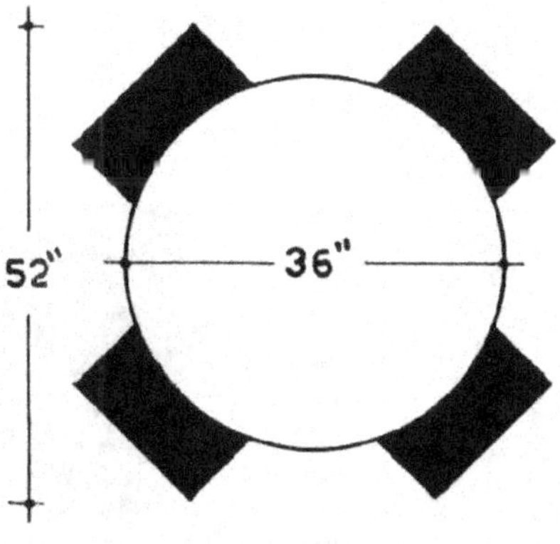

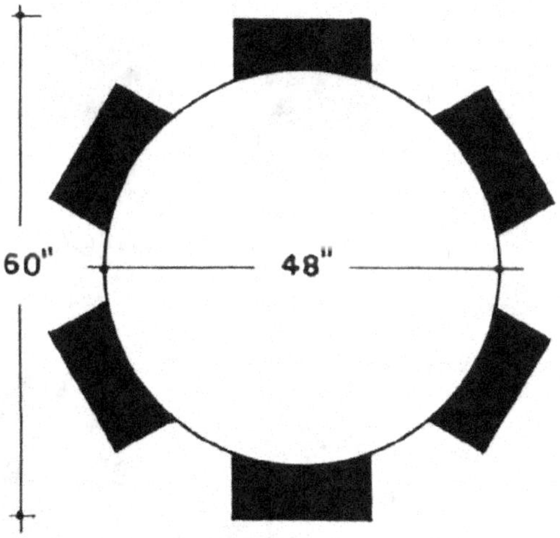

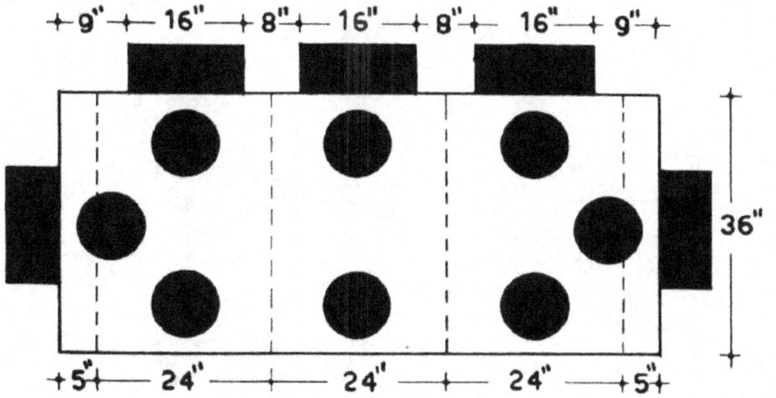

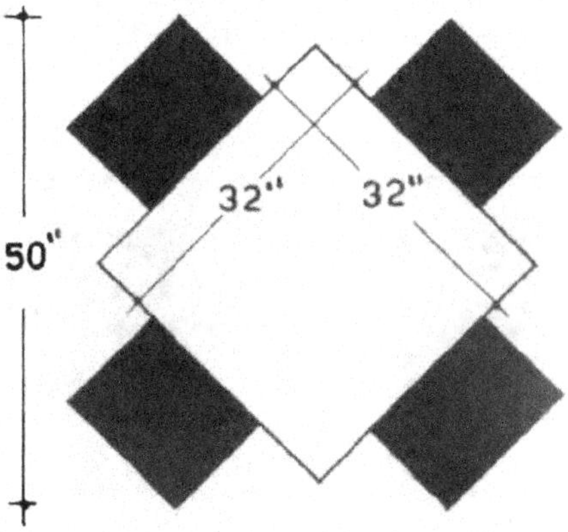

DESK

THE DESK CAN BE CONSIDERED IN THE SAME CATEGORY AS THE TABLE. ITS PRIMARY FUNCTION IS ITS USE AS A WORK TABLE. IT IS IMPORTANT TO NOTE THAT THE SPACE BETWEEN THE LEGS MUST NEVER MEASURE LESS THAN 22" TO ALLOW ROOM FOR A DESK CHAIR TO BE TUCKED AWAY WHEN NOT IN USE.

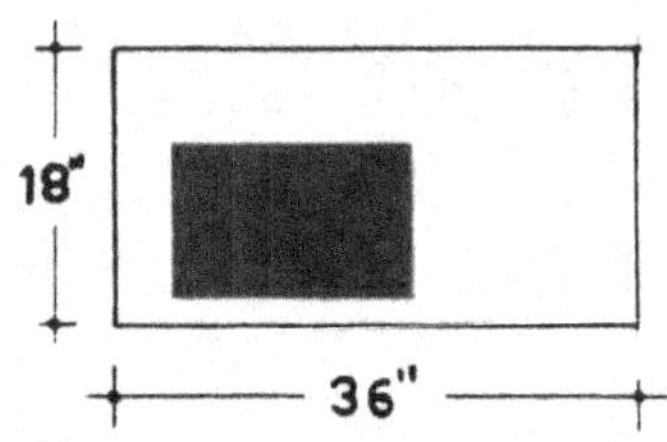

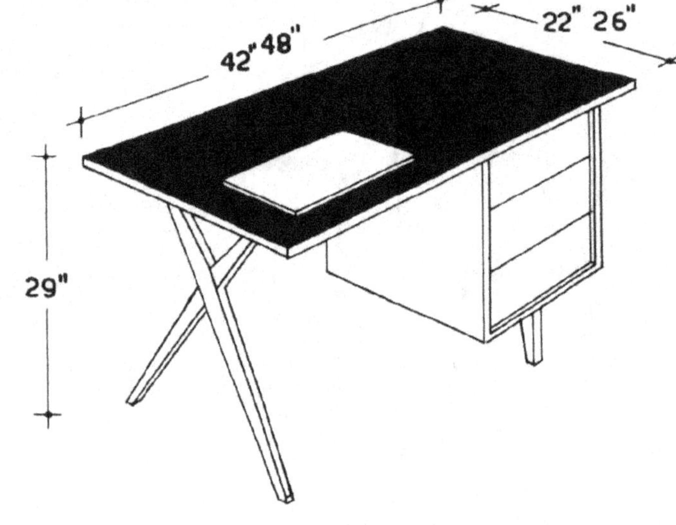

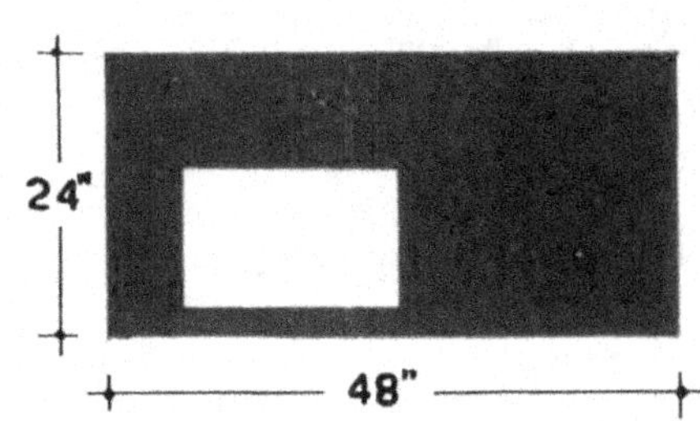

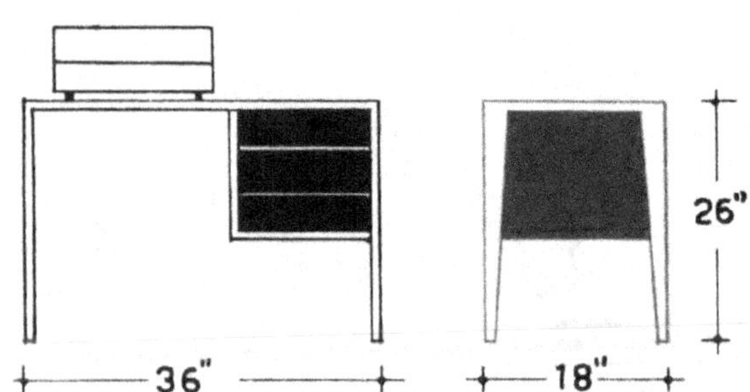

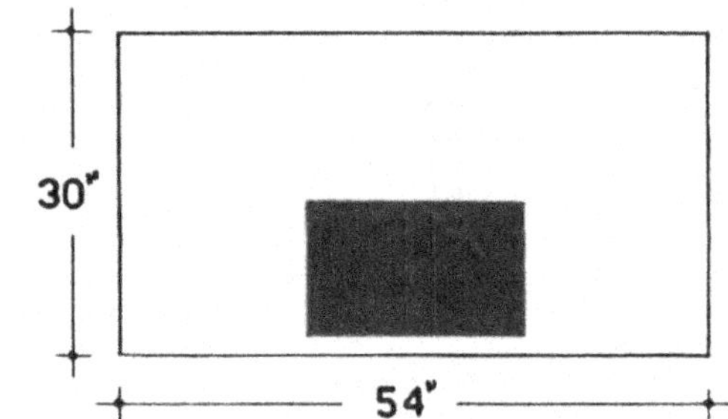

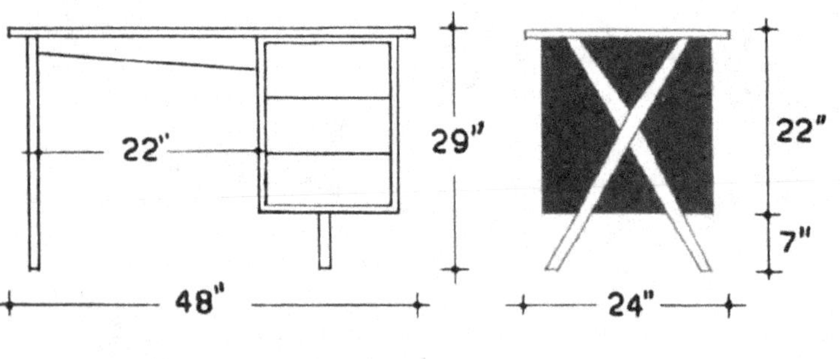

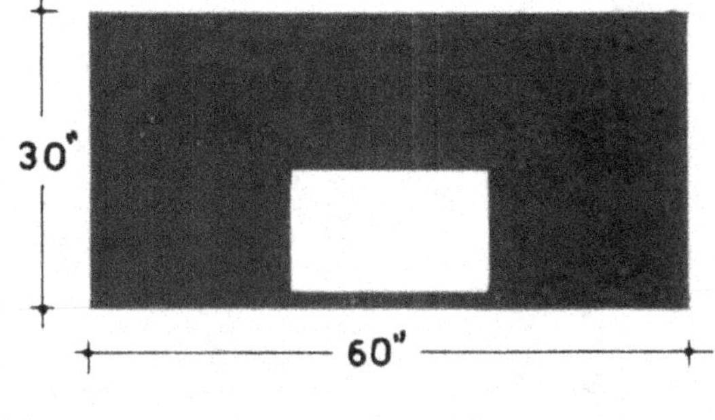

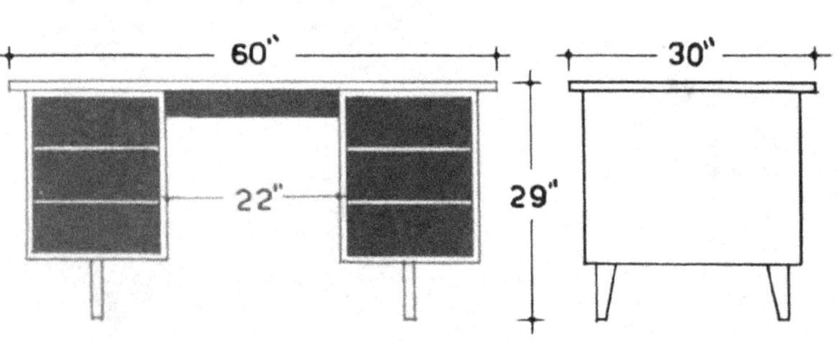

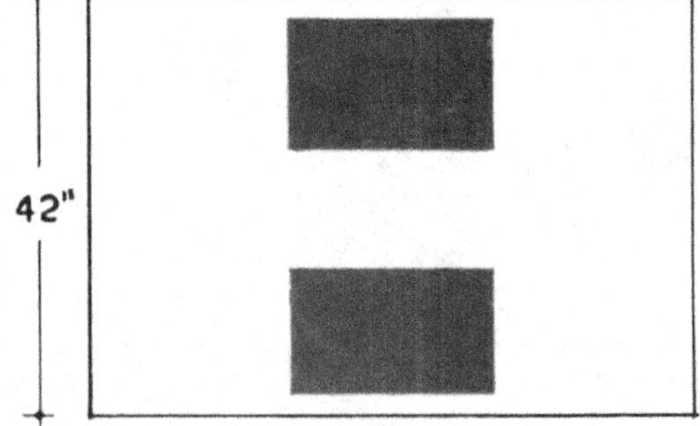

BOOKCASE

THE MAIN FUNCTION OF A BOOKCASE IS TO STORE BOOKS AND MAGAZINES. THEREFORE ITS DEPTH MUST GENERALLY BE ABOUT 12". THE MAXIMUM HEIGHT SHOULD NEVER BE HIGHER THAN MAN'S REACH. REMOVABLE SHELVES ARE A GREAT CONVENIENCE. THE MAGAZINE RACK MAY BE CONSIDERED A SMALL PORTABLE BOOKCASE.

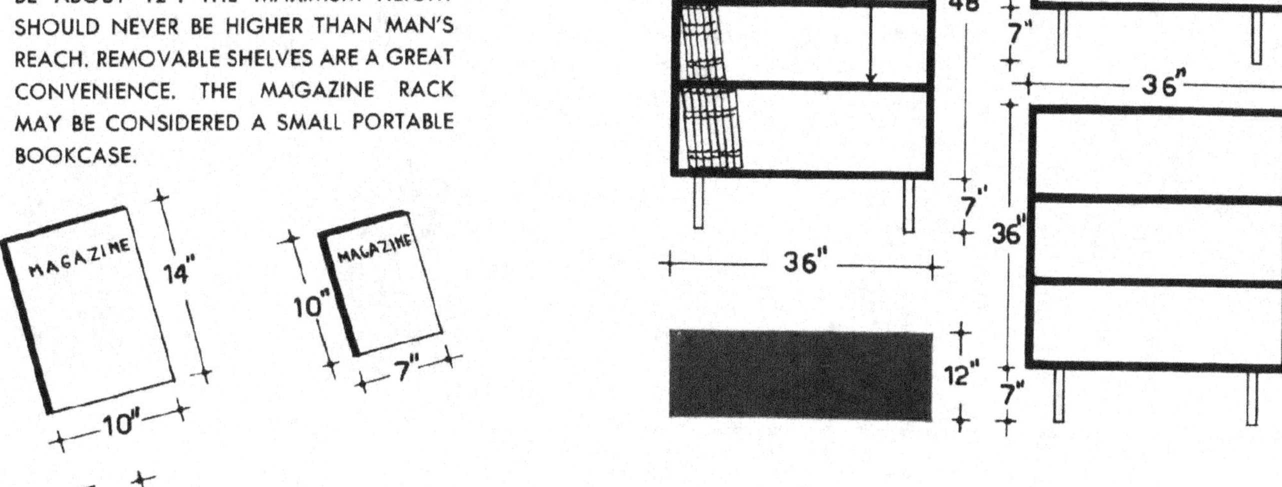

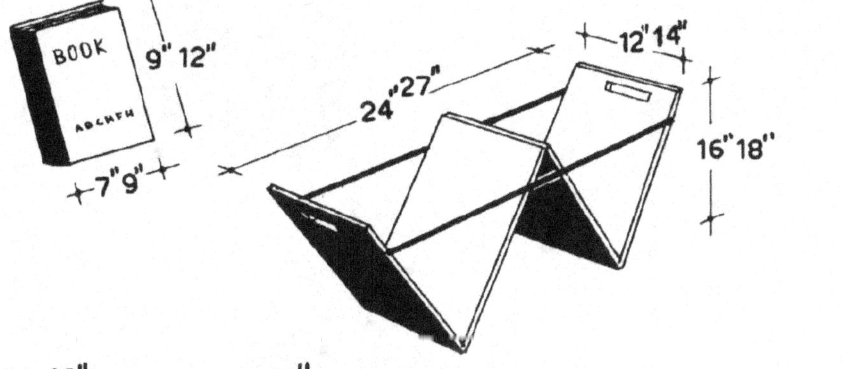

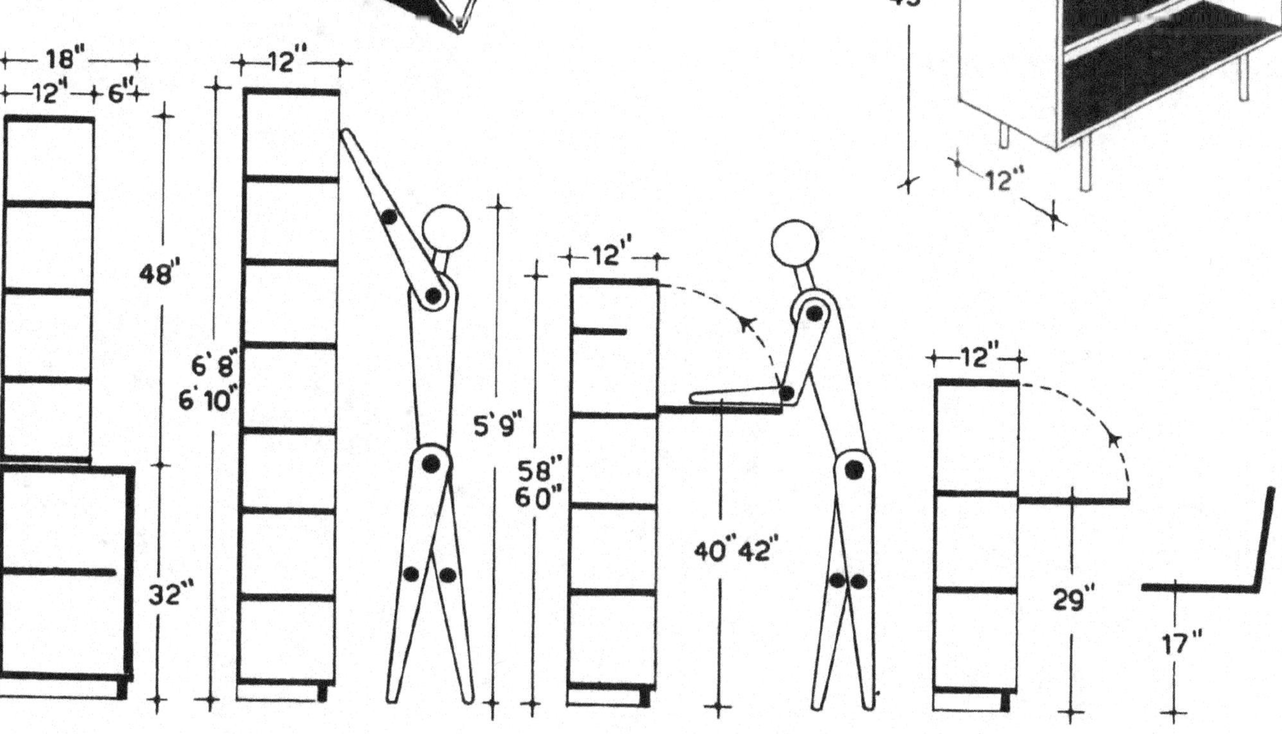

KITCHEN FURNITURE

KITCHEN FURNITURE INCLUDES CABINETS WITH DRAWERS FOR SILVERWARE, SHELVES FOR DISHES, AND COMPARTMENTS FOR OTHER TYPES OF EQUIPMENT. THE DRAWINGS ON THIS PAGE SHOW THE SPACE TO BE ALLOWED FOR THE VARIOUS ARTICLES STORED.

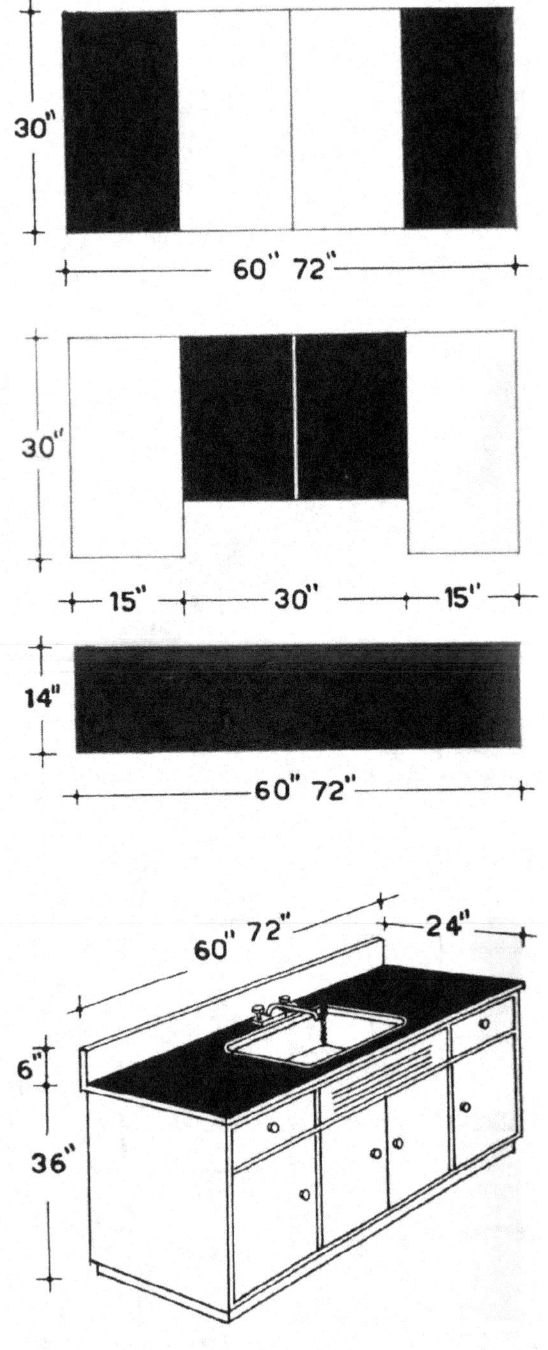

22"
10"
72"
18"
60" 72"
32"
15" 18"
CABINETS
THESE ARE IN VARIOUS SIZES ACCORD-
ING TO THEIR USE IN THE DINING ROOM,
OFFICE, ETC. IN THESE TYPES THE STAND-
ARD MEASUREMENTS ARE UP TO 32" IN
HEIGHT. WHILE THE DEPTH IS GENERALLY
15", IT CAN VARY UP TO 21".
21"
26"
15"
30" 36"
24" 28"
32"
7"
15"
36"
48"
5"
15" 18"
10"
5"
6"
4"
3"
5"
6"
8"
10"
7" 8"
10" 13"
18"
18"
65"
5' 9"
36"
29"
15"
18"
14"
32"
60"

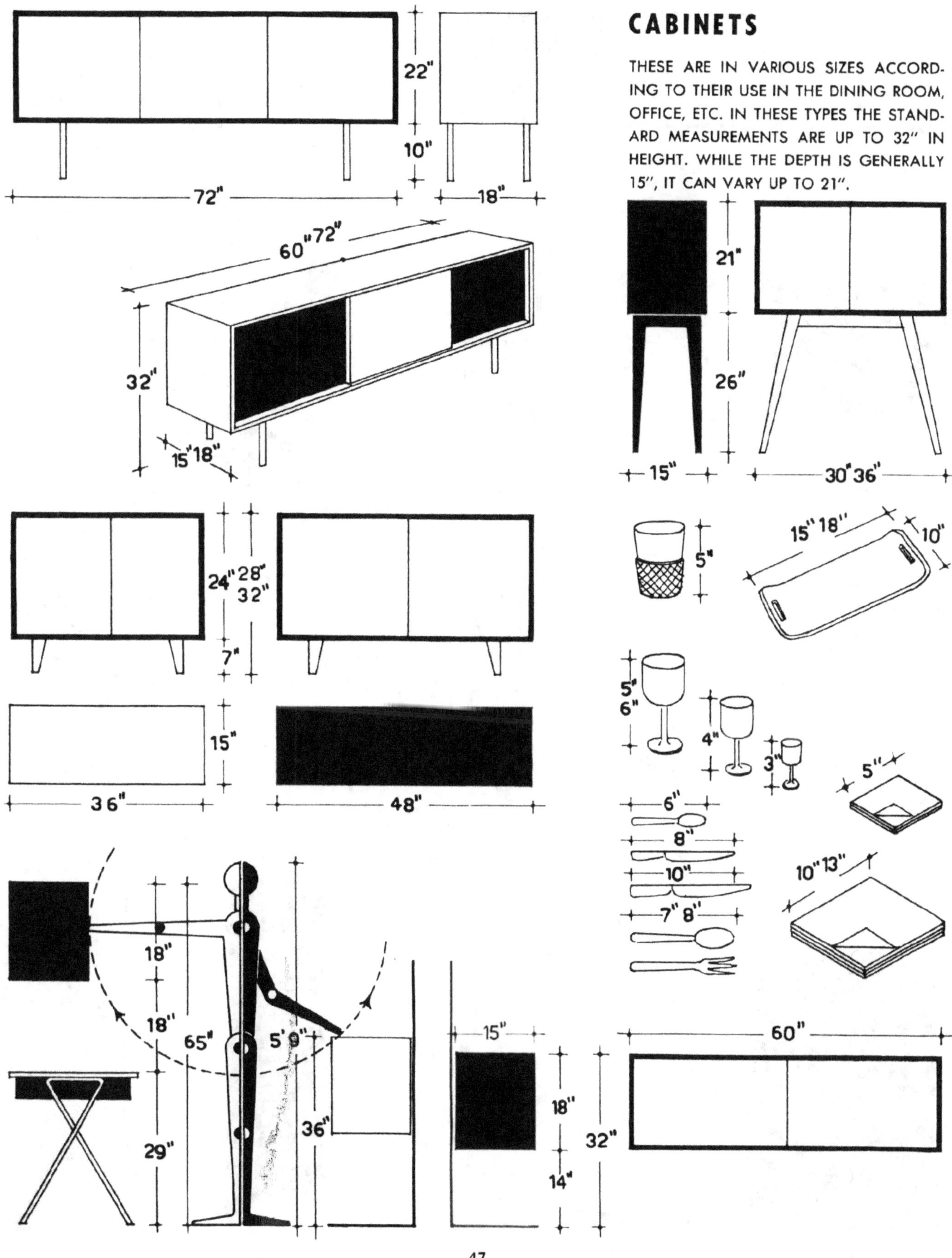

47

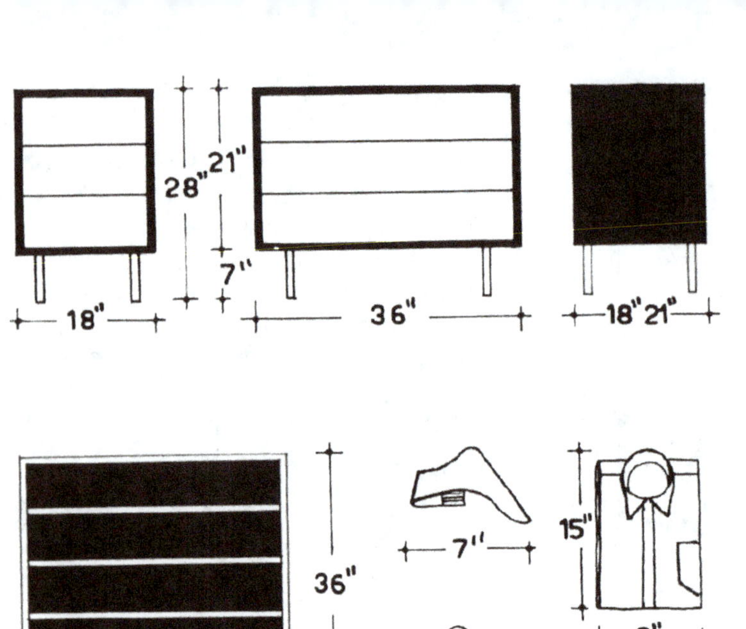

CHESTS

THE HEIGHT OF A CHEST MUST NEVER BE MORE THAN 54" SO THAT THE CONTENTS OF EACH DRAWER MAY BE EASILY SEEN WHEN THE DRAWER IS OPENED. IN MODERN CHESTS THE STANDARD MEASUREMENTS ARE GENERALLY 28" TO 36" IN HEIGHT AND 18" TO 21" IN DEPTH. IN CARD FILES FOR OFFICE USE THE DEPTH IS 15" AND THE WIDTH MAY VARY ACCORDING TO THE INDIVIDUAL USE.

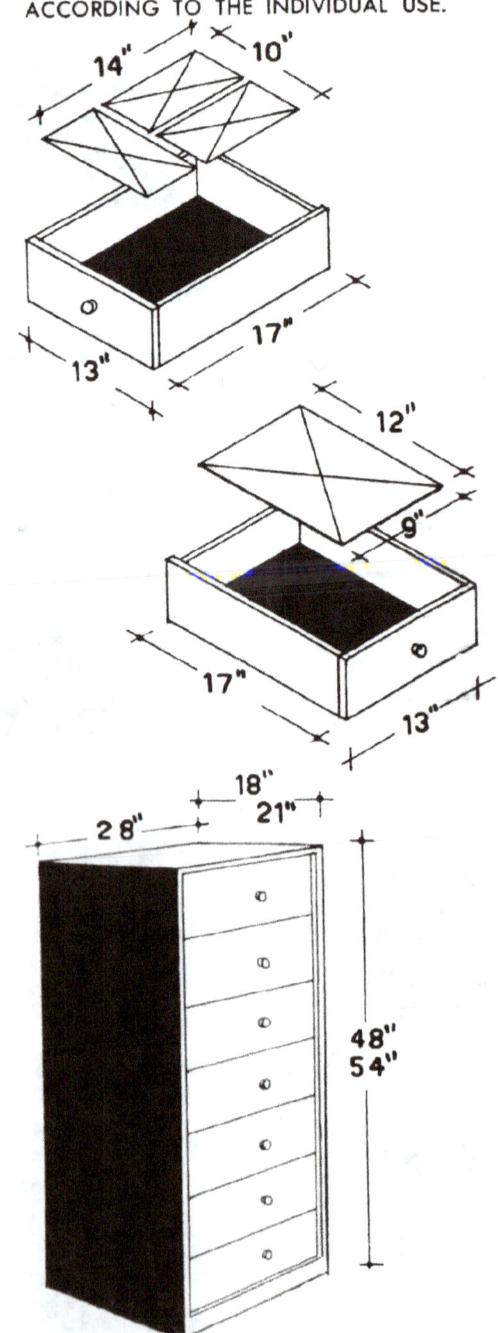

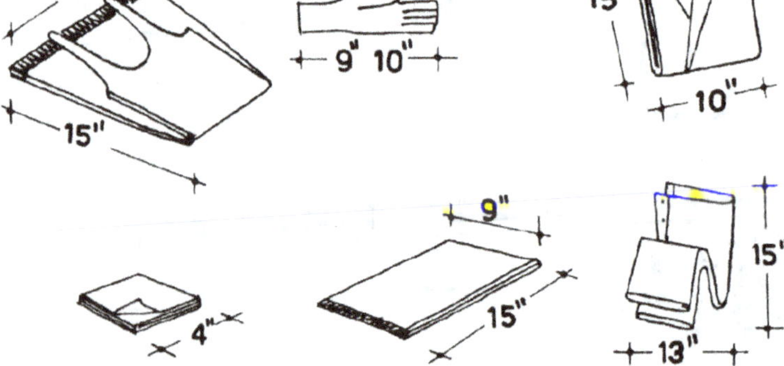

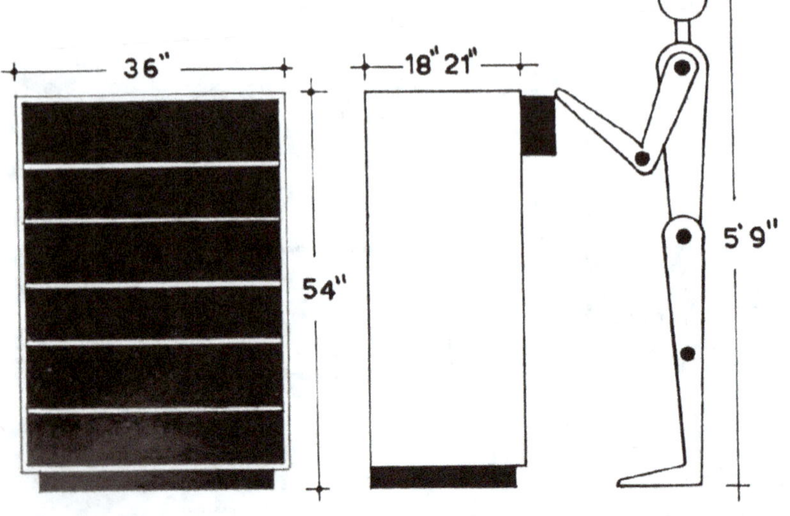

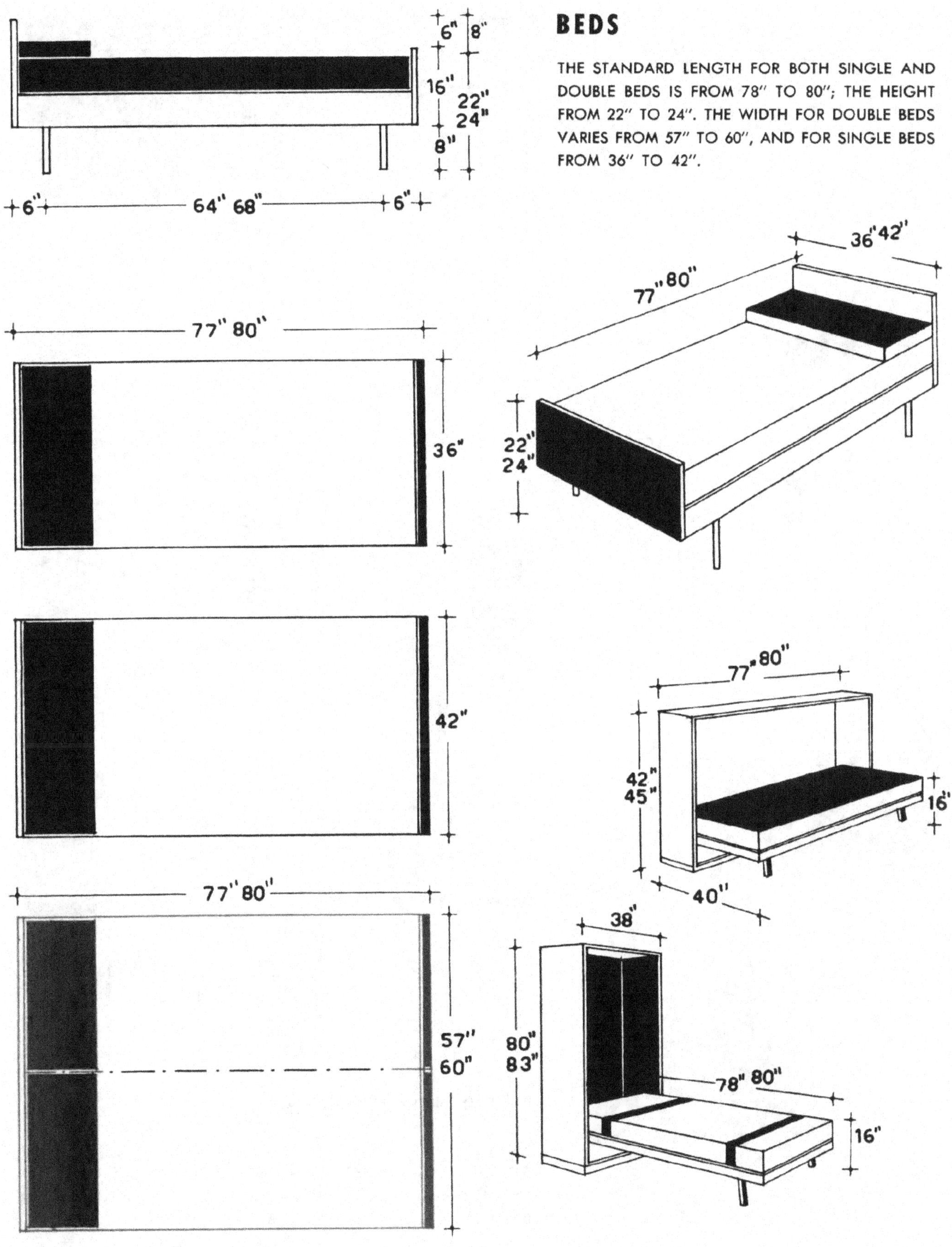

BEDS

THE STANDARD LENGTH FOR BOTH SINGLE AND DOUBLE BEDS IS FROM 78″ TO 80″; THE HEIGHT FROM 22″ TO 24″. THE WIDTH FOR DOUBLE BEDS VARIES FROM 57″ TO 60″, AND FOR SINGLE BEDS FROM 36″ TO 42″.

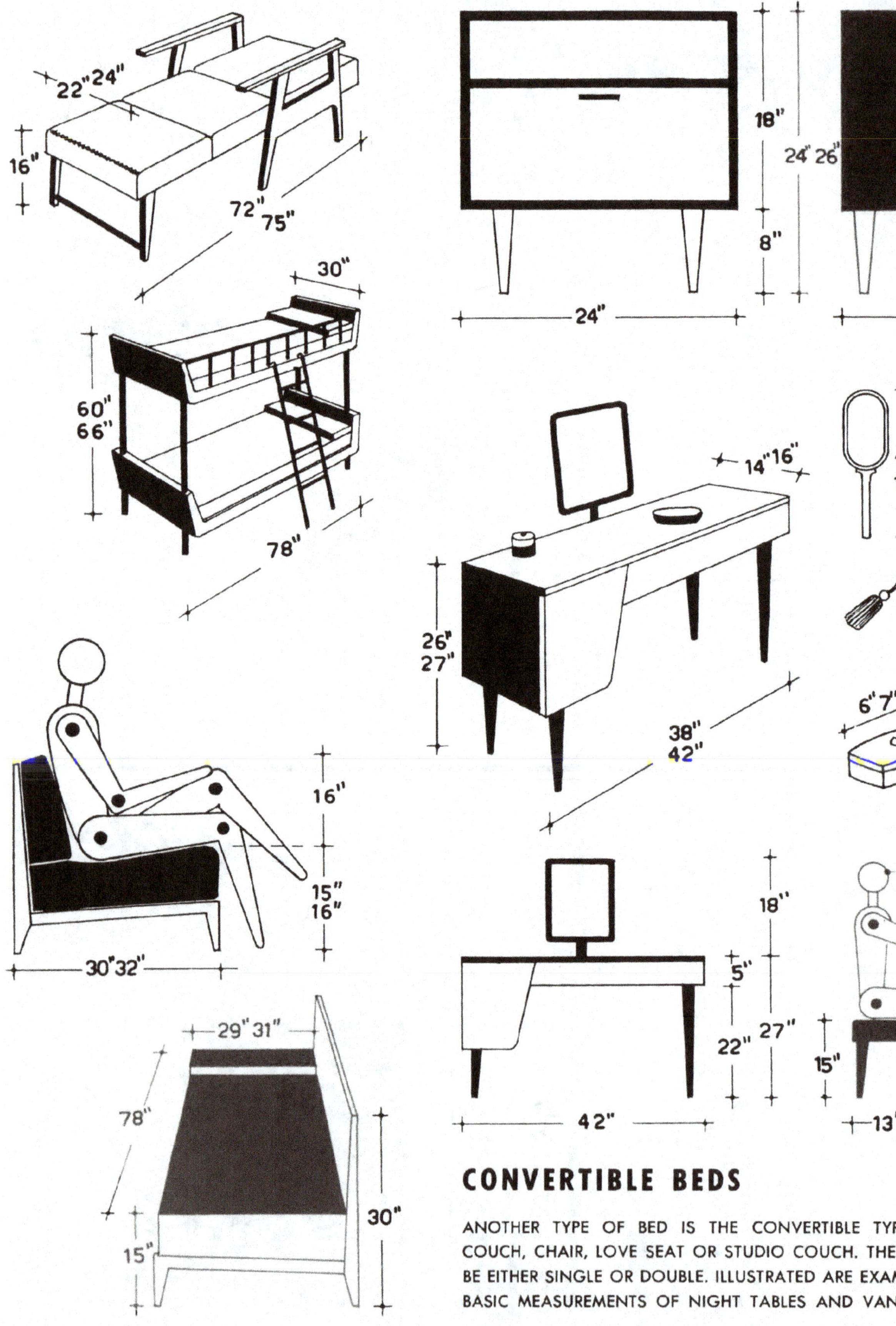

CONVERTIBLE BEDS

ANOTHER TYPE OF BED IS THE CONVERTIBLE TYPE, SUCH AS COUCH, CHAIR, LOVE SEAT OR STUDIO COUCH. THESE BEDS MAY BE EITHER SINGLE OR DOUBLE. ILLUSTRATED ARE EXAMPLES OF THE BASIC MEASUREMENTS OF NIGHT TABLES AND VANITIES.

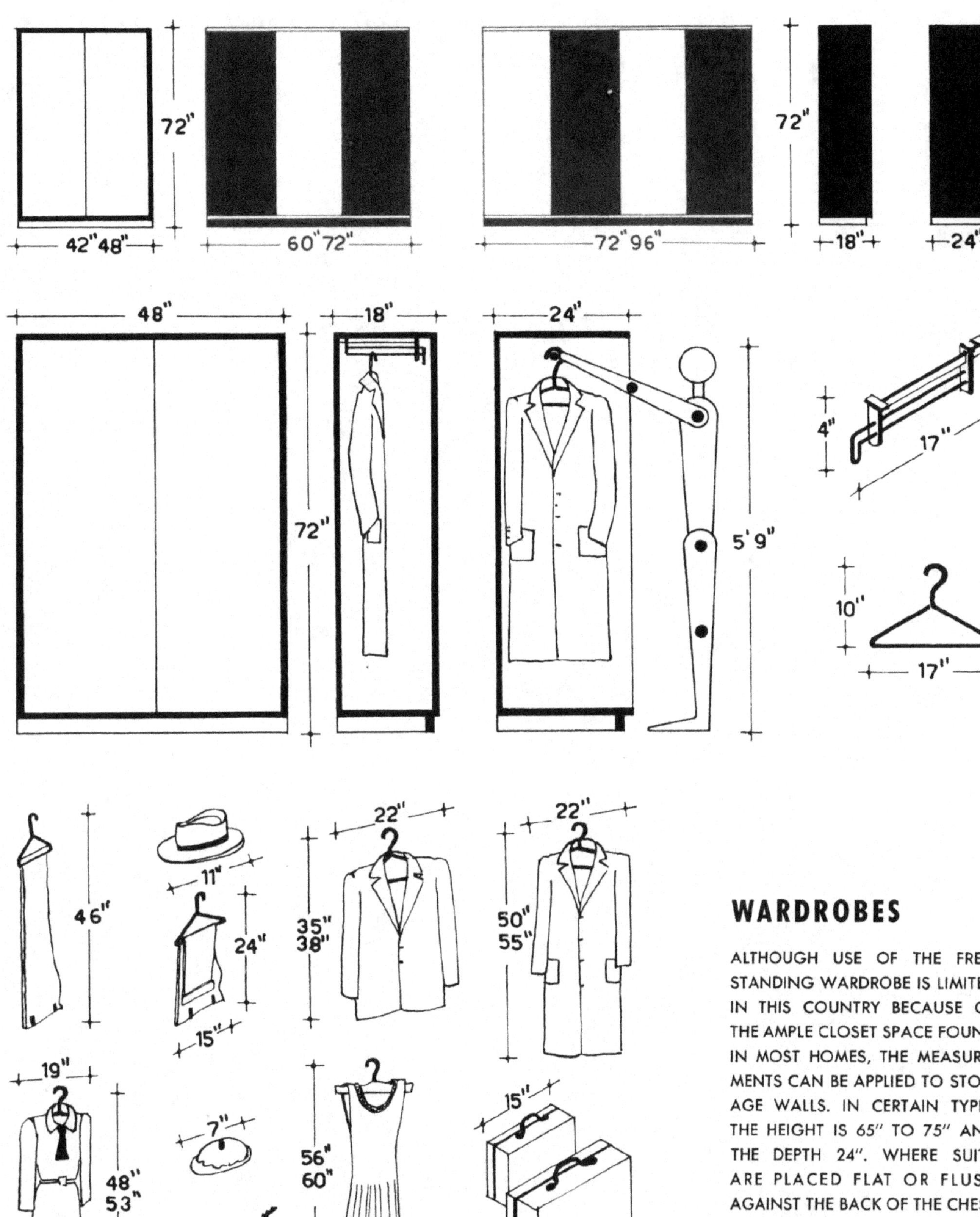

WARDROBES

ALTHOUGH USE OF THE FREE-STANDING WARDROBE IS LIMITED IN THIS COUNTRY BECAUSE OF THE AMPLE CLOSET SPACE FOUND IN MOST HOMES, THE MEASUREMENTS CAN BE APPLIED TO STORAGE WALLS. IN CERTAIN TYPES THE HEIGHT IS 65" TO 75" AND THE DEPTH 24". WHERE SUITS ARE PLACED FLAT OR FLUSH AGAINST THE BACK OF THE CHEST THE DEPTH IS 15" TO 18". THE WIDTH VARIES ACCORDING TO INDIVIDUAL NEEDS. THERE MAY BE TWO OR THREE DOORS.

FURNITURE YOU CAN BUILD

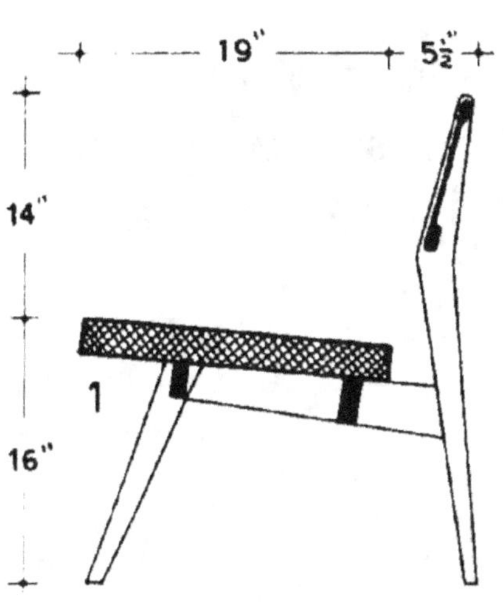

CONSTRUCTION PROCEDURES

IN THIS FINAL SECTION OF HOW TO BUILD MODERN FURNITURE WILL BE FOUND INSTRUCTIONS FOR BUILDING 60 DIFFERENT PIECES OF FURNITURE, AND THE OPPORTUNITY TO APPLY THE INFORMATION ON TOOLS, WOODWORKING METHODS, AND STANDARD MEASUREMENTS PRESENTED IN SECTIONS I, II AND III. PHOTOGRAPHS OF MANY OF THE PIECES IN MODEL ROOM ARRANGEMENTS WILL HELP THE CRAFTSMAN TO VISUALIZE THE WORK IN HIS OWN HOME.

AFTER YOU HAVE SELECTED THE PIECE OF FURNITURE YOU WANT TO BUILD, THE NEXT STEP IS TO ORDER THE LUMBER. ONE WAY IS TO COPY A LIST OF THE MATERIALS REQUIRED AND ASK ANY LUMBER DEALER TO CUT THE PIECES FOR YOU. ANOTHER WAY IS TO USE LUMBER CUT IN STANDARD SIZES.

IF THE MATERIAL IS PURCHASED IN THE SECOND WAY, IT IS ADVISABLE TO DRAW AN OUTLINE OF THE PIECES DIRECTLY ON THE WOOD. CUT OUT WITH A SAW, PLANE THE SAWED PIECES AND USE A FILE ON THE CURVED SURFACES. MARK AND EXECUTE THE JOINTS OF THE VARIOUS PIECES, CHECKING TO SEE THAT EVERYTHING FITS CORRECTLY. THIS DONE, PROCEED WITH THE ASSEMBLING AS SHOWN IN THE DRAWINGS, USING GLUE AND SCREWS. BE SURE TO FOLLOW THE DIRECTIONS INDICATED IN THE LEGEND. AFTER USING SANDPAPER, PAINT EDGE OF PLYWOOD TO MATCH THE REST OF THE WOOD.

FURTHER INFORMATION ON SPECIAL JOINTS, UPHOLSTERY, AND WORK WITH GLASS, METAL, AND PLASTIC WILL BE FOUND IN VOLUME I OF THIS SERIES, *PRACTICAL CONSTRUCTION METHODS.*

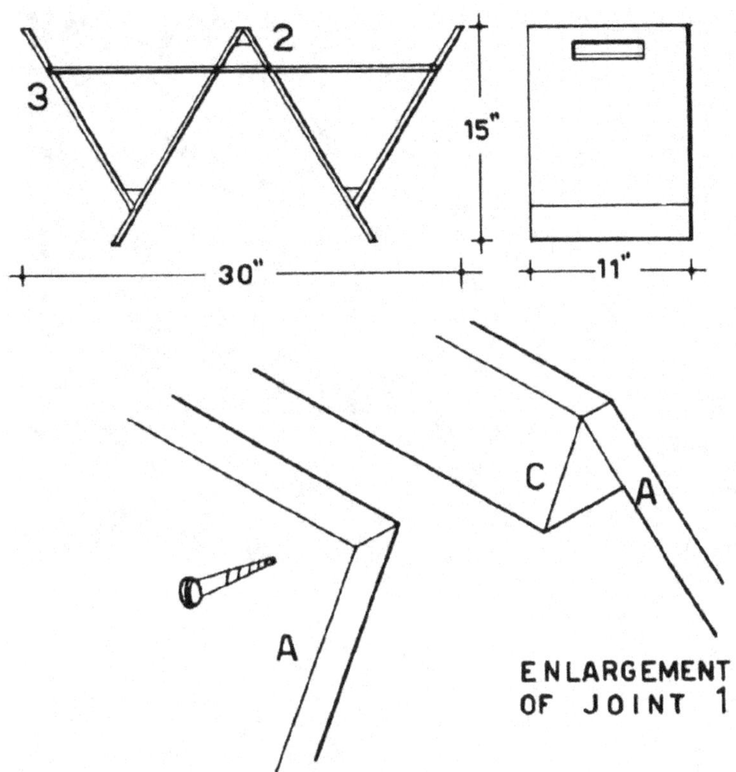

MAGAZINE RACK

A — 2 PIECES OF WOOD ¾" THICK AND 11" x 17". B — 2 PIECES ¾" THICK AND 11" x 14". C — 3 PIECES 1¼" THICK AND 11" x 1¼". D — 2 PIECES ⅜" THICK AND 27" x 1". SEE PAGE 54 FOR GENERAL INSTRUCTIONS. AFTER MATERIAL IS READY FOR ASSEMBLING JOIN AS FOLLOWS:

(1) "A" AND "B" WITH "C"; (2) "A" AND "A" WITH "C;" (3) "A, B" WITH "D."

SEE PAGE 14 FOR FINISH.

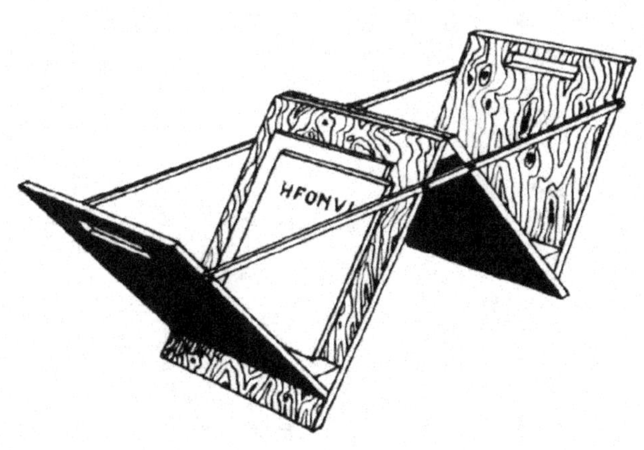

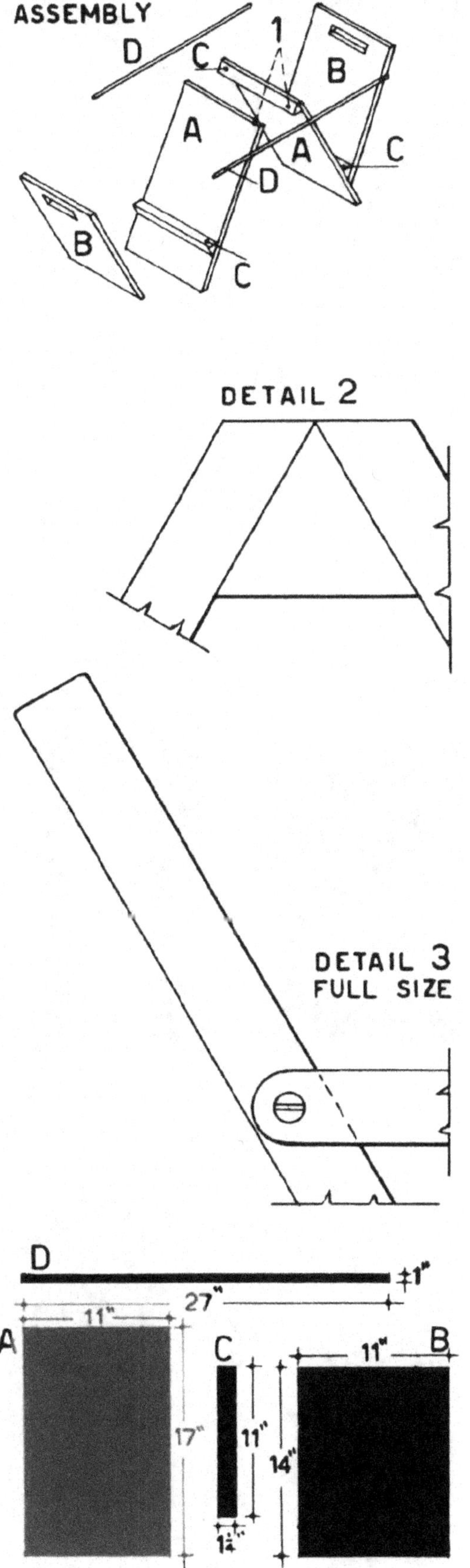

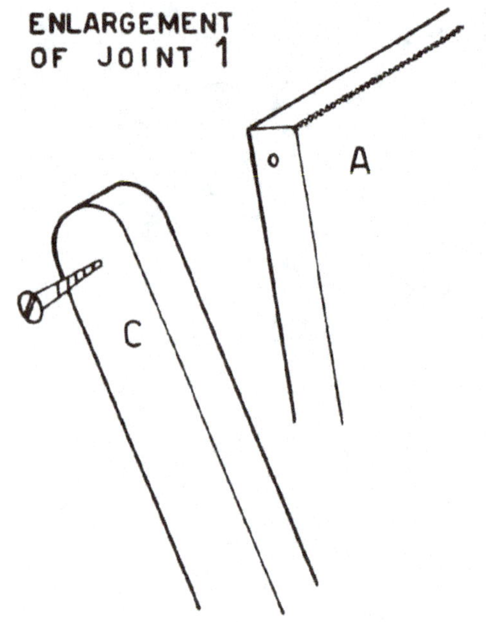

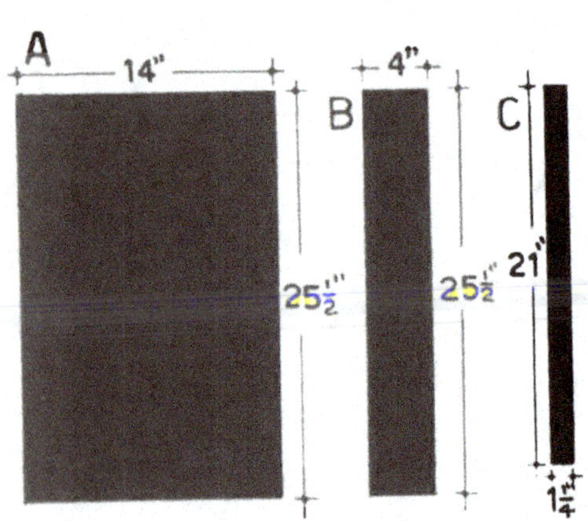

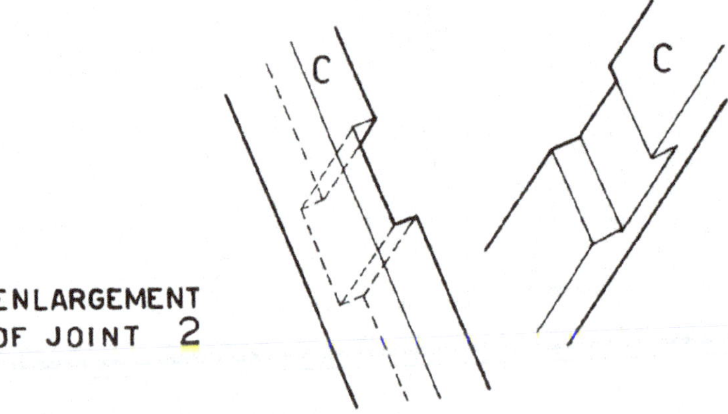

MAGAZINE RACK

A — 2 PIECES ¾" THICK AND 25½" x 14". B — 1 PIECE ¾" THICK AND 25½" x 4". C — 4 PIECES ¾" THICK AND 21" x 1¼". FOR GENERAL INSTRUCTIONS SEE PAGE 54. AFTER MATERIAL IS READY FOR ASSEMBLING PROCEED AS FOLLOWS:

JOIN (1) "A" WITH "B;" (2) "C" WITH "C"; (3) "A,B" WITH "C," AND YOU HAVE COMPLETED THE MAGAZINE RACK. FOR FINISH SEE PAGE 14.

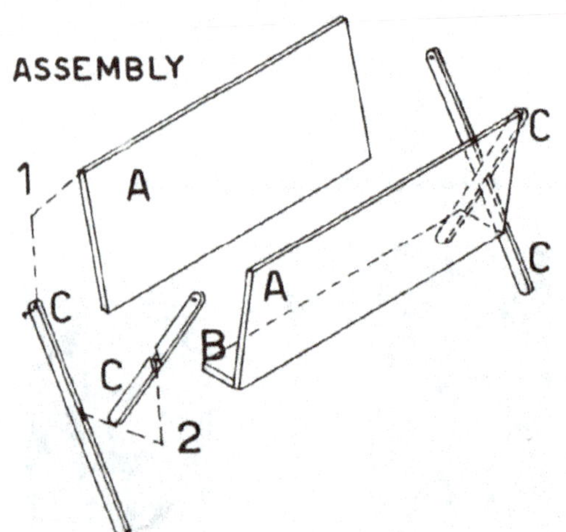

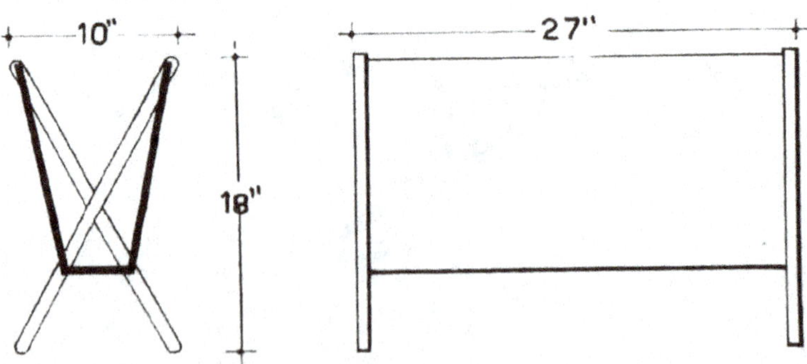

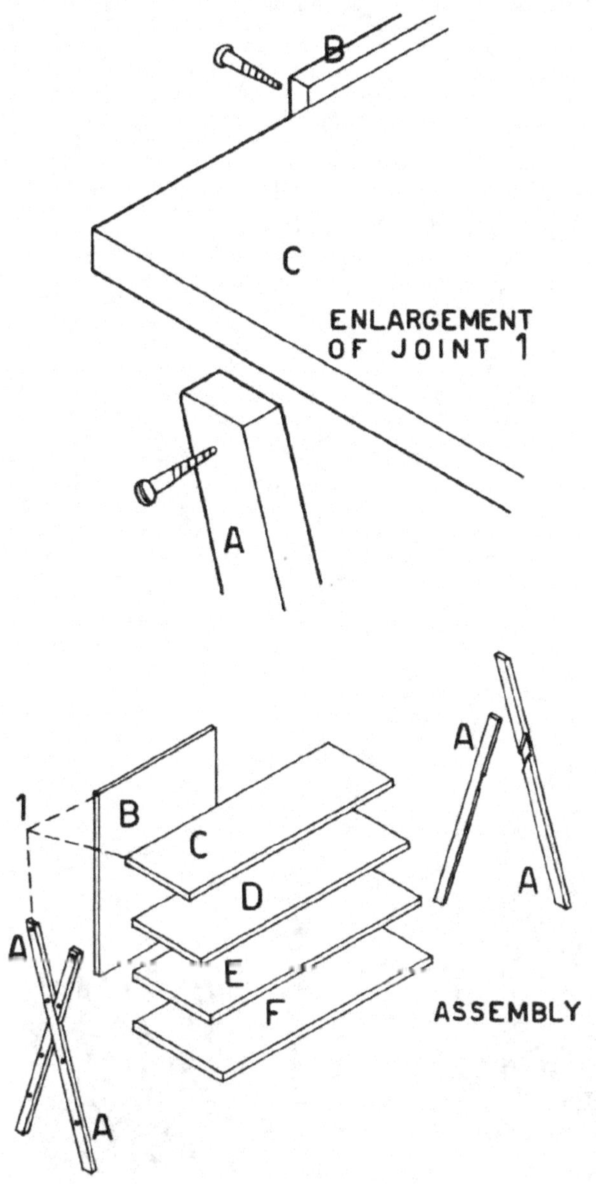

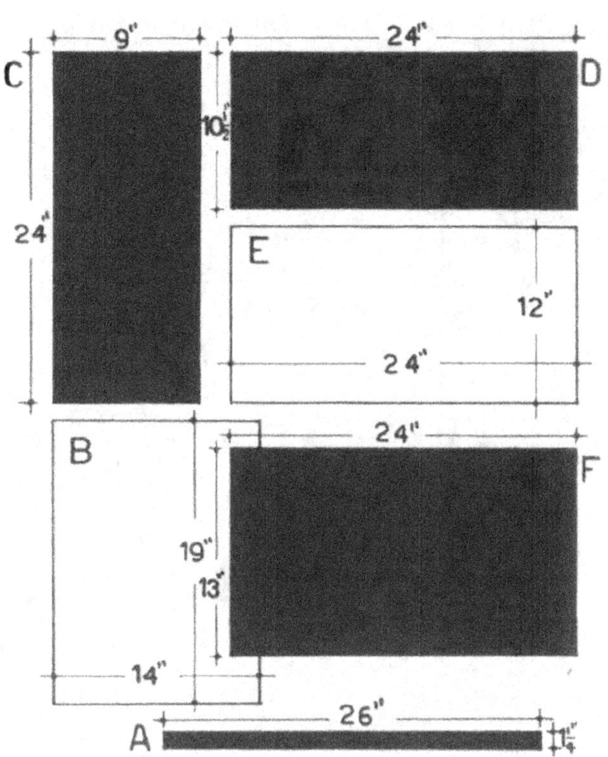

MAGAZINE STORAGE RACK

LIST OF MATERIALS.

A — 4 PIECES 1" THICK AND 26" x 1¼". B — 1 PIECE ½" THICK AND 14" x 19". C — 1 PIECE ¾" THICK AND 9" x 24". D — 1 PIECE ¾" THICK AND 10½" x 24". E — 1 PIECE ¾" THICK AND 12" x 24". F — 1 PIECE ¾" THICK AND 13" x 24". SEE PAGE 54 FOR GENERAL INSTRUCTIONS. AFTER MATERIAL IS READY FOR ASSEMBLING PROCEED AS FOLLOWS: JOIN (1) "A" WITH "A" (2) "A" WITH "C," "D," "E," "F" (3) "B" WITH "C," "D," "E," "F." SEE PAGE 14 FOR NATURAL FINISH.

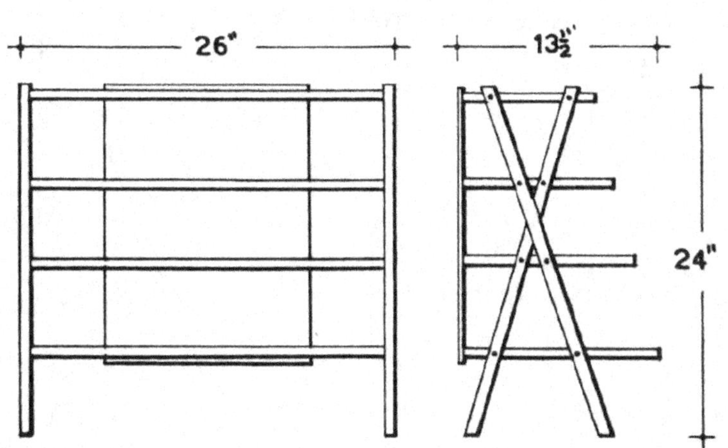

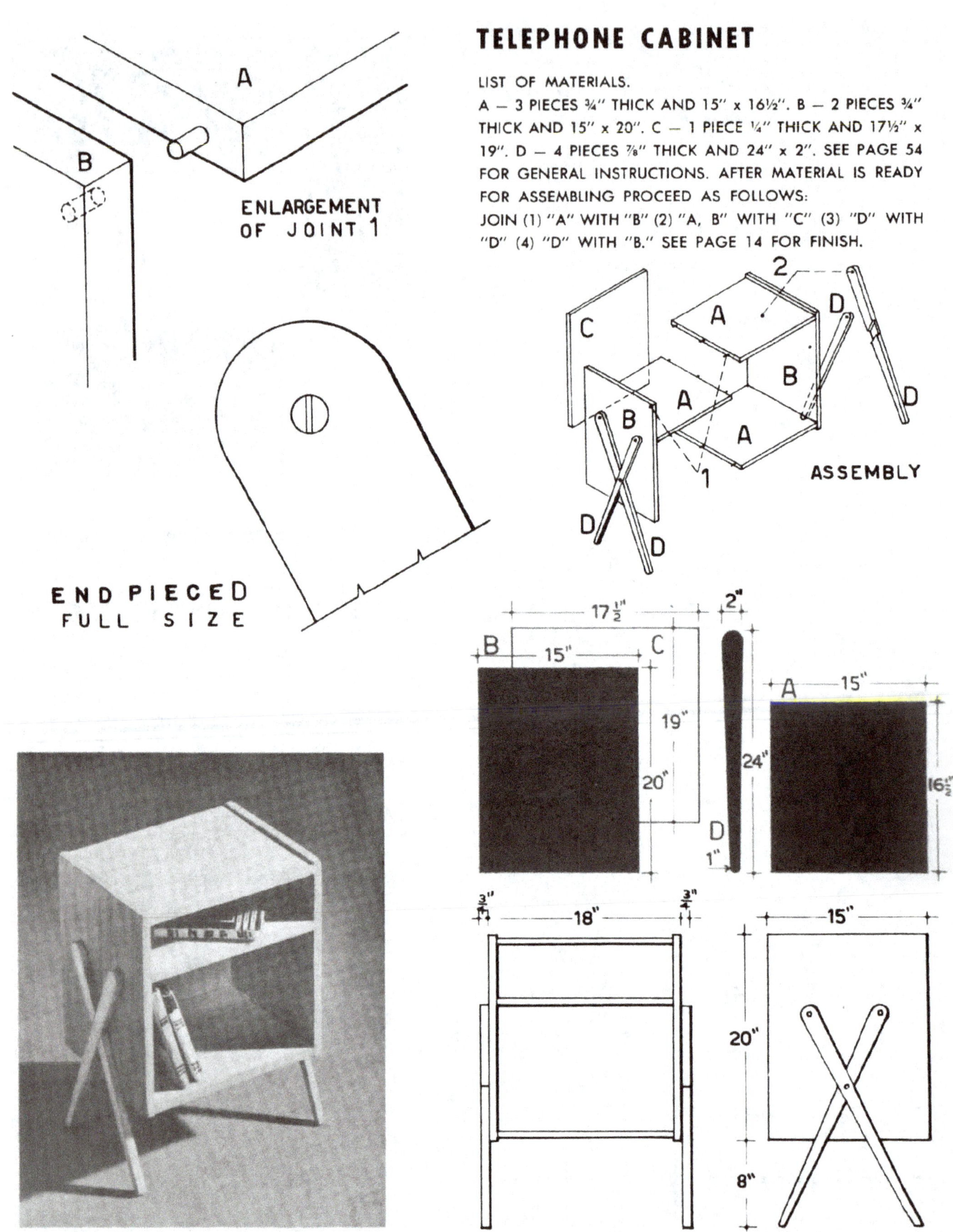

TELEPHONE CABINET

LIST OF MATERIALS.

A — 3 PIECES ¾" THICK AND 15" x 16½". B — 2 PIECES ¾" THICK AND 15" x 20". C — 1 PIECE ¼" THICK AND 17½" x 19". D — 4 PIECES ⅞" THICK AND 24" x 2". SEE PAGE 54 FOR GENERAL INSTRUCTIONS. AFTER MATERIAL IS READY FOR ASSEMBLING PROCEED AS FOLLOWS:

JOIN (1) "A" WITH "B" (2) "A, B" WITH "C" (3) "D" WITH "D" (4) "D" WITH "B." SEE PAGE 14 FOR FINISH.

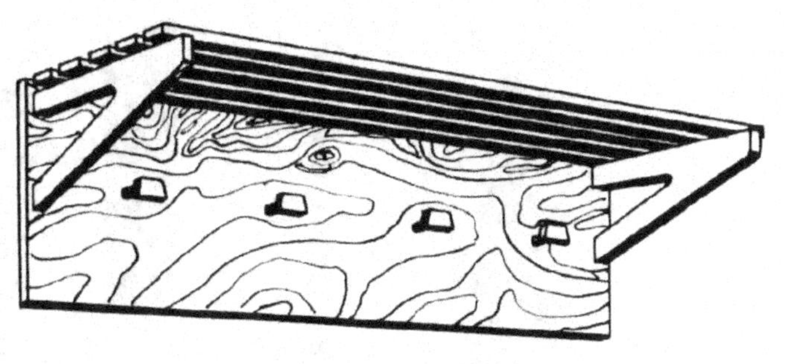

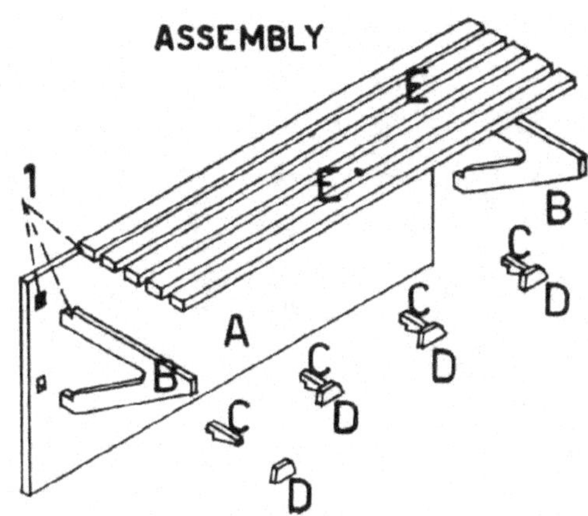

EXPOSED WARDROBE

LIST OF MATERIALS.

A — 1 PIECE ¾" THICK AND 15" x 40". B — 2 PIECES ¾" THICK AND 12¾" x 9". C — 4 PIECES ¾" THICK AND 3" x 1½". D — 4 PIECES ¾" THICK AND 2½" x 1¾". E — 5 PIECES ¾" THICK AND 40" x 1½". SEE PAGE 54 FOR GENERAL INSTRUCTIONS. AFTER MATERIAL IS READY FOR ASSEMBLING PROCEED AS FOLLOWS:
JOIN (1) "C" WITH "D" (2) "C" WITH "A" (3) "A" WITH "B" (4) "B" WITH "E." SEE PAGE 14 FOR NATURAL FINISH.

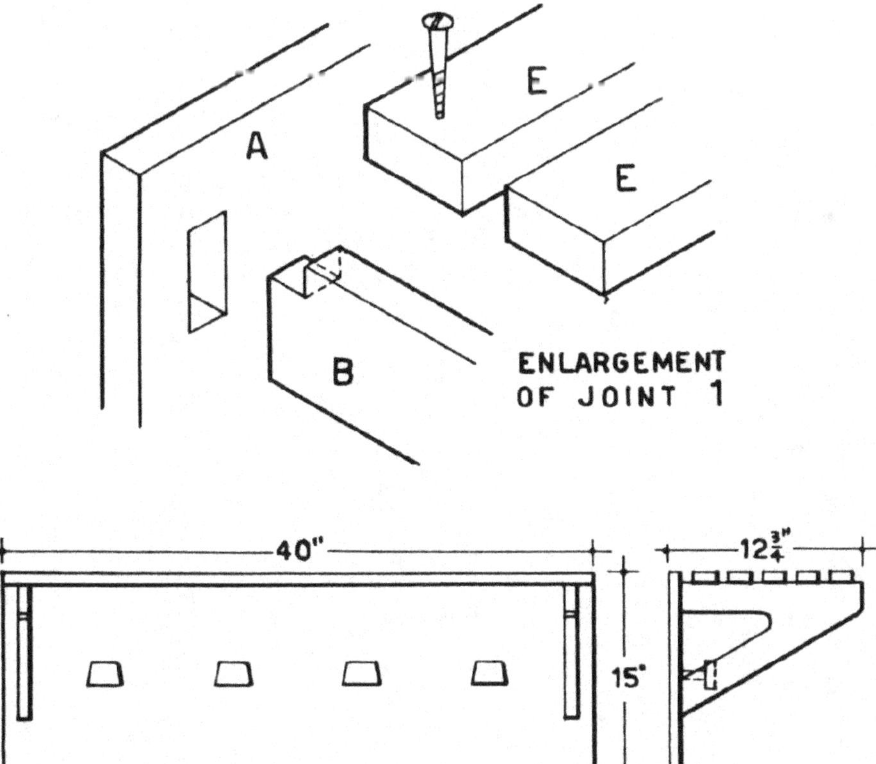

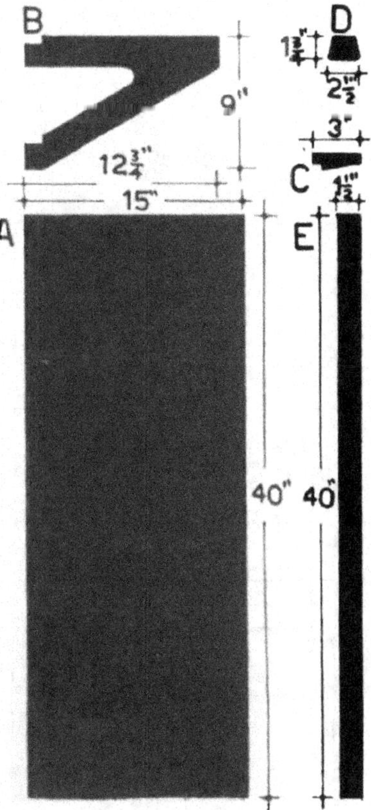

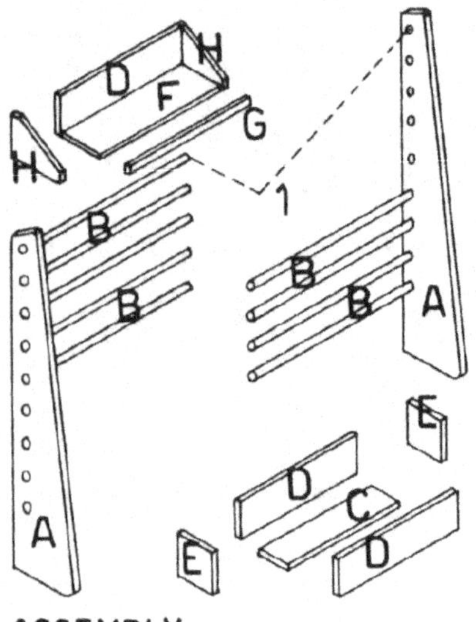

ASSEMBLY

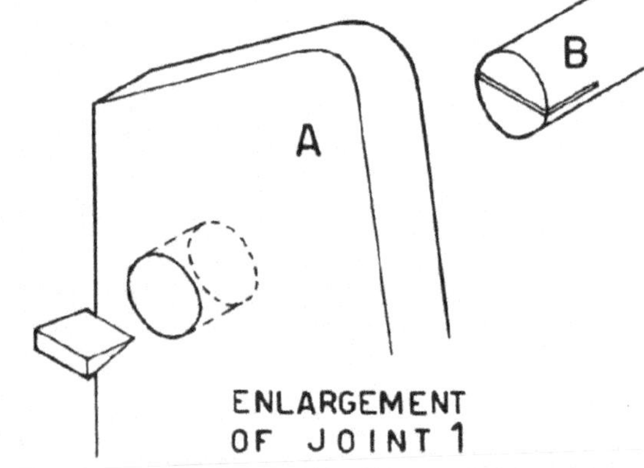

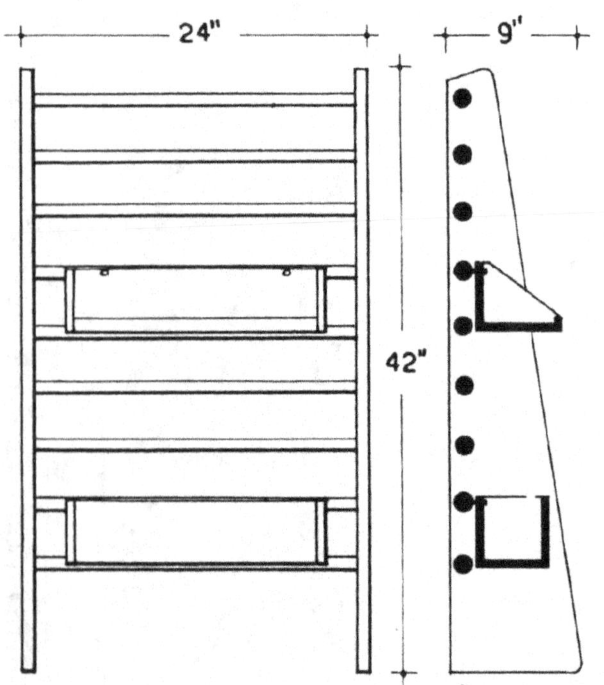

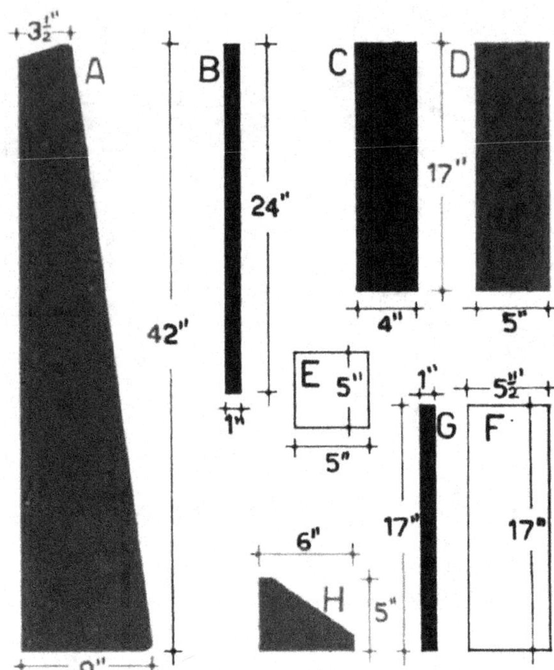

FLOWER STAND

LIST OF MATERIALS.

A — 2 PIECES 1" THICK AND 42" x 9". B — 9 PIECES 1" IN DIAMETER AND 24" LONG. C — 1 PIECE ½" THICK AND 17" x 4". D — 3 PIECES ½" THICK AND 17" x 5". E — 2 PIECES ½" THICK AND 5" x 5". F — 1 PIECE ½" THICK AND 17" x 5½". G — 1 PIECE ½" THICK AND 17" x 1". H — 2 PIECES ½" THICK AND 6" x 5". SEE PAGE 54 FOR GENERAL INSTRUCTIONS. AFTER MATERIAL IS READY FOR ASSEMBLING PROCEED AS FOLLOWS:

JOIN (1) "A" WITH "B" (2) "C" WITH "D" (3) "E" WITH "C, D" (4) "F" WITH "D" AND "G" (5) "H" WITH "D, F, G" (6) "D" WITH "B."

FINISH WITH EXTERIOR OR INTERIOR PAINT.

ASSEMBLY

ENLARGEMENT OF JOINT 1

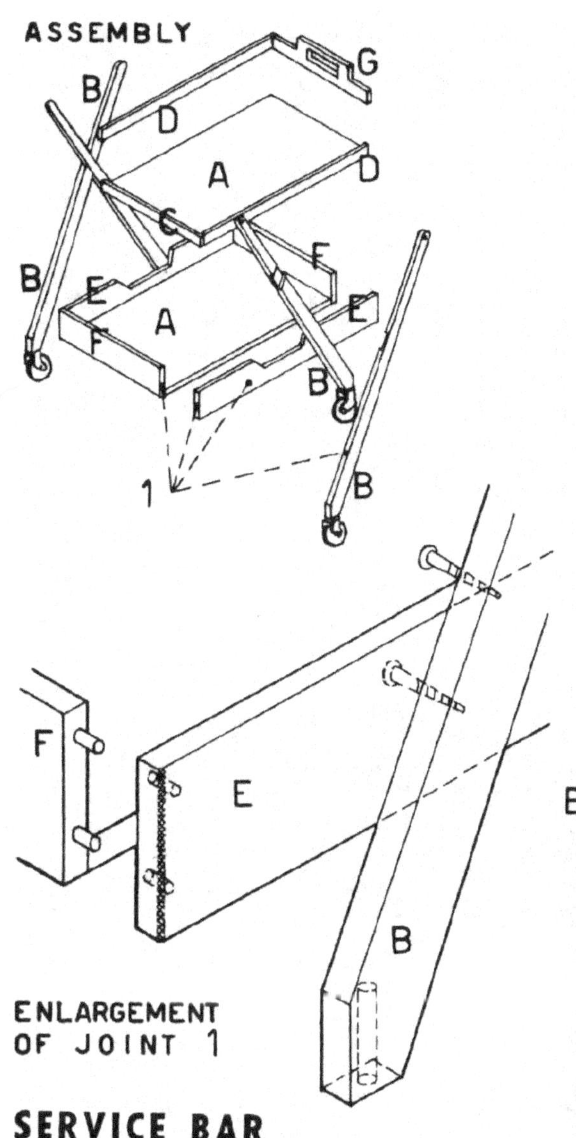

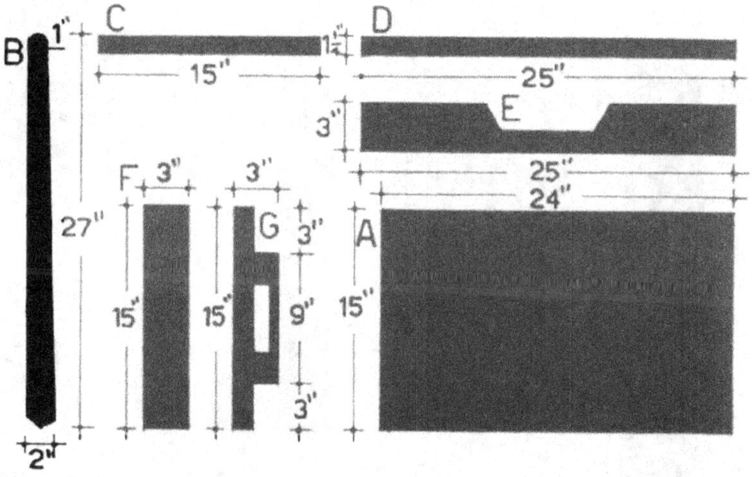

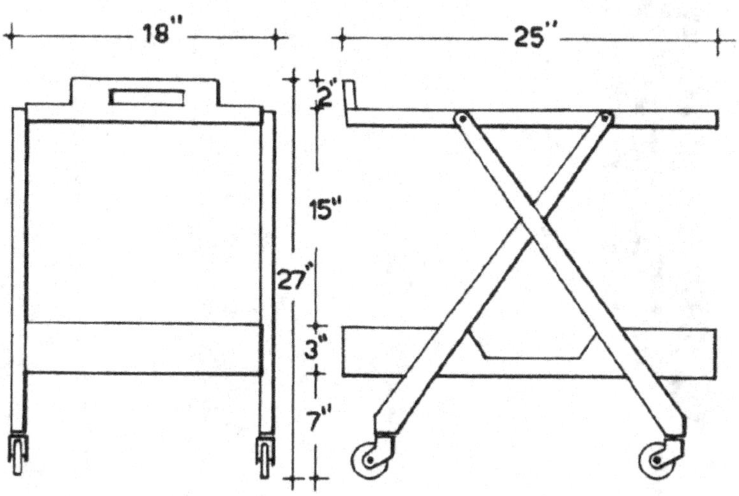

SERVICE BAR

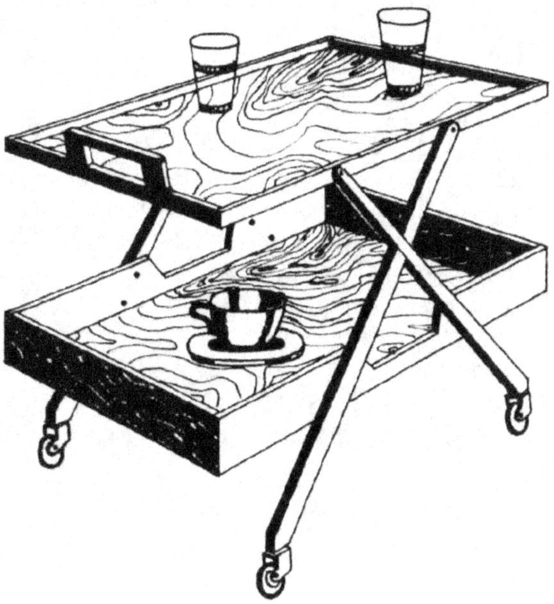

LIST OF MATERIALS.

A — 2 PIECES ½" THICK AND 15" x 24".
B — 4 PIECES ⅞" THICK AND 27" x 2".
C — I PIECE ½" THICK AND 15" x 1¼".
D — 2 PIECES ½" THICK AND 25" x 1¼".
E — 2 PIECES ½" THICK AND 25" x 3".
F AND G — 3 PIECES ½" THICK AND 15" x 3". ADD FOUR CASTERS. SEE PAGE 54 FOR GENERAL INSTRUCTIONS.

WHEN MATERIAL IS READY FOR ASSEMBLING PROCEED AS FOLLOWS:
JOIN (1) "A" WITH "C" AND "G" (2) "A" WITH "D" (3) "A" WITH "F" (4) "A" WITH "E" (5) "B" WITH "B" (6) "B" WITH "D" AND "E." APPLY CASTERS TO COMPLETE SERVICE BAR. FOR VARIOUS METHODS OF FINISHING SEE PAGE 14.

BOOKCASE WITH ADJUSTABLE SHELVES

LIST OF MATERIALS.

A — 2 PIECES 1" THICK AND 61" x 8". B — 4 PIECES ¾" THICK AND 35" x 11". C — 1 PIECE 1" THICK AND 34" x 4". D — 1 PIECE 1" THICK AND 34" x 3½" E — 2 PIECES 1" THICK AND 16" x 2¼".

SEE PAGE 54 FOR GENERAL INSTRUCTIONS.

AFTER MATERIAL IS READY FOR ASSEMBLING PROCEED AS FOLLOWS:

JOIN (1) "A" WITH "E" (2) "A" WITH "C" AND "D." APPLY THE REMOVABLE- SHELVES ("B") TO COMPLETE BOOKCASE. NATURAL FINISH IS ADVISABLE. SEE PAGE 14.

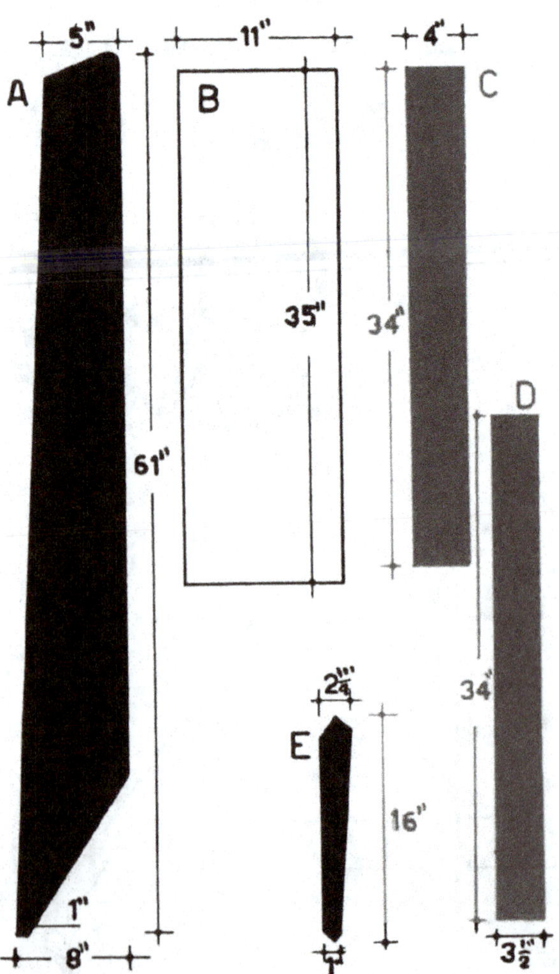

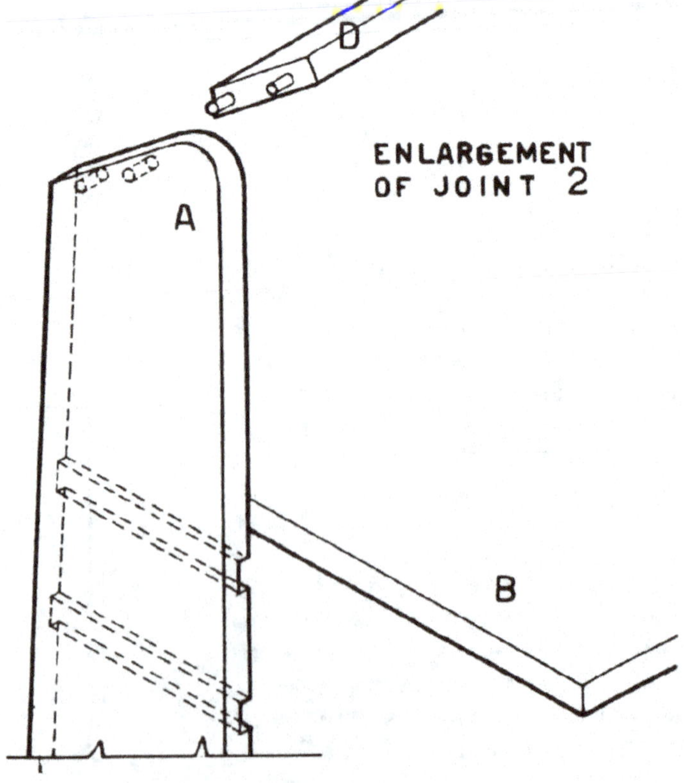

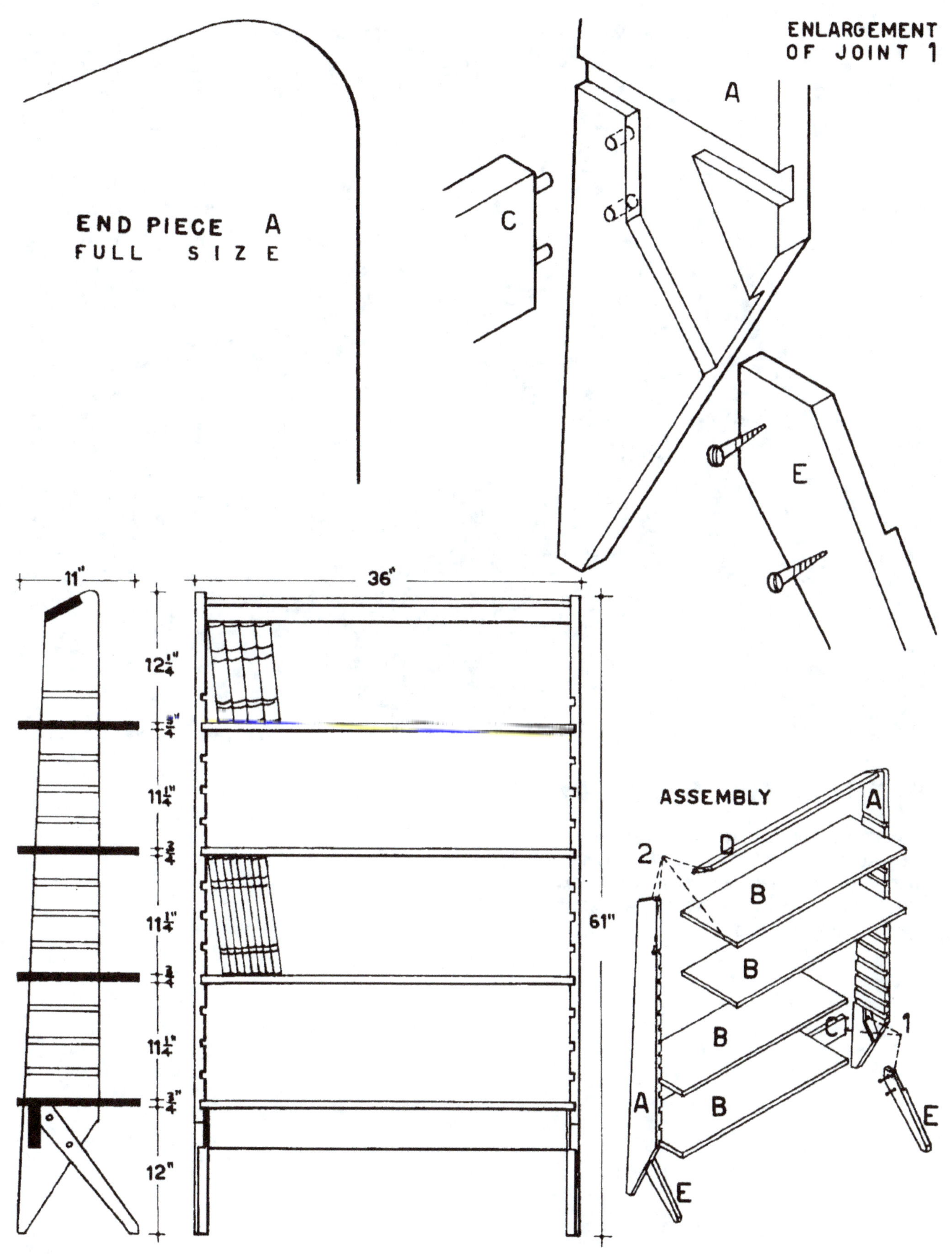

ENLARGEMENT
OF JOINT 1
A
C
E
END PIECE A
FULL SIZE
11"
36"
12 1/4"
3/4"
11 1/4"
3/4"
11 1/4"
3/4"
11 1/4"
3/4"
12"
61"
ASSEMBLY
A
D
2
B
B
B
C
1
B
A
E
E

FURNITURE FOR THE STUDY

INSTRUCTIONS FOR BUILDING THE PIECES SHOWN
HERE WILL BE FOUND ON THE FOLLOWING PAGES:
CHAIR, PAGE 101; ARMCHAIR, PAGE 104; BOOK-
SHELF, PAGE 62; TABLE, PAGE 92; MAGAZINE
STORAGE RACK, PAGE 58.

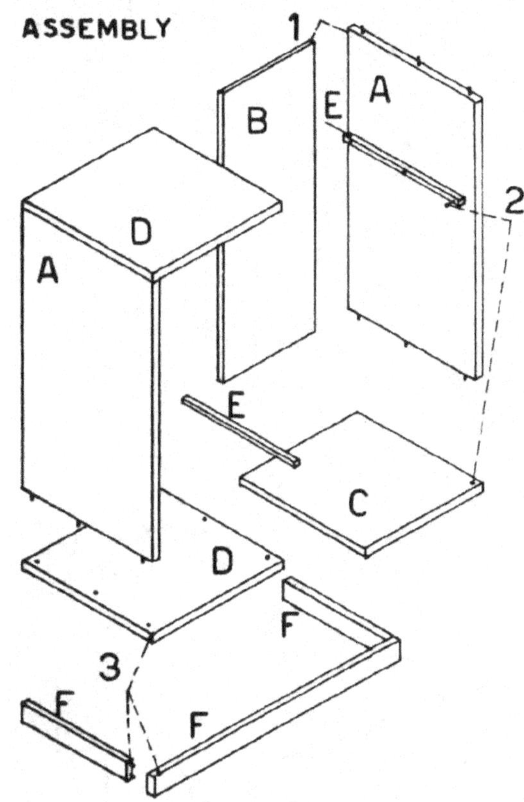

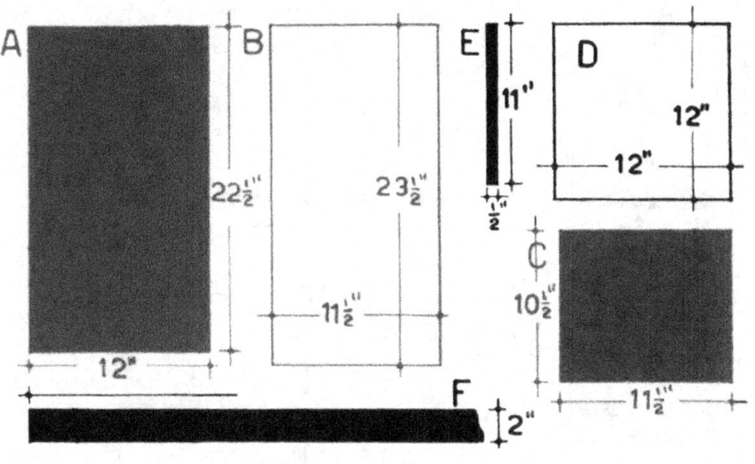

MODULAR BOOKCASE

LIST OF MATERIALS.

A — 2 PIECES ¾" THICK AND 22½" x 12". B — 1 PIECE ½" THICK AND 23" x 11½". C — 1 PIECE ¾" THICK AND 10½" x 11½". D — 2 PIECES ¾" THICK AND 12" x 12". E — 2 PIECES ½" THICK AND 11" x ½". F — 1 PIECE 1" THICK AND 2" IN HEIGHT. LENGTH DEPENDS ON THE NUMBER OF UNITS TO BE ALIGNED. 2 ADDITIONAL PIECES 10" LONG FOR SIDES. SEE PAGE 54 FOR GENERAL INSTRUCTIONS. WHEN MATERIAL IS READY FOR ASSEMBLING PROCEED AS FOLLOWS:

JOIN (1) "A" WITH "D" (2) "A,D" WITH "B" (3) "A" WITH "E" (4) "C" WITH "E" (5) "F" WITH "F" (6) "D" WITH "F." FOR FINISH SEE PAGE 14.

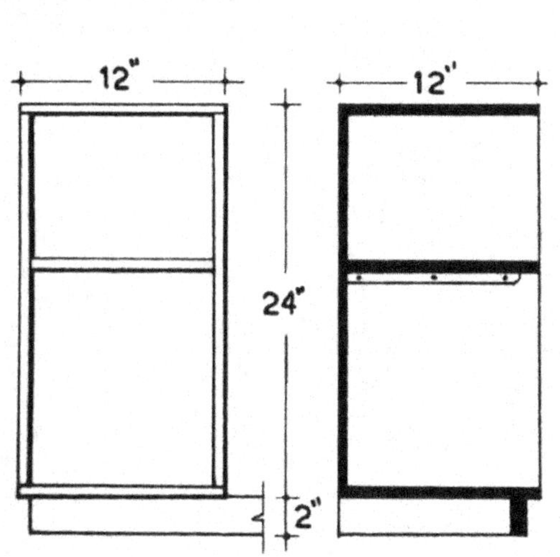

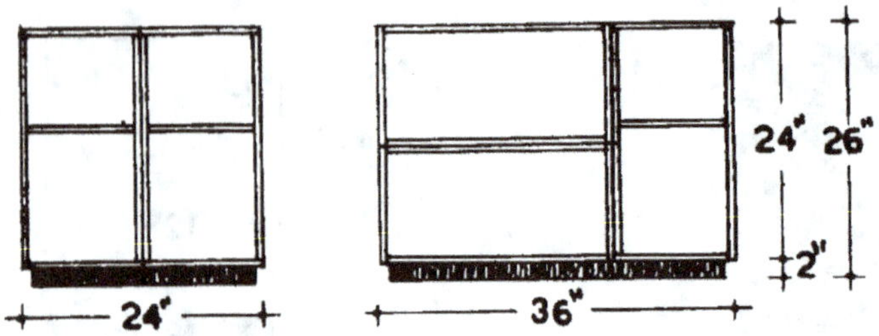

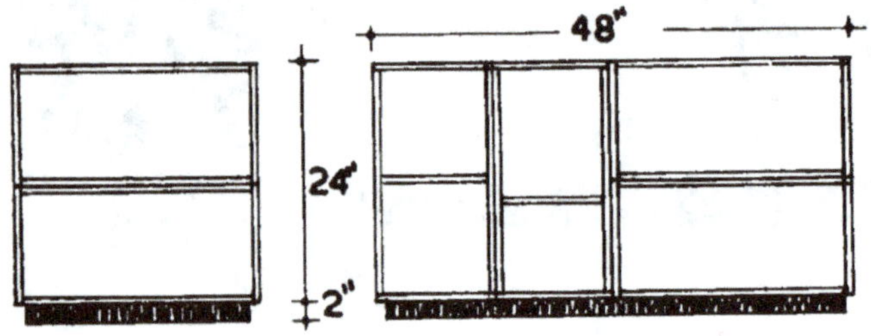

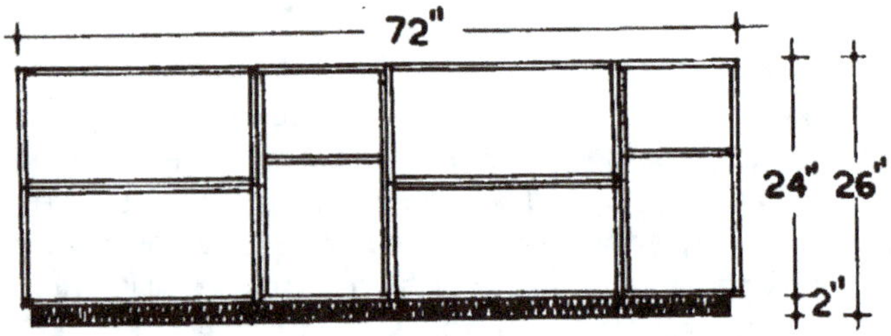

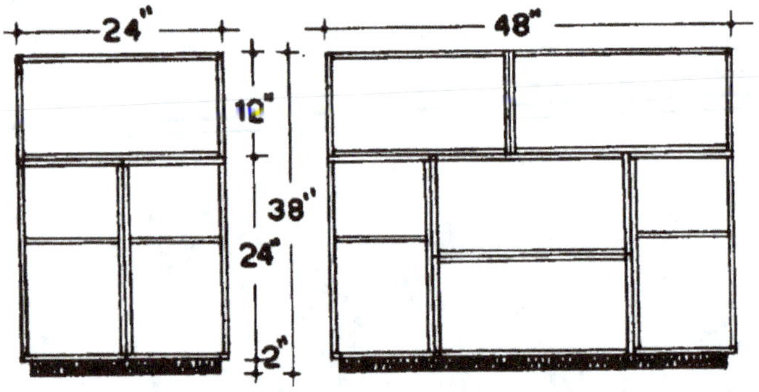

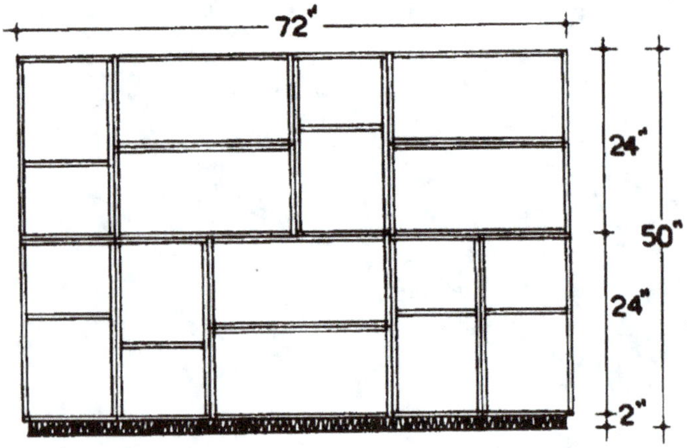

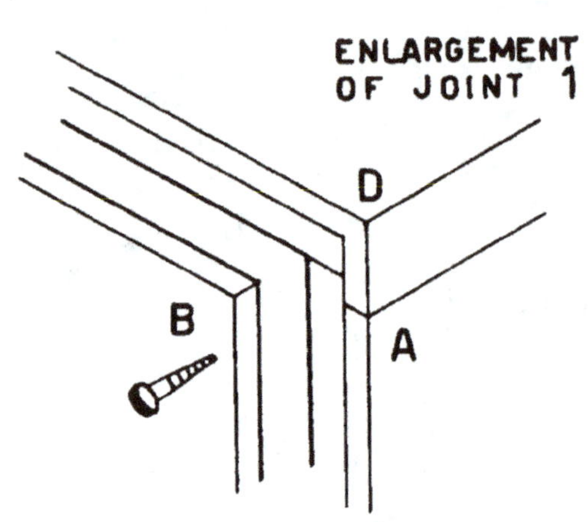

ENLARGEMENT
OF JOINT 1
D
B
A

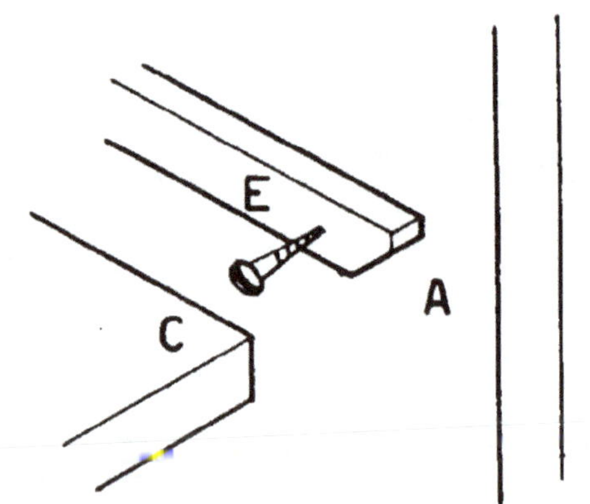

ENLARGEMENT
OF JOINT 2
E
A
C

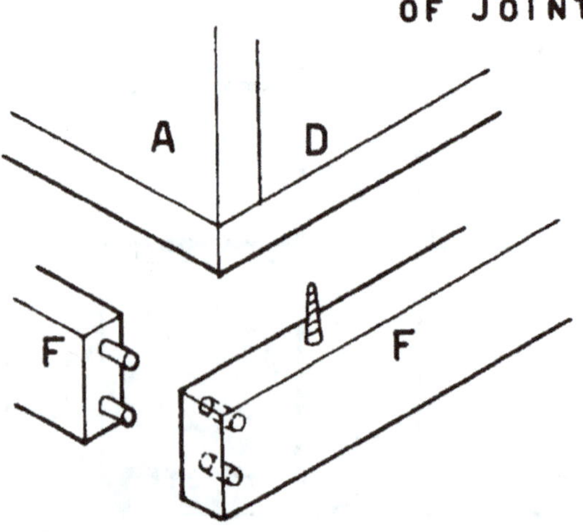

ENLARGEMENT
OF JOINT 3
A
D
F
F

BOOKCASE WITH DESK

LIST OF MATERIALS.

A — 3 PIECES ¾" THICK AND 36" x 12". A1 —
1 PIECE ¾" THICK AND 34½" x 12". B — 2 PIECES
¾" THICK AND 34½" x 11¾". C — 1 PIECE ½"
THICK AND 24" x 9". D — 2 PIECES ½" THICK
AND 5" x 9". E — 1 PIECE ¼" THICK AND 35½"
x 35½". F — 1 PIECE ¾" THICK AND 11¾" x 14".
G — 1 PIECE ¾" THICK AND 24" x 14". H — 4
PIECES OF STEEL PIPE 1" IN DIAMETER AND 7"
LONG. H1 — 4 PIECES ⅞" IN DIAMETER AND 5"
LONG. SEE GENERAL INSTRUCTION ON PAGE
54. AFTER MATERIAL IS READY FOR ASSEMBLING
PROCEED AS FOLLOWS:

JOIN (1) "B" WITH "F" (2) "A" WITH "A," "A1,"
"B" (3) "A,A1" WITH "E" (4) "C" WITH "D" (5)
"C,D" WITH "A,F" (6) "A1" WITH "H1" AND "H."
APPLY WITH HINGES THE DOOR "G" TO COM-
PLETE BOOKCASE. FOR FINISH SEE INSTRUC-
TIONS ON PAGE 14.

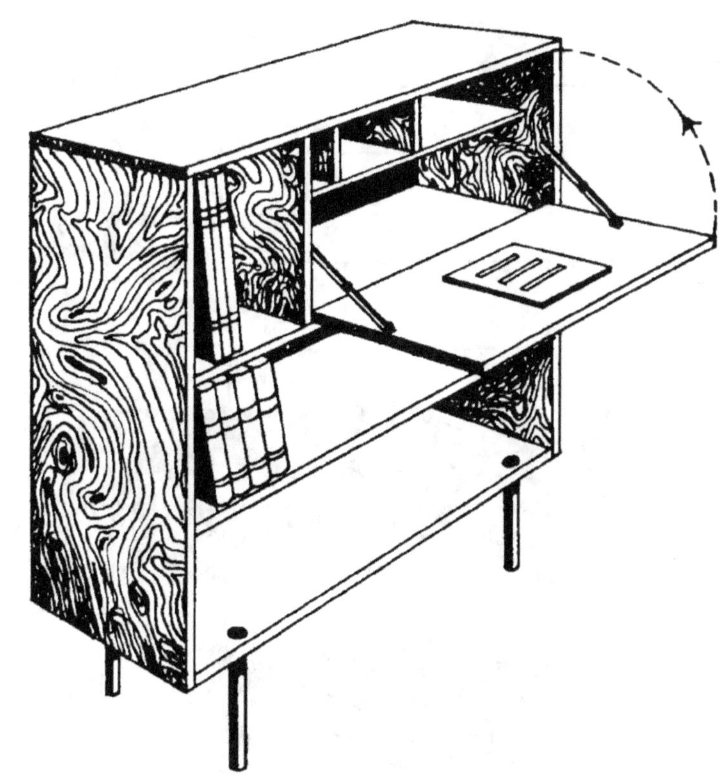

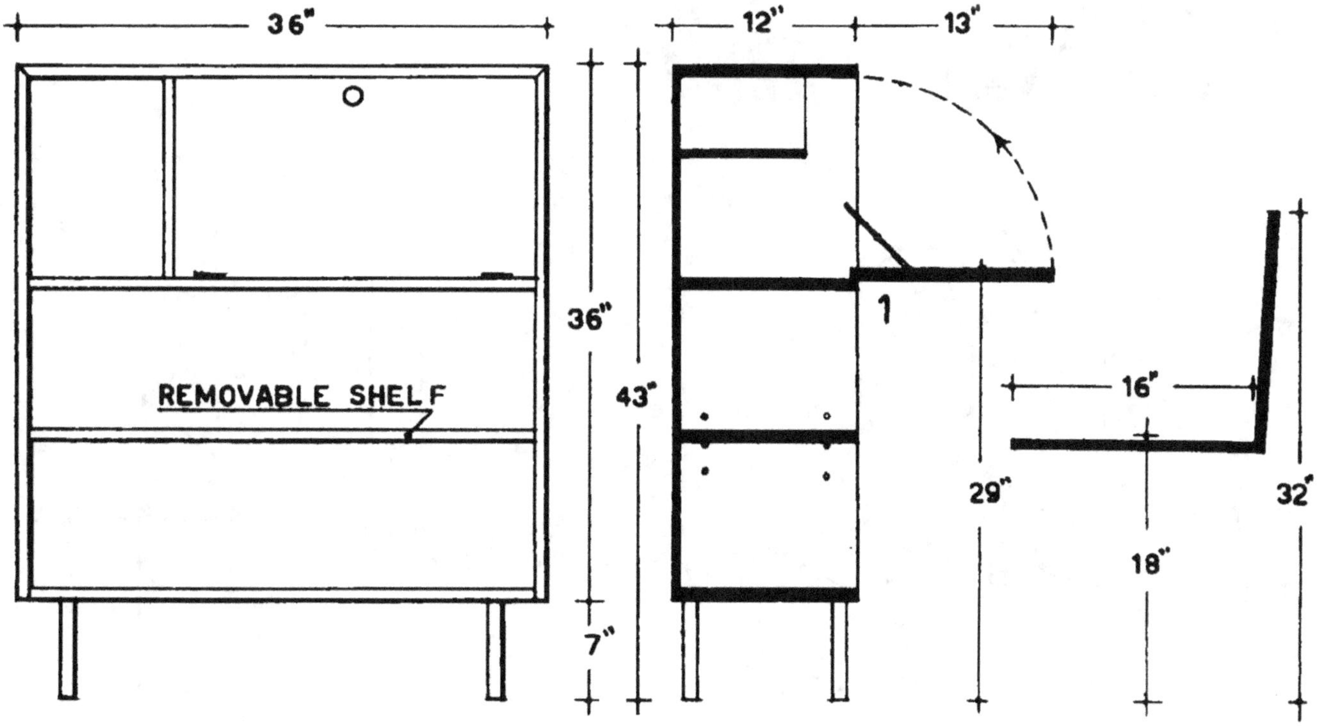

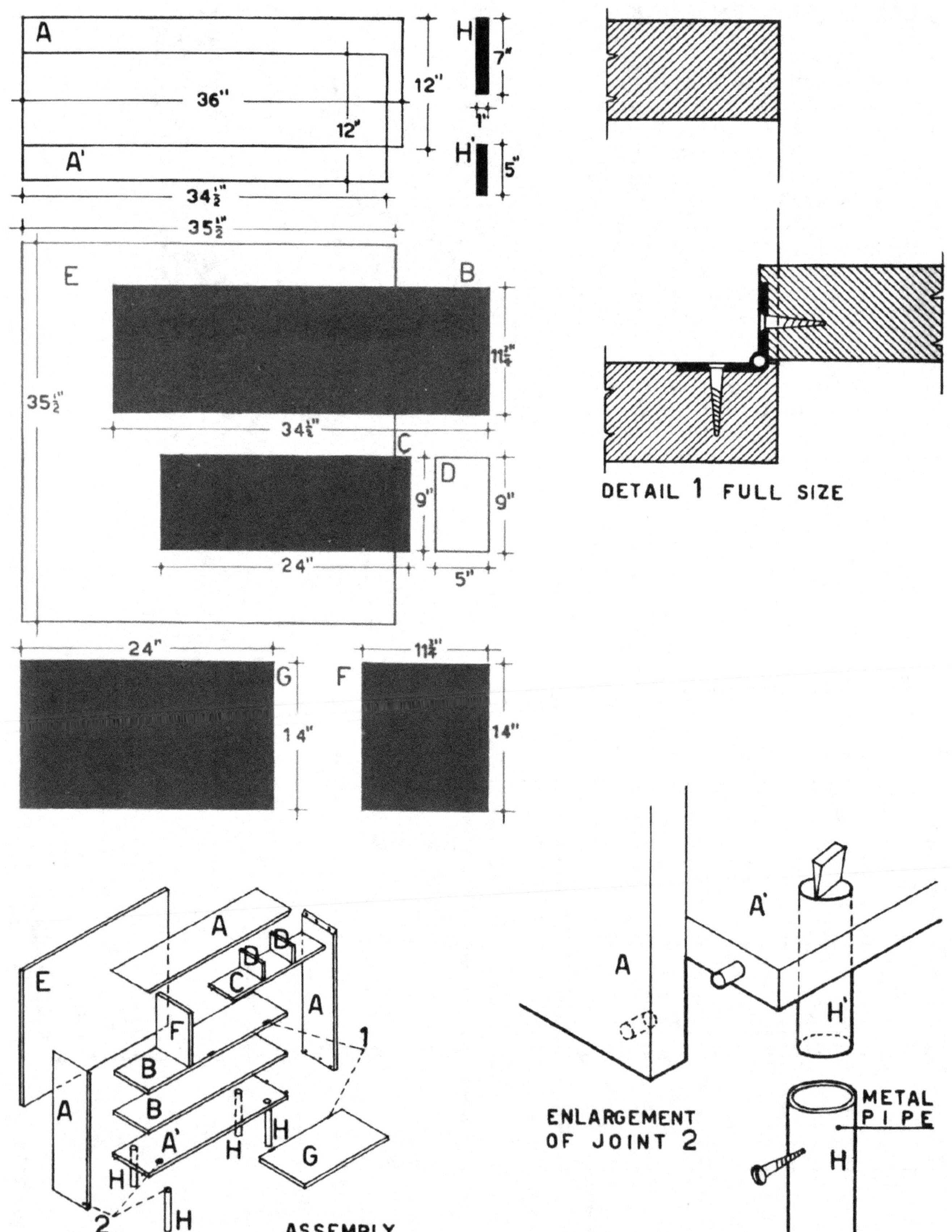

A
A'
36"
12"
12"
34½"
H
7"
1"
H'
5"
35½"
E
B
11¾"
34½"
35½"
C
D
9"
9"
24"
5"
24"
G
11¾"
F
14"
14"
DETAIL 1 FULL SIZE
E
A
D
C
F
A
B
B
A'
H
H
H
G
2
H
ASSEMBLY
A
A'
H'
ENLARGEMENT
OF JOINT 2
METAL
PIPE
H

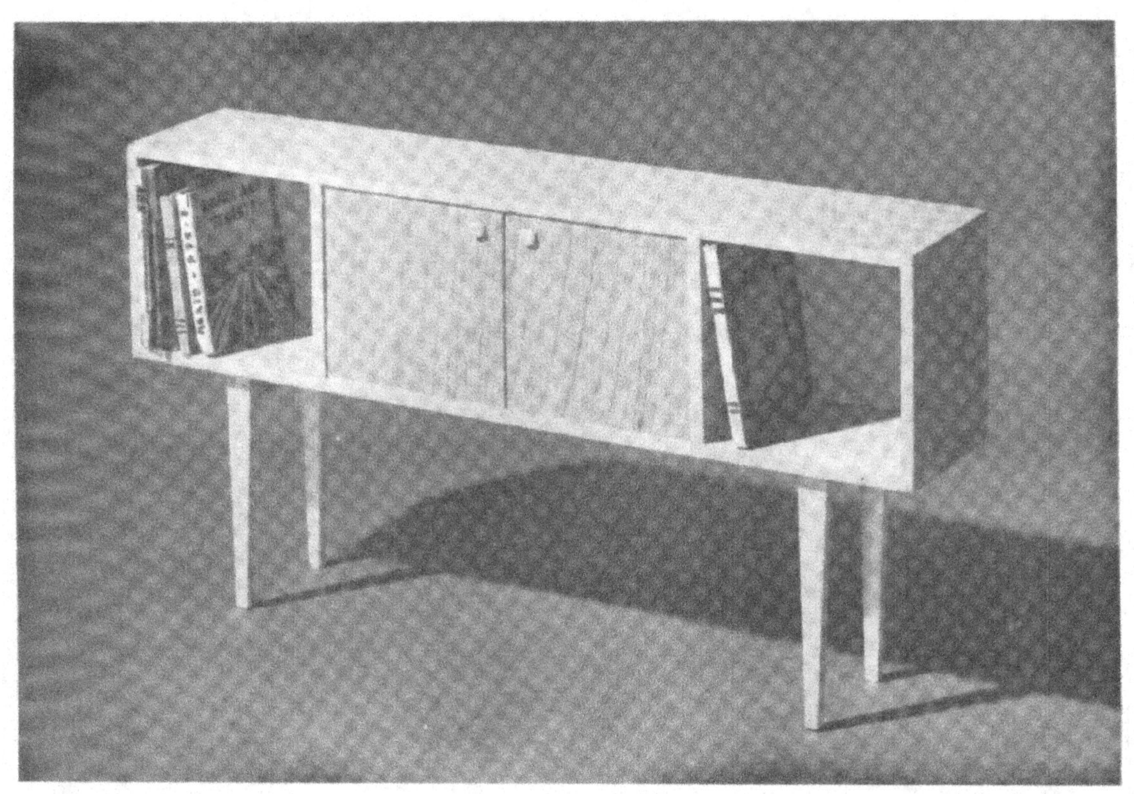

HANGING BOOKCASE

LIST OF MATERIALS.

A — 1 PIECE ¾" THICK AND 60" x 12". B — 1 PIECE ¾" THICK AND 58½" x 12". C — 2 PIECES ¾" THICK AND 12" x 14¼". D — 1 PIECE ¼" THICK AND 59½" x 14½". E — 2 PIECES ¾" THICK AND 13½" x 11¾". F — 1 PIECE 1" THICK AND 43½" x 2". G — 4 PIECES 1" THICK AND 17" x 2". H — 2 PIECES 1" THICK AND 8" x 2". VARIATION: L — 2 OR 4 PIECES ¾" THICK AND 13½" x 14¼". K (PAGE 70) — 1 PIECE ¾" THICK AND 28½" x 11¾". SEE GENERAL INSTRUCTIONS ON PAGE 54. AFTER MATERIAL IS READY FOR ASSEMBLING PROCEED AS FOLLOWS: JOIN (1) "A" AND "B" WITH "C" AND "E" (2) "A,B,-C" WITH "D" (3) "G" WITH "H" (4) "H" WITH "F" (5) "F,H" WITH "B." APPLY THE DOORS ("L") WITH HINGES AND SHELF ("K") TO COMPLETE YOUR BOOKCASE. FOR FINISH SEE PAGE 14.

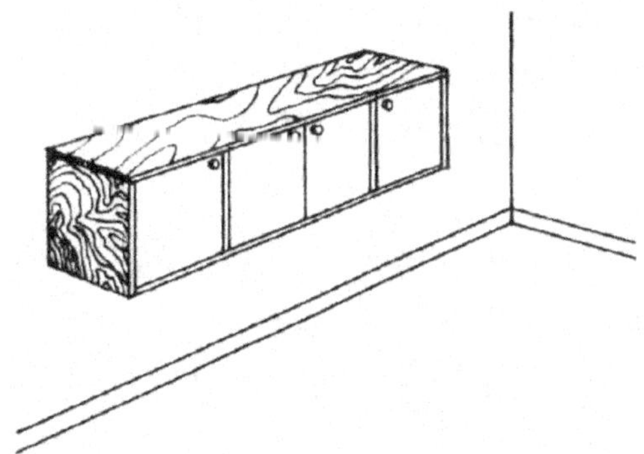

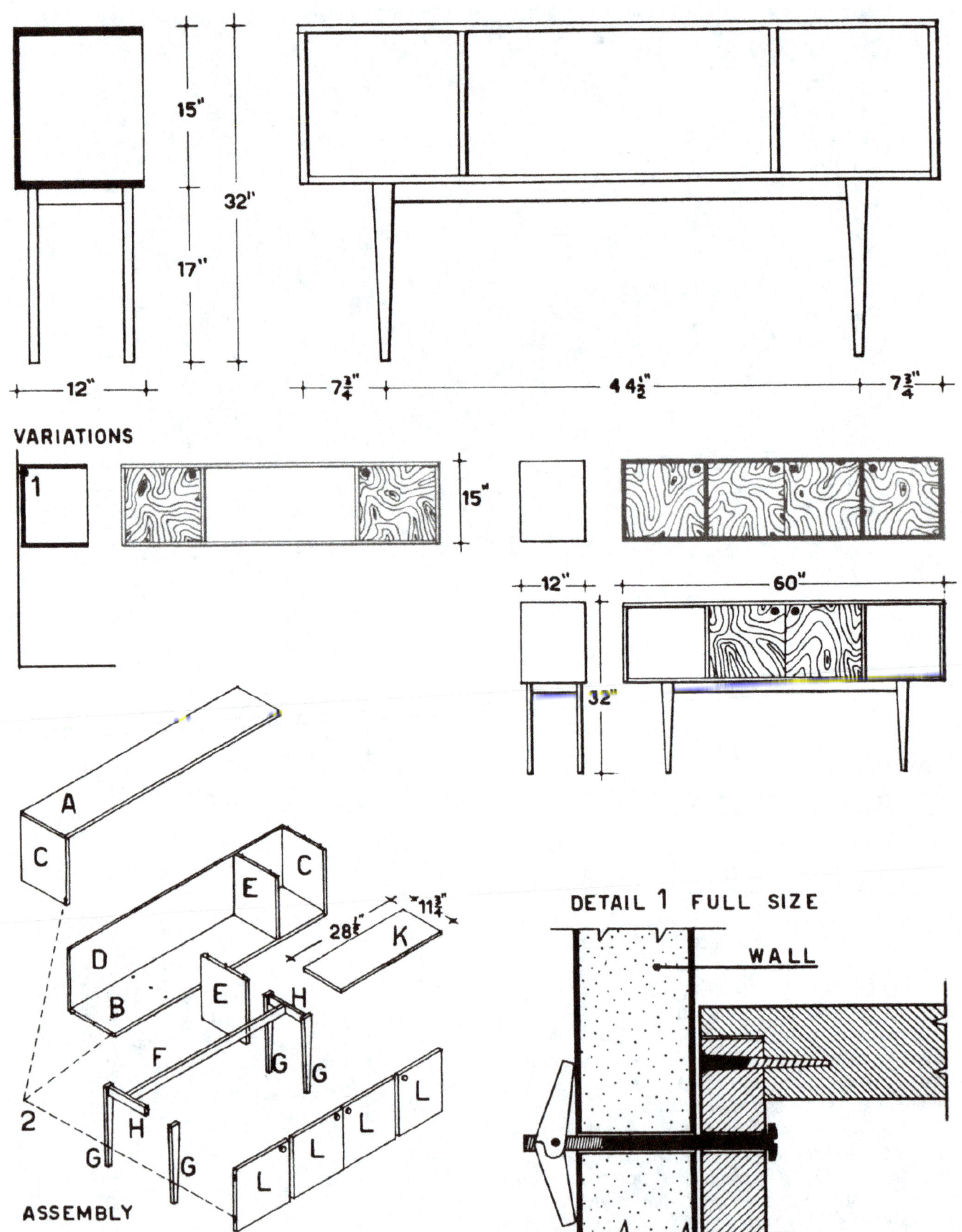

15"
32"
17"
12"
7 3/4"
4 4 1/2"
7 3/4"
VARIATIONS
1
15"
12"
60"
32"
A
C
C
E
D
B
E
K
11 3/4"
28"
H
G
G
F
G
H
G
2
H
L
L
L
L
L
ASSEMBLY
DETAIL 1 FULL SIZE
WALL

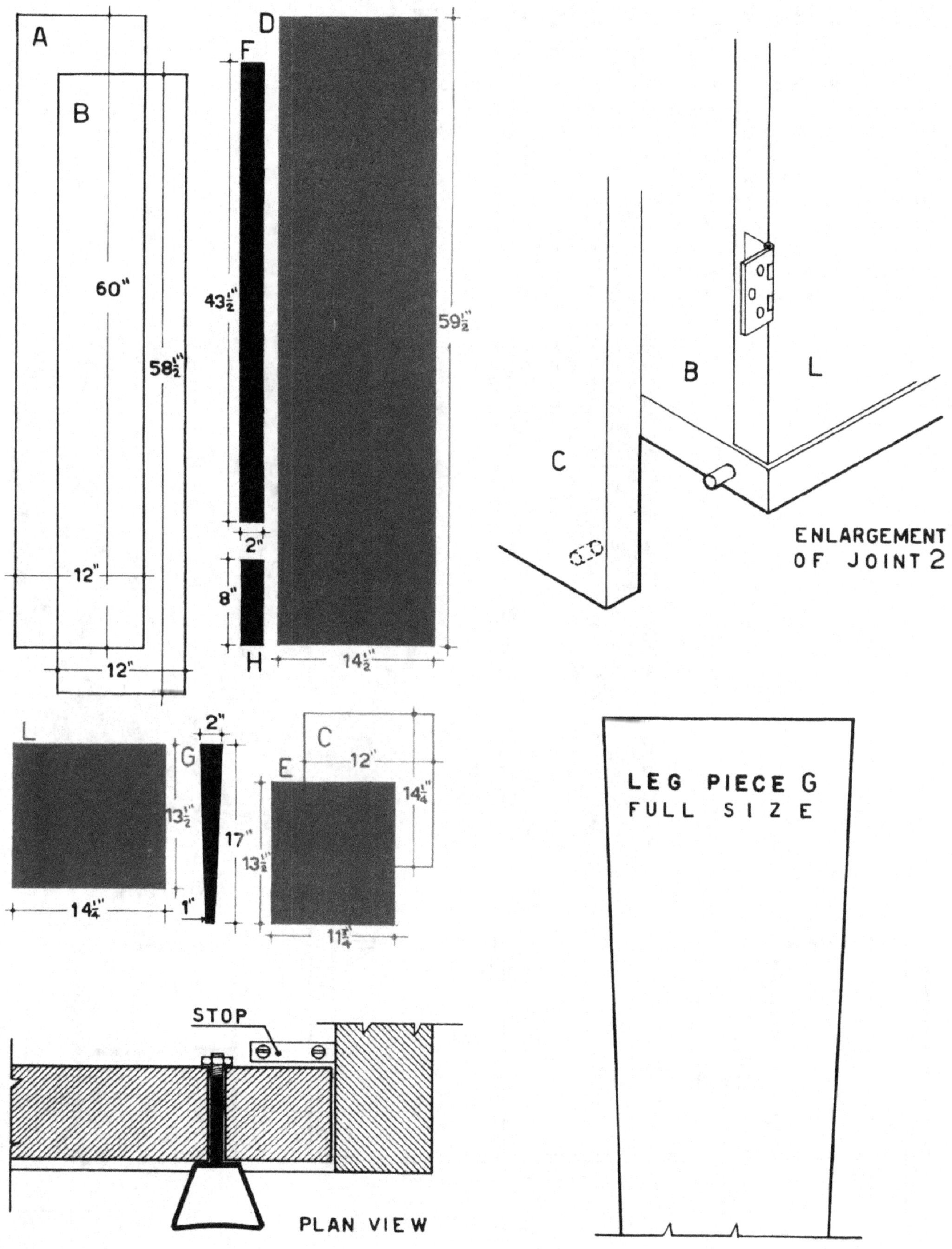

A
B
D
F
60"
43½"
58½"
59½"
12"
2"
8"
12"
H
14½"
L
G
2"
C
E
13½"
17"
13½"
14¼"
14¼"
1"
11¾"
12"
STOP
PLAN VIEW
ENLARGEMENT
OF JOINT 2
B
L
C
LEG PIECE G
FULL SIZE

SHOE CABINET OR SERVING CABINET

LIST OF MATERIALS.

A — 1 PIECE ¾" THICK AND 36" x 15". B — 1 PIECE ¾" THICK AND 34½" x 15".
C — 6 PIECES 1" DIAMETER AND 35½" LONG. D — 1 PIECE ½" THICK AND 35½" x
20½". E — 2 PIECES ¾" THICK AND 20¼" x 15". F — 2 PIECES ¾" THICK AND 19½"
x 17¼" G — 4 PIECES 1" THICK AND 7" x 2". H — 1 PIECE 1" THICK AND 25" x 2".
K — 2 PIECES 1" THICK AND 11" x 2". SEE GENERAL INSTRUCTIONS ON PAGE 54.
AFTER MATERIAL IS READY FOR ASSEMBLING PROCEED AS FOLLOWS:
JOIN (1) "A" AND "B" WITH "C" AND "E" (2) "A,E" WITH "D" (3) "G" WITH "K" (4)
"K" WITH "H" (5) "H,K" WITH "B." APPLY THE DOORS WITH HINGES TO COMPLETE
SHOE CABINET. FOR FINISH SEE PAGE 14.
VARIATION: SHELF MAY BE INSTALLED INSTEAD OF SHOE POLES.

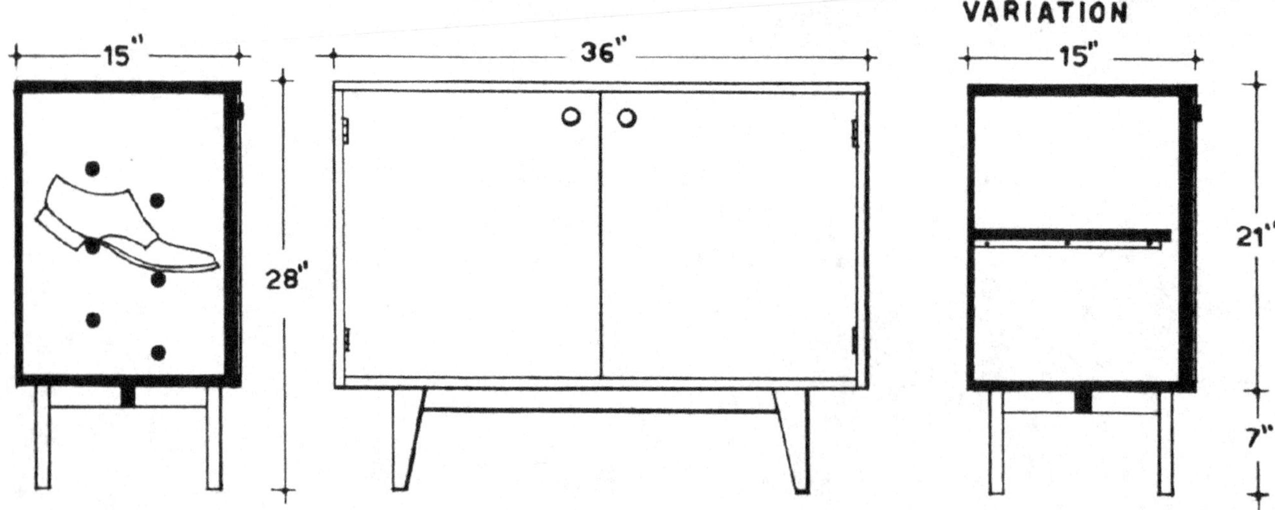

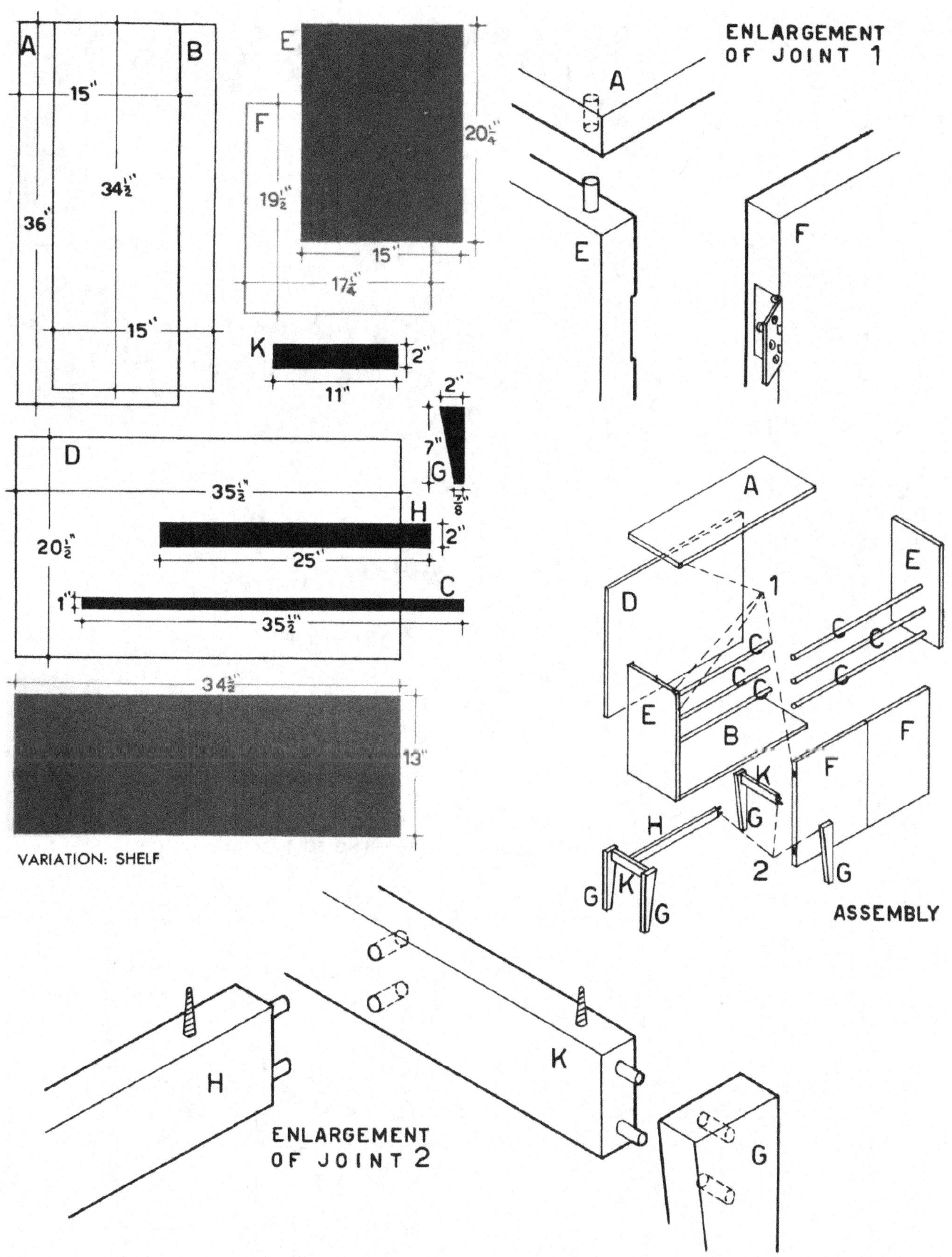

A
B
15"
34½"
36"
15"
15"
E
F
20¼"
19½"
15"
17¼"
K
2"
11"
2"
7"
G
H
⅛"
2"
D
35½"
20½"
25"
C
1"
35½"
34½"
13"
VARIATION: SHELF
ENLARGEMENT
OF JOINT 1
A
E
F
A
1
D
E
C
C
C
C
C
C
E
B
K
F
F
H
G
2
G
G
K
G
G
ASSEMBLY
H
K
G
ENLARGEMENT
OF JOINT 2

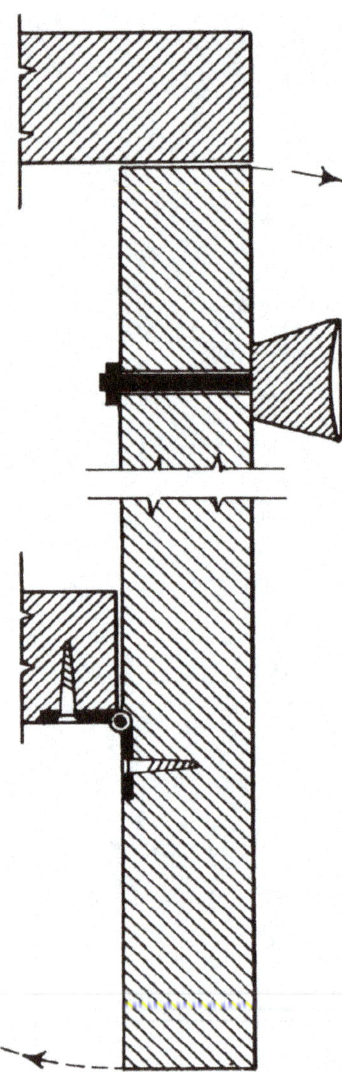

DETAIL 1
FULL SIZE

DROP-FRONT CABINET

LIST OF MATERIALS.

A — 1 PIECE ¾" THICK AND 54" x 15". B — 1 PIECE ¾" THICK AND 52½" x 14¼".
C — 2 PIECES ¾" THICK AND 15¼" x 14¼". D — 2 PIECES ¾" THICK AND 14½" x 14".
E — 1 PIECE ¼" THICK AND 53½" x 15½". F — 1 PIECE ¾" THICK AND 21¼" x 13".
G — 2 PIECES ¾" THICK AND 17¼" x 16". H — 1 PIECE ¾" THICK AND 22" x 17¼".
K — 4 PIECES 1¼" THICK AND 16" x 2½". L — 2 PIECES 1¼" THICK AND 11" x 2½".
M — 1 PIECE 1¼" THICK AND 38" x 2½". FOR GENERAL INSTRUCTION SEE PAGE 54.
AFTER MATERIAL IS READY FOR ASSEMBLING PROCEED AS FOLLOWS:
JOIN (1) "A" AND "B" WITH "C" AND "D" (2) "A,B,C,D" WITH "E" (3) "F" WITH "D"
(4) "L" WITH "K" (5) "M" WITH "L" (6) "M,L" WITH "B." APPLY DOORS ("G" AND "H")
TO COMPLETE CABINET. FOR FINISHING SEE PAGE 14.

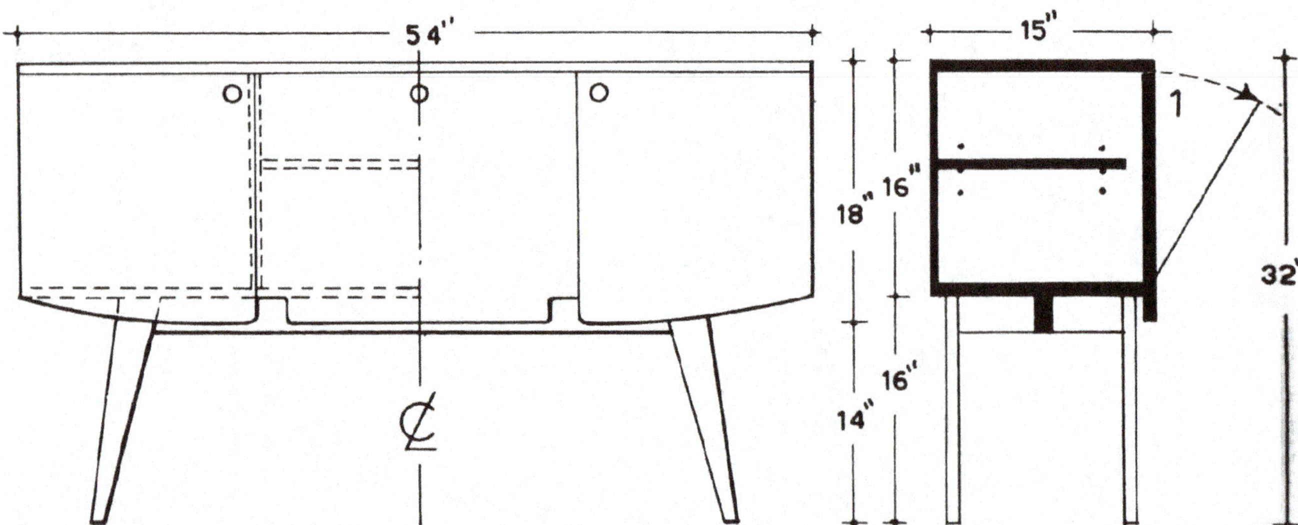

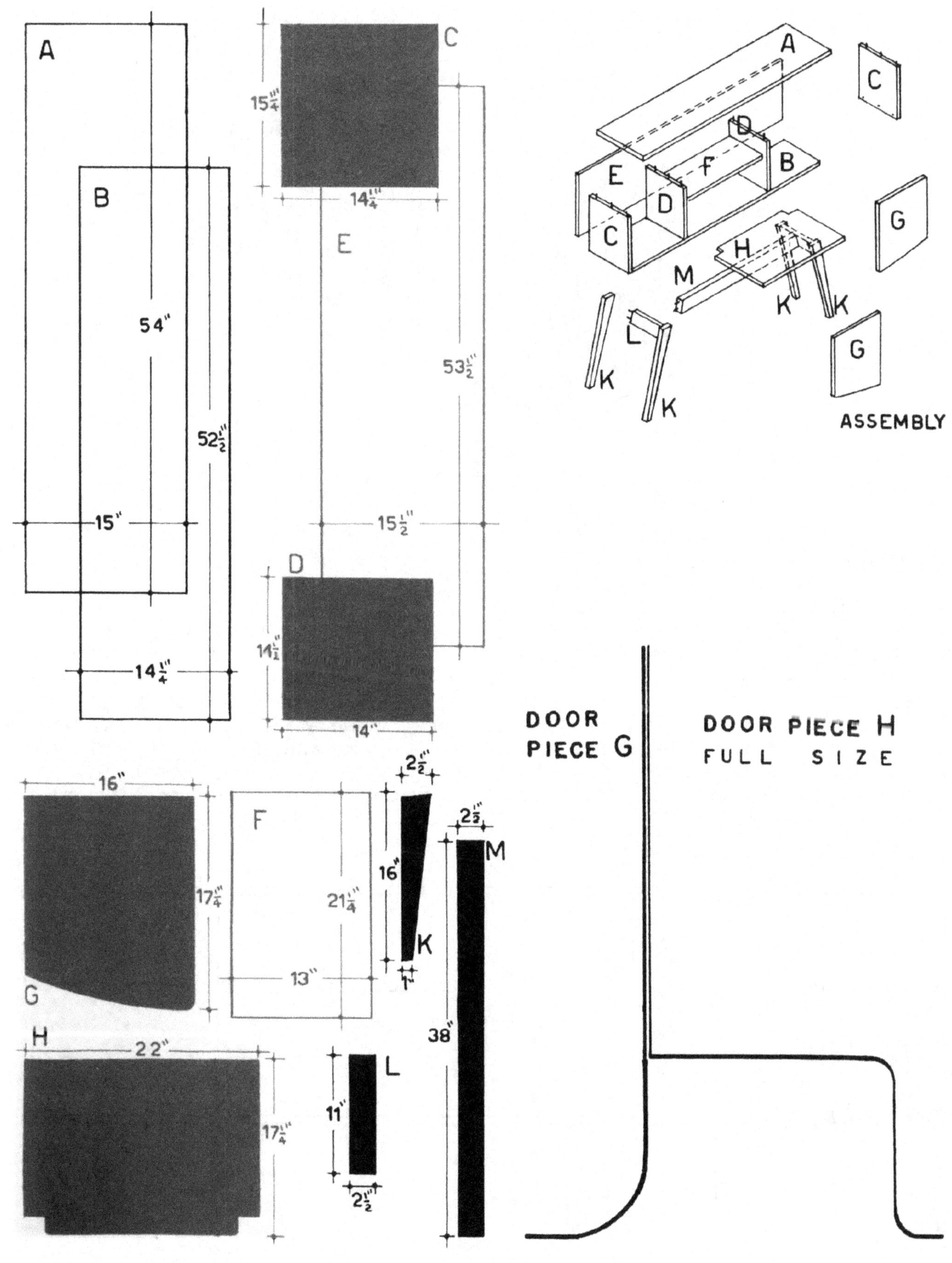

A
B
C
E
D
F
G
G
H
M
K
L
K
K
ASSEMBLY
54"
52½"
15"
14¼"
15¼"
14¼"
53½"
15½"
14½"
14"
16"
17¼"
G
F
21¼"
13"
H
22"
17¼"
2½"
16"
K
1"
2½"
M
38"
L
11"
2½"
DOOR PIECE G
DOOR PIECE H
FULL SIZE

CABINET

LIST OF MATERIALS.

A — 1 PIECE ¾" THICK AND 60" x 15". B — 1 PIECE ¼" THICK AND 58½" x 15". C — 1 PIECE ¼" THICK AND 59½" x 21½". D — 2 PIECES ¾" THICK AND 21¼" x 15". E — 2 PIECES ¾" THICK AND 20½" x 14¾". F — 2 PIECES ¾" THICK AND 20½" x 16½". G — 1 PIECE ¾" THICK AND 24" x 14¾". H — 2 PIECES ¾" THICK AND 16½" x 13". K — 1 PIECE ¾" THICK AND 24" x 2". L — 4 PIECES 2" IN DIAMETER AND 11" LONG. J — 2 PIECES ¼" THICK AND 23½" x 14½". O — 4 PIECES ½" THICK AND 14½" x 5½". P — 2 PIECES ½" THICK AND 23½" x 4½". R — 2 PIECES ¾" THICK AND 24" x 5½". FOR GENERAL INSTRUCTIONS SEE PAGE 54. AFTER MATERIAL IS READY FOR ASSEMBLING PROCEED AS FOLLOWS:

JOIN (1) "A" AND "B" WITH "D," "E" AND "K" (2) "A,D,E" WITH "C" (3) "B" WITH "L" (4) "H" WITH "D" AND "E" (5) "P" AND "R" WITH "O" (6) "J" WITH "O,P,R." TO COMPLETE THE DRAWER. APPLY DOOR "F" WITH NORMAL HINGE. FOR FINISH SEE PAGE 14.

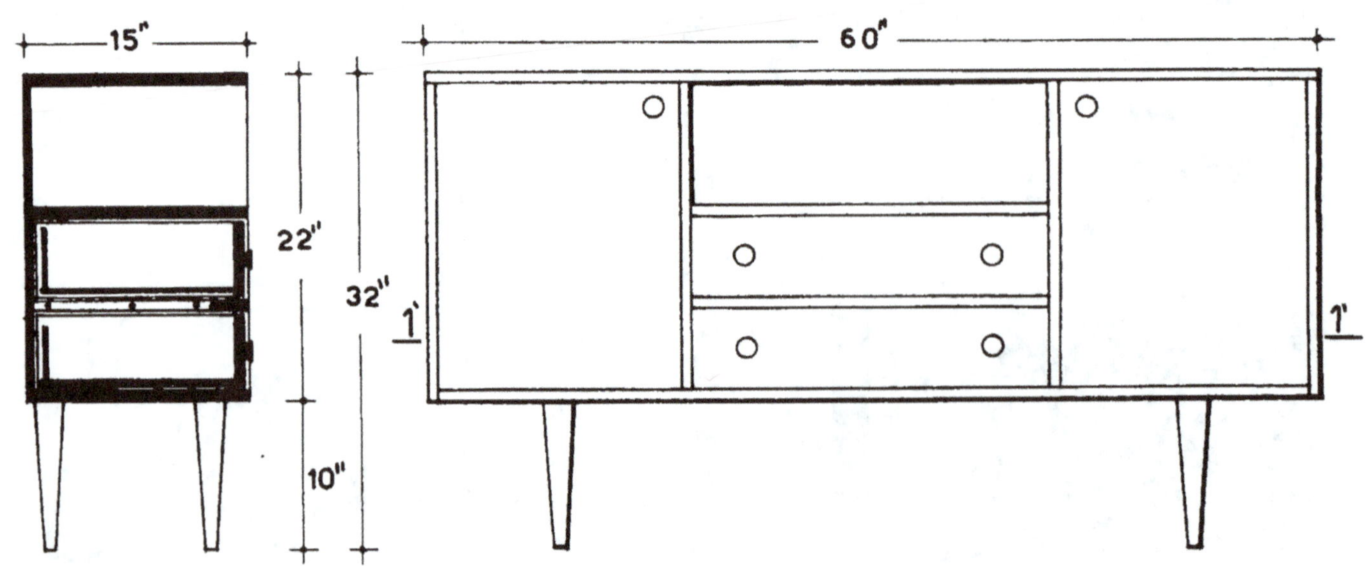

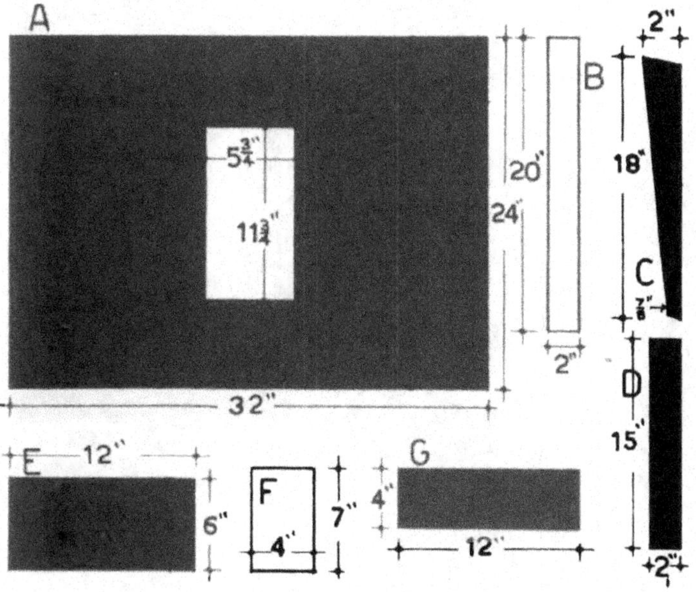

COFFEE TABLE

A — 1 PIECE ¾" THICK AND 32" x 24". B — 2 PIECES 1" THICK AND 20" x 2". C — 4 PIECES 1" THICK AND 18" x 2". D — 2 PIECES 1" THICK AND 15" x 2". E — 1 PIECE ½" THICK AND 12" x 6". F — 2 PIECES ½" THICK AND 7" x 4". G — 2 PIECES ½" THICK AND 12" x 4". SEE GENERAL INSTRUCTION ON PAGE 54. AFTER MATERIAL IS READY FOR ASSEMBLING PROCEED AS FOLLOWS:

JOIN (1) "B" WITH "C" (2) "D" WITH "B,C" (3) "E" WITH "G" (4) "F" WITH "E,G" (5) "F,G" WITH "A" (6) "B,D" WITH "A." FOR NATURAL FINISH SEE INSTRUCTIONS ON PAGE 14.

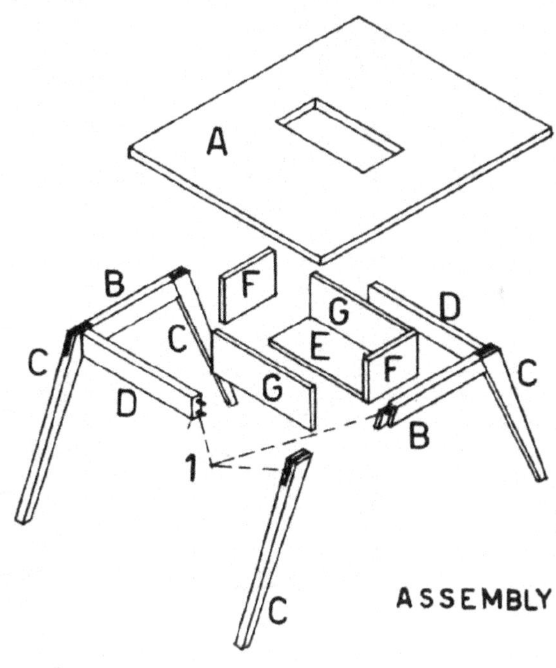

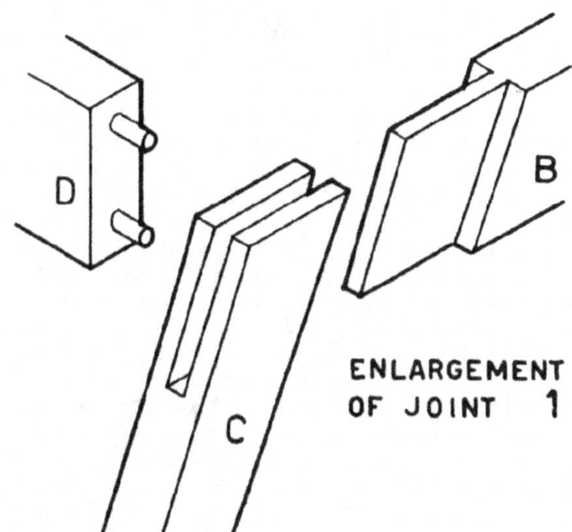

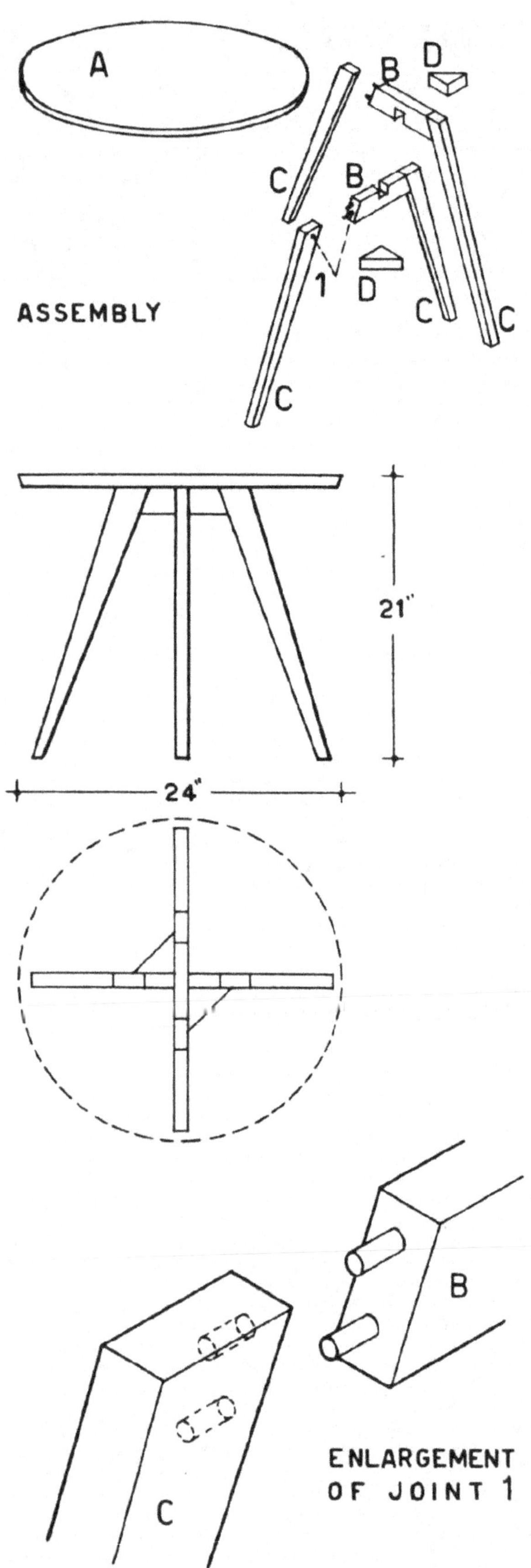

ROUND TABLE

LIST OF MATERIALS.

A — 1 PIECE ¾" THICK AND 24" DIAMETER. B — 2 PIECES 1" THICK AND 7" x 2". C — 4 PIECES 1" THICK AND 22" x 2". D — 2 PIECES 1" THICK AND 3" x 3". SEE GENERAL INSTRUCTIONS ON PAGE 54. AFTER MATERIAL IS READY FOR ASSEMBLING PROCEED AS FOLLOWS:

JOIN (1) "C" WITH "B" (2) "B" WITH "B" (3) "D" WITH "B" (4) "A" WITH "B." FOR FINISH SEE INSTRUCTIONS ON PAGE 14.

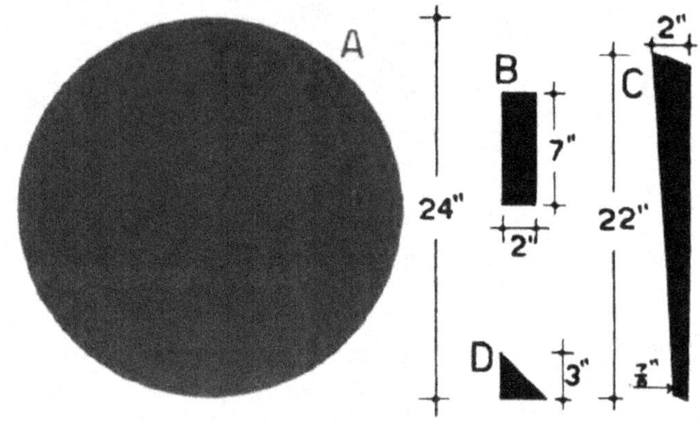

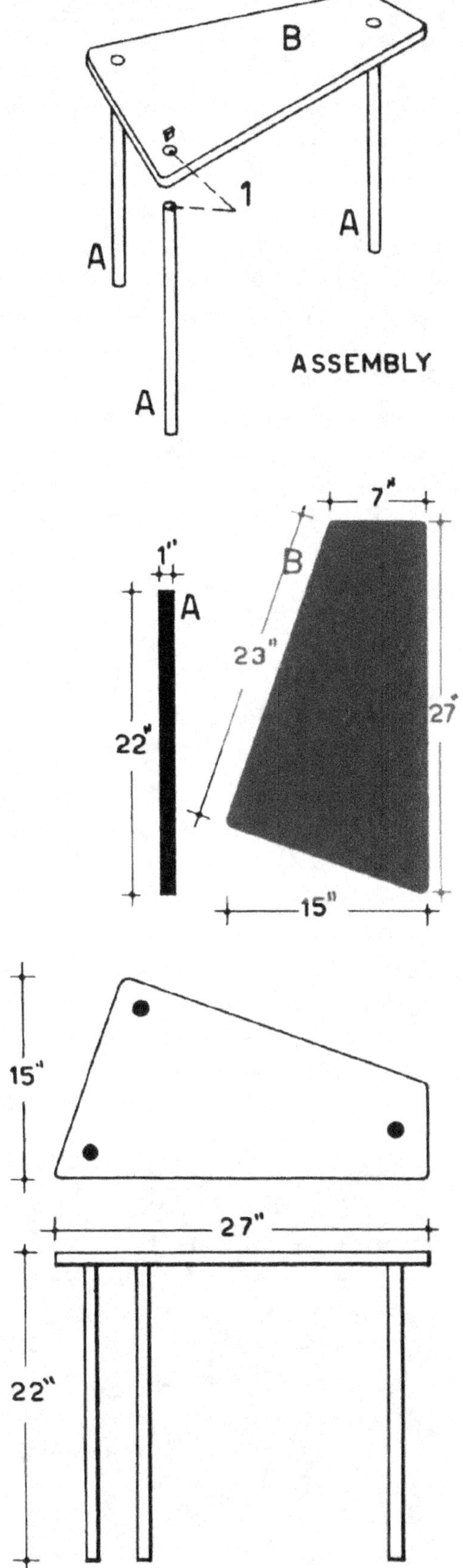

SIDE TABLE

LIST OF MATERIALS.

A — 3 PIECES 1" OR 1⅛" DIAMETER AND 22" LONG. B — 1 PIECE ¾" THICK AND 27" x 15". SEE GENERAL INSTRUCTIONS ON PAGE 54.

AFTER MATERIAL IS READY FOR ASSEMBLING PROCEED AS FOLLOWS:

JOIN "A" WITH "B" AND YOU HAVE COMPLETED YOUR SIDE TABLE. FOR FINISH SEE PAGE 14.

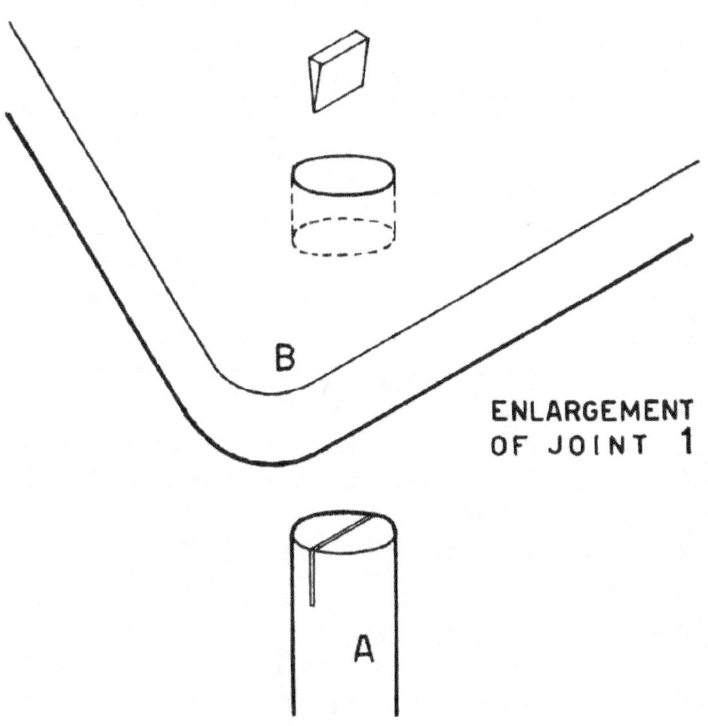

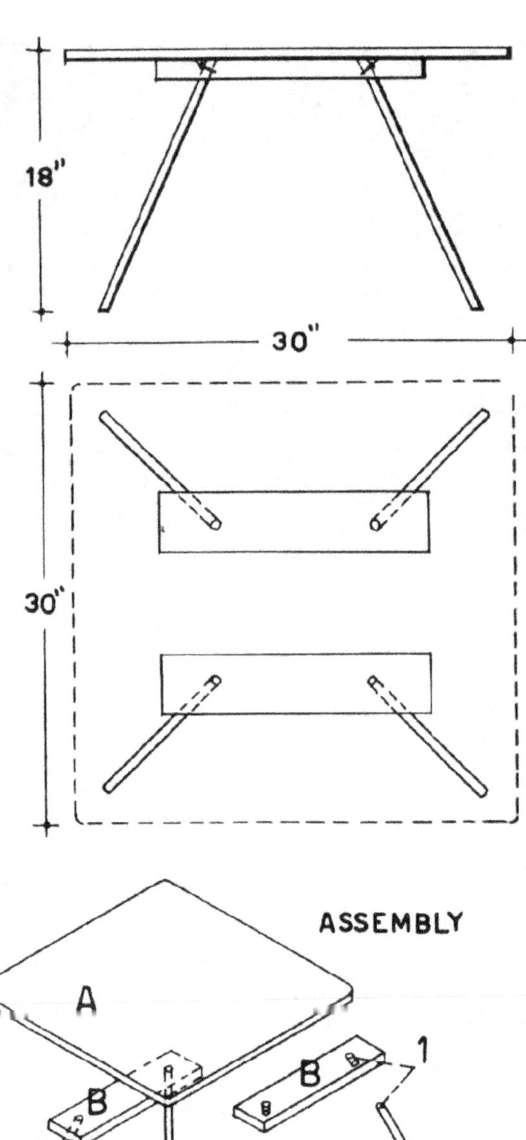

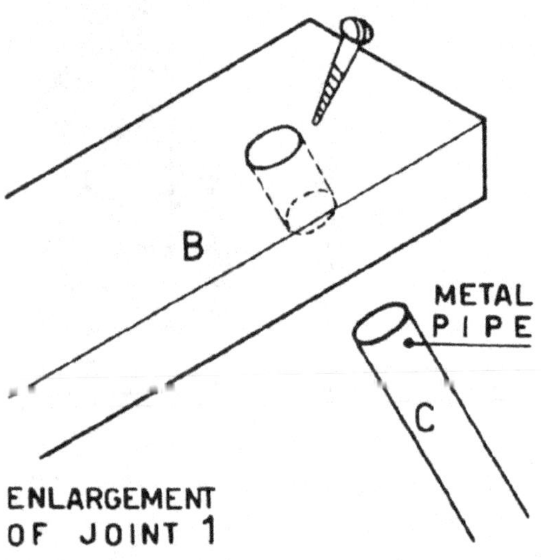

ENLARGEMENT
OF JOINT 1

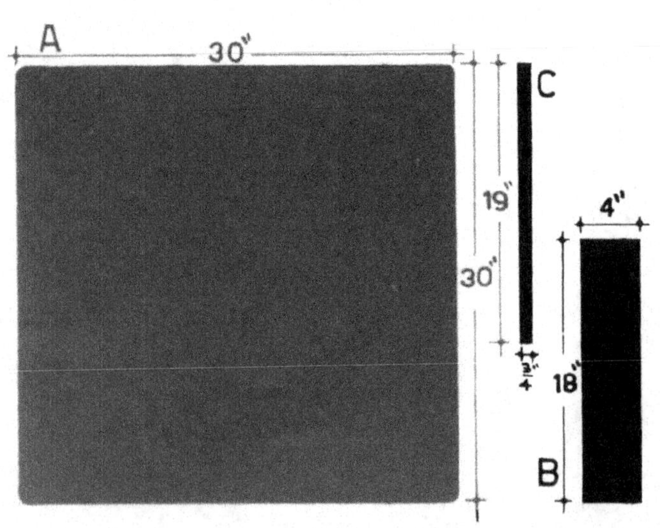

MAGAZINE TABLE

LIST OF MATERIALS.

A — 1 PIECE ¾" THICK AND 30" x 30". B — 2 PIECES 1¼" THICK AND 18" x 4". C — 4 PIECES OF METAL PIPE ¾" IN DIAMETER AND 19" LONG. FOR GENERAL INSTRUCTIONS SEE PAGE 54.

AFTER MATERIAL IS READY FOR ASSEMBLING PROCEED AS FOLLOWS:

JOIN (1) "C" WITH "B" (FORCED JOINT) (2) "A" WITH "B." FOR FINISH SEE PAGE 14.

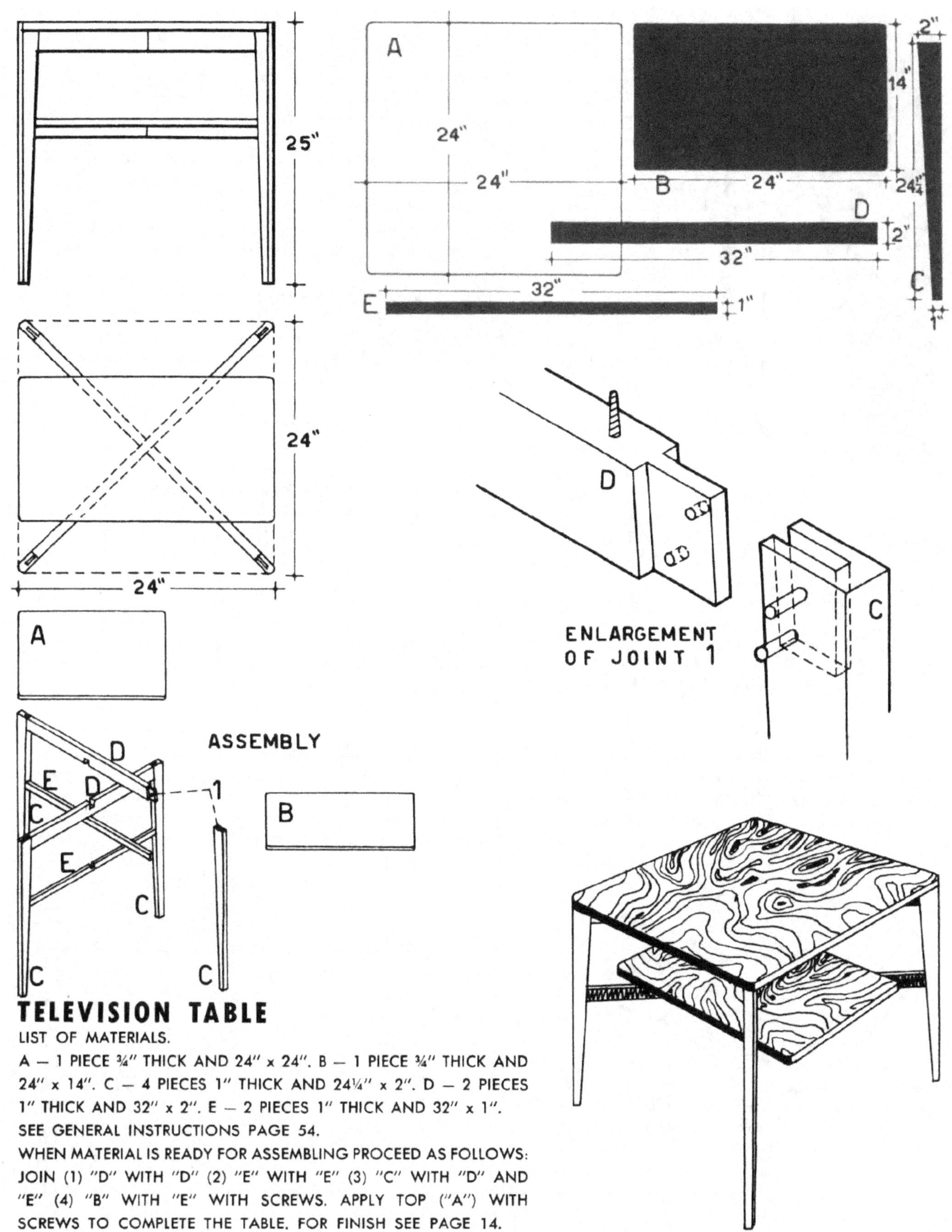

TELEVISION TABLE

LIST OF MATERIALS.

A — 1 PIECE ¾" THICK AND 24" x 24". B — 1 PIECE ¾" THICK AND 24" x 14". C — 4 PIECES 1" THICK AND 24¼" x 2". D — 2 PIECES 1" THICK AND 32" x 2". E — 2 PIECES 1" THICK AND 32" x 1". SEE GENERAL INSTRUCTIONS PAGE 54.

WHEN MATERIAL IS READY FOR ASSEMBLING PROCEED AS FOLLOWS: JOIN (1) "D" WITH "D" (2) "E" WITH "E" (3) "C" WITH "D" AND "E" (4) "B" WITH "E" WITH SCREWS. APPLY TOP ("A") WITH SCREWS TO COMPLETE THE TABLE. FOR FINISH SEE PAGE 14.

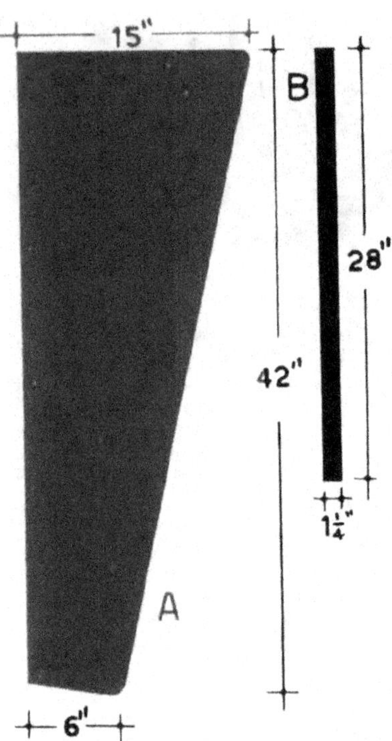

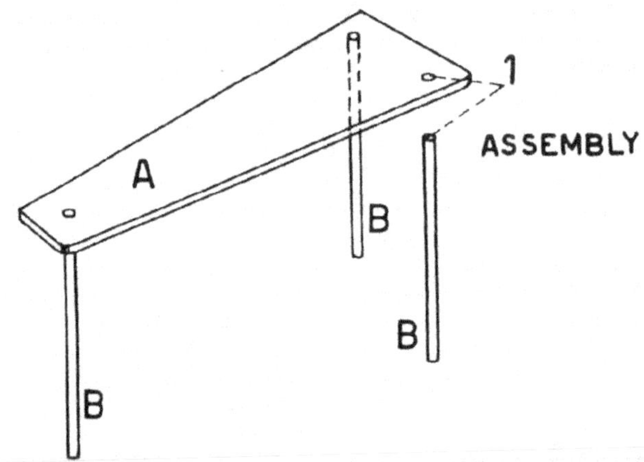

WALL TABLE

LIST OF MATERIALS.
A — 1 PIECE ¾" THICK AND 42" x 15".
B — 3 PIECES 1¼" IN DIAMETER AND 28" LONG.
FOR GENERAL INSTRUCTION SEE PAGE 54.
AFTER MATERIAL IS READY FOR ASSEMBLING PROCEED AS FOLLOWS:
JOIN "A" WITH "B." SEE FINISH PAGE 14.

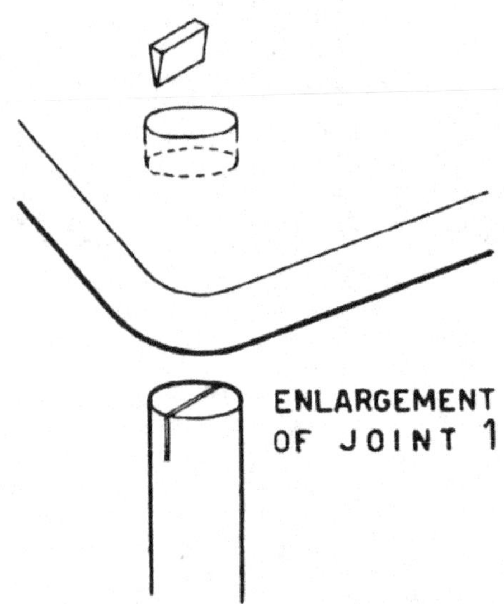

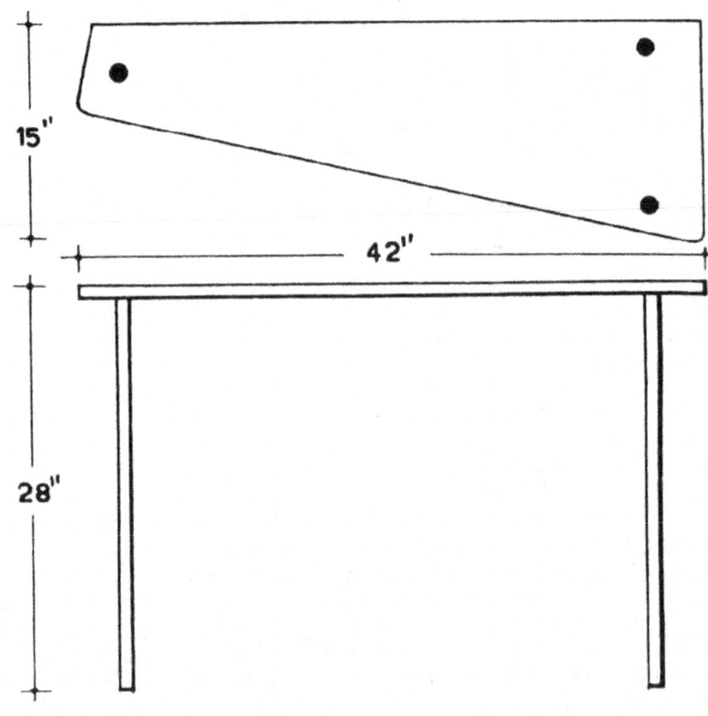

WALL TABLE

LIST OF MATERIALS.

A — 1 PIECE ¾" THICK AND 42" x 15". B — 1 PIECE 1" THICK AND 23" x 4". C — 2 PIECES 1" THICK AND 11" x 4". D — 4 PIECES 1" THICK AND 30" x 2¼". E — 1 PIECE ½" THICK AND 13" x 11½". F — 2 PIECES ½" THICK AND 11½" x 4". G — 1 PIECE ¾" THICK AND 14" x 4". H — 2 PIECES ½" THICK AND 12" x 3½". K — 1 PIECE ½" THICK AND 12½" x 3". L — 1 PIECE ¼" THICK AND 12½" x 12". SEE GENERAL INSTRUCTION ON PAGE 54. AFTER MATERIAL IS READY FOR ASSEMBLING PROCEED AS FOLLOWS:

JOIN (1) "C" WITH "D" (2) "B" WITH "C,D" (3) "A" WITH "B,C" (4) "E" WITH "F" (5) "F" WITH "A,B" (6) "G" WITH "H" (7) "L" WITH "H,G." FOR NATURAL FINISH SEE PAGE 14.

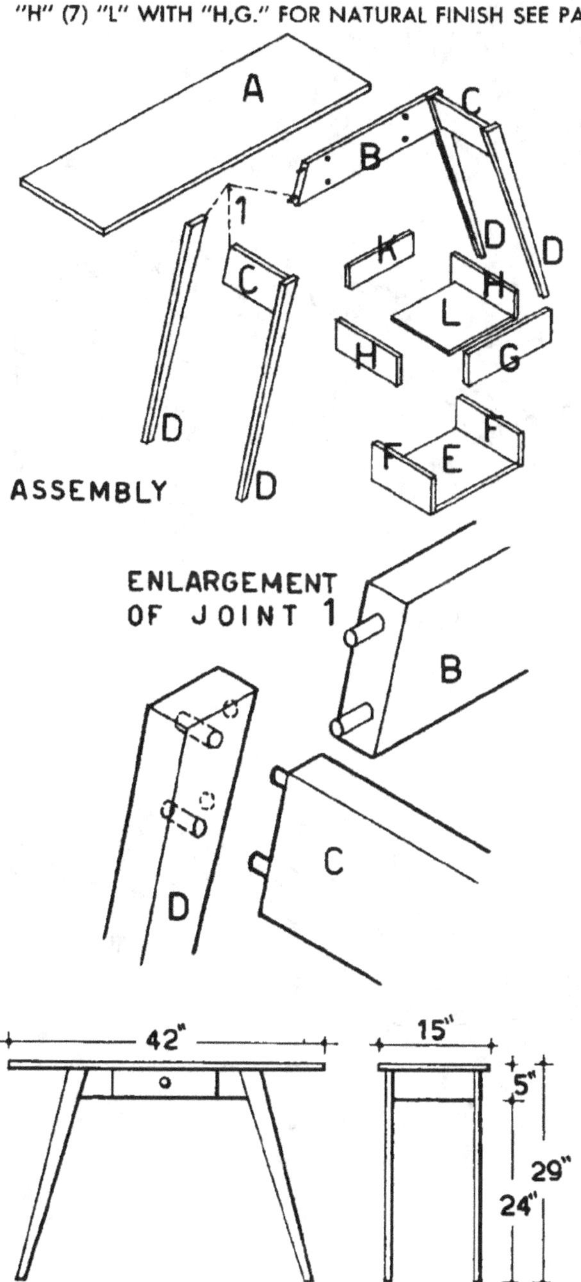

ASSEMBLY

ENLARGEMENT OF JOINT 1

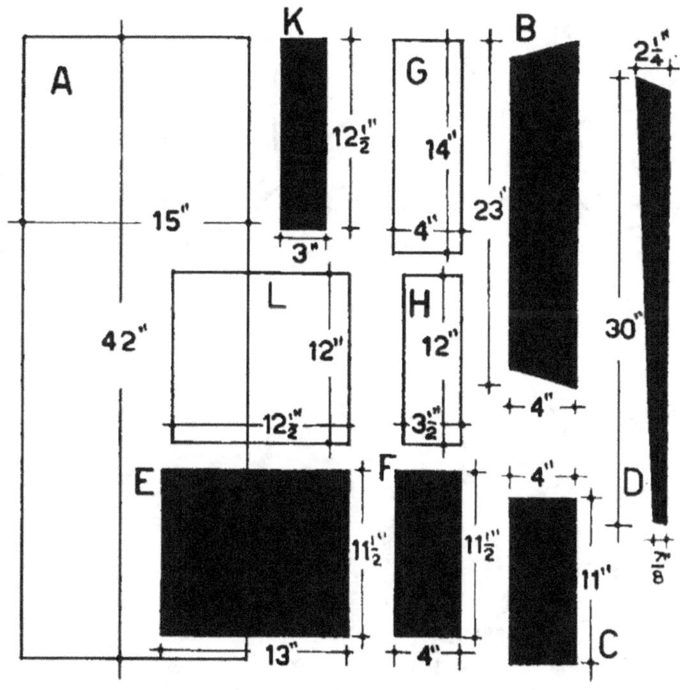

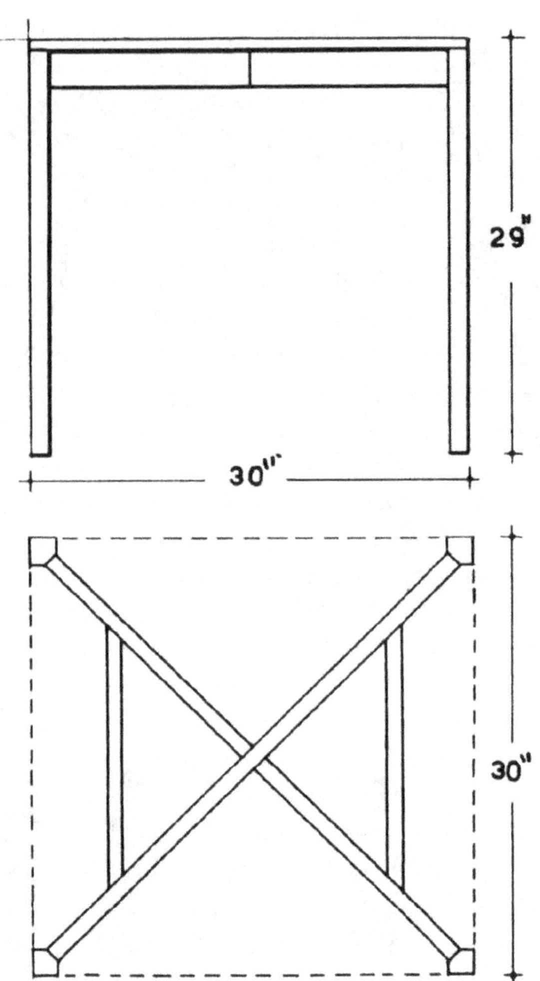

EXTENSION DINING TABLE

LIST OF MATERIALS.

A — 1 PIECE ¾" THICK AND 30" x 30".
B — 2 PIECES 1¼" THICK AND 42" x 2½".
C — 2 PIECES 1¼" THICK AND 20" x 2½".
D — 4 PIECES 1⅜" THICK AND 28" x 1⅜".
FOR GENERAL INSTRUCTIONS SEE PAGE
54. AFTER MATERIAL IS READY FOR ASSEM-
BLING PROCEED AS FOLLOWS:
JOIN (1) "B" WITH "D" (2) "B" WITH "B"
(3) "B" WITH "C." APPLY TOP ("A") WITH
SCREWS TO COMPLETE TABLE. FOR FINISH
SEE PAGE 14.

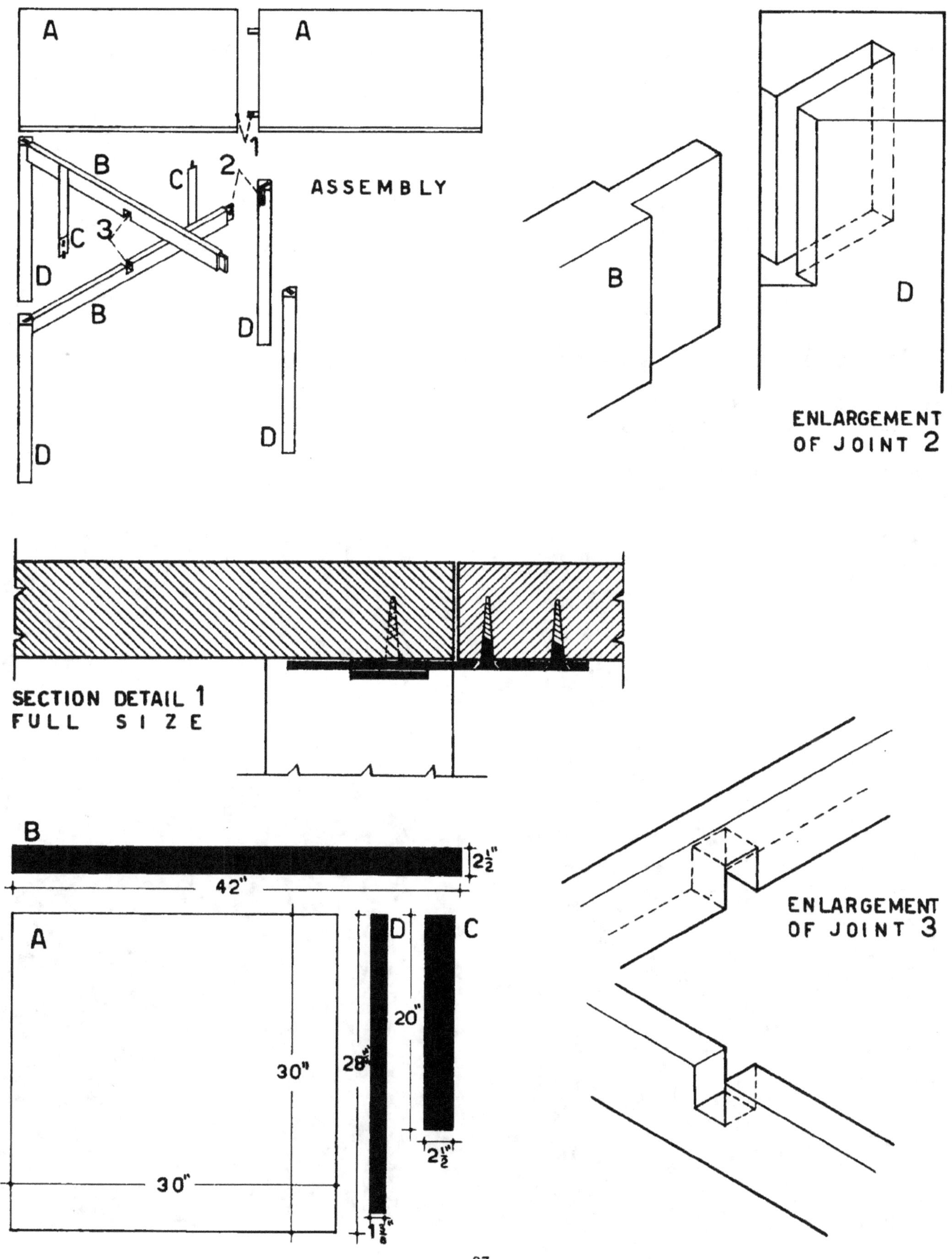

A
A
B
C
2
3
C
D
D
B
D
D
D
ASSEMBLY
B
ENLARGEMENT
OF JOINT 2
D
SECTION DETAIL 1
FULL SIZE
B
2½"
42"
A
D
C
30"
28"
20"
30"
2½"
1⅛"
ENLARGEMENT
OF JOINT 3

FURNITURE FOR THE DINING AREA

INSTRUCTIONS FOR BUILDING THE PIECES SHOWN
HERE WILL BE FOUND ON THE FOLLOWING PAGES:
SERVING TABLE, PAGE 72; CHAIR, PAGE 103; TABLE,
PAGE 86; BENCH, PAGE 100; MAGAZINE STORAGE
RACK, PAGE 58.

DINING TABLE

LIST OF MATERIALS.

A — 1 PIECE ¾" THICK AND 60" x 32". B — 1 PIECE 1¼" THICK AND 44" x 3". C —
2 PIECES 1¼" THICK AND 22" x 3". D — 4 PIECES 1⅜" THICK AND 29" x 2½".
E — 4 PIECES 1⅜" THICK AND 4" x 4". SEE GENERAL INSTRUCTIONS PAGE 54.
AFTER MATERIAL IS READY FOR ASSEMBLING PROCEED AS FOLLOWS:
JOIN (1) "C" WITH "D" (2) "B" WITH "C" (3) "E" WITH "B,C." APPLY TOP ("A") TO
COMPLETE THE TABLE. FOR FINISH SEE PAGE 14.

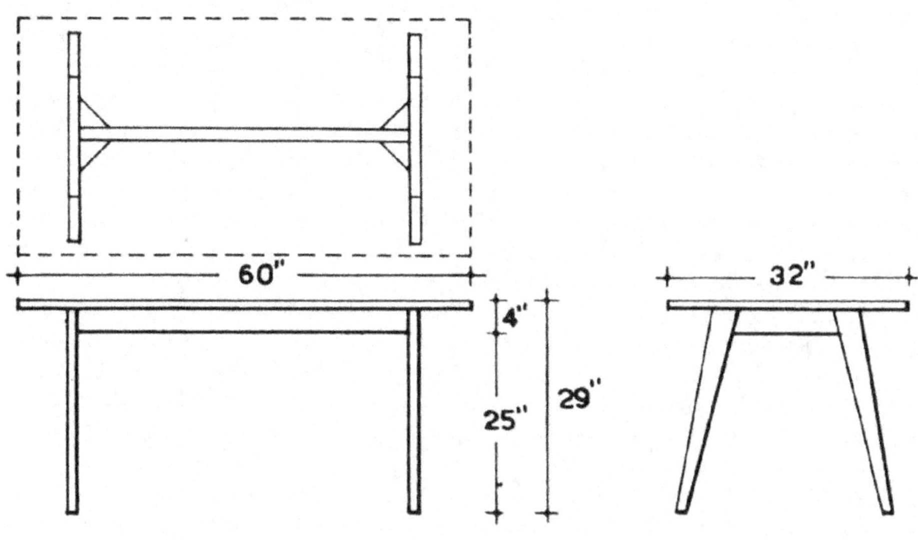

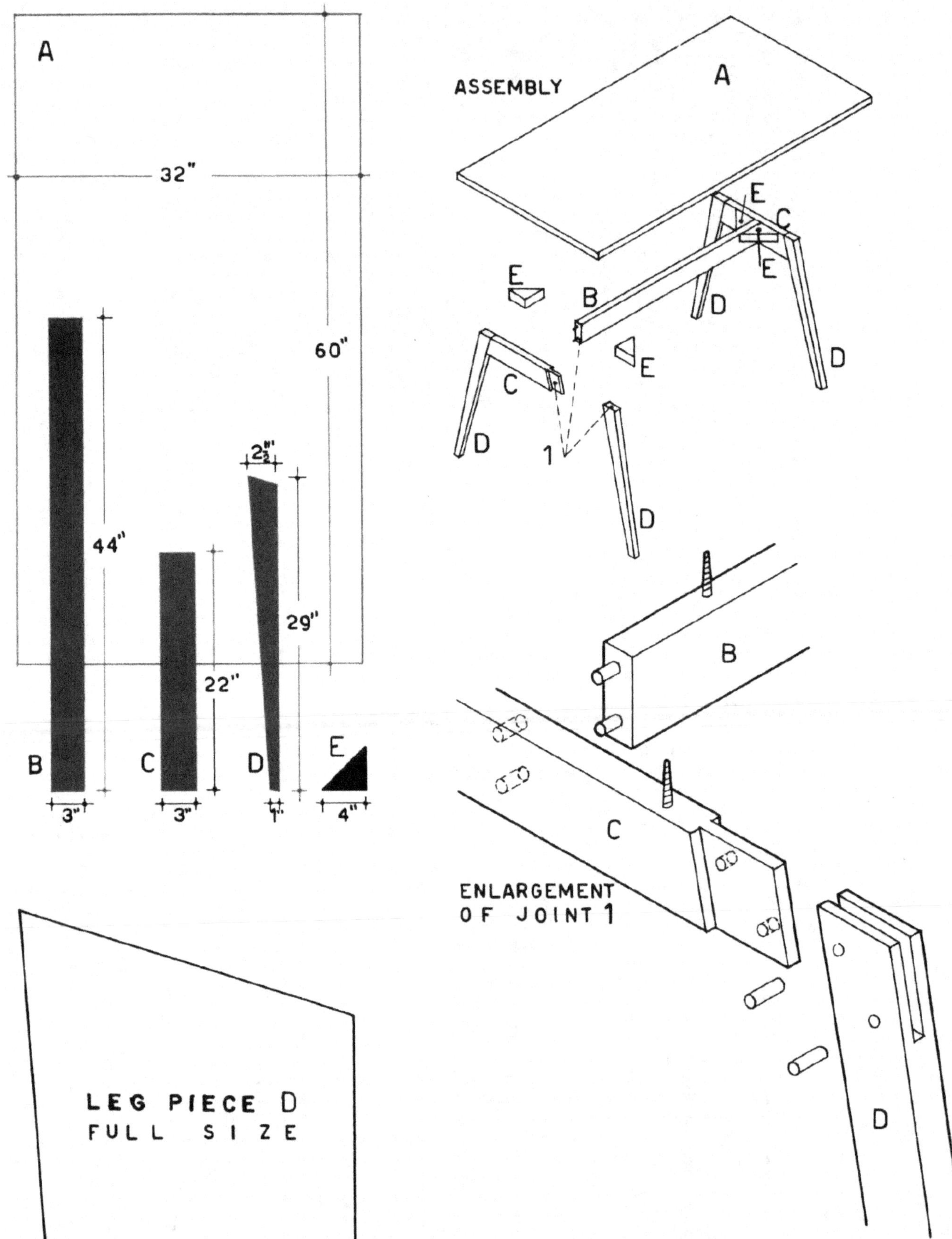

A
ASSEMBLY
32"
60"
44"
29"
22"
2½"
B
C
D
E
3"
3"
1"
4"
E
C
B
D
1
LEG PIECE D
FULL SIZE
B
C
D
ENLARGEMENT
OF JOINT 1

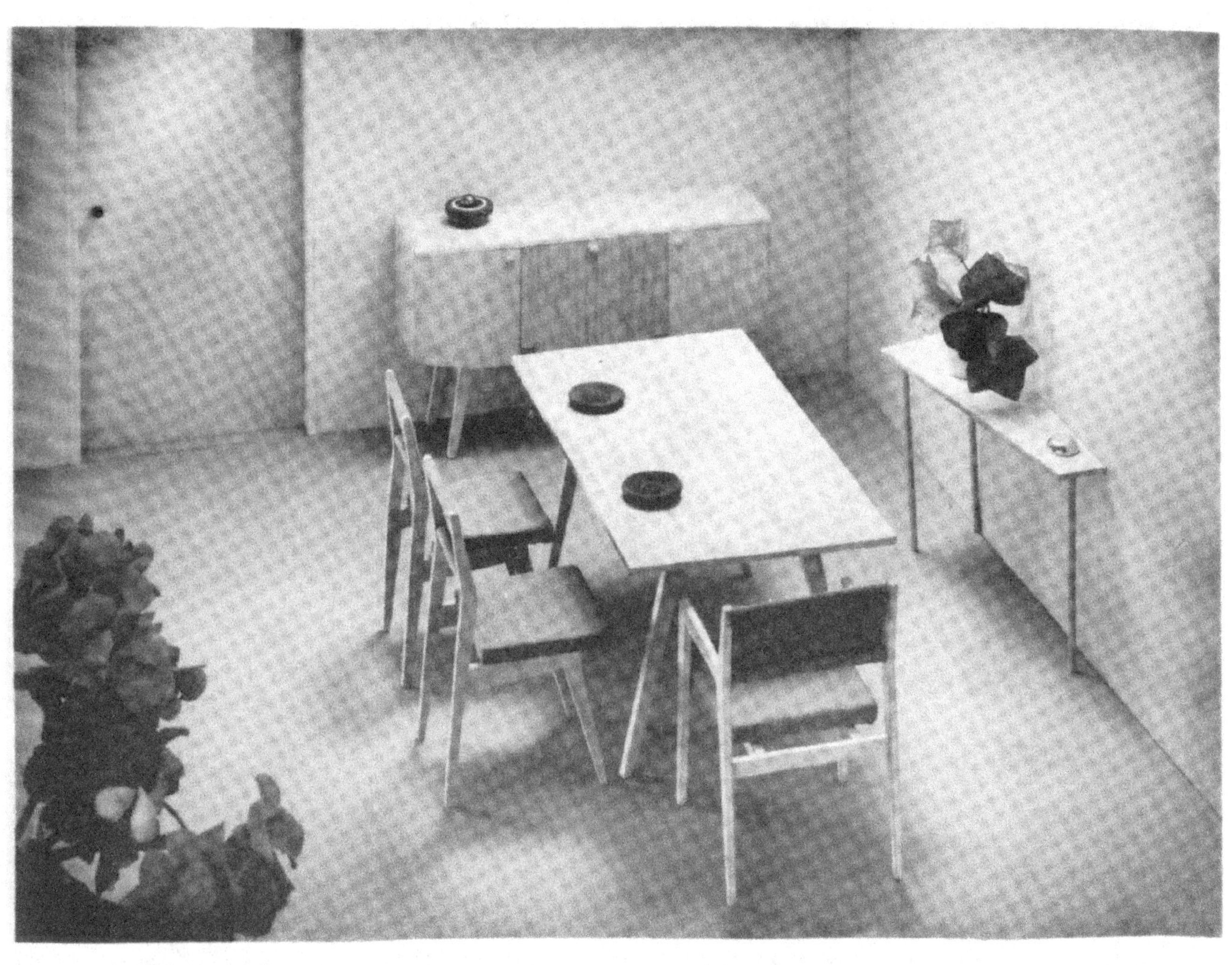

FURNITURE FOR THE DINING ROOM

INSTRUCTIONS FOR BUILDING THE PIECES SHOWN
HERE WILL BE FOUND ON THE FOLLOWING PAGES:
CHAIR, PAGE 103; DROP-FRONT CABINET, PAGE 74;
TABLE, PAGE 89; ARMCHAIR, PAGE 104; SIDE TABLE,
PAGE 84.

WORK TABLE

LIST OF MATERIALS.

A — 1 PIECE ¾" THICK AND 48" x 24". B — 2 PIECES 1¼" THICK AND 13" x 2¼". C — 2 PIECES 1¼" THICK AND 35" x 2¼". D — 4 PIECES 1¼" THICK AND 29" x 2½". E — 2 PIECES ½" THICK AND 19½" x 5". F — 2 PIECES ½" THICK AND 15" x 5". G — 2 PIECES ½" THICK AND 19½" x 14". H — 1 PIECE ½" THICK AND 13½" x 3½". K — 2 PIECES ½" THICK AND 20" x 4". L — 1 PIECE ¼" THICK AND 19½" x 13½". SEE GENERAL INSTRUCTIONS ON PAGE 54. AFTER THE MATERIAL IS READY, ASSEMBLE THE JOINTS AS FOLLOWS:

(1) "B" WITH "D" (2) "C" WITH "B" (3) "A" WITH "B,C,D" (4) "G" WITH "E" AND "F" FOR DRAWER. (5) "K" WITH "F" AND "H" (6) "L" WITH "H,K,F" TO COMPLETE THE TABLE.

FOR FINISH SEE GENERAL INSTRUCTIONS ON PAGE 14.

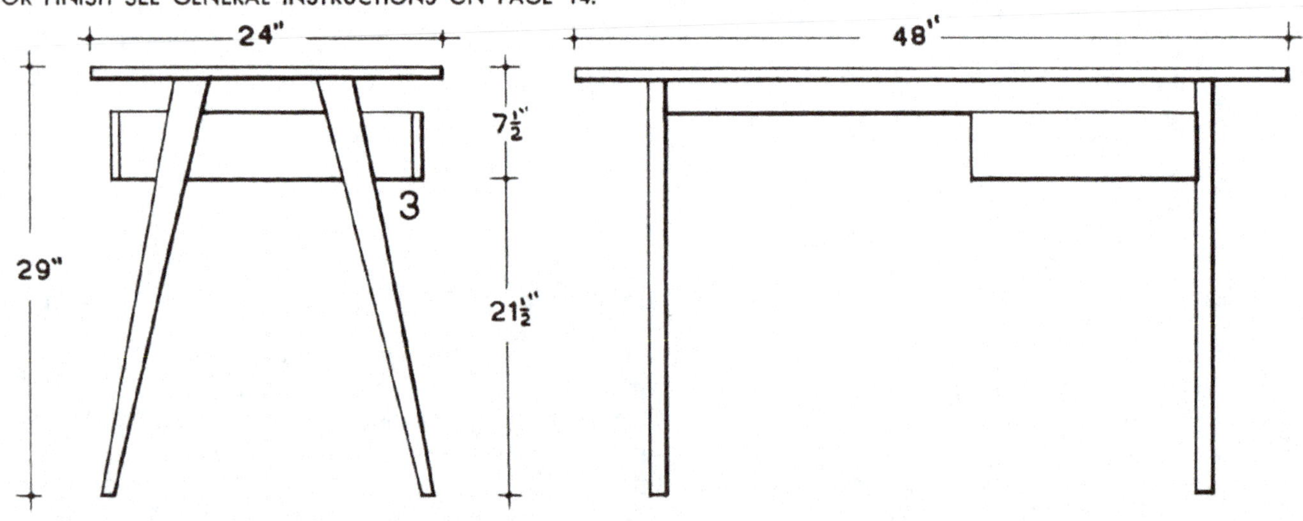

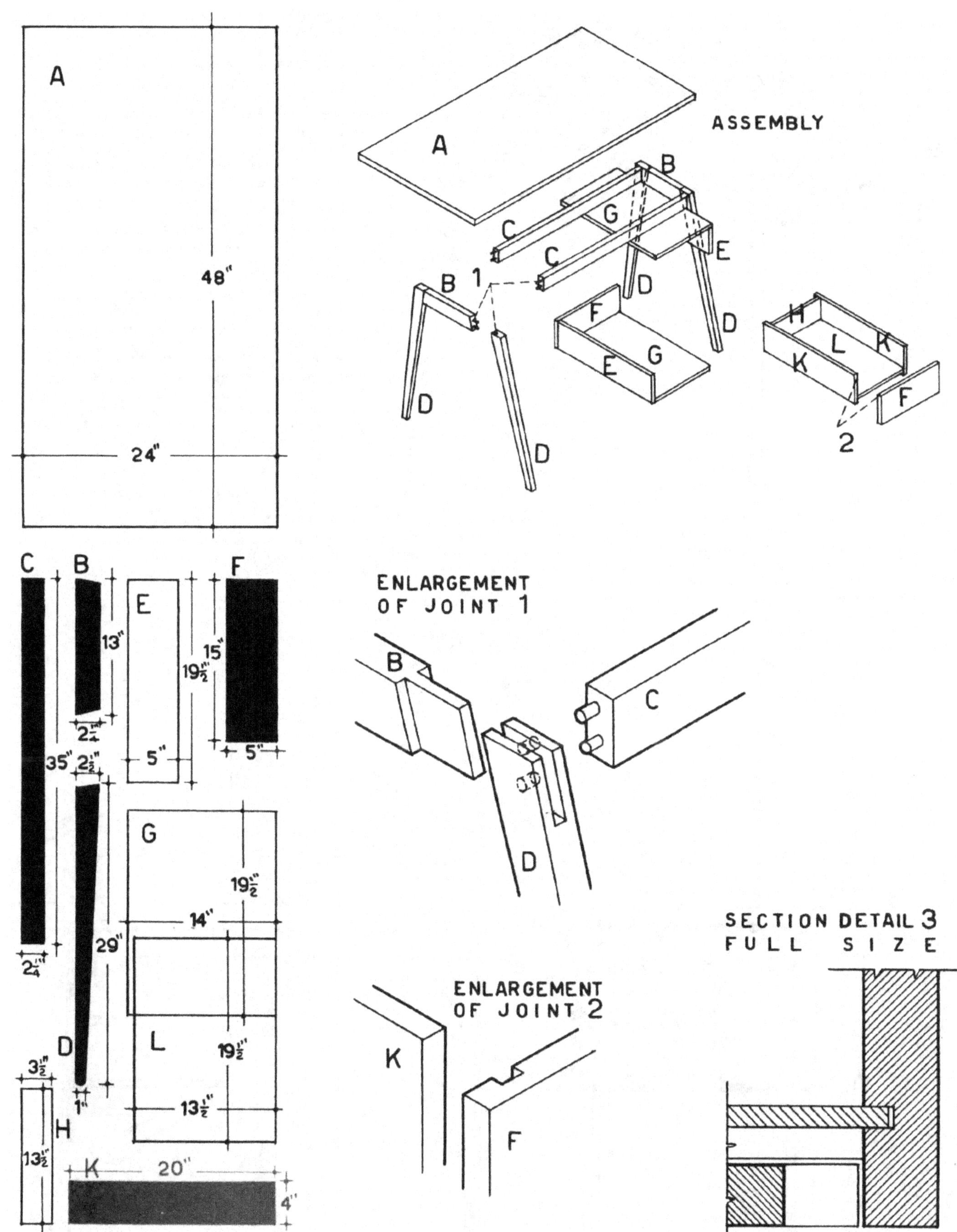

A
48"
24"
ASSEMBLY
A
B
C
G
C
E
B
1
D
D
F
E
G
D
H
L
K
K
F
2
C
B
F
E
13"
15"
19½"
2¼"
2½"
5"
5"
35"
G
19½"
14"
29"
L
19½"
D
3½"
13½"
1"
H
13½"
K
20"
4"
ENLARGEMENT
OF JOINT 1
B
C
D
ENLARGEMENT
OF JOINT 2
K
F
SECTION DETAIL 3
FULL SIZE

DESK

A — 1 PIECE ¾″ THICK AND 45″ x 24″.
B — 2 PIECES 1¼″ THICK AND 43″ x 2½″.
C — 2 PIECES 1″ THICK AND 13″ x 2½″.
D — 4 PIECES 1¼″ THICK AND 28¼″ x 2¼″.
E — 4 PIECES ¾″ THICK AND 23″ x 12″.
F — 1 PIECE ¾″ THICK AND 12″ x 10½″.
G — 1 PIECE ¾″ THICK AND 12″ x 2″. H —
2 PIECES ¾″ THICK AND 12″ x 5″. K — 4
PIECES ½″ THICK AND 13½″ x 5″. O — 2
PIECES ¼″ THICK AND 13″ x 11½″. P —
2 PIECES ½″ THICK AND 11½″ x 4″.

FOR GENERAL INSTRUCTIONS SEE PAGE
54. AFTER THE MATERIAL IS READY FOR
ASSEMBLING, JOIN AS FOLLOWS:
(1) "B" WITH "D" (2) "C" WITH "B" (3) "A"
WITH "B" AND "C" (4) "E" WITH "F" AND
"G" (5) "K" WITH "H,P" (6) "O" WITH
"H,K" (7) "E" TO "B" WITH SCREWS AND
YOU HAVE COMPLETED YOUR DESK.
FOR FINISH SEE GENERAL INSTRUCTIONS
ON PAGE 14.

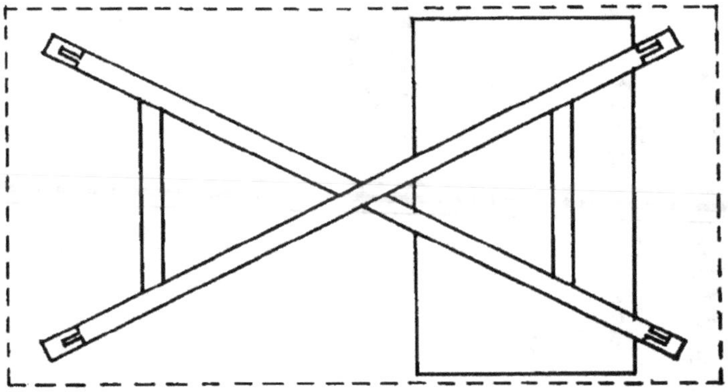

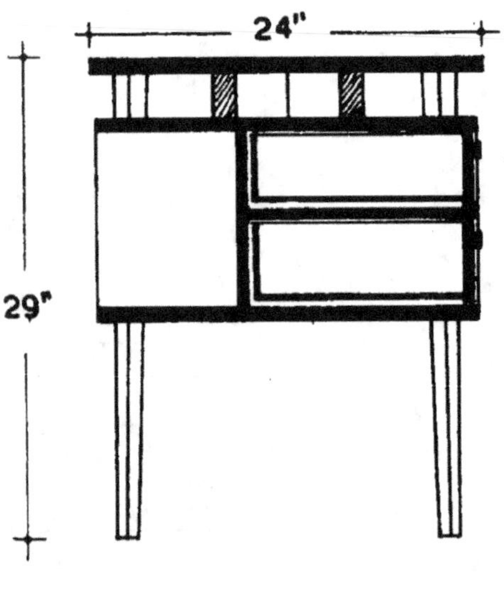

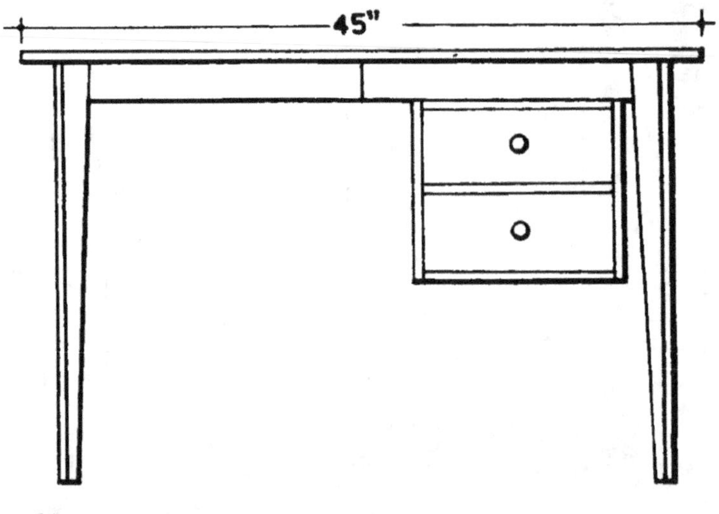

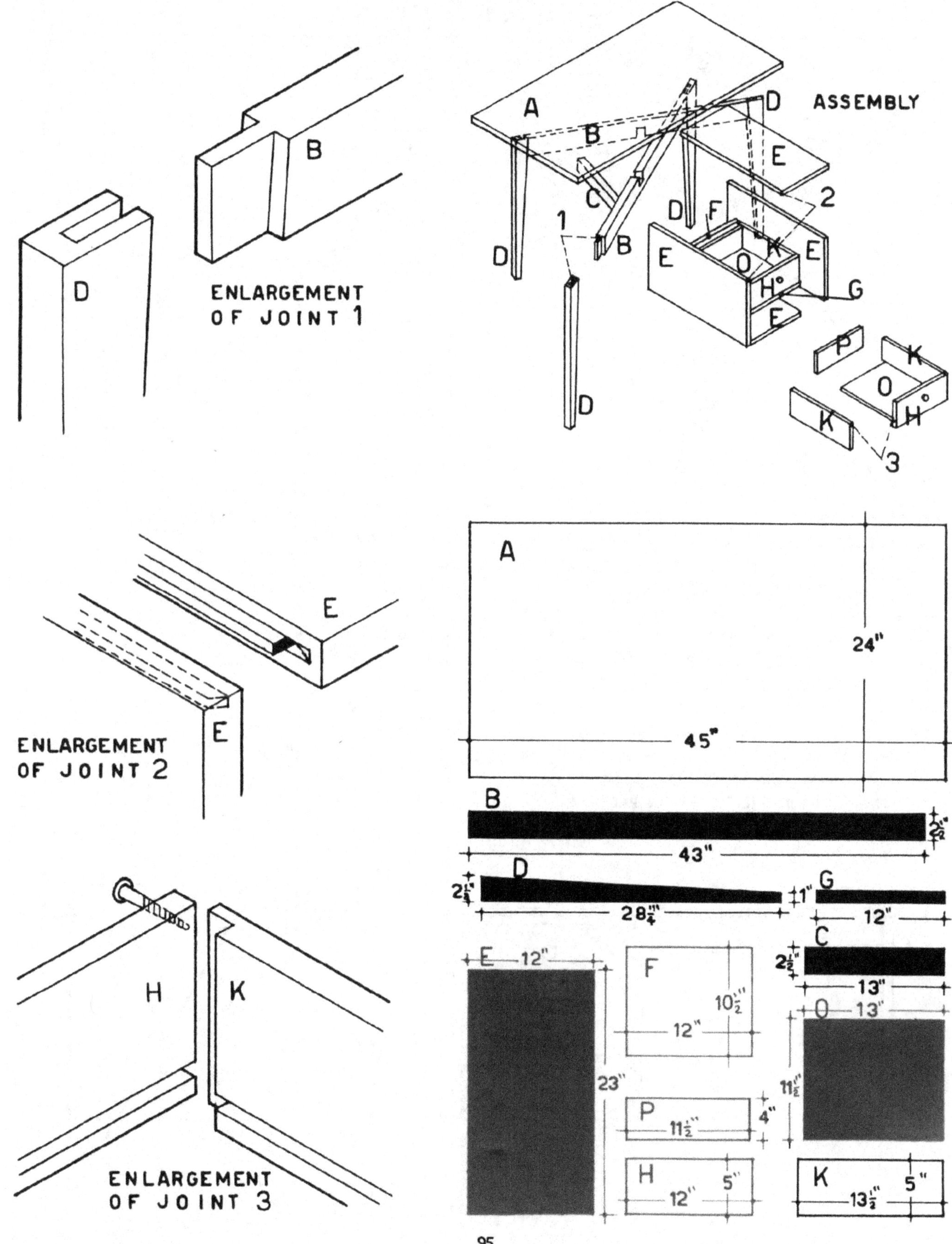

ENLARGEMENT
OF JOINT 1
B
D
ENLARGEMENT
OF JOINT 2
E
E
ENLARGEMENT
OF JOINT 3
H
K
ASSEMBLY
A
B
D
E
C
D
F
2
1
B
D
E
O
K
E
H°
G
E
D
P
K
O
K
H°
3
A
24"
45"
B
43"
D
G
2¼"
1"
28¾"
12"
E
12"
F
12"
10½"
C
2½"
13"
O
13"
11½"
23"
P
11½"
4"
H
12"
5"
K
13½"
5"

DESK

LIST OF MATERIALS.

A — 1 PIECE ¾" THICK AND 48" x 24". B — 2 PIECES ¾" THICK AND 20" x 19½".
C — 2 PIECES ¾" THICK AND 20" x 16". D — 4 PIECES 1¼" THICK AND 34" x 2½".
E — 1 PIECE 1¼" THICK AND 22½" x 3½". F — 1 PIECE ¾" THICK AND 18" x 16".
G — 2 PIECES ¾" THICK AND 16" x 2". H — 4 PIECES ¾" THICK AND 17" x 1".
K — 6 PIECES ½" THICK AND 19" x 5½". L — 3 PIECES ¾" THICK AND 16" x 5½".
M — 3 PIECES ¼" THICK AND 18½" x 15½". O — 3 PIECES ½" THICK AND 15½" x 4½".
SEE GENERAL INSTRUCTIONS ON PAGE 51.
WHEN THE MATERIAL IS READY FOR ASSEMBLING PROCEED AS FOLLOWS:
(1) "D" WITH "D" (2) "B" WITH "C," "F" AND "G" (3) "B" WITH "H" (4) "K" WITH
"L" AND "O" (5) "M" WITH "K,L" (6) "D" WITH "B" AND "E" (7) APPLY THE TOP ("A")
AND YOU HAVE COMPLETED YOUR DESK.
FOR FINISH SEE INSTRUCTIONS ON PAGE 14.

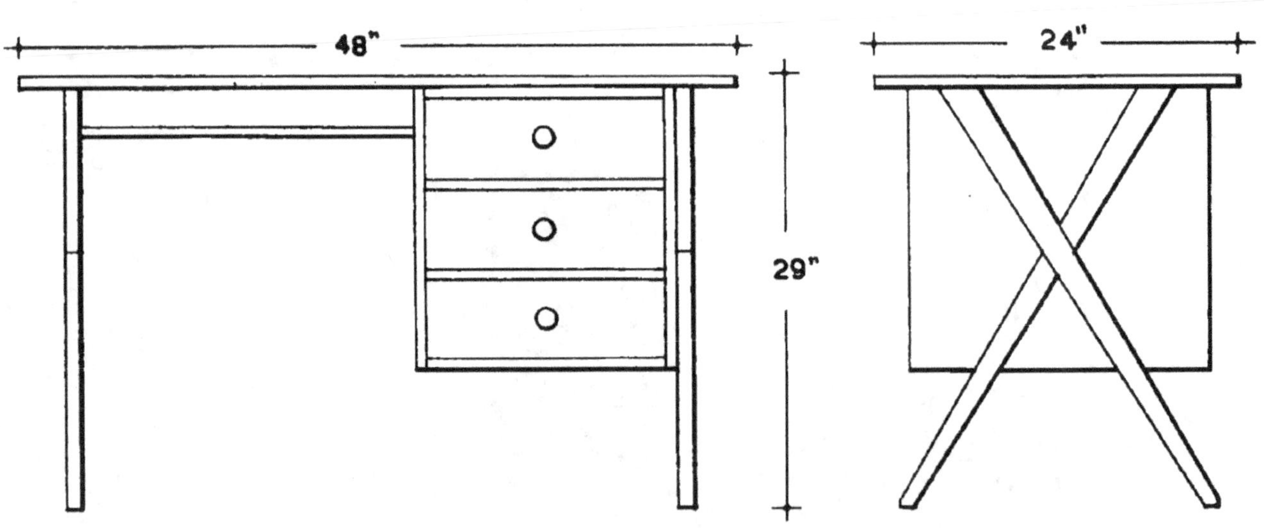

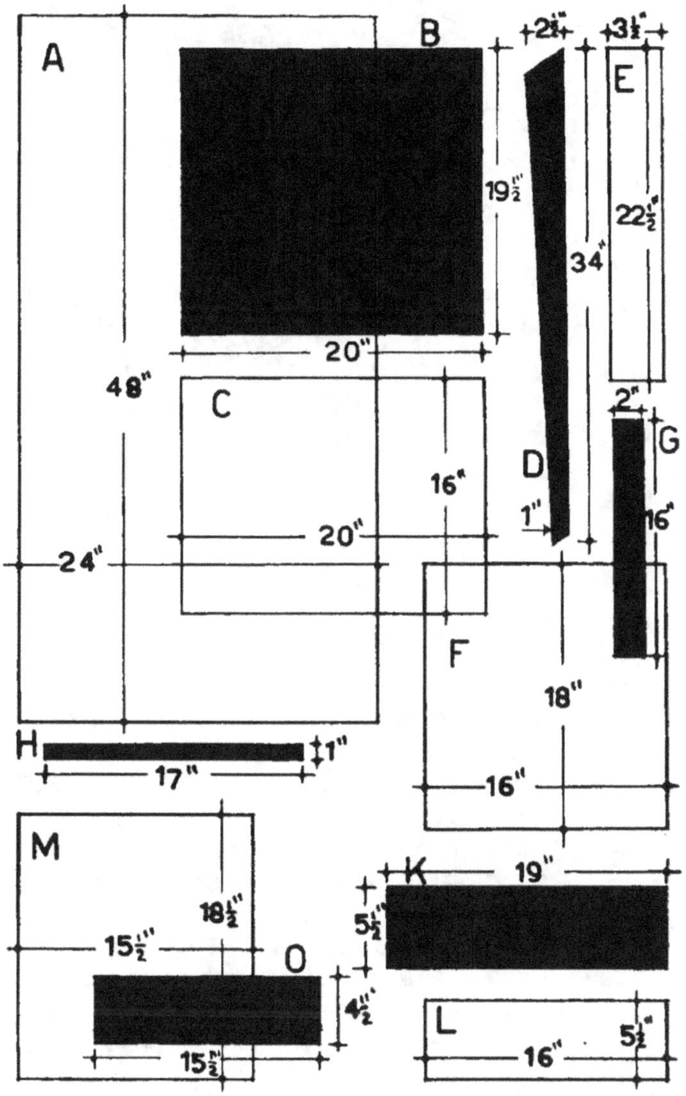

A

B

C

D

E

F

G

H

M

O

K

L

48"

24"

20"

20"

16"

19½"

34"

22½"

2¼"

3½"

2"

16"

1"

18"

16"

1"

17"

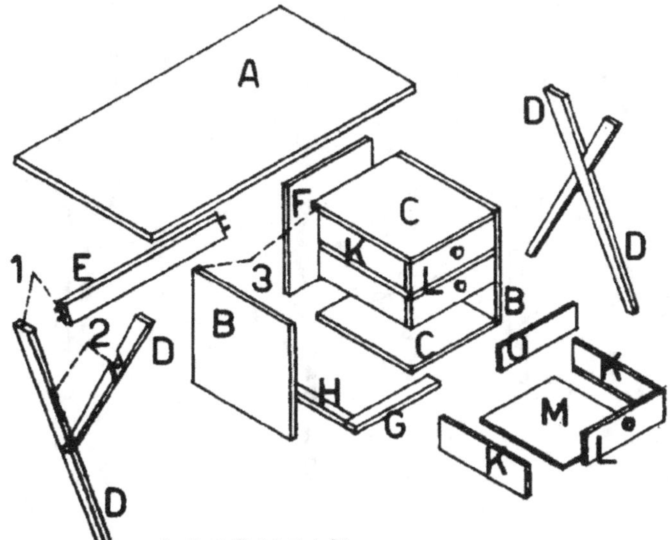

18½"

15½"

15½"

4½"

5½"

5½"

19"

16"

ASSEMBLY

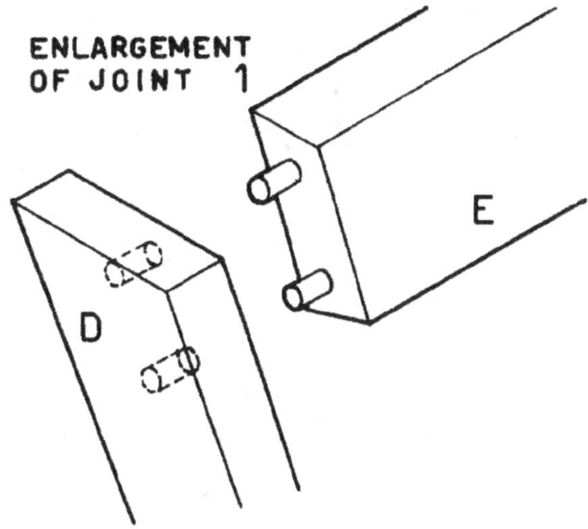

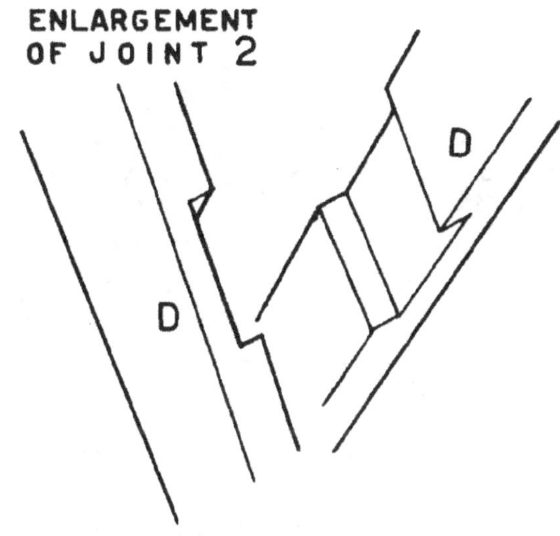

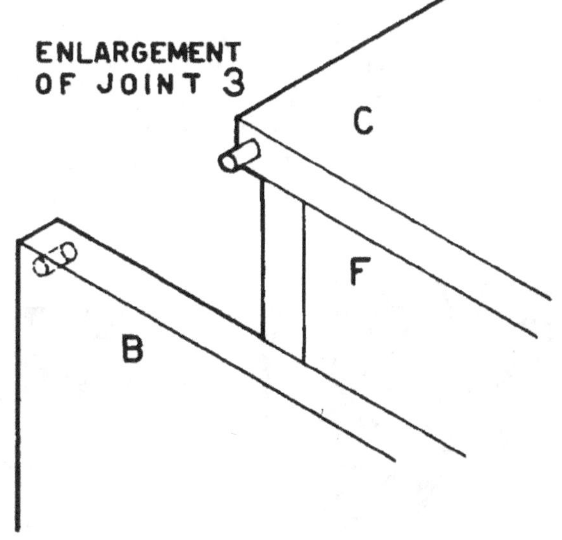

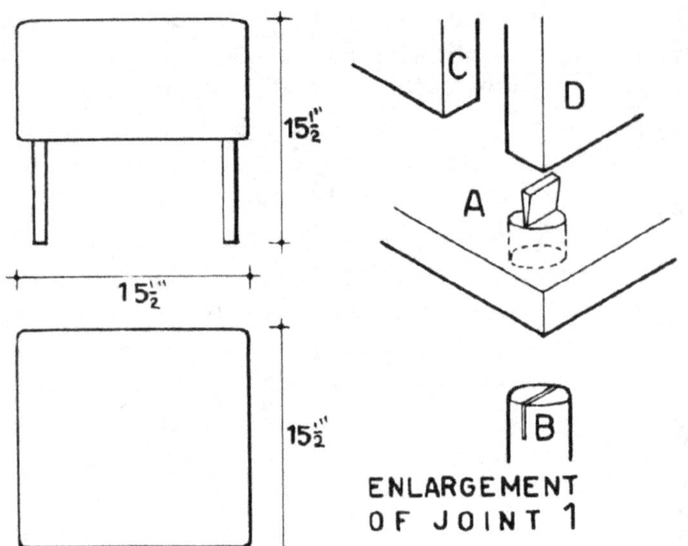

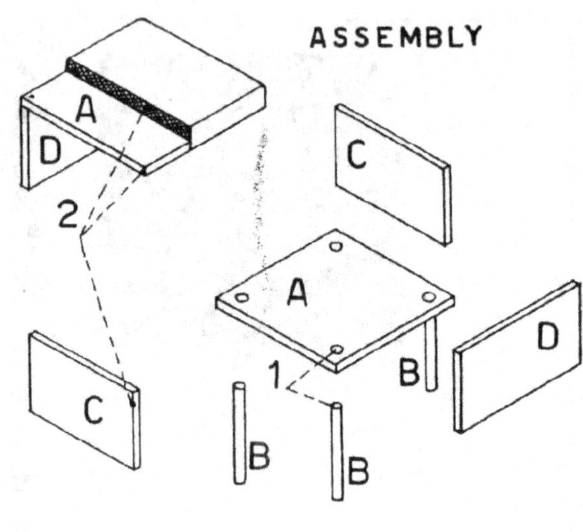

STOOL

LIST OF MATERIALS.

A — 2 PIECES ¾" THICK AND 15" x 15". B — 4 PIECES 1" OR 1⅛" DIAMETER AND 8" LONG. C — 2 PIECES ¾" THICK AND 13½" x 5½". D — 2 PIECES ¾" THICK AND 15" x 5½". ONE PIECE RUBBER 1" THICK AND 15½" x 15½". ONE YARD OF FABRIC. SEE GENERAL INSTRUCTIONS ON PAGE 54.

AFTER THE MATERIAL IS READY TO BE ASSEMBLED, JOIN AS FOLLOWS:

(1) "A" WITH "B" (2) "A" WITH "C" AND "D." APPLY THE UPHOLSTERY MATERIAL (SEE ENLARGEMENT 2) AND YOU HAVE COMPLETED YOUR STOOL.

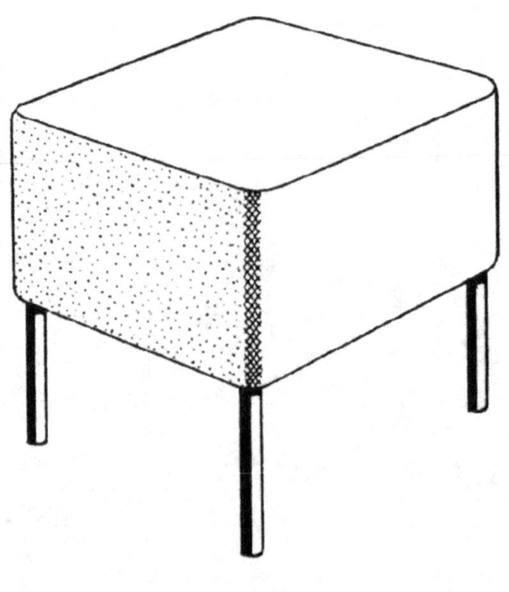

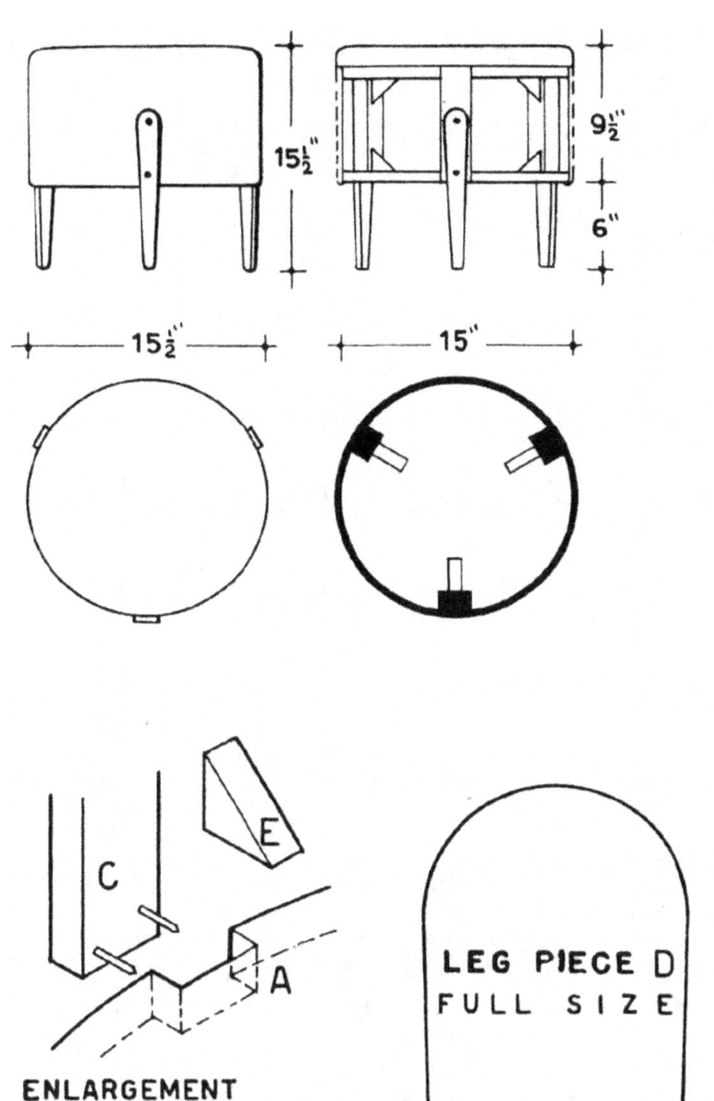

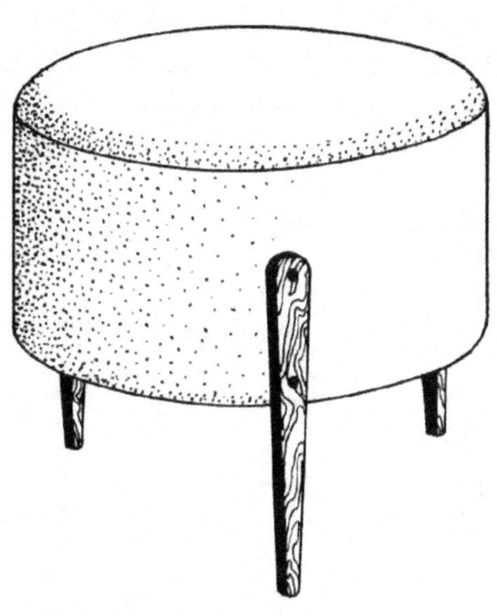

STOOL

LIST OF MATERIALS.

A — 2 PIECES ¾" THICK AND 15" DIAMETER. B — 1 PIECE CARDBOARD 50" x 8". C — 3 PIECES ¾" THICK AND 8" x 2". D — 3 PIECES ⅞" THICK AND 11" x 1½". E — 6 PIECES 1" THICK AND 3" x 3". ONE PIECE RUBBER 1" THICK AND 15½" IN DIAMETER. ONE YARD OF FABRIC.

SEE GENERAL INSTRUCTIONS ON PAGE 54.

WHEN THE MATERIAL IS READY FOR ASSEMBLING PROCEED AS FOLLOWS:

JOIN (1) "A" WITH "C" (2) "E" WITH "A,C" (3) "B" WITH "A,C" (4) APPLY THE UPHOLSTERY MATERIAL (SEE ENLARGEMENT 2 PAGE 98) (5) FINISH THE LEGS IN A NATURAL FINISH (SEE PAGE 14) AND APPLY THEM TO COMPLETE THE STOOL.

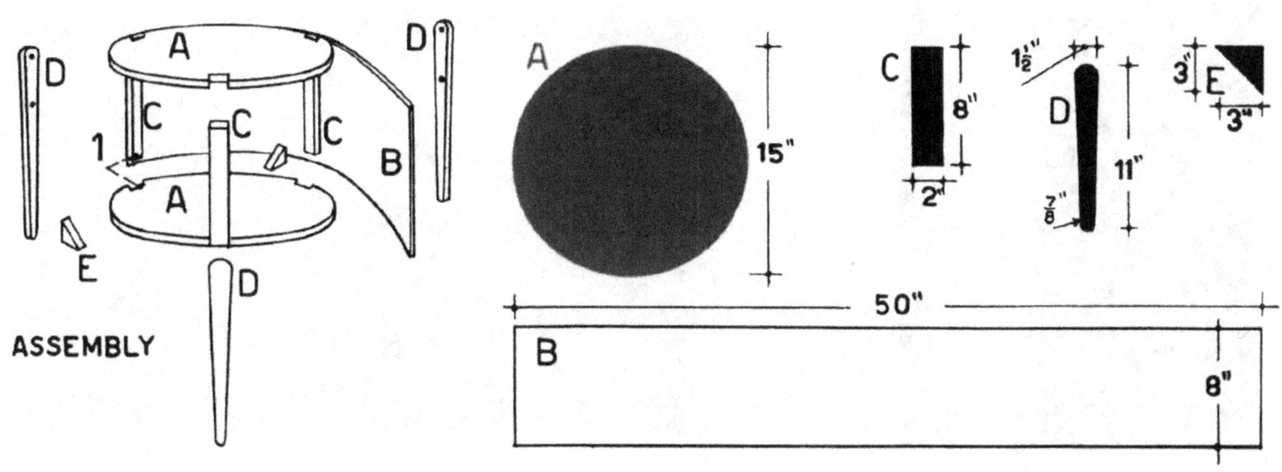

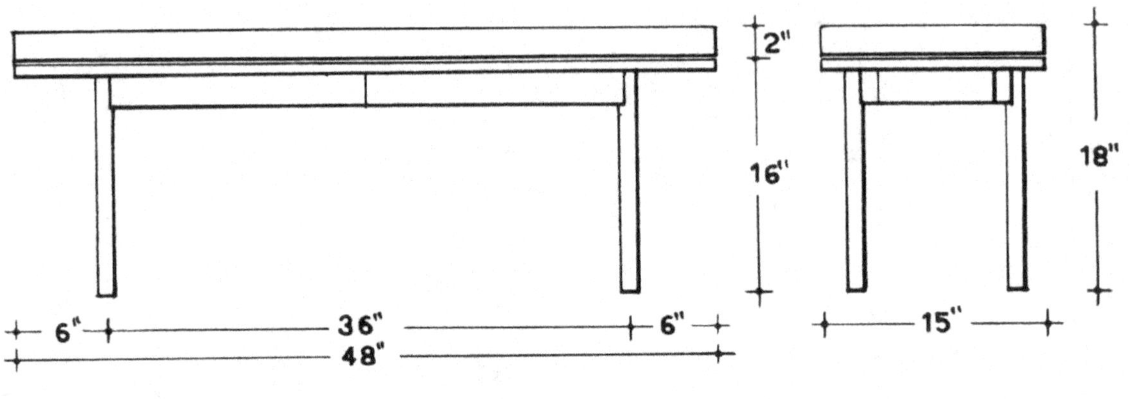

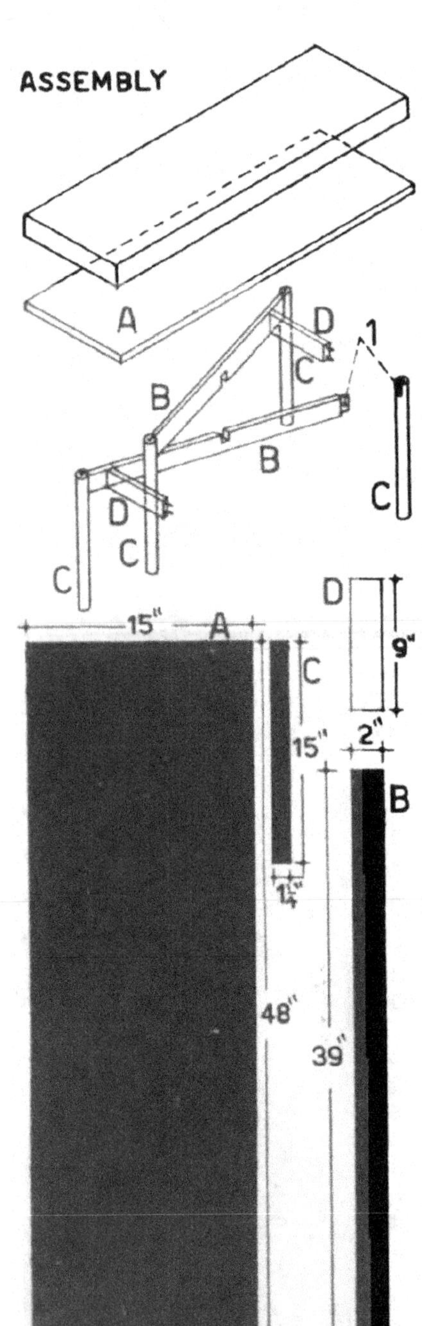

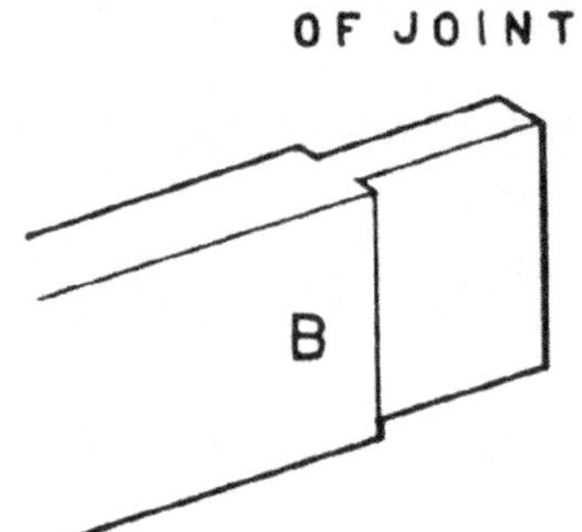

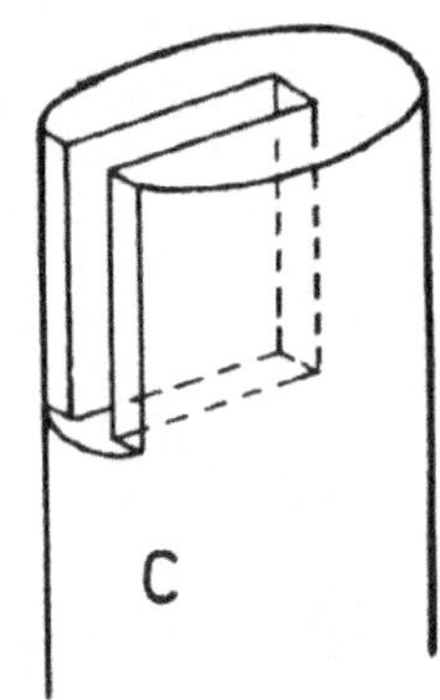

BENCH

LIST OF MATERIALS.

A — 1 PIECE ¾" THICK AND 48" x 15". B — 2 PIECES 1" THICK AND 39" x 2". C — 4 PIECES 1¼" DIAMETER AND 15" LONG. D — 2 PIECES 1" THICK AND 9" x 2". ONE PIECE RUBBER 2" THICK AND 15" x 48". FABRIC 1½ YARDS.

FOR GENERAL INSTRUCTIONS SEE PAGE 54.

WHEN THE MATERIAL IS READY, ASSEMBLE AS FOLLOWS:

JOIN (1) "B" WITH "C" (2) "B" WITH "B" (3) "B" WITH "D" (4) "A" WITH "B,D" (5) MAKE THE RUBBER CUSHION AND YOU HAVE COMPLETED THE BENCH. FOR NATURAL FINISH SEE PAGE 14.

CHAIR

LIST OF MATERIALS.

1 PIECE OF PLYWOOD ¾" THICK AND 30" x 36". FROM THIS PIECE MAY BE DERIVED ALL THE COMPONENT PARTS OF THE CHAIR AS INDICATED IN THE SIDE DRAWING. NOTE "E" AND "F" REQUIRE TWO PIECES EACH.

SEE GENERAL INSTRUCTIONS ON PAGE 54.

AFTER THE MATERIAL IS READY TO BE ASSEMBLED, PROCEED TO JOIN AS FOLLOWS:

(1) "A" WITH "F" (2) "A" WITH "B" (3) "E" WITH "A,B" (4) "C" WITH "A,F" (5) "D" WITH "A,B" TO COMPLETE YOUR CHAIR.

FOR FINISH SEE INSTRUCTIONS ON PAGE 14.

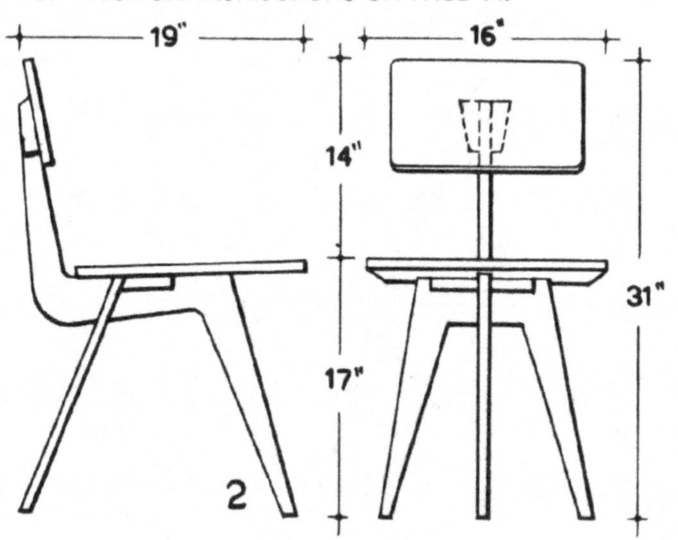

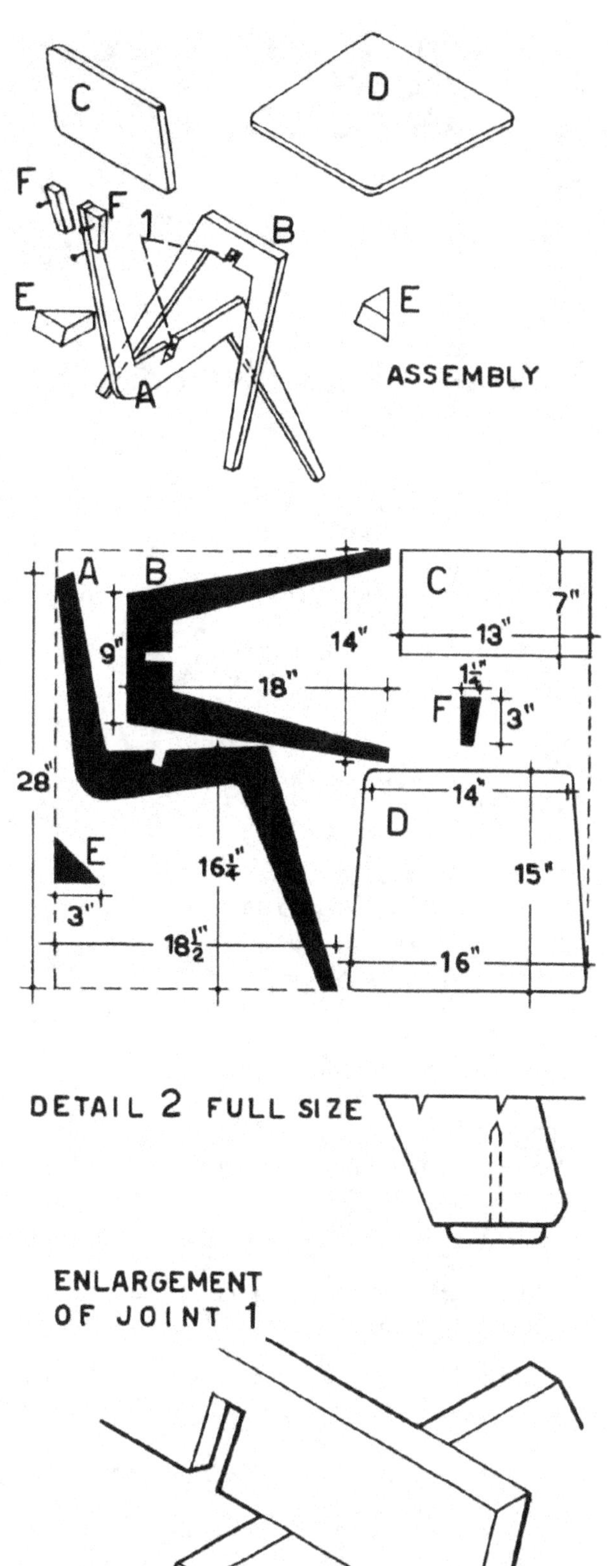

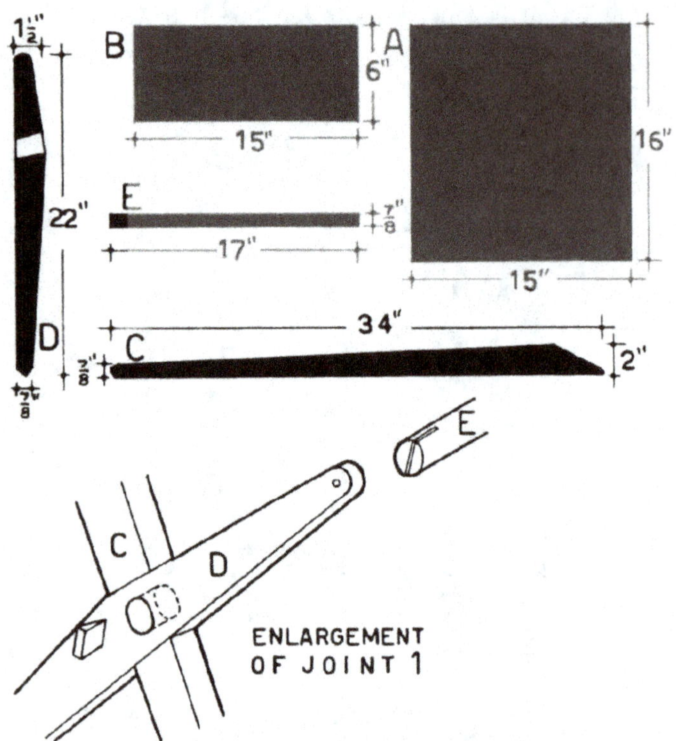

ENLARGEMENT OF JOINT 1

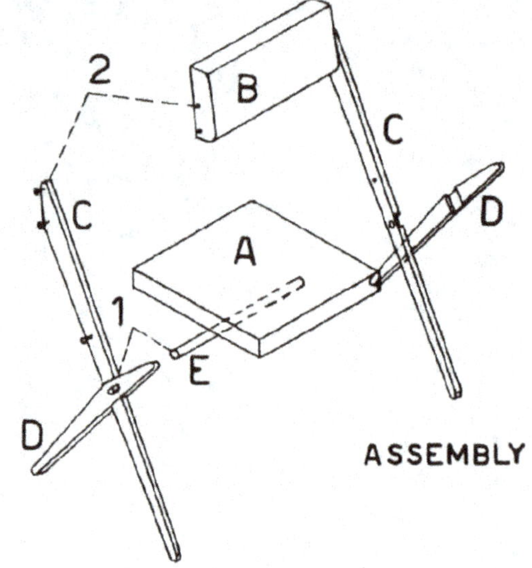

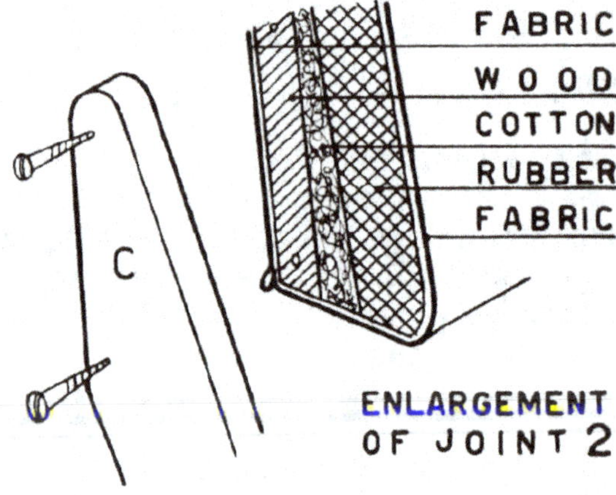

ENLARGEMENT OF JOINT 2

CHAIR

LIST OF MATERIALS.

A — 1 PIECE ½" THICK AND 15" x 16". B — 1 PIECE ½" THICK AND 15" x 6". C — 2 PIECES 1" THICK AND 34" x 2". D — 2 PIECES 1" THICK AND 22" x 1½". E — 1 PIECE ⅞" DIAMETER AND 17" LONG. ONE PIECE RUBBER 1" THICK AND 16" x 24". FABRIC ¾ YARDS.

SEE GENERAL INSTRUCTIONS ON PAGE 54.

WHEN THE MATERIAL IS READY TO BE ASSEMBLED, PROCEED AS FOLLOWS:

JOIN (1) "C" WITH "D" (2) "E" WITH "C,D" (3) COMPLETE THE FRAME WITH NATURAL FINISH (SEE PAGE 14) (4) APPLY THE UPHOLSTERY MATERIAL ON PIECES "A" AND "B" (SEE ENLARGEMENT AND DETAIL 1 ON PAGE 103) (5) APPLY THE SEAT AND BACK ON THE FRAME AND YOU HAVE COMPLETED YOUR CHAIR.

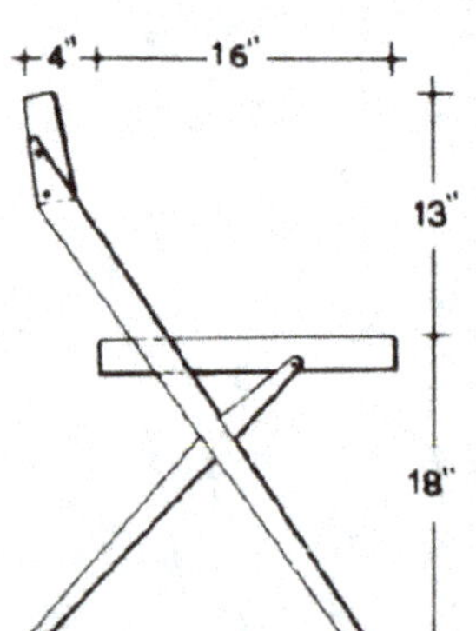

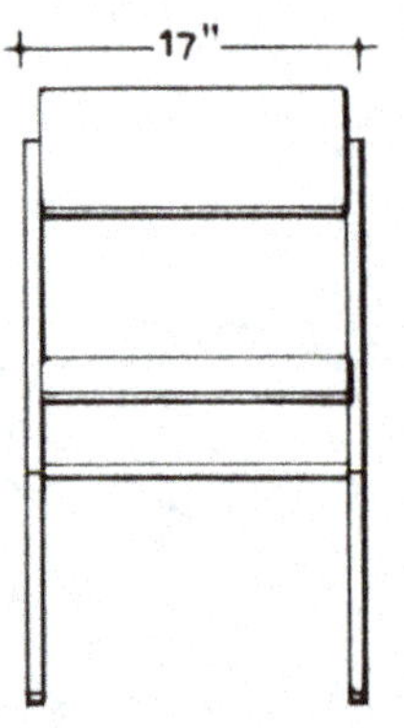

CHAIR

LIST OF MATERIALS.

A — 2 PIECES ⅞″ THICK AND 32½″ x 3″. B — 2 PIECES ⅞″ THICK AND 15″ x 2½″. C — 2 PIECES ⅞″ THICK AND 13″ x 2″. D — 2 PIECES ¾″ THICK AND 13″ x 1¼″. E — 2 PIECES ⅞″ THICK AND 17″ x 2¼″. F — 1 PIECE ½″ THICK AND 17″ x 15″. ONE PIECE RUBBER 1″ THICK AND 18″ x 16″. FABRIC 1 YARD.

SEE GENERAL INSTRUCTIONS ON PAGE 54.

WHEN THE MATERIAL IS READY TO ASSEMBLE, PROCEED AS FOLLOWS:

JOIN (1) "A" WITH "B" (2) "B" WITH "E" (3) "C" AND "D" WITH "A,B,E" (4) COMPLETE THE FRAME WITH NATURAL FINISH (5) APPLY THE UPHOLSTERY MATERIAL ON THE SEAT (6) JOIN "F" WITH "C" (7) APPLY THE UPHOLSTERY MATERIAL ON THE BACK (SEE PAGE 108) AND YOU HAVE COMPLETED YOUR CHAIR.

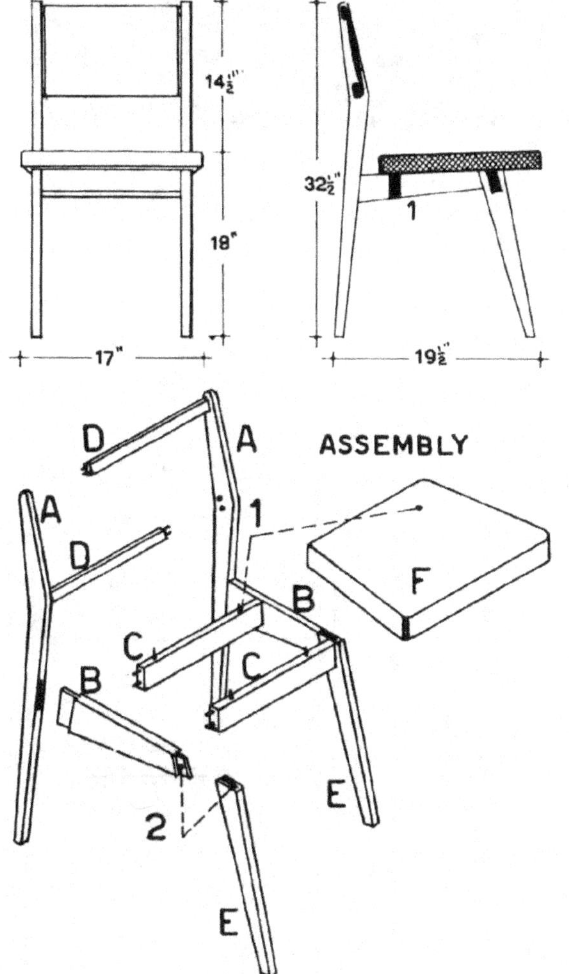

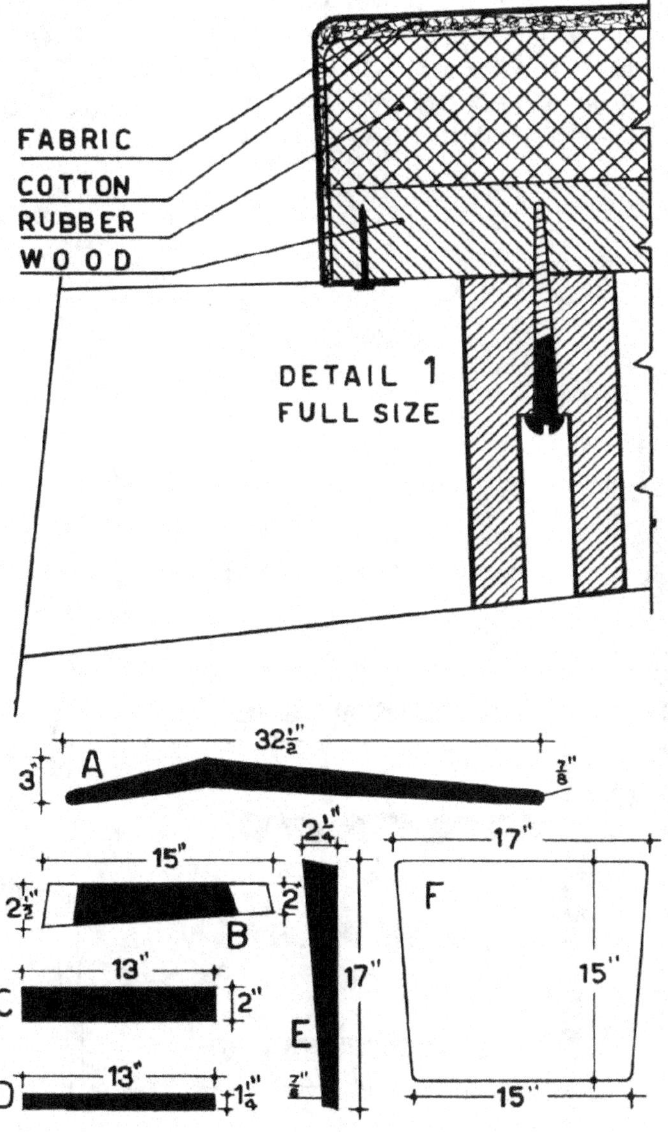

ARM CHAIR

LIST OF MATERIALS.

A — 2 PIECES 1⅛" THICK AND 31½" x 3".
B — 1 PIECE ½" THICK AND 17" x 19".
C — 2 PIECES 1⅛" THICK AND 24" x 2".
D — 2 PIECES 1⅛" THICK AND 14" x 1½".
E — 2 PIECES ¾" THICK AND 19" x 1¼".
F — 2 PIECES 1" THICK AND 19" x 2". G —
2 PIECES 1" THICK AND 15" x 1½". ONE
PIECE RUBBER 1" THICK AND 17½" x 19½".
FABRIC 1⅜ YARDS.

SEE GENERAL INSTRUCTIONS ON PAGE 54.
AFTER THE MATERIAL IS READY TO BE
ASSEMBLED, JOIN AS FOLLOWS:

(1) "D" WITH "A" AND "C" (2) "G" WITH
"F" (3) "A,D,C" WITH "E,F" (4) FINISH THE
FRAME WITH NATURAL FINISH (SEE PAGE
14) (5) APPLY THE UPHOLSTERY MATERIAL
ON THE SEAT "B" (SEE DETAIL 1 PAGE 103)
(6) JOIN "B" WITH "F,G" (7) APPLY UP-
HOLSTERY TO BACK (SEE PAGE 108) AND
YOU HAVE COMPLETED YOUR ARM CHAIR.

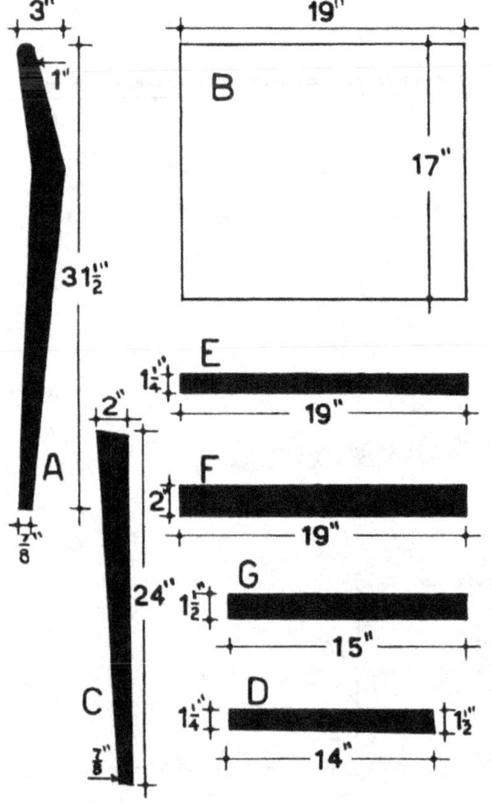

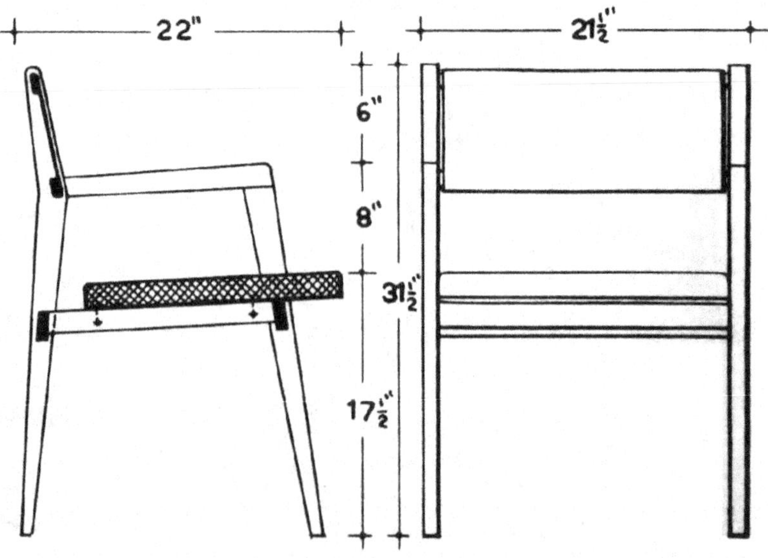

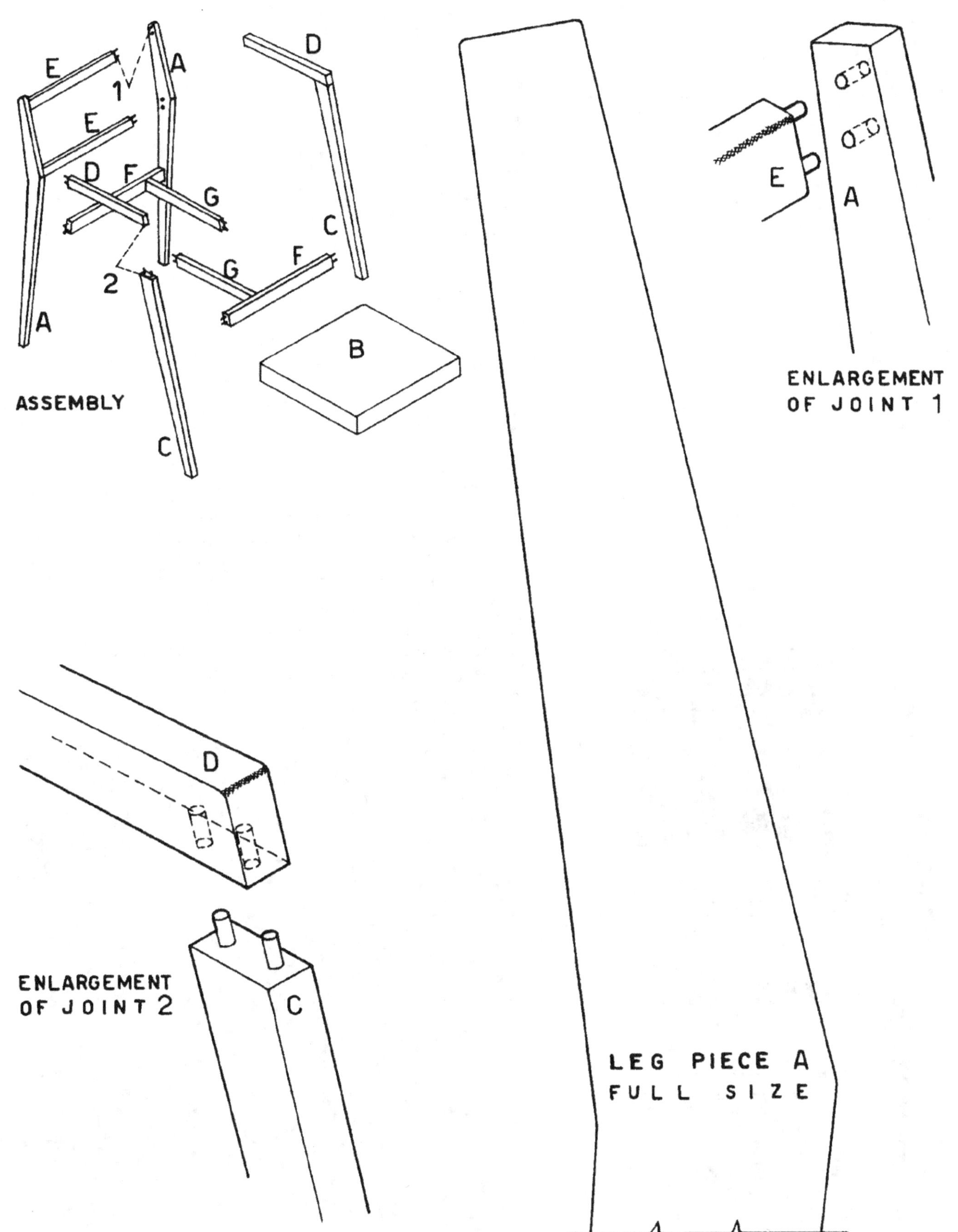

E
A
1
E
D
D
F
G
A
G
F
C
2
B
C
ASSEMBLY
C
ENLARGEMENT
OF JOINT 1
E
A
D
ENLARGEMENT
OF JOINT 2
C
LEG PIECE A
FULL SIZE

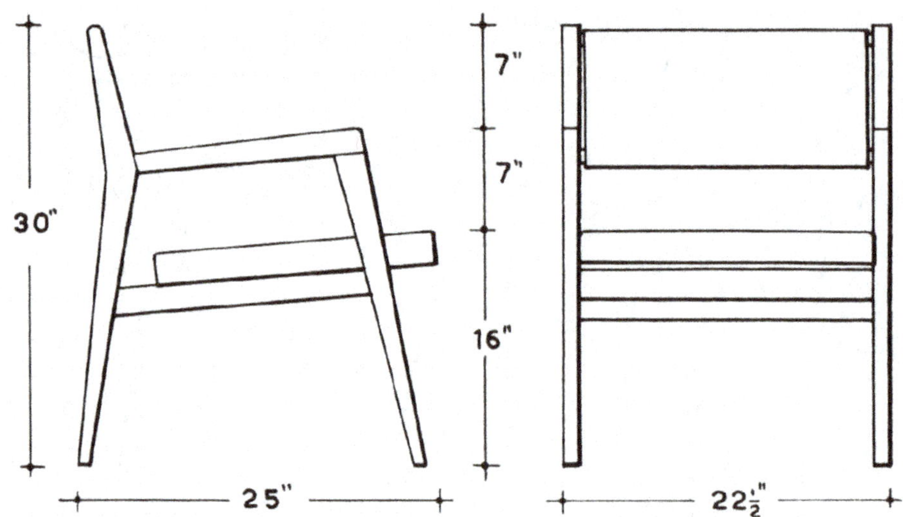

ARM CHAIR

LIST OF MATERIALS.

A — 2 PIECES 1⅛″ THICK AND 30″ x 4″. B — 1 PIECE ½″ THICK AND 20″ x 19″. C — 2 PIECES 1⅛″ THICK AND 22″ x 2″. D — 2 PIECES 1⅛″ THICK AND 16″ x 1½″. E — 2 PIECES ¾″ THICK AND 20″ x 1¼″. F — 2 PIECES 1″ THICK AND 20″ x 2″. G — 2 PIECES 1″ THICK AND 18″ x 2″. ONE PIECE RUBBER 1″ THICK AND 20½″ x 19½″. FABRIC 1⅜ YARDS.

FOR GENERAL INSTRUCTIONS SEE PAGE 54.

WHEN THE MATERIALS ARE READY FOR ASSEMBLING, JOIN THE PIECES FOLLOWING THE SAME DIRECTIONS AS FOR THE ARM CHAIR ON PAGE 104.

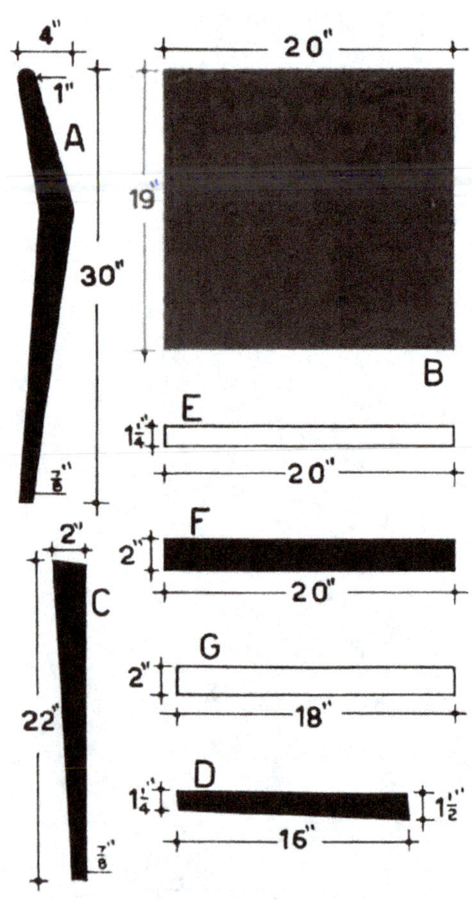

ARMLESS CHAIR

LIST OF MATERIALS.

A — 2 PIECES 1″ THICK AND 30″ x 3½″. B — 2 PIECES 1″ THICK AND 15″ x 2″. C — 1 PIECE ½″ THICK AND 20″ x 19″. D — 2 PIECES 1″ THICK AND 19½″ x 3″. E — 1 PIECE 1″ THICK AND 16″ x 2½″. F — 1 PIECE 1″ THICK AND 16″ x 2″. G — 2 PIECES ¾″ THICK AND 19″ x 1¼″. ONE PIECE RUBBER 1″ THICK AND 20½″ x 19½″. FABRIC 1⅜ YARDS.

FOR GENERAL INSTRUCTIONS SEE PAGE 54.

WHEN THE MATERIAL IS READY TO BE ASSEMBLED, JOIN AS FOLLOWS:

(1) "D" WITH "B" (2) "D" WITH "A" (3) "E," "F" AND "G" WITH "A,B,D" (4) COMPLETE THE FRAME IN NATURAL FINISH (SEE PAGE 14) (5) APPLY THE UPHOLSTERY MATERIAL ON SEAT ("C") (6) JOIN "C" WITH "E,F" (7) APPLY THE UPHOLSTERY TO BACK AND YOU HAVE COMPLETED YOUR ARMLESS CHAIR.

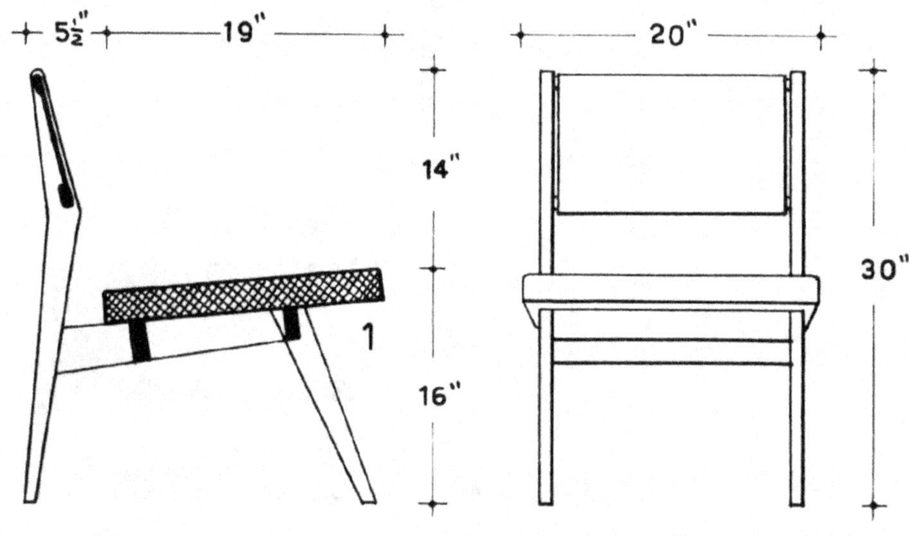

DETAIL 1 FULL SIZE

ASSEMBLY

ENLARGEMENT OF JOINT 2

ENLARGEMENT OF JOINT 3

UPHOLSTERED BACK

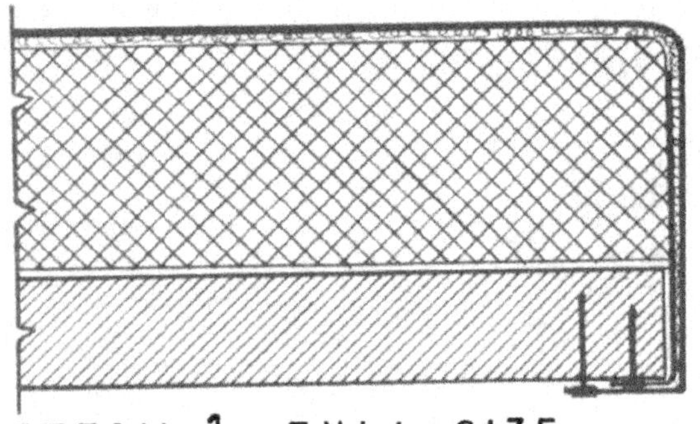

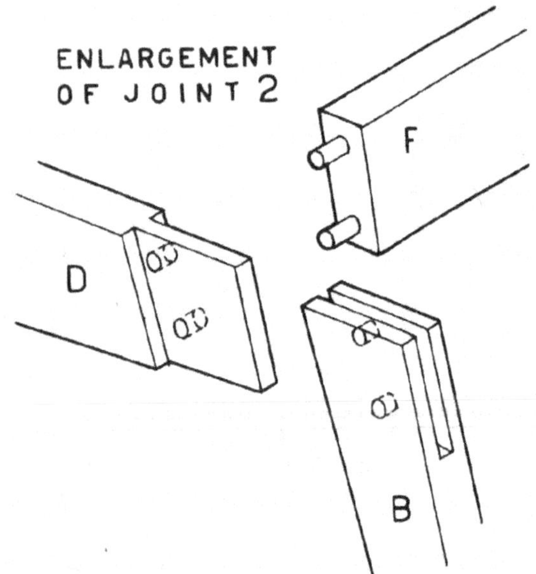

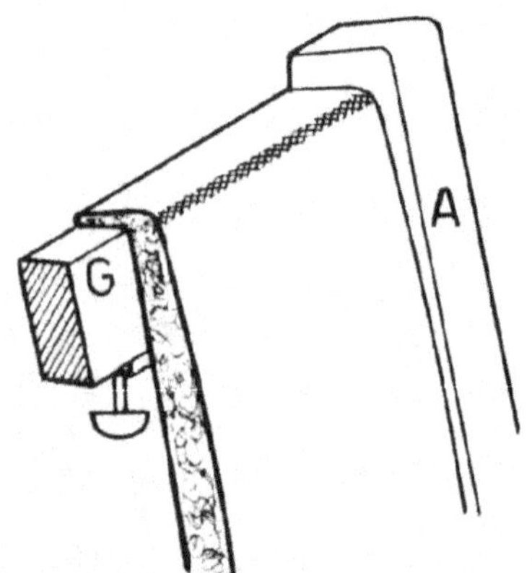

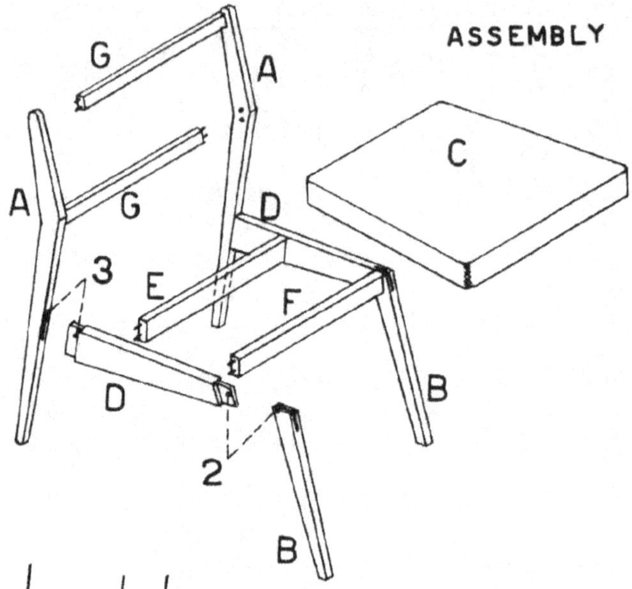

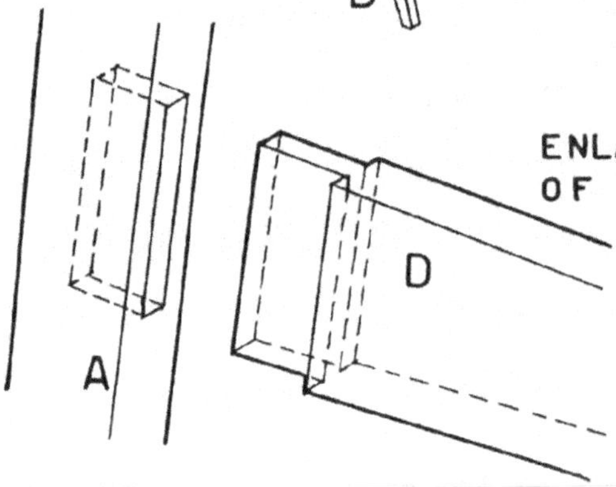

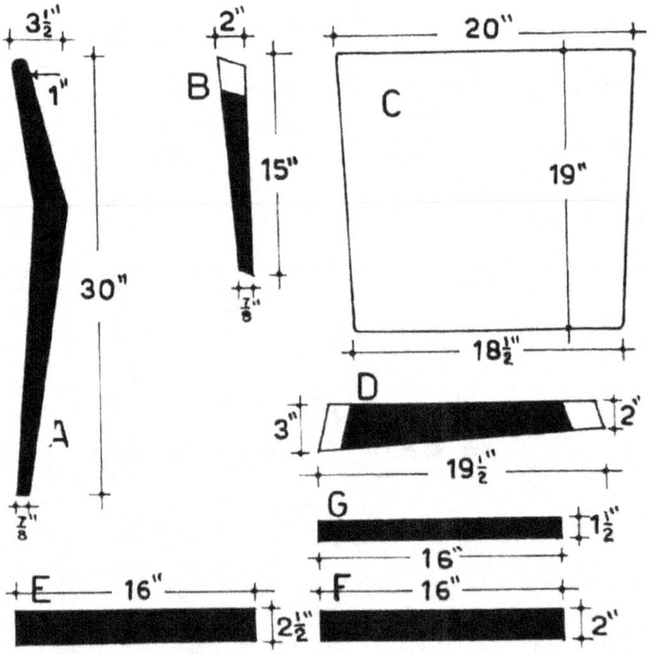

LIVING ROOM   GROUP I

INSTRUCTIONS FOR BUILDING THE PIECES SHOWN
HERE WILL BE FOUND ON THE FOLLOWING PAGES:
END (OR CORNER) TABLE, PAGE 82; ARMCHAIR,
PAGE 106; SOFA, PAGE 118; COFFEE TABLE, PAGE
100 (WITHOUT CUSHION); ARMLESS CHAIR, 107.

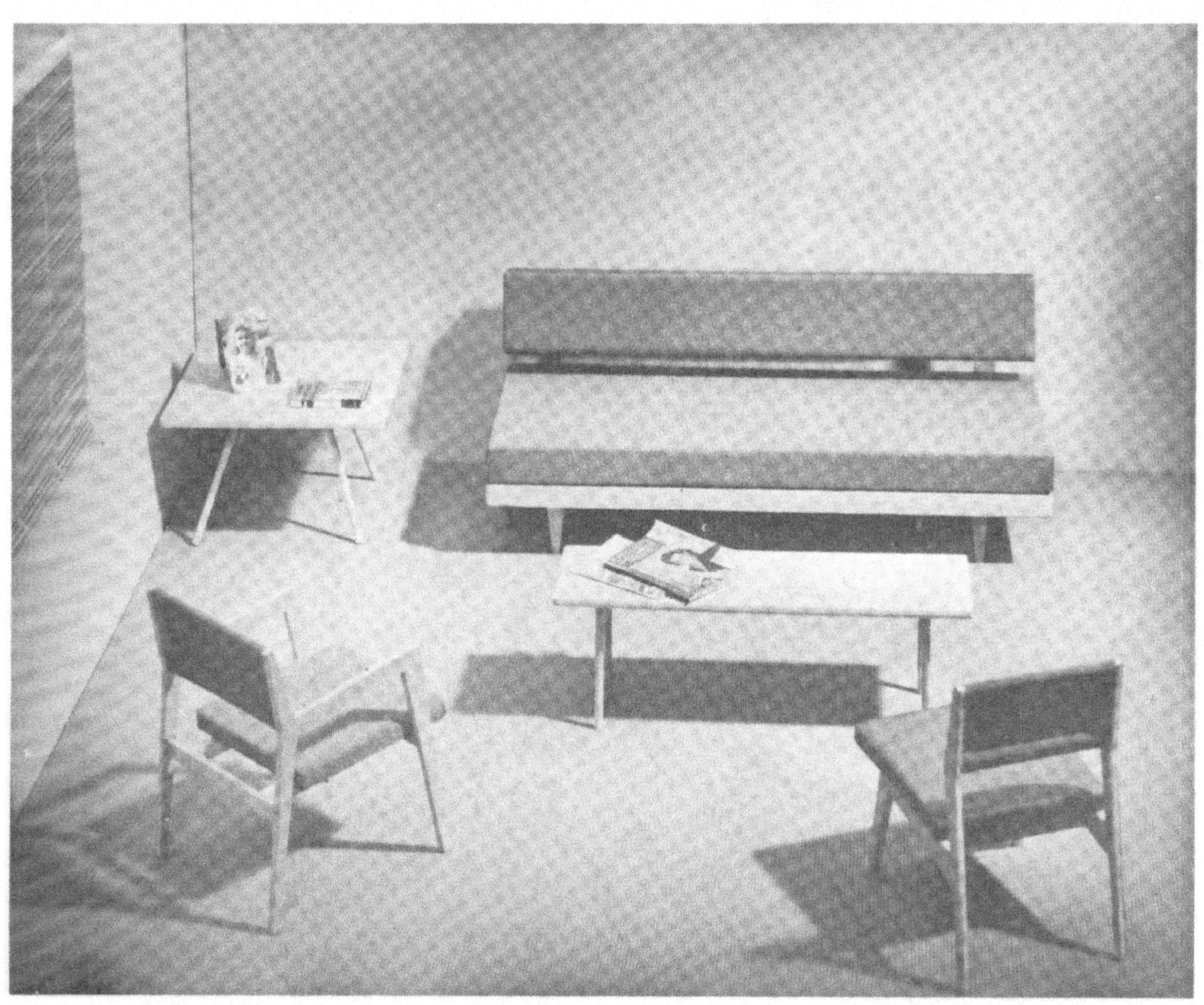

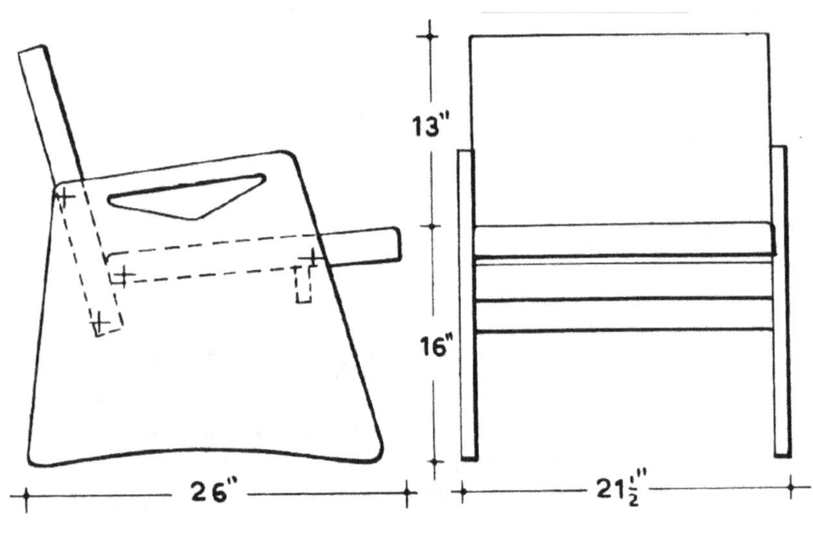
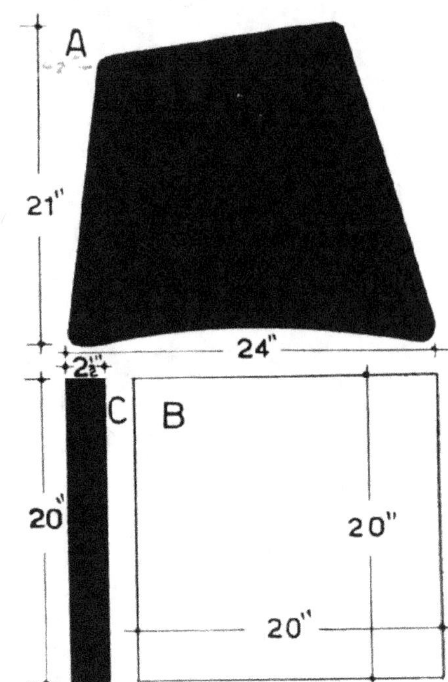

ARM CHAIR

LIST OF MATERIALS.

A — 2 PIECES ¾" THICK AND 24" x 21". B — 2 PIECES ¾" THICK AND 20" x 20". C — 1 PIECE 1" THICK AND 20" x 2½". ONE PIECE RUBBER 1" THICK AND 21" x 42". TWO YARDS OF FABRIC.

FOR GENERAL INSTRUCTIONS SEE PAGE 54. WHEN THE MATERIAL IS READY, PROCEED TO JOIN THE PIECES IN THE FOLLOWING MANNER:

(1) APPLY THE UPHOLSTERY MATERIAL ON SEAT AND BACK ("B"). (SEE PAGE 108, DETAIL 1) (2) COMPLETE THE "A" PIECES WITH THE NATURAL FINISH. (3) JOIN "A" WITH "B" AND "C" AND YOU HAVE COMPLETED YOUR ARM CHAIR.

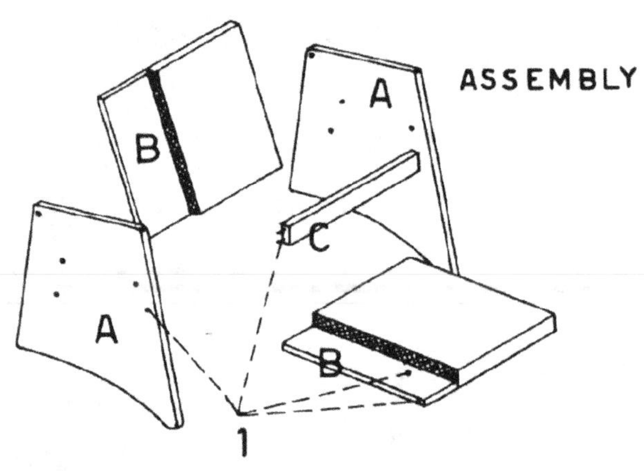

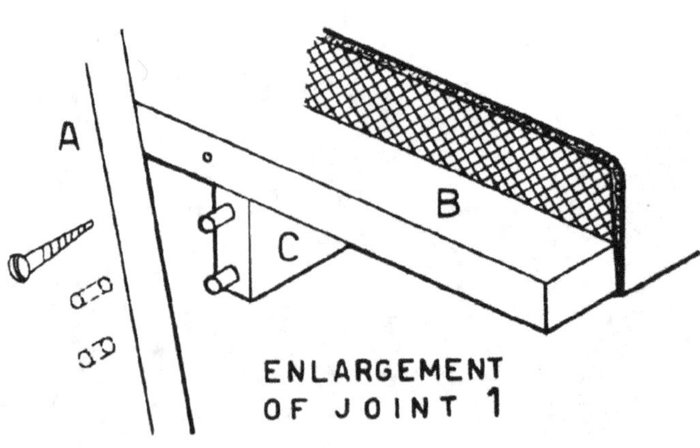

ARM CHAIR

LIST OF MATERIALS.
(USE HARDWOOD FOR VIEW PART AND SOFT WOOD FOR COVERED PART.)
A — 2 PIECES 1⅜" THICK AND 19½" x 2". B — 2 PIECES 1⅜" THICK AND 21" x 2". C — 2 PIECES 1⅜" THICK AND 20½" x 1½". D — 1 PIECE 1⅜" THICK AND 22½" x 2". E — 1 PIECE 1" THICK AND 20½" x 2½". F — 1 PIECE 1" THICK AND 22" x 4". G — 2 PIECES 1" THICK AND 20½" x 6½". H — 2 PIECES 1" THICK AND 19½" x 4". K — 2 PIECES 1" THICK AND 26" x 4". ALSO 7 YARDS COMMON WEBBING, 4 YARDS NO-SAG SPRINGS, 20 EXTENSION SPRINGS. ONE PIECE RUBBER 1" THICK AND 23" x 40", FABRIC, 2½ YARDS.

FOR GENERAL INSTRUCTIONS SEE PAGE 54.
WHEN THE MATERIAL IS READY TO BE ASSEMBLED, JOIN THE PIECES IN THE FOLLOWING MANNER:
(1) "C" WITH "A" AND "B" (2) "D" WITH "B" (3) COMPLETE THE FRAME WITH NATURAL FINISH (SEE PAGE 14). (4) JOIN "H" WITH "E" AND "G." (5) "K" WITH "F" AND "G" (SEE PAGES 112 AND 117) (6) APPLY THE WEBBING ON THE BACK AND NO-SAG SPRINGS ON THE SEAT AND ALSO UPHOLSTERY MATERIAL (SEE DETAIL PAGES 112 AND 113). JOIN (7) "G" WITH "G" WITH BOLTS (8) "A, B, C" WITH "H" AND "K" AND YOU HAVE COMPLETED YOUR ARM CHAIR.

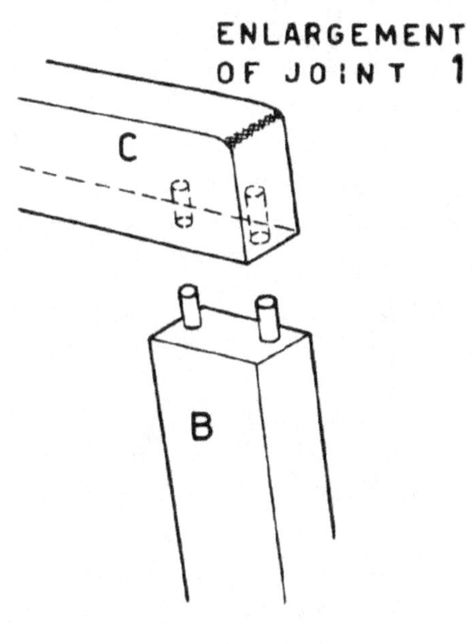

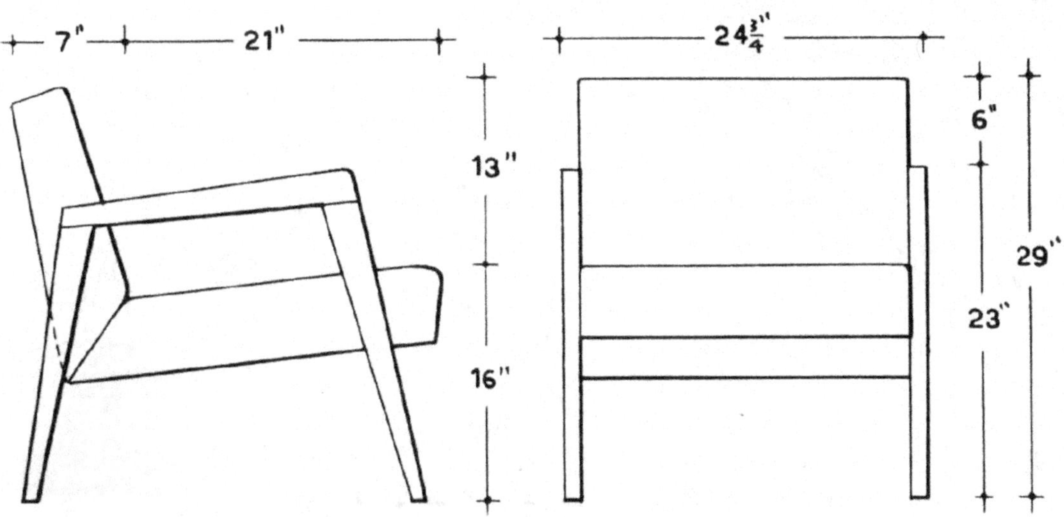

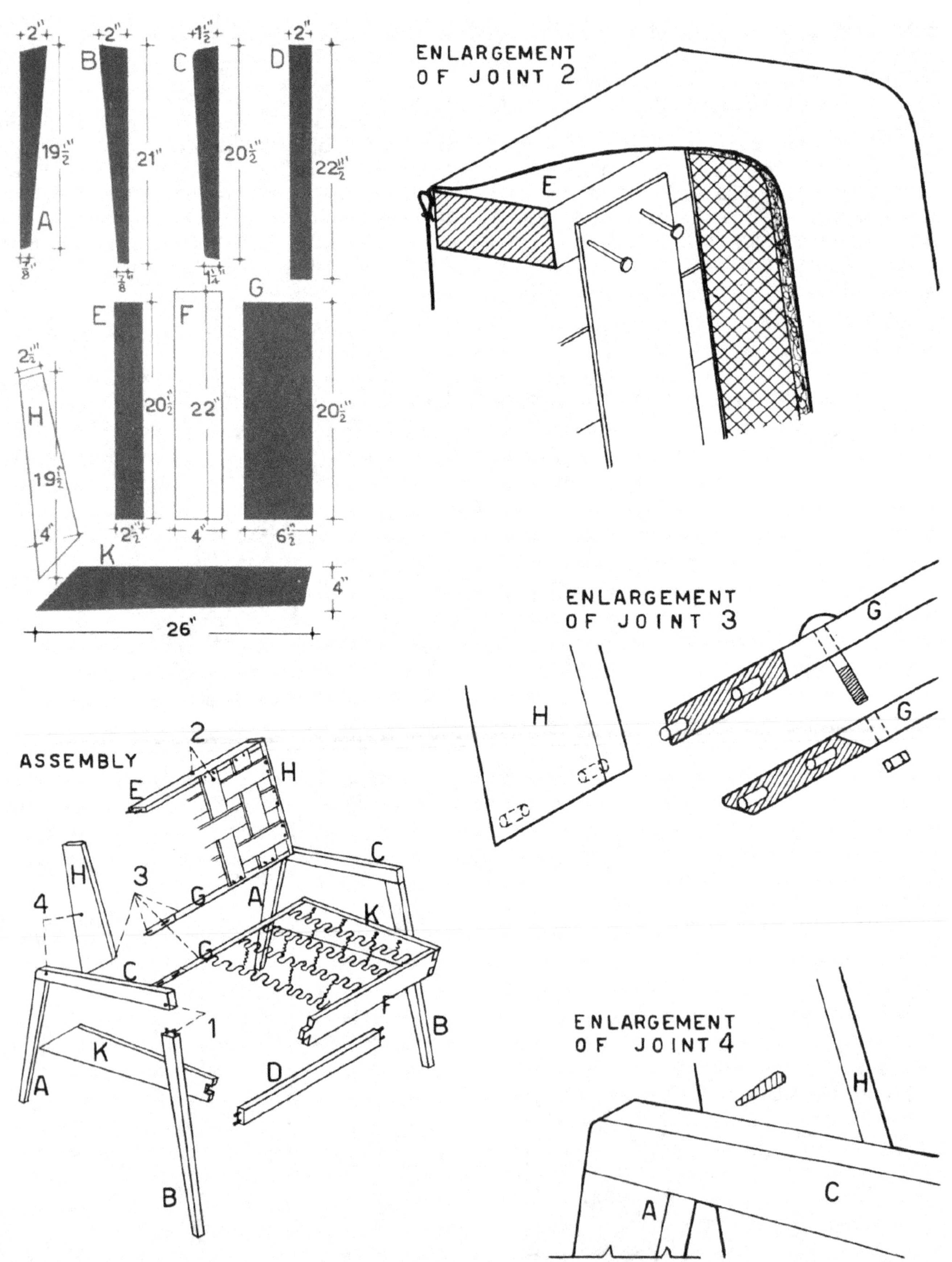

2"
B 2"
C 1½"
D 2"
19½"
21"
20½"
22½"
A
⅞
⅞
1¼
E
F
G
2½"
H
20½"
22"
20½"
19½"
4"
2½"
4"
6½"
K
4"
26"

ENLARGEMENT OF JOINT 2
E

ENLARGEMENT OF JOINT 3
G
H
G

ENLARGEMENT OF JOINT 4
H
A
C

ASSEMBLY
2
E
H
H
C
3
G
A
4
G
K
C
1
K
D
F
B
A
B

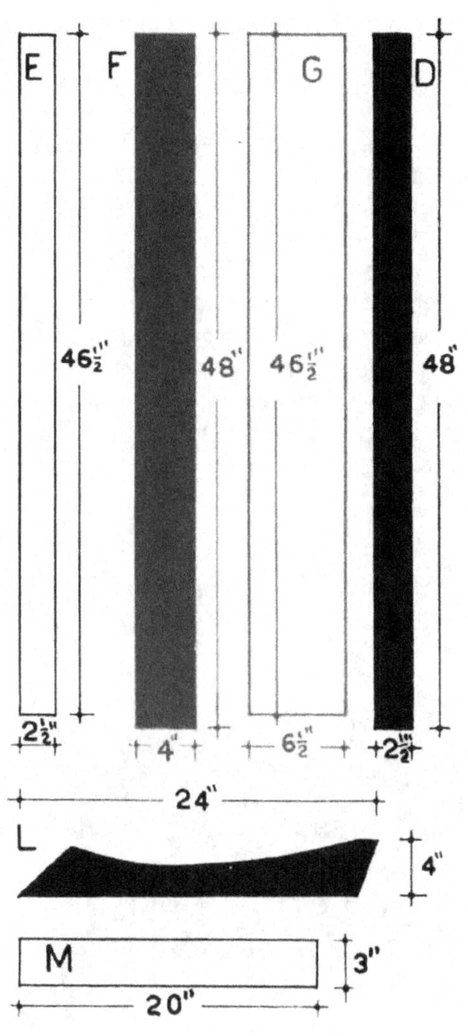

LOVE SEAT

LIST OF MATERIALS.

USE SAME LIST OF MATERIALS AS APPLIED TO ARMCHAIR ON PAGE 111, EXCEPT FOR THE FOLLOWING VARIATIONS:

E — 1 PIECE 1" THICK AND 46½" x 2½". F — 1 PIECE 1" THICK AND 48" x 4". G — 2 PIECES 1" THICK AND 46½" x 6½". D — 1 PIECE 1¼" THICK AND 48" x 2½". L — 1 PIECE 1" THICK AND 24" x 4". M — 1 PIECE 1" THICK AND 20" x 3". THIRTEEN YARDS OF WEBBING, 8 YARDS OF NO-SAG SPRING, 30 EXTENSION SPRINGS, ONE PIECE OF RUBBER 1¼" THICK AND 49" x 40". FABRIC 4½ YARDS.

FOR GENERAL INSTRUCTIONS SEE PAGE 54.

WHEN THE MATERIAL IS READY FOR ASSEMBLING, JOIN THE PARTS USING THE SAME PROCEDURE AS FOR ARM CHAIR SHOWN ON PAGE 111.

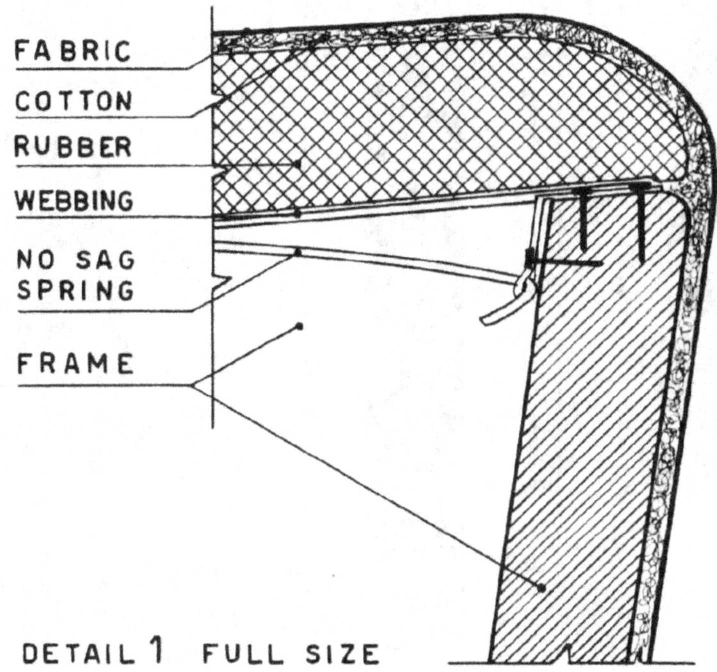

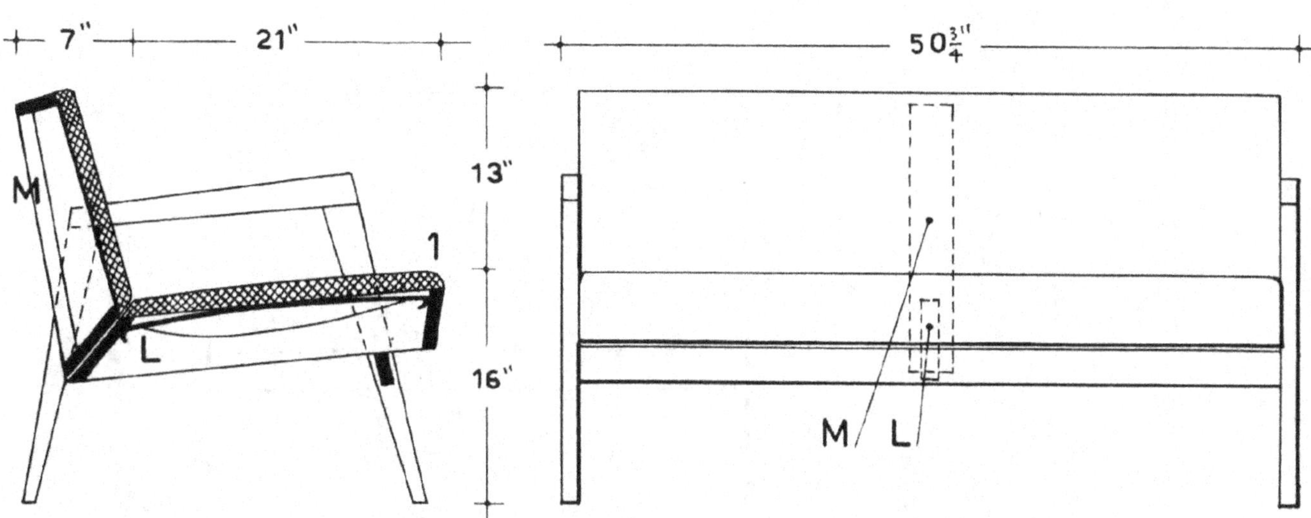

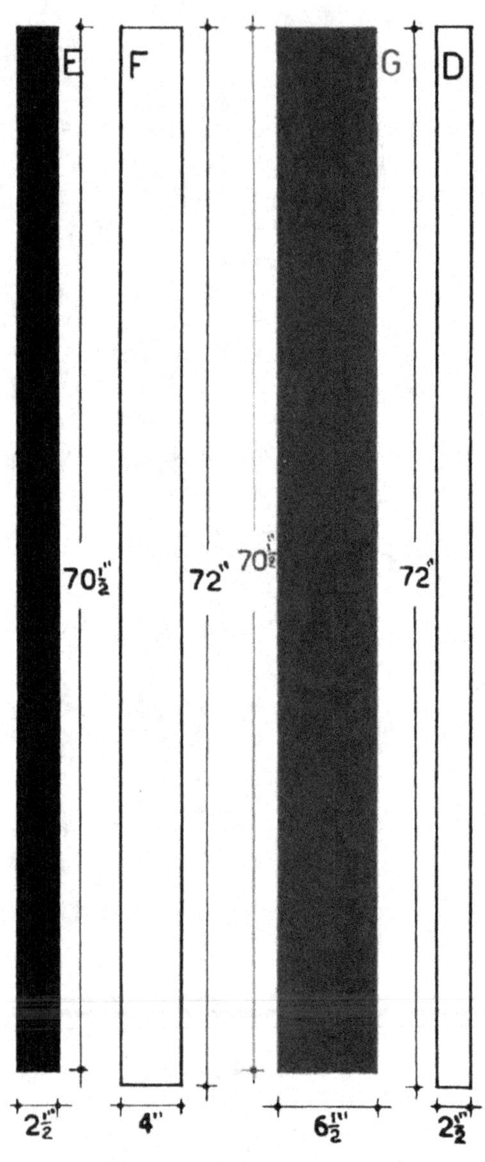

SOFA

LIST OF MATERIALS.

USE THE SAME LIST AS FOR ARM CHAIR ON PAGE 111 EXCEPT FOR THE FOLLOWING VARIATIONS:

E — 1 PIECE 1" THICK AND 70½" x 2½". F — 1 PIECE 1" THICK AND 72" x 4". G — 2 PIECES 1" THICK AND 70½" x 6½". D — 1 PIECE 1¼" THICK AND 72" x 2½". L — 2 PIECES 1" THICK AND 24" x 4". M — 2 PIECES 1" THICK AND 20" x 3" (SEE PAGE 113). TWENTY YARDS OF WEBBING, 12 YARDS OF NO-SAG SPRING, AND 50 EXTENSION SPRINGS. ONE PIECE OF RUBBER 1¼" THICK AND 73" x 40". FABRIC 6½ YARDS FOR GENERAL INSTRUCTIONS SEE PAGE 54. AFTER THE MATERIAL IS READY FOR ASSEMBLING, USE SAME PROCEDURE AS FOR ASSEMBLING OF ARM CHAIR ON PAGE 111. SEE PAGE 14 FOR FINISH.

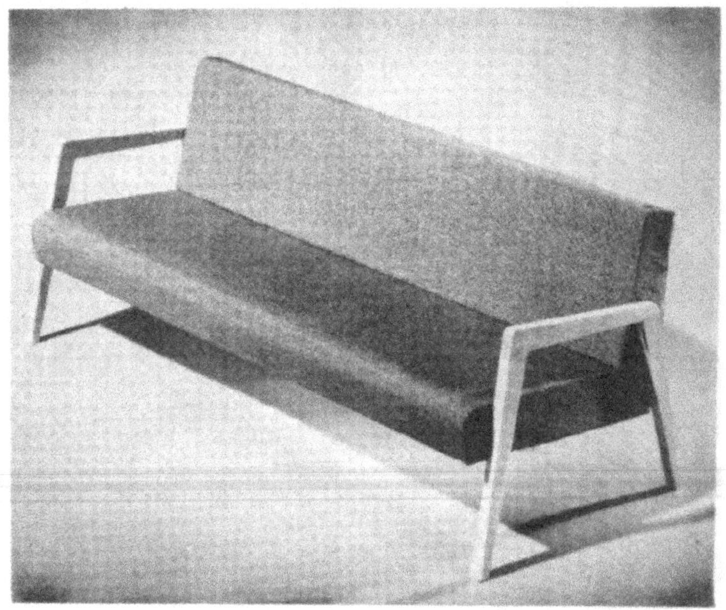

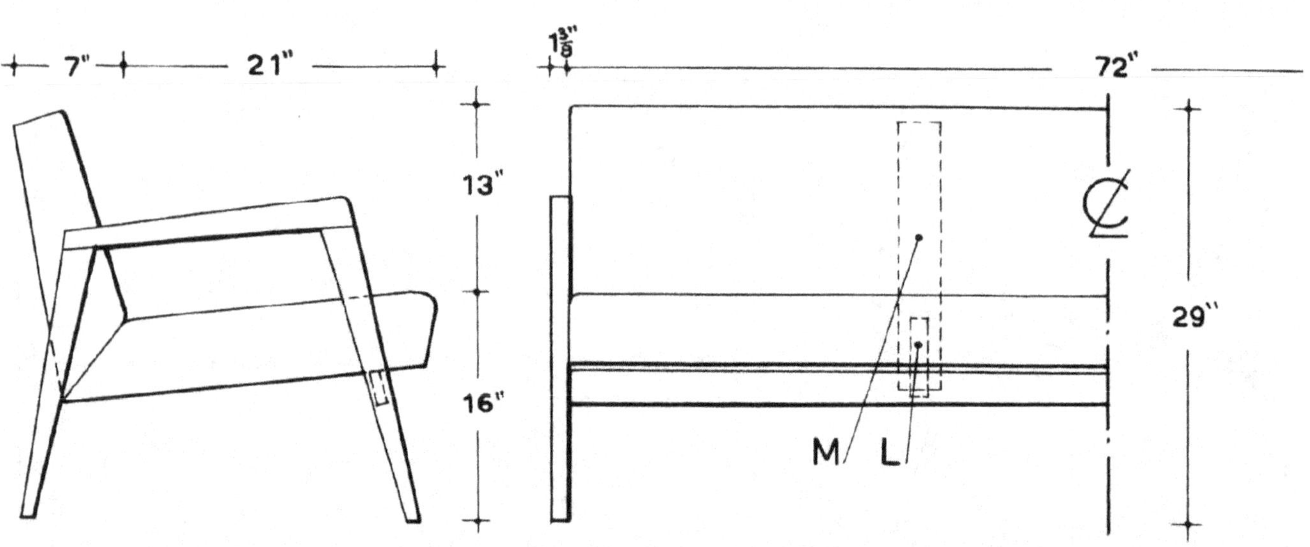

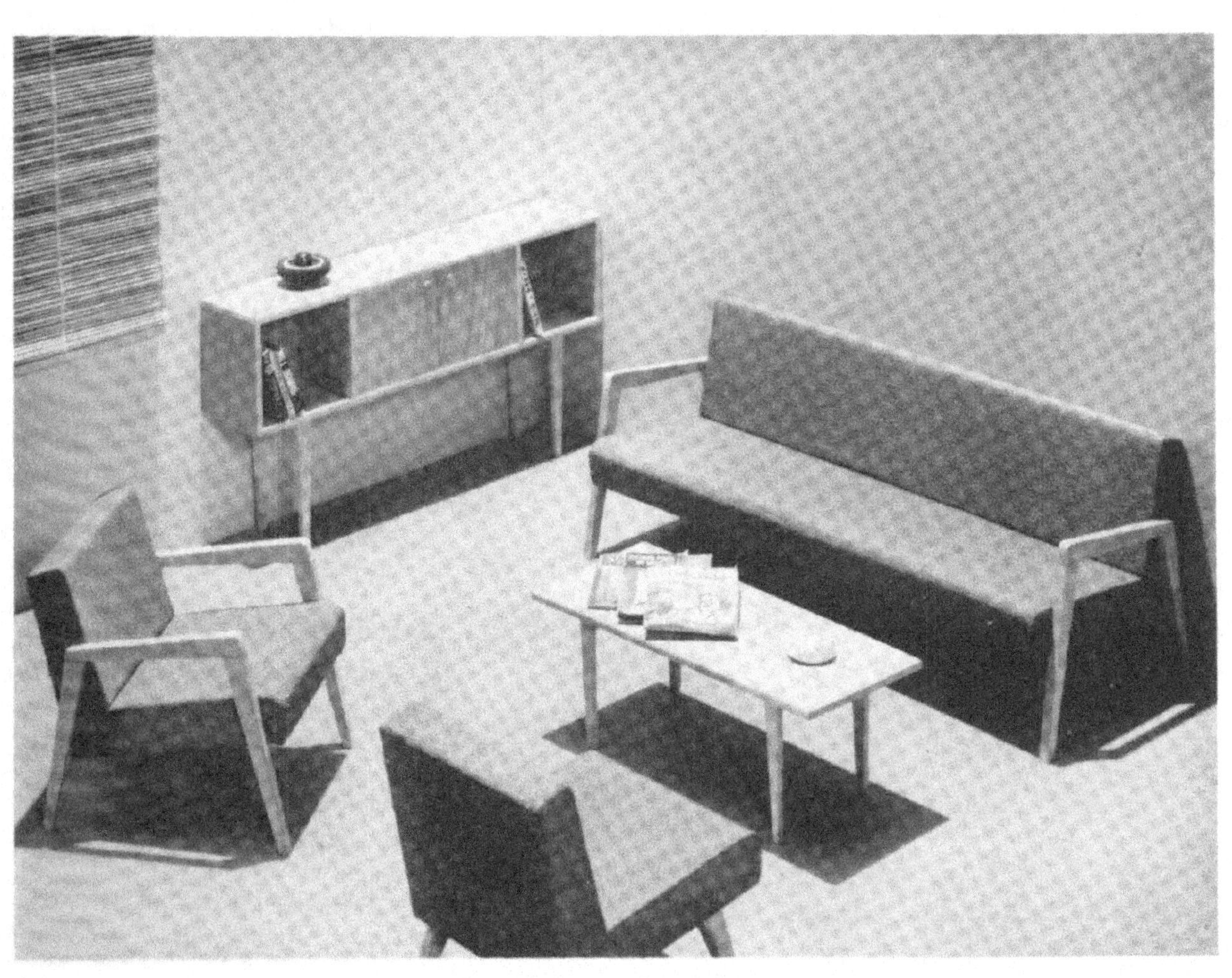

LIVING ROOM   GROUP II

INSTRUCTIONS FOR BUILDING THE PIECES SHOWN
HERE WILL BE FOUND ON THE FOLLOWING PAGES:
ARMCHAIR, PAGE 111; BOOKCASE, PAGE 69; COF-
FEE TABLE, PAGE 78; SOFA, PAGE 114; ARMLESS
CHAIR, PAGE 116.

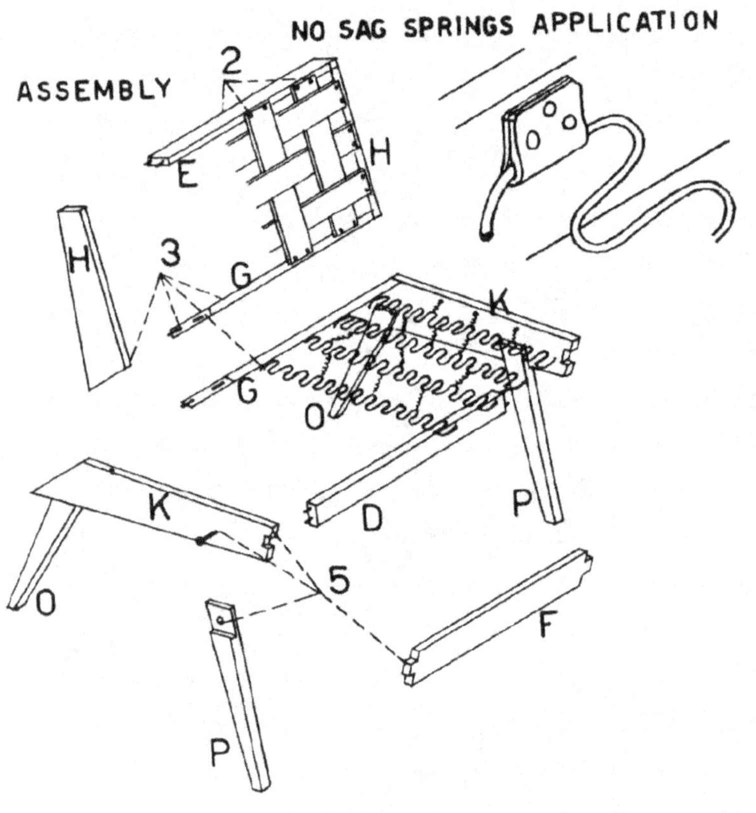

ARMLESS CHAIR

FOR "D, E, F, G, H, K" AND WEBBING, NO-SAG SPRING, EXTENSION SPRING, RUBBER, FABRIC, USE SAME LIST AS ARM CHAIR, PAGE 111. O — 2 PIECES 1¼" THICK AND 14" x 2½". P — 2 PIECES 1¼" THICK AND 14" x 2½".

LOVE SEAT (ARMLESS)

FOR "H" AND "K" USE SAME LIST AS ARM CHAIR, PAGE 111. FOR "E, F, G, D, L, M" AND WEBBING, NO-SAG SPRINGS, EXTENSION SPRING, RUBBER AND FABRIC, USE SAME LIST AS FOR LOVE SEAT PAGE 113. FOR "O" AND "P" USE SAME LIST AS ARMLESS CHAIR ABOVE.

SOFA (ARMLESS)

FOR "H" AND "K" USE SAME LIST AS ARM CHAIR PAGE 111. FOR "E, F, G, D, L, M" AND WEBBING, NO-SAG SPRING, EXTENSION SPRING, RUBBER, AND FABRIC, USE SAME LIST AS SOFA PAGE 114. FOR "O" AND "P" USE SAME LIST AS FOR ARMLESS CHAIR ABOVE.

SEE GENERAL INSTRUCTIONS ON PAGE 54. ASSEMBLY INSTRUCTIONS FOR PIECES SHOWN ON THIS PAGE.

WHEN THE MATERIAL IS READY TO BE ASSEMBLED, JOIN AS FOLLOWS:
(1) "H" WITH "E,G" (2) "K" WITH "F,G" (SEE PAGE 112 AND PAGE 117). (3) APPLY THE WEBBING ON BACK AND NO-SAG SPRING ON THE SEAT (SEE DETAILS PAGE 112 AND PAGE 113) AND COMPLETE WITH UPHOLSTERY MATERIAL. (4) JOIN "G" WITH "G" WITH BOLTS (5) COMPLETE THE LEGS "O" AND "P" WITH NATURAL FINISH (6) JOIN "K" WITH "O" AND "P" WITH BOLTS, AND YOU HAVE COMPLETED YOUR ARMLESS CHAIR, LOVE SEAT, OR SOFA.

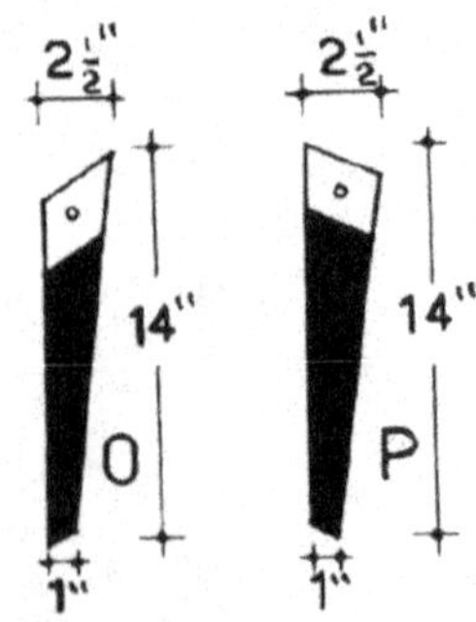

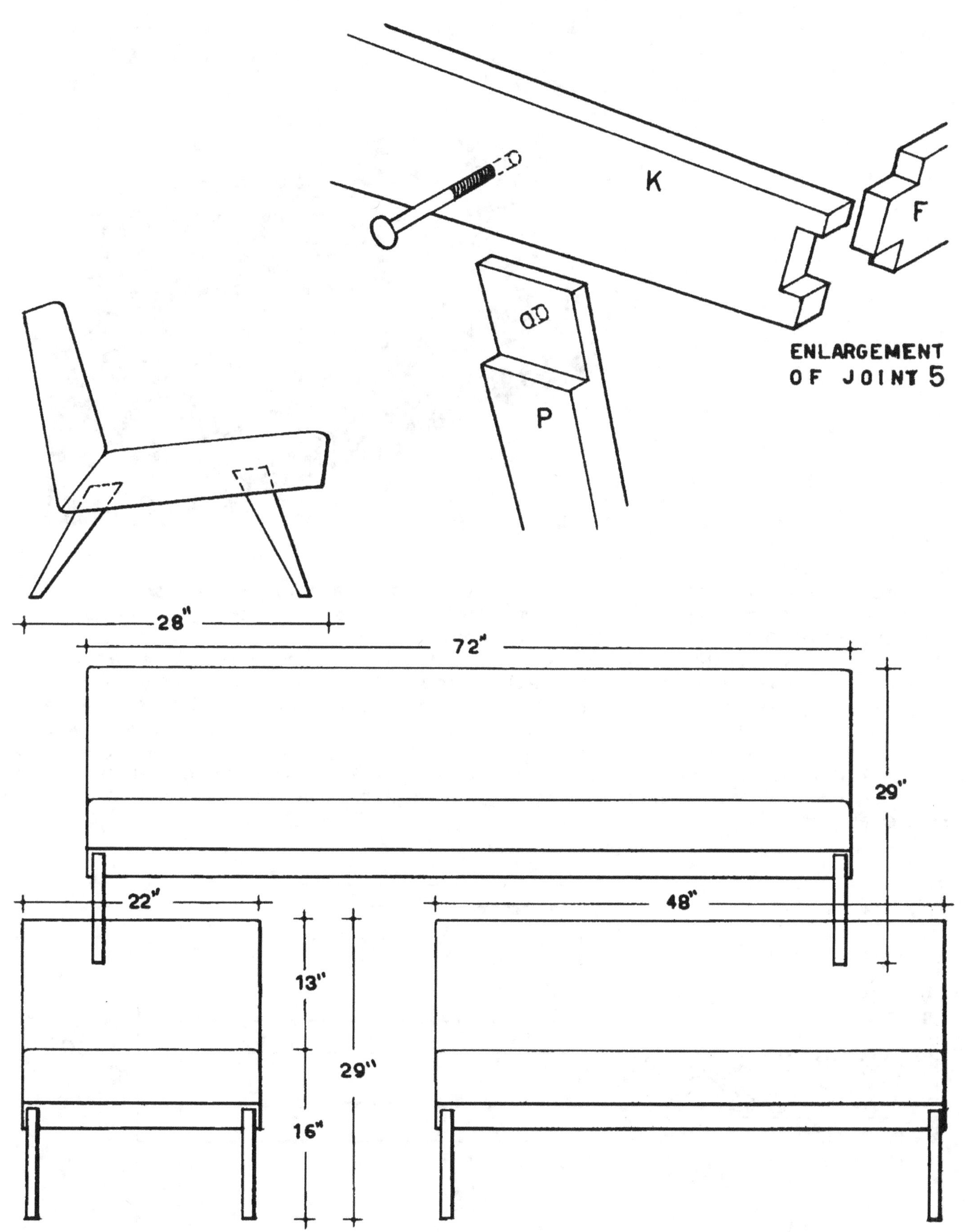

K
F
ENLARGEMENT OF JOINT 5
P
28"
72"
29"
22"
48"
13"
29"
16"

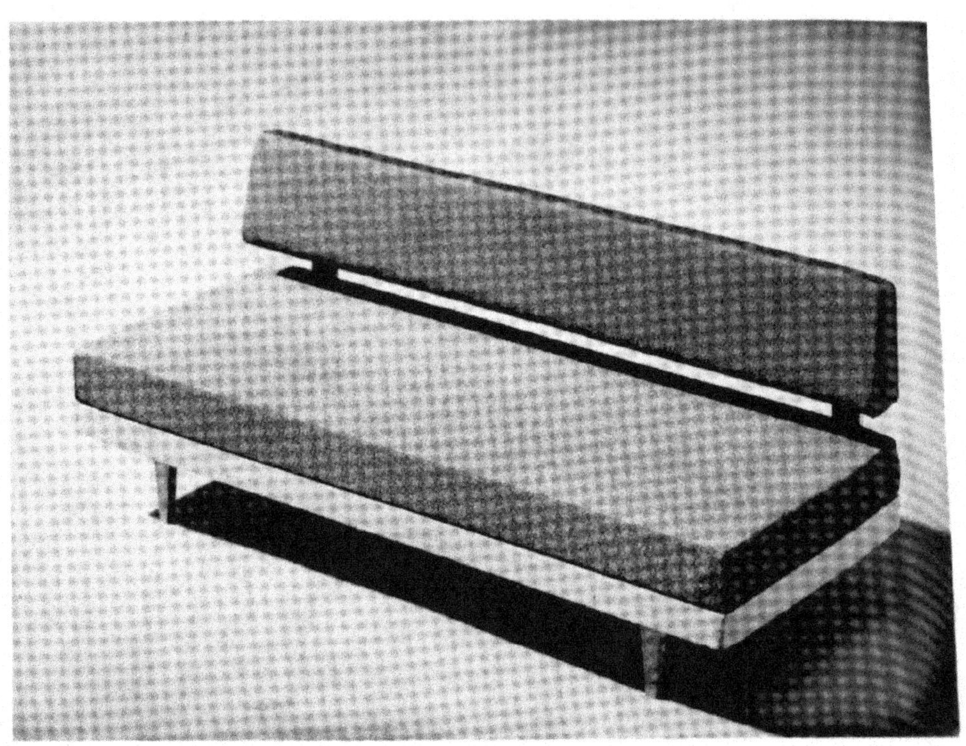

SOFA

LIST OF MATERIALS.

A — 2 PIECES 1" THICK AND 74" x 3½". B — 2 PIECES 1" THICK AND 30" x 3½". C — 1 PIECE ½" THICK AND 72" x 28". E — 2 PIECES 1" THICK AND 72" x 1". F — 2 PIECES 1" THICK AND 28" x 1". G — 4 PIECES 1¼" THICK AND 8½" x 2½". H — 2 PIECES 1" THICK AND 19" x 3". K — 2 PIECES 1" THICK AND 11" x 5½". L — 2 PIECES 1" THICK AND 11" x 4". M — 1 PIECE 1" THICK AND 72" x 3½". N — 1 PIECE 1" THICK AND 72" x 5½". P — 4 PIECES 1½" THICK AND 3" x 3". TEN YARDS OF WEBBING. ONE PIECE RUBBER 1¼" THICK AND 73" x 12". ONE RUBBER CUSHION 5" THICK AND 29" x 74". SEVEN YARDS OF FABRIC.

SEE GENERAL INSTRUCTIONS ON PAGE 54.

WHEN THE MATERIAL IS READY TO BE ASSEMBLED, JOIN AS FOLLOWS:

(1) "A" WITH "B" (2) "D" WITH "G" (3) "D" WITH "A" (4) "E,F" AND "D" WITH "A,B" (5) "C" WITH "A,B" (6) "K,L" WITH "M" AND "N" (7) APPLY THE UPHOLSTERY MATERIAL ON THE BACK (8) COMPLETE THE FRAME WITH NATURAL FINISH ON THE VIEW PART (9) JOIN TOGETHER SEAT AND BACK WITH PIECE "H" AND BOLTS (9) APPLY THE RUBBER MATTRESS AND YOU HAVE COMPLETED YOUR SOFA.

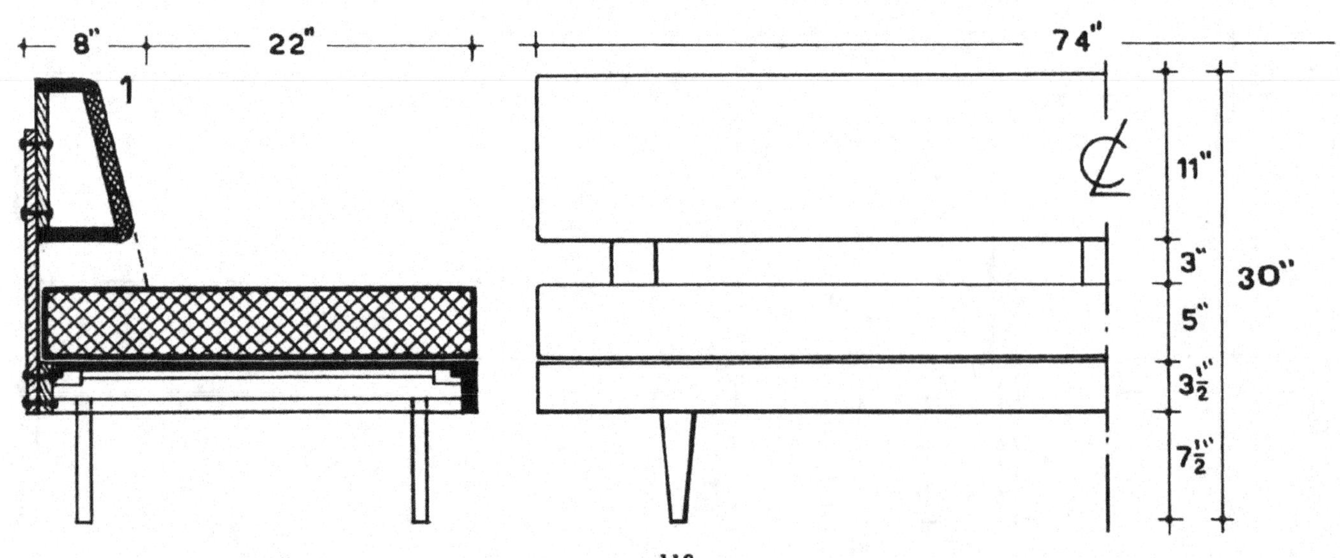

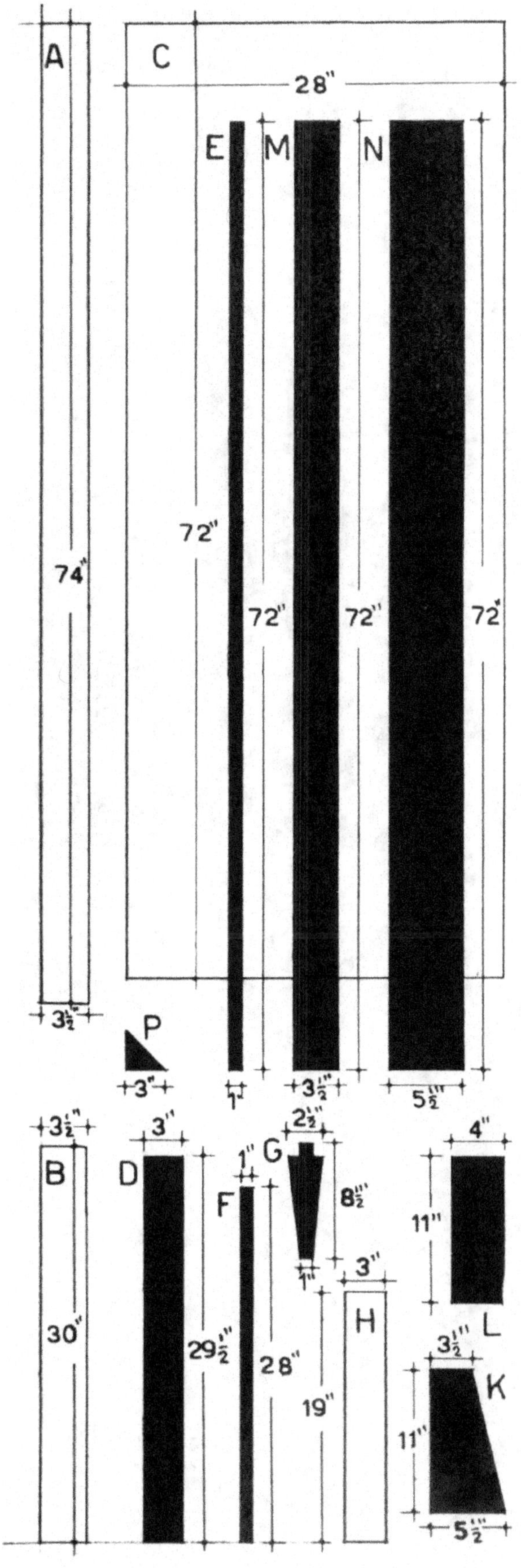

A
C
28"
E M N
72"
72" 72" 72"
74"
3½"
P
3"
1"
3½"
5½"
B
30"
D
3"
F
G
1"
2½"
8½"
3"
1"
H
3½"
L
K
29½"
28"
19"
11"
5½"
4"
11"
ASSEMBLY
H
K M L K
N
B F
L
D
H A E G
G
C
P
D
G
G
1
B
A
B
DETAIL 1 FULL SIZE
ENLARGEMENT
OF JOINT 1
H A
E
P
D
B
G

119

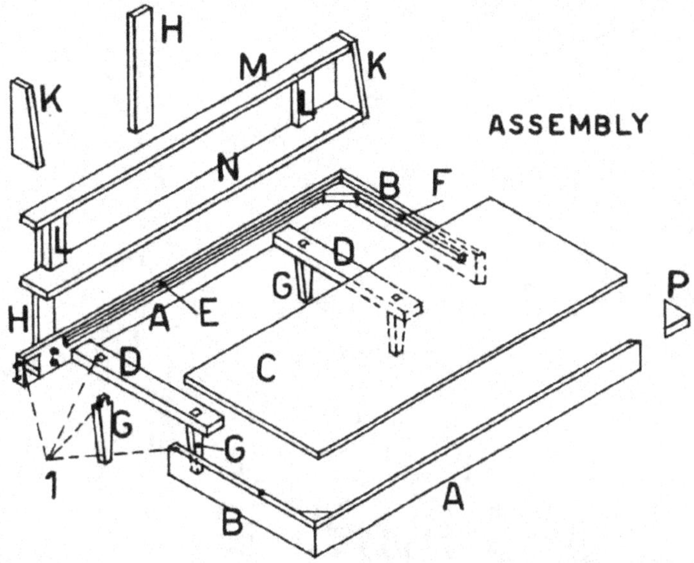

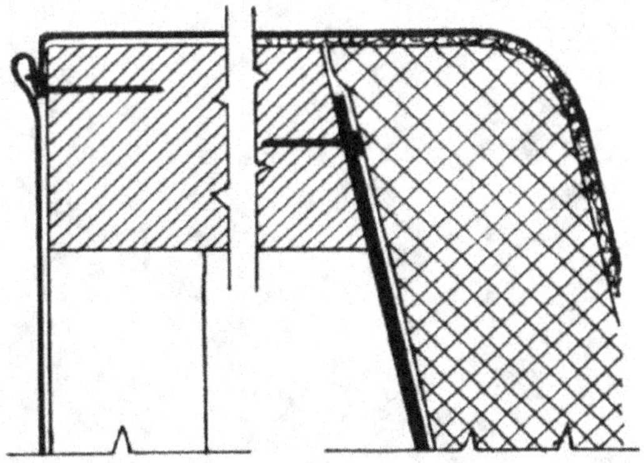

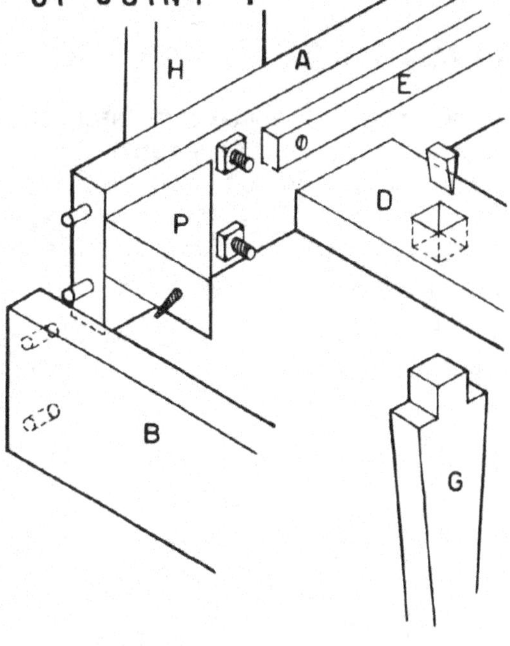

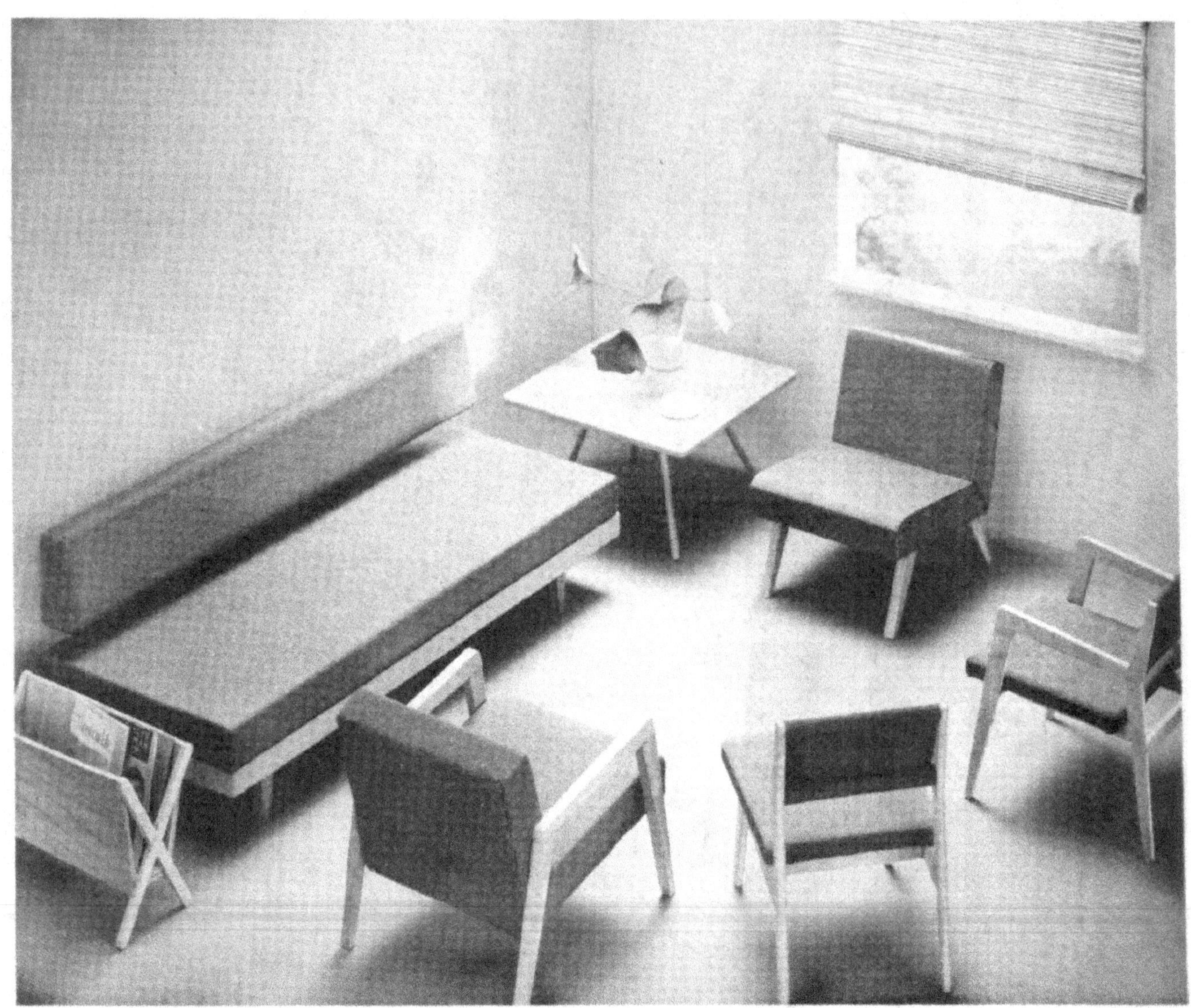

LIVING ROOM   GROUP III

INSTRUCTIONS FOR BUILDING THE PIECES SHOWN
HERE WILL BE FOUND ON THE FOLLOWING PAGES:
MAGAZINE RACK, PAGE 56; SOFA, PAGE 118; END
(OR CORNER) TABLE, PAGE 82; ARMCHAIR, PAGE
111; CHAIR, PAGE 107; ARMLESS CHAIR, PAGE
116; ARMCHAIR, PAGE 106.

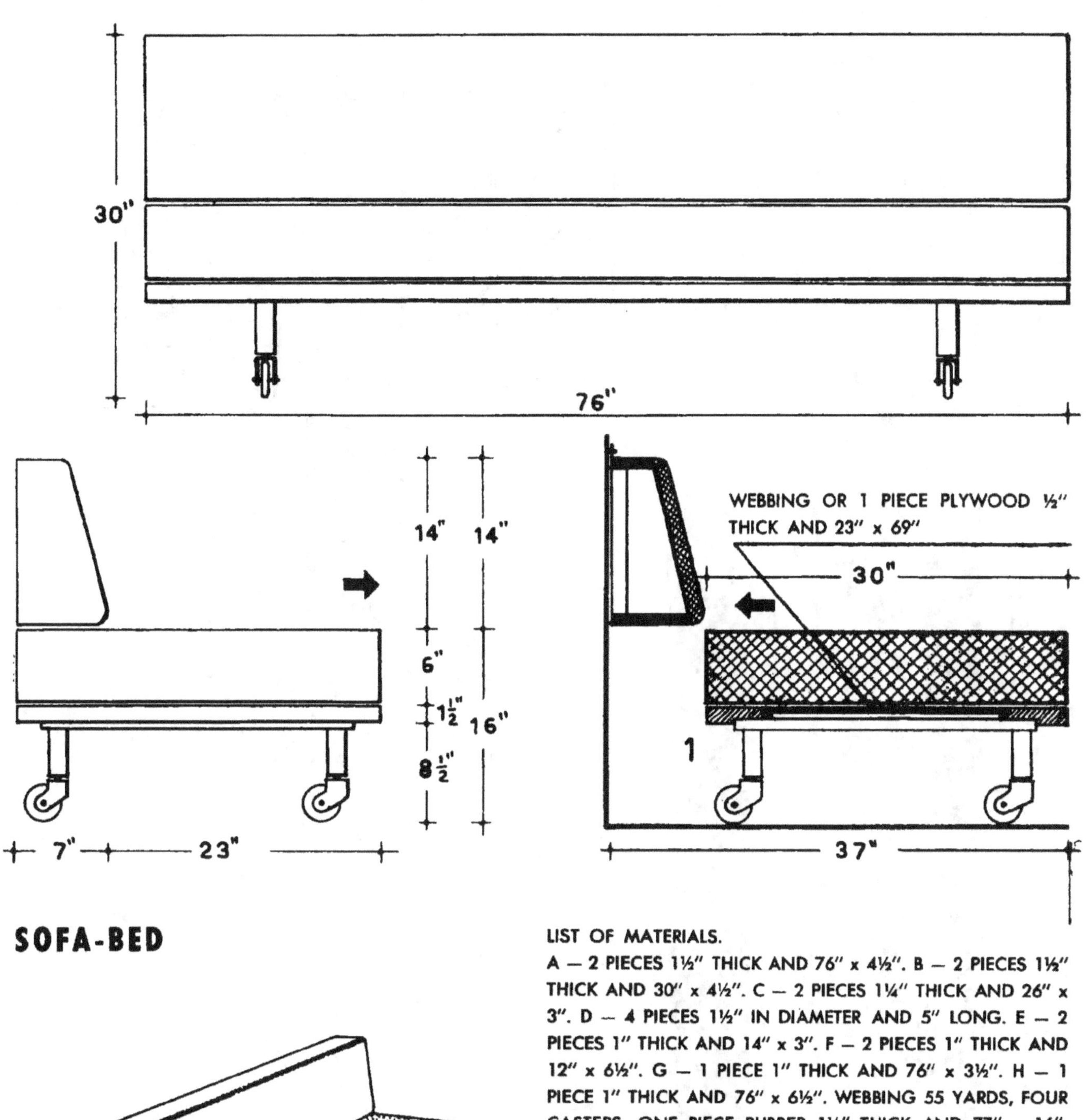

SOFA-BED

LIST OF MATERIALS.

A — 2 PIECES 1½" THICK AND 76" x 4½". B — 2 PIECES 1½" THICK AND 30" x 4½". C — 2 PIECES 1¼" THICK AND 26" x 3". D — 4 PIECES 1½" IN DIAMETER AND 5" LONG. E — 2 PIECES 1" THICK AND 14" x 3". F — 2 PIECES 1" THICK AND 12" x 6½". G — 1 PIECE 1" THICK AND 76" x 3½". H — 1 PIECE 1" THICK AND 76" x 6½". WEBBING 55 YARDS, FOUR CASTERS. ONE PIECE RUBBER 1¼" THICK AND 77" x 16". ONE RUBBER OR CONVENTIONAL MATTRESS 5" THICK AND 30" x 76".

SEE GENERAL INSTRUCTIONS ON PAGE 54.

AFTER THE MATERIAL IS READY, PROCEED AS FOLLOWS: JOIN (1) "A" WITH "B" (2) "D" WITH "C" (3) "A" WITH "C" (4) APPLY THE CASTERS (5) COMPLETE WITH NATURAL FINISH (6) APPLY THE WEBBING (7) JOIN "F" AND "E" WITH "G" AND "H" (8) APPLY THE UPHOLSTERY MATERIAL ON BACK (SEE PAGE 112) AND MATTRESS ON THE SEAT AND YOU HAVE COMPLETED YOUR SOFA BED. NOTE: THE BACK MUST BE ATTACHED TO THE WALL.

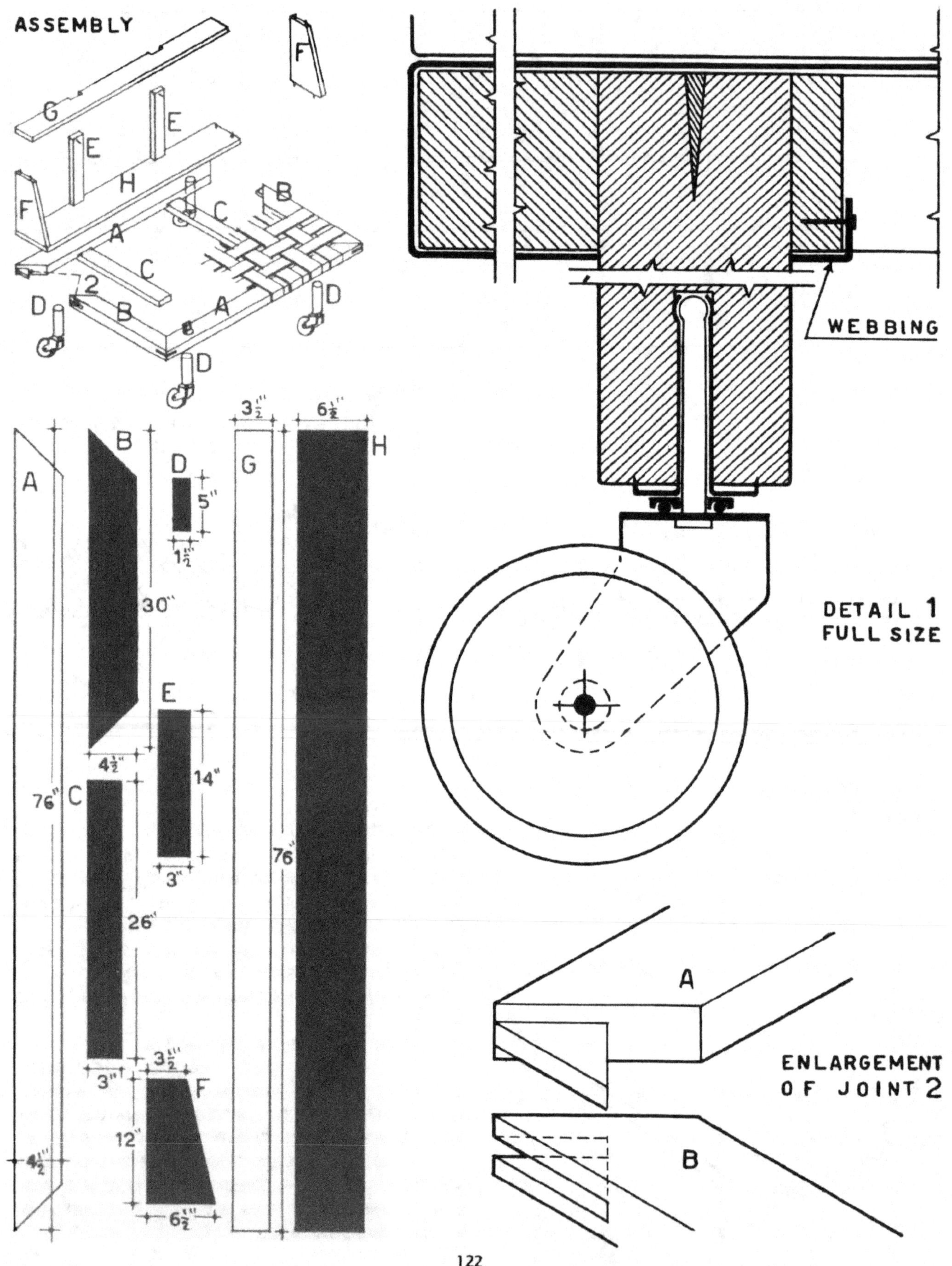

ASSEMBLY
G
E
E
H
F
C
B
C
A
D
2
B
A
B
D
D
F
A
B
D
5"
1½"
30"
4½"
E
14"
3"
76"
C
26"
G
76"
H
3½"
6½"
3½"
3"
F
12"
6½"
4½"
WEBBING
DETAIL 1
FULL SIZE
A
ENLARGEMENT
OF JOINT 2
B

BED

LIST OF MATERIALS.

A — 2 PIECES 1¼" THICK AND 76" x 5½". B — 2 PIECES 1¼" THICK AND 40" x 5½". C — 2 PIECES 1¼" THICK AND 26" x 3½". D — 4 PIECES 1¼" THICK AND 30" x 2½". E — 2 PIECES 1¼" THICK AND 39" x 3". F — 4 PIECES 1½" THICK AND 5" x 5". TWELVE YARDS OF NO-SAG SPRING, 60 EXTENSION SPRINGS, AND ONE SINGLE MATTRESS.

SEE GENERAL INSTRUCTIONS ON PAGE 54.

AFTER THE MATERIAL IS READY, PROCEED AS FOLLOWS:

JOIN (1) "A" WITH "B" (2) "E" AND "F" WITH "A,B" (3) APPLY NO-SAG SPRING AND COVER WITH MUSLIN TACKED TO "A" AND "B" TO PROTECT MATTRESS (4) JOIN "C" WITH "D" AND (5) JOIN "D" WITH "B" USING BOLTS. APPLY THE MATTRESS AND YOU HAVE COMPLETED THE BED.

NIGHT TABLE

LIST OF MATERIALS.

G — 1 PIECE ¾" THICK AND 24" x 12". J — 1 PIECE ¾" THICK AND 22½" x 12". H — 2 PIECES ¾" THICK AND 12" x 8¼". K — 1 PIECE ¼" THICK AND 23½" x . 8½". L — 1 PIECE 1" THICK AND 9" x 1½". M — 2 PIECES 1" THICK AND 13" x 1½". P — 4 PIECES 1" THICK AND 19" x 1½".

SEE GENERAL INSTRUCTIONS ON PAGE 54.

AFTER THE MATERIAL IS READY, PROCEED AS FOLLOWS:

JOIN (1) "H" WITH "G" AND "J" (2) "K" WITH "G,H,J" (3) "M" WITH "P" (4) "L" WITH "M,P" (5) "L,M" WITH "J," AND YOU HAVE COMPLETED THE NIGHT TABLE.

FOR FINISH SEE INSTRUCTIONS ON PAGE 14.

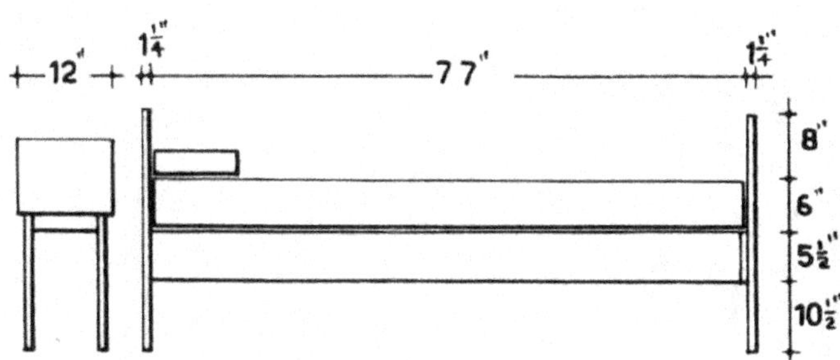

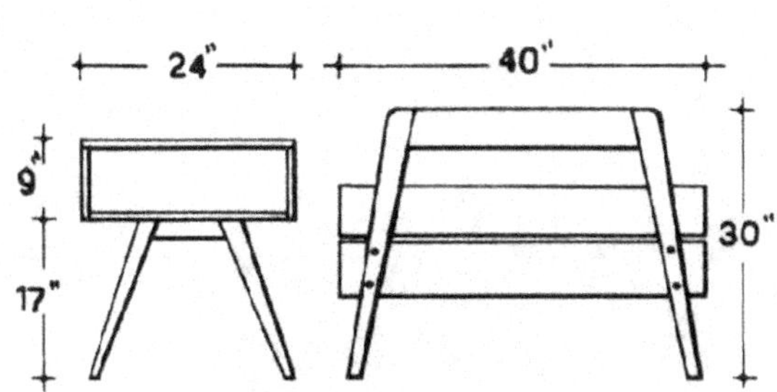

A
B
E
C
26"
39"
40"
76"
3½"
2½"
5½"
3"
D
30"
5"
F
1"
L
9"
1½"
M
13"
19"
P
1½"
H
12"
5½"
8¼"
1½"
¾"
G
24"
J
12"
12"
22½"
23½"
K
8½"
ASSEMBLY
1
D
C
B
D
A
C
E
E
F
D
F
B
F
A
D
G
K
H
J
H
2
M
M
L
P
P
P
P
SCREWS
A
F
B
D
ENLARGEMENT
OF JOINT 1
F
H
ENLARGEMENT
OF JOINT 2

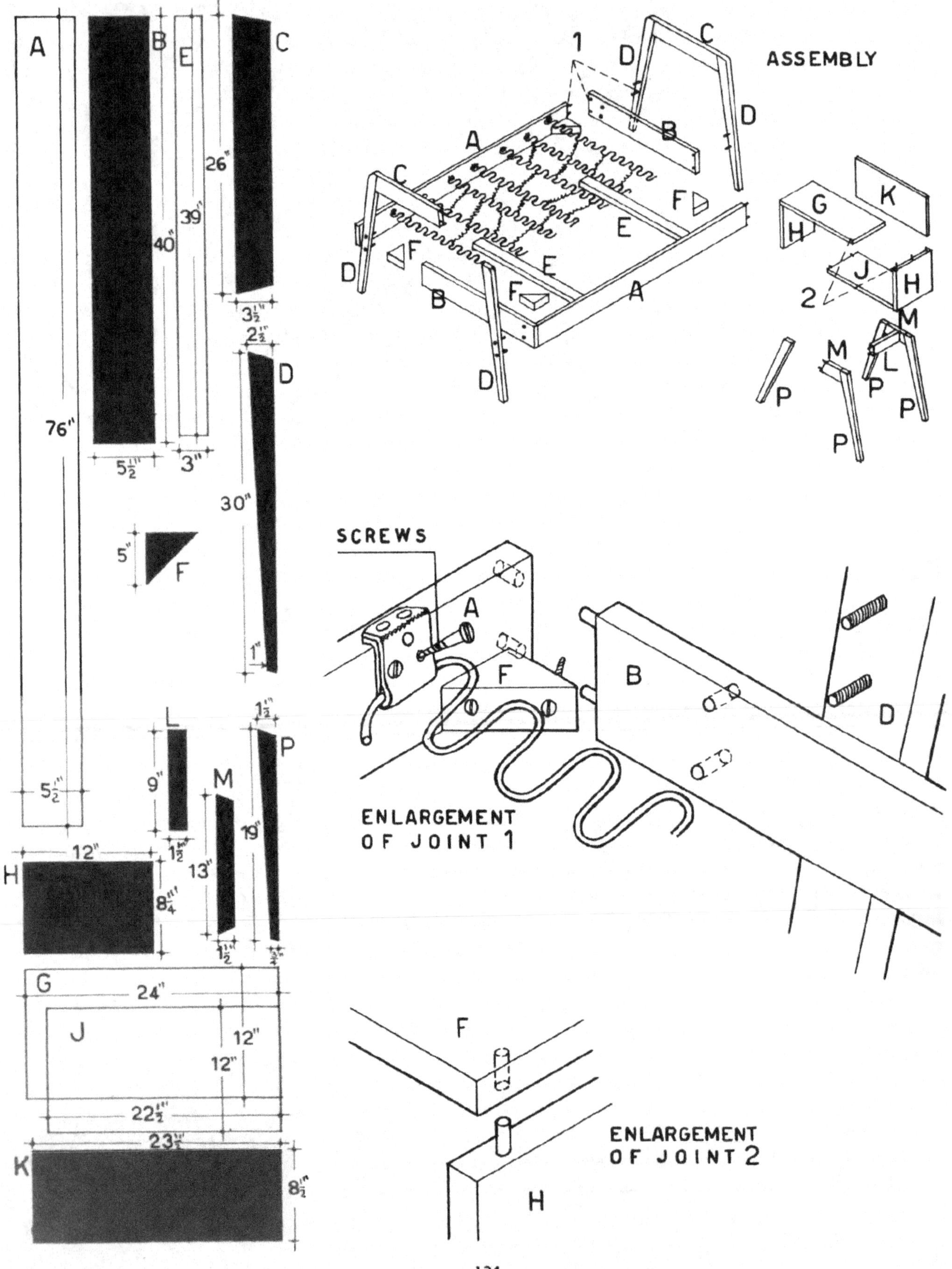

124

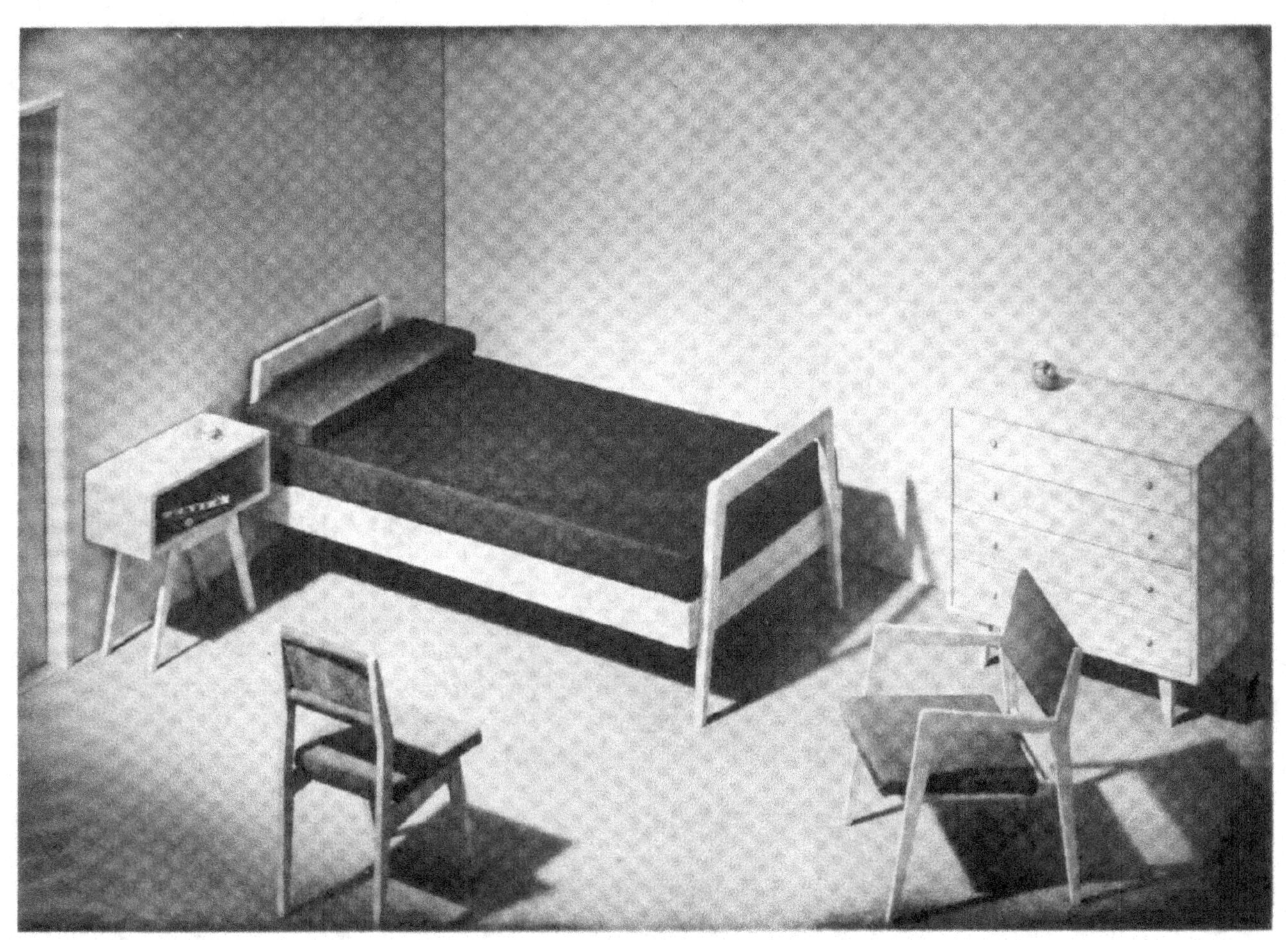

BEDROOM GROUP I (SINGLE)

INSTRUCTIONS FOR BUILDING THE PIECES SHOWN
HERE WILL BE FOUND ON THE FOLLOWING PAGES:
NIGHT TABLE, PAGE 123; CHAIR, PAGE 103; SINGLE
BED, PAGE 123; ARMCHAIR, PAGE 106; CHEST,
PAGE 107; BED, PAGE 128.

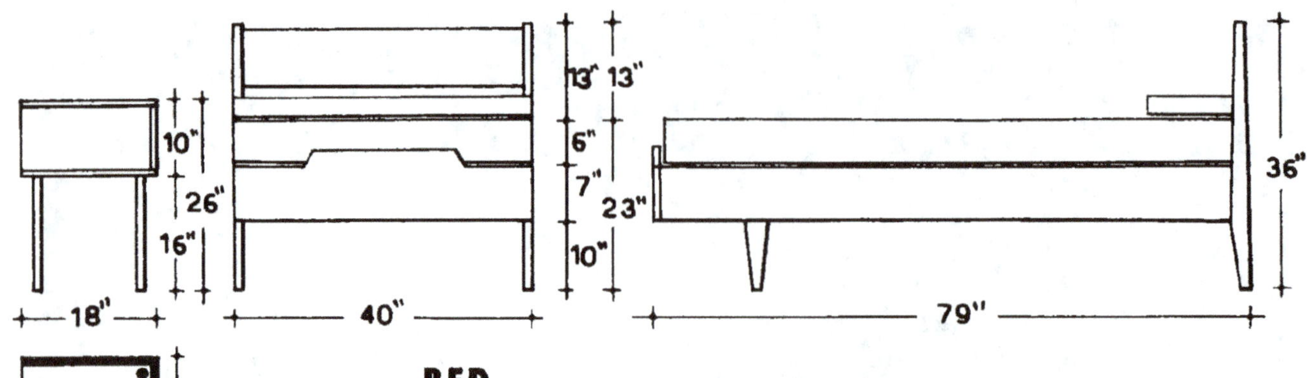

ENLARGEMENT OF JOINT 1

BED

A — 2 PIECES 1" THICK AND 76" x 7". B — 1 PIECE 1" THICK AND 40" x 9". C — 3 PIECES ¾" THICK AND 40" x 7". D — 2 PIECES 1¼" THICK AND 36" x 2½". E — 2 PIECES 1" THICK AND 12" x 2½". F — 2 PIECES 1" THICK AND 75" x 1¼". G — 3 PIECES 1" THICK AND 38" x 2½". ONE SINGLE BOX SPRING AND ONE SINGLE MATTRESS.

FOR GENERAL INSTRUCTIONS SEE PAGE 54.

AFTER THE MATERIAL IS READY, PROCEED AS FOLLOWS:

JOIN (1) "C" WITH "D" (2) "A" WITH "E" (3) "F" WITH "A" (4) "A" WITH "B,D" (FOR DEMOUNTABLE JOINTS SEE ENLARGEMENT 2) (5) APPLY PIECES "G," BOX SPRING, AND MATTRESS TO COMPLETE THE BED.

FOR FINISH SEE GENERAL INSTRUCTIONS ON PAGE 14.

NIGHT TABLE

LIST OF MATERIALS.

H — 2 PIECES ¾" THICK AND 18" x 14". K — 3 PIECES 1" OR 1⅛" IN DIAMETER AND 17" LONG. L — 1 PIECE ¾" THICK AND 8½" x 4". M — 1 PIECE ¾" THICK AND 17¼" x 8½".

FOR GENERAL INSTRUCTIONS SEE PAGE 54.

AFTER THE MATERIAL IS READY, PROCEED TO JOIN AS FOLLOWS:

JOIN (1) "H" WITH "K" (SEE DETAIL PAGE 81) (2) "L" WITH "M" (3) "H" WITH "L,M" AND THE NIGHT TABLE IS COMPLETED.

FOR FINISH SEE GENERAL INSTRUCTIONS ON PAGE 14.

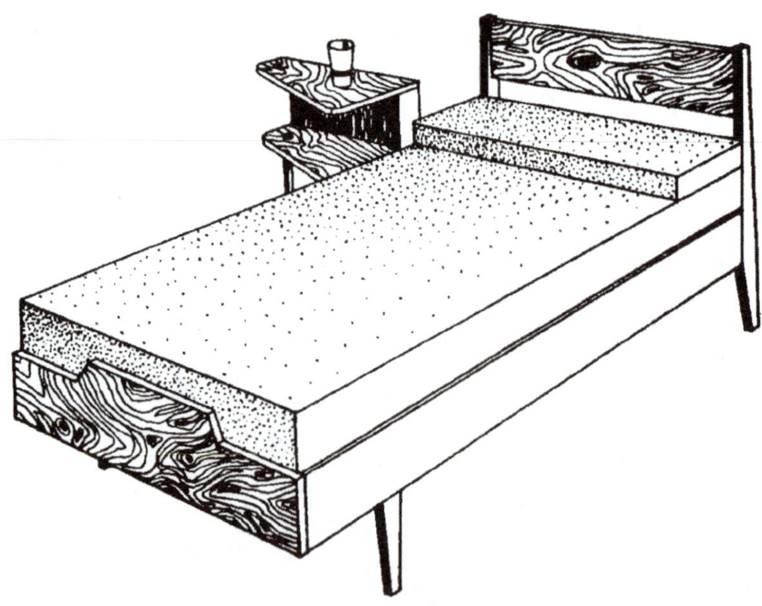

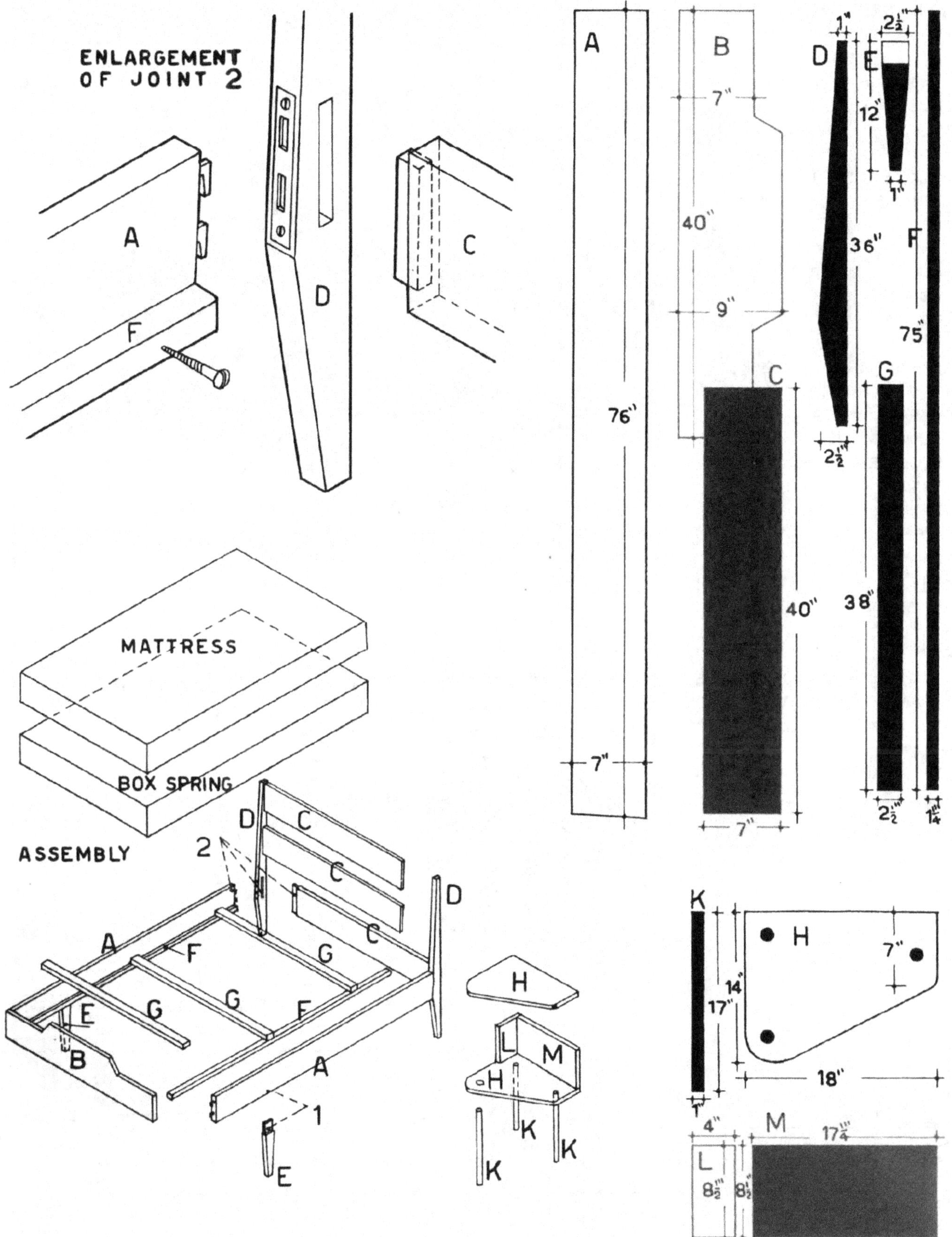

ENLARGEMENT
OF JOINT 2
A
F
D
C
MATTRESS
BOX SPRING
ASSEMBLY
D
C
2
A
F
G
E
G
G
F
B
A
D
C
C
C
H
L
M
H
E
1
K
K
K
A
76"
7"
7"
B
7"
40"
9"
C
40"
7"
D
1"
12"
1"
E
2½"
36"
75"
2½"
F
1¼"
G
38"
2½"
K
14"
17"
1"
H
7"
18"
4"
M
17¼"
L
8½"
8½"

DOUBLE BED

LIST OF MATERIALS.

A — 1 PIECE ¾" THICK AND 92½" x 26". B — 2 PIECES 1" THICK AND 76" x 6". C — 2 PIECES 1" THICK AND 55" x 6". D — 2 PIECES ⅜" THICK AND 93" x 1". E — 2 PIECES ⅜" THICK AND 27" x 1". F — 2 PIECES ¾" THICK AND 15" x 12". G — 4 PIECES 1½" THICK AND 4" x 4". H — 2 PIECES 1¼" THICK AND 54½" x 4". L — 2 PIECES 1¼" THICK AND 54" x 1". M — 2 PIECES 1¼" THICK AND 75" x 1". P — 16 PIECES ½" THICK AND 53" x 4". K — 4 PIECES METAL PIPE 1¼" IN DIAMETER AND 9" LONG. ONE DOUBLE MATTRESS.

SEE GENERAL INSTRUCTIONS ON PAGE 54.

AFTER THE MATERIAL IS READY PROCEED AS FOLLOWS:

JOIN (1) "A" WITH "F" (2) "A" WITH "D" AND "E" (3) "K" WITH "H" (SEE DETAIL PAGE 68) (4) "B" WITH "H" AND "C" (5) "L,M,G" WITH "B,C" (6) "P" WITH "M" (7) "C" WITH "D" USING BOLTS (8) APPLY THE MATTRESS AND YOU HAVE COMPLETED YOUR BED.

FOR NATURAL FINISH SEE IN-STRUCTIONS ON PAGE 14.

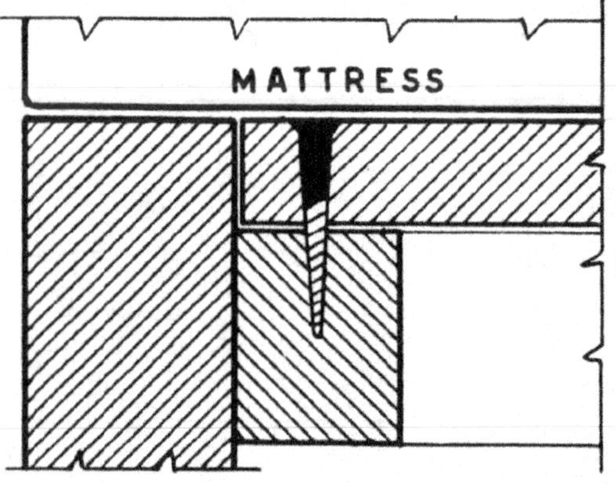

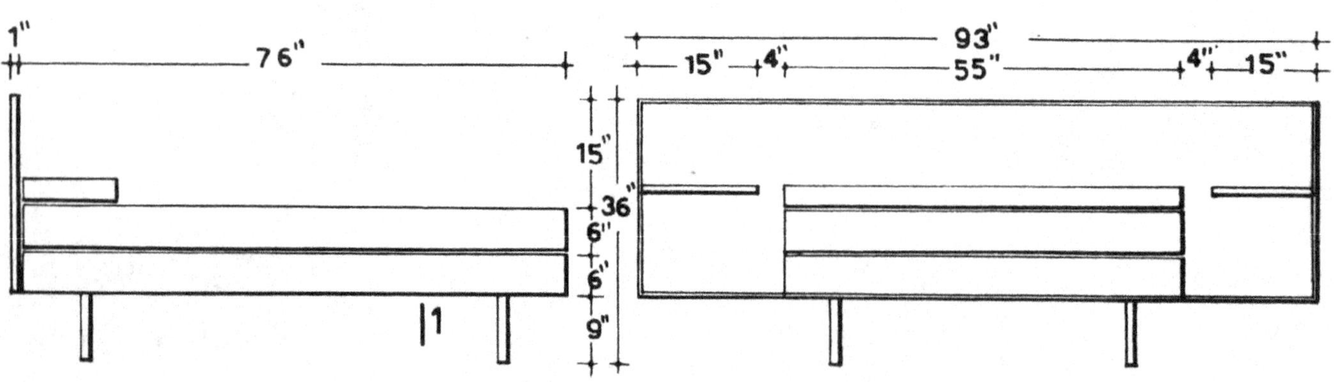

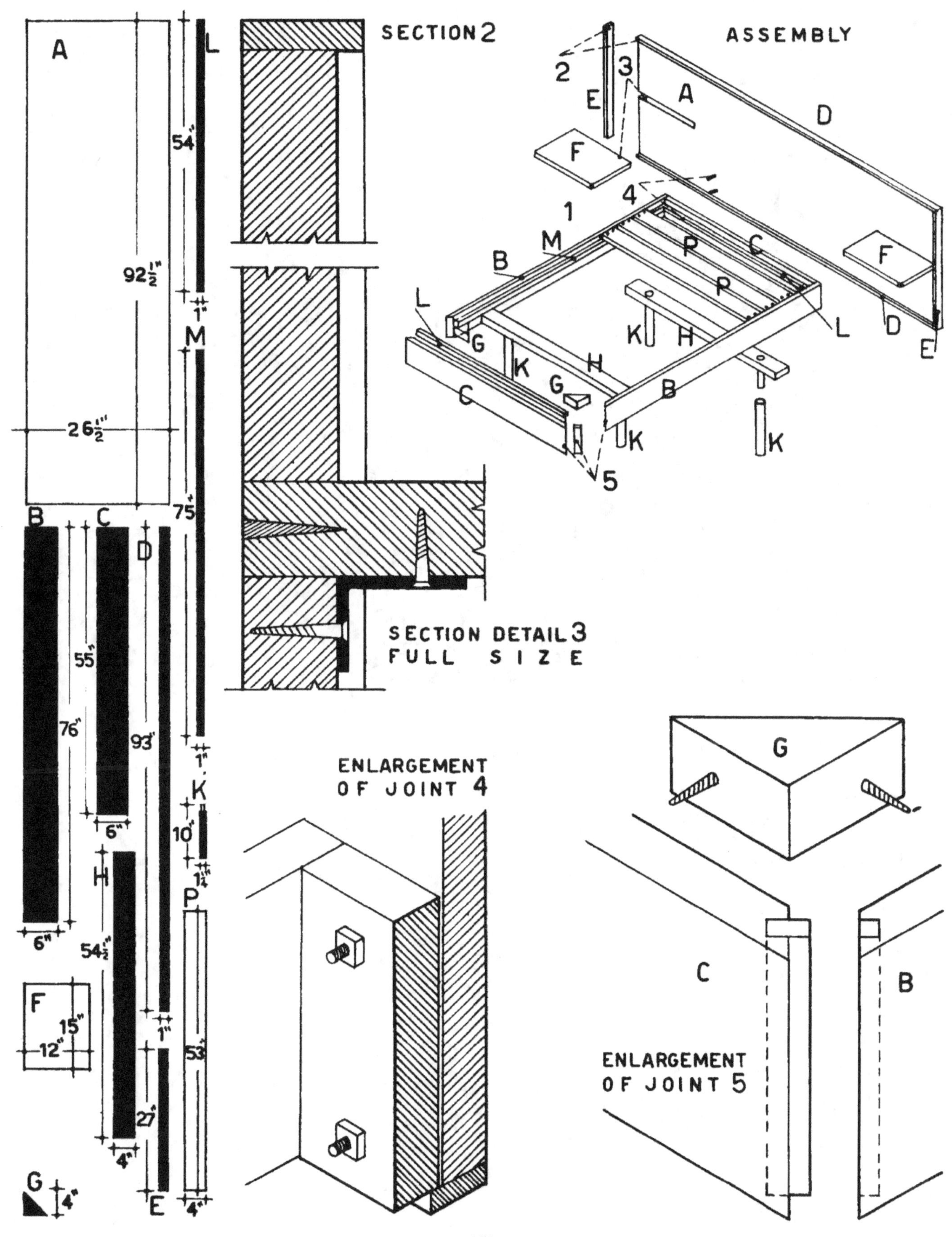

A
L
54"
M
92 1/2"
1"
26 1/2"
75"
B
C
D
M
55"
76"
93"
6"
K
H
6"
54 1/2"
P
10"
1 1/4"
F
15"
12"
1"
53"
G
4"
27"
4"
E
4"
SECTION 2
ASSEMBLY
2
3
E
A
F
D
1
4
M
B
P
C
L
K
H
G
P
K
H
L
K
G
D
C
B
E
S
K
K
5
SECTION DETAIL 3
FULL SIZE
ENLARGEMENT OF JOINT 4
G
ENLARGEMENT OF JOINT 5
C
B

BEDROOM   GROUP II   (DOUBLE)

INSTRUCTIONS FOR BUILDING THE PIECES SHOWN
HERE WILL BE FOUND ON THE FOLLOWING PAGES:
VANITY, PAGE 137; BENCH, PAGE 137; CHAIR,
PAGE 107; BED, PAGE 128.

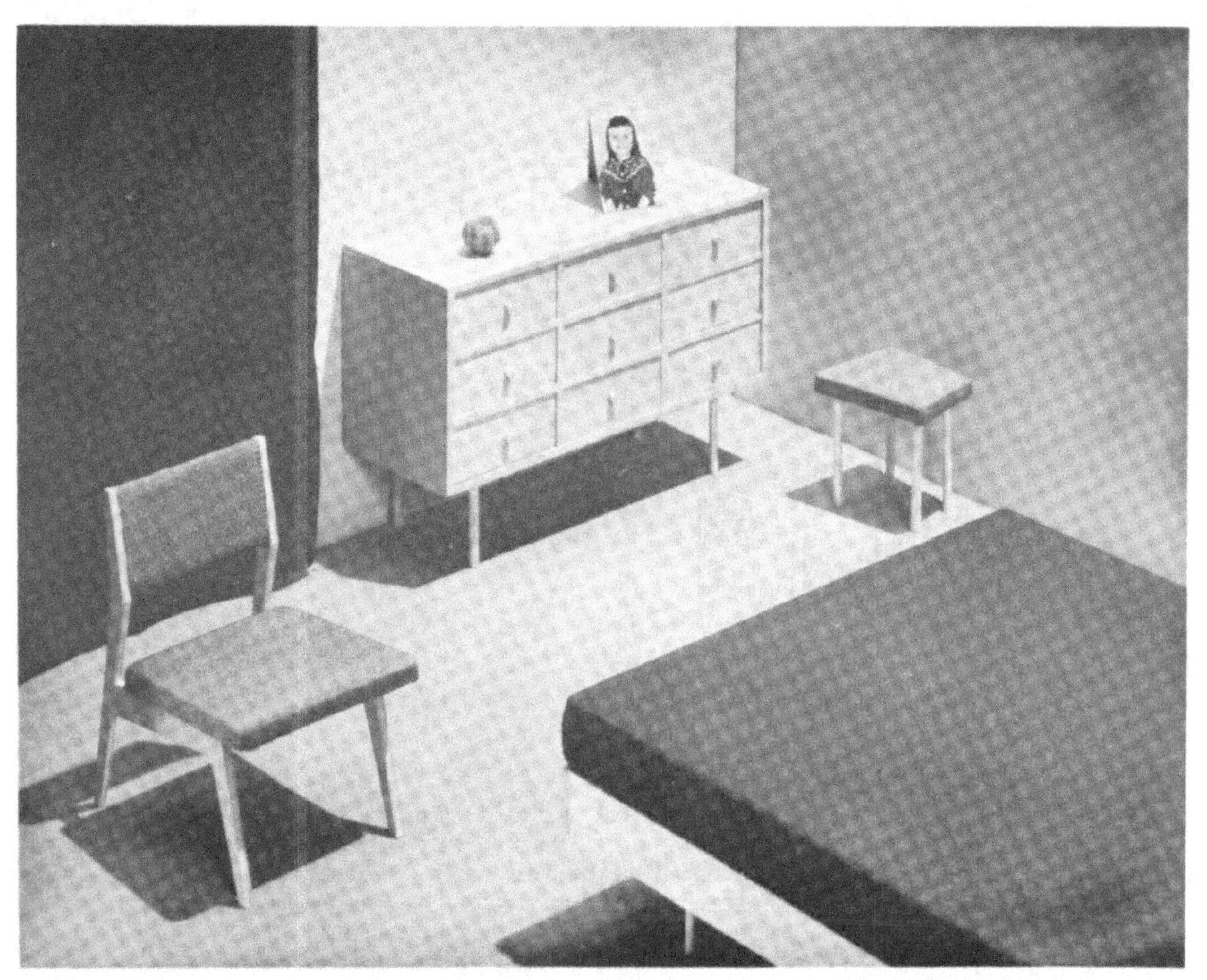

BEDROOM GROUP III (DOUBLE)

INSTRUCTIONS FOR BUILDING THE PIECES SHOWN HERE WILL BE FOUND ON THE FOLLOWING PAGES: CHAIR, PAGE 107; CHEST, PAGE 145; BENCH, PAGE 137; BED, PAGE 128.

DOUBLE BED

LIST OF MATERIALS.

A — 1 PIECE ¾" THICK AND 57" x 23". B — 1 PIECE ¾" THICK AND 57" x 15".
C — 4 PIECES ½" THICK AND 23" x 1". D — 4 PIECES ½" THICK AND 15" x 1".
E — 4 PIECES ½" THICK AND 57" x 2". F — 2 PIECES ½" THICK AND 23" x 2".
G — 2 PIECES ½" THICK AND 15" x 2". H — 4 PIECES 1¼" THICK AND 11" x 2½".
K — 3 PIECES 1" THICK AND 55" x 2". L — 2 PIECES 1¼" THICK AND 77" x 1½".
M — 2 PIECES 1" THICK AND 77" x 7". ONE DOUBLE BOX SPRING AND ONE DOUBLE
MATTRESS.

SEE GENERAL INSTRUCTIONS ON PAGE 54.

AFTER THE MATERIAL IS READY, PROCEED AS FOLLOWS:

JOIN (1) "A" WITH "E" AND "F" (2) "A" WITH "C" (3) "B" WITH "E" AND "G" (4)
"B" WITH "D" (5) "M" WITH "H" AND "L" (6) "M" WITH "A" AND "G" (FOR
DEMOUNTABLE JOINTS SEE ENLARGEMENT 3). APPLY THE "K" PIECES, BOX SPRING,
AND MATTRESS TO COMPLETE YOUR BED.

FOR FINISH SEE GENERAL INSTRUCTIONS ON PAGE 14.

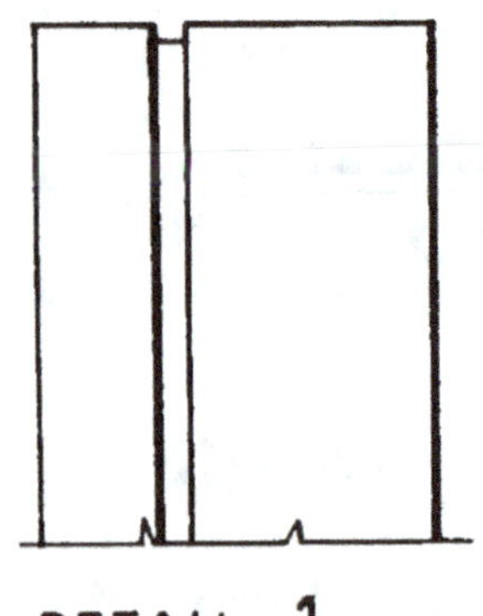

DETAIL 1
FULL SIZE

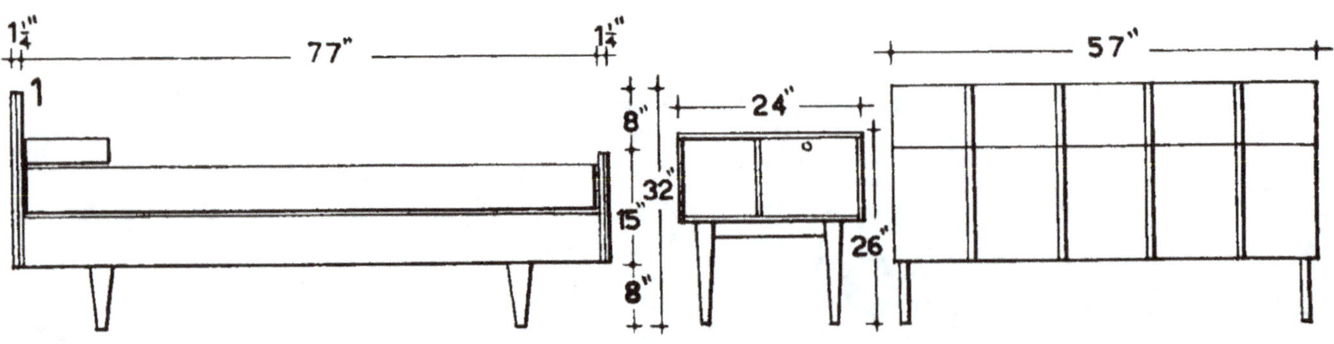

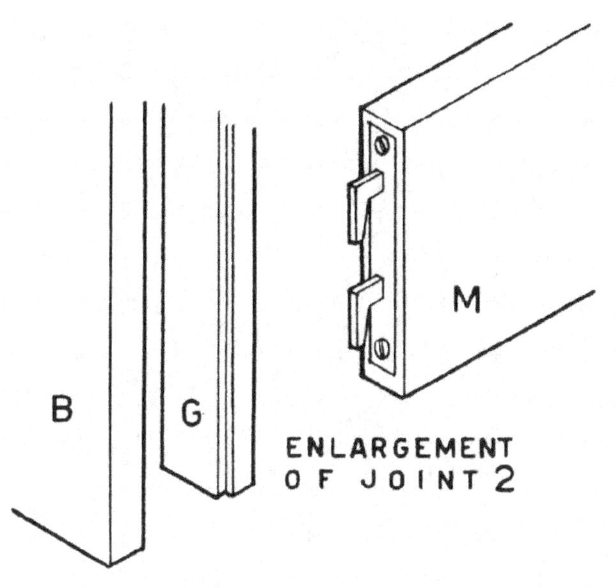

B
G
M
ENLARGEMENT
OF JOINT 2

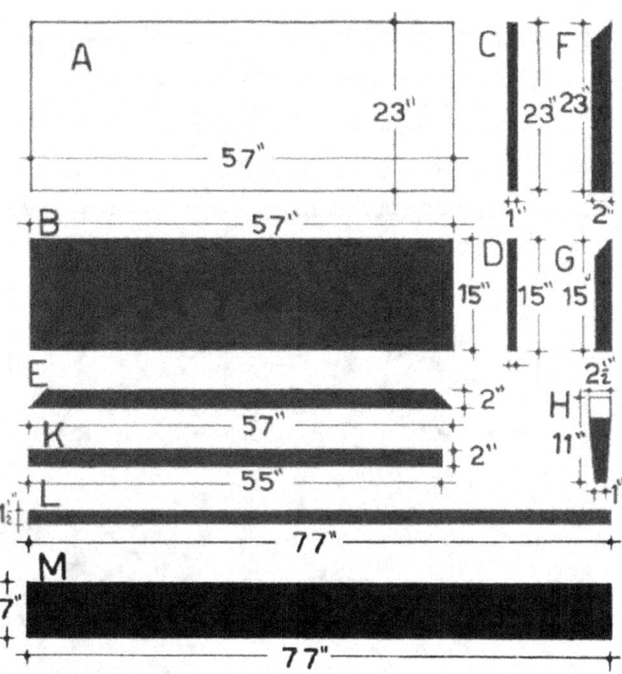

A
C
F
23"
23"
23
57"
B
57"
D
G
15"
15"
15
E
2"
57"
H
2½
K
2"
11"
55"
L
1½"
77"
M
7"
77"
1"
1"
2½

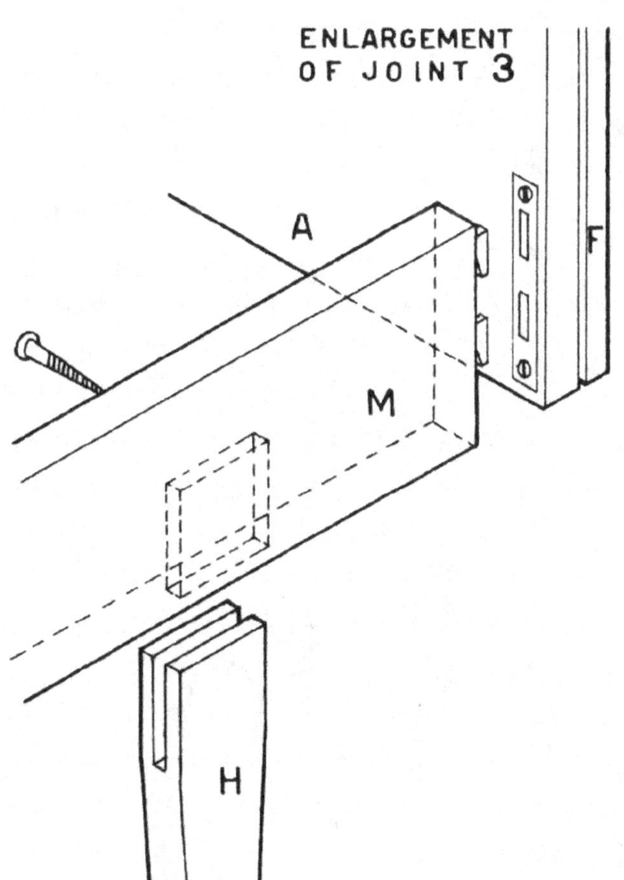

ENLARGEMENT
OF JOINT 3
A
F
M
H

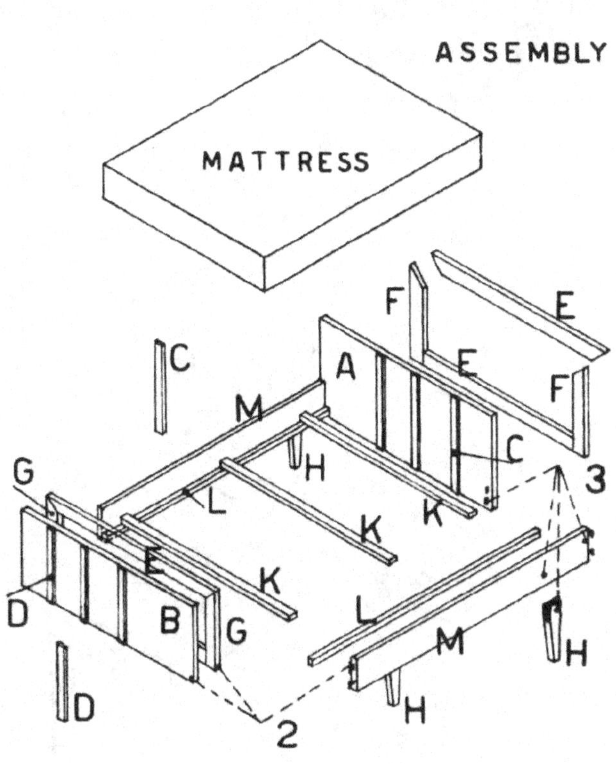

ASSEMBLY
MATTRESS
C
F
E
A
E
F
E
M
C
G
H
3
L
K
K
E
K
D
B
G
L
M
H
D
H
2
H

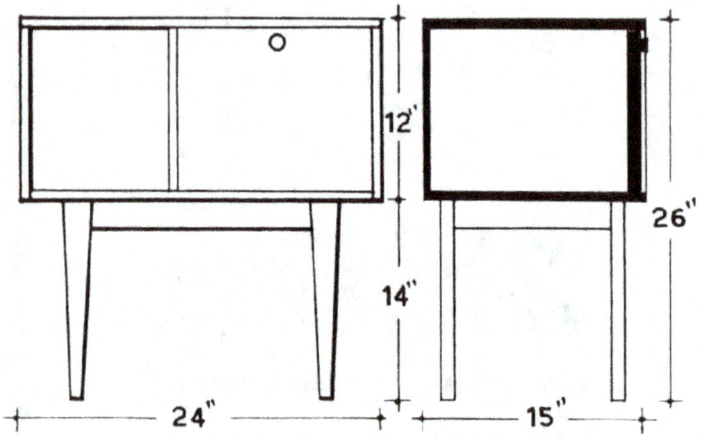

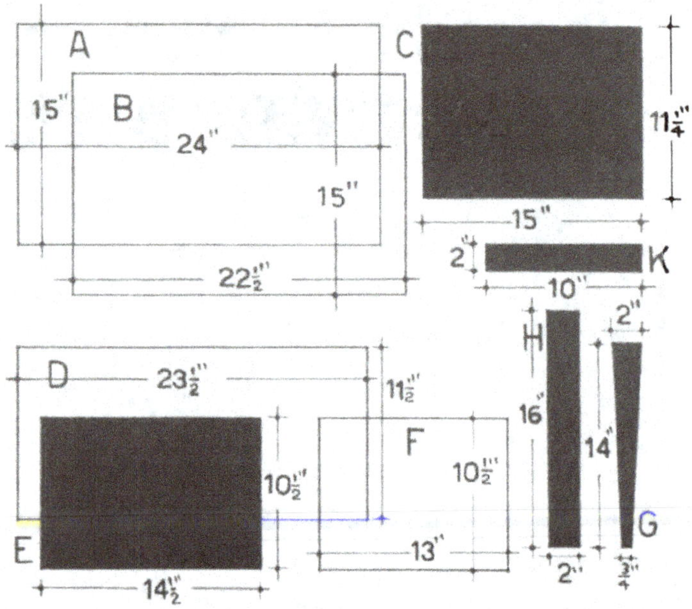

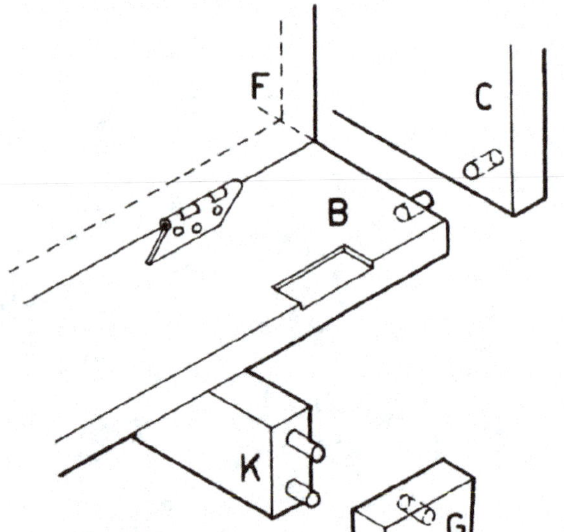

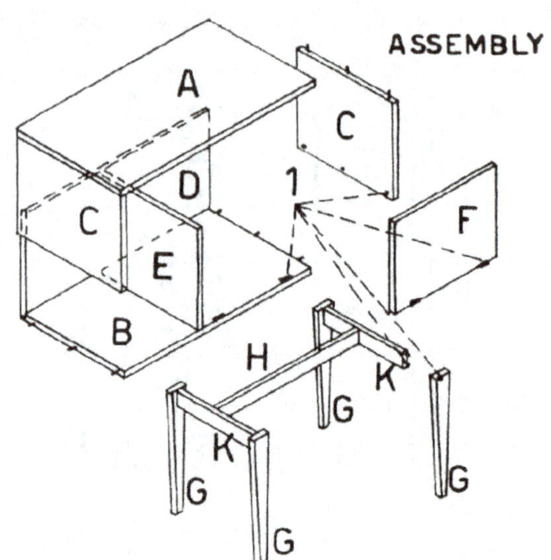

NIGHT TABLE

LIST OF MATERIALS.

A — 1 PIECE ¾" THICK AND 24" x 15". B — 1 PIECE ¾" THICK AND 22½" x 15". C — 2 PIECES ¾" THICK AND 15" x 11¼". D — 1 PIECE ½" THICK AND 23½" x 11½". E — 1 PIECE ¾" THICK AND 14½" x 10½". F — 1 PIECE ¾" THICK AND 13" x 10½". G — 4 PIECES 1" THICK AND 14" x 2". H — 1 PIECE 1" THICK AND 16" x 2". K — 2 PIECES 1" THICK AND 10" x 2".

FOR GENERAL INSTRUCTIONS SEE PAGE 54.

AFTER THE MATERIAL IS READY, PROCEED AS FOLLOWS:

JOIN (1) "A" AND "B" WITH "C" AND "E" (2) "D" WITH "A,B,C" (3) APPLY THE DOOR "F" WITH ORDINARY HINGES. JOIN (4) "K" WITH "G" (5) "H" WITH "K" (6) "H,K" WITH "B" AND YOU HAVE COMPLETED THE NIGHT TABLE.

FOR FINISH SEE GENERAL INSTRUCTIONS PAGE 14.

ENLARGEMENT OF JOINT 1

VANITY

A — 2 PIECES 1" THICK AND 43" x 2½". B — 2 PIECES 1" THICK AND 33" x 2½". C — 4 PIECES 1" IN DIAMETER AND 36" LONG. D — 1 PIECE ¾" THICK AND 34" x 15". E — 1 PIECE ¾" THICK AND 32½" x 15". F — 2 PIECES ¾" THICK AND 15" x 6¼". G — 2 PIECES ¾" THICK AND 14½" x 5½". H — 1 PIECE ½" THICK AND 33½" x 6½". K — 2 PIECES ½" THICK AND 16½" x 5½". L — 2 PIECES ½" THICK AND 14½ " x 5½". M — 1 PIECE ¼" THICK AND 16" x 14". ONE MIRROR 18" x 14".

SEE GENERAL INSTRUCTIONS ON PAGE 54.

AFTER THE MATERIAL IS READY FOR ASSEMBLING, PROCEED AS FOLLOWS:

JOIN (1) "A" WITH "B" (2) "D" AND "E" WITH "F" AND "G" (3) "H" WITH "D,E,F,G" (4) "K" WITH "L" (5) "M" WITH "K,L" (6) "A,B" WITH "C,F" (7) APPLY THE MIRROR AND YOU HAVE COMPLETED THE VANITY.

FOR FINISH SEE GENERAL INSTRUCTIONS ON PAGE 14.

BENCH

Q — 1 PIECE ¾" THICK AND 18" x 12". O — 2 PIECES ¾" DIAMETER AND 12" LONG. R — 4 PIECES 1" THICK AND 14" x 2". ONE PIECE RUBBER 1" THICK AND 18½" x 16½". FABRIC ½ YARD.

SEE GENERAL INSTRUCTIONS ON PAGE 54.

AFTER THE MATERIAL IS READY FOR ASSEMBLING, PROCEED AS FOLLOWS:

JOIN (1) "R" WITH "Q" AND "O" (2) APPLY THE UPHOLSTERY MATERIAL (SEE PAGE 103) AND THE BENCH IS READY.

FOR FINISH SEE GENERAL INSTRUCTIONS ON PAGE 14.

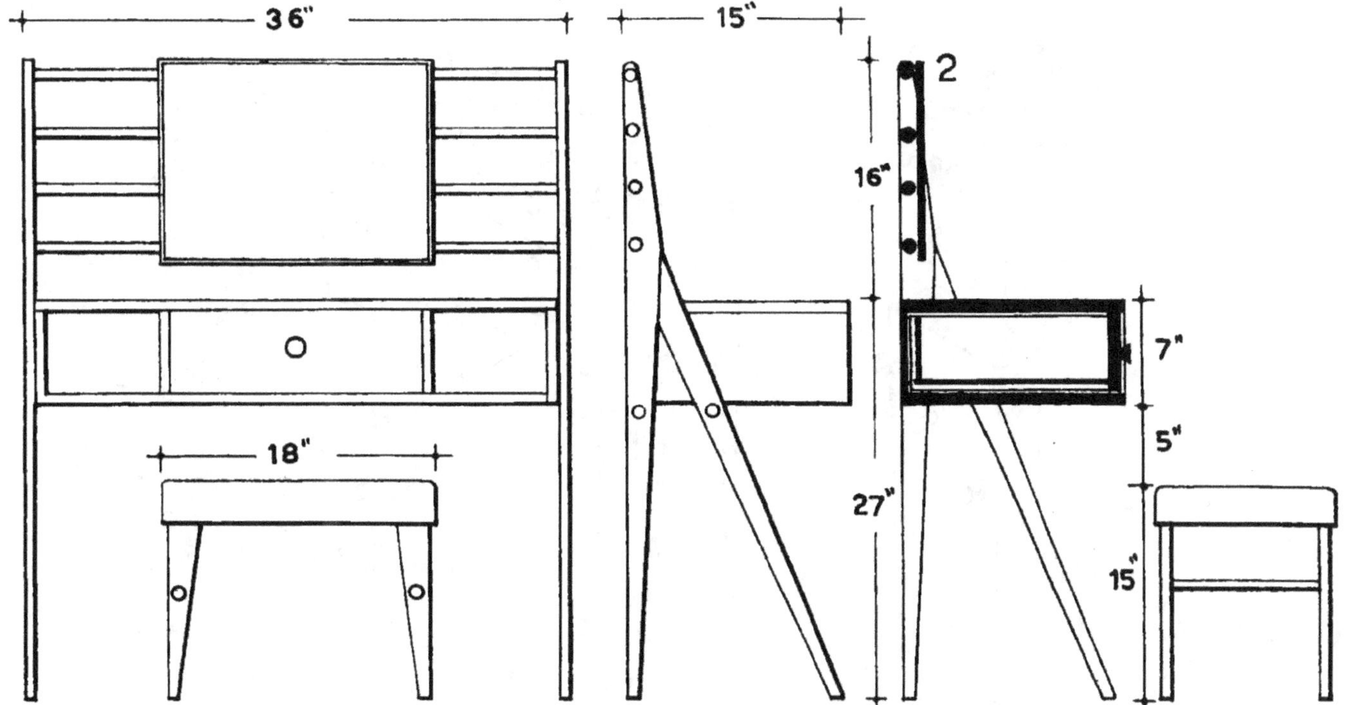

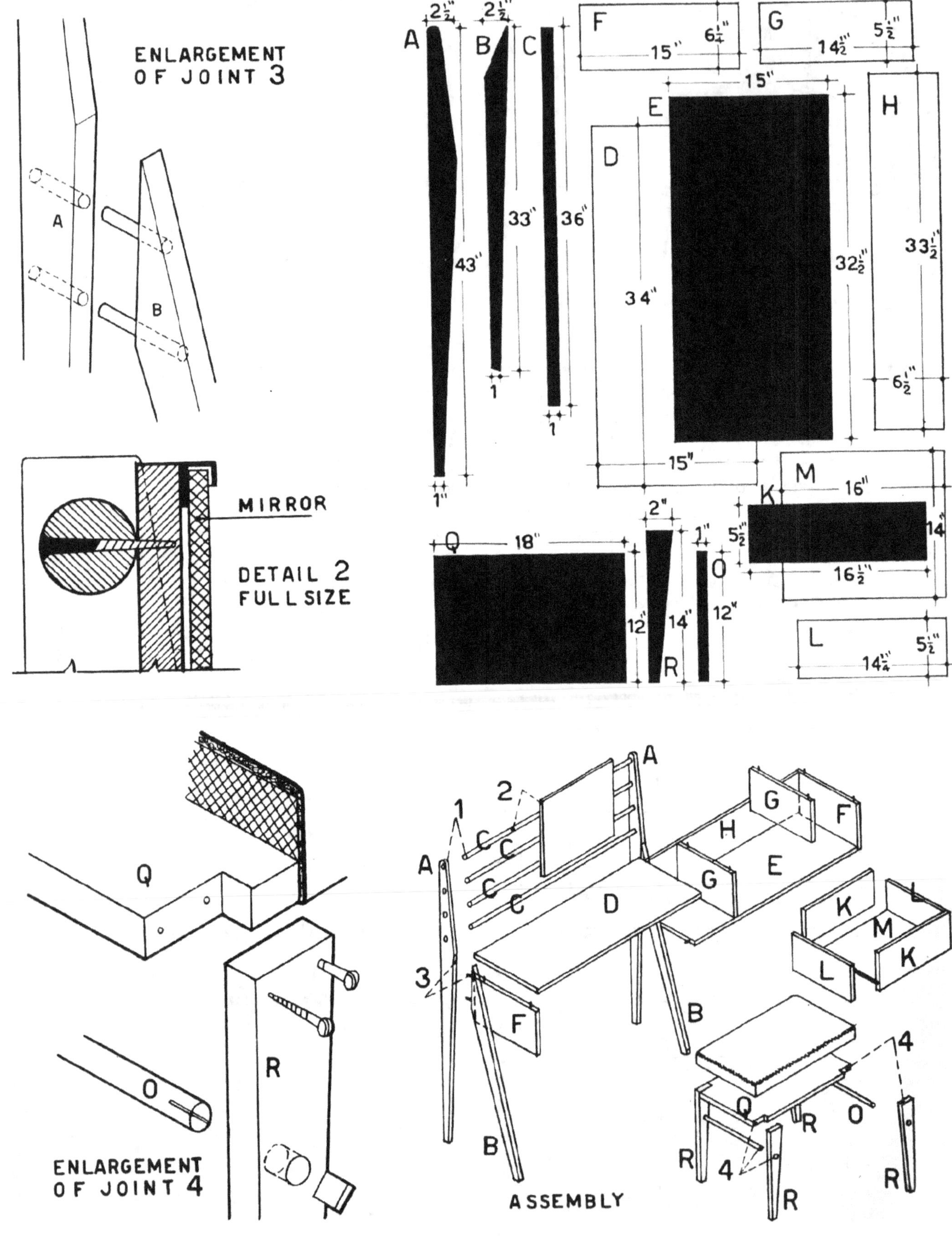

ENLARGEMENT OF JOINT 3
A
B
MIRROR
DETAIL 2 FULL SIZE
ENLARGEMENT OF JOINT 4
Q
O
R
A 2½"
B 2½"
C
43"
33"
36"
1"
1"
1"
F 15" 6¼"
G 14½" 5½"
15"
E
D
34"
32½"
H 33½"
6½"
15"
M 16"
K 5½"
14"
16½"
L 14¼" 5½"
Q 18"
2"
1"
12"
14"
12"
R
O
1
2
A
C
C
C
C
A
D
3
F
B
B
H
G
E
G
F
K
M
L
K
Q
R
O
R
R
R
4
4
ASSEMBLY

VANITY

LIST OF MATERIALS.

A — 1 PIECE ¾" THICK AND 42" x 15".
B — 4 PIECES 1¼" IN DIAMETER AND 27"
LONG. C — 2 PIECES ¾" DIAMETER AND
18" LONG. D — 2 PIECES ¾" THICK AND
11" x 12". E — 2 PIECES ¾" THICK AND
11" x 10½". F — 1 PIECE ½" THICK AND
11½" x 11½". G — 1 PIECE ½" THICK AND
10½" x 9". H — 1 PIECE ¾" THICK AND
10½" x 10½". ONE MIRROR 17" x 15".
SEE GENERAL INSTRUCTIONS ON PAGE 54.
AFTER THE MATERIAL IS READY FOR AS-
SEMBLING, PROCEED AS FOLLOWS:
JOIN (1) "A" WITH "B" (2) "C" WITH "A"
(3) "D" WITH "E" AND "G" (4) "D,E" WITH
"F" (5) APPLY THE DOOR "H" WITH
NORMAL HINGES (6) JOIN "E" WITH "A"
(7) APPLY THE MIRROR AND YOU HAVE
COMPLETED THE VANITY.
FOR NATURAL FINISH SEE PAGE 14.

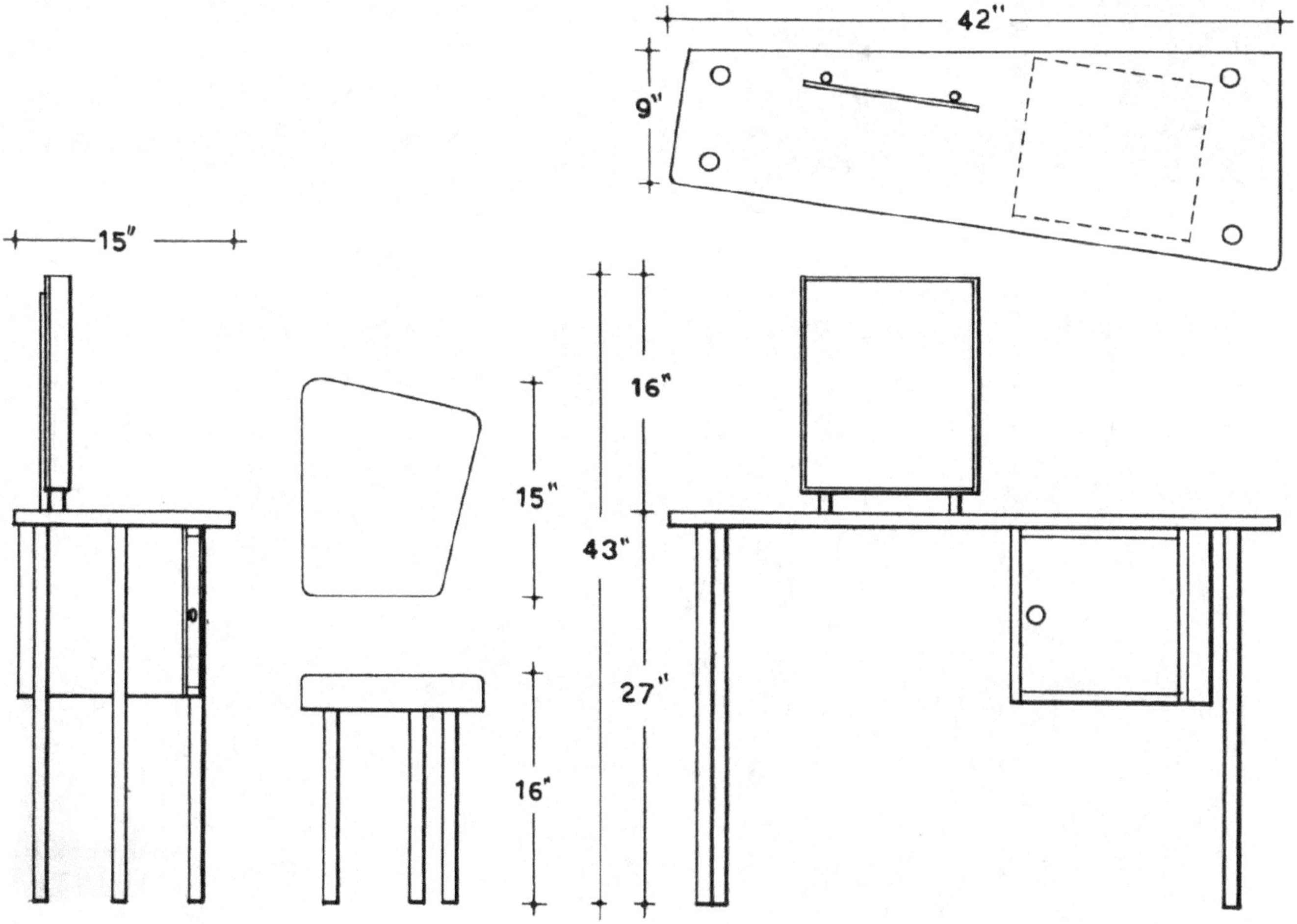

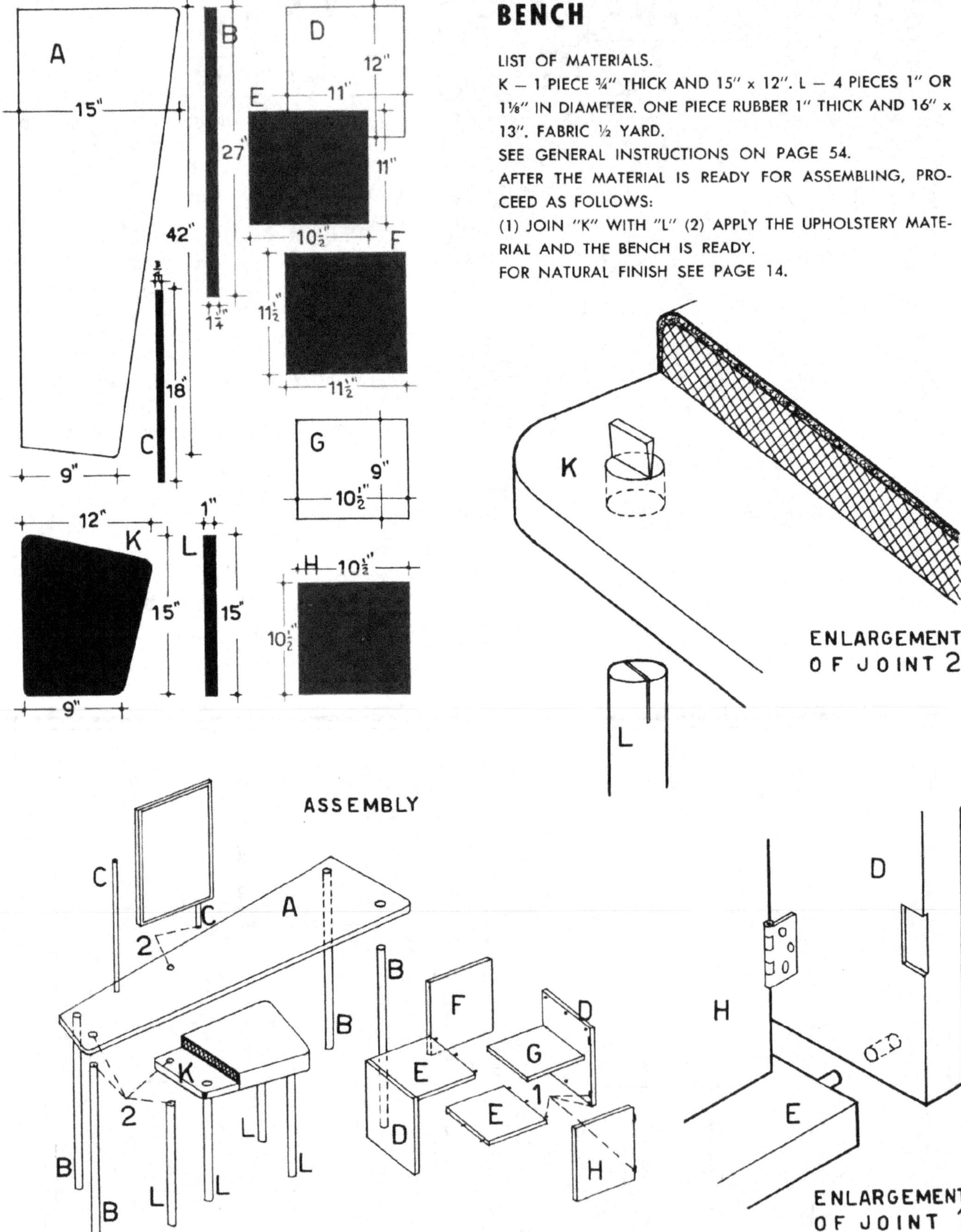

BENCH

LIST OF MATERIALS.

K — 1 PIECE ¾" THICK AND 15" x 12". L — 4 PIECES 1" OR 1⅛" IN DIAMETER. ONE PIECE RUBBER 1" THICK AND 16" x 13". FABRIC ½ YARD.

SEE GENERAL INSTRUCTIONS ON PAGE 54.

AFTER THE MATERIAL IS READY FOR ASSEMBLING, PROCEED AS FOLLOWS:

(1) JOIN "K" WITH "L" (2) APPLY THE UPHOLSTERY MATERIAL AND THE BENCH IS READY.

FOR NATURAL FINISH SEE PAGE 14.

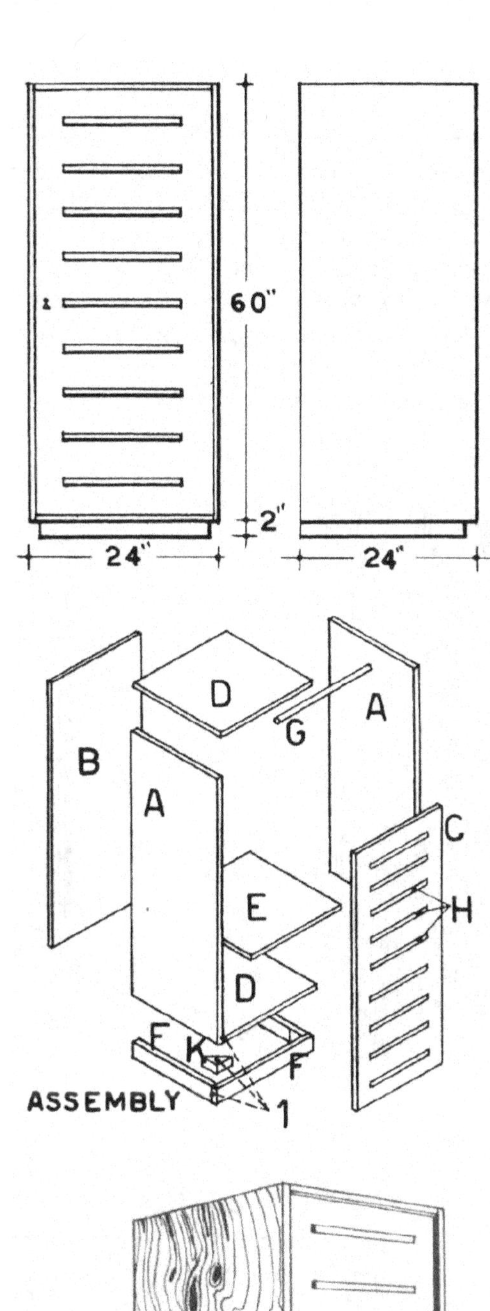

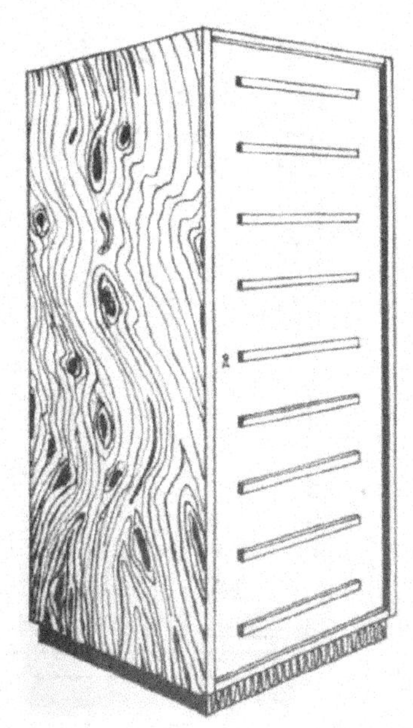

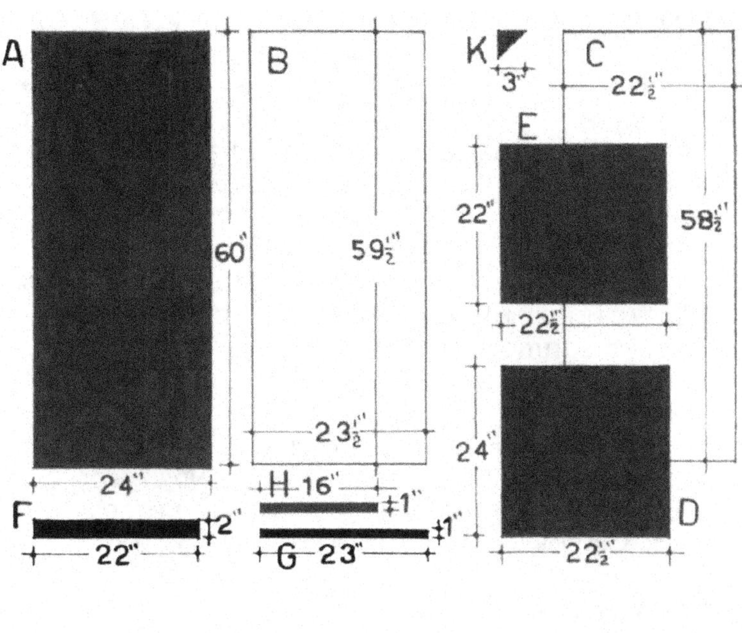

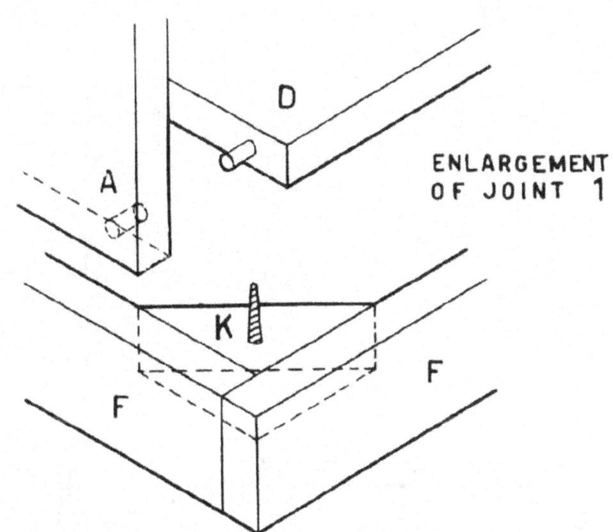

WARDROBE

LIST OF MATERIALS.

A — 2 PIECES ¾" THICK AND 60" x 24". B — 1 PIECE ½" THICK AND 59½" x 23½". C — 2 PIECES ¾" THICK AND 22½" x 58½". D — 2 PIECES ¾" THICK AND 24" x 22½". E — 1 PIECE ¾" THICK AND 22½" x 22". F — 3 PIECES 1¼" THICK AND 22" x 2". G — 1 PIECE 1" IN DIAMETER AND 23" LONG. H — 9 PIECES ½" THICK AND 16" x 1". K — 2 PIECES 1½" THICK AND 3" x 3".

SEE GENERAL INSTRUCTIONS ON PAGE 54.

AFTER THE MATERIAL IS READY FOR ASSEMBLING, PROCEED AS FOLLOWS:

JOIN (1) "A" WITH "D" (2) "B" WITH "A,D" (3) "F" WITH "F,K" (4) "F" WITH "D" (5) "G" WITH "A" (6) "E" (REMOVABLE) WITH "D" (7) "H" WITH "C" (8) "C" WITH "A" USING NORMAL HINGES TO COMPLETE YOUR WARDROBE.

FOR FINISH SEE GENERAL INSTRUCTIONS ON PAGE 14.

WARDROBE

LIST OF MATERIALS.

FIRST SOLUTION.

A — 2 PIECES ¾" THICK AND 60" x 24". B — 2 PIECES ¾" THICK AND 58½" x 23¼". C — 1 PIECE ¼" THICK AND 59½" x 47½". D — 2 PIECES ¾" THICK AND 24" x 46½". F — 4 PIECES 1¼" THICK AND 8" x 2½". G — 1 PIECE 1¼" THICK AND 36" x 2". H — 2 PIECES 1¼" THICK AND 18" x 2". E — 1 PIECE METAL PIPE 1" IN DIAMETER AND 46½" LONG.

FOR SECOND SOLUTION:

ADD K — 3 PIECES ¾" THICK AND 46½" x 22½".

FOR THIRD SOLUTION:

OMIT SHELVES "K" AND ADD THE FOLLOWING: O — 1 PIECE ¾" THICK AND 21" x 22". P — 1 PIECE ¾" THICK AND 22" x 19½". Q — 2 PIECES ¾" THICK AND 18½" x 22". R — 1 PIECE ½" THICK AND 20½" x 19". T — 3 PIECES ¼" THICK AND 21" x 19". U — 3 PIECES ¾" THICK AND 19½" x 5½". V — 6 PIECES ½" THICK AND 21½" x 5½". W — 3 PIECES ½" THICK AND 19" x 4½". X — 6 PIECES ¾" THICK AND 20" x 1". Y — 3 PIECES ¾" THICK AND 19½" x 2".

FOR GENERAL INSTRUCTIONS SEE PAGE 54.

AFTER THE MATERIAL IS READY, ASSEMBLE, FOLLOWING INSTRUCTIONS FOR WARDROBE PAGE 139 AND CHEST PAGE 143.

FOR FINISH SEE INSTRUCTIONS ON PAGE 14.

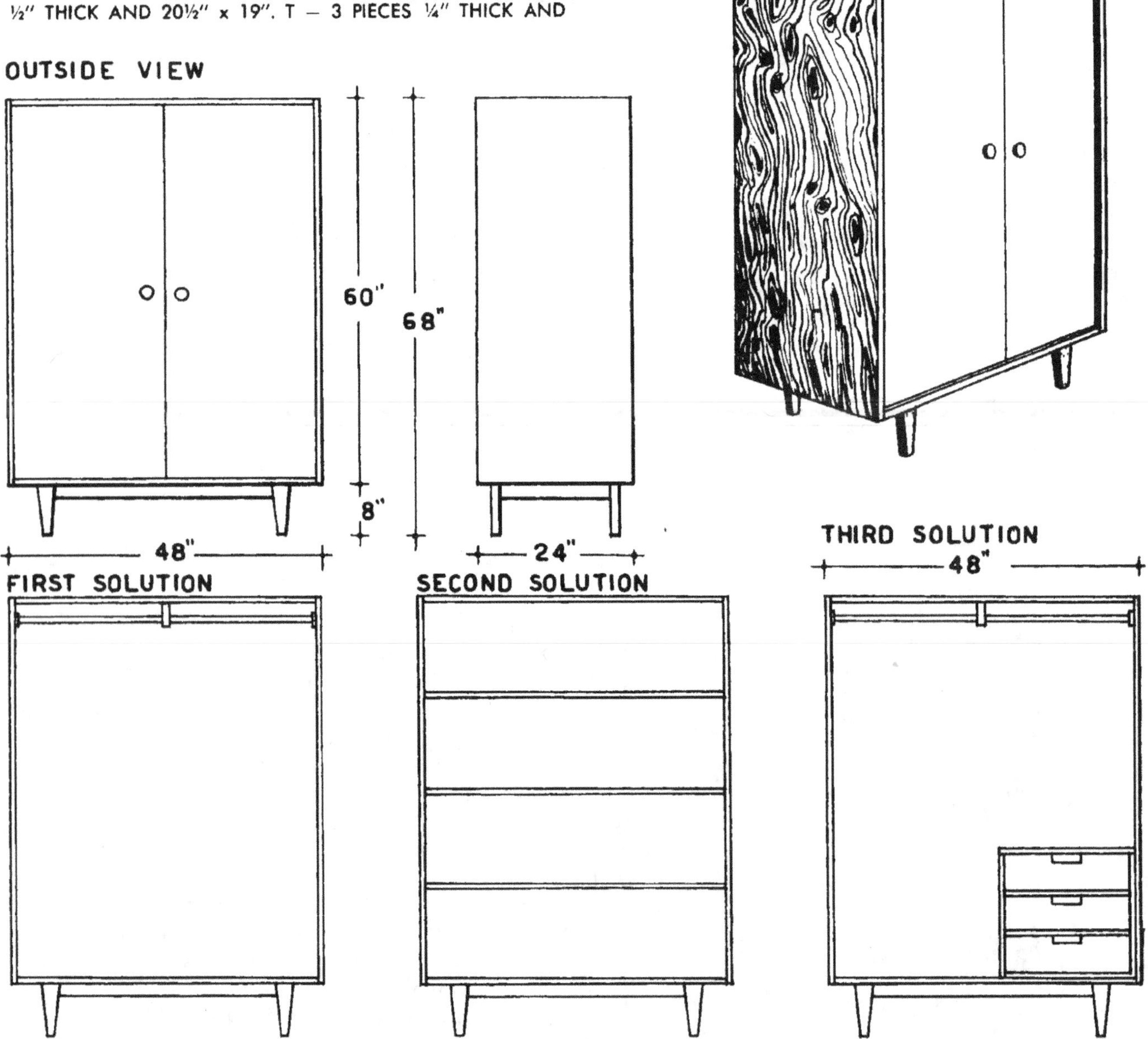

OUTSIDE VIEW

60"

68"

8"

48"

24"

FIRST SOLUTION

SECOND SOLUTION

THIRD SOLUTION

48"

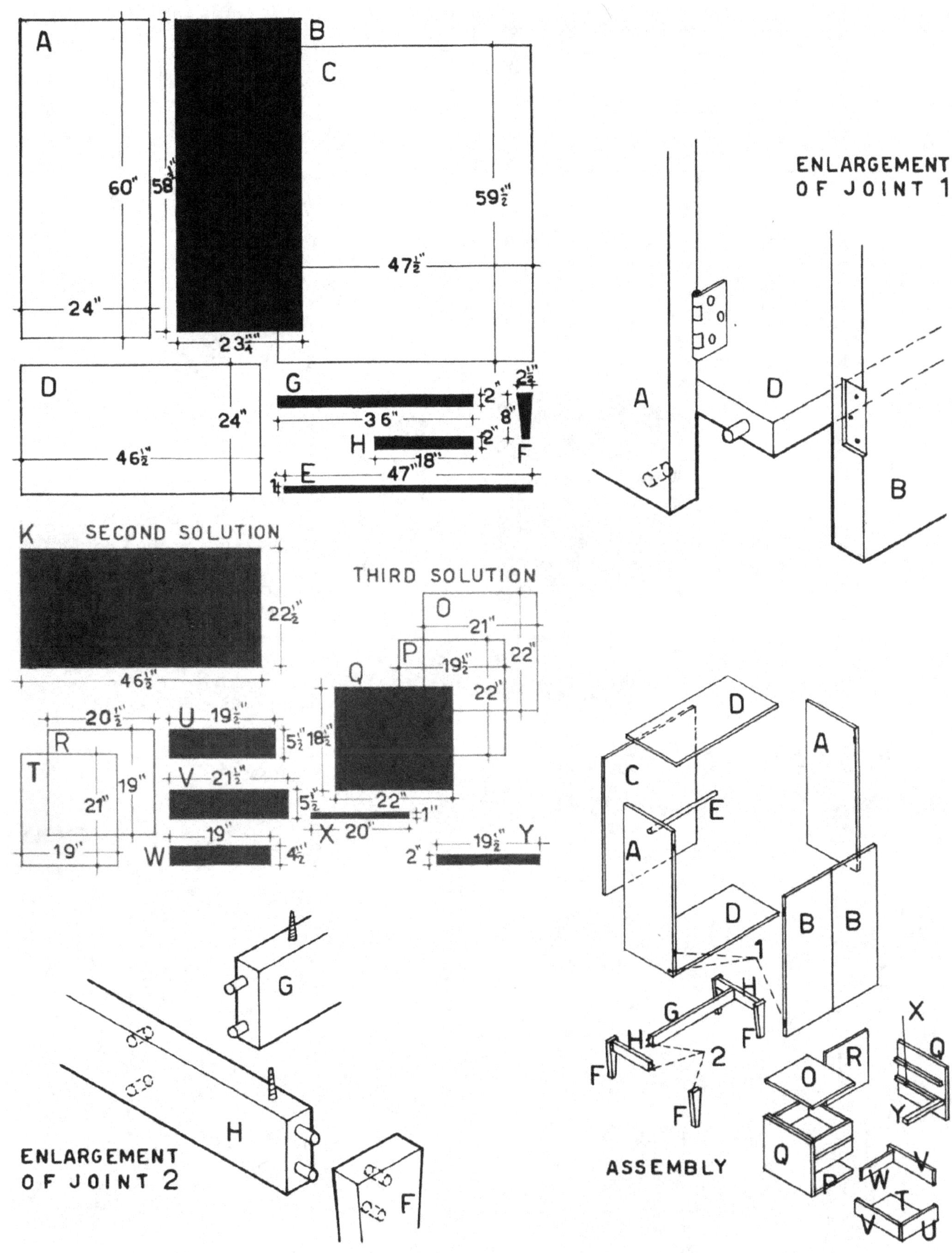

A
B
C
60"
58½"
59½"
47½"
24"
23¾"
D
24"
46½"
G
36"
2"
2½"
8"
2"
H
18"
F
E
47"
¼"
ENLARGEMENT
OF JOINT 1
A
D
B
K
SECOND SOLUTION
22½"
46½"
THIRD SOLUTION
O
21"
P
19½"
22"
22"
Q
18"
22"
1"
20½"
U
19½"
5½"
R
T
19"
V
21½"
21"
5½"
19"
19"
W
4½"
X
20"
2"
19½"
Y
ENLARGEMENT
OF JOINT 2
G
H
F
ASSEMBLY
D
C
A
A
E
D
B
B
1
G
H
F
H
F
2
F
X
O
R
Q
Y
Q
P
W
V
T
U
V

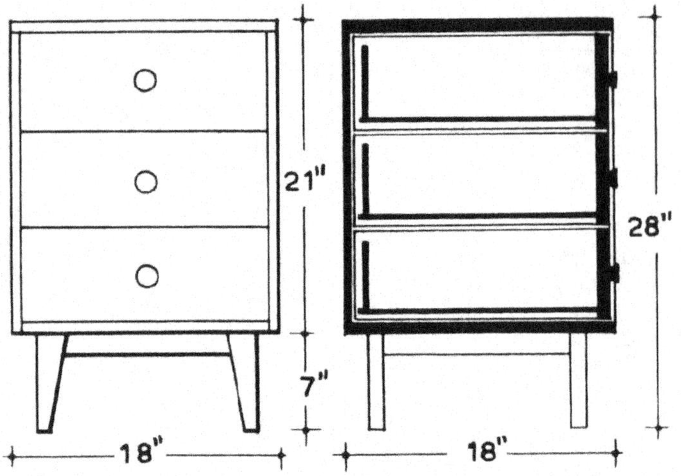

CHEST

LIST OF MATERIALS.

A — 1 PIECE ¾" THICK AND 18" x 18". A1 — 1 PIECE ¾" THICK AND 18" x 16½". B — 2 PIECES ¾" THICK AND 18" x 20¼". C — 1 PIECE ¼" THICK AND 20½" x 17½". D — 3 PIECES ¾" THICK AND 16½" x 6½". E — 3 PIECES ½" THICK AND 16" x 5½". F — 6 PIECES ½" THICK AND 17½" x 6½". G — 3 PIECES ¼" THICK AND 17¼" x 16". H — 4 PIECES 1¼" THICK AND 7" x 2". K — 3 PIECES 1¼" THICK AND 13" x 2". L — 6 PIECES ¼" THICK AND 17½" x ½".

SEE GENERAL INSTRUCTIONS ON PAGE 54.

AFTER THE MATERIAL IS READY FOR ASSEMBLING, USE THE SAME PROCEDURE AS CHEST, PAGE 143. SEE PAGE 14 FOR FINISH.

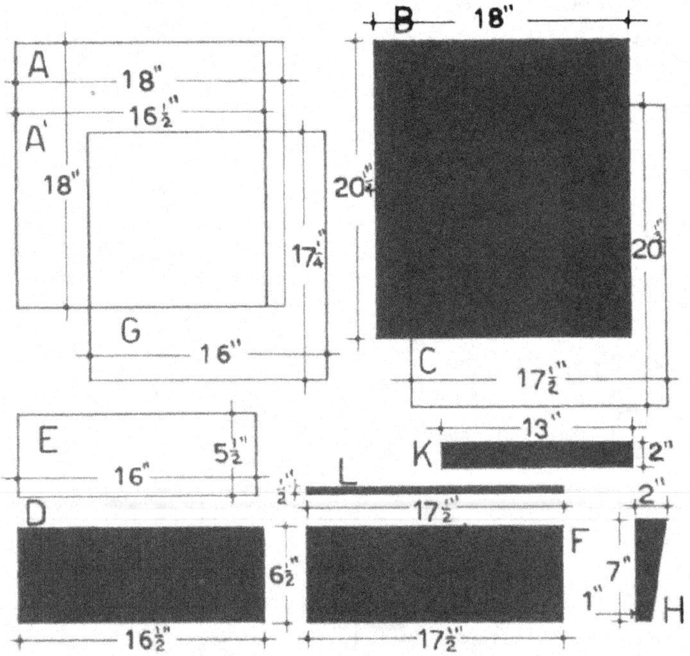

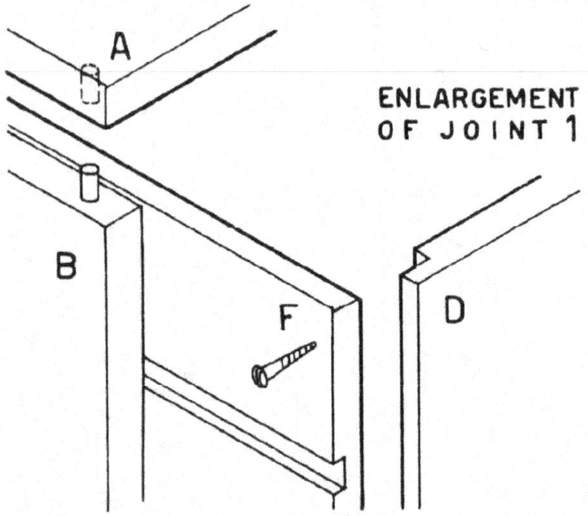

ENLARGEMENT OF JOINT 1

ASSEMBLY

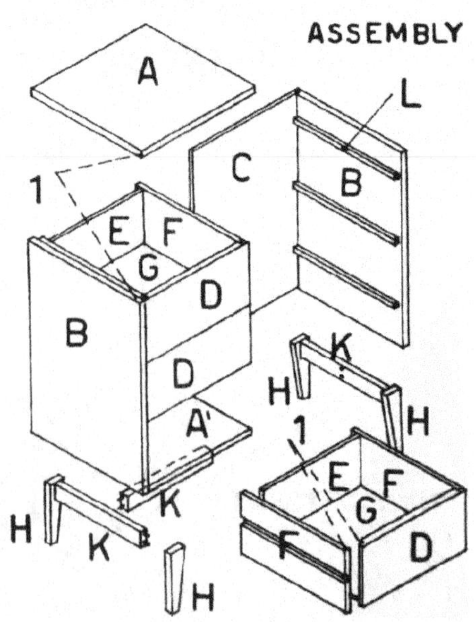

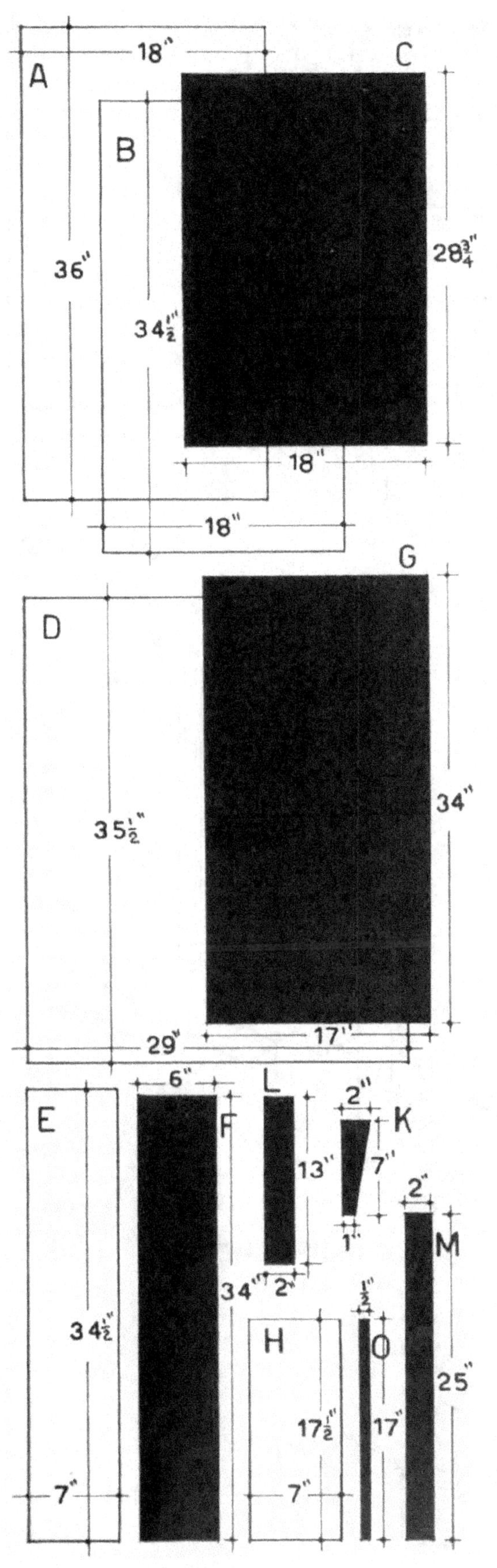

CHEST

LIST OF MATERIALS.

A — 1 PIECE ¾" THICK AND 18" x 36". B — 1 PIECE ¾" THICK AND 18" x 34½". C — 2 PIECES ¾" THICK AND 28¾" x 18". D — 1 PIECE ¼" THICK AND 35½" x 29". E — 4 PIECES ¾" THICK AND 34½" x 7". F — 4 PIECES ½" THICK AND 34" x 6". G — 4 PIECES ¼" THICK AND 34" x 17". H — 8 PIECES ½" THICK AND 17½" x 7". K — 4 PIECES 1¼" THICK AND 7" x 2". L — 2 PIECES 1¼" THICK AND 13" x 2". M — 1 PIECE 1¼" THICK AND 25" x 2". O — 8 PIECES ¼" THICK AND 17" x ½".

FOR GENERAL INSTRUCTIONS SEE PAGE 54.

WHEN THE MATERIAL IS READY FOR ASSEMBLING, PROCEED AS FOLLOWS:

JOIN (1) "A" AND "B" WITH "C" (2) "A,B,C" WITH "D" (3) "O" WITH "C" (4) "K" WITH "L" (5) "L" WITH "M" (6) "L,M" WITH "B" (7) "H" WITH "E,F" (8) "G" WITH "E,F,H" (9) APPLY THE DRAWERS AND YOU HAVE COMPLETED YOUR CHEST.

FOR NATURAL FINISH SEE INSTRUCTIONS ON PAGE 14.

29½"
7"
36"
36½"
18"
1¾"
14½"
2"
A
O
D
C
H
F G
C
E
E
E
B
K
L
K
M
K
K
1
F G H
E
ASSEMBLY
H
C
E
B
M
L
K
ENLARGEMENT
OF JOINT 1

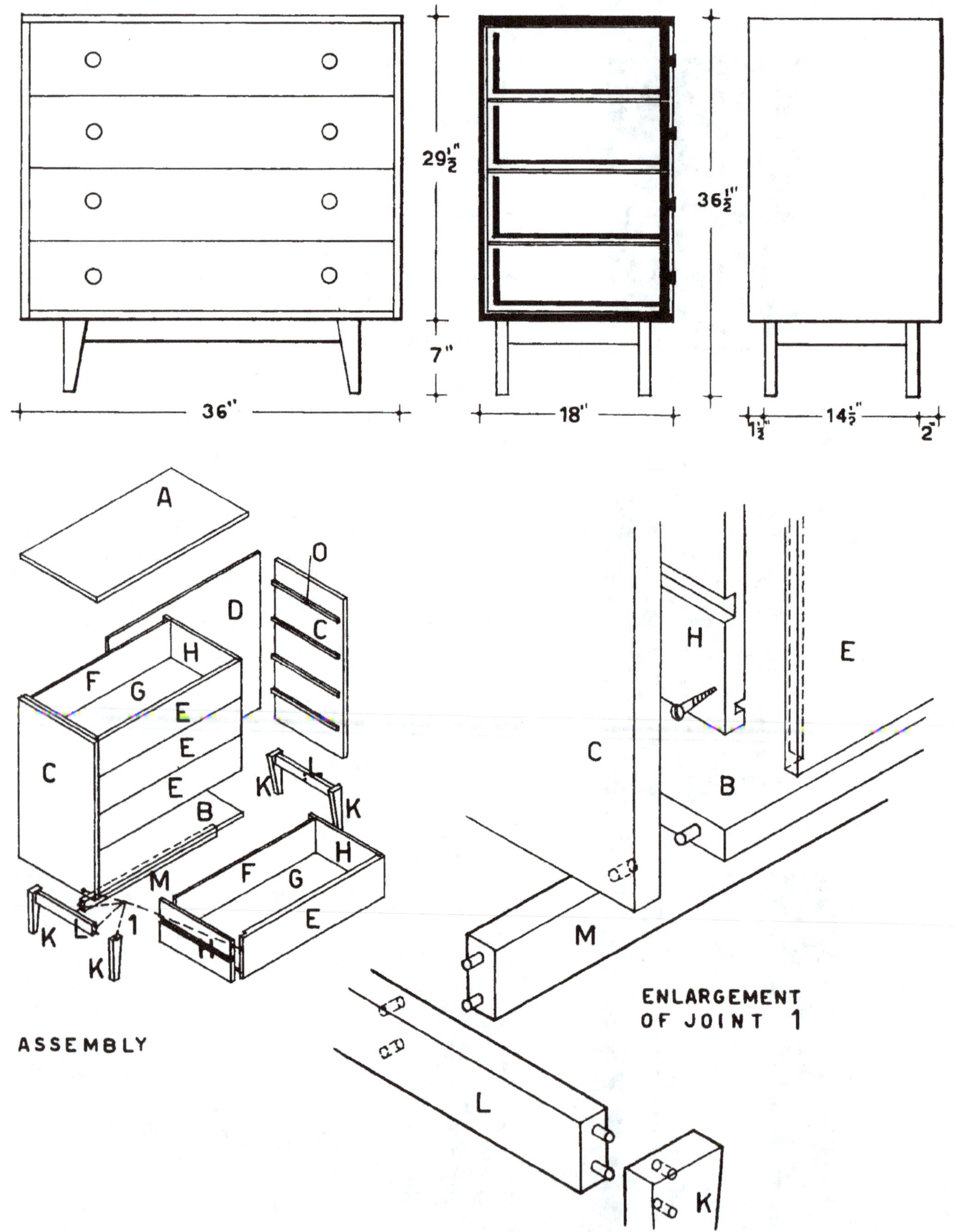

144

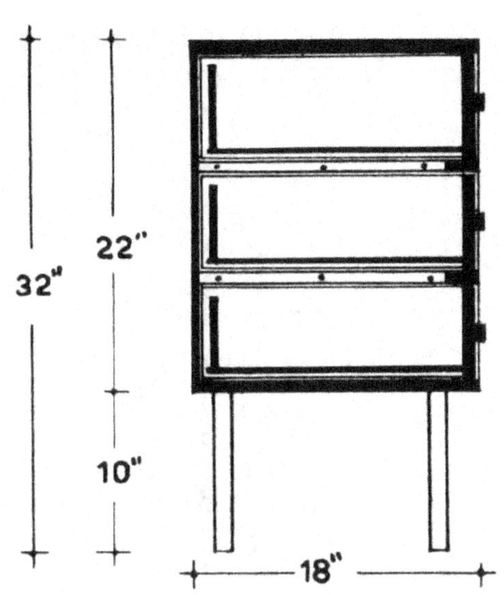
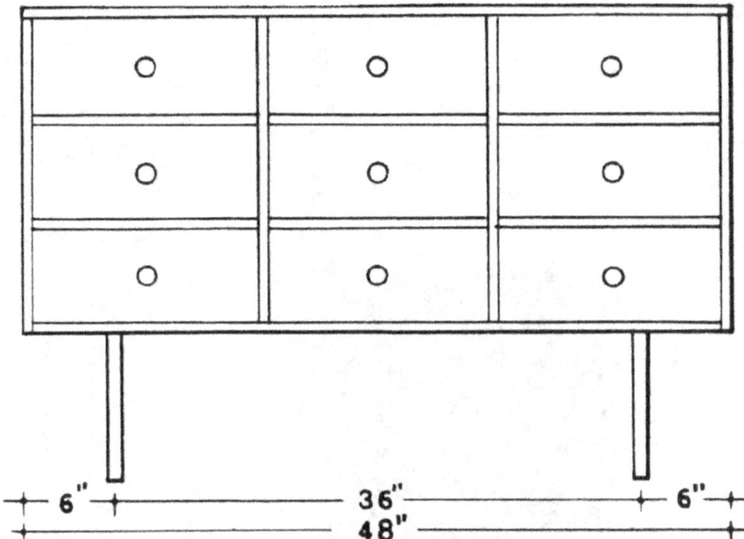

CHEST

A — 1 PIECE ¾" THICK AND 48" x 18". B — 1 PIECE ¾" THICK AND 18" x 46½". C — 1 PIECE ¼" THICK AND 47½" x 21½". D — 2 PIECES ¾" THICK AND 18" x 21¼". E — 2 PIECES ¾" THICK AND 20½" x 17¾". F — 6 PIECES ¾" THICK AND 15" x 2". G — 12 PIECES ¾" THICK AND 16" x 1". H — 4 PIECES 1¼" IN DIAMETER AND 11" LONG. K — 9 PIECES ¾" THICK AND 15" x 6½". L — 18 PIECES ½" THICK AND 17½" x 6½". M — 9 PIECES ½" THICK AND 14½" x 5½". O — 9 PIECES ¼" THICK AND 17½" x 14½".

FOR GENERAL INSTRUCTION SEE PAGE 54.

WHEN THE MATERIAL IS READY FOR ASSEMBLING, PROCEED AS FOLLOWS:

JOIN (1) "A" AND "B" WITH "D," "E" AND "F" (2) "A,B,D,E" WITH "C" (3) "B" WITH "H" (4) "G" WITH "D" AND "E" (5) "L" WITH "K" AND "M" (6) "O" WITH "L,K,M" AND YOU HAVE COMPLETED YOUR CHEST.

FOR FINISH SEE GENERAL INSTRUCTIONS ON PAGE **14.**

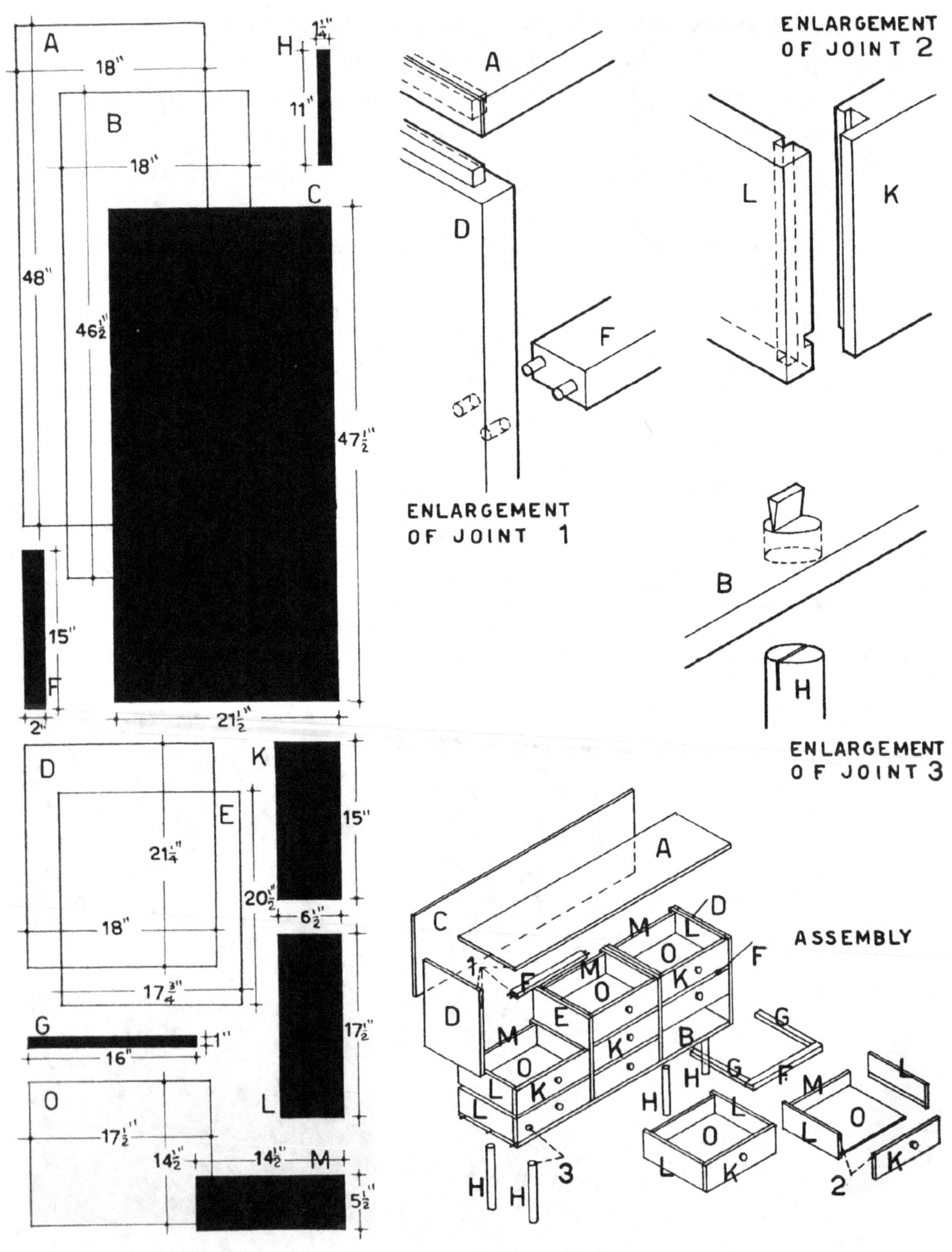

A
18"
B
18"
H
1 1/4"
11"
C
48"
46 1/2"
47 1/2"
F
15"
2"
21 1/2"
ENLARGEMENT
OF JOINT 1
ENLARGEMENT
OF JOINT 2
A
D
F
L
K
B
H
ENLARGEMENT
OF JOINT 3
D
E
21 1/4"
18"
17 3/4"
K
15"
20 1/2"
6 1/2"
L
17 1/2"
G
16"
1"
O
17 1/2"
14 1/2"
14 1/2"
M
5 1/2"
A
C
D
M
L
O
K
F
E
M
O
K
D
M
E
K
B
L
K
G
G
F
M
H
H
L
K
L
O
L
K
2
H
H
3
L
O
K
L
K
ASSEMBLY